AF473944

Remarkable Graphic Styles

# CHAOTIC

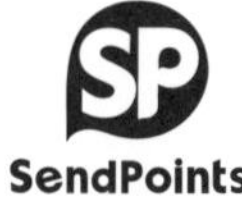

SendPoints

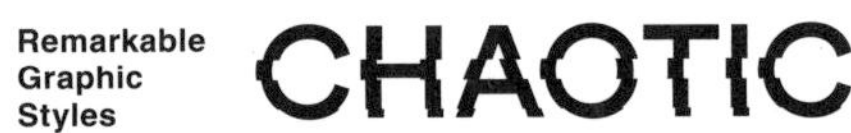


Second printing of the first edition, April 2020

**EDITED & PUBLISHED BY** SendPoints Publishing Co., Ltd.
**PUBLISHER:** Lin Gengli
**PUBLISHING DIRECTOR:** Lin Shijian
**ASSISTANT PUBLISHING-DIRECTOR:** Chen Ting
**CHIEF EDITOR:** Lin Shijian
**LEAD EDITOR:** Li Weiji
**EXECUTIVE EDITOR:** Huang Qian
**DESIGN DIRECTOR:** Lin Shijian
**EXECUTIVE ART EDITOR:** Ding Jiaxin
**PROOFREADING:** James N. Powell, Li Weiji

**REGISTERED ADDRESS:** Room 15A Block 9 Tsui Chuk Garden, Wong Tai Sin, Kowloon, Hong Kong
**TEL:** +852-35832323 / FAX: +852-35832448
**OFFICE ADDRESS:** 7F, No.9-1 Anning Street, Jinshazhou Road, Baiyun District, Guangzhou, China
**TEL:** +86-20-89095121 / FAX: +86-20-89095206
**BEIJING OFFICE:** Flat 1701, Block C, BBMG International, Wangjing West Road no.48, Chaoyang District, Beijing, China
**TEL:** +86-10-84139071 / FAX: +86-10-84139071
**SHANGHAI OFFICE:** Room 302, Floor 3, Ningbo Road no.349, Huangpu District, Shanghai, China
**TEL:** +86-21-63523469 / FAX: +86-21-63523469

**SALES TEAM**
UK, Europe, Africa, Oceania: Sunnie sales02@sendpoints.cn
America, the Middle East: Mia sales03@sendpoints.cn
Asia: Hedy sales01@sendpoints.cn
**TEL:** +86-20-81007895
**EMAIL:** sales@sendpoints.cn
**WEBSITE:** www.sendpoints.cn / www.spbooks.cn

**ISBN** 978-988-78494-6-9

Printed and bound in China

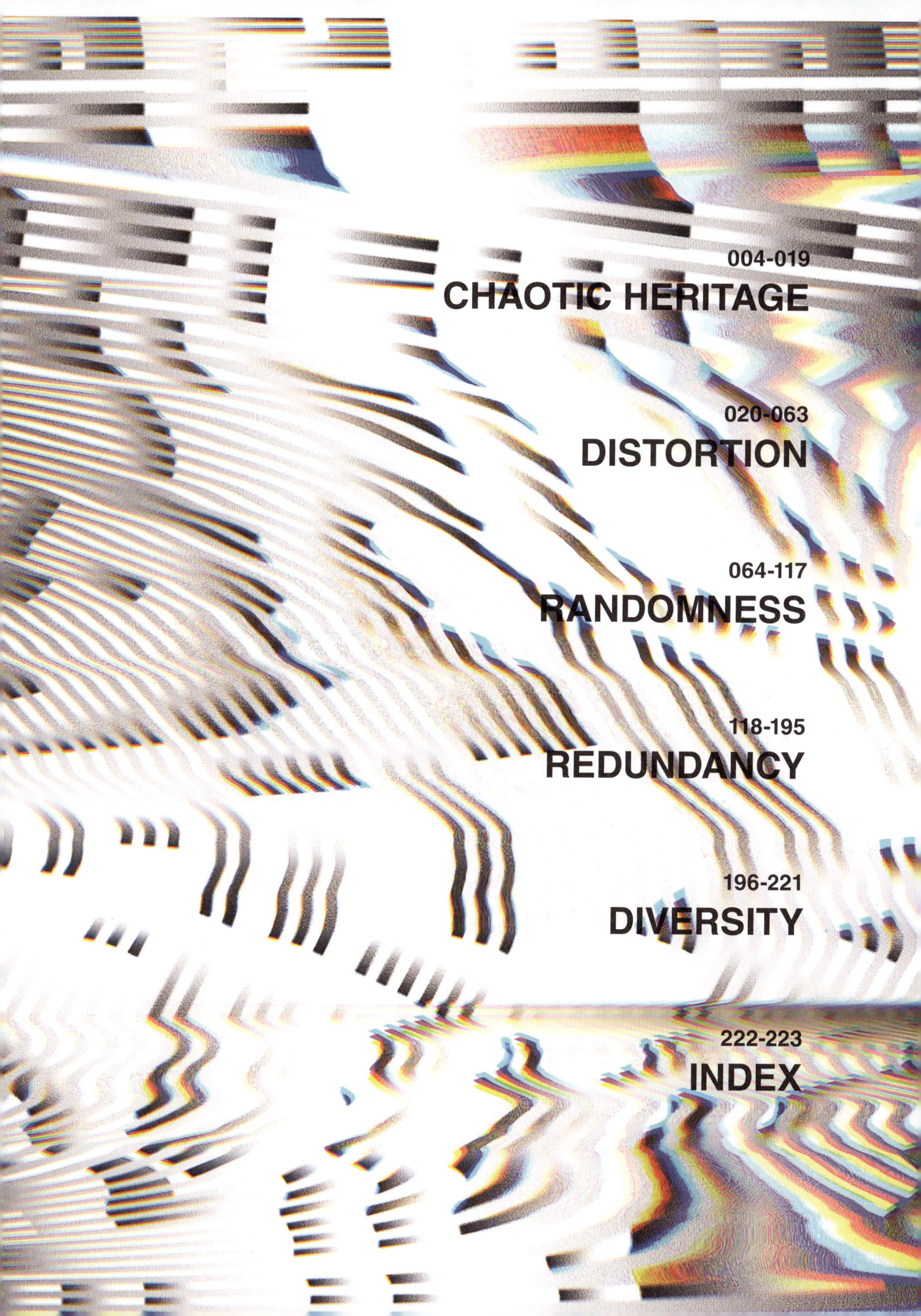

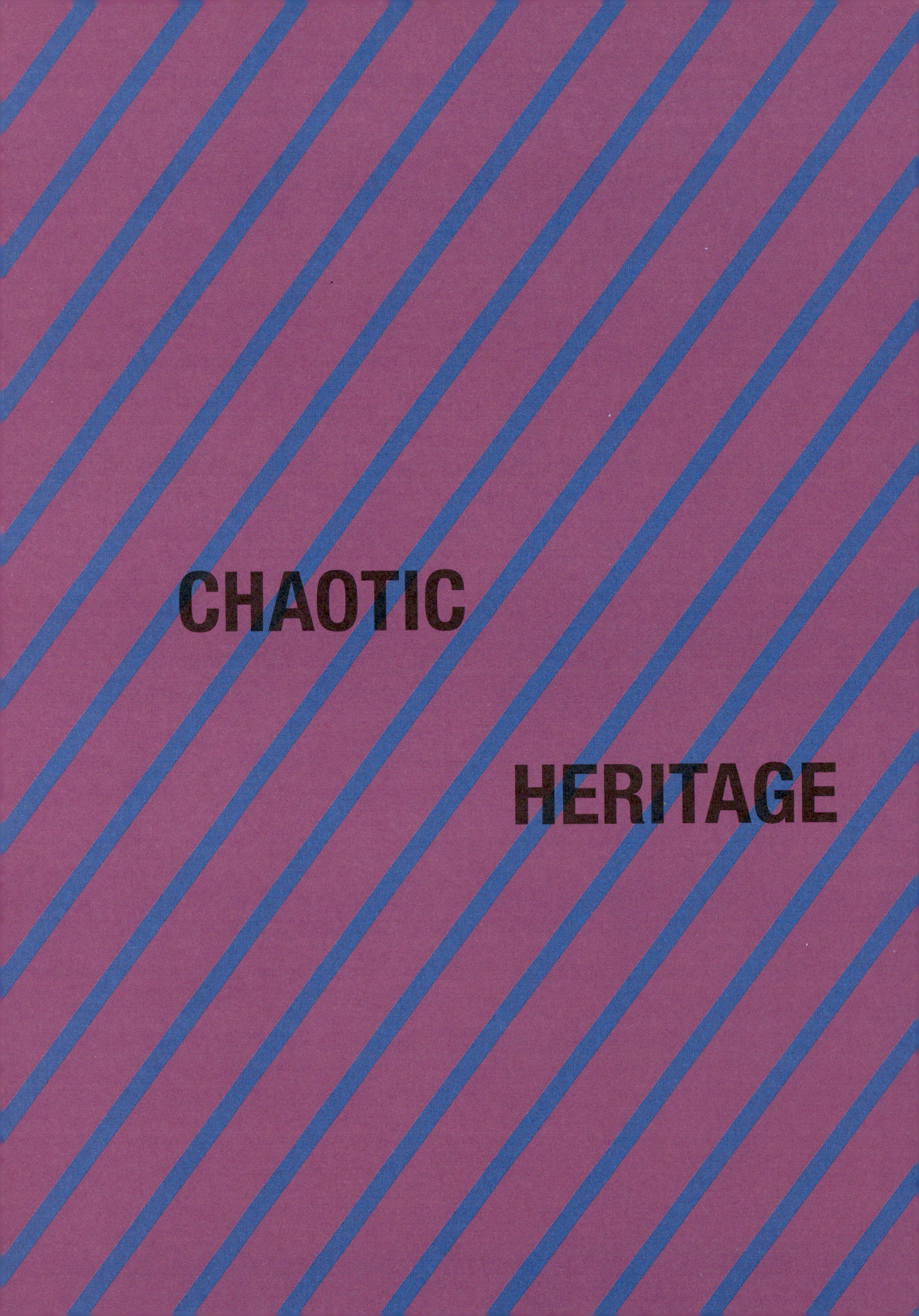
CHAOTIC
HERITAGE

Celebrated as the most powerful style of Chinese calligraphy, the cursive script exemplifies the unorthodox aesthetics of chaos. As an abstract art of lines, it allows calligraphers to explore and demonstrate the energetics of gesture through recreating the lines and spacing of characters. Some Western abstract expressionists or action painters have embraced an approach similar to that of East Asian calligraphy, from which some of them have drawn inspiration. The American artist Jackson Pollock's signature method of dripping painting, like Chinese cursive script, exhibits creator's state of mind in a vigorous and forceful way, but with order and control.

This chapter, *Chaotic Heritage*, chronologically presents "chaotic" works of art from the past before we step into the contemporary graphic design world where all sorts of "chaotic" creations have been pushing the boundaries of visual communication. These creations combine various tools and approaches—distortion, randomness, redundancy, and diversity—to willfully and freely express the artist's mind and emotions. The frequent appearance of chaos reminds us that chaotic effects have evolved into a distinct visual language.

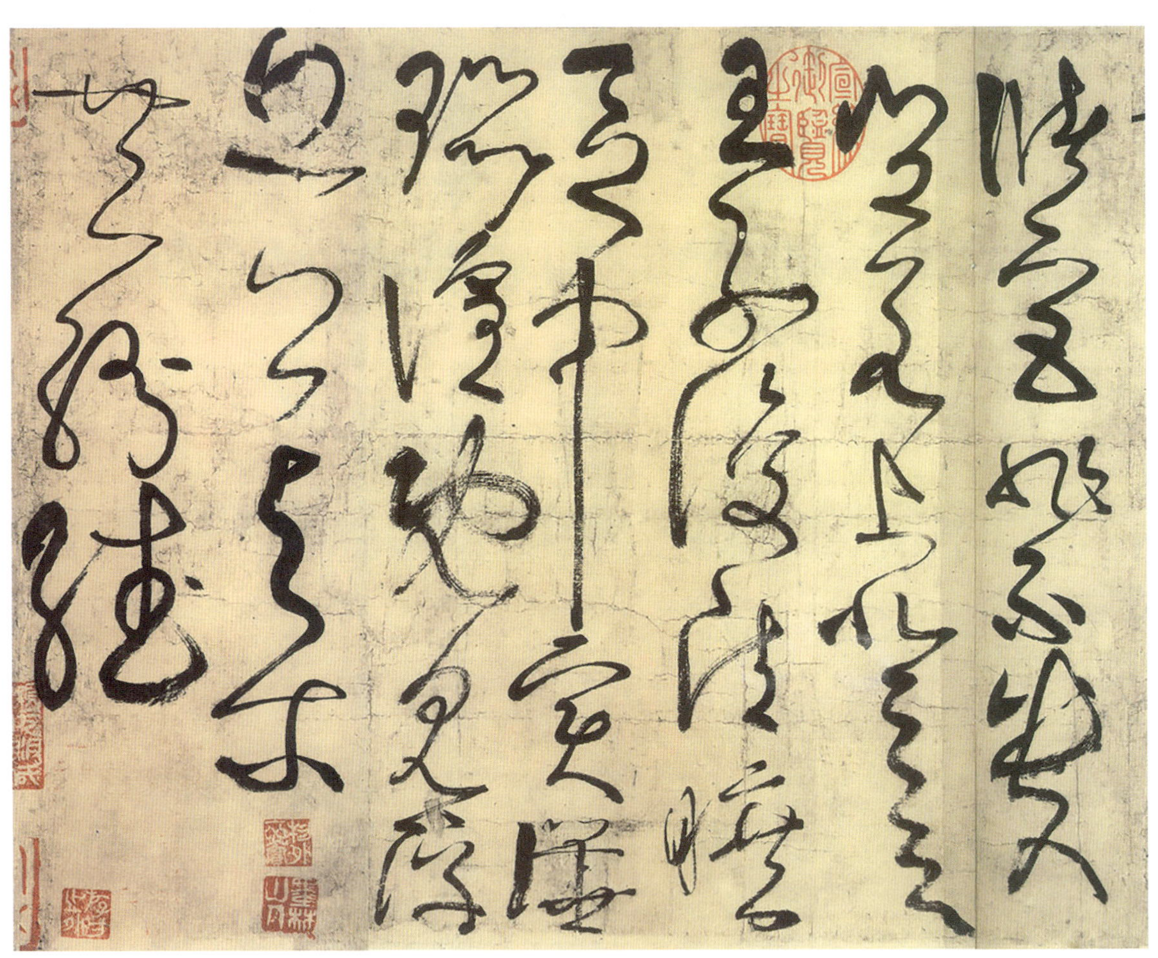

Cursive script *Four Ancient Poems* (detail), Zhang Xu, Tang Dynasty (618-907)

# Chinese Cursive Script

As one of the five categories of Chinese calligraphy, cursive script is written quickly but is difficult to comprehend. Such a highly fluid approach is realized by omitting, merging, and abbreviating parts of the characters or even changing their style.

Originating during the Han dynasty (202BC-220AD), Chinese cursive script preserves an ancient form named *zhangcao* as well as offering modern cursive. In addition to these two forms, a more uninhibited style of cursive script, dubbed "wild cursive," hovers somewhere between Being and Non-Being. It was initiated by Zhang Xu (675- fl. 750), who was said to have written it—when drunk—using his long hair as his brush.

The modern scholar Han Yutao has accurately delineated the three basic characteristics embodied in Zhang Xu's calligraphic works: wild, strange and varied, and formidable. Its wildness lies in its explosive power released in one random sweep; It is as strange, unpredictable, and diverse as a changing cloud; In contrast to the tender delicacy of most Chinese calligraphy, it is as sharp and threatening as a sword. In spite of being wild and crazy, one can sense the rules in his every dot and line. It is thus justifiable to say that Zhang's calligraphy has significantly transformed chaos into visual art.

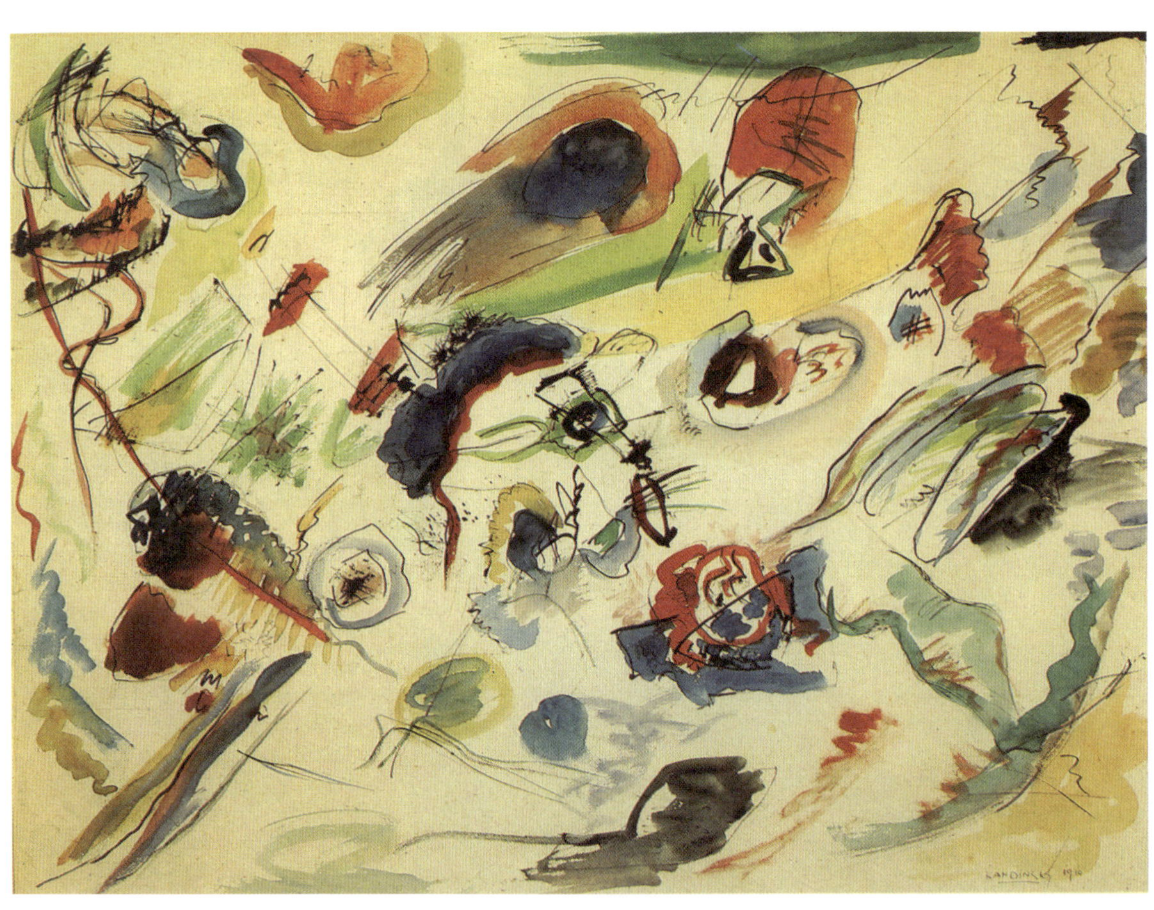


*Untitled (First Abstract Watercolor)*, Wassily Kandinsky, 1910

## Kandinsky's First Abstract Watercolor

The year 1910 saw the emergence of abstract art within the Western art scene, when Russian-born artist Wassily Kandinsky's (1866-1944) first abstract watercolor was initially recognized as the first, and later, as one of the most important exemplars of purely abstract painting. Escaping the conventions of figurative painting, the flat surface offers disordered composition of lines, shapes, and colors that stand on their own— without any representational objects.

With its lines and colors functioning in a way similar to notes, the piece suggests analogies between painting and music. After all, the artist believed that our visual language, instead of being a tool for the faithful rendering of reality, could form a general imagery within the viewer's mind as does music. In this way an image deeply affects a person spiritually.

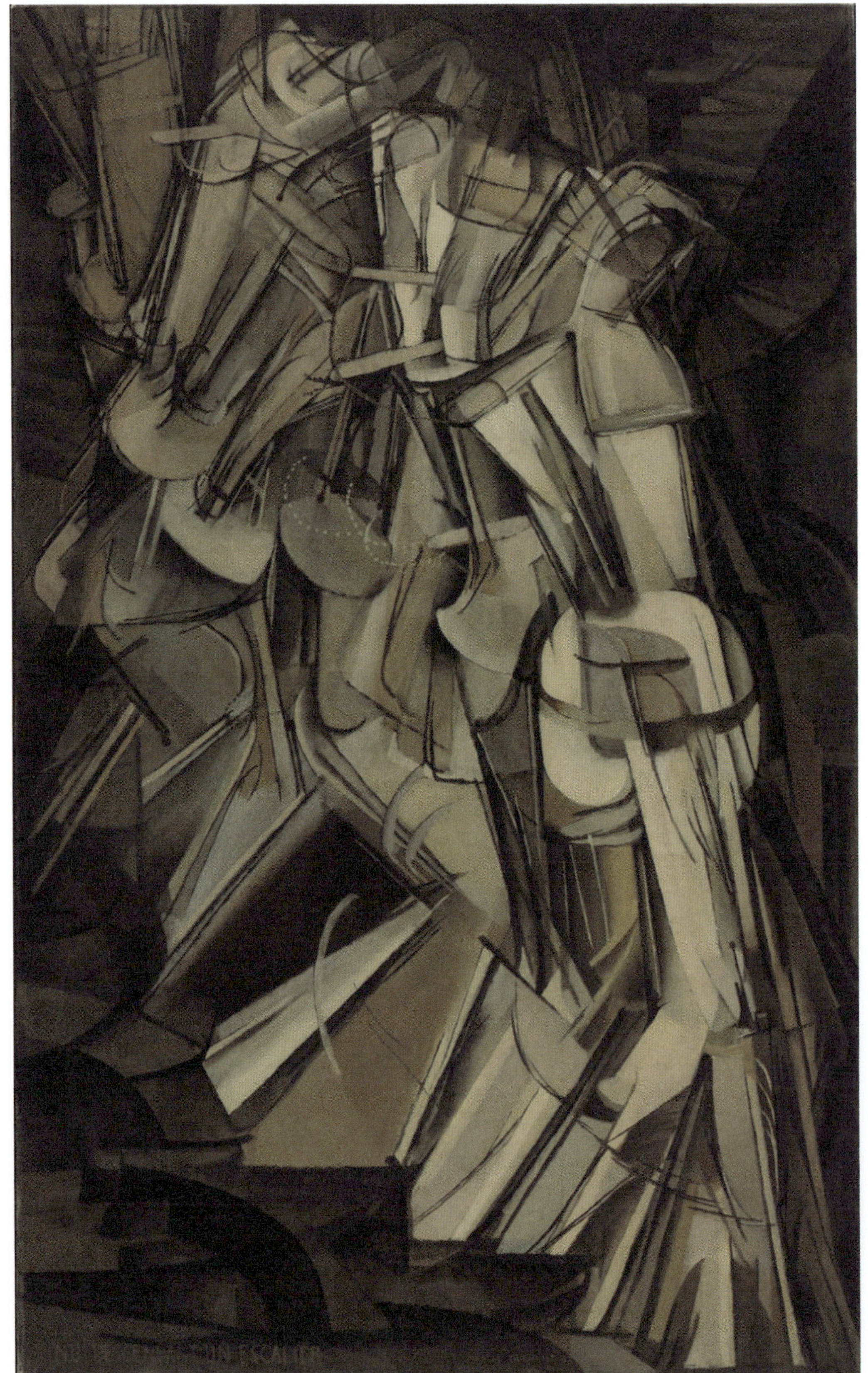

*Nude Descending a Staircase, No. 2*, Marcel Duchamp, 1912

# Nude Descending a Staircase, No.2

After the tepid response to its first showing in France in 1912, the oil painting *Nude Descending a Staircase, No. 2*, by French artist Marcel Duchamp (1887-1968), caused a huge stir at the 1913 Armory Show in New York when realistic practices still prevailed in America. Its unorthodox rendition of the nude presented an extreme of modern art at the time: capturing a walking nude in motion rather than a static one in an elegant pose.

The canvas is filled with angular shapes, an iconic cubist approach of shattered planes, superimposed images, and motion lines for dynamics. The motion it suggests often reminds viewers of time-lapse photography or of works of the avant-garde movement Futurism. This now famous modernist classic showcases Duchamp's use of satire, which is more widely known through his later readymade works. The artist refused to create just to please the eyes. He once said that he painted "to put art back in the service of the mind."

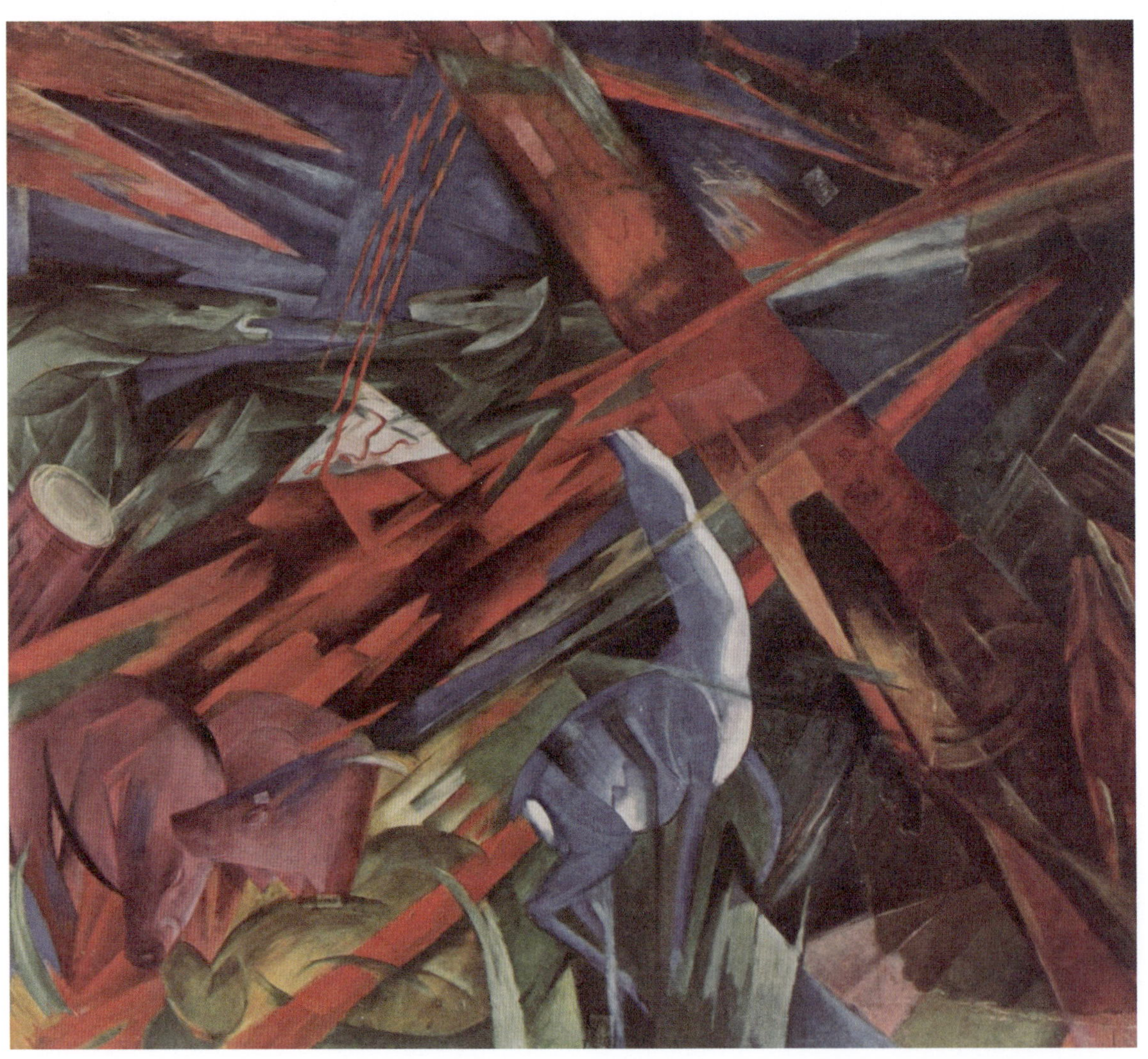

*Tierschicksale*, Franz Marc, 1913

# An Expressionist's Premonition of War

*Tierschicksale*, known as *Fate of the Animals* in English, is an oil painting completed in 1913 by German expressionist Franz Marc (1880-1916), who in his mature works exhibited a strong preference for portraying animals. However, instead of presenting animals in a pacific way, as in the artist's previous paintings, *Tierschicksale* demonstrates a wild style by depicting a chaotic scene where several animals scatter in a flaming forest, including a blue deer, two boars, two horses, and four unidentified animals: each escaping or accepting the fate of death. The work proved to be a portent of World War I, as Marc wrote to his wife about the painting during his service in the army, "[It] is like a premonition of this war—horrible and shattering. I can hardly conceive that I painted it."

The painting is full of oblique lines—the postures of the animals, the fires, and the falling tree are diagonal, which highlight the tension of those lives while imparting power into this torn-apart vision. Despite the chaos, optimism and order can be found in the work: the blue deer in the center foreground symbolizes hope.

kp' erioUM lp'er ioum

Nm' periii pERnoooum

bprEtiBerreeeRREbee e e

ONNOo gplanpouk

konmpout pERIKOUL

RrEEeeEEee rrrreeeeA

oapAerrre EE E

mgl ed padANou

MTNOU tnoum t

*Kp'erioum*, Raoul Hausmann, 1919

# Kp' erioum

Known as a pioneer of Berlin Dada, Austrian artist Raoul Hausmann (1886-1971) was inexhaustible in his artistic pursuit of dealing with new materials in innovative ways. His unique approach to typography stemmed from chance letter arrangements from which he created sound poems he called "phonemes" or "poster poems".

*Kp'erioum* is a sound poem created in 1919. As a relatively mature work of this artistic form, its typography turned to a system of sound symbols. The letters of various typefaces and sizes seem random and wild, but are in fact placed across the paper under certain rules. The artist once said, "The characters of the acoustic poem are arranged so that their visual appearance directly represents their sound. The flow of the vowels appears to be visually blocked by the consonants; the graphical differences mediate spontaneously the representation of phonetic signs in the mind which our memory has become accustomed to translate into phonemes without difficulty."

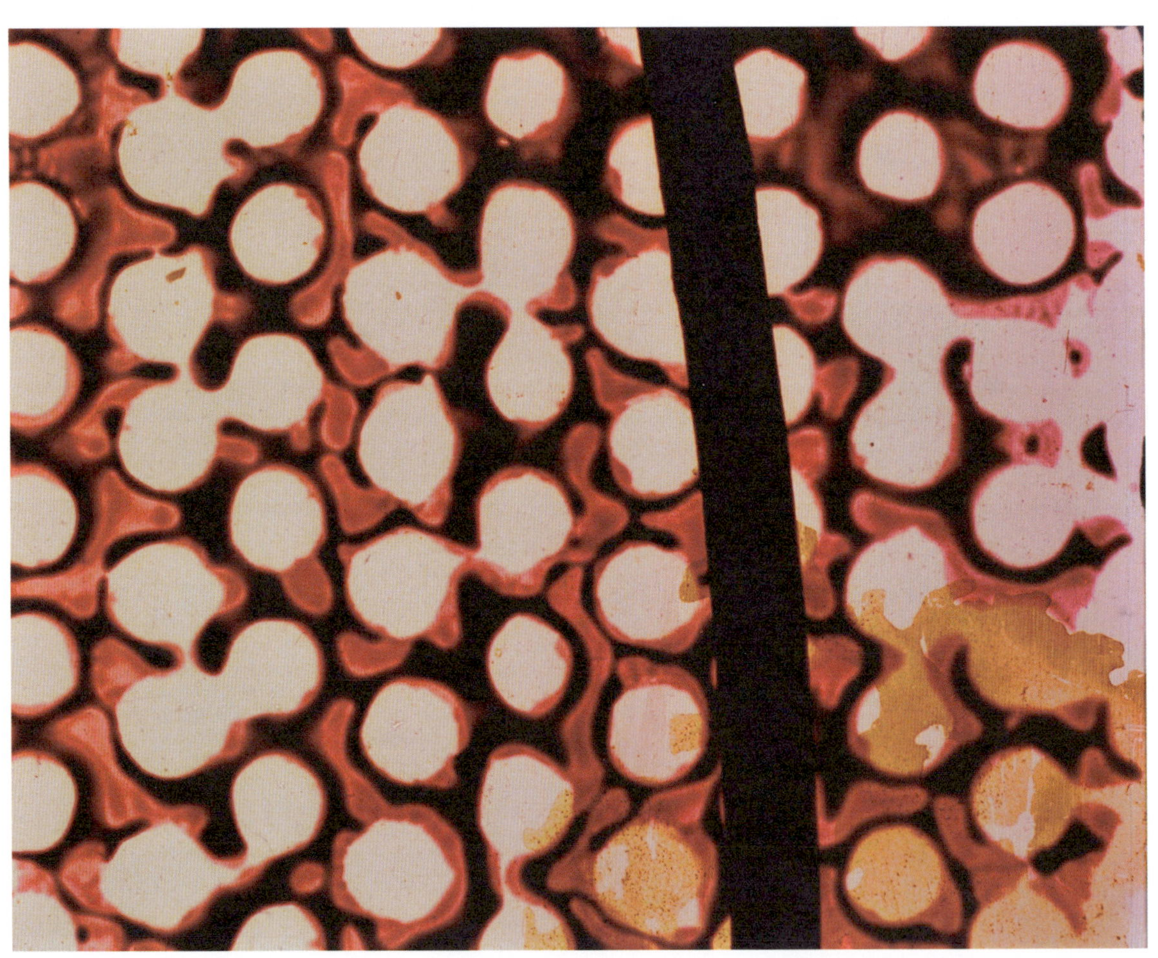

*A Colour Box (Screenshot from the film)*, Len Lye, 1935

# Glitch Pioneer—A Colour Box

*A Colour Box* was reported to be the first preserved direct animation, a form of animation where footage is produced directly on the film itself. This 4-minute film for GPO (general post office) was made in 1935 by Len Lye (1901-1980), a New Zealand-born artist who took an interest in a "pre-rational" artistic tradition and won prestige at home and abroad for his experimental films and kinetic sculptures. Lye had always favored motion, and he believed that motion is part of the language of art.

In the film colorful lines and other abstract patterns dance to popular Cuban music. These vibrant hand-painted images are present in a dynamic and jumbled way instead of following one line of motion, as opposed to those story-based, black-and-white films of that era. All the innovative ideas involved made this animation one of the most significant artworks in the history of animation and a pioneer of so-called glitch art.

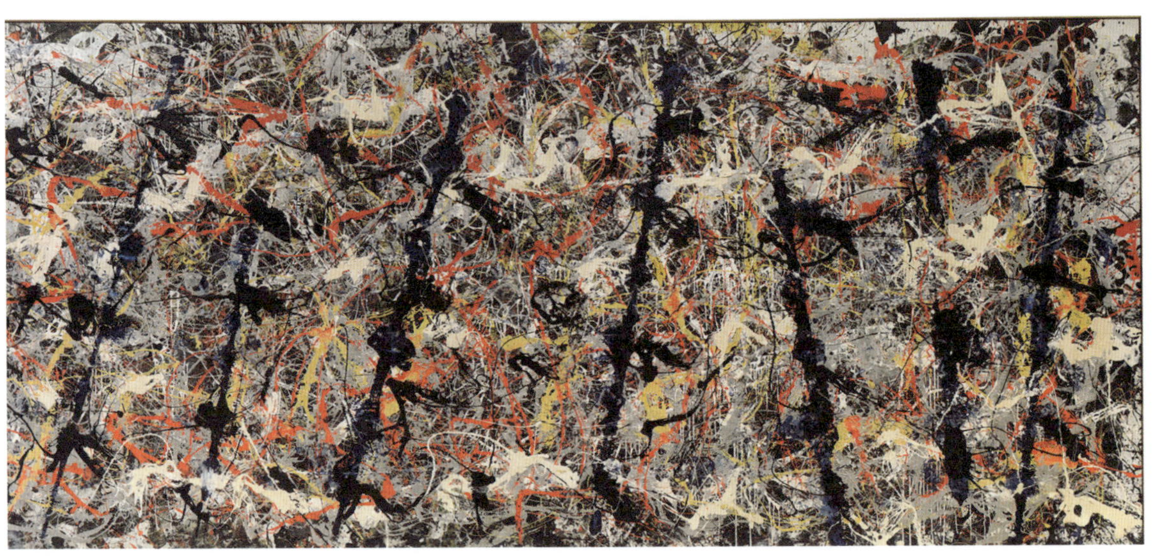

*Blue Poles*, Jackson Pollock, 1952

## Drip Painting—Blue Poles

*Blue Poles*, originally named *Number 11, 1952*, is an abstract expressionist painting by Jackson Pollock (1912-1956), an American artist who was famous for his nearly exclusive technique of drip painting.

Across the canvas appear numerous wild, twisted lines of yellow, orange, silver, and other colors. Apart from these, there are eight blue pole-like lines at different angles, conveying a sense of discernible order to the chaotic backdrop. Unlike a conventional painting, *Blue Poles* is neither made with brushes nor aimed to symbolize something in our real life. It was painted when Pollock was in a state of alcoholic intoxication. The artist underwent depression at that time, thus his works were intended to express his thinking and emotional states while he painted. Pollock once described his expression of inner world as "energy and motion made visible—memories arrested in space."

Pausa

Pausa

Pausa

Pausa

# DISTORTION

The deformation of the object by means of twisting, stretching, squeezing or turning, thus making it somewhat unrecognizable for a chaotic and exaggerated effect.

# WYSIWYG

The poster was designed for photographer Vincent Paul Yong's solo exhibition—WYSIWYG, which aimed to question the viewer's perception and to break one's ability to see, hear and become aware of something through their senses. Thus, the designers created an unusual poster that can be folded in multiple ways, yet the information still can be obtained.

Studio: LIE
Designer: Driv Loo, Iris Martens

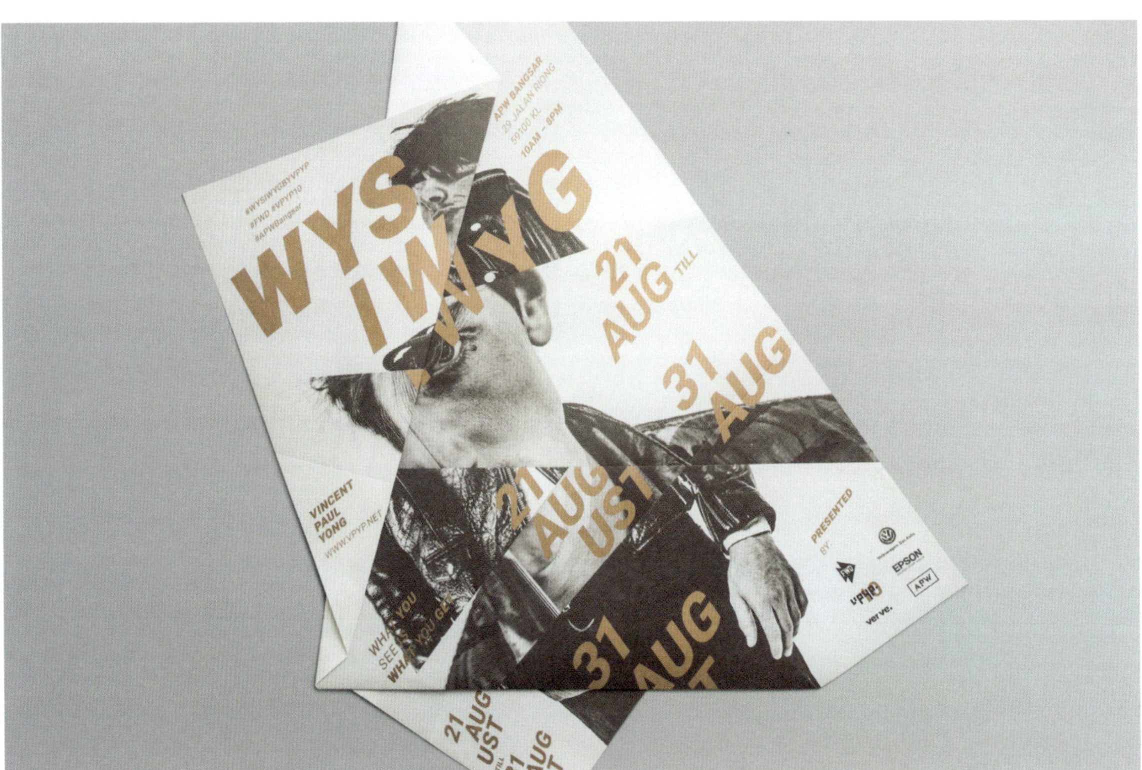


### *As a kind of visual experience, what do you think about the "chaos" in graphic design?*

In contrast to the minimalist and modernistic approaches which are very popular in design nowadays, "chaotic" provides a new perspective and causes a more attractive visual impression for the audience. There's no right or wrong way for this visual language, just a different approach to solve some design issues.

### *What are your common approaches to produce a "chaotic" visual effect?*

There's no certain logic or rule when creating a chaotic design. In some ways it is more experimental, just like a free jam session. The process of construction and deconstruction is endless until a satisfying result turns up.

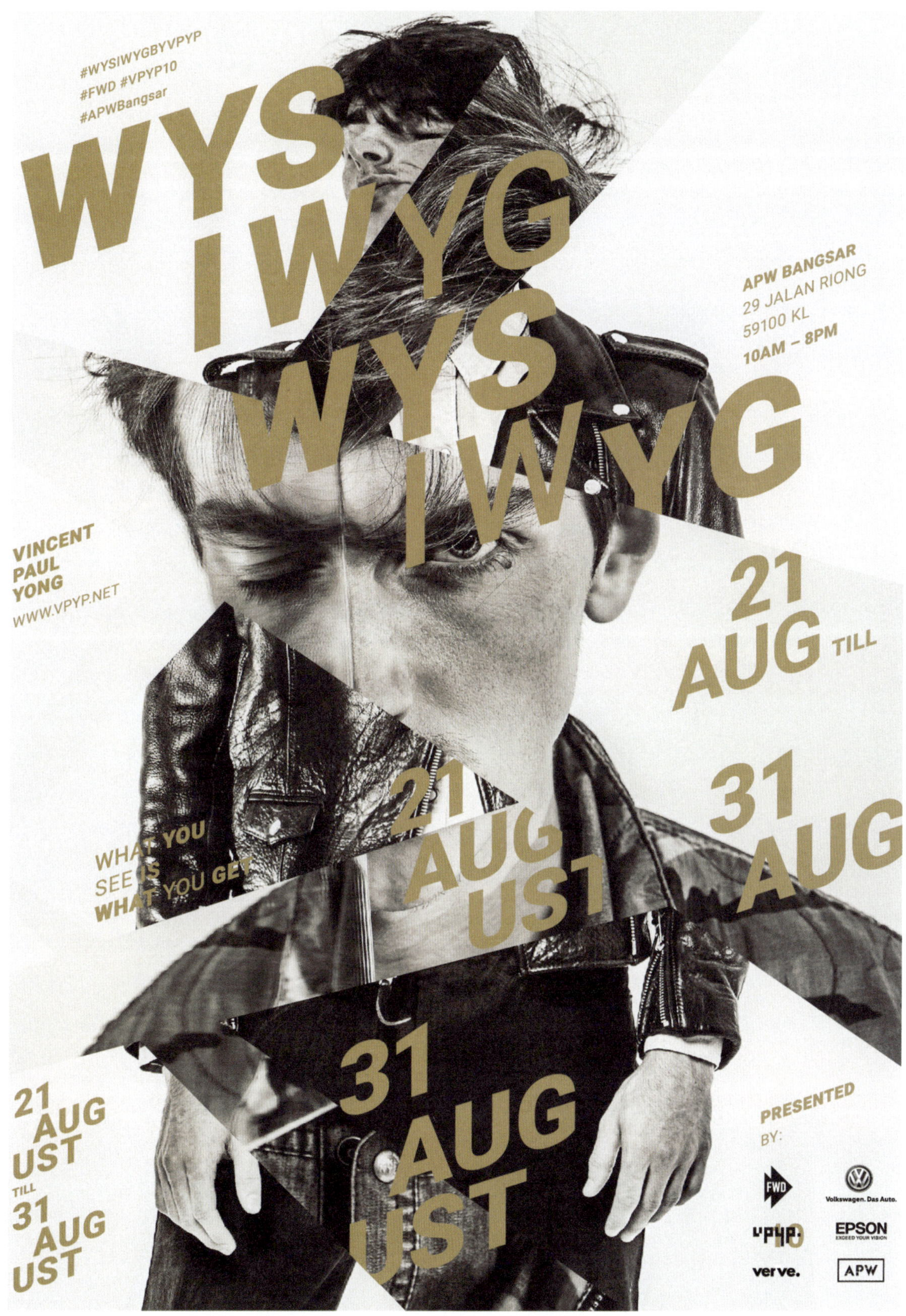
#WYSIWYGBYVPYP
#FWD #VPYP10
#APWBangsar
WYS
IWYG
WYS
IWYG
APW BANGSAR
29 JALAN RIONG
59100 KL
10AM – 8PM
VINCENT
PAUL
YONG
WWW.VPYP.NET
21
AUG TILL
21
AUG
UST1
31
AUG
WHAT YOU
SEE IS
WHAT YOU GET
21
AUG
UST
TILL
31
AUG
UST
31
AUG
UST
PRESENTED
BY:
FWD
Volkswagen. Das Auto.
EPSON
EXCEED YOUR VISION
verve.
APW

# PARABOLIKA

The idea behind this project was to create an art book, which transferred usually static typography into motion through all elements. The content of the book contained only images of the artwork *Schleudertrauma Nr.11*, which had been photographed in different angles and modified digitally.

Studio: Hubert & Fischer
Designer: Phillipp Hubert, Sebastian Fischer

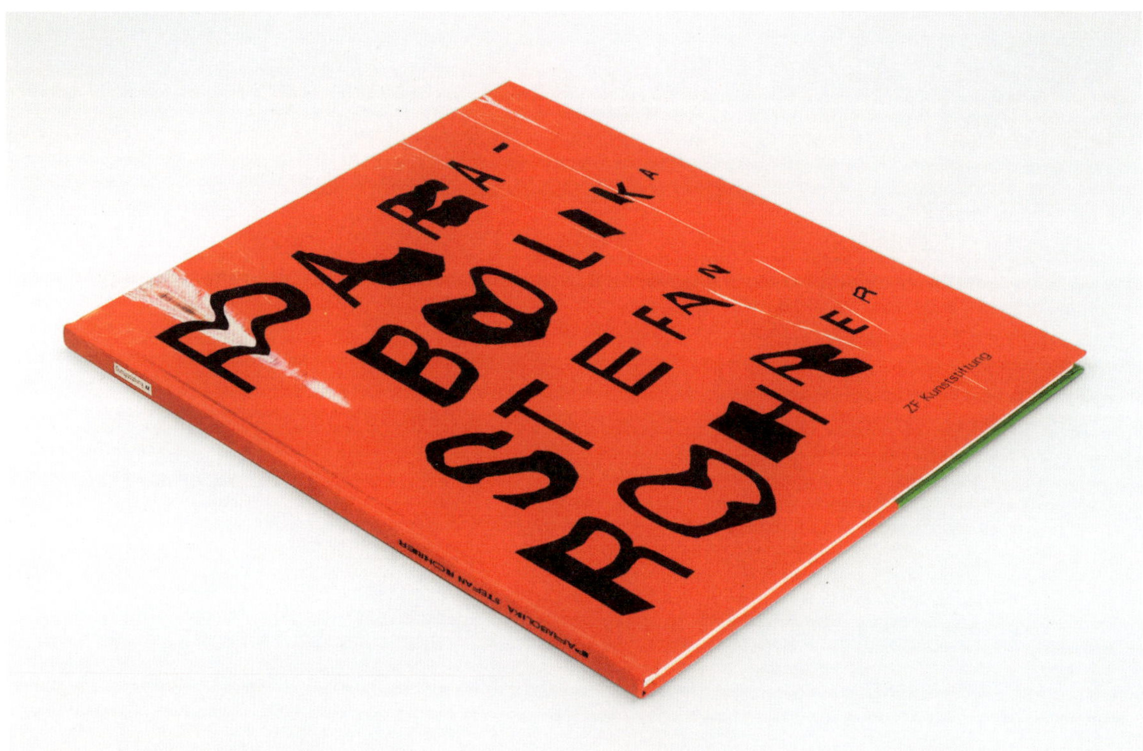


*As a kind of visual experience, what do you think about the "chaos" in graphic design?*

It can look beautiful or it can look ugly. But the visual experience of chaos is a matter of interpreting the nature of chaos. Design is mostly interpreted individually and everyone probably has his own definition where chaos starts and where it ends.

*What are your common approaches to produce a "chaotic" visual effect?*

It has all to do with the information you would like to provide in your design. If you have some elements you want to use in your design, to push them into extremes and you will cause the effect of chaos. Or you sit in front of your final design and you start to destroy it, ripping it apart in all elements. But in chaos there is a specific order, so there is no certain approach to produce chaos.

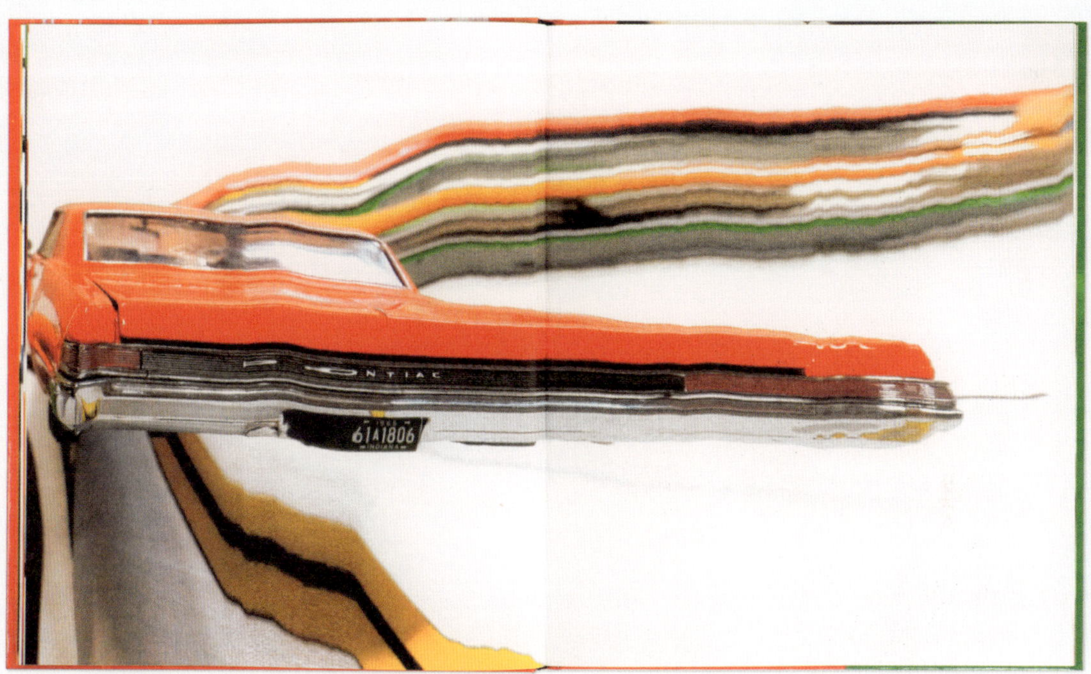


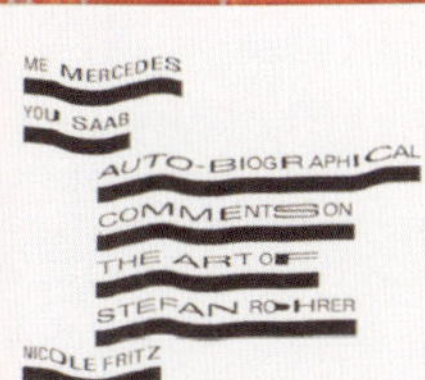


In a jury session on art in public space the works of Stefan Rohrer are presented to the president. At the sight of the grotesquely distorted Vespas and automobiles, the seasoned district administrator bursts out laughing, whereupon the atmosphere among those present feels palpably relaxed at a stroke.

This scene is no isolated case. Even at vernissages and in exhibitions of Stefan Rohrer, time and again I could observe visitors of every age breaking out into spontaneous laughter on viewing his work. But what or who were they laughing about, and why? I decided on an *auto-biographical* approach to track down the secret behind the automobile sculptures.

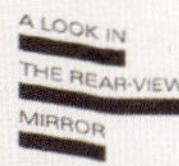


Automobiles have been a lifelong passion both for the artist and for the author from an early age. Whereas Stefan Rohrer was interested in gender-specific Carrera tracks and toy cars as is proper, my early childhood experience, whether I wanted it or not, also included fast cars with trees, houses and people flashing by. As the daughter of an automobile designer in a big German car company, I already had the pleasure of sitting at the wheel of a Mercedes at the age of five; and at ten I had tried driving not only box cars, but also on steep banks and off-road. Father's fascination with speed was especially obvious on Sundays when motor racing was being broadcast on television. Hour after hour the racing cars went round, uselessly in my view, but I regarded them with disinterested pleasure, and often wondered how anyone could fall into a rapt trance from the droning sound of racing car engines that made one oblivious to everything and everyone around.

However, one advantage of my socialisation with automobiles was that I was given my own car on passing my Abitur high school exam, as was the norm at the time, so that I could be mobile and flexible. One day, on my way to university, I underestimated the winter road conditions, with the result that I came in contact with the drawbacks of motoring early on. I overturned on an icy country road worthy of a stunt film, but by a wonder I climbed out unscathed from the vehicle, which was still new. What was previously a proud shiny black Ford Fiesta (1989 model) had been transformed from one second to the next, although that seemed like hours to me at the time of the rollover, into a sorrowful, battered total wreck on four wheels. Fully incapable of moving on its own, my first car, after just a short life, was towed by a recovery truck back in the direction it had come from shortly before. From then on I regarded the automobile as cult object with even greater mistrust, and increasingly devoted myself as an art and cultural historian to the symbolic significance of things in consumer culture from a discreet distance.

Stefan Rohrer, born in 1968, and like me a member of the *Generation Golf*, also corresponded in no way to the stereotype of a juvenile representative of the egoistic society, striving for success and consumption, in the way Florian Illies characterised teenagers of the 1980s in his bestseller *Generation Golf*[1]. Completely untypical of his generation, he also distanced himself from the automobile as a status symbol early on. "As a child I wanted to be a car designer. As an adult that was no longer acceptable for me politically. For me the subject was very ambivalent; later the fascination of the car was for me also somehow painful, and I questioned the car as a prestige object". Instead of single-mindedly pursuing a streamlined career as a car designer, Stefan Rohrer therefore began down-to-earth training as a stonemason, only afterwards deciding to

22

trace his inner creative instincts, first as an art student at the Burg Giebichenstein University of Art and Design in Halle, and later at the Academy of Art and Design in Stuttgart.

Possibly because he was spared the experience of a motor accident, and the real whiplash that not uncommonly accompanies it, Stefan Rohrer was able to keep his childhood fascination for the car into adulthood. With great momentum this then takes an affective course in the early artistic works.

Already during his studies the artist gave free rein to his childhood desire to find creative forms. Carried and attracted by the desire for movement, he developed his own individual DIY fantasy vehicle, using the ideas of toy cars and Vespas that he found discarded, as well as real car bodies.

An example is *Strudel* from 2004. In this case Rohrer single-handedly extended the roof and hood parts of a blue VW Golf 2 (in production 1983 – 1992) skyward in expressionist forms. By contrast, the work *Schleudertrauma Nr. 11* documented in this artist book shows a collision between two differently colored model cars, a Pontiac GTO (in production 1964 – 1965) and a Ford Mustang (in production 1964 – 1973), typical representatives of American Muscle Cars[2], at the moment when their wheels, rear ends, and miniature drivers are flung through the air by the impact, like a gloriole or halo. Similar to an instantaneous photograph, the climax of the centrifugal forces is frozen in a sculpture. Even though the artist lets the movement of the cars run on and does not show the collision, the catastrophe nevertheless ultimately resonates in the thoughts, and like a religious *Memento Mori*, continues inescapably in the minds of the viewers – with or without the whiplash experience.

Rohrer's graceful, strongly colored *Memento Mori* out of sheet metal are on the one hand in the tradition of Pop Art, since real everyday objects are transformed into art. However, the elegant painterly lines of *Schleudertrauma Nr. 11* and his other wall reliefs are in addition also reminiscent of the futurists, who glorified the automobile and the associated exhilaration of speed at the beginning of the last century. To this fascination for the movement and surface aesthetics of goods, the artist has now added with this artist book a further facet: he has scanned photographic images of the work *Schleudertrauma Nr. 11*, and reproduced them distorted and alienated, like the real work.

By grotesquely exaggerating the dynamic movement patterns of automobiles in his works, Rohrer overshoots in the truest sense of the word the positivistic faith in technology of the modern age directed toward the future. From a postmodern stance, he takes a sceptical and ironic view of the forward looking positivistic optimization paradigm of the performance society: *faster, higher, further* in the here and now. One possible explanation for the laughter of the district administrator?

The postmodern distance of the artist from the sham of the affluent society with its standardized facade identities is also clear in the work *Lothar 2007* in a humorous way. In an allusion to hurricane Lothar, Rohrer subverts the uniformity of lower-middle class suburban estates by formally *really sorting out* the miniature model terraced cottages, to use a colloquial expression.

While Stefan Rohrer, still relatively almost unnoticed by the public, step by step continued to develop for himself and refine his constructive language of form using scrap parts, and invented forms of his own design, I was at the University of Tübingen as an intellectual. To the chagrin of my father, at an advanced stage I came in contact with culture critical ideas that in the 1980s were increasingly dealing with the ambivalence of a construction of reality centered around the automobile.

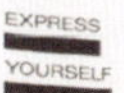


Particularly formative for me were the French sociologists, with books like *Distinction*[3] by Pierre Bourdieu, and *The System of Objects*[4] by Jean Baudrillard, that show how people in the modern consumer society look to the culture of things for identity construction and self-expression. Along the lines of *Me Prada, You Armani*[5] the functional and utility value of things falls increasingly into the background in lifestyle capitalism. More important than the function of things is what the goods signify, and the emotions they arouse among consumers. "We are what we buy"[6], according to the latest feuilleton-style edition of the writer Robert Misik on this insight. "I am what I am because I wear Prada and not Armani". With products we buy lifestyles that fit to us, and model our own identity. "People", writes the cultural theorist Hartmut Böhme "expand their ego boundaries to ever more object realms. Never before was the world of things so dense, diverse, seductive, artificial, fascinating..."[7].

It is obvious that the automobile in particular possesses great potential for ego tuning, and is exactly predestined for an outwardly oriented interpretation in such a way. Along the lines *Me Mercedes, You Porsche*, the automobile industry offers a whole collection of automobile identities, off the shelf so to speak: from tough SUV driver to the intellectual with a Swedish car.

23

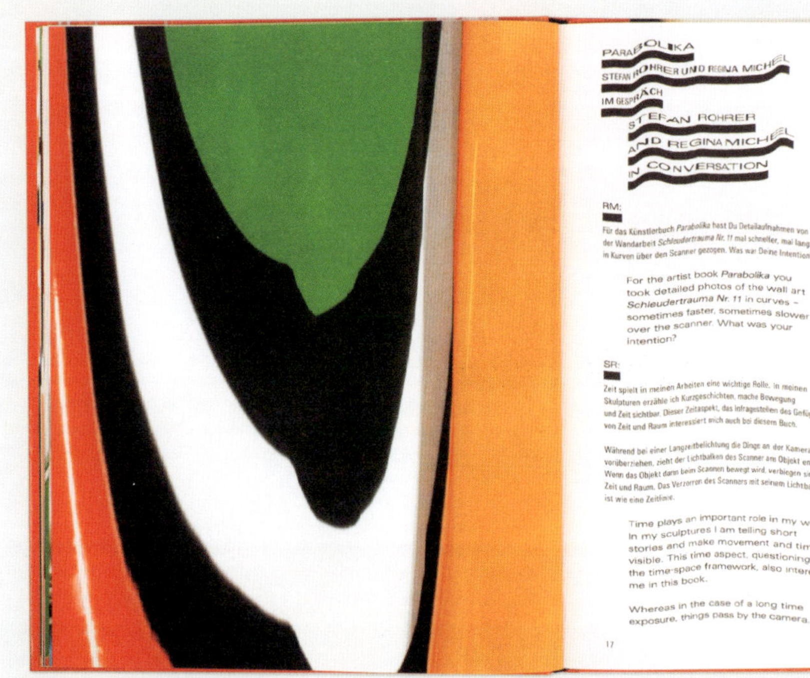

PARABOLIKA
STEFAN ROHRER UND REGINA MICHEL
IM GESPRÄCH

STEFAN ROHRER
AND REGINA MICHEL
IN CONVERSATION

RM:

Für das Künstlerbuch *Parabolika* hast Du Detailaufnahmen von der Wandarbeit *Schleudertrauma Nr. 11* mal schneller, mal langsamer in Kurven über den Scanner gezogen. Was war Deine Intention?

For the artist book *Parabolika* you took detailed photos of the wall art *Schleudertrauma Nr. 11* in curves – sometimes faster, sometimes slower – over the scanner. What was your intention?

SR:

Zeit spielt in meinen Arbeiten eine wichtige Rolle. In meinen Skulpturen erzähle ich Kurzgeschichten, mache Bewegung und Zeit sichtbar. Dieser Zeitaspekt, das Infragestellen des Gefüges von Zeit und Raum interessiert mich auch bei diesem Buch.

Während bei einer Langzeitbelichtung die Dinge an der Kamera vorüberziehen, zieht der Lichtbalken des Scanner am Objekt entlang. Wenn das Objekt dann beim Scannen bewegt wird, verbiegen sich Zeit und Raum. Das Verzerren des Scanners mit seinem Lichtbalken ist wie eine Zeitlinie.

Time plays an important role in my work. In my sculptures I am telling short stories and make movement and time visible. This time aspect, questioning the time-space framework, also interests me in this book.

Whereas in the case of a long time exposure, things pass by the camera, the light bar of the scanner is drawn along the object. If the object is then moved during scanning, time and space warp. The distortion of the scanner with its light bar is like a timeline.

RM:

Manche dieser Scans erinnern auf den ersten Blick an abstrakte Gemälde …

At first glance, some of these scans are reminiscent of abstract paintings –

SR:

Für mich wird der malerische Aspekt in meinen Objekten immer wichtiger. Bereits meine Entwürfe, die als erster Schritt zu meinen Skulpturen entstehen, sind eigentlich *informelle Zeichnungen*. Es gibt für mich immer einen Anlass aus dem heraus die Bewegung in meinen Arbeiten entsteht. Diese Bewegung finde und entwickle ich durch gestische Zeichnungen, die ich dann in Skulpturen übersetze.

Dieses Buch ist nun der Versuch, durch den Einsatz eines Scanners, neue Bilder von meinen Skulpturen zu generieren, die die malerische Qualität meiner Arbeiten hervorheben und von der vordergründigen Dinglichkeit wegführen.

Viele der Scans sind trotz ihrer Verfremdung immer noch als Details meiner Arbeit zu lesen. Selbst die auf den ersten Blick völlig abstrakten Bilder, lassen sich beispielsweise durch die Reflektionen in der Wandarbeit *Schleudertrauma Nr. 11* verorten. Wenn wir etwas sehen und nicht gleich verstehen, dreht und schraubt unser Gehirn solange an den Stellschrauben, bis es unserem Verstand

17

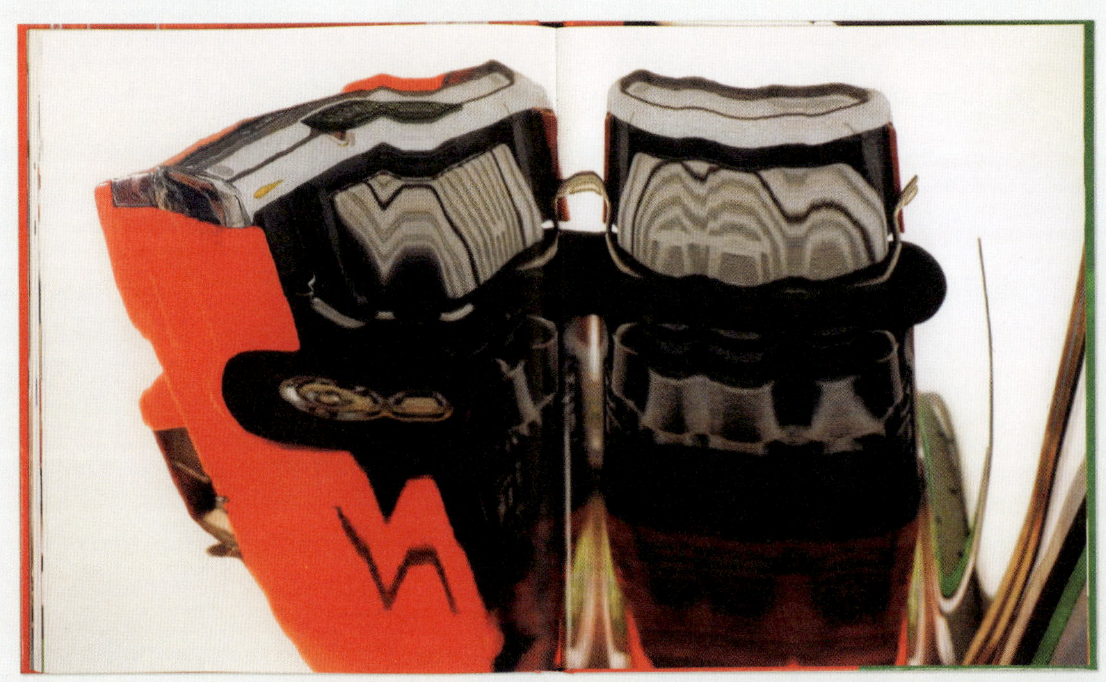

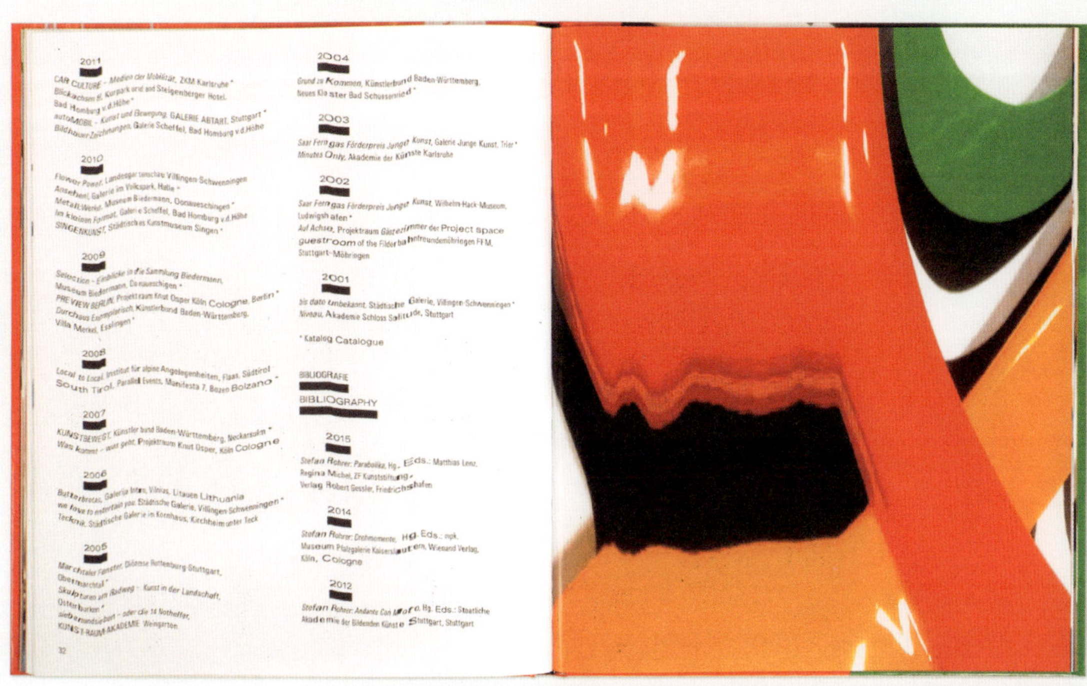

2011

CAR CULTURE – Medien der Mobilität, ZKM Karlsruhe *
Blickachsen 8, Kurpark und and Steigenberger Hotel, Bad Homburg v.d.Höhe *
autoMOBIL – Kunst und Bewegung, GALERIE ABTART, Stuttgart *
Bildhauer Zeichnungen, Galerie Scheffel, Bad Homburg v.d.Höhe

2010

Flower Power, Landesgartenschau Villingen-Schwenningen
Ansehen!, Galerie im Volkspark, Halle *
Metall:Werke, Museum Biedermann, Donaueschingen *
Im kleinen Format, Galerie Scheffel, Bad Homburg v.d.Höhe
SINGENKUNST, Städtisches Kunstmuseum Singen *

2009

Selection – Einblicke in die Sammlung Biedermann, Museum Biedermann, Donaueschigen *
PREVIEW BERLIN, Projektraum Knut Osper Köln Cologne, Berlin *
Durchaus Exemplarisch, Künstlerbund Baden-Württemberg, Villa Merkel, Esslingen *

2008

Local to Local, Institut für alpine Angelegenheiten, Flaas, Südtirol South Tirol, Parallel Events, Manifesta 7, Bozen Bolzano *

2007

KUNSTBEWEGT, Künstlerbund Baden-Württemberg, Neckarsulm *
Was kommt – was geht, Projektraum Knut Osper, Köln Cologne

2006

Butterbrotas, Galerija Intro, Vilnius, Litauen Lithuania
we love to entertain you, Städtische Galerie, Villingen-Schwenningen *
Tecknik, Städtische Galerie im Kornhaus, Kirchheim unter Teck

2005

Marchtaler Fenster, Diözese Rottenburg-Stuttgart, Obermarchtal *
Skulpturen am Radweg – Kunst in der Landschaft, Osterburken *
siebenundsiebzig – oder die 14 Nothelfer, KUNST-RAUM-AKADEMIE Weingarten

32

2004

Grund zu Kommen, Künstlerbund Baden-Württemberg, Neues Kloster Bad Schussenried *

2003

Saar Ferngas Förderpreis Junger Kunst, Galerie Junge Kunst, Trier *
Minutes Only, Akademie der Künste Karlsruhe

2002

Saar Ferngas Förderpreis Junger Kunst, Wilhelm-Hack-Museum, Ludwigshafen *
Auf Achse, Projektraum Gästezimmer der Project space guestroom of the Filderbahnfreundemöhringen FFM, Stuttgart-Möhringen

2001

bis dato unbekannt, Städtische Galerie, Villingen-Schwenningen *
Niveau, Akademie Schloss Solitude, Stuttgart

* Katalog Catalogue

BIBLIOGRAFIE

BIBLIOGRAPHY

2015

Stefan Rohrer: Parabolika, Hg., Eds.: Matthias Lenz, Regina Michel, ZF Kunststiftung, Verlag Robert Gessler, Friedrichshafen

2014

Stefan Rohrer: Drehmomente, Hg. Eds.: mpk, Museum Pfalzgalerie Kaiserslautern, Wienand Verlag, Köln, Cologne

2012

Stefan Rohrer: Andante Con Moto, Hg. Eds.: Staatliche Akademie der Bildenden Künste Stuttgart, Stuttgart

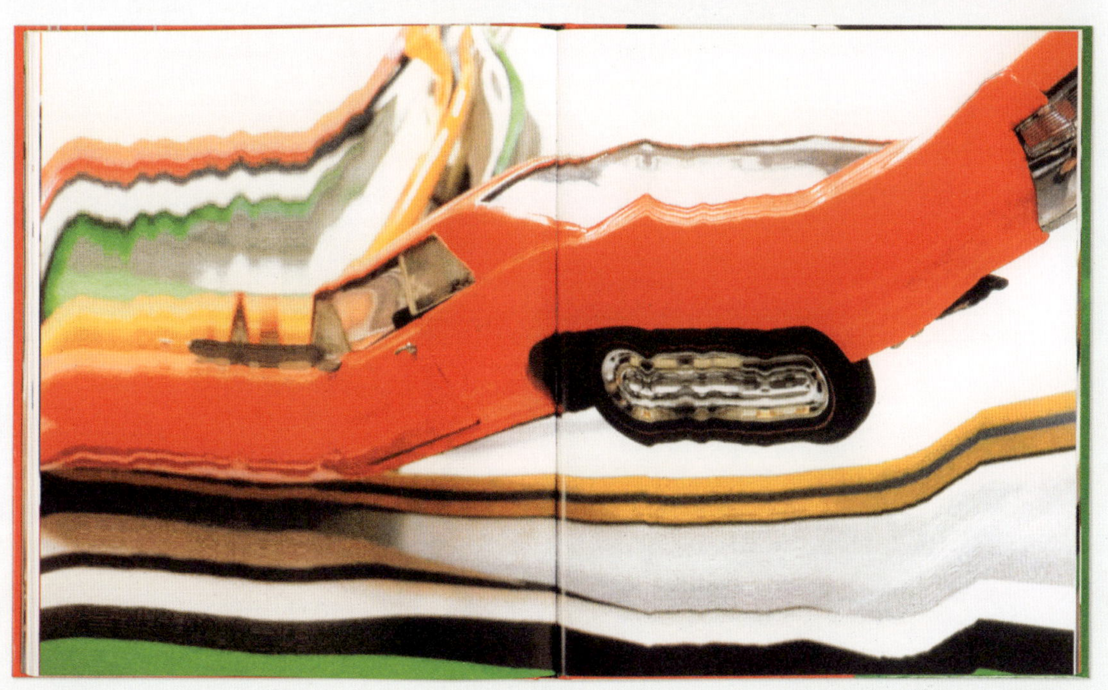

# UNSOUND FESTIVAL 2016

The design was made to reflect the theme of Unsound Music Festival 2016—Discolation. The artist used computer glitches and distortions to remind individuals of electronic music which was important for the whole event. Besides, the poster was made unreadable at first sight in order to get people closer to it.

Designer: Dawid Koruszowic

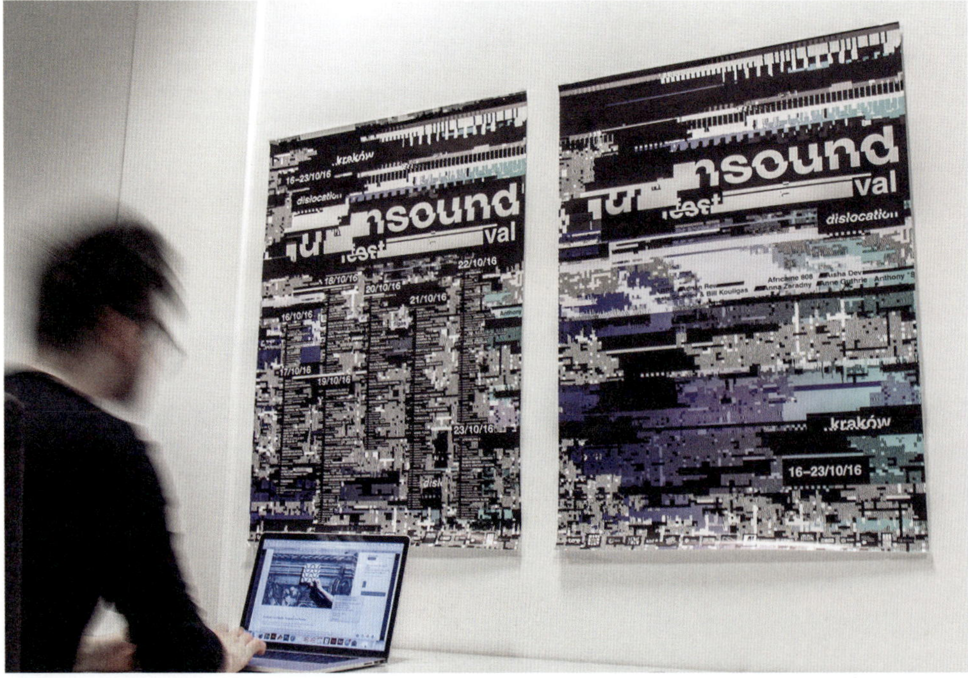

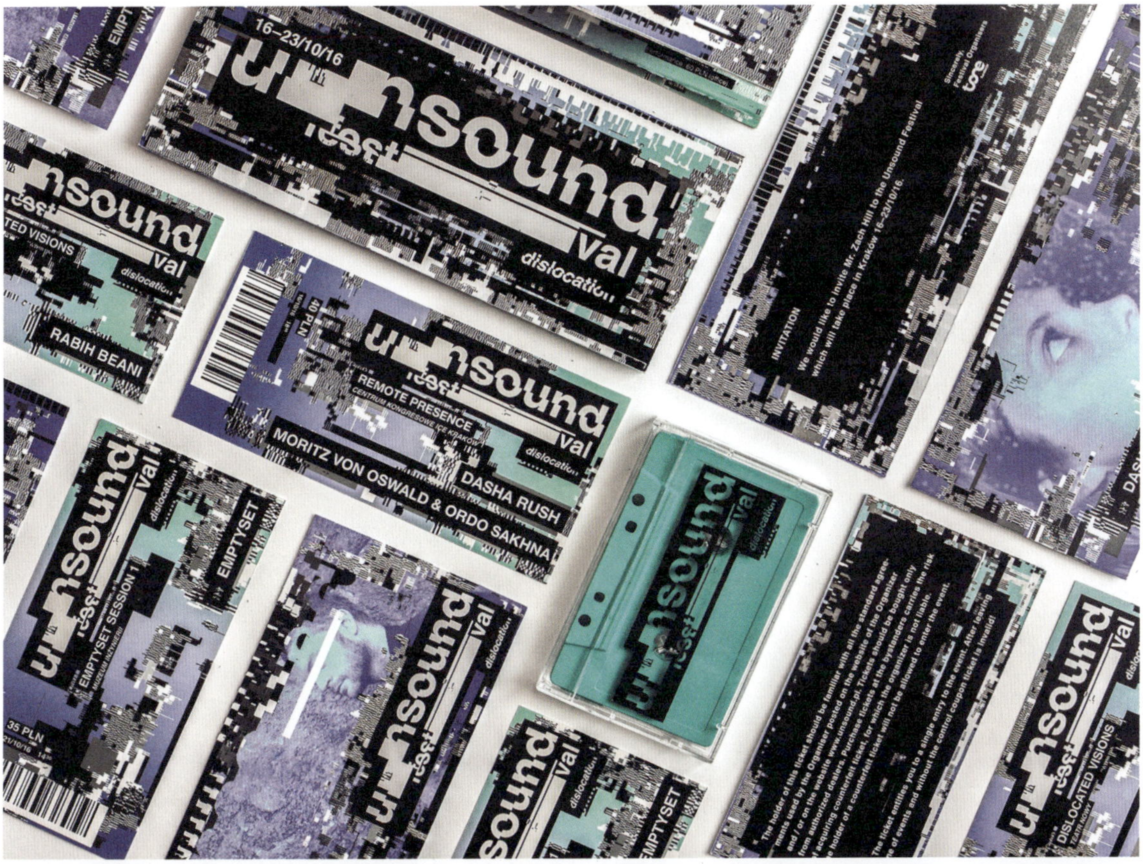
16–23/10/16
unsound
val
dislocation
DISLOCATED VISIONS
RABIH BEANI
REMOTE PRESENCE
DASHA RUSH
MORITZ VON OSWALD & ORDO SAKHNA
EMPTYSET SESSION 1
EMPTYSET
35 PLN
40 PLN
INVITATION
We would like to invite Mr. Zach Hill to the Unsound Festival
which will take place in Kraków 16–23/10/16.

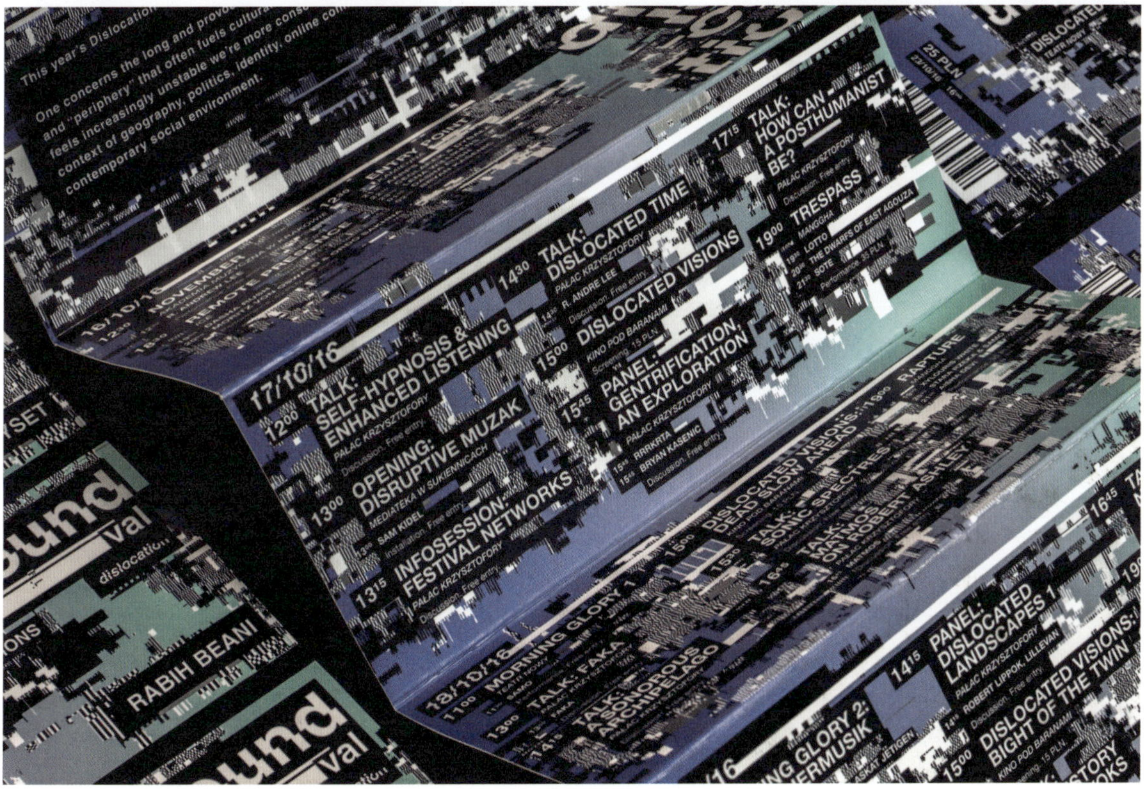
This year's Dislocation
17/10/16
TALK: SELF-HYPNOSIS & ENHANCED LISTENING
PAŁAC KRZYSZTOFORY
OPENING: DISRUPTIVE MUZAK
INFOSESSION: FESTIVAL NETWORKS
TALK: DISLOCATED TIME
DISLOCATED VISIONS
KINO POD BARANAMI
PANEL: GENTRIFICATION, AN EXPLORATION
TALK: HOW CAN A POSTHUMANIST BE?
TRESPASS
18/10/16
MORNING GLORY 1
TALK: FAKA
PANEL: DISLOCATED LANDSCAPES 1
DISLOCATED VISIONS: BIGHT OF THE TWIN
RABIH BEANI
25 PLN

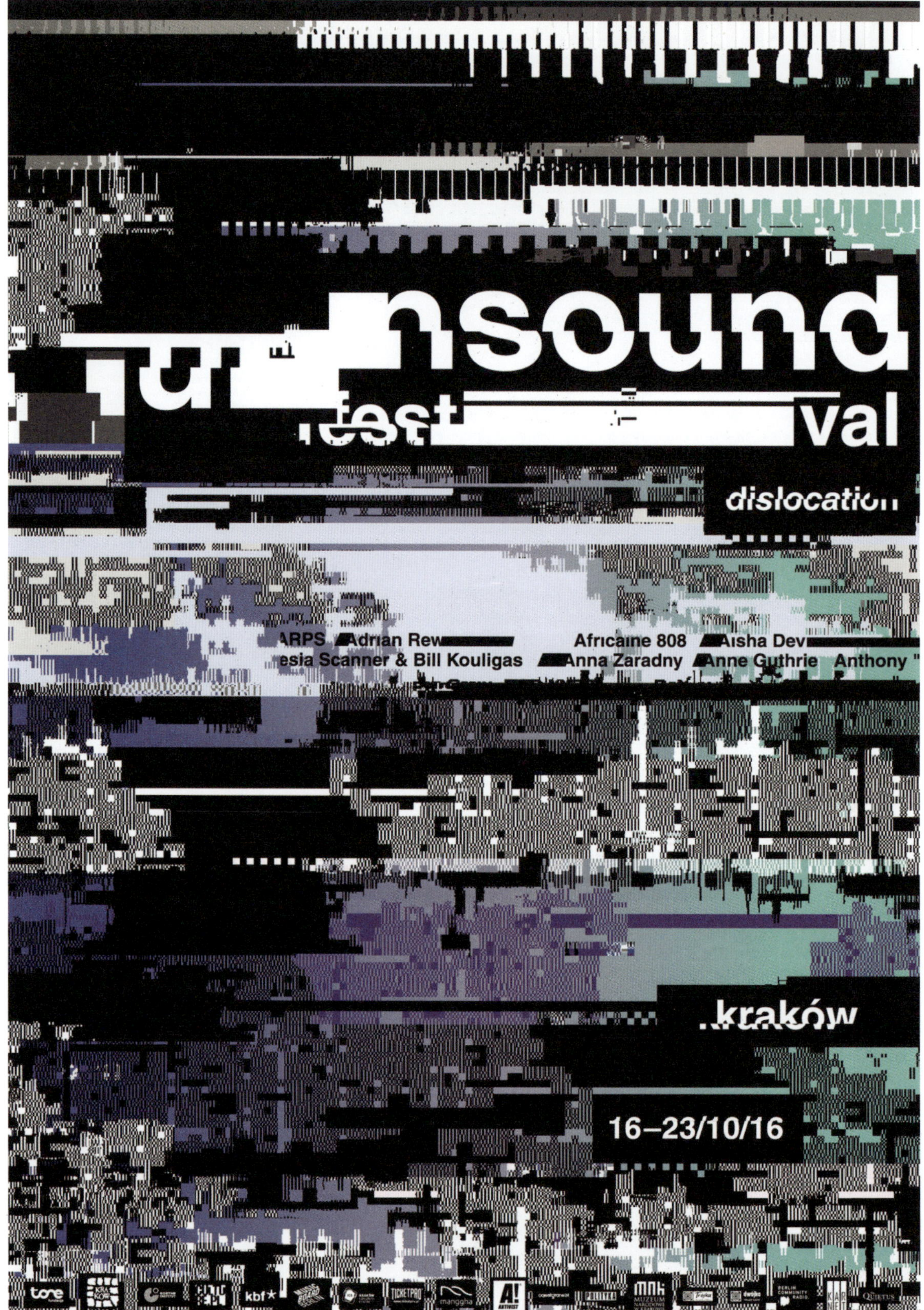
nsound
val
dislocation
Africaine 808
Anna Zaradny
Anne Guthrie
Anthony
Scanner & Bill Kouligas
kraków
16–23/10/16

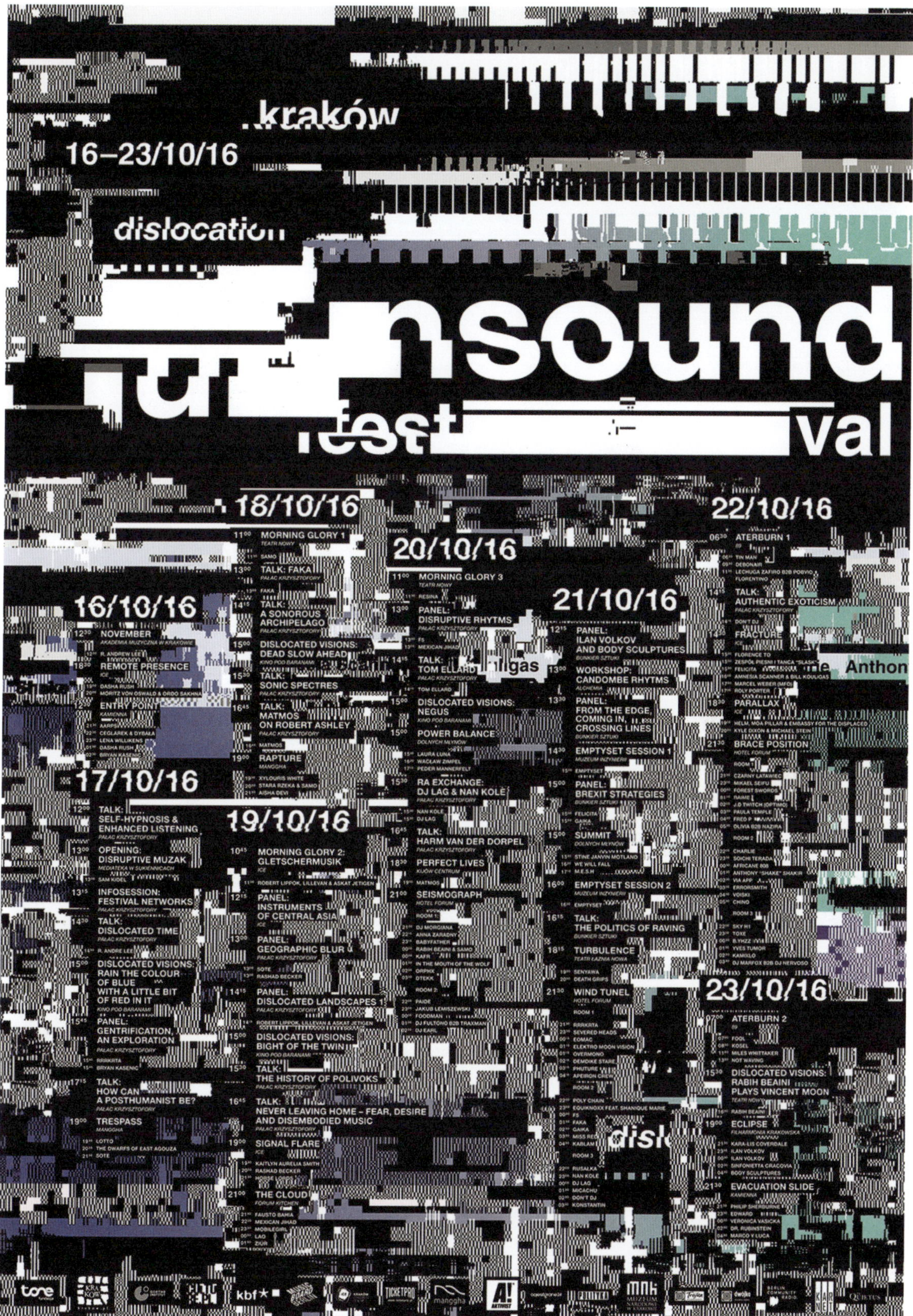
kraków
16–23/10/16
dislocation
nsound
val
18/10/16
MORNING GLORY 1
TALK: FAKA
TALK: A SONOROUS ARCHIPELAGO
DISLOCATED VISIONS: DEAD SLOW AHEAD
TALK: SONIC SPECTRES
TALK: MATMOS ON ROBERT ASHLEY
RAPTURE
20/10/16
MORNING GLORY 3
PANEL: DISRUPTIVE RHYTMS
TALK: TOM ELLARD
DISLOCATED VISIONS: NEGUS
POWER BALANCE
RA EXCHANGE: DJ LAG & NAN KOLÈ
TALK: HARM VAN DER DORPEL
PERFECT LIVES
SEISMOGRAPH
22/10/16
ATERBURN 1
TALK: AUTHENTIC EXOTICISM
FRACTURE
PARALLAX
BRACE POSITION
16/10/16
NOVEMBER
REMOTE PRESENCE
ENTRY POINT
21/10/16
PANEL: ILAN VOLKOV AND BODY SCULPTURES
WORKSHOP: CANDOMBE RHYTMS
PANEL: FROM THE EDGE, COMING IN, CROSSING LINES
EMPTYSET SESSION 1
PANEL: BREXIT STRATEGIES
SUMMIT
EMPTYSET SESSION 2
TALK: THE POLITICS OF RAVING
TURBULENCE
WIND TUNEL
17/10/16
TALK: SELF-HYPNOSIS & ENHANCED LISTENING
OPENING: DISRUPTIVE MUZAK
INFOSESSION: FESTIVAL NETWORKS
TALK: DISLOCATED TIME
DISLOCATED VISIONS: RAIN THE COLOUR OF BLUE WITH A LITTLE BIT OF RED IN IT
PANEL: GENTRIFICATION, AN EXPLORATION
TALK: HOW CAN A POSTHUMANIST BE?
TRESPASS
19/10/16
MORNING GLORY 2: GLETSCHERMUSIK
PANEL: INSTRUMENTS OF CENTRAL ASIA
PANEL: GEOGRAPHIC BLUR
PANEL: DISLOCATED LANDSCAPES
DISLOCATED VISIONS: BIGHT OF THE TWIN
TALK: THE HISTORY OF POLIVOKS
TALK: NEVER LEAVING HOME – FEAR, DESIRE AND DISEMBODIED MUSIC
SIGNAL FLARE
THE CLOUD
23/10/16
ATERBURN 2
DISLOCATED VISIONS: RABIH BEAINI PLAYS VINCENT MOON
ECLIPSE
EVACUATION SLIDE
kbf
manggha

# EN ATTENDANT NORDIK IMPAKT

To cause a surprise amongst electronic music lovers, the festival team hosted a pre-event entitled "En attendant Nördik Impakt" (Pending Nördik Impakt) at the Cargö Concert Hall. The agency has designed a powerful, electronic and modern black and white visual identity. The festival's major principles regarding typography and layout have been kept and reused for consistency.

Studio: Murmure
Designer: Julien Alirol, Paul Ressencourt

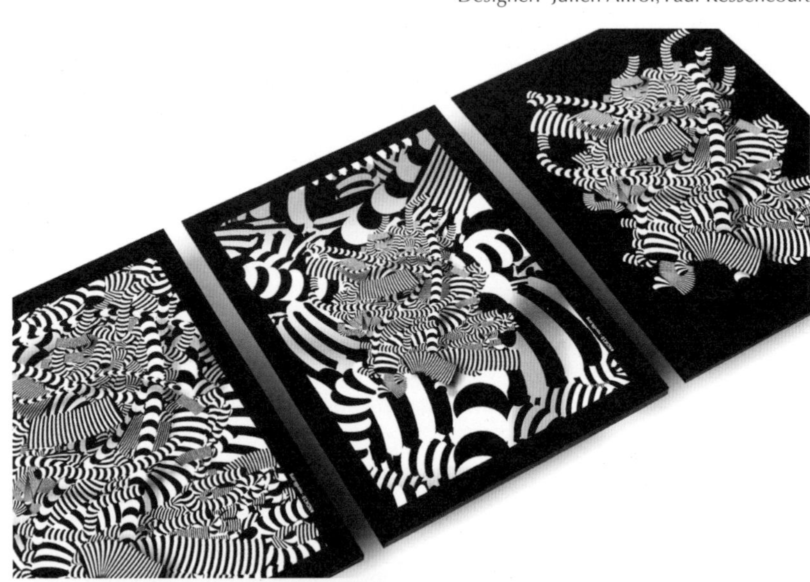

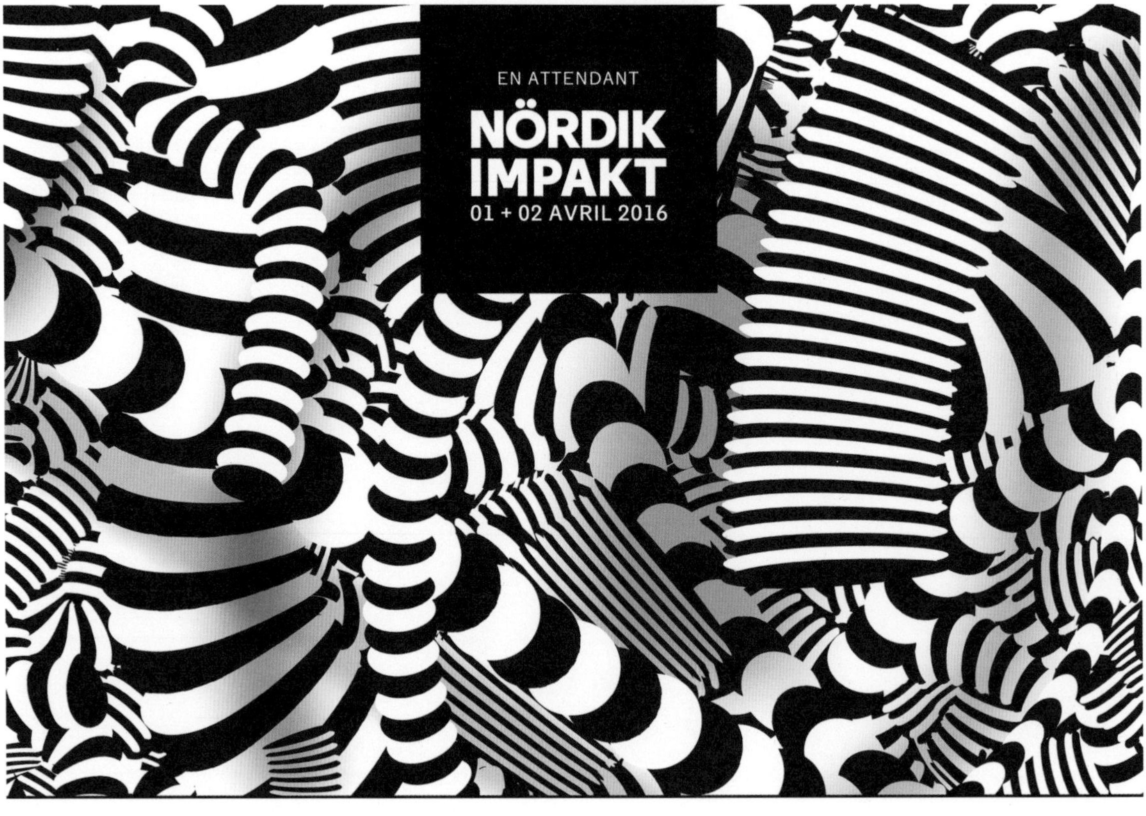

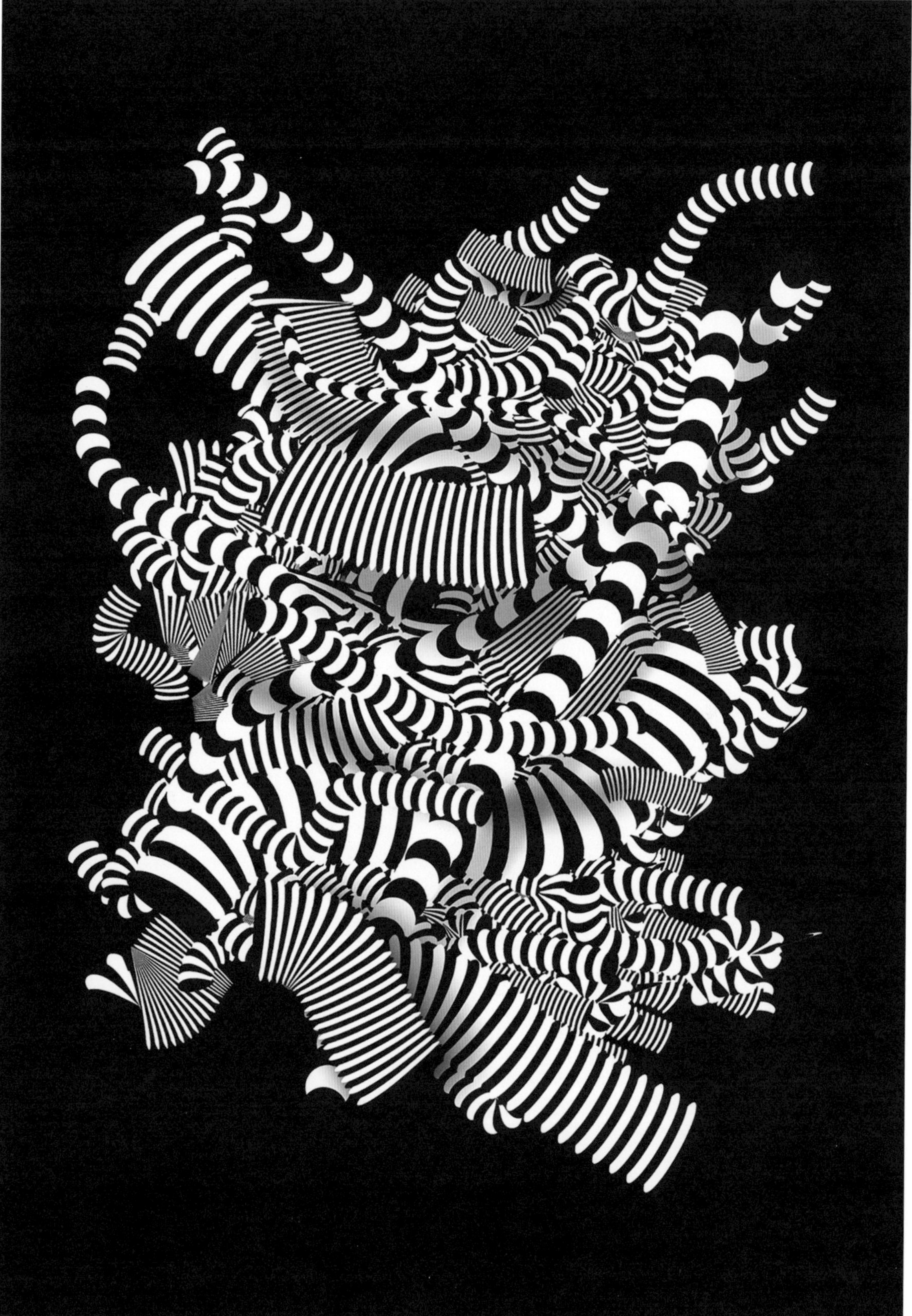

# SPEAK TO THE EYES

The research exhibition "Speak to the Eye" studies information visualization with a specific focus on the Late Ottoman and the Early Turkish Republic periods while also taking into account the history of information design in the West.

Designer: Erman Yilmaz, Sarp sozd inler

# MURAL ISTANBUL 2017

Mural Istanbul is one of the city's most prominent street art festivals. Bringing in amazing street artists from abroad to paint building-sized murals, the Yeldegirmeni neighborhood has been turned into an open-air museum since the festival's inception in 2012.

Designer: Erman Yilmaz

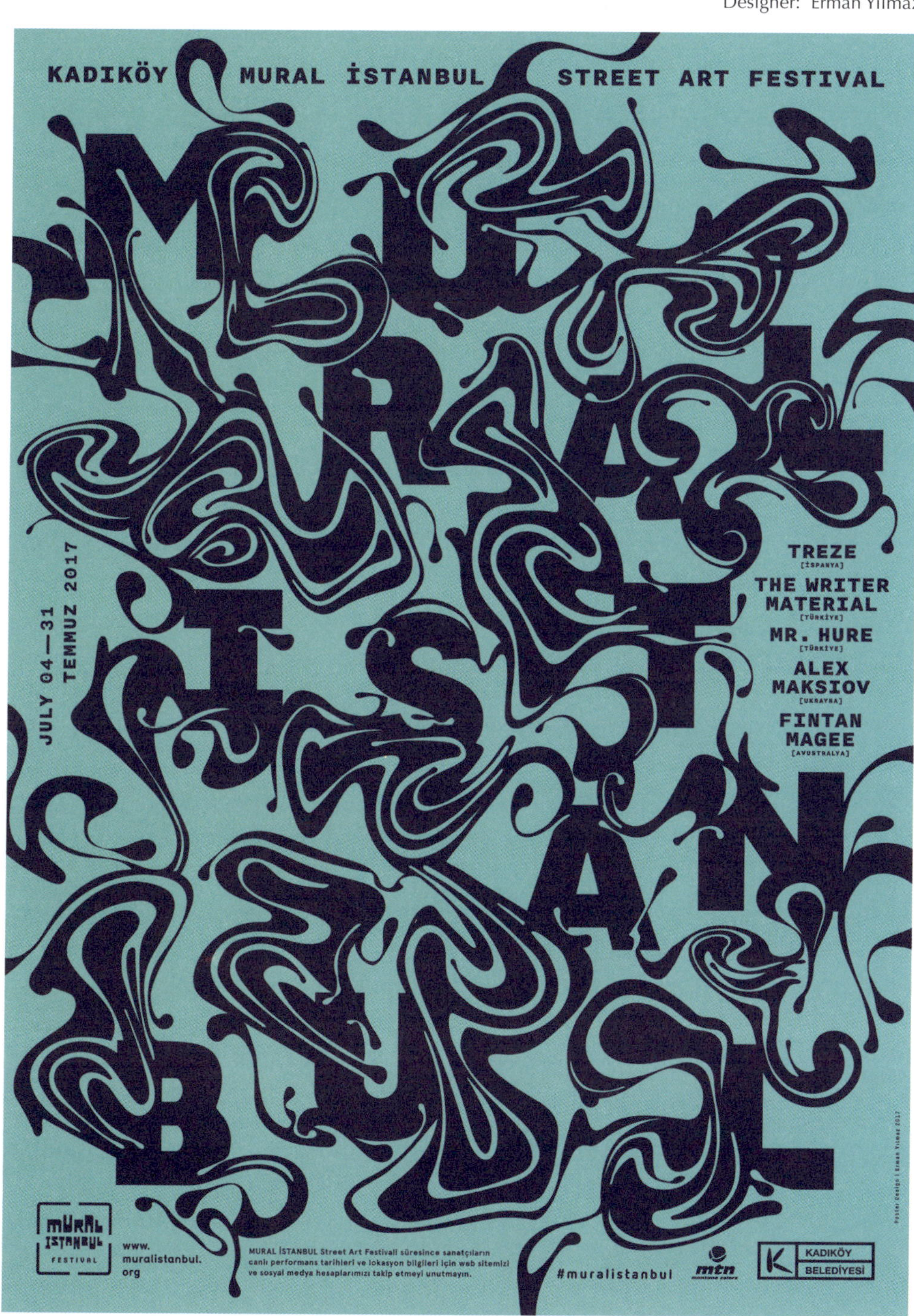

# EARTH AND AIR AND RAIN

This is an artwork and design for EARTH AND AIR AND RAIN, a new EP collaborated by Microburst and My Panda Shall Fly.

Designer: Emir Šehanović

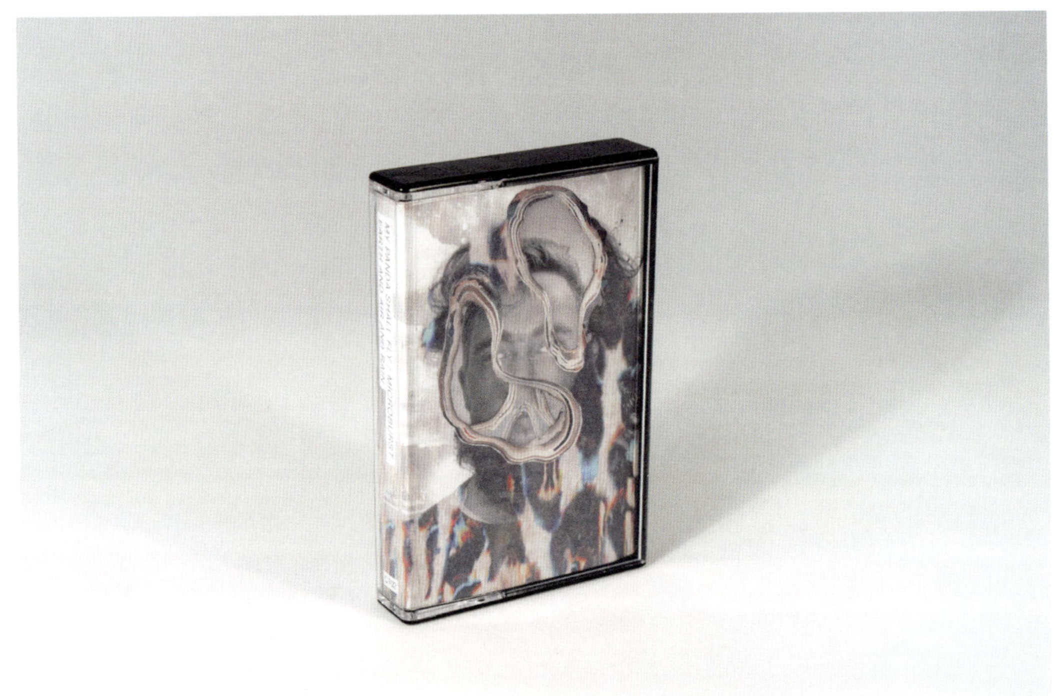

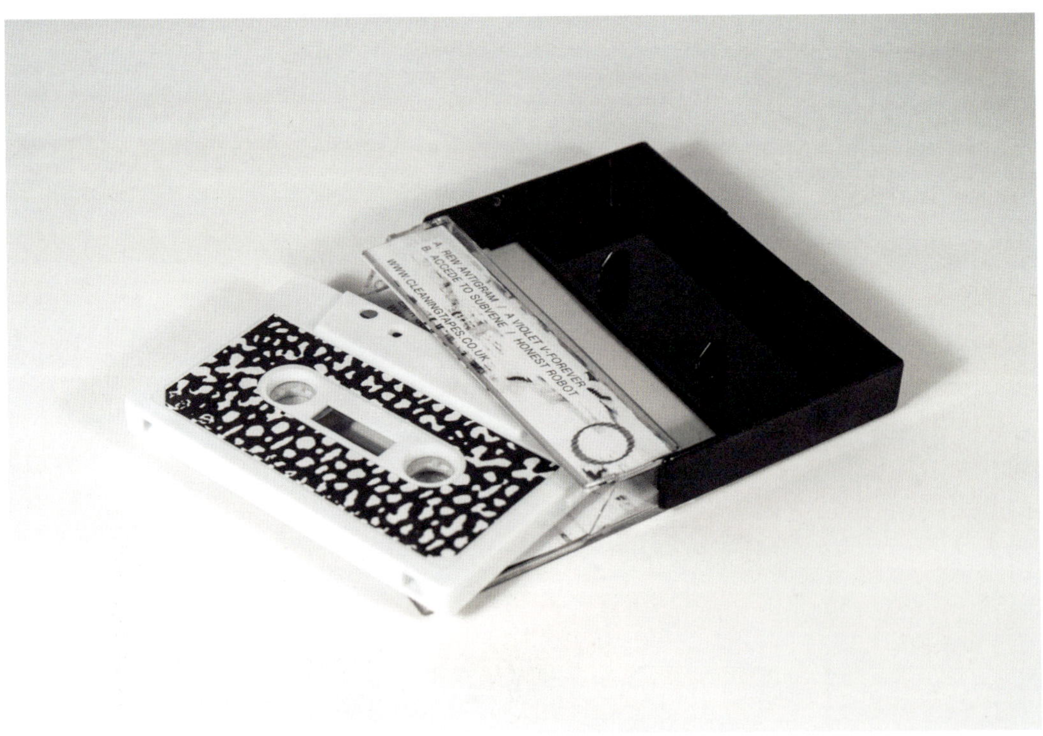

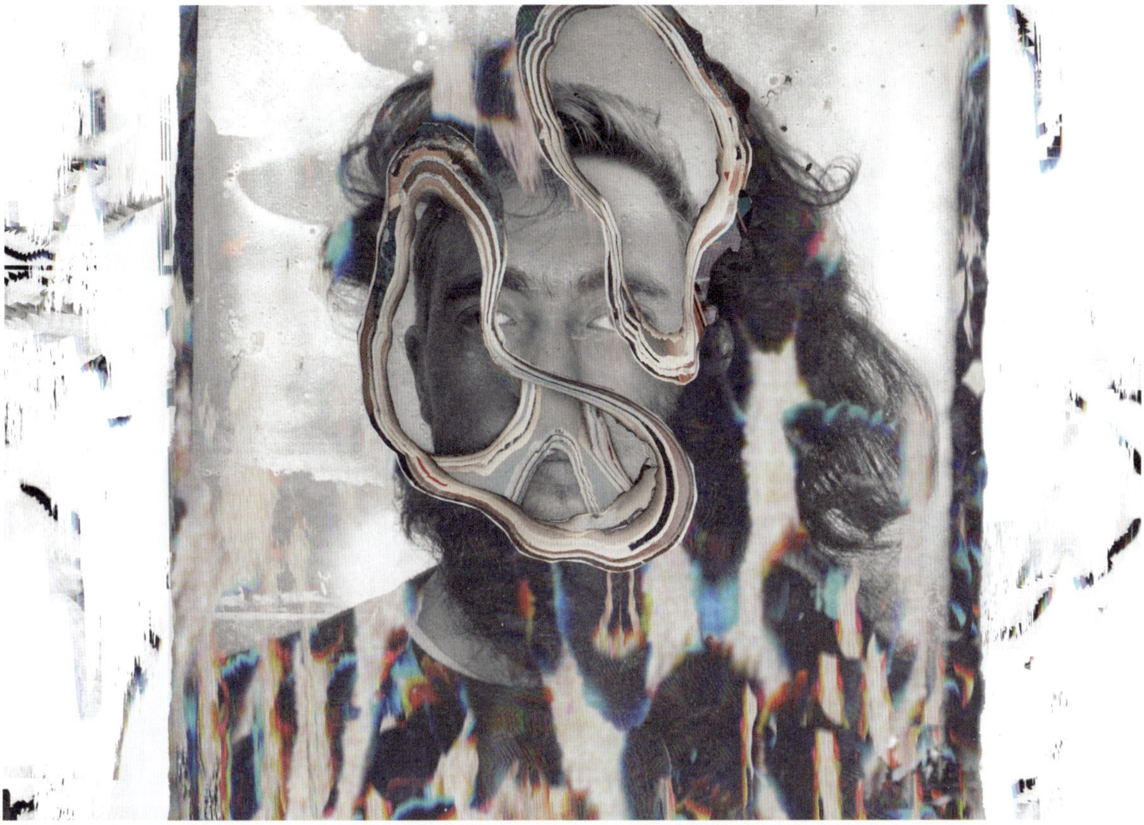

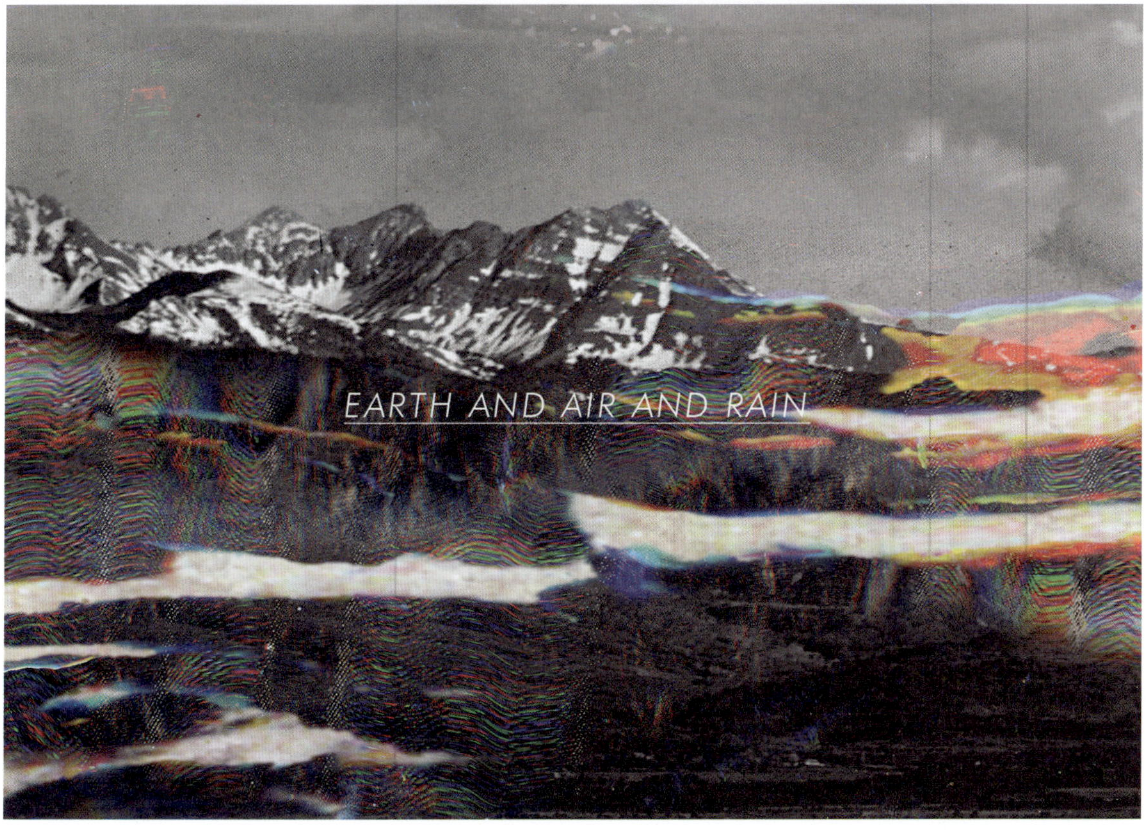

EARTH AND AIR AND RAIN

# NUITS SONORES

Nuits Sonores is an electronic music festival held annually in Lyon, France. The designers prensented Lyon the way they envisioned it, just like the visitors of the festival shaped Lyon the way they envisioned it—it is a city that is constantly changing and adapting to the rhythms and melodies of music.

Studio: Feixen

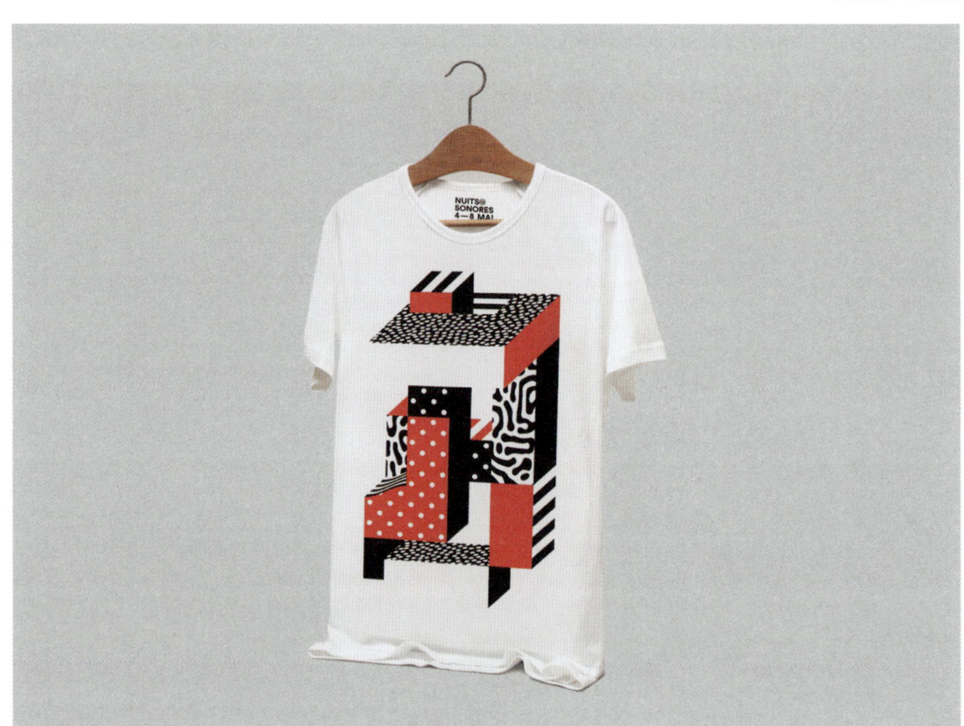


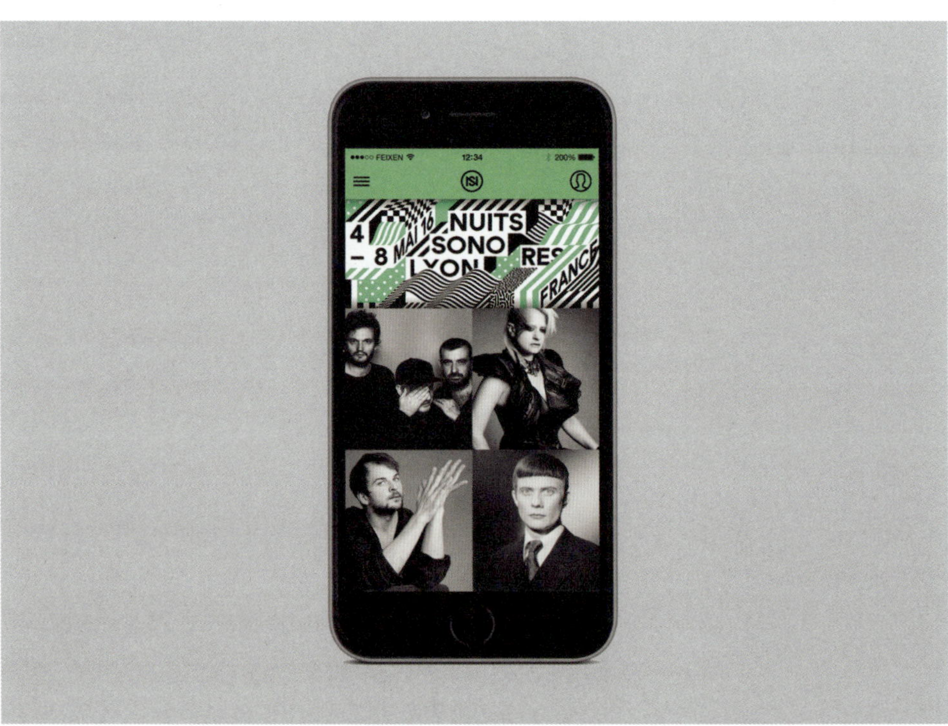

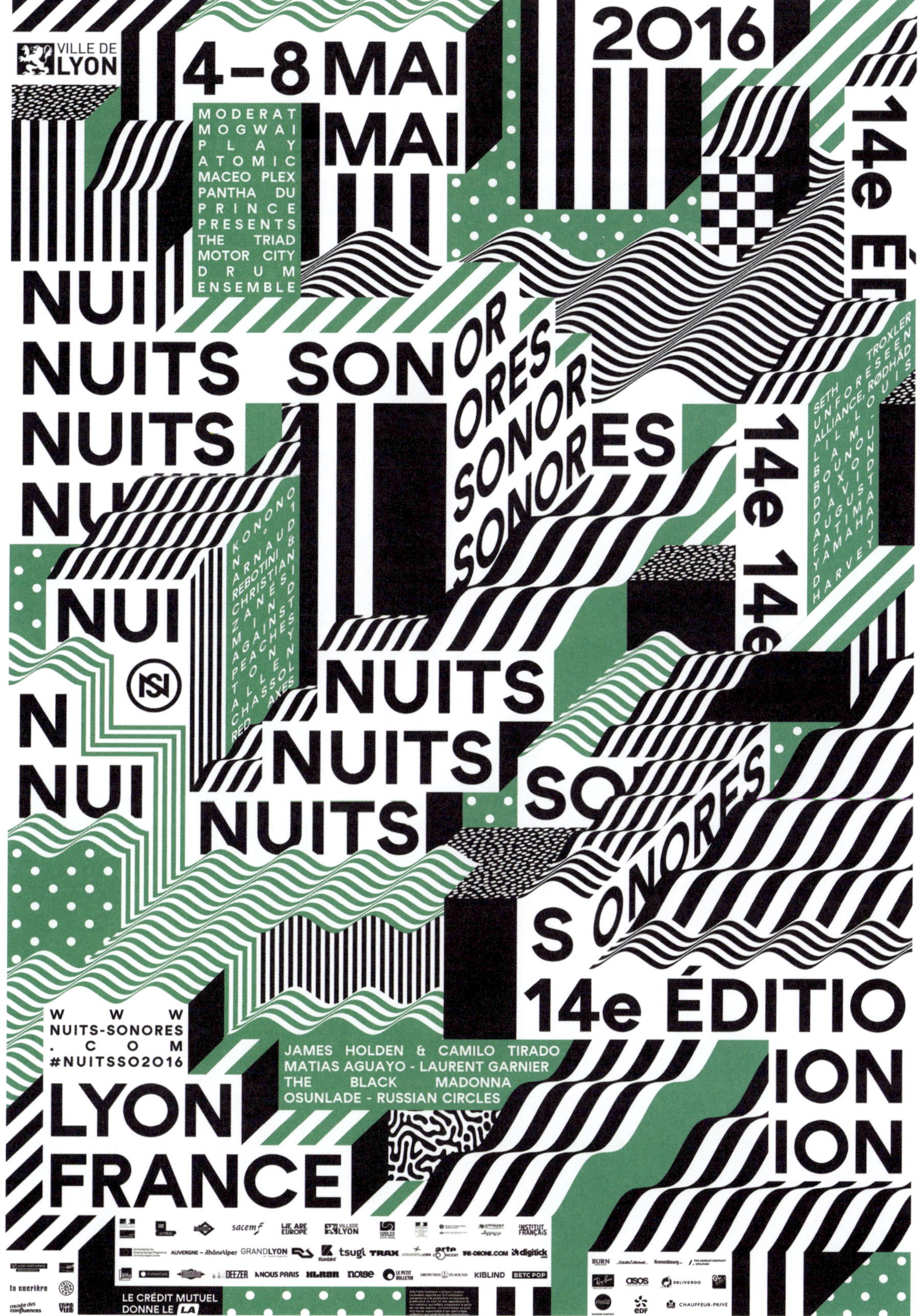
VILLE DE LYON
4–8 MAI
MAI
2016
14e ÉDITION
MODERAT
MOGWAI
PLAY
ATOMIC
MACEO PLEX
PANTHA DU PRINCE PRESENTS THE TRIAD
MOTOR CITY DRUM ENSEMBLE
NUI
NUITS SON
NUITS
NU
OR
ORES
SONOR
SONORES
SONORES
14e 14e 14e
SETH TROXLER
UNFORESEEN ALLIANCE, RØDHÅD
LIL LOUIS
BADBOUNOU
DIXON
DAVID AUGUST
FATIMA YAMAHA
JD HARVEY
KONONO N°1
ARNAUD REBOTINI & CHRISTIAN ZANÉSI
MIND AGAINST
PEACHES
TALE OF US
CHASSOL
RED AXES
NUI
N
NUI
NUITS
NUITS
NUITS
SO
SONORES
S ONORES
14e ÉDITIO
ION
ION
WWW.NUITS-SONORES.COM
#NUITSSO2016
JAMES HOLDEN & CAMILO TIRADO
MATIAS AGUAYO - LAURENT GARNIER
THE BLACK MADONNA
OSUNLADE - RUSSIAN CIRCLES
LYON
FRANCE
LE CRÉDIT MUTUEL DONNE LE LA

## RUÍDO

This series of posters investigates how a day-to-day aesthetic experience can be configured as noise. The typographic work was done manually with the use of collage and Letraset, in addition to digital.

Designer: Fernanda Gontijo

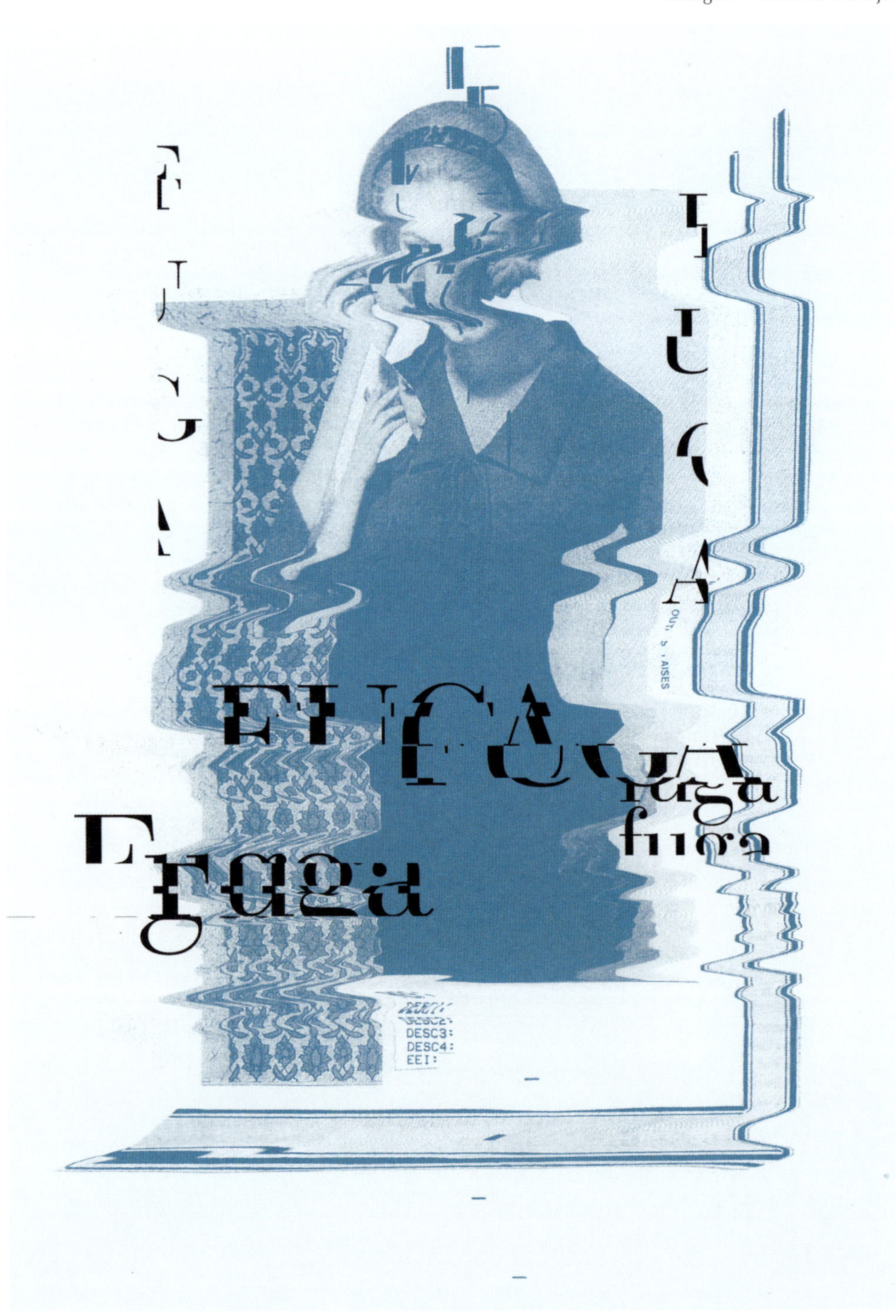

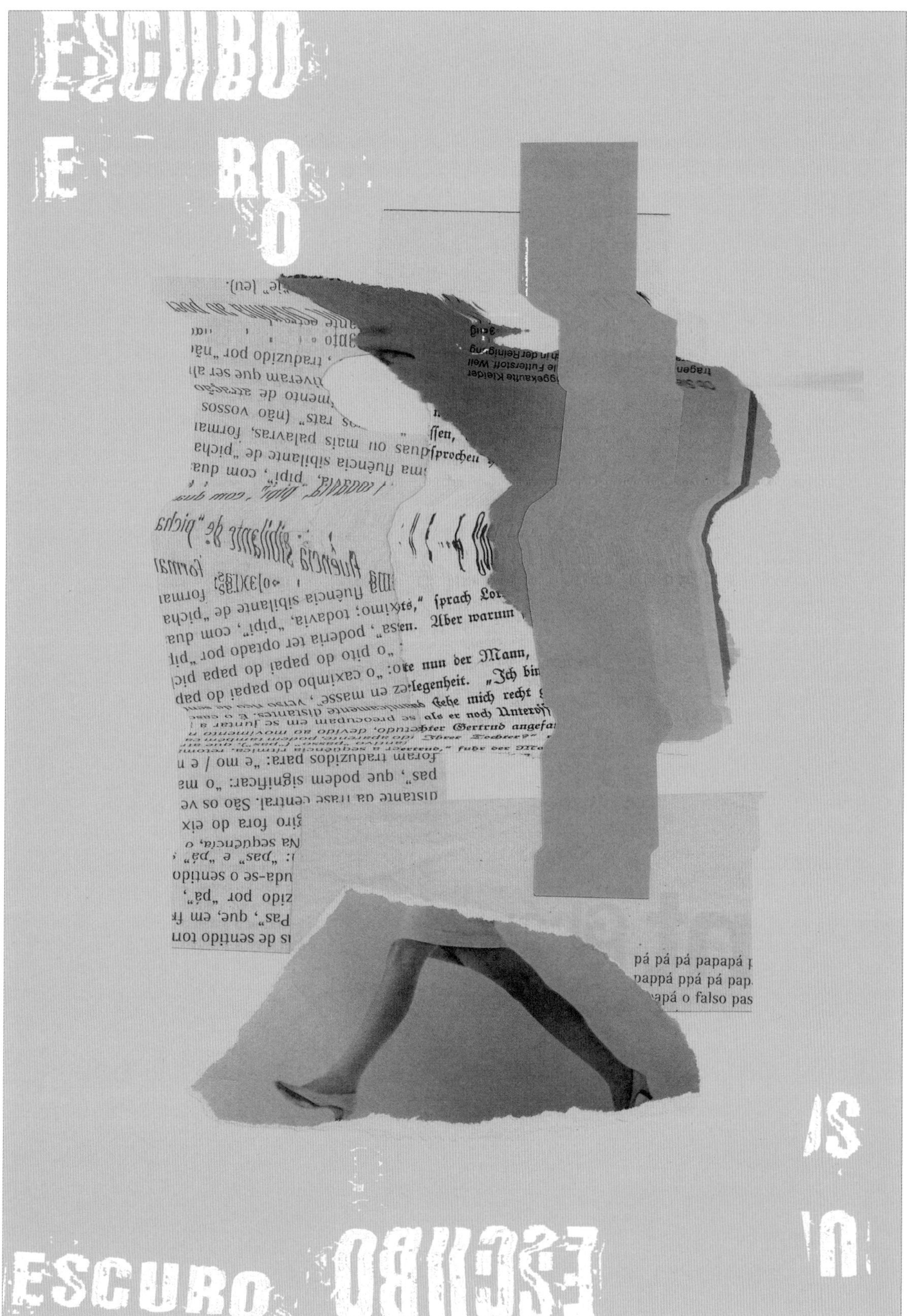
ESCURO
pá pá pá papapá
pappá ppá pá pap.
papá o falso pas

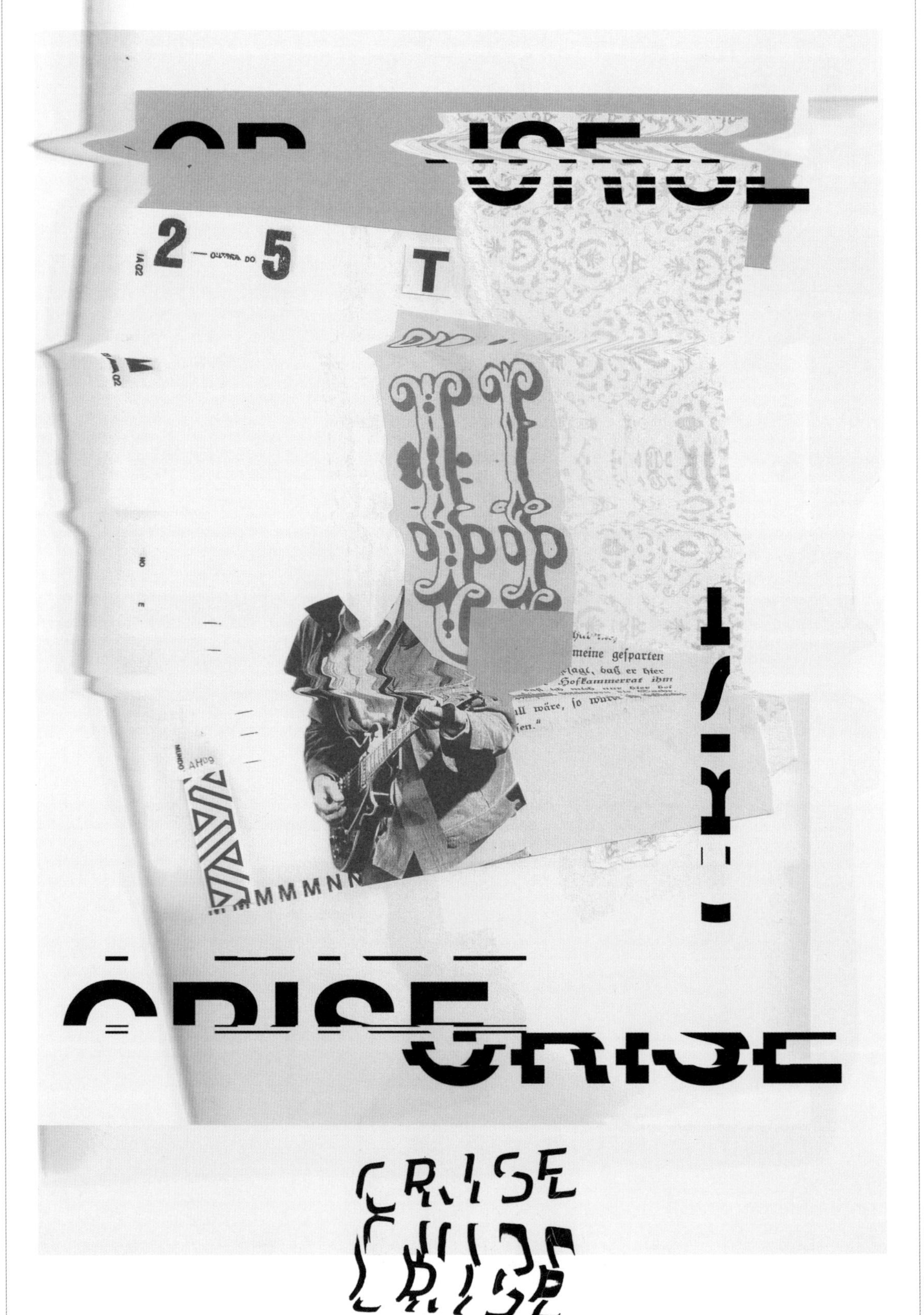
2
5
T
meine gesparten
Hofkammerrat ihm
MMMMN
CRISE
CRISE

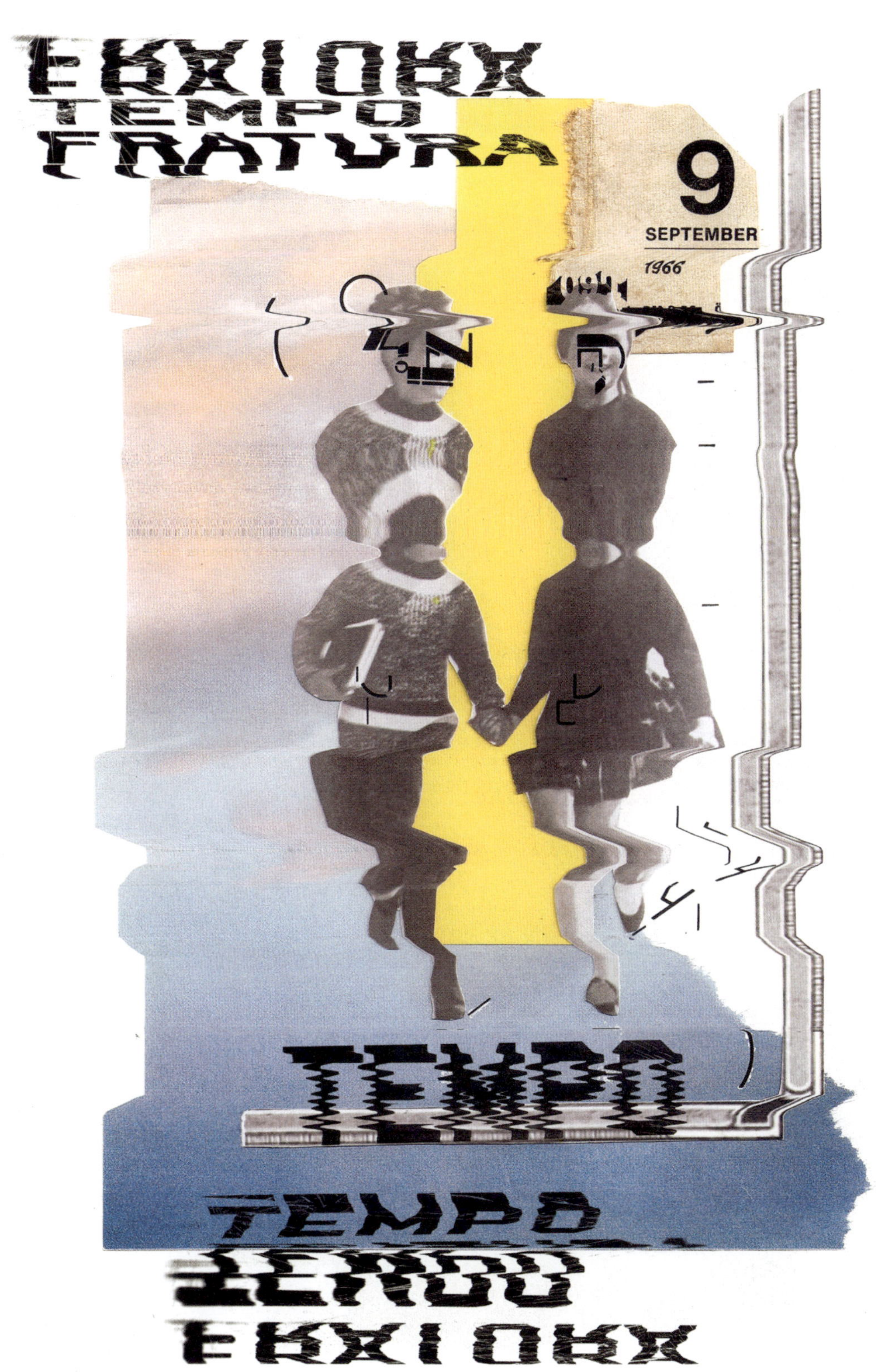
TEMPO
FRATURA
9
SEPTEMBER
1966
TEMPO
TEMPO

# LORD OF THE FLIES

This is a design for the book *Lord of the Flies*, which depicts a group of British boys stranded on an uninhabited island and their attempt to govern themselves, with disastrous results.

Designer: Yasemin Cakir

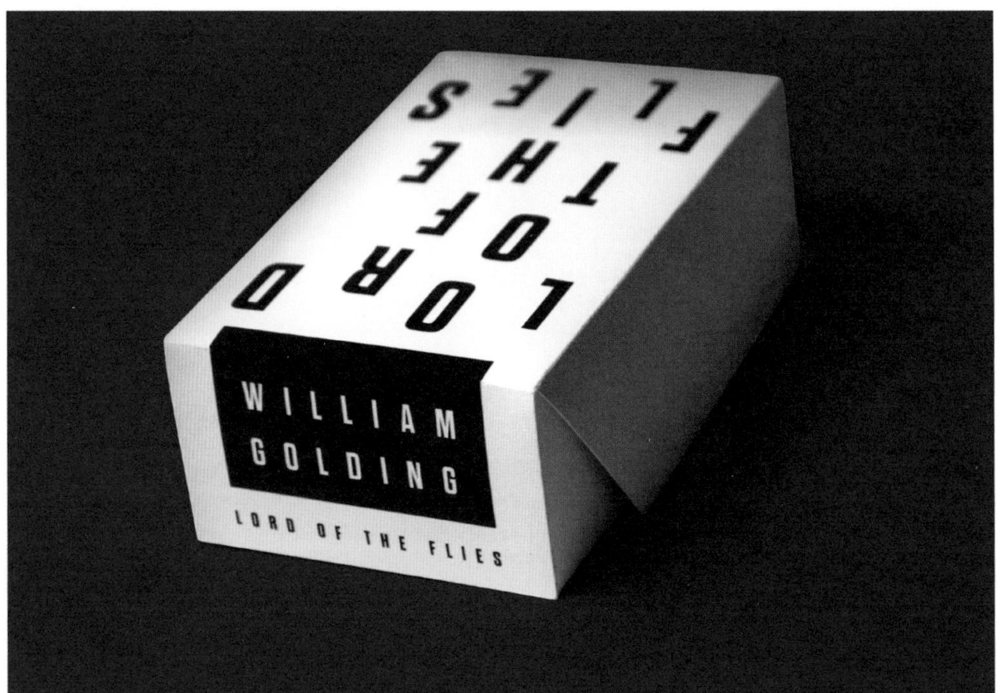


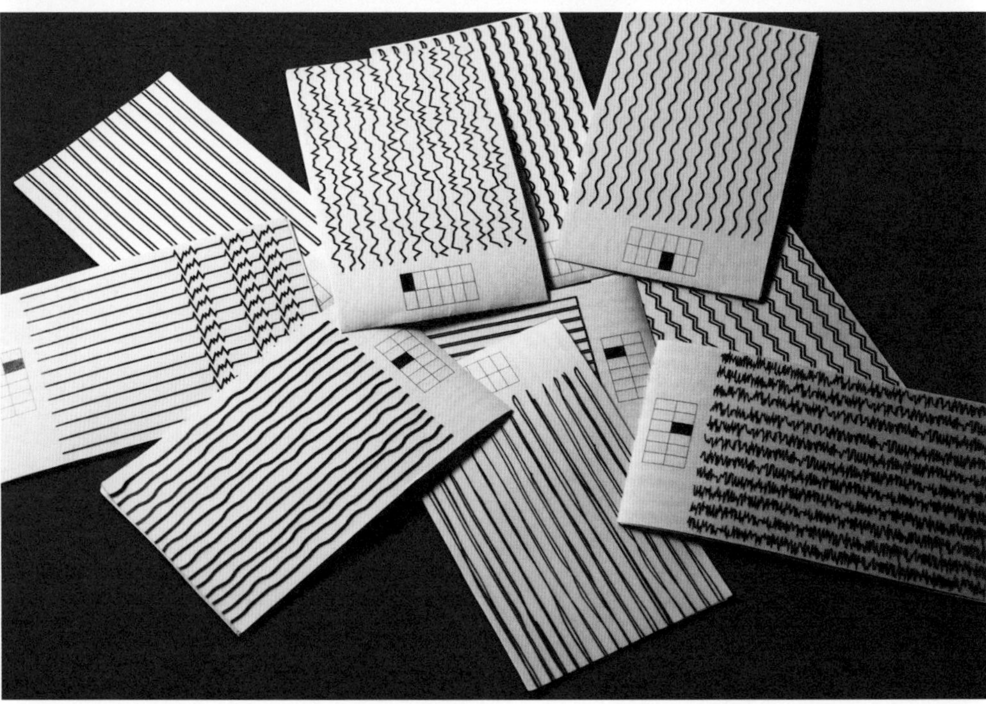

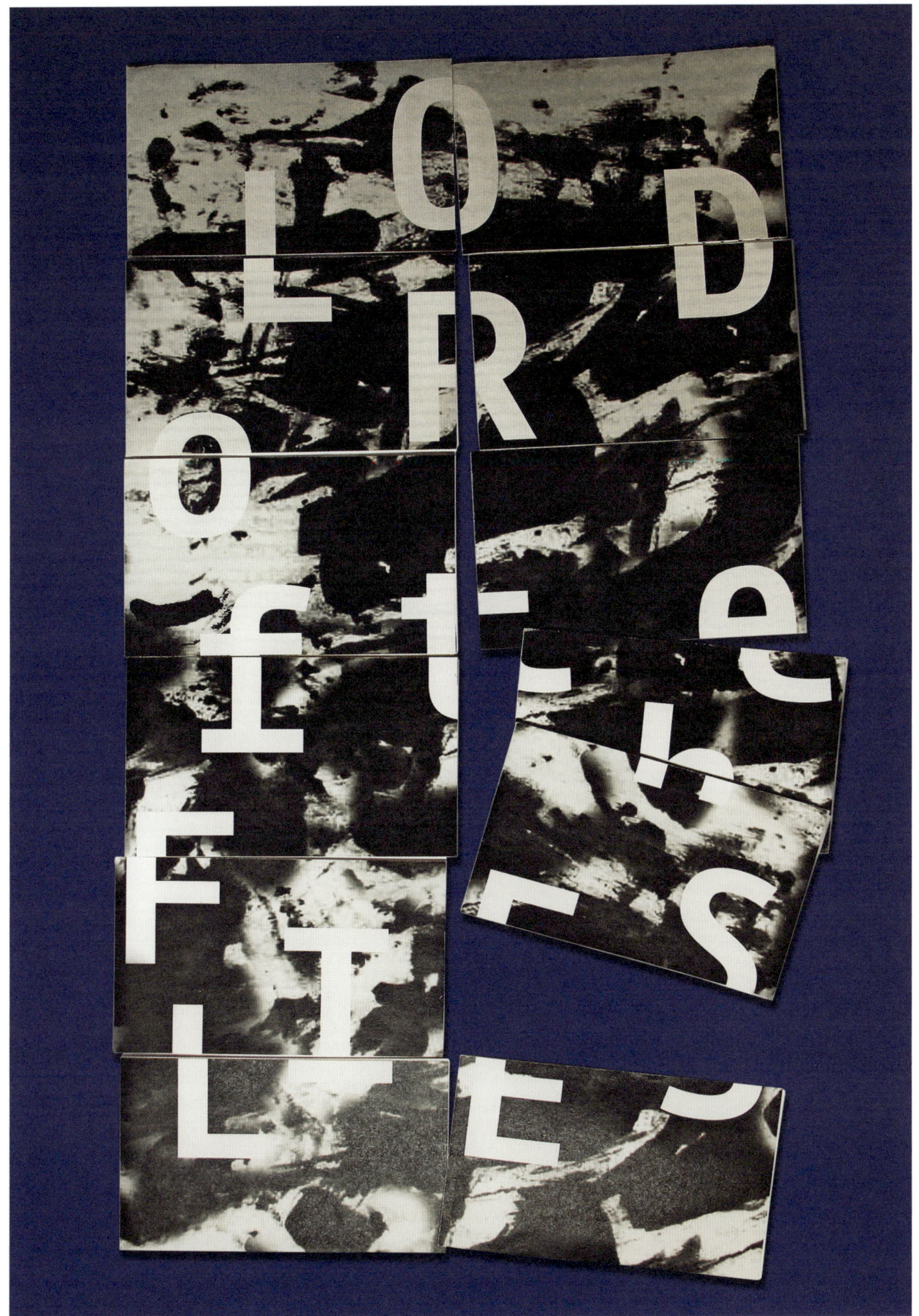

# ALWAYS WANT THE SPACE TO REAPPEAR

Art3, a non-profit organization, has developed a program of events related to experimental projects. This is a design for the exhibitions organized at art3 and elsewhere with various partners, which reflected the diversity of artistic creation at present.

Studio: My Name is Wendy

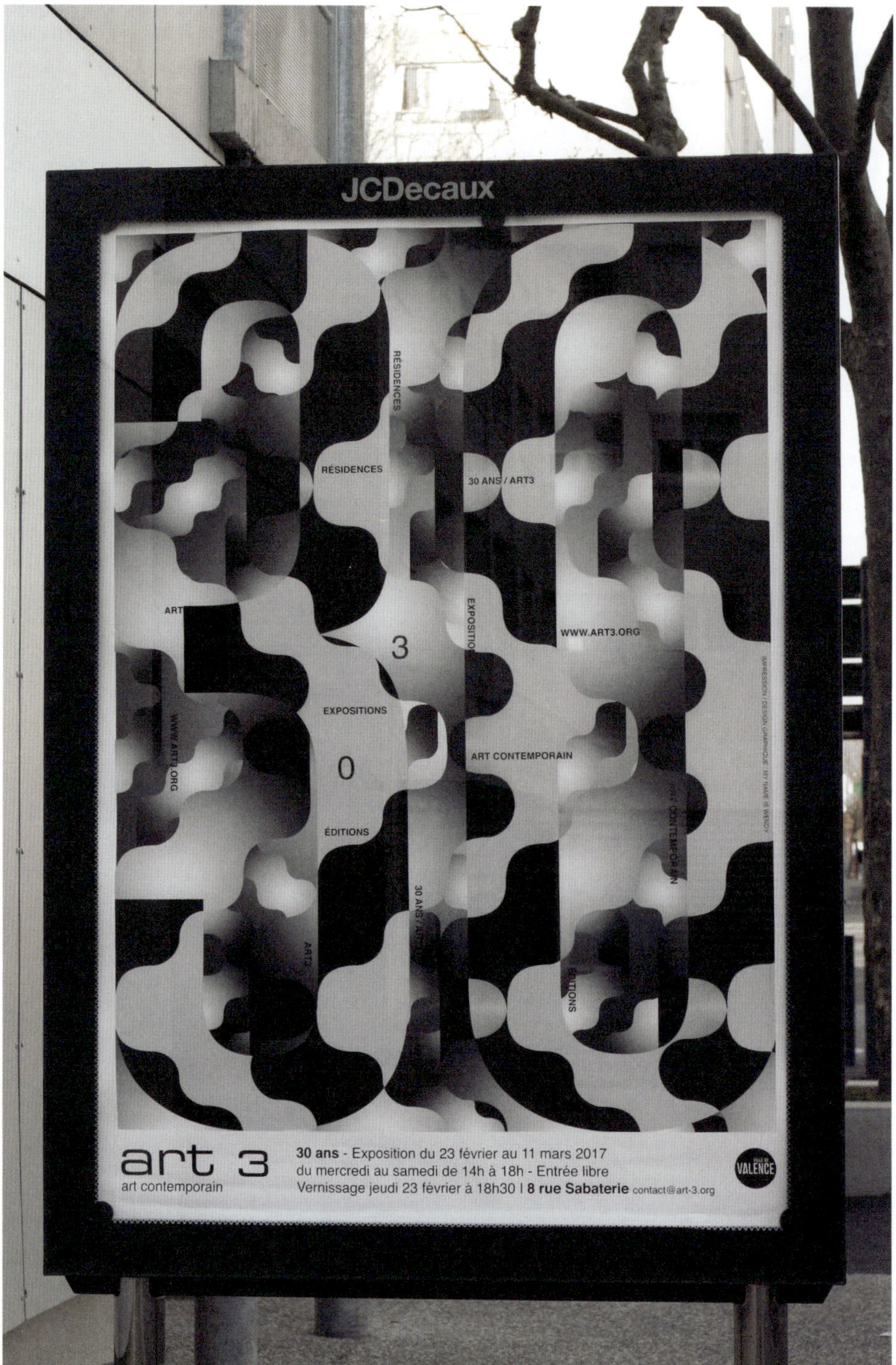

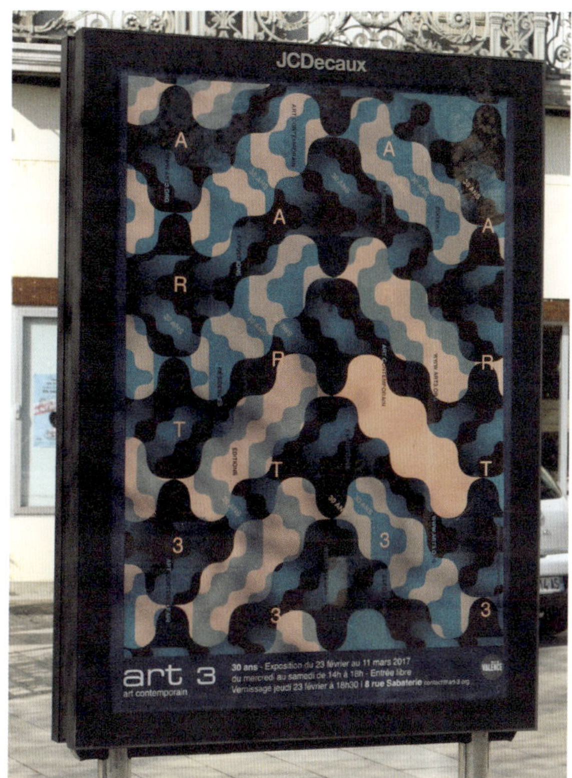
JCDecaux
art 3
art contemporain
30 ans - Exposition du 23 février au 11 mars 2017
du mercredi au samedi de 14h à 18h - Entrée libre
Vernissage jeudi 23 février à 18h30 | 8 rue Sabaterie

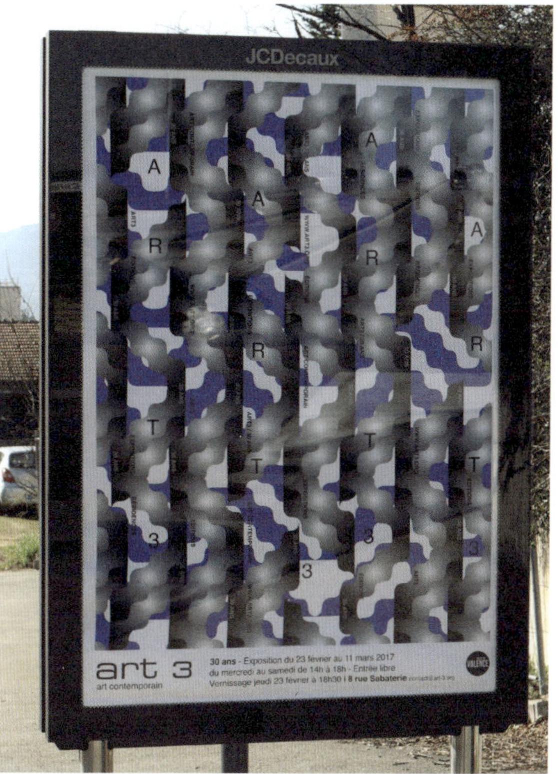
JCDecaux
art 3
art contemporain
30 ans - Exposition du 23 février au 11 mars 2017
du mercredi au samedi de 14h à 18h - Entrée libre
Vernissage jeudi 23 février à 18h30 | 8 rue Sabaterie

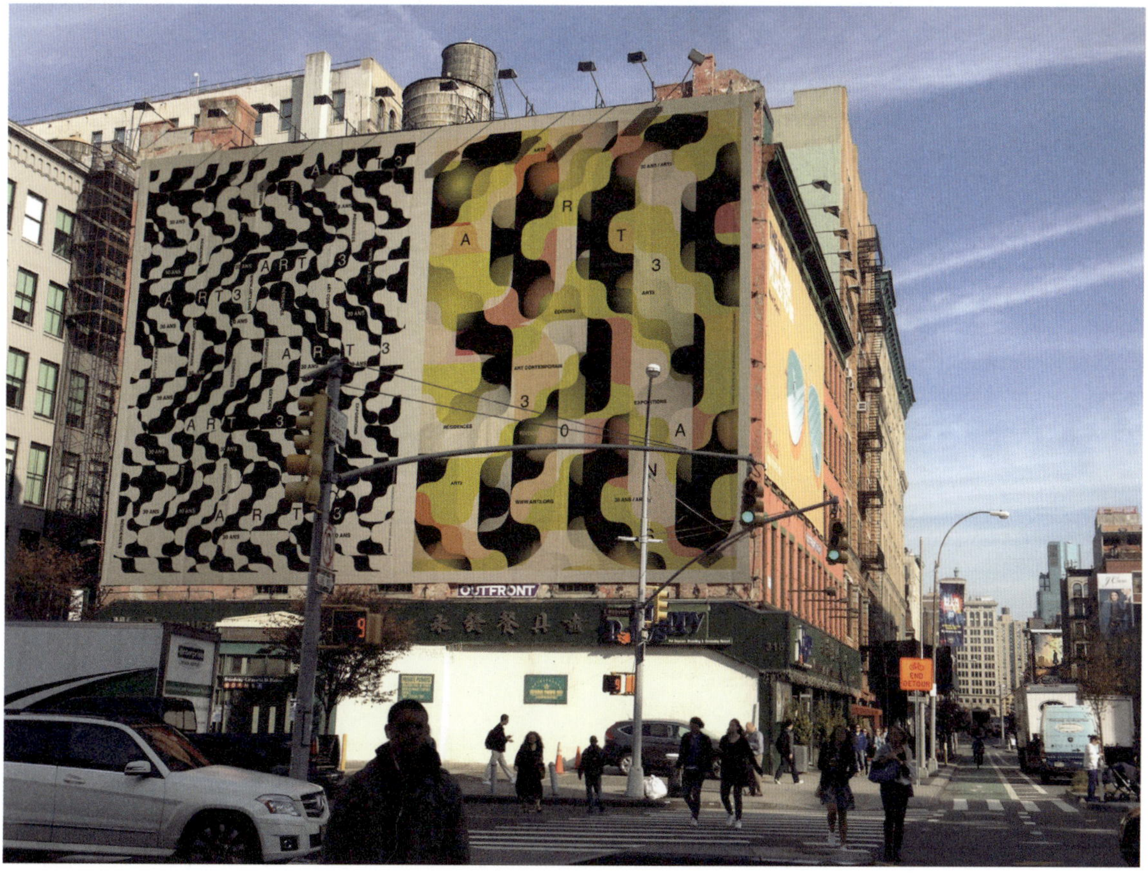

# EGO DISTORTION FESTIVAL

The idea behind the design is that even a mature person can use a pathological or immature defense mechanism. The designer would like to learn about mature defense mechanism through this work.

Designer: Gwak Min Yeong

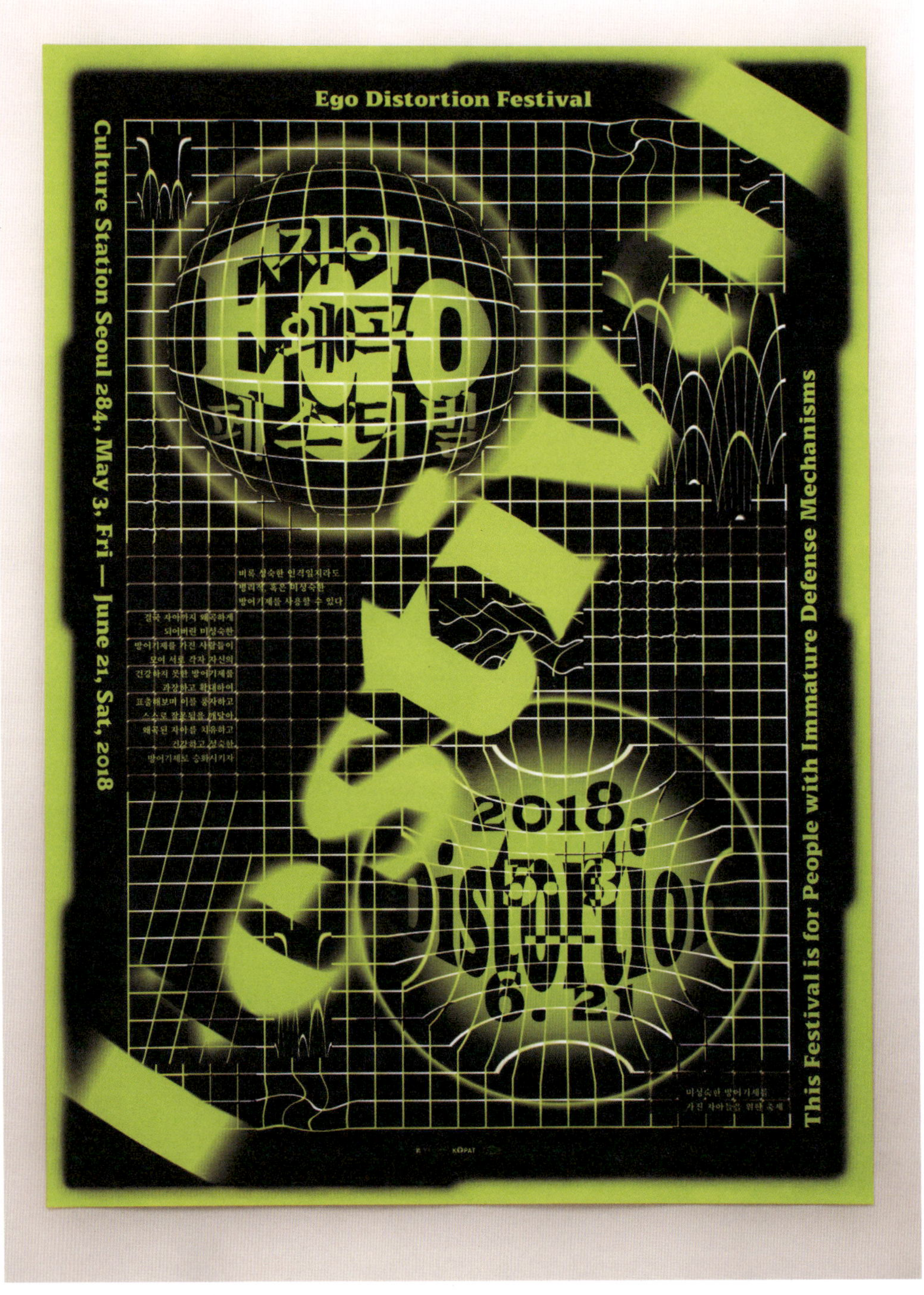

# THE SCIENCE OF SLEEP

The designer intended to express the ambiguity of the boundary between dream and reality, since he believed that a dream is a simulacrum, not an imperfect replica of reality.

Designer: Gwak Min Yeong

# THINK—ART WITH IBM WATSON

This poster belongs to IBM's "THINK" poster series. The designer used unconventional elements of light and reflection to feed his natural curiosity and exploration desire.

Studio: Ogilvy New York
Designer: Ruslan Khasanov

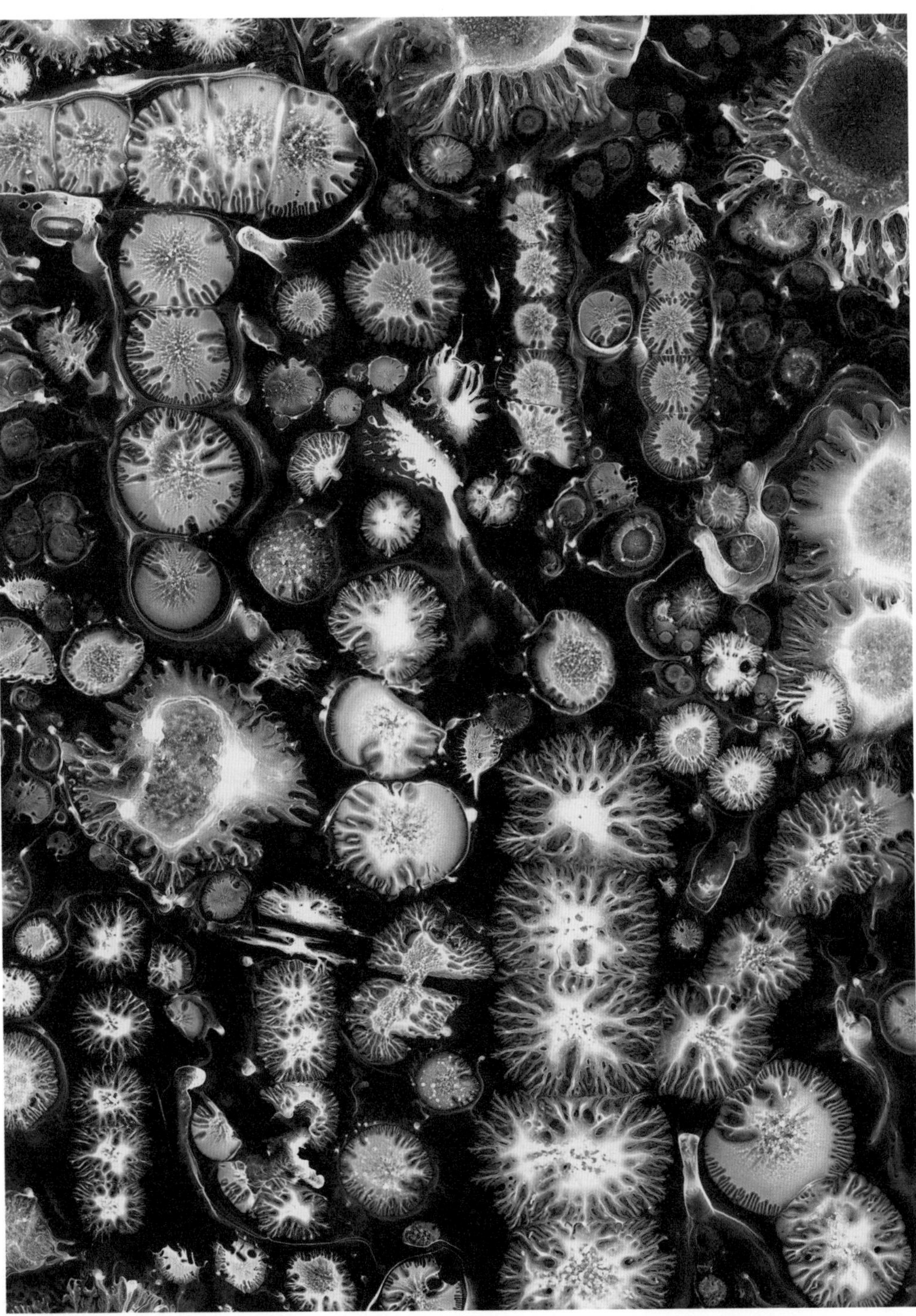

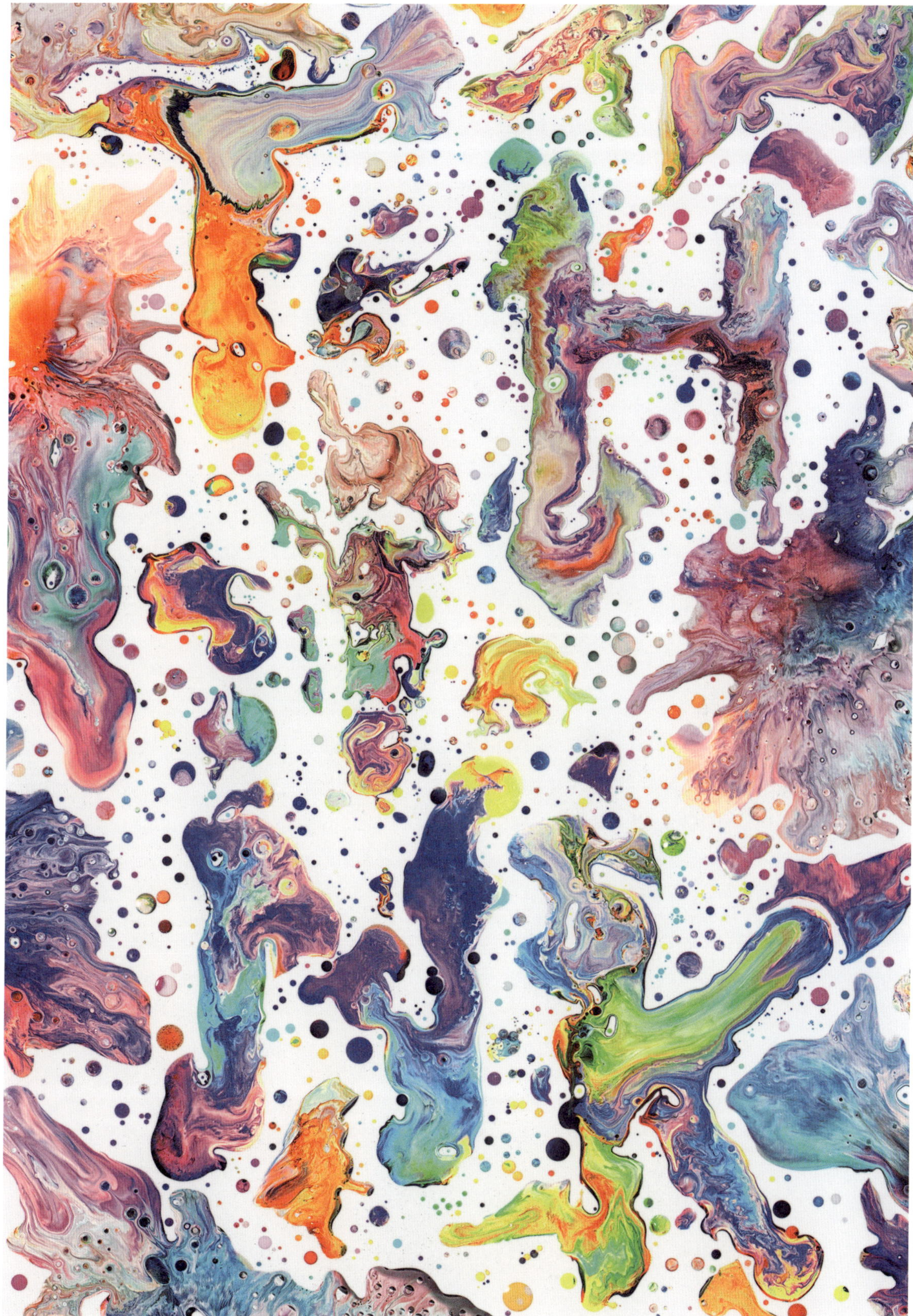

# PERDICION—PLAQUETA LITERARIA

This is a personal project on *Perdición* – a short text written by Sergio Bizzio. The designer edited the text and made this low-cost book by hand.

Designer: Maria Lucila Quintana

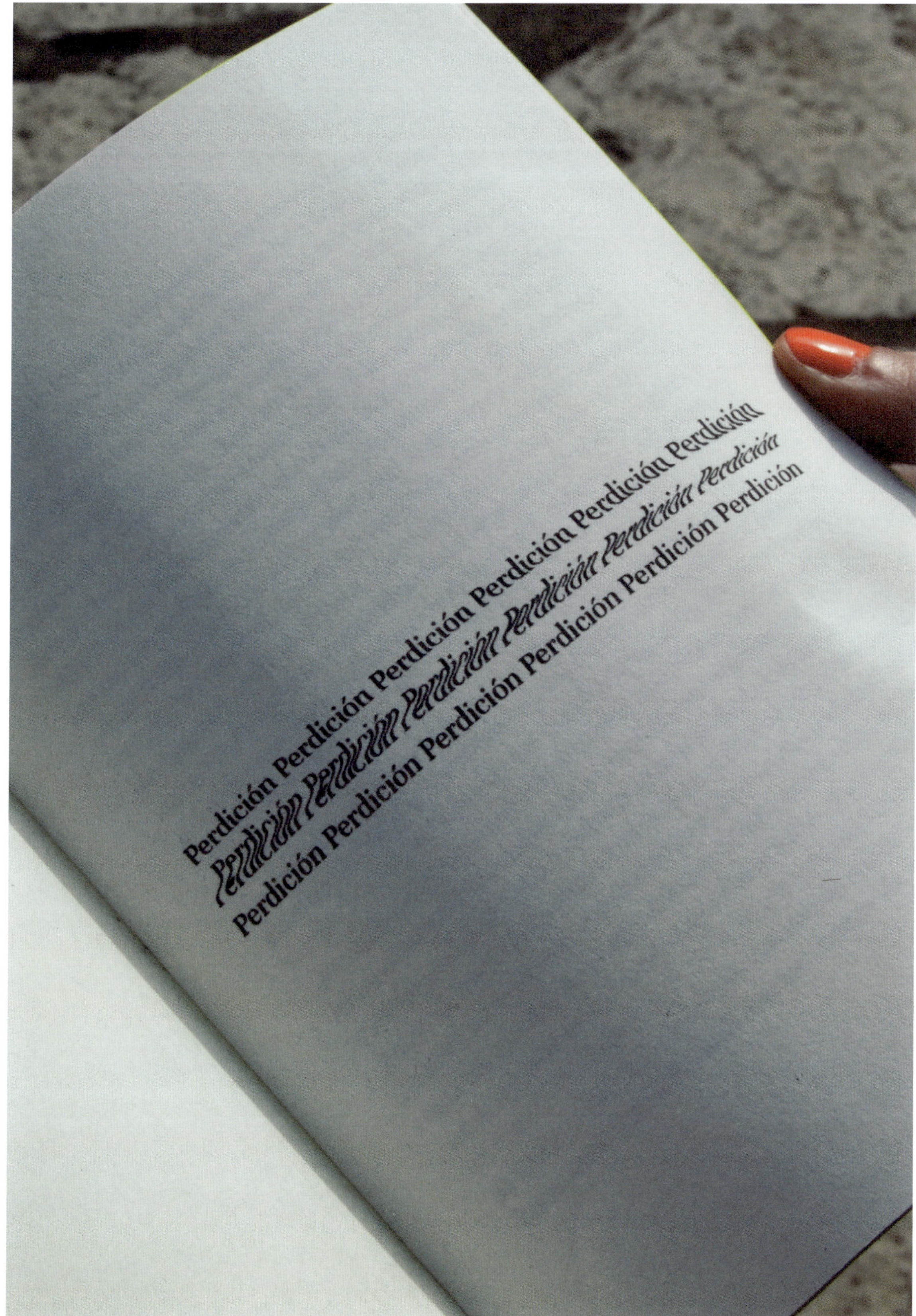
Perdición Perdición Perdición Perdición Perdición Perdición
Perdición Perdición Perdición Perdición Perdición Perdición

# DEFORM

DEFORM is a fanzine about the trend of glitches, deforming shapes and type distorting. It seeks answers for questions such as: Why is glitch art so popular?

Designer: Lilla Tóth

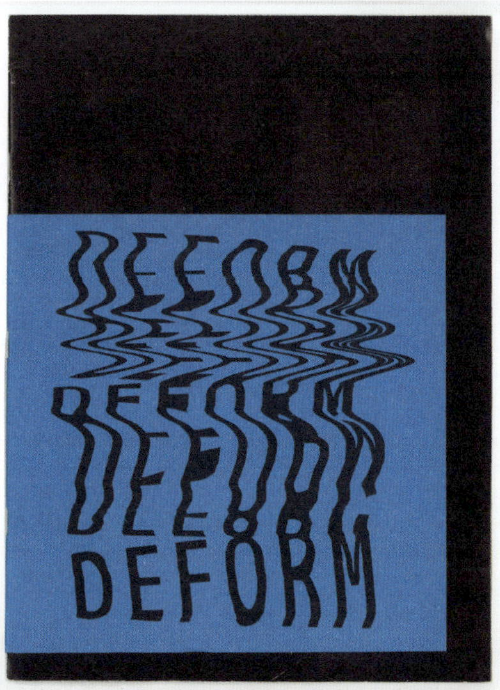


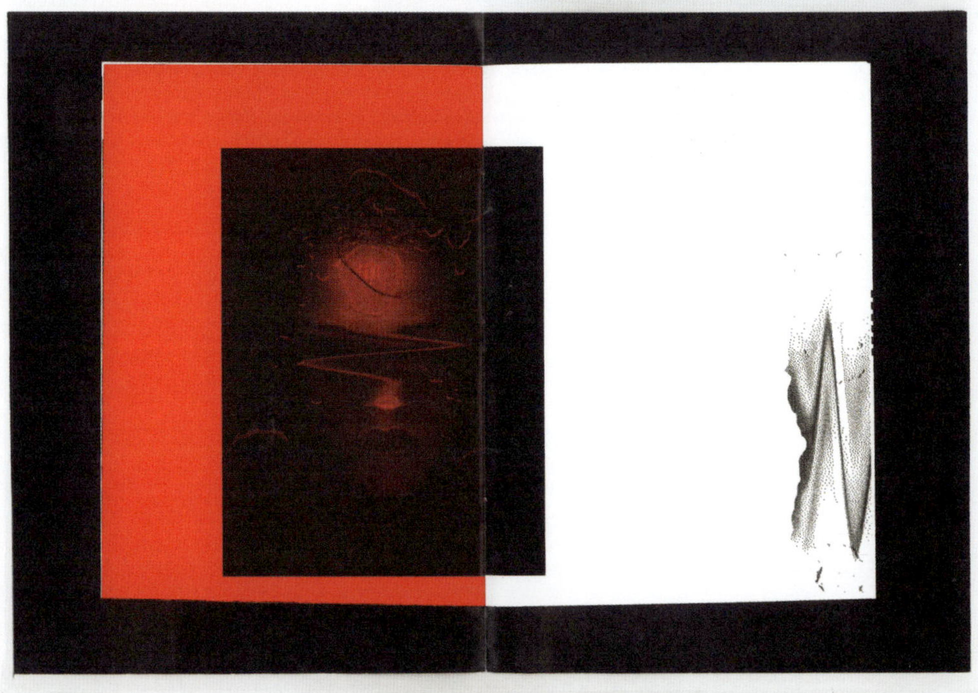

### The Art of the Unexpected

It started out as a software malfunction - now it is a design genre. Instead of holding their hands up in horror and crying: "Oh, oh, we have a glitch!", the artists featured in this article say: "Whoopee! We have a glitch!" - and proceed to make the most of it

The use of the world "glitch" - derived from the German (or Yiddish) for "a slip" - to describe a design genre is a tribute to serendipity (a happy accident). This "sudden irregularity or malfunction", as the dictionary definition has it, has been welcomed by some in the creative community as a way of turning an unintended fault to its advantage - in other words, making a virtue out of what could have been a setback.

As Doug Black put in his review of Glitch: Designing Imperfection in Design magazine: "When viewed in their own right, seemingly randomised visual abstraction become fascinating designs that represents a unique hybrid of human intention and mechanical failure."

Mindflash Advertising summed it up as "that annoying thing that happens on your PC when you keep clicking and clicking and the machine provides you with increasingly odd colour variations that just seem to slow everything down." And described the glitch generation of designers as "free-wheeling spirits who didn't throw their hands up in the air and slam their mouse against the table when their computer froze. Instead, they stared at the screen and made_art.

The ultimate visual impact of today's glitch could be said to lie somewhere between collage and pattern design, with both of which it has a lot in common. The difference being, of course, that the former is bulit on making creative use of whatwere, in the first instance, software errors, while the other two are usually meticulously pre-planned.

One thing is for sure: even if the initial inspiration stems from something going wrong, what these artists subsequently make from mistakes, or glitches, requires just as much hard work and talent to convert into a viable aesthetic offering as more conventional works of art. And the name they have earned for themselves by doing it is no accident!

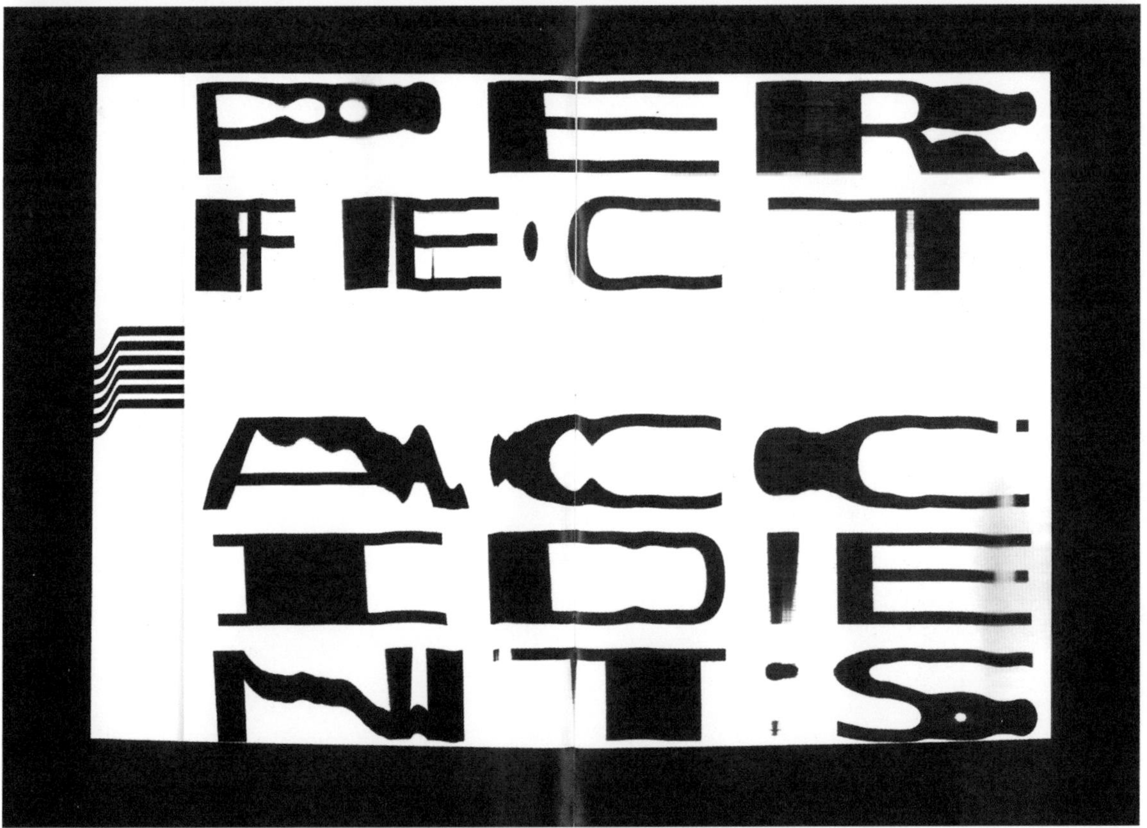

# MULTIVERSO

This visual identity for Icograda Design Week Torino was developed around the theme "Multiverso", a hypothetical world of possibilities which is a collage of many cultures and various behaviors. In the work, the artists gathered a variety of faces, giving Torino life thoughts and sounds.

Studio: ZUP
Designer: Andrea Medri, Lucia Roscini

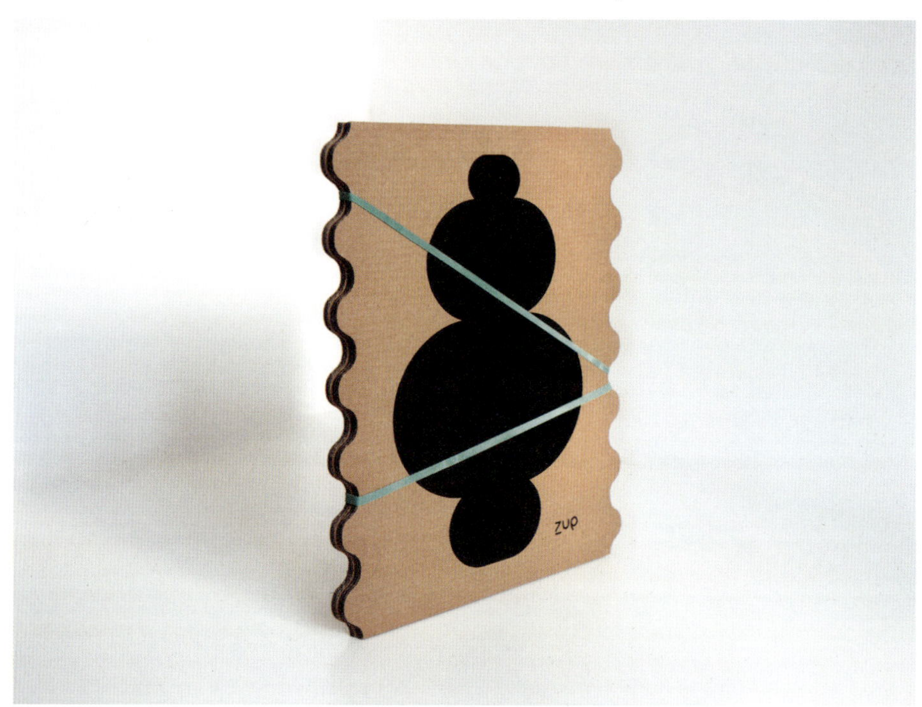


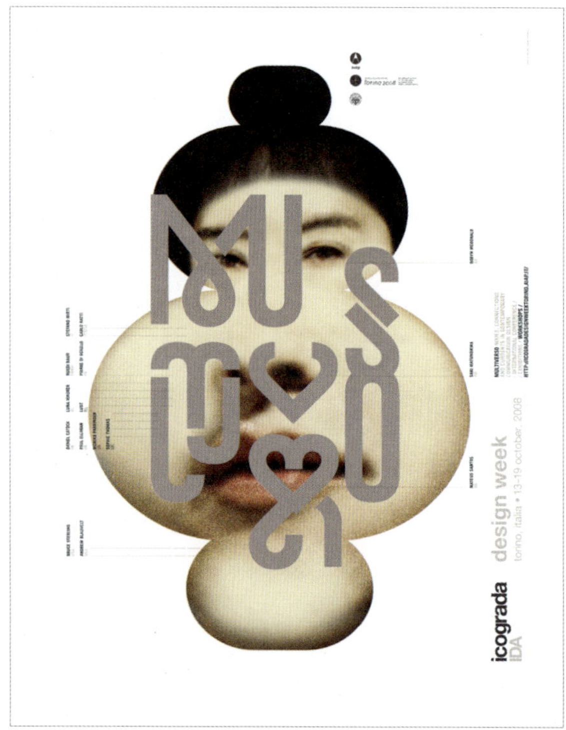


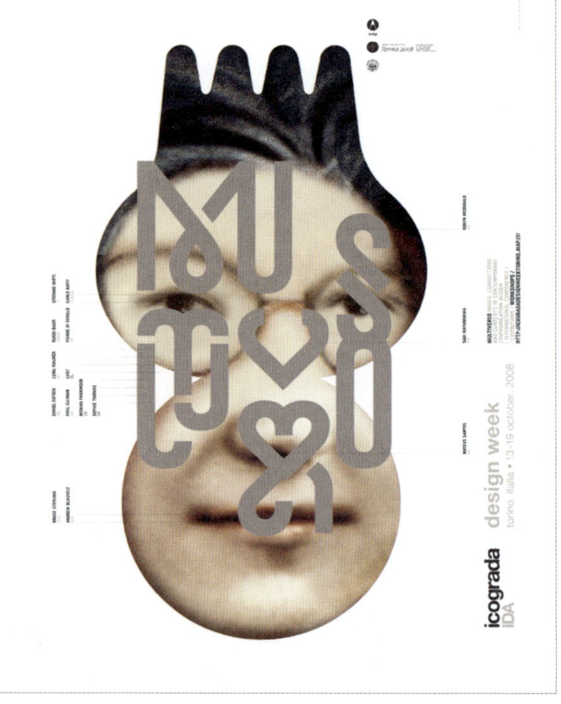

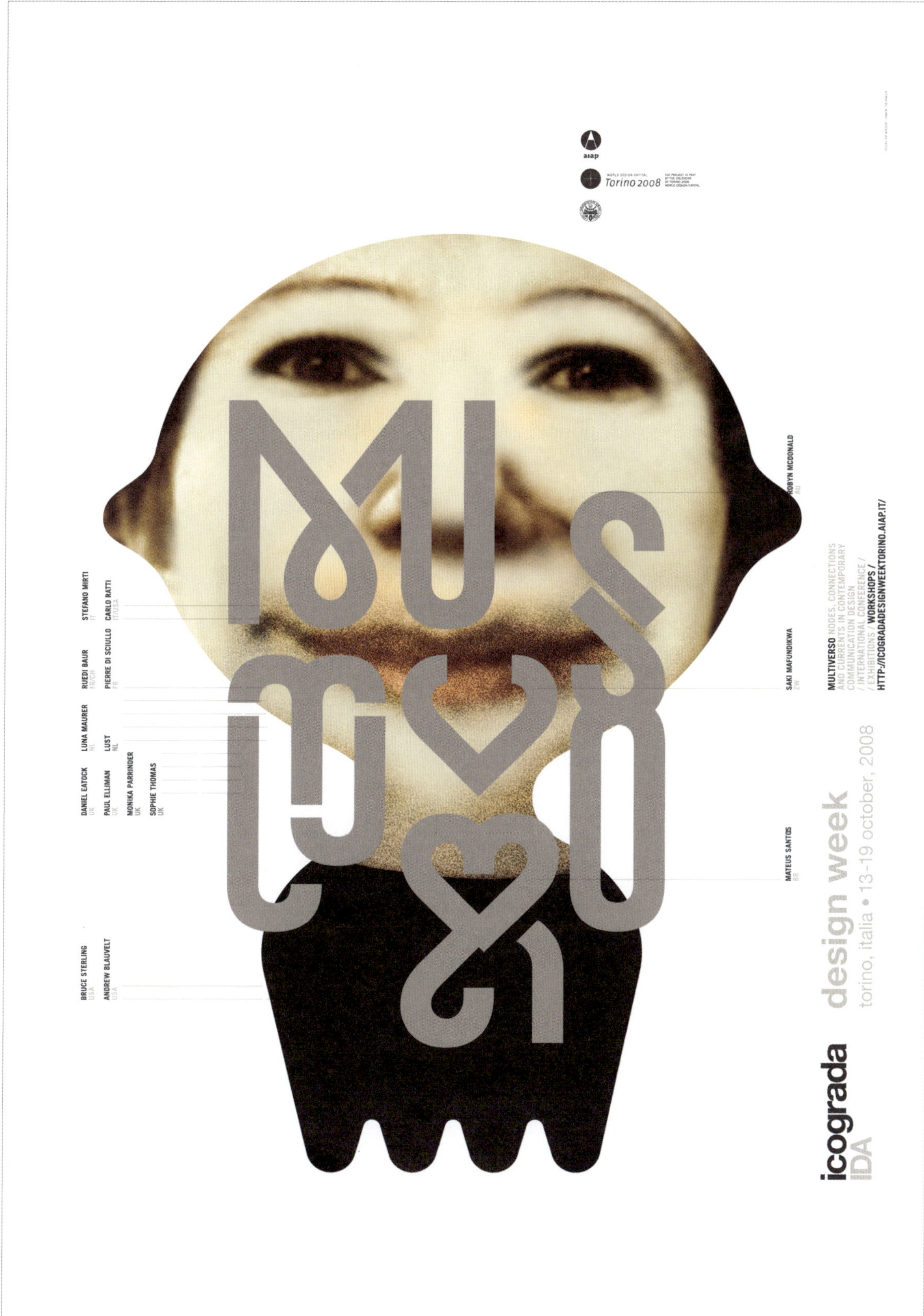
aiap
WORLD DESIGN CAPITAL
Torino 2008
BRUCE STERLING
USA
ANDREW BLAUVELT
USA
DANIEL EATOCK
UK
PAUL ELLIMAN
UK
MONIKA PARRINDER
UK
SOPHIE THOMAS
UK
LUNA MAURER
NL
LUST
NL
RUEDI BAUR
FR/CH
PIERRE DI SCIULLO
FR
STEFANO MIRTI
IT
CARLO RATTI
IT/USA
ROBYN MCDONALD
AU
SAKI MAFUNDIKWA
ZW
MATEUS SANTOS
BR
MULTIVERSO NODES, CONNECTIONS AND CURRENTS IN CONTEMPORARY COMMUNICATION DESIGN / INTERNATIONAL CONFERENCE / EXHIBITIONS / WORKSHOPS / HTTP://ICOGRADADESIGNWEEKTORINO.AIAP.IT/
icograda
IDA
design week
torino, italia • 13-19 october, 2008

icograda
IDA

design week
torino, italia • 13-19 october, 2008

MULTIVERSO

ANNA NAUMOVA RUS
RUEDI BAUR FR/CH
STEFANO MIRTI IT
CARLO RATTI IT/USA
LUNA MAURER NL
LUST NL
DANIEL EATOCK UK
PAUL ELLIMAN UK
MONIKA PARRINDER UK
SOPHIE THOMAS UK
ANDREW BLAUVELT USA
BRUCE STERLING USA
SUSAN SELLERS USA

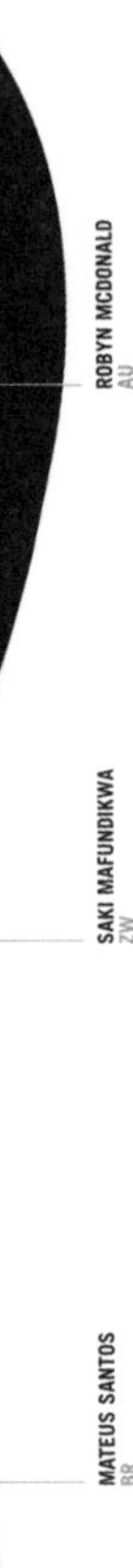


MULTIVERSO
TORINO
OCT 13/19

MULTIVERSO NODES, CONNECTIONS AND CURRENTS
IN CONTEMPORARY COMMUNICATION DESIGN
/ INTERNATIONAL CONFERENCE /
/ EXHIBITIONS / WORKSHOPS /
HTTP://ICOGRADADESIGNWEEKTORINO.AIAP.IT/

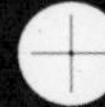


THE PROJECT IS PART
OF THE CALENDAR
OF TORINO 2008
WORLD DESIGN CAPITAL

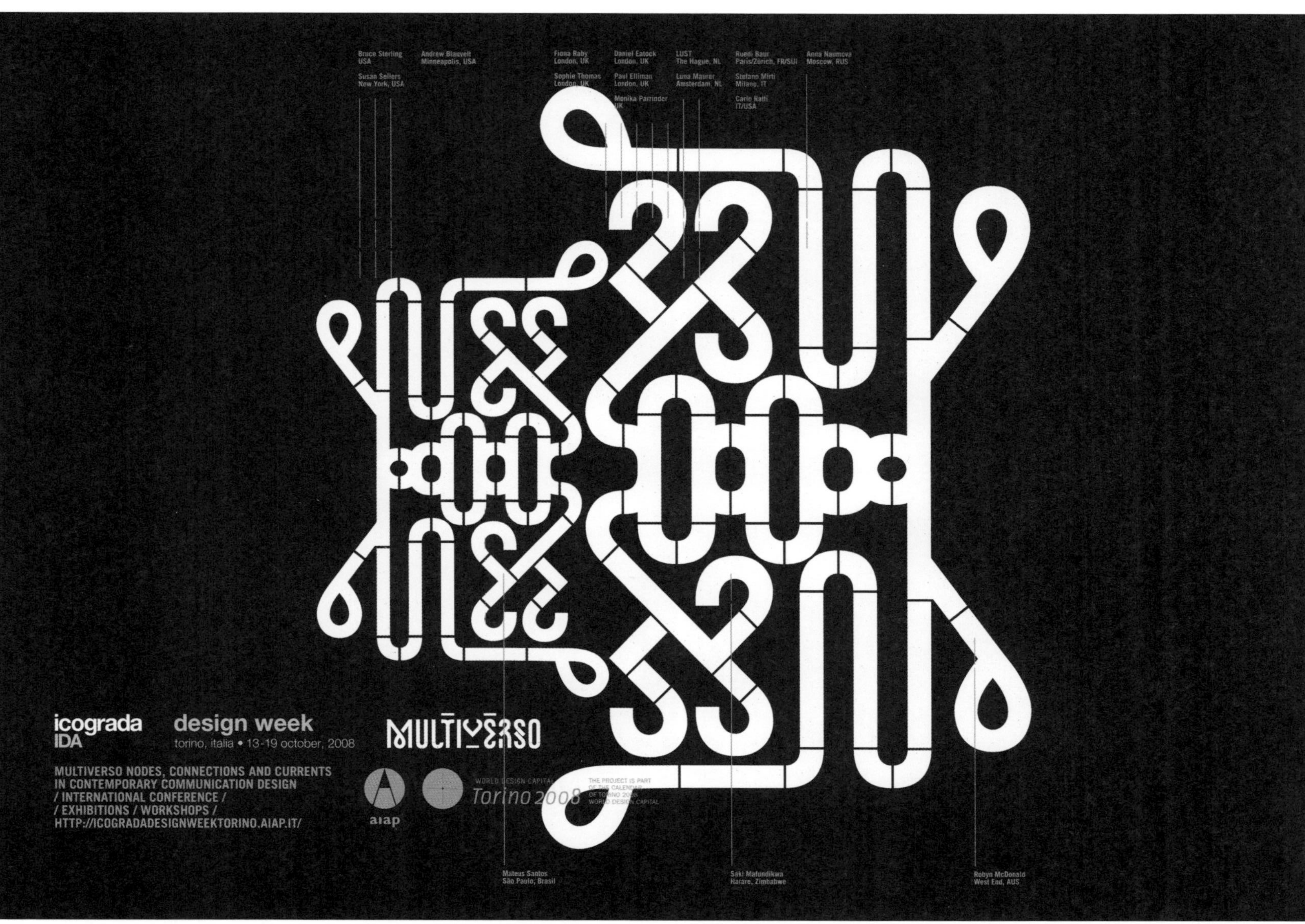
Bruce Sterling
USA
Susan Sellers
New York, USA
Andrew Blauvelt
Minneapolis, USA
Fiona Raby
London, UK
Sophie Thomas
London, UK
Daniel Eatock
London, UK
Paul Elliman
London, UK
Monika Parrinder
UK
LUST
The Hague, NL
Luna Maurer
Amsterdam, NL
Ruedi Baur
Paris/Zurich, FR/SUI
Stefano Mirti
Milano, IT
Carlo Ratti
IT/USA
Anna Naumova
Moscow, RUS
icograda
IDA
design week
torino, italia • 13-19 october, 2008
MULTIVERSO
MULTIVERSO NODES, CONNECTIONS AND CURRENTS
IN CONTEMPORARY COMMUNICATION DESIGN
/ INTERNATIONAL CONFERENCE /
/ EXHIBITIONS / WORKSHOPS /
HTTP://ICOGRADADESIGNWEEKTORINO.AIAP.IT/
aiap
WORLD DESIGN CAPITAL
Torino 2008
THE PROJECT IS PART
OF THE CALENDAR
OF TORINO 2008
WORLD DESIGN CAPITAL
Mateus Santos
São Paulo, Brasil
Saki Mafundikwa
Harare, Zimbabwe
Robyn McDonald
West End, AUS

# QUICKSILVER ANNIVERSARY PARTY

This poster was designed for Quicksilver 40th Anniversary Wake Party which aimed at fans of extreme water sports. It demonstrated the course of integrating the typography into the dangerous but fascinating quicksilver.

Designer: Boris Alaev

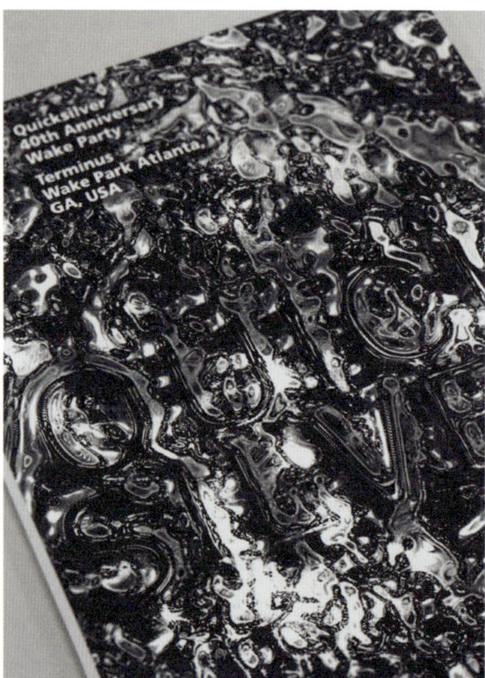


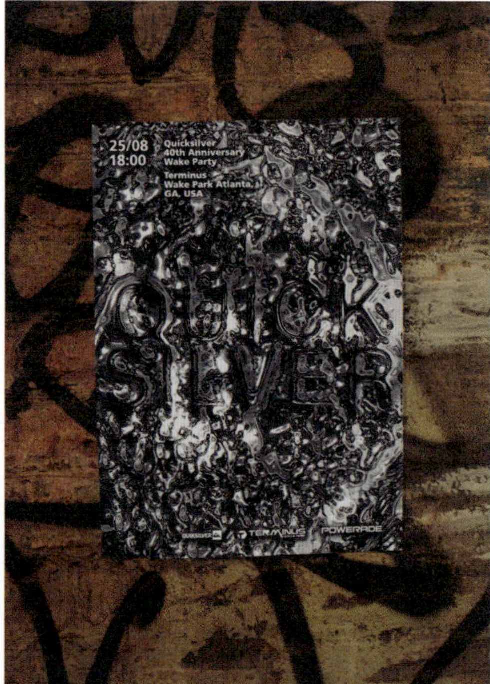


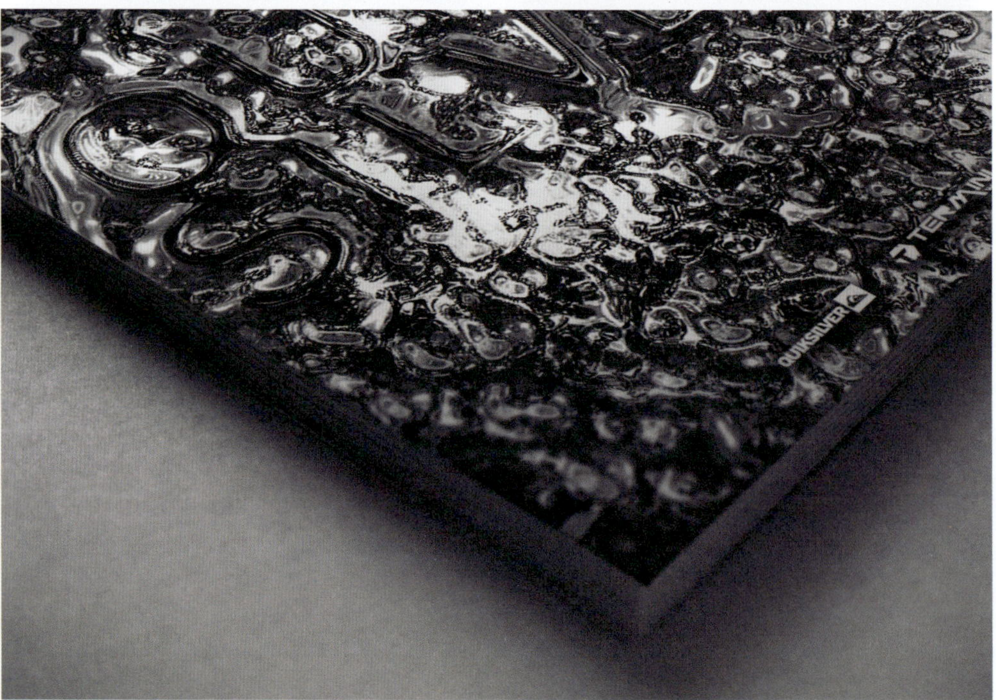

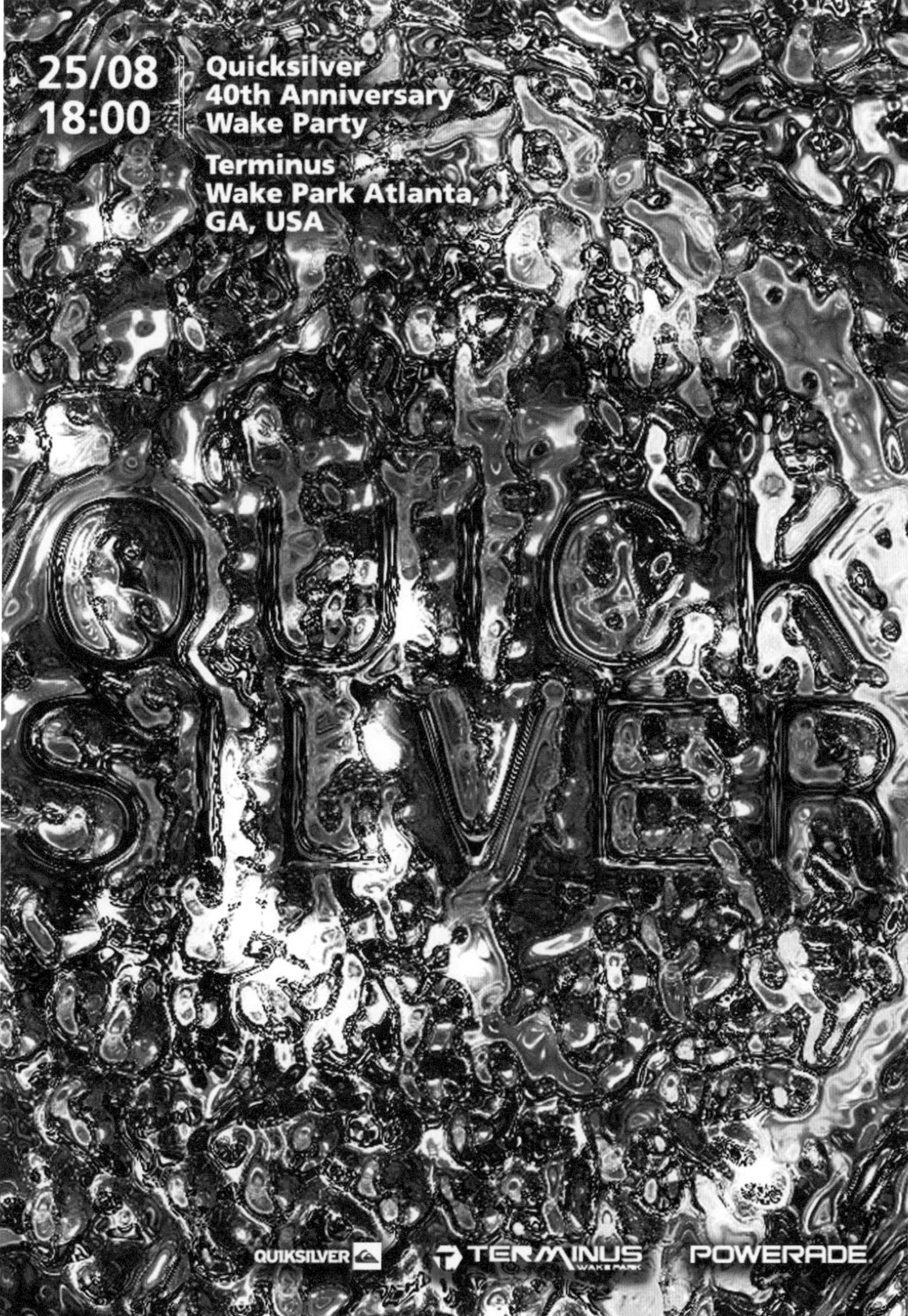
25/08
18:00
Quicksilver
40th Anniversary
Wake Party
Terminus
Wake Park Atlanta,
GA, USA
QUICK
SILVER
QUIKSILVER
TERMINUS
WAKE PARK
POWERADE

# C41 MAGAZINE ISSUE 03—CHANGE

C41 Magazine presented their third issue with the theme of change, which was inspired by the 2016 presidential election in the Uniterd States, as they believed that it's time for change after 8 years of Barack Obama as president. Moreover, they took this chance to make a change since they called upon a non-photographer to create the magazine cover for the first time.

Studio: C41
Designer: Luca A. Caizzi, Federico Cavalieri
Cover Artist: Kensuke Koike

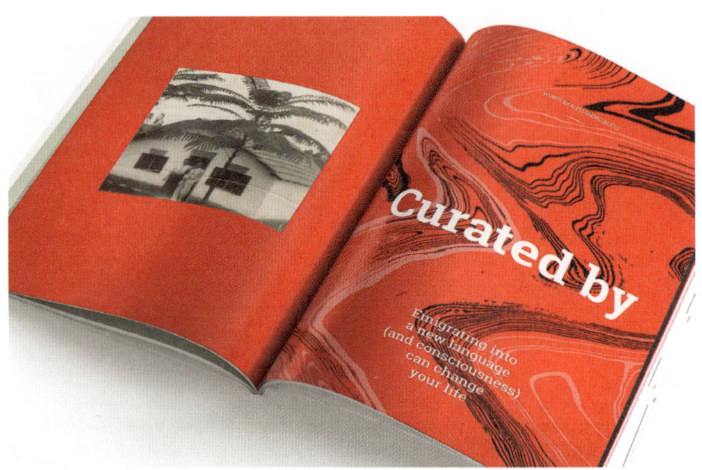


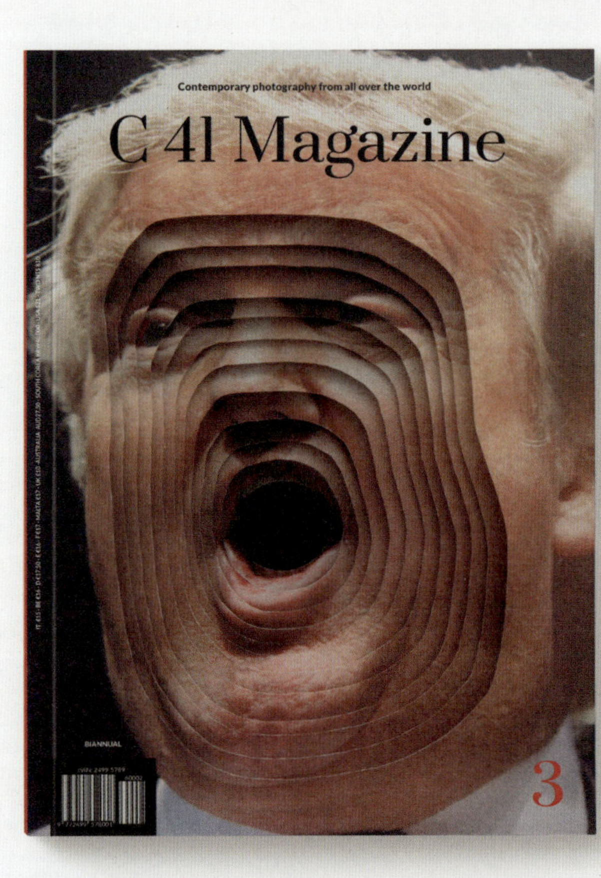

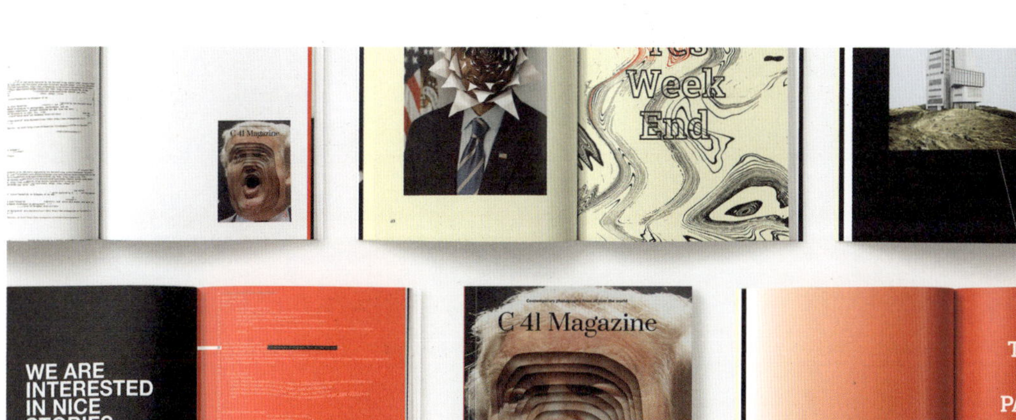
C 4l Magazine
Week
End

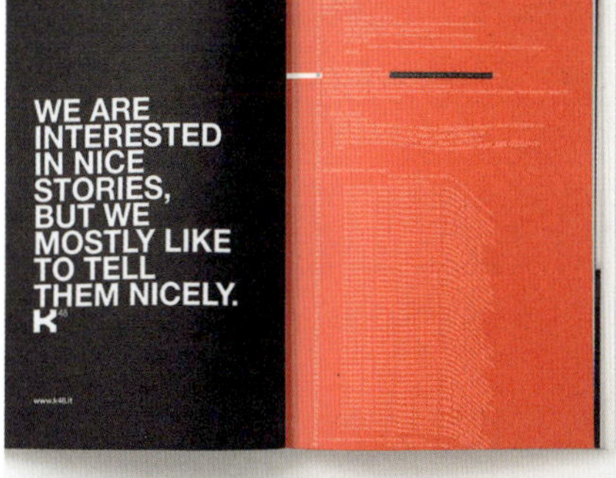
WE ARE INTERESTED IN NICE STORIES, BUT WE MOSTLY LIKE TO TELL THEM NICELY.
www.k48.it

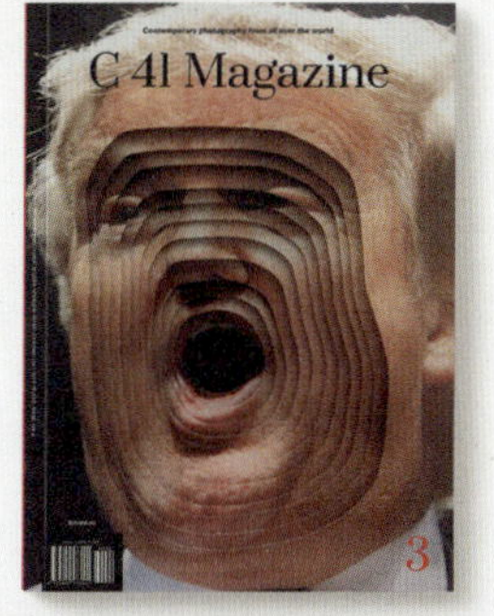
C 4l Magazine
3

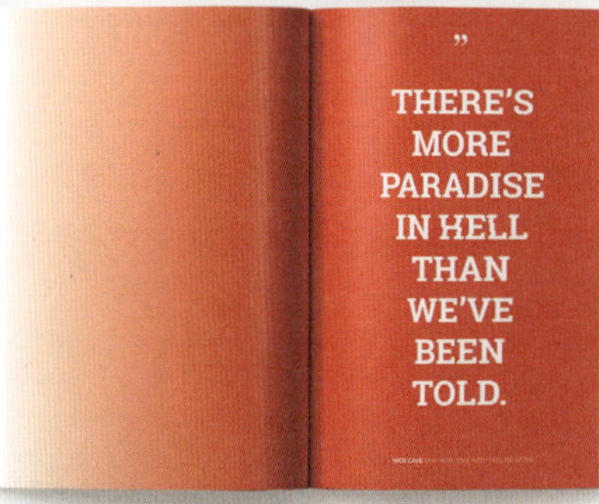
THERE'S MORE PARADISE IN HELL THAN WE'VE BEEN TOLD.

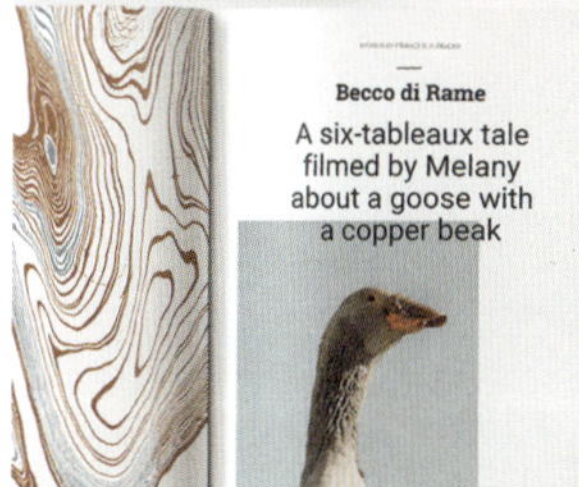
Becco di Rame
A six-tableaux tale filmed by Melany about a goose with a copper beak

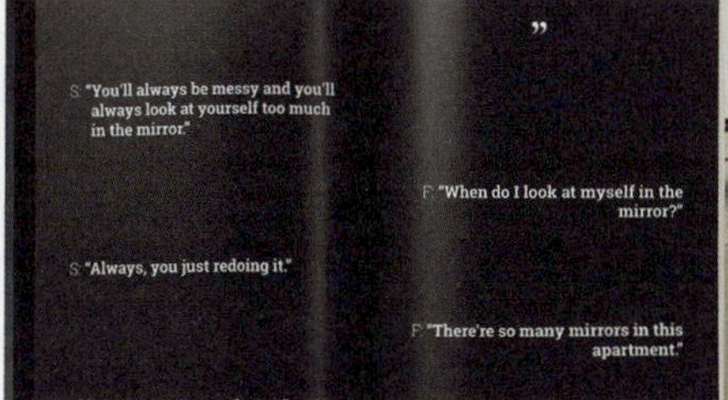
S: "You'll always be messy and you'll always look at yourself too much in the mirror."
F: "When do I look at myself in the mirror?"
S: "Always, you just redoing it."
F: "There're so many mirrors in this apartment."

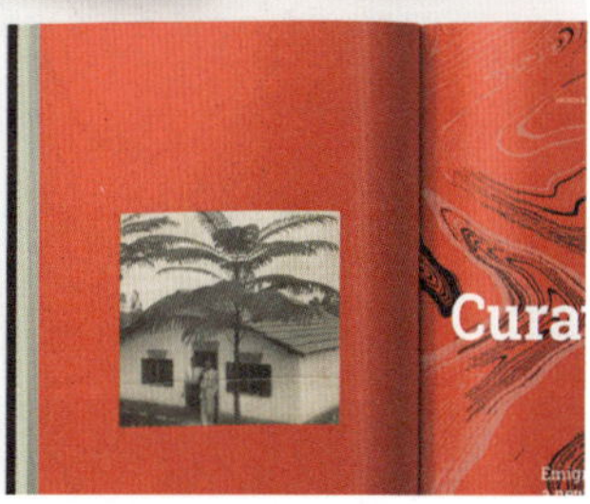

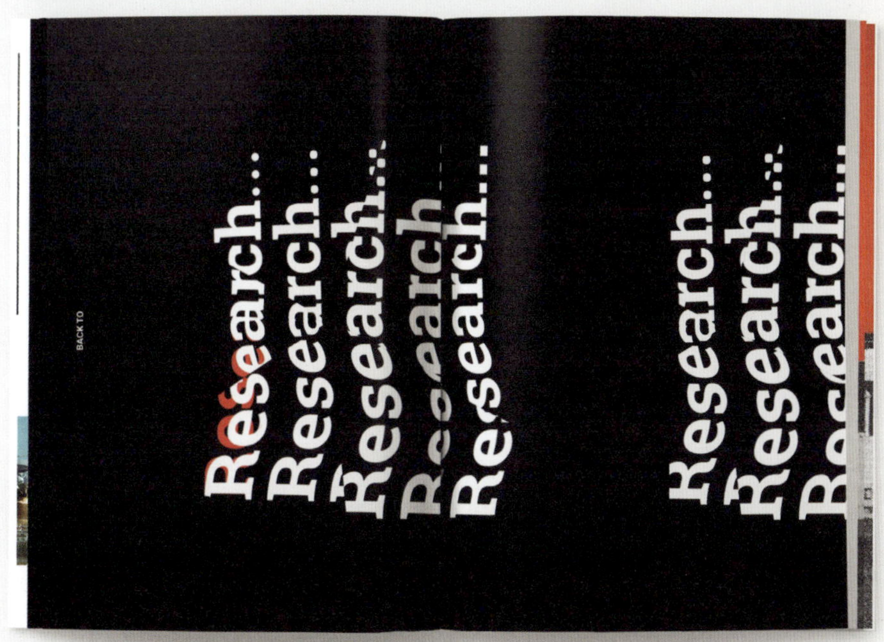
BACK TO
Research...
Research...
Research...
Research...
Research...
Research...

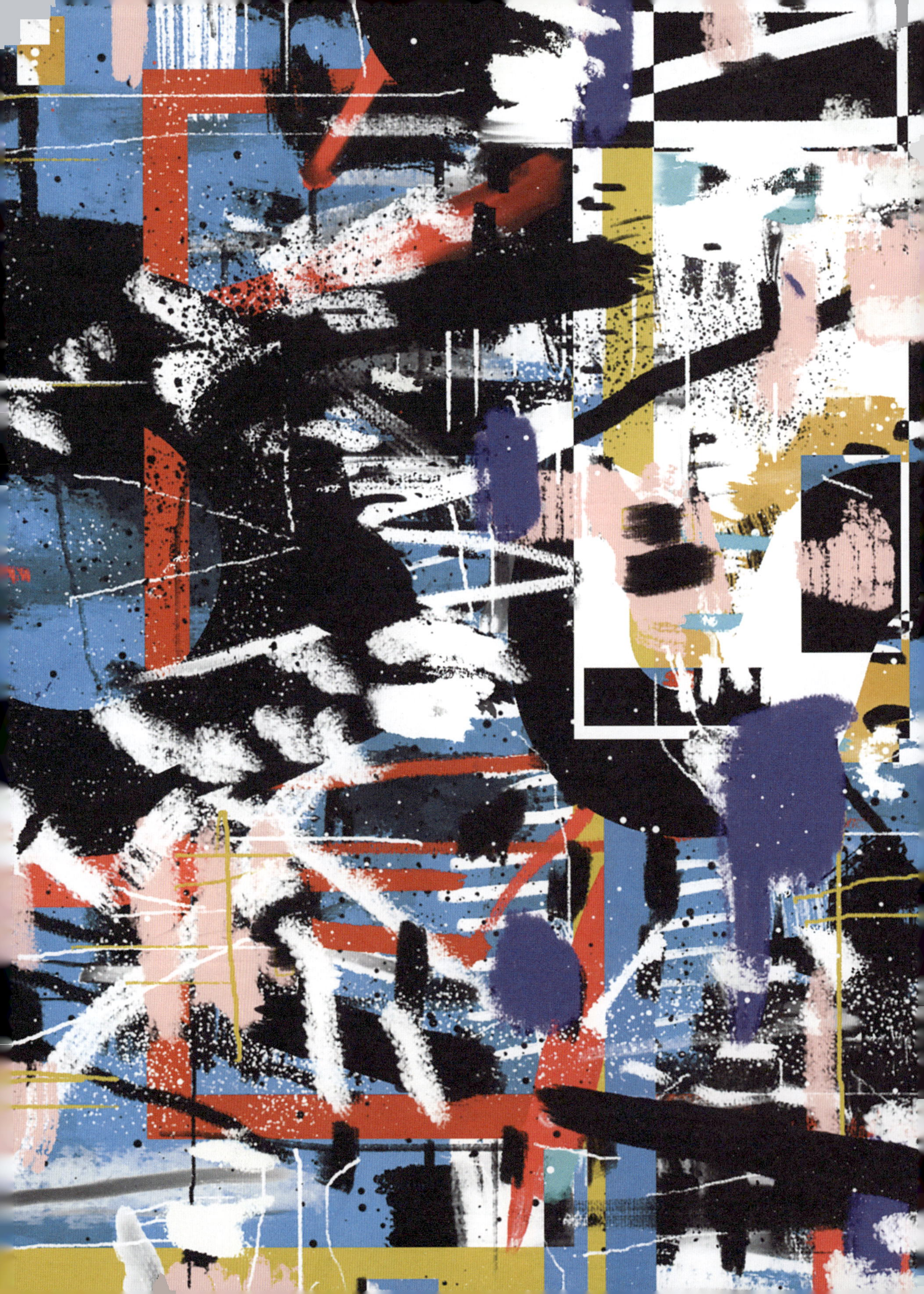

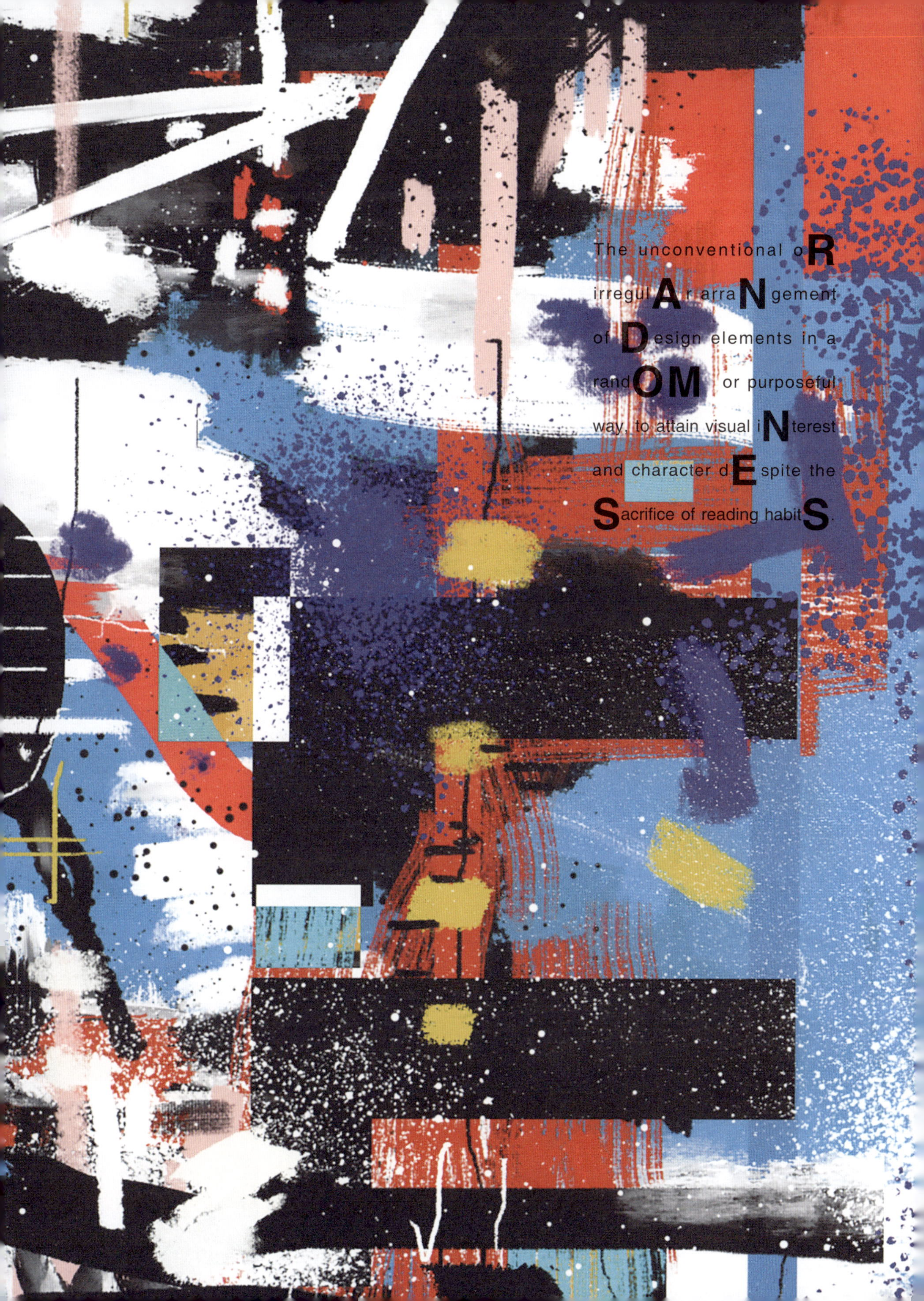
The unconventional oR
irregulAr arraNgement
of Design elements in a
randOM or purposeful
way, to attain visual iNterest
and character dEspite the
Sacrifice of reading habitS.

# # KOOOLLEKTOOR 2017

This is the designer's portfolio which includes projects' basic concept development and journey of execution. It has challenged the common knowledge as a visual designer to reverse the common issues/ideas to another possible direction.

Designer: Kristine H. Kawakubo

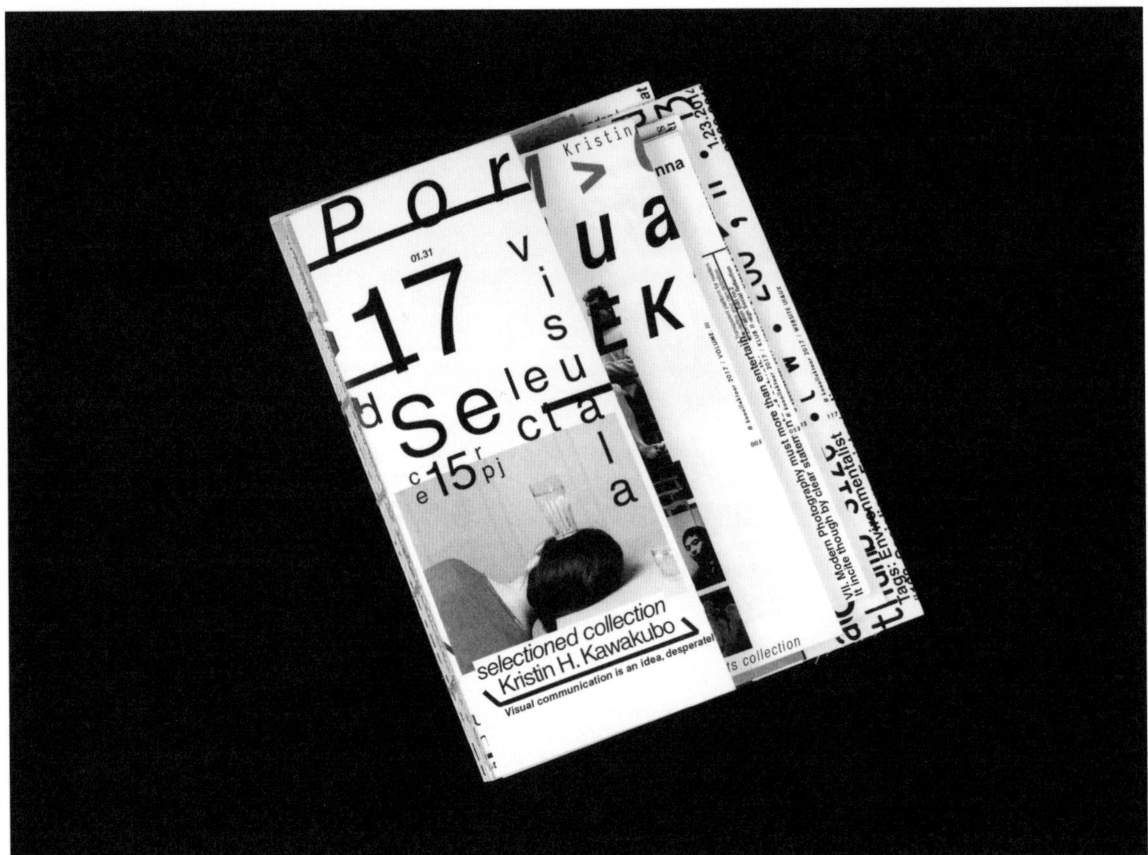


*As a kind of visual experience, what do you think about the "chaos" in graphic design?*

It's common that a creative would challenge the visual method while developing a new concept. For me it's the most essential part of the journey of visual communication. Sometimes chaos brings diversity, sometimes confusion and disorder. However, the accomplishment of great works is often the result of the collision of different perspectives and countless contradictions and confusions. In the field of graphic design, "chaos" has a unique position. It exists in the very beginning of concept development, and it does not go away after we finish the project. To some extent, it reveals the core element of visual communication.

*What are your common approaches to produce a "chaotic" visual effect?*

The chaos is not the kind of beauty that designers are against but conversely it leads us to beauty. It is the interaction between the creator and the project. Then the form of such conversation gets re-constructed between the project (as well as the designer) and the audience. I think this is the most beautiful "chaotic" approach—through the project itself and brings a great influence on the public.

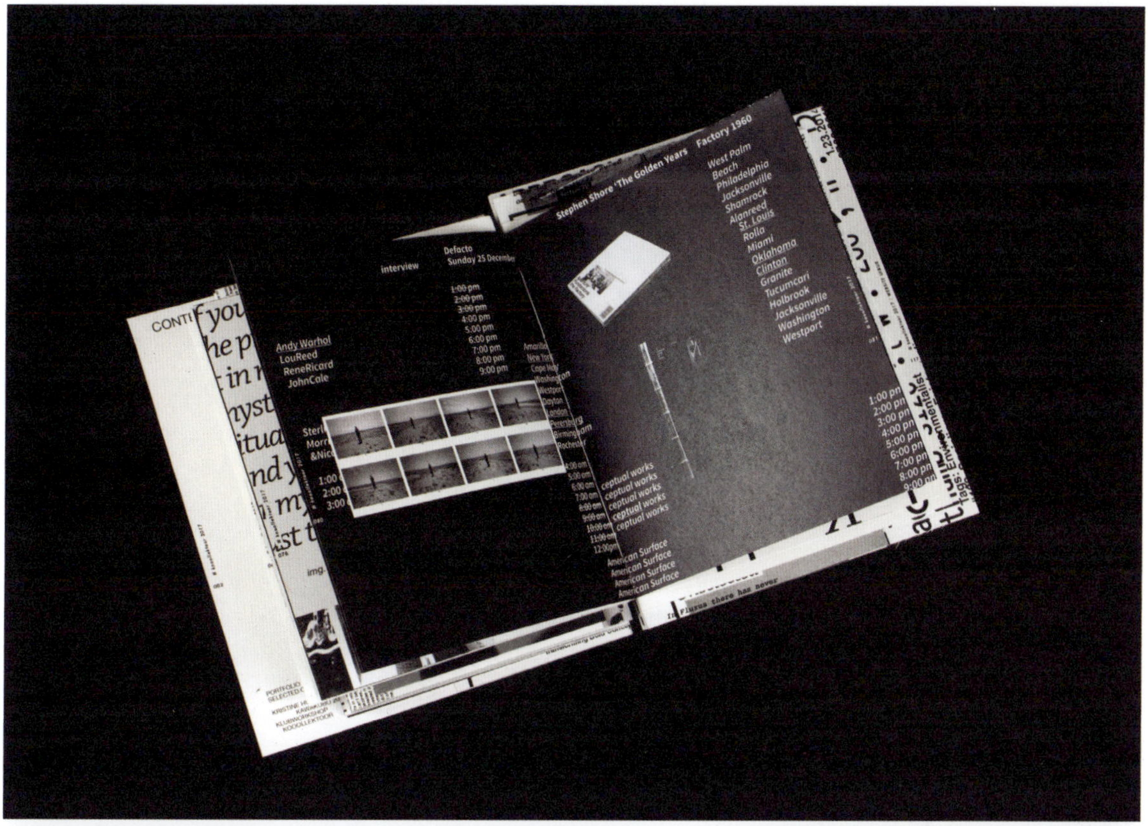
Stephen Shore 'The Golden Years   Factory 1960
West Palm Beach
Philadelphia
Jacksonville
Shamrock
Alanreed
St. Louis
Rolla
Miami
Oklahoma
Clinton
Granite
Tucumcari
Holbrook
Jacksonville
Washington
Westport
Defacto
Sunday 25 December
interview
Andy Warhol
LouReed
ReneRicard
JohnCale
ceptual works
American Surface

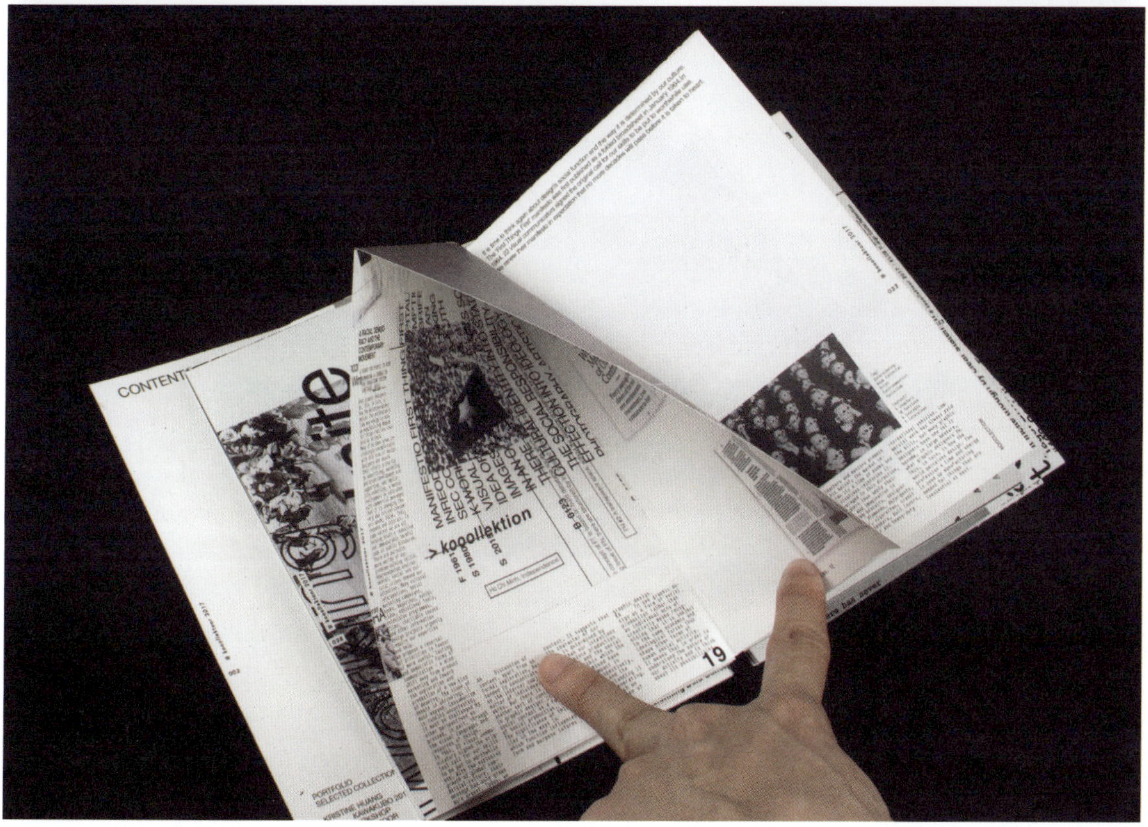
CONTENT
koollektion
19

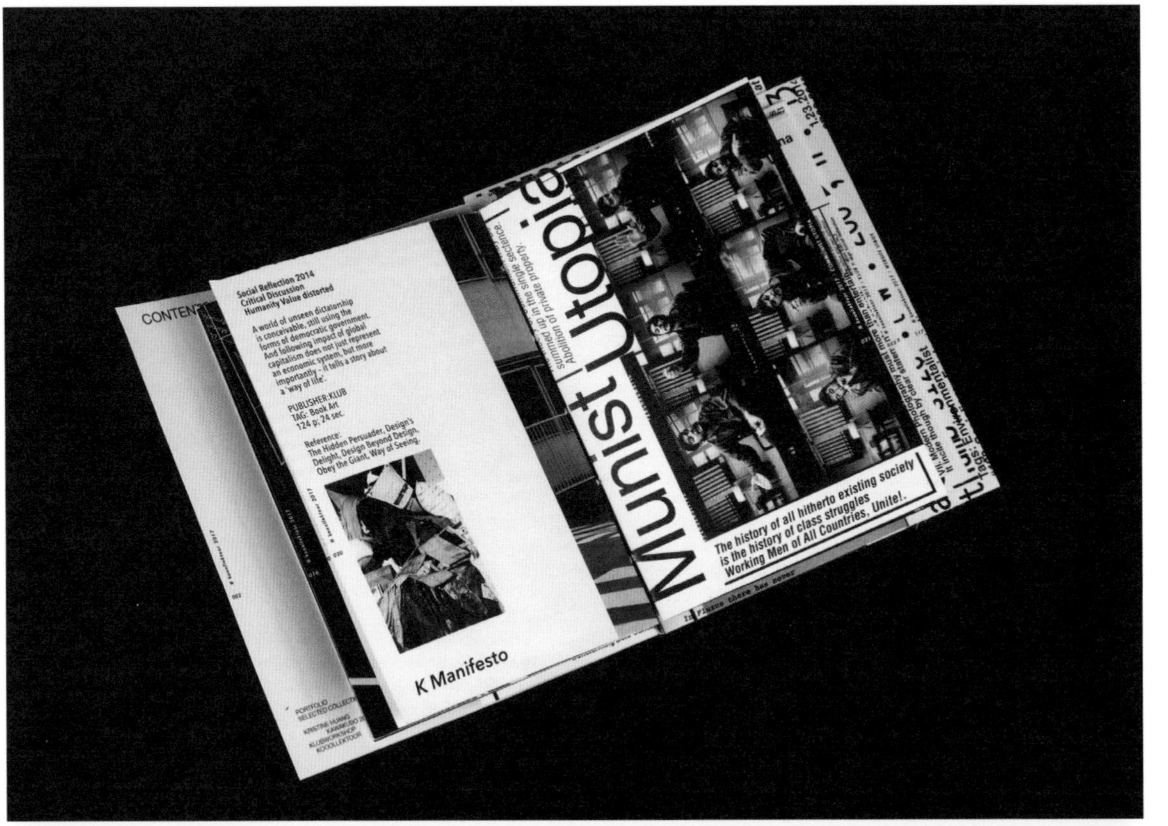

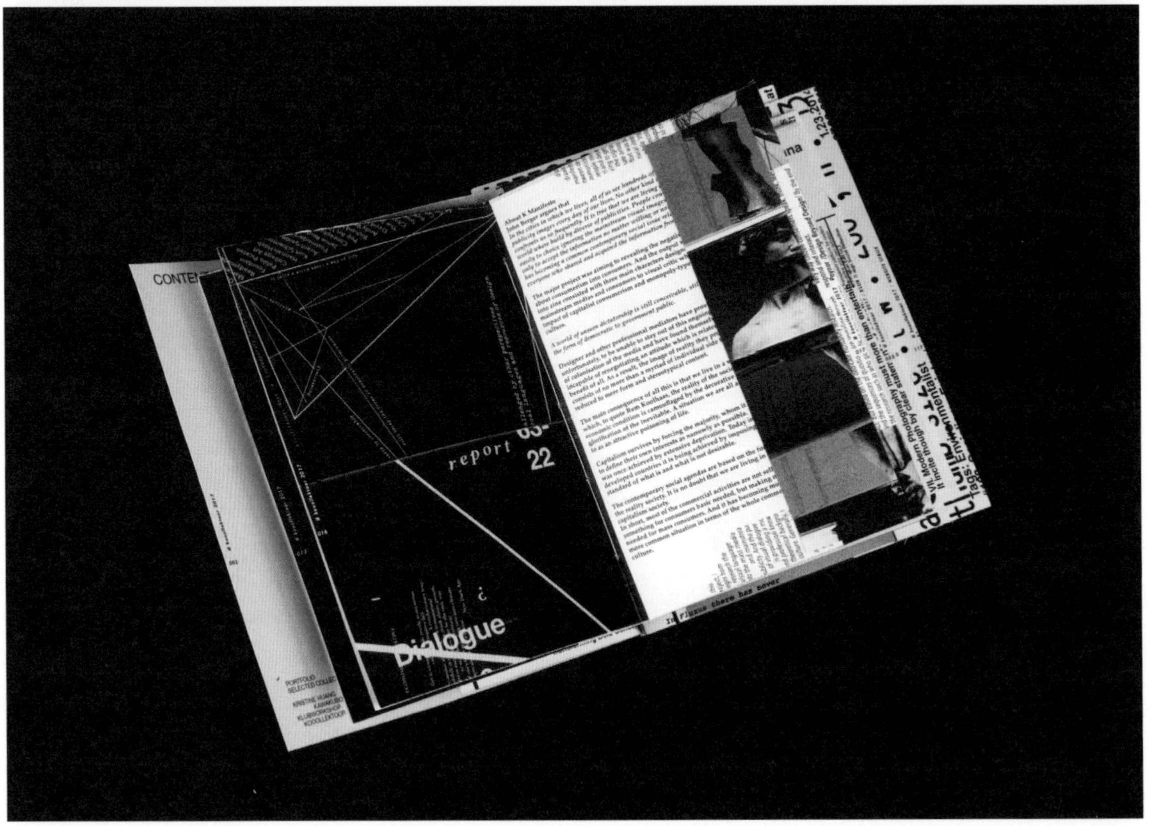

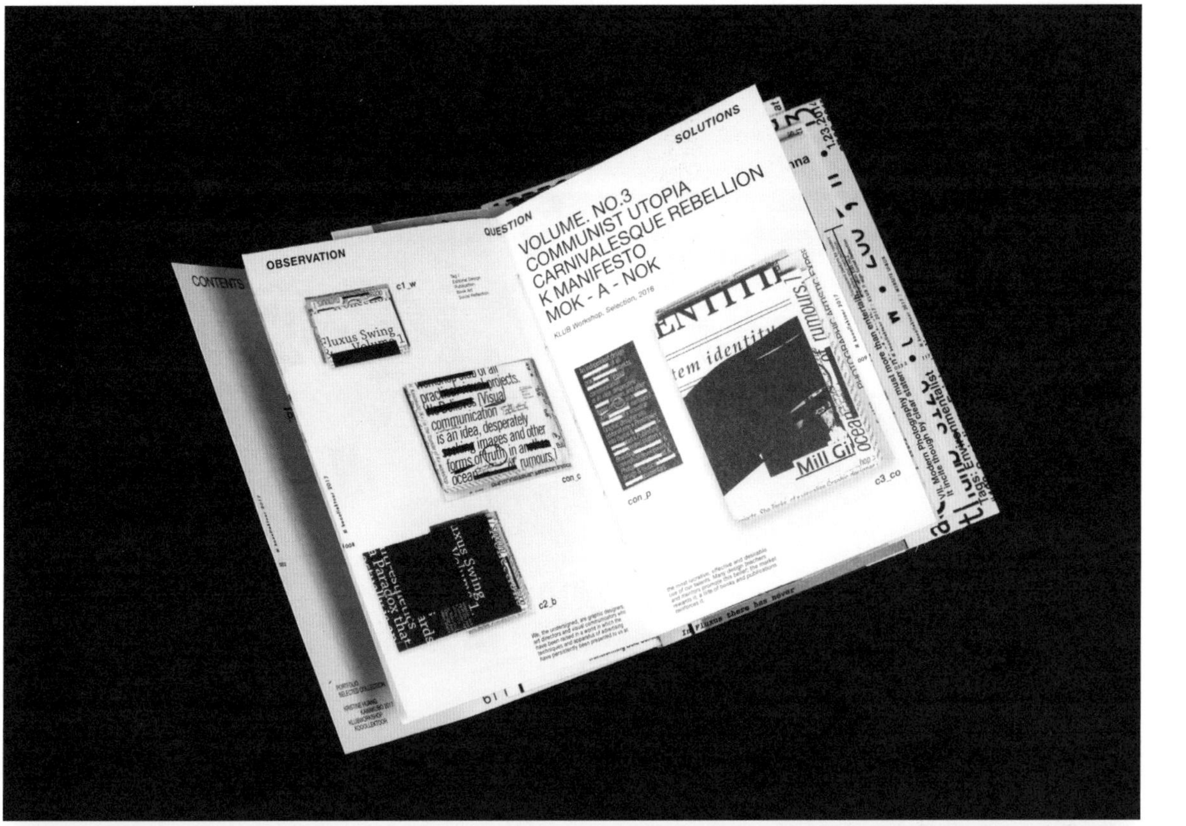
OBSERVATION
QUESTION
SOLUTIONS
VOLUME. NO.3
COMMUNIST UTOPIA
CARNIVALESQUE REBELLION
K MANIFESTO
MOK - A - NOK
KLUB Workshop, Selection, 2016
CONTENTS

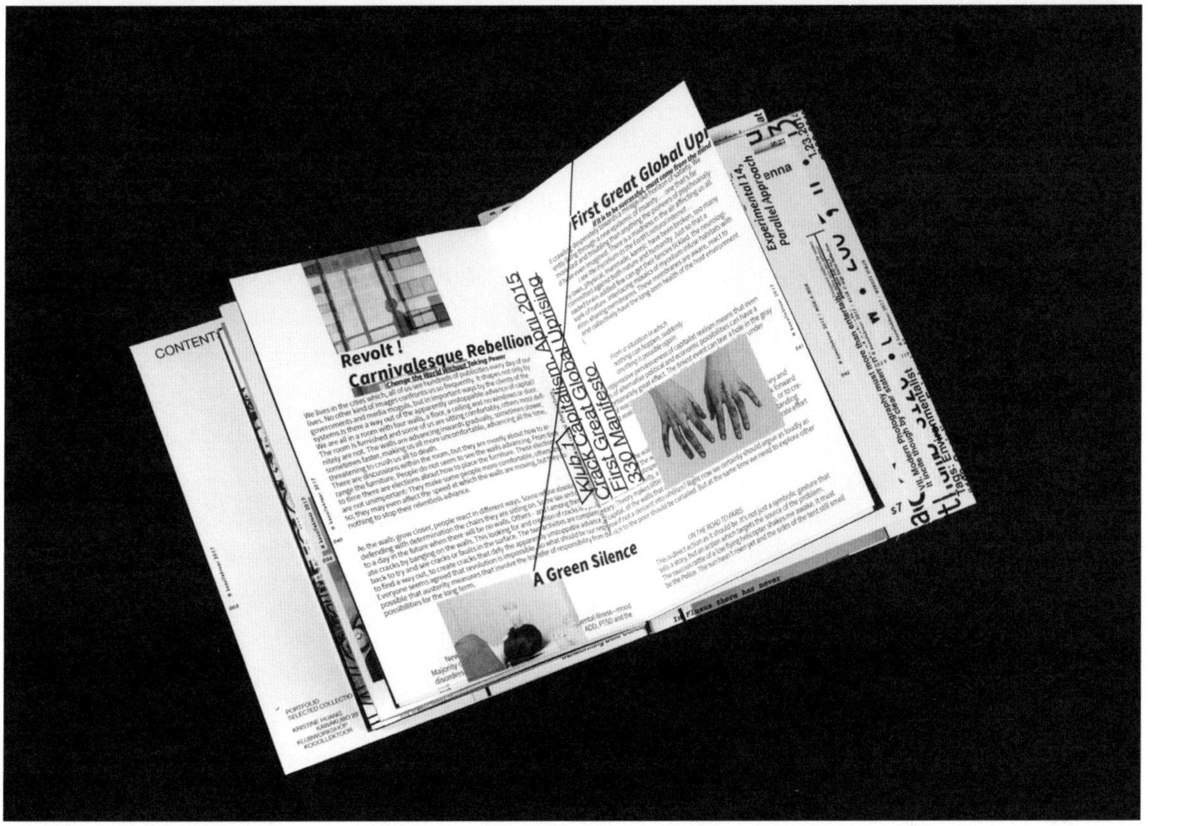
Revolt !
Carnivalesque Rebellion
First Great Global Up
Klub 1 Capitalism, April 2015
Crack Great Global Uprising
First Manifesto
330 Manifesto
A Green Silence
Experimental 14,
Parallel Approach
CONTENT

# NO NAME

The designer would like to change the thoughts and feelings in his daily life into images. The images, just like their paper counterparts, can record the details of life.

Designer: Yang Shi Ching

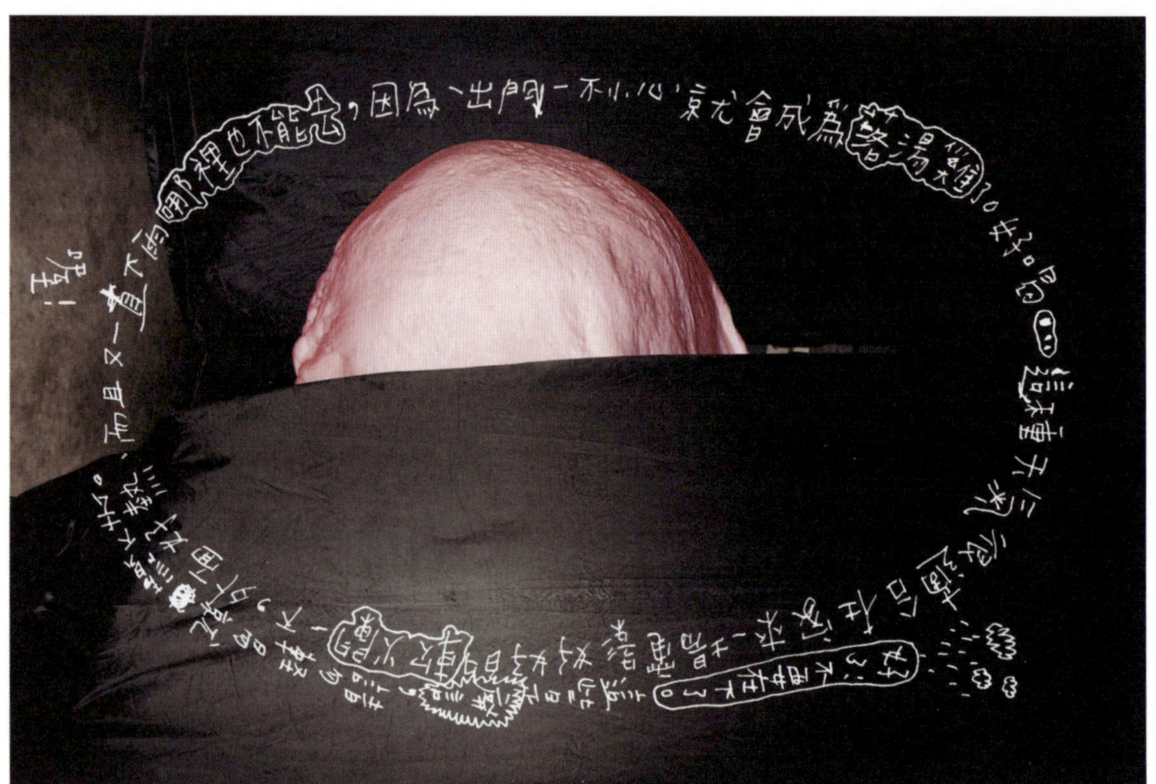


*As a kind of visual experience, what do you think about the "chaos" in graphic design?*

For me, "Chaos" in graphic design is an experimental and destructive way of visual presentation.

*What are your common approaches to produce a "chaotic" visual effect?*

In my works, I prefer to dismantle the bits of resource materials and to reorganize them. In this process, I would like to keep making experiments to excavate the materials' many possibilities.

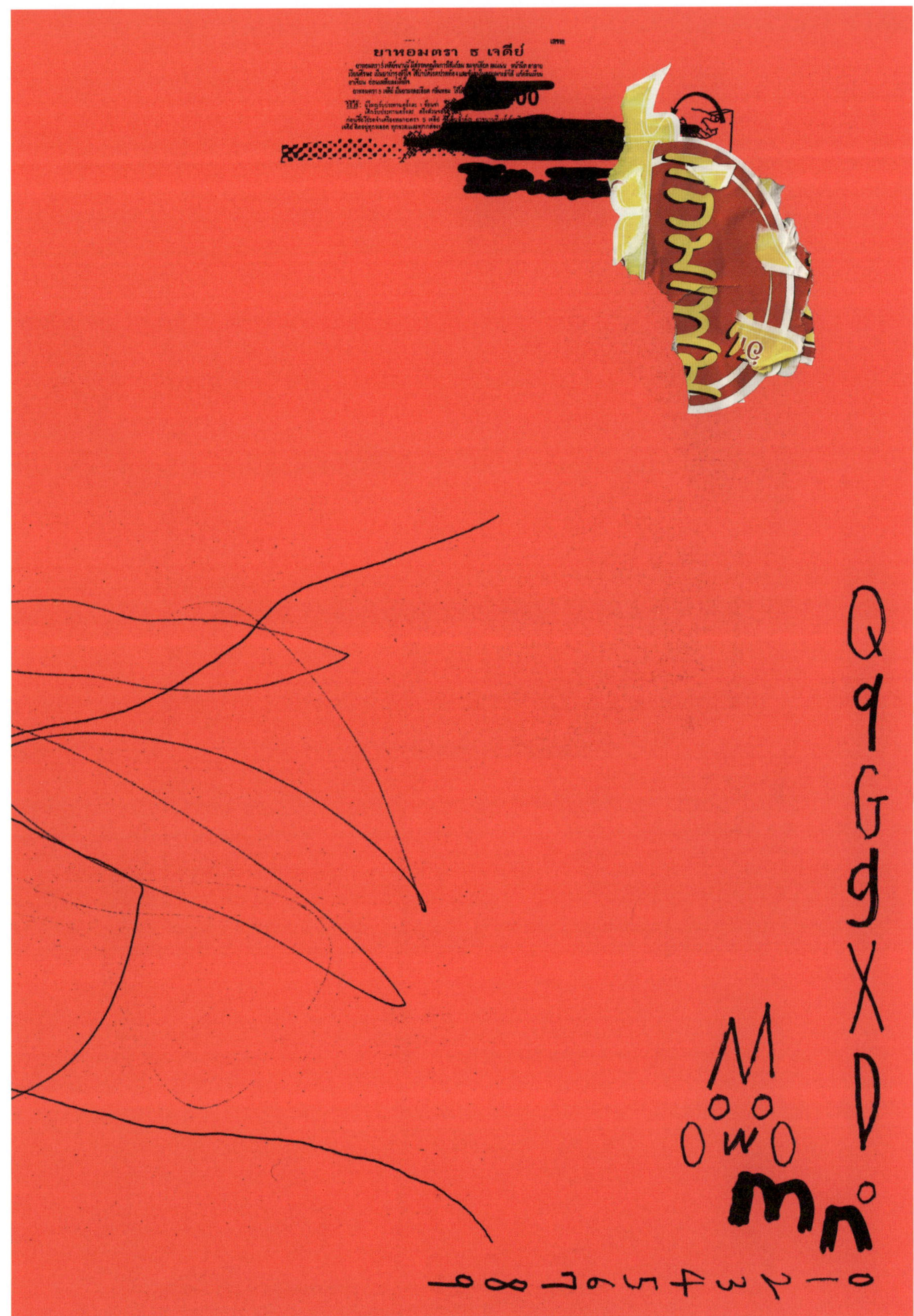

# MOI

Visual exercises and experiments are part of the creative process. MOI is a project from "I" to "We": to disassemble and reconstruct ourselves, and finally combine and become "us."

Designer: Yang Shi Ching , Zih Yu-Liu

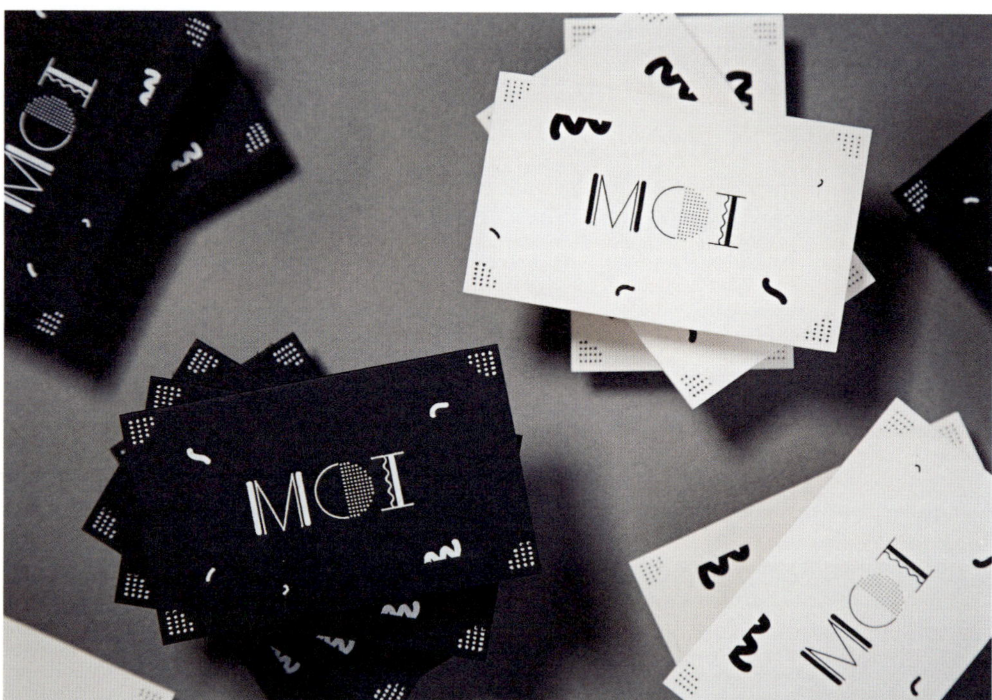


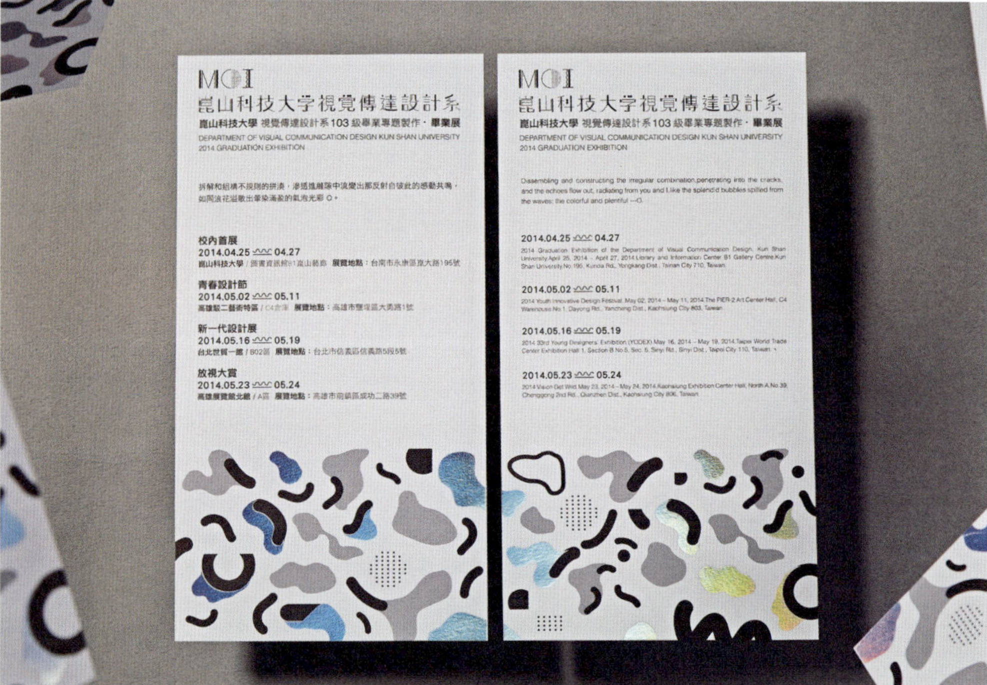

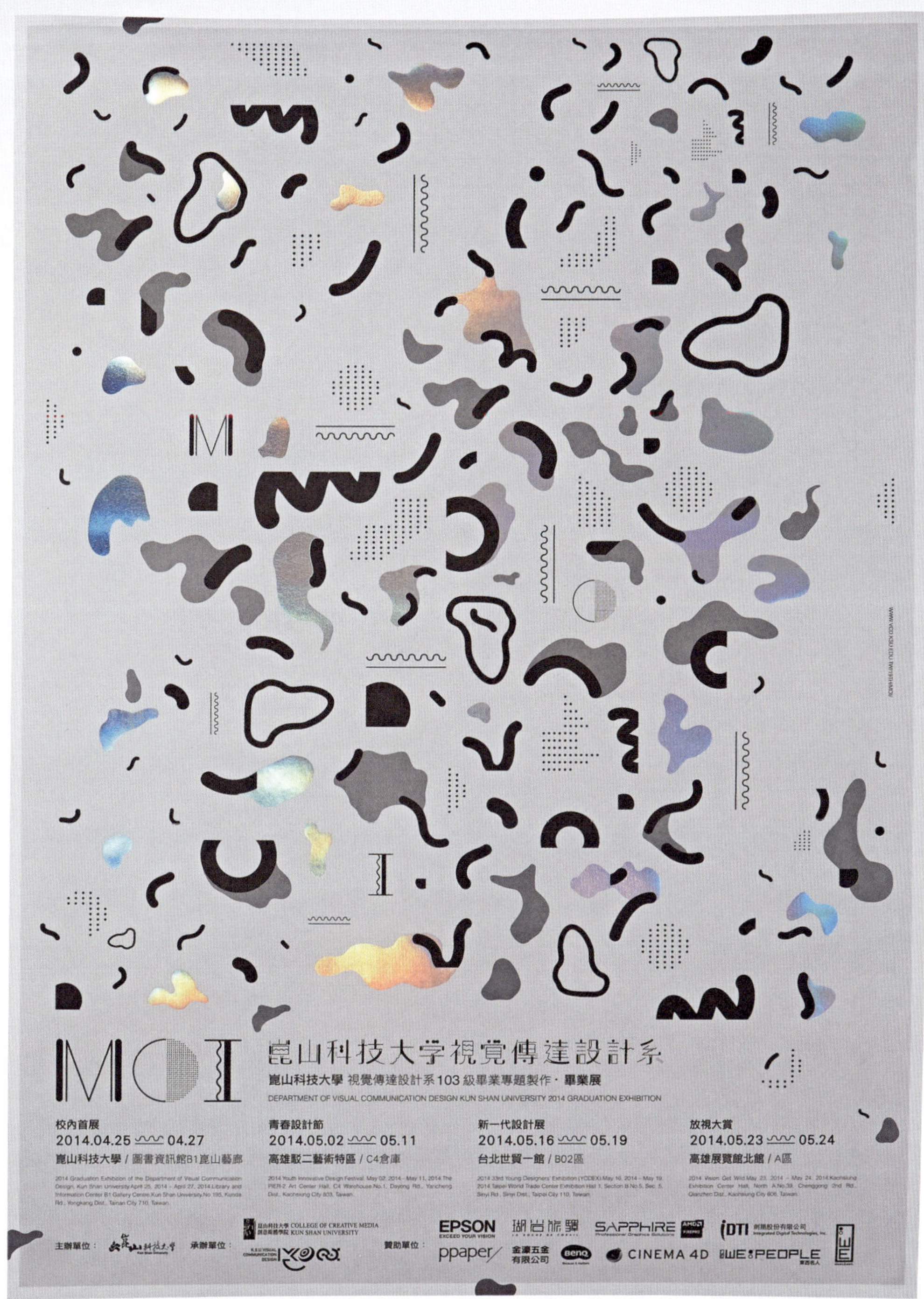
MOI
崑山科技大學視覺傳達設計系
崑山科技大學 視覺傳達設計系103級畢業專題製作 · 畢業展
DEPARTMENT OF VISUAL COMMUNICATION DESIGN KUN SHAN UNIVERSITY 2014 GRADUATION EXHIBITION
校內首展
2014.04.25 ~ 04.27
崑山科技大學 / 圖書資訊館B1崑山藝廊
青春設計節
2014.05.02 ~ 05.11
高雄駁二藝術特區 / C4倉庫
新一代設計展
2014.05.16 ~ 05.19
台北世貿一館 / B02區
放視大賞
2014.05.23 ~ 05.24
高雄展覽館北館 / A區
主辦單位：
承辦單位：
COLLEGE OF CREATIVE MEDIA KUN SHAN UNIVERSITY
贊助單位：
EPSON
EXCEED YOUR VISION
SAPPHIRE
iDTI
ppaper
金濠五金有限公司
BenQ
CINEMA 4D
WE PEOPLE

# 1991-2015 PORTFOLIO POSTER

The designer tried to eliminate his own personality traits to get inspirations. The posters themes include: neurotic, paranoia and obsession.

Designer: Yang Shi Ching

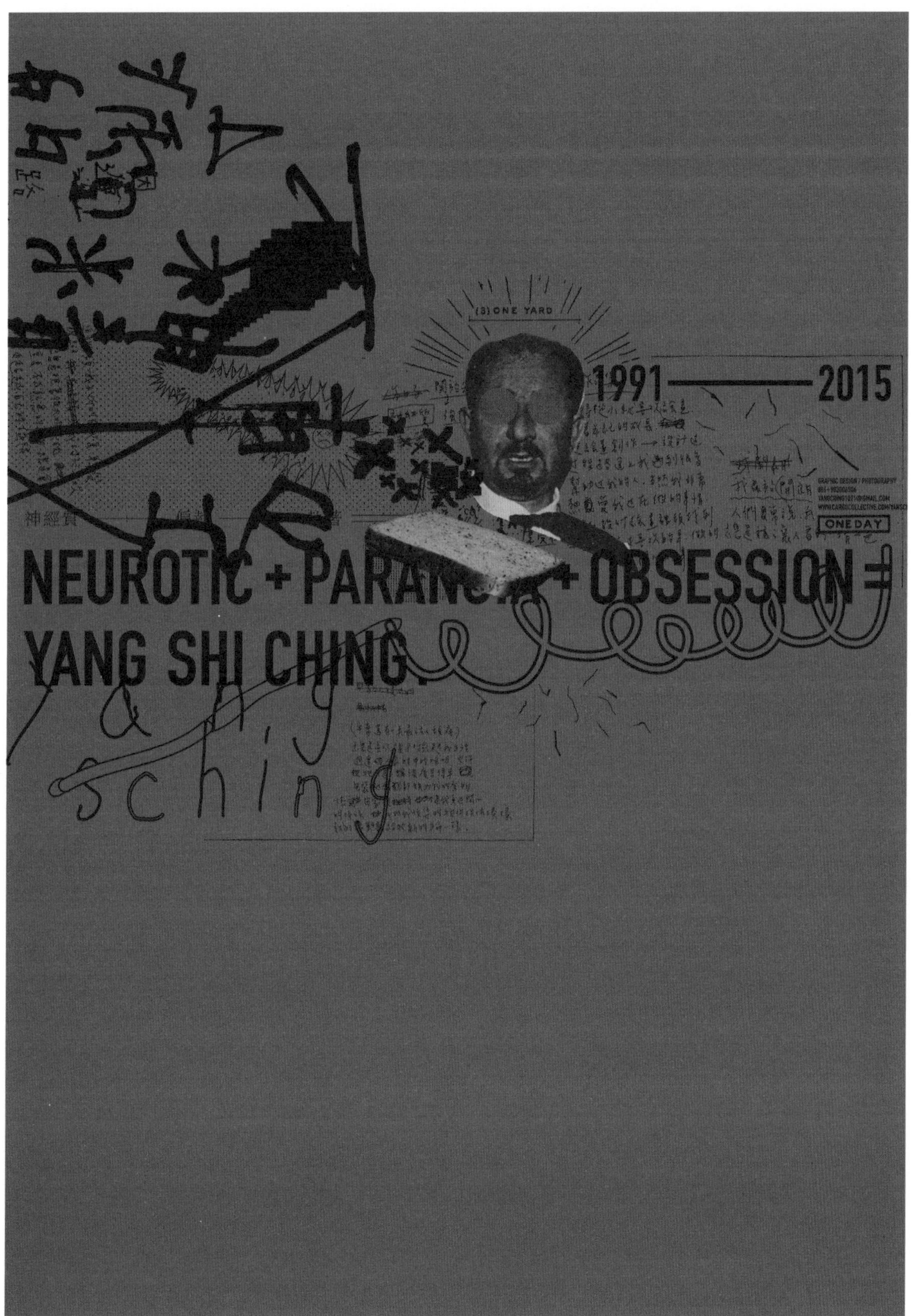
(3) ONE YARD
1991——2015
ONEDAY
NEUROTIC + PARANOIA + OBSESSION =
YANG SHI CHING
神經質

# PAKHO CHAU BOXED SET

This is a boxed set for Pakho Chau, known as a recording artist in Hong Kong. The designer has made artworks utilizing Pakho's lyrics and positive messages for the cover, poster and post cards.

Designer: Glenn Wolk

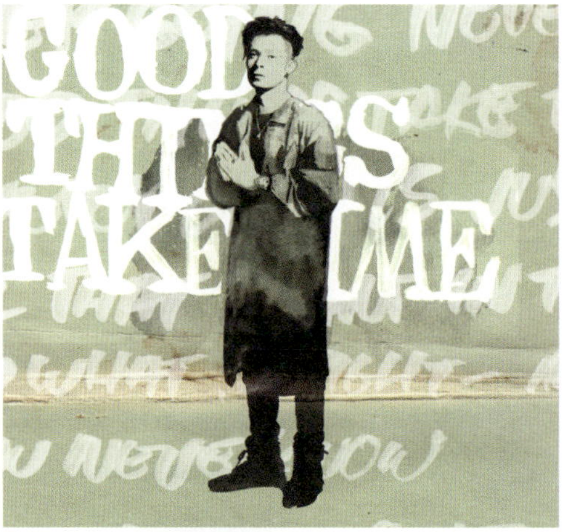

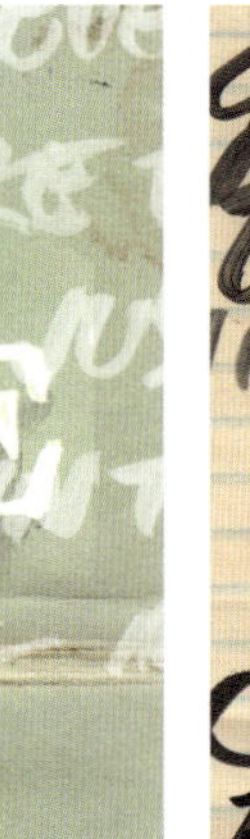

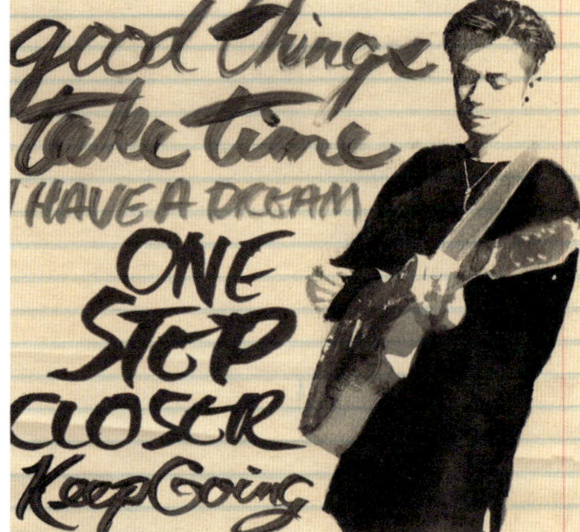

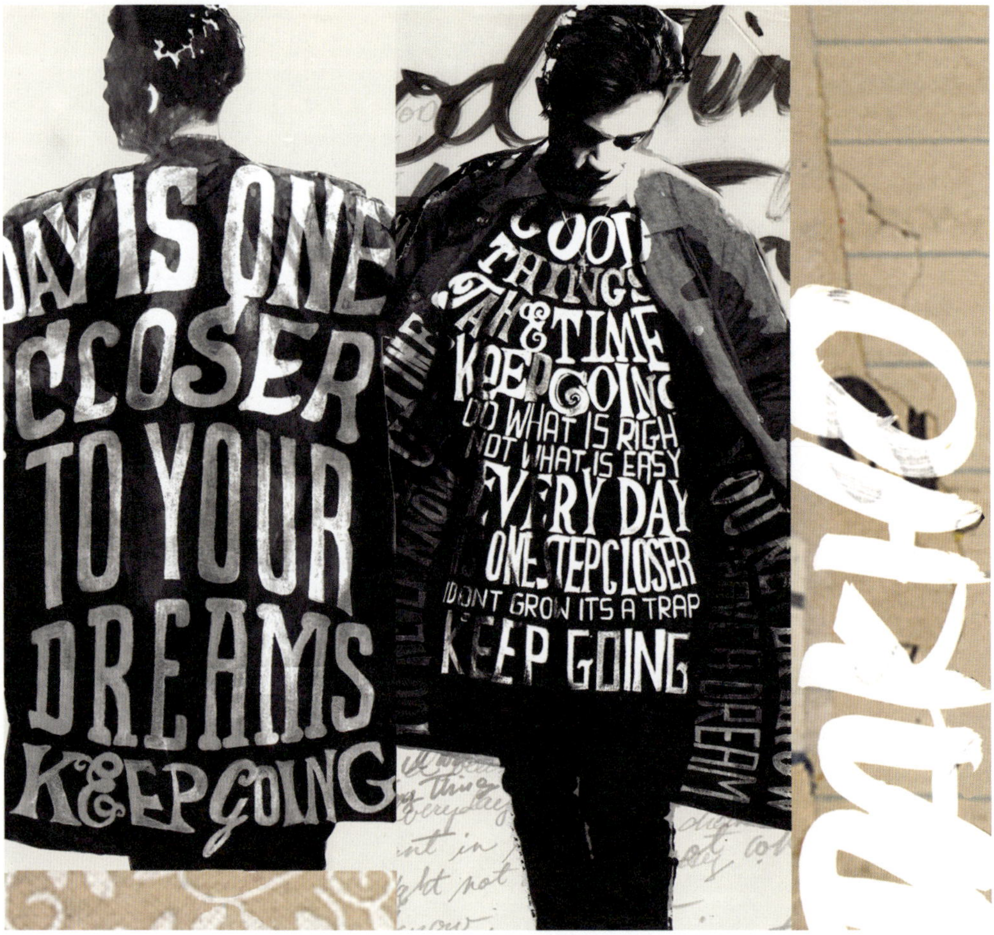

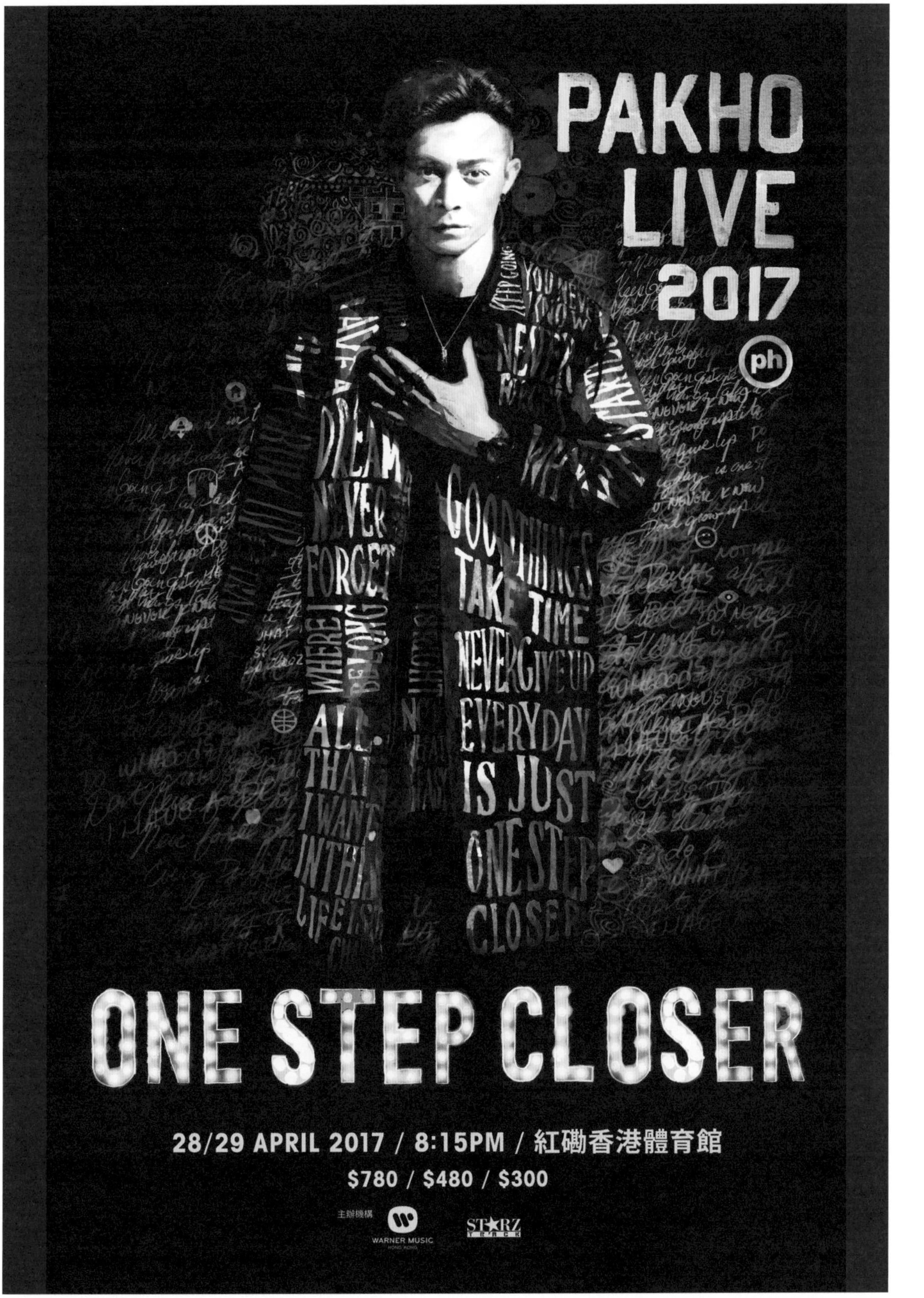

PAKHO
LIVE
2017

ONE STEP CLOSER

28/29 APRIL 2017 / 8:15PM / 紅磡香港體育館

$780 / $480 / $300

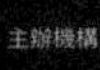

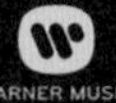

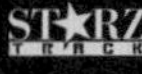

# SAMTHEAGENCY

This is an identity design for SAMTHEAGENCY model management agency based in Budapest. The logo is a modular and geometrical typographic work inspired by the agency owner's tattoo and his black and white photos.

Studio: HOOH
Designer: Anna Rozsa, Norbert Mayer

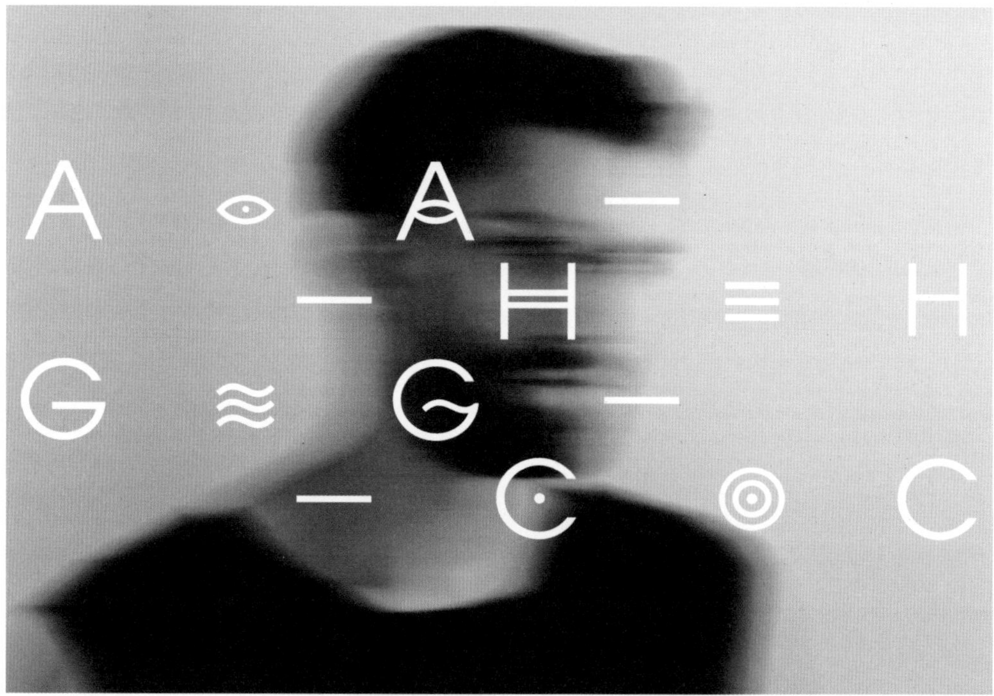

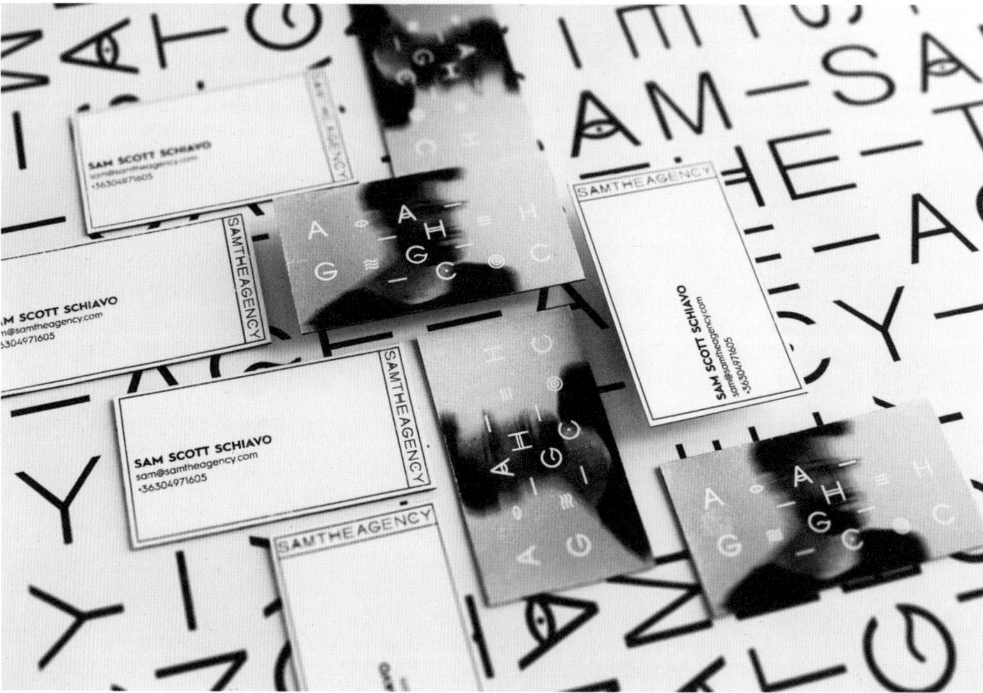

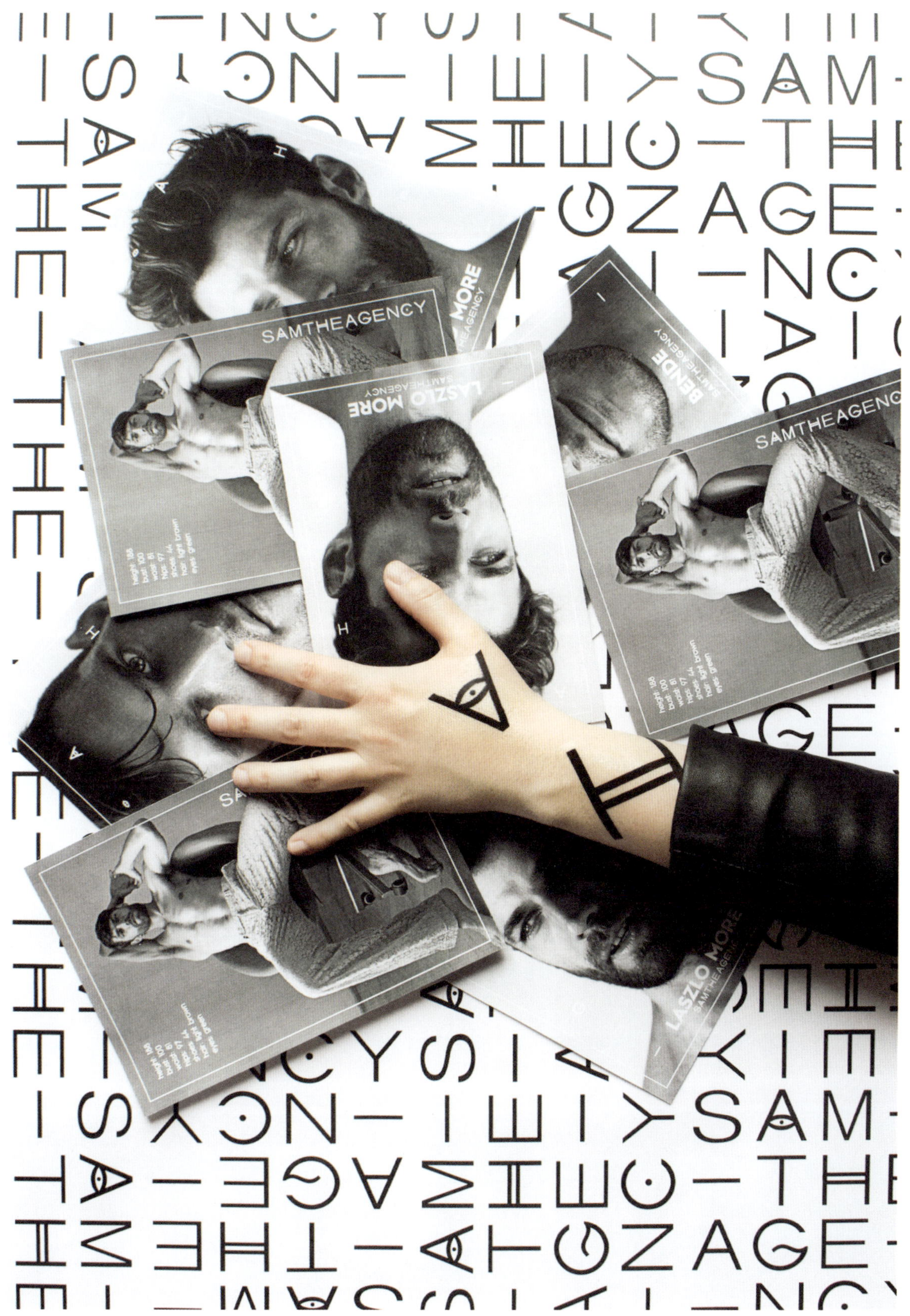
SAMTHEAGENCY
LASZLO MORE
SAMTHEAGENCY
BENDE
SAMTHEAGENCY
height 188
bust 100
waist 81
hips 97
shoes 44
hair light brown
eyes green

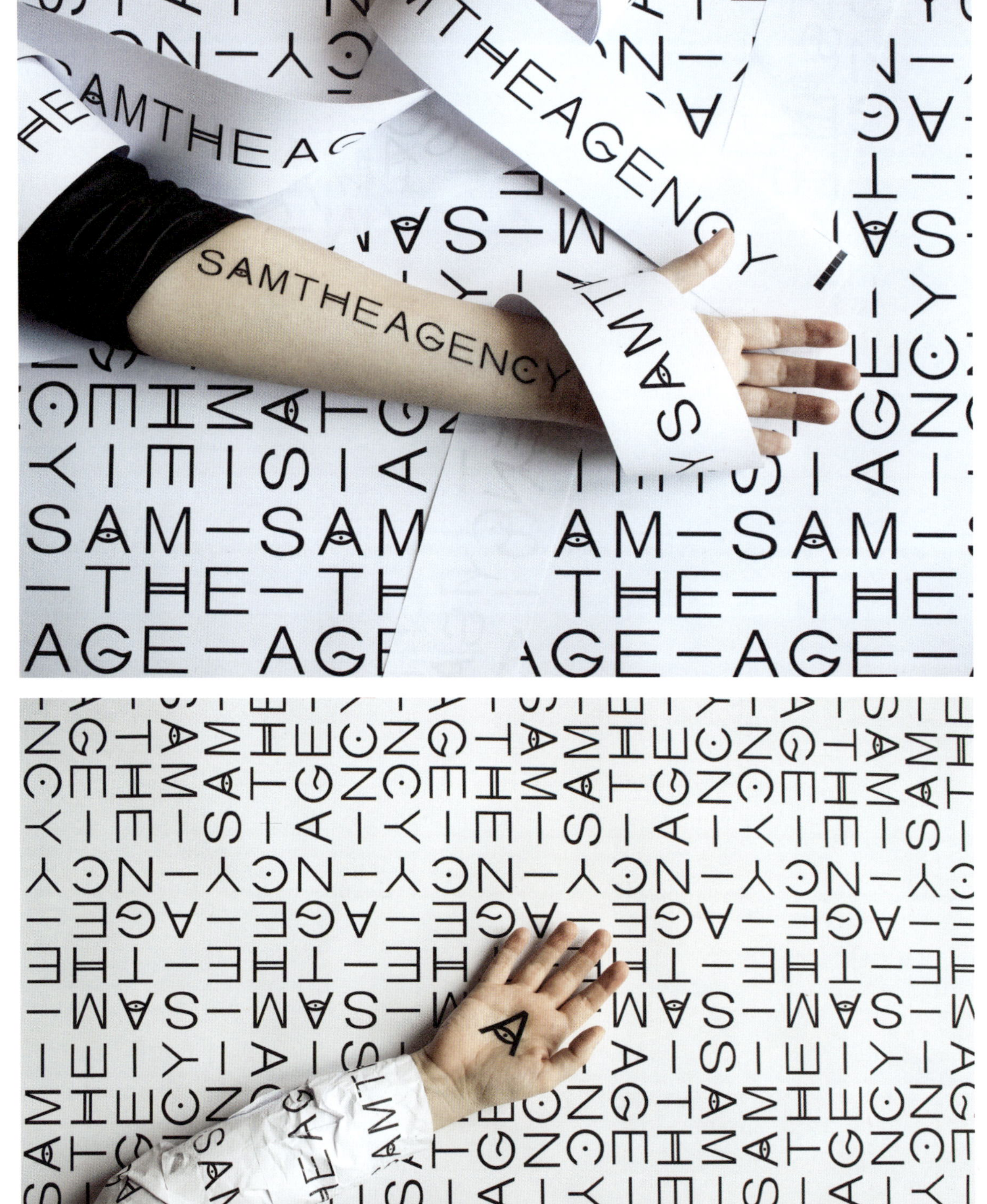
SAMTHEAGENCY
SAM–SAM
–THE–TH
AGE–AGE
SAM–SAM–SAM–SAM–SA
–THE–THE–THE–THE–T
AGE–AGE–AGE–AGE–AG

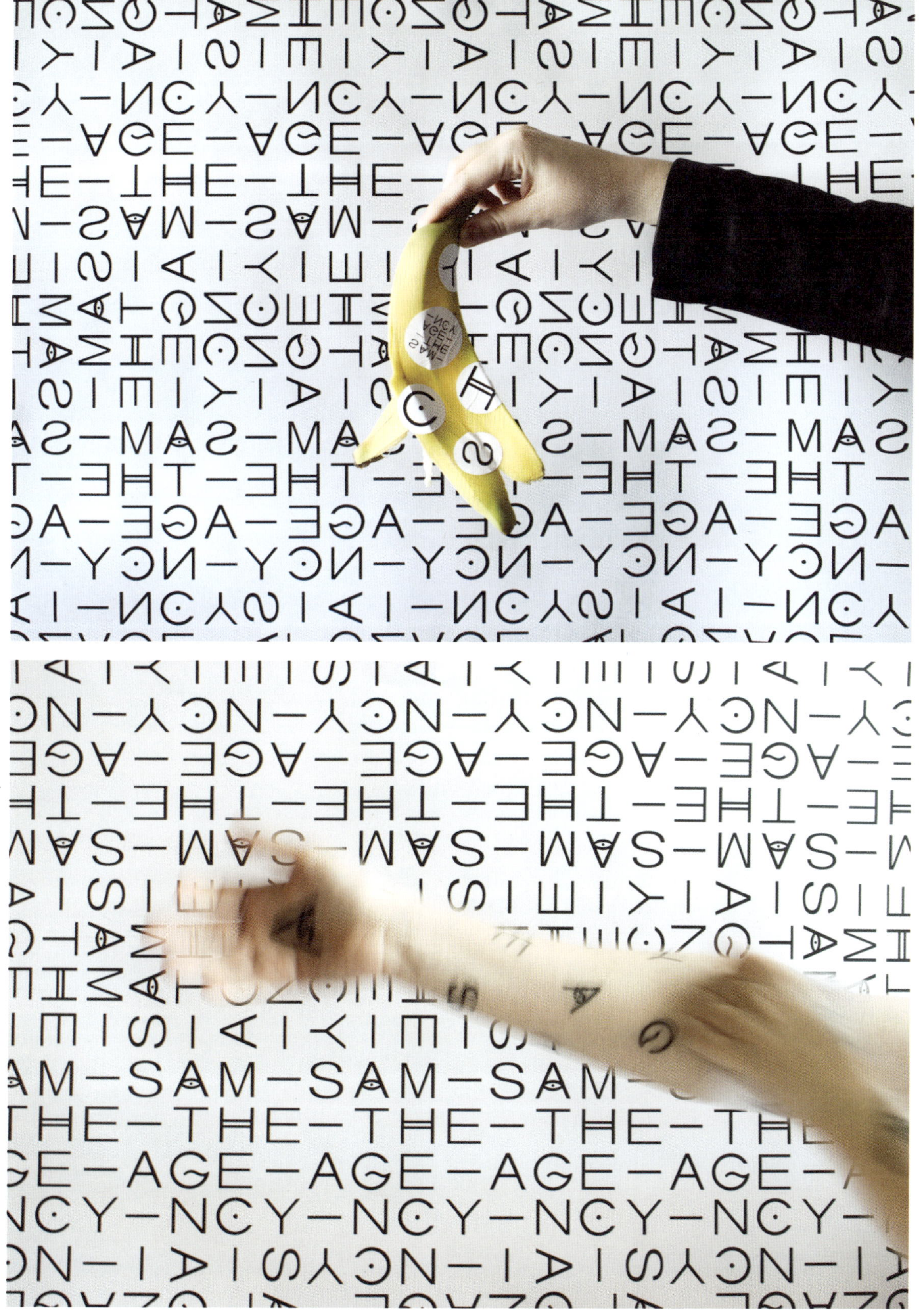

# HV—100 GLITCH EXPERIMENT

Inspired by the lettering of Vilmos Huszar, a painter and designer who was a founding member of De Stijl movement, the artist created this experimental glitch series based on a regular grid system between 2014 and 2017.

Studio: Dora Balla

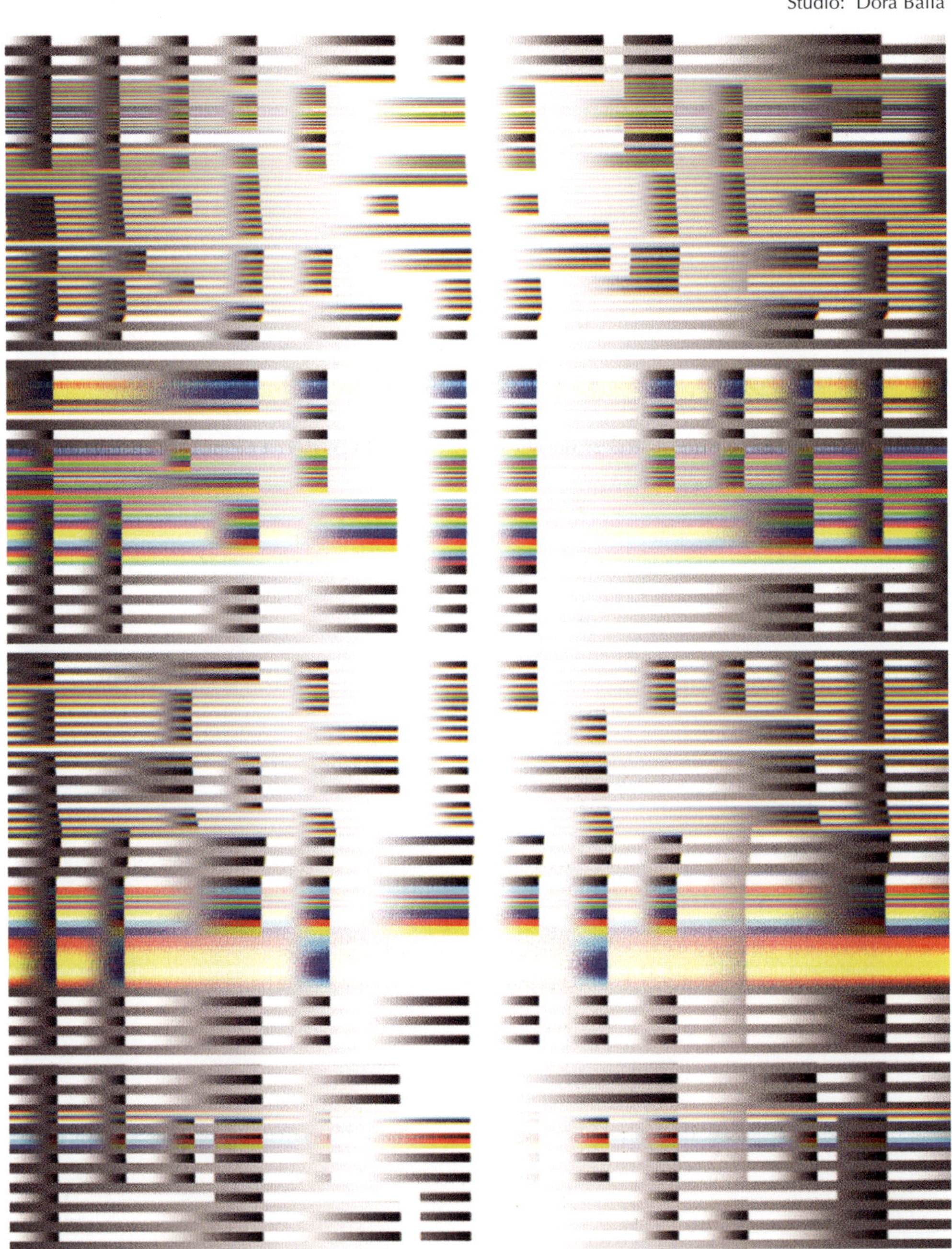

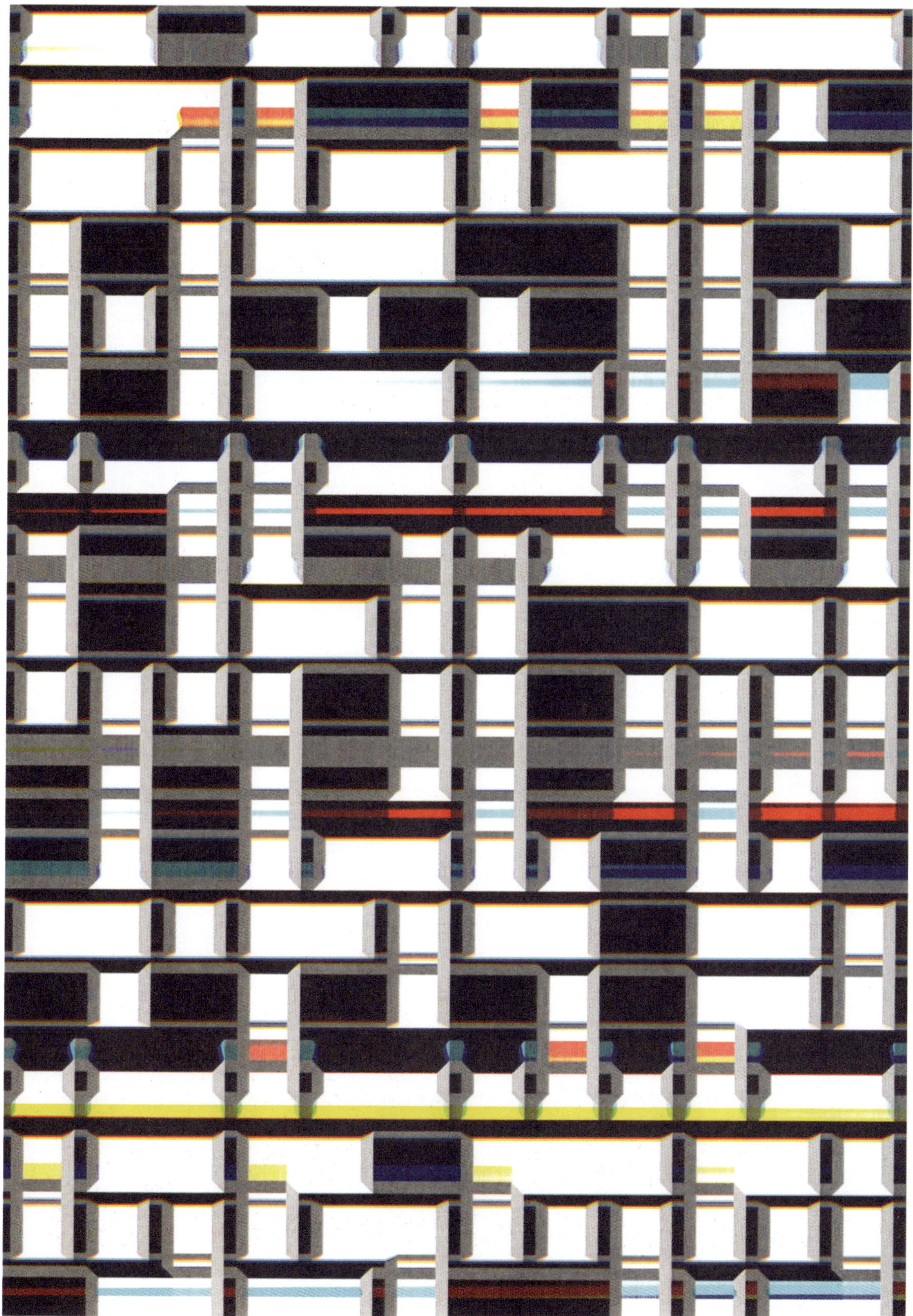

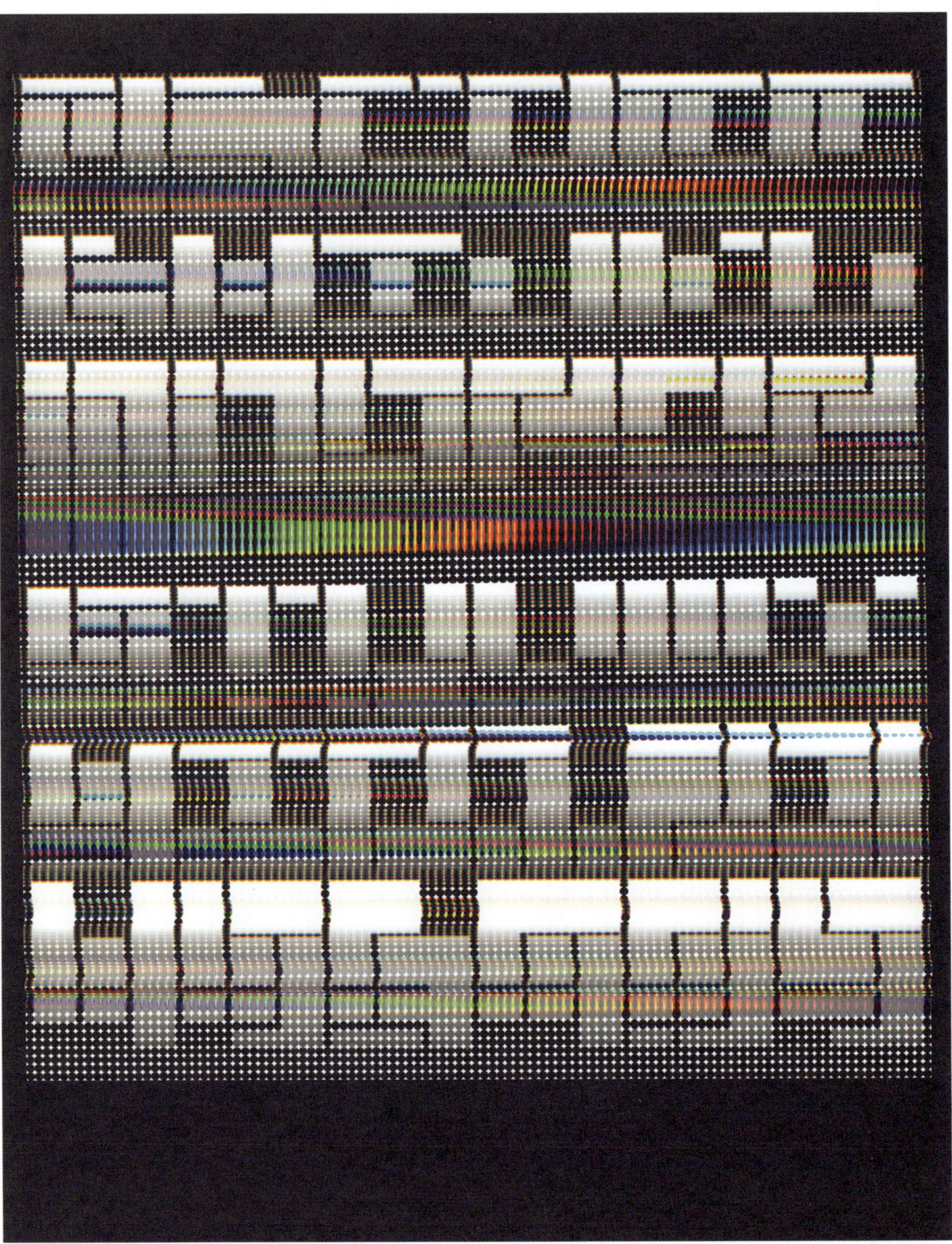

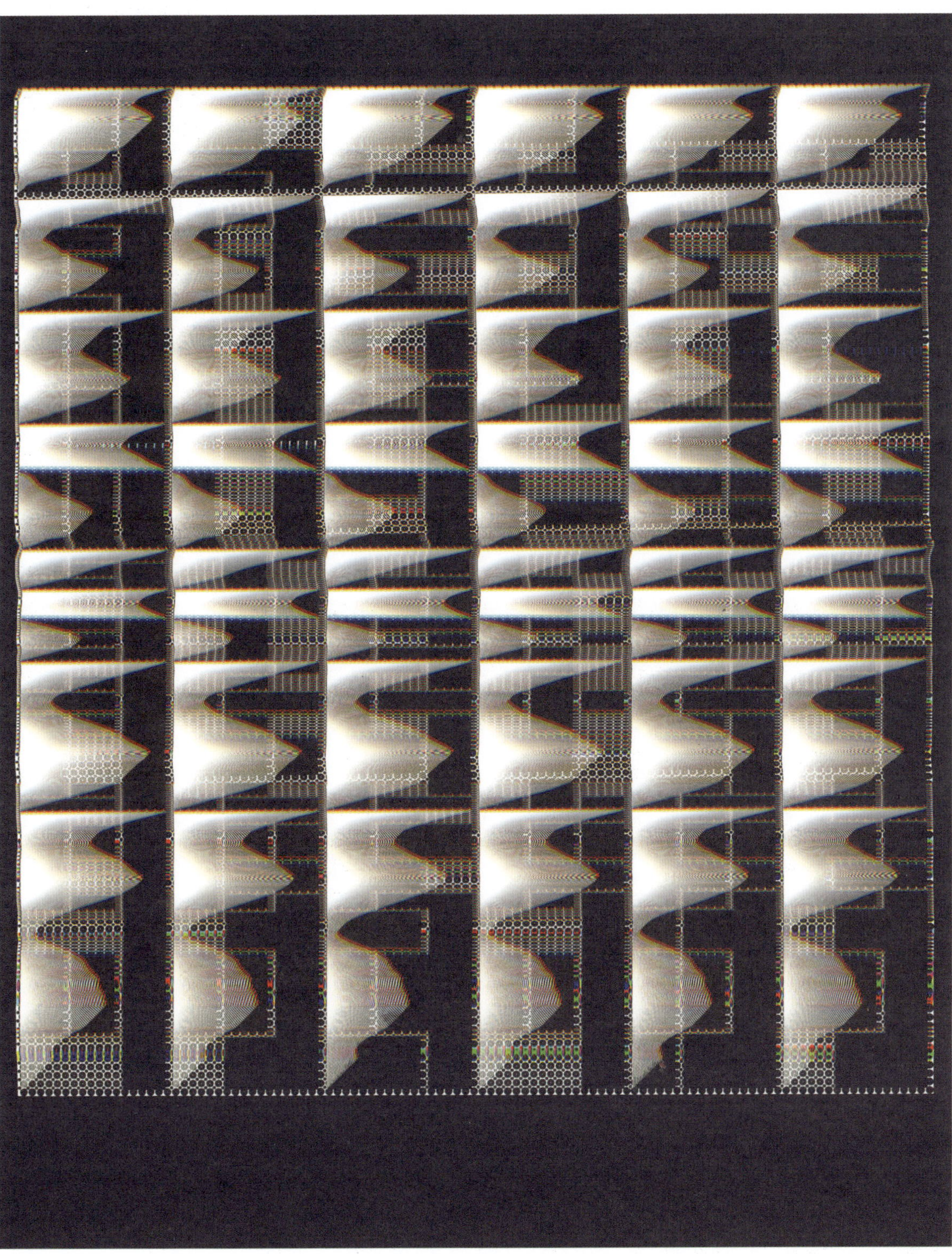

# BLACK HAND PATH—OBFUSCANT

"Obfuscant", which refers to the act of obfuscating content, is a word coined by the rap group Blackhandpath. Being transparent to the content, the artwork derives from the actual lyrics. As the lyrics get mashed, the information gets destroyed, the digital comes into play and the cover is an algorithmic dance between its own corruption obfuscating the artwork and building identity.

Studio: Royal

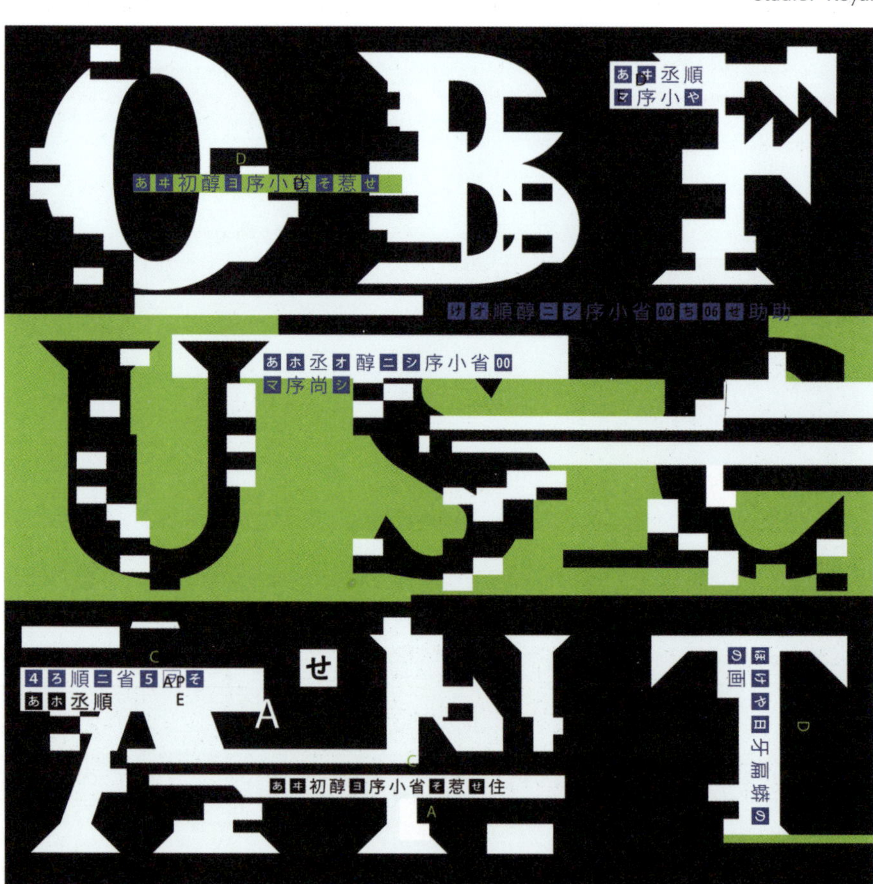

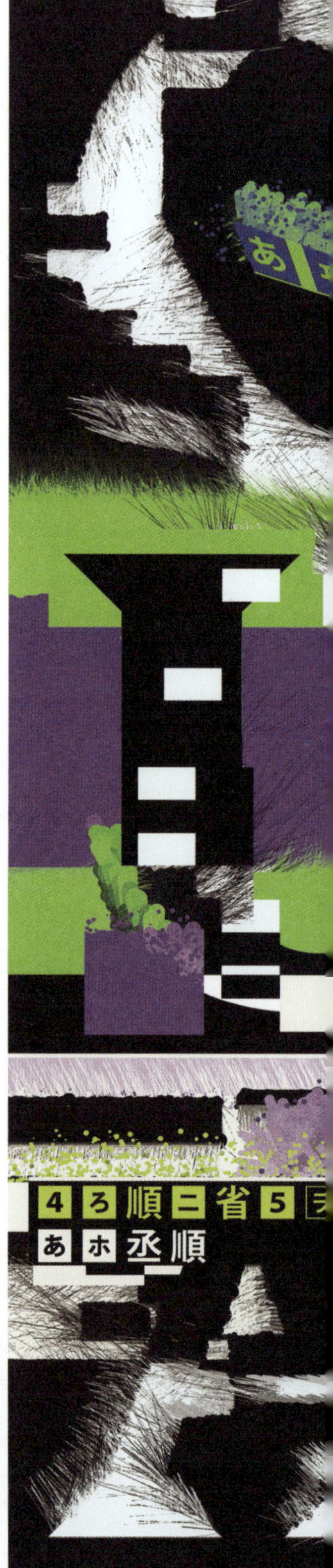

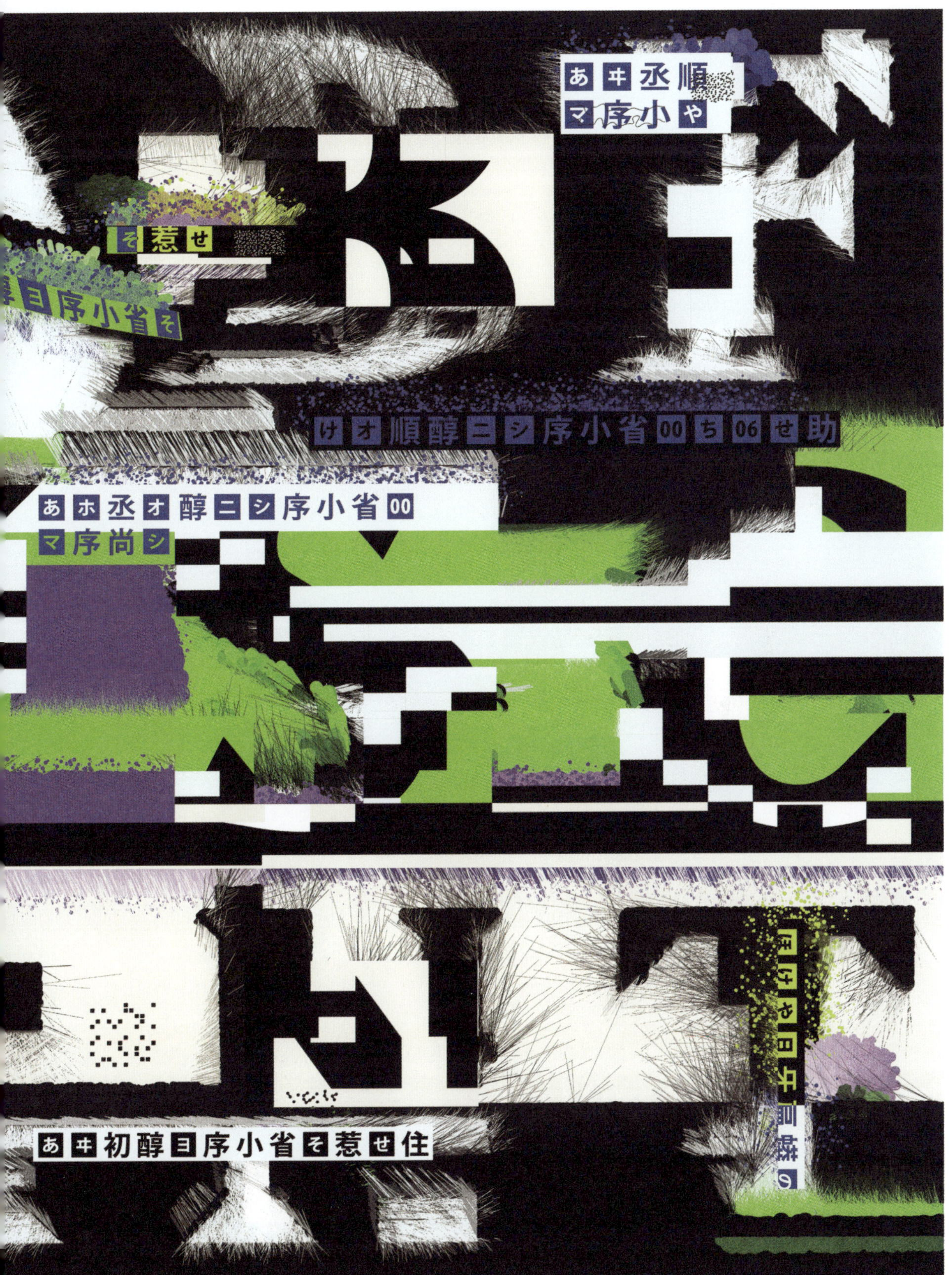

# SEWOON PLAZA AND MAKERS

Sewoon Plaza is an electronic products shopping mall in Seoul. And "Makers" are the young people who generate different ideas by using the electronic devices. Sewoon Plaza and Makers is an event to the public that showcases the result of the collaboration between young "Makers" and the people working at Sewoon Plaza. For the event's graphic design, the designer used some electronic devices as the main visual elements.

Studio: TRIANGLE-STUDIO
Designer: Kisung Jang

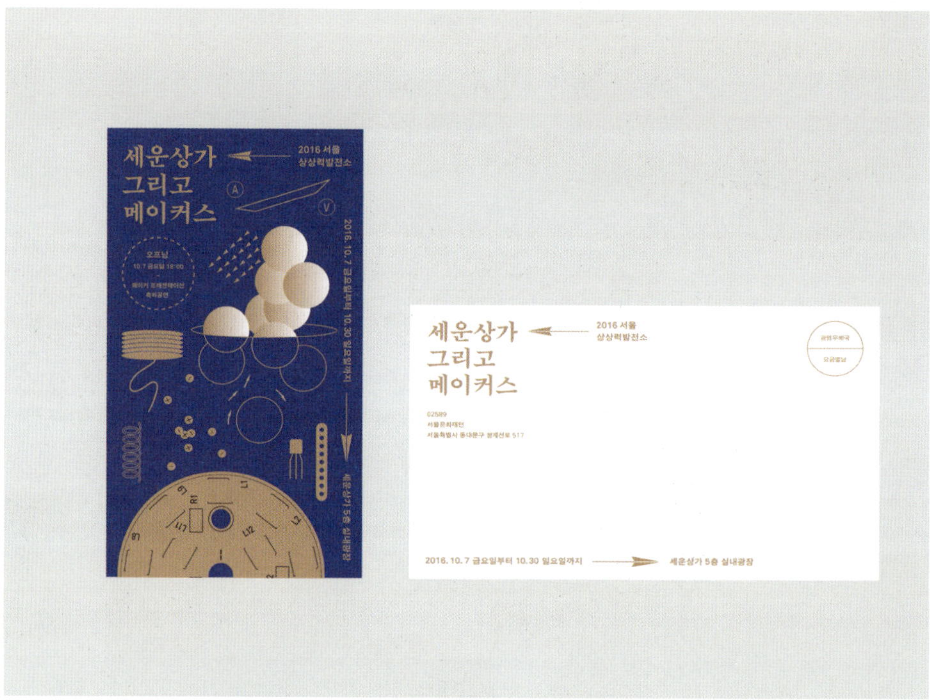


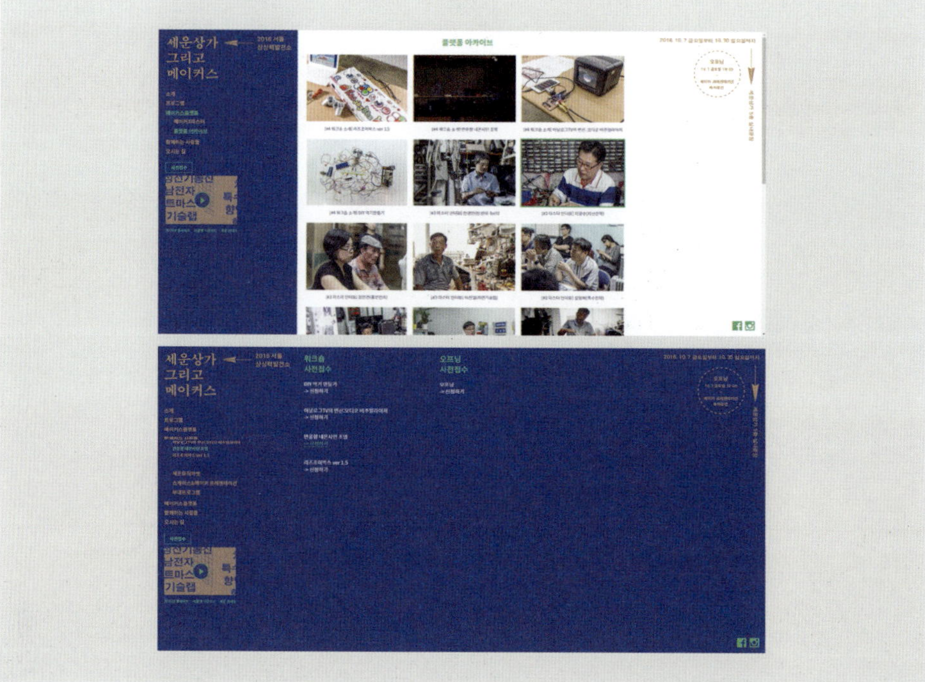

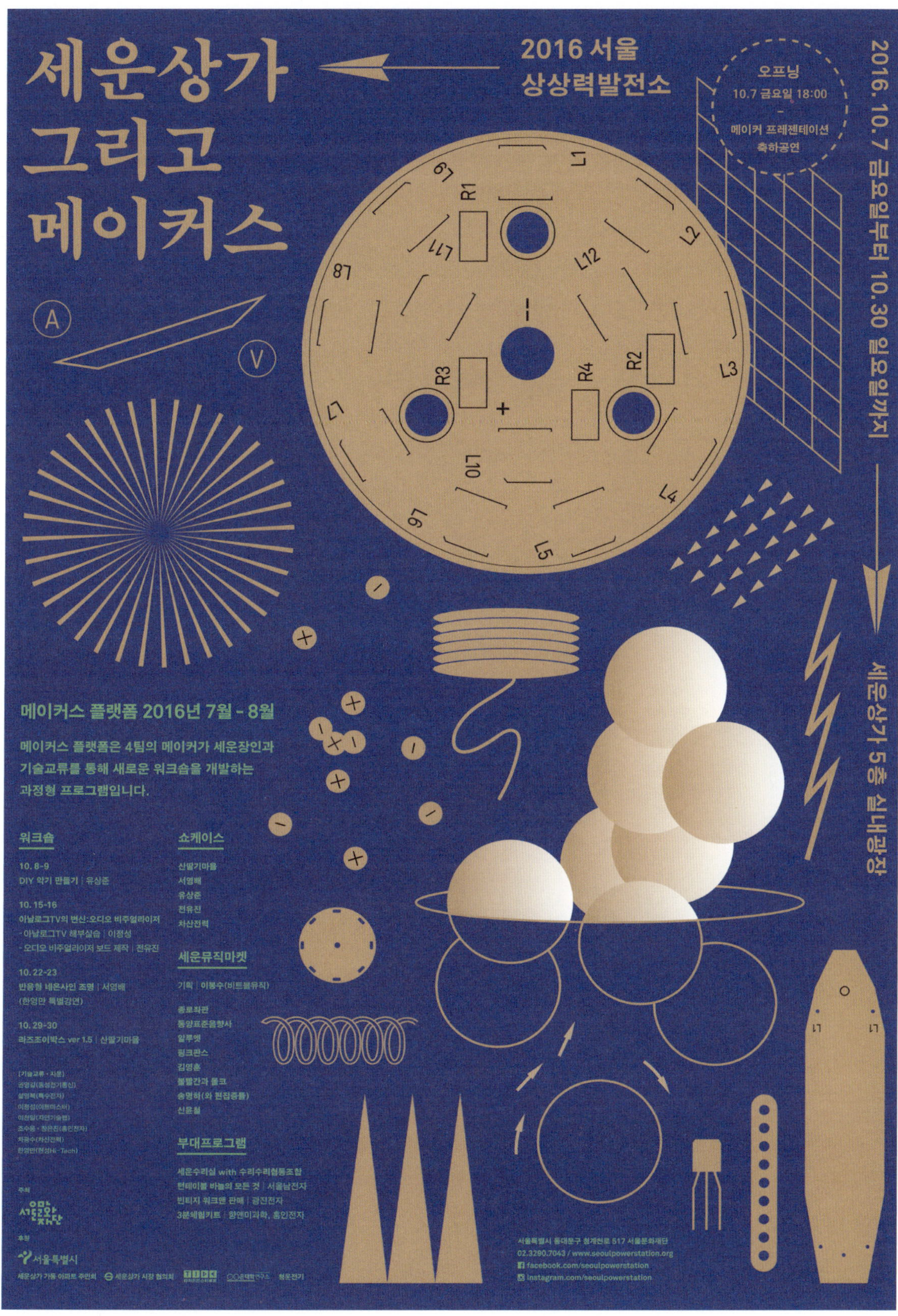

세운상가
그리고
메이커스
2016 서울
상상력발전소
오프닝
10.7 금요일 18:00
-
메이커 프레젠테이션
축하공연
2016. 10. 7 금요일부터 10. 30 일요일까지
세운상가 5층 실내광장
메이커스 플랫폼 2016년 7월 - 8월
메이커스 플랫폼은 4팀의 메이커가 세운장인과
기술교류를 통해 새로운 워크숍을 개발하는
과정형 프로그램입니다.
워크숍
10. 8-9
DIY 악기 만들기 | 유상준
10. 15-16
아날로그TV의 변신:오디오 비주얼라이저
- 아날로그TV 해부실습 | 이정성
- 오디오 비주얼라이저 보드 제작 | 전유진
10. 22-23
반응형 네온사인 조명 | 서영배
(한영만 특별강연)
10. 29-30
라즈조이박스 ver 1.5 | 산딸기마을
쇼케이스
산딸기마을
서영배
유상준
전유진
차산전력
세운뮤직마켓
기획 | 이봉수(비트볼뮤직)
종로좌판
동양표준음향사
알루엣
핑크판스
김영춘
빨간과 울코
송명하(와 편집중들)
신윤철
부대프로그램
세운수리실 with 수리수리협동조합
턴테이블 바늘의 모든 것 | 서울남전자
빈티지 워크맨 판매 | 광진전자
3분체험키트 | 황앤미과학, 홍인전자
주최
후원
서울특별시
세운상가 가동 아파트 주민회
세운상가 시장 협의회
청운전기
서울특별시 동대문구 청계천로 517 서울문화재단
02.3290.7043 / www.seoulpowerstation.org
facebook.com/seoulpowerstation
instagram.com/seoulpowerstation

# WEIWUYIN

The shapes of the three Chinese characters in the program guide—Wei, Wu and Ying—were inspired by the outline of the building of Wei-Wu-Ying Center for the Arts. Moreover, as an avant-garde symbol of the building, the bold colors overlap represents the shadows of the building and trees in the garden.

Studio: Onion Design Associates
Creative Director: Andrew Wong
Designer: Jay Song

## 1月

**1/1**
榕園 Outdoor Plaza
免費入場 Free Admission

**維也納新年音樂會**
**Vienna Philharmonic Orchestra New Year's Concert**

全球衛星直播
Live Broadcast with Maestro Mariss Jansons

1/1 維也納新年音樂會

## 1月—6月

榕園 Outdoor Plaza
免費入場 Free admission

**榕樹下音樂系列**
**Banyan Tree Music Series**

拒絕點播 我們給你Live開唱
Presenting Musical Matinees for Families and Friends

原民的聲音系列

- 1/17 桑布伊及專屬樂團《桑布伊古謠分享會》
- 2/20 蘇瓦那與 CMO樂團《自由的旅程》
- 3/6 嵐馨樂團《我們的生活 · 我們的歌》

人聲系列

- 2/21 SURE 人聲樂團《歌暖聲響迎春風》
- 4/10 高雄室內合唱團《榕樹下的光合作用》
- 4/24 瑞士 Bliss 人聲樂團《阿卡貝拉瘋臺灣》

世界的音樂系列

- 1/24 海馬樂團《旅人 · 出走》
- 5/29 泥灘地浪人《寶島賣藥秀》
- 6/5 科羅曼德融合樂團《印度樂遊 · 即興神遊》

音樂實驗場系列

- 3/20 笙根閣陽《嘿！武營來坐啊》
- 5/15 午後之樹爵士樂團《仲夏午後之夢》
- 6/12 玩弦四度爵士弦樂團《玩弦四度》

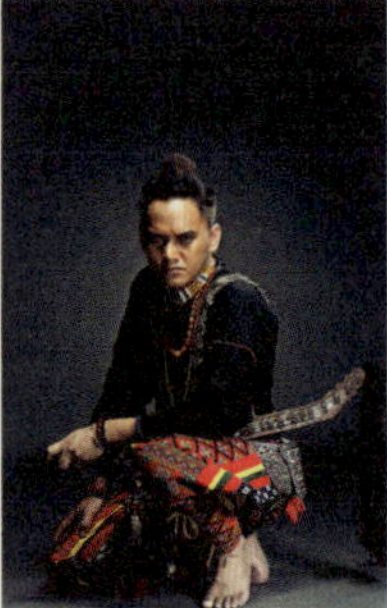
1/17 桑布伊及專屬樂團《桑布伊古謠分享會》

## 2月

**2/11, 2/12**
戶外園區 Outdoor Plaza
免費入場 Free admission

**臺灣國際鼓樂節**
**Taiwan International Drum Festival**

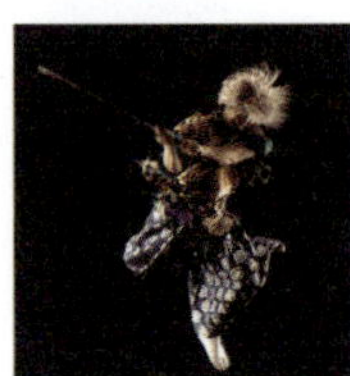
2/11 臺灣國際鼓樂節 - 日本我龍太鼓團

## 2月—3月

戶外園區 Outdoor Plaza
免費入場 Free admission

**歌仔戲系列**
**Taiwanese Opera Series**

- 2/27 春美歌劇團《悍動天下》
- 3/4 明華園天字戲劇團《宮變》
- 3/19 秀琴歌劇團《魅湖咒》

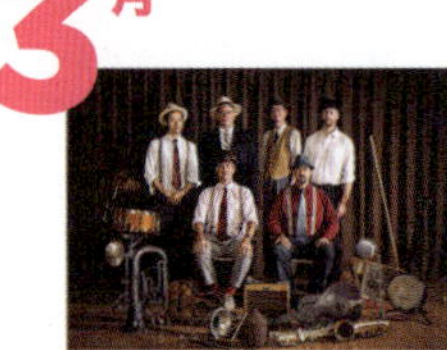
5/29 榕樹下音樂系列 - 泥灘地浪人《寶島賣藥秀》

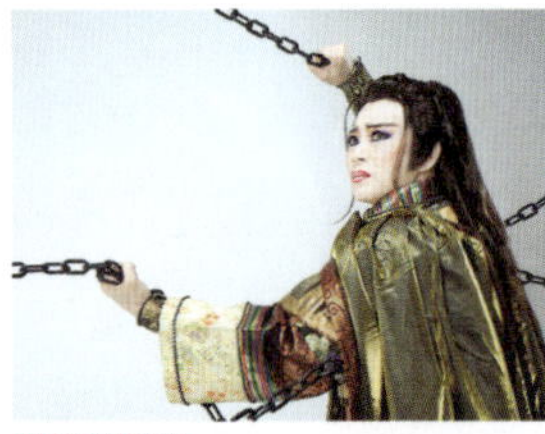
3/19 秀琴歌劇團《魅湖咒》

## 4月

**4/15, 4/16**
281棟 Building 281
售票節目 Ticket Required

**楊輝《邊界》**
**New Work by Yeung Faï**

五代操偶傳人
呈現大時代小人物的悲歌
See The Changes and Turbulences of Time Through Puppetry

**4/27**
高雄市音樂館 Kaohsiung Music Hall
售票節目 Ticket Required

**齊瑪諾夫斯基弦樂四重奏**
**Szymanowski Quartet**

感受當今頂尖弦樂四重奏魅力
Experience One of The World's Best String Quartet

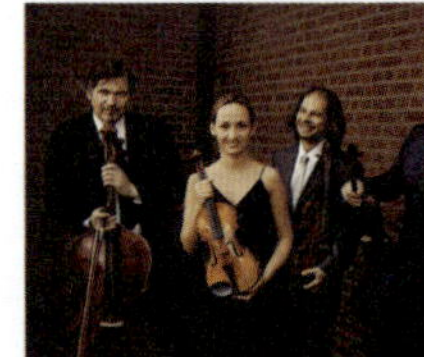
4/27 齊瑪諾夫斯基弦樂四重奏

## 5月

**5/6—5/8**
281 棟 Building 281
售票節目 Ticket Required

**無垢舞蹈劇場《緩行中的漫舞》演出暨工作坊**
**Legend Lin Dance Theatre Poetry in Motion**

5/6-5/8 無垢舞蹈劇場《緩行中的漫舞》演出暨工作坊

## 6月

**6/3, 6/5**
高雄至德堂 Jhihde Hall
售票節目 Ticket Required

衛武營2016音樂劇場

**茶花女 歌劇**
**La Traviata**

首度與高雄春天藝術節攜手合作
Giuseppe Verdi's acclaimed opera with Soprano Valentina Farcas and Tenor Andrei Dunaev only in Kaohsiung

## 7月

衛武營
童樂節

7月衛武營童樂節

衛武營 Weiwuying

**衛武營童樂節**
一年一度的親子藝術遊樂園
**Weiwuying Children's Festival**

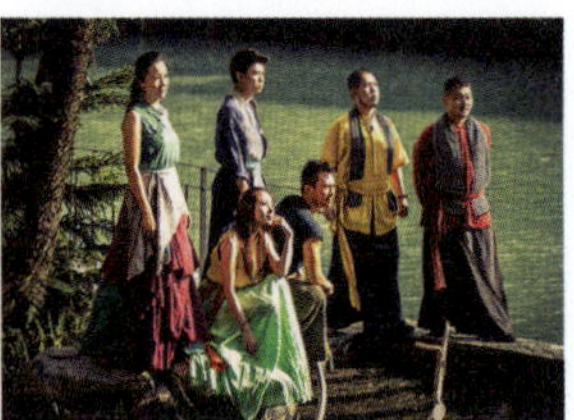
1/24 海馬樂團《旅人 · 出走》

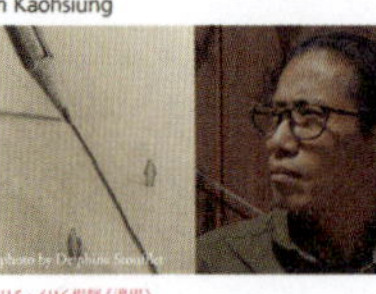
4/15、4/16 楊輝《邊界》

## 8月

衛武營 Weiwuying

**青少年戲劇營**
**Youth Theater Camp**

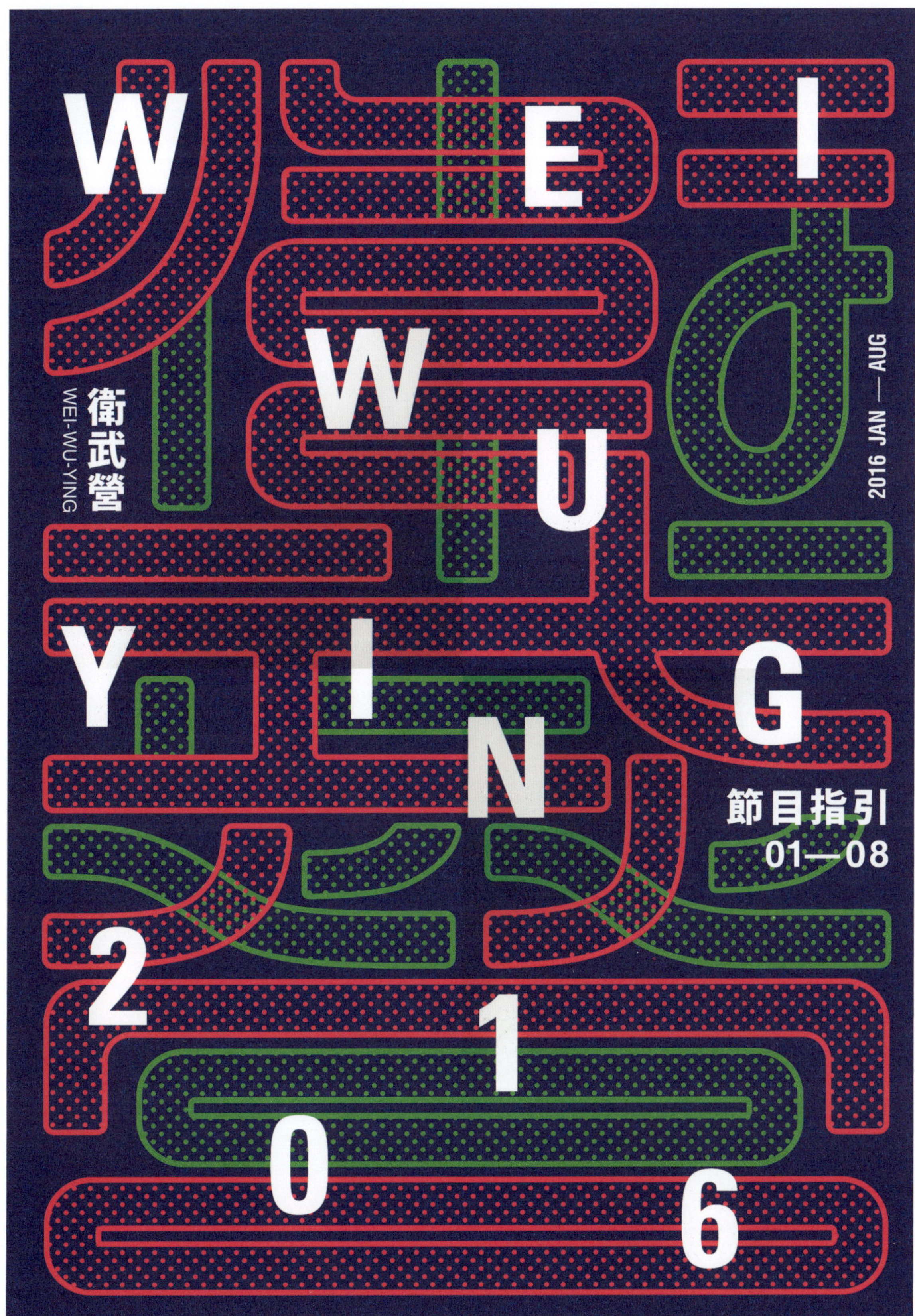
WEI
WU
YING
2016
衛武營
WEI-WU-YING
2016 JAN — AUG
節目指引
01—08

# ANXIETY DIARY

This is part of a studio-published visual essay exploring the visual limits of communication when the designer becomes the author, bridging the intentions of art and design in the context of the project Thatcouldbe.com. The content of each poster came from the moments that triggered anxiety-attack-like behaviors of the studio founder João Castro.

Studio: Royal

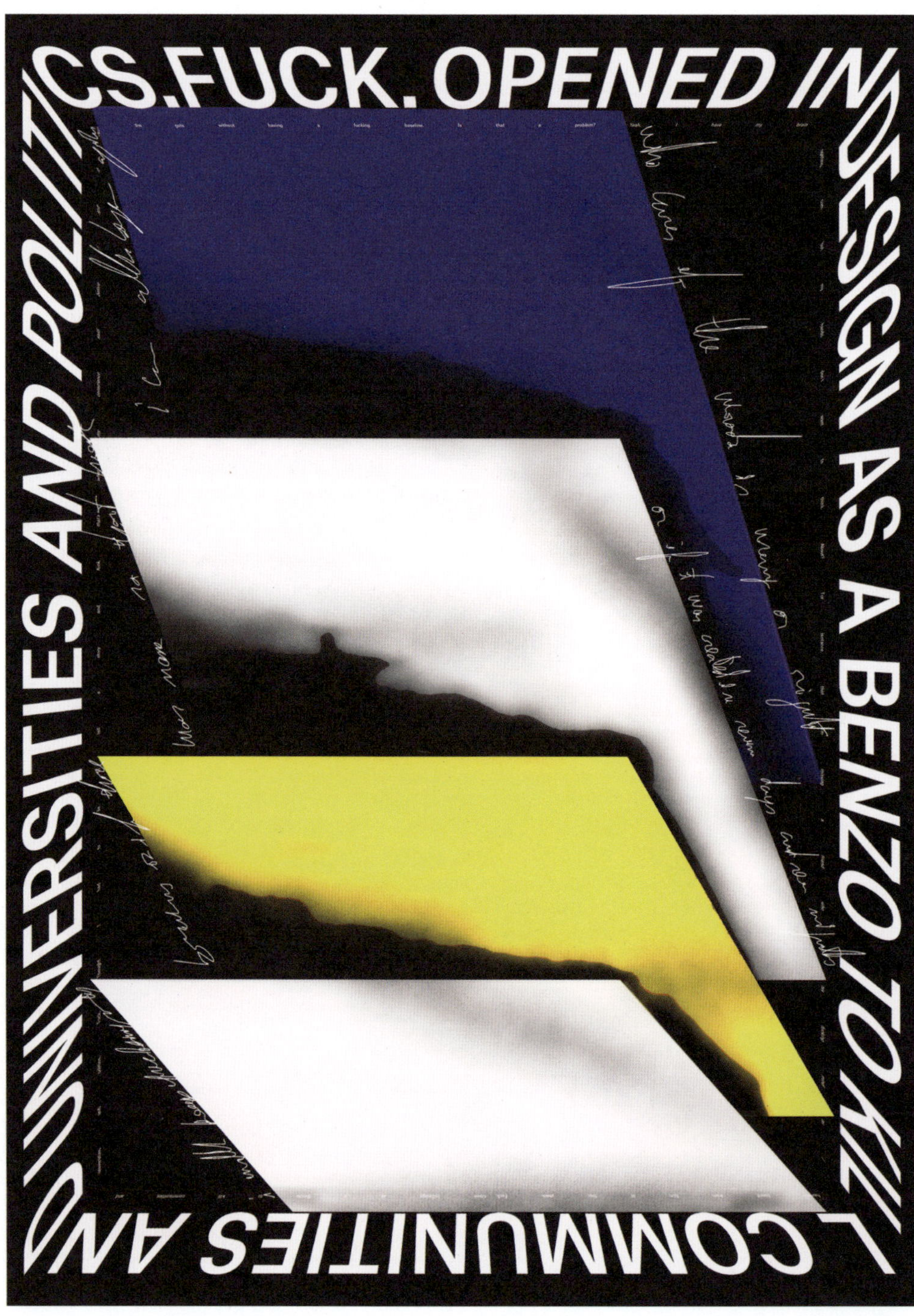

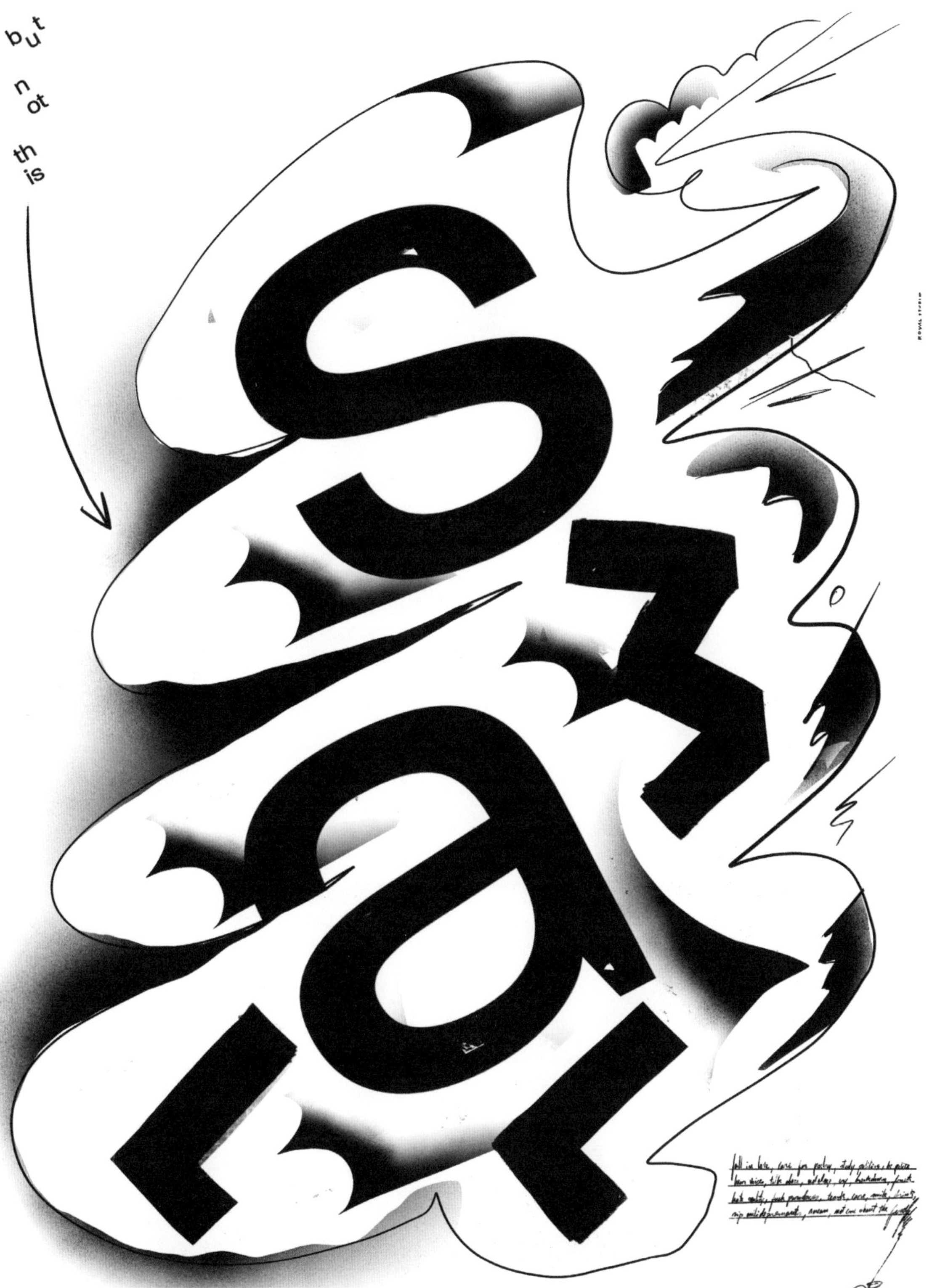
but not this
fall in love, care for poetry, study politics, be polite

# ASLEEP—FESTIVAL SONAMBULO

In this personal project, the designer created a festival including its name, song, graphic design and illustrations. The festival is named "Asleep" and is related to dreams.

Designer: Maria Lucila Quintana

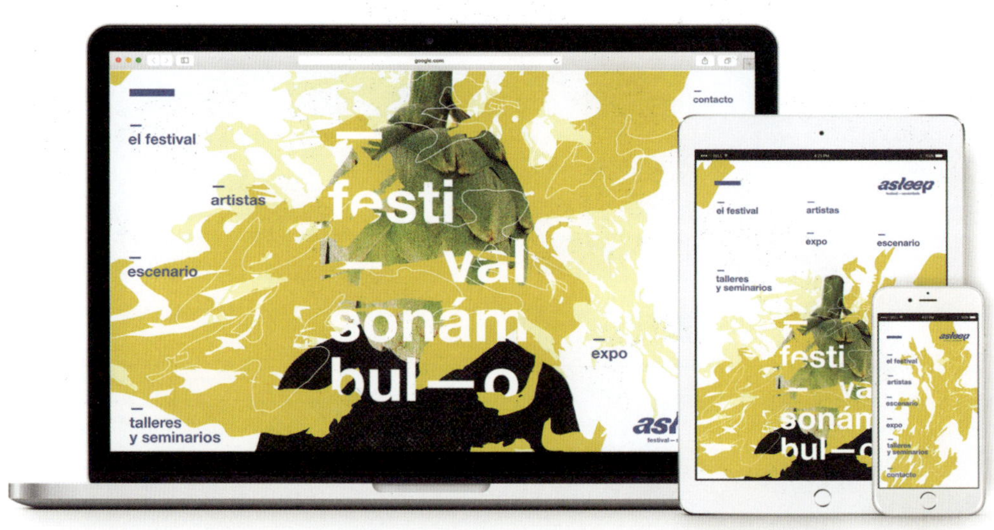

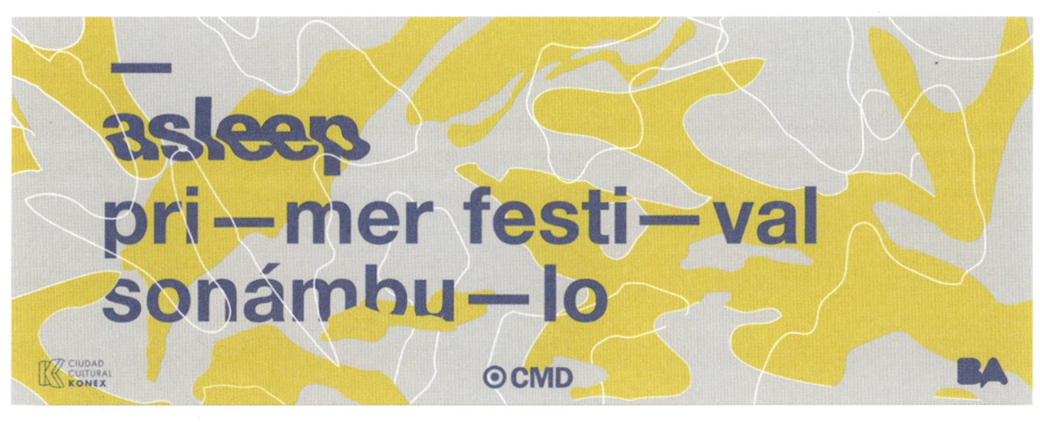
—
asleep
pri—mer festi—val
sonámbu—lo
CIUDAD
CULTURAL
KONEX
CMD
BA

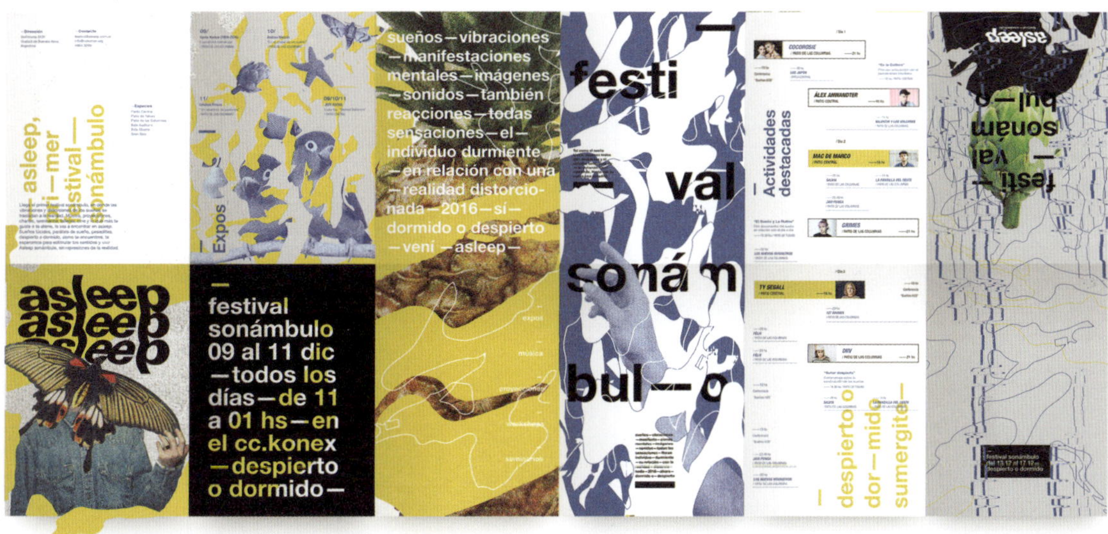
asleep, pri—mer festival—sonámbulo
Expos
sueños—vibraciones—manifestaciones mentales—imágenes—sonidos—también reacciones—todas sensaciones—el—individuo durmiente—en relación con una—realidad distorcio-nada—2016—sí—dormido o despierto—vení—asleep—
festi
val
sonám
bul—o
Actividades destacadas
despierto o dor—mido sumergite—
asleep
asleep
asleep
festival sonámbulo 09 al 11 dic—todos los días—de 11 a 01 hs—en el cc.konex—despierto o dormido—

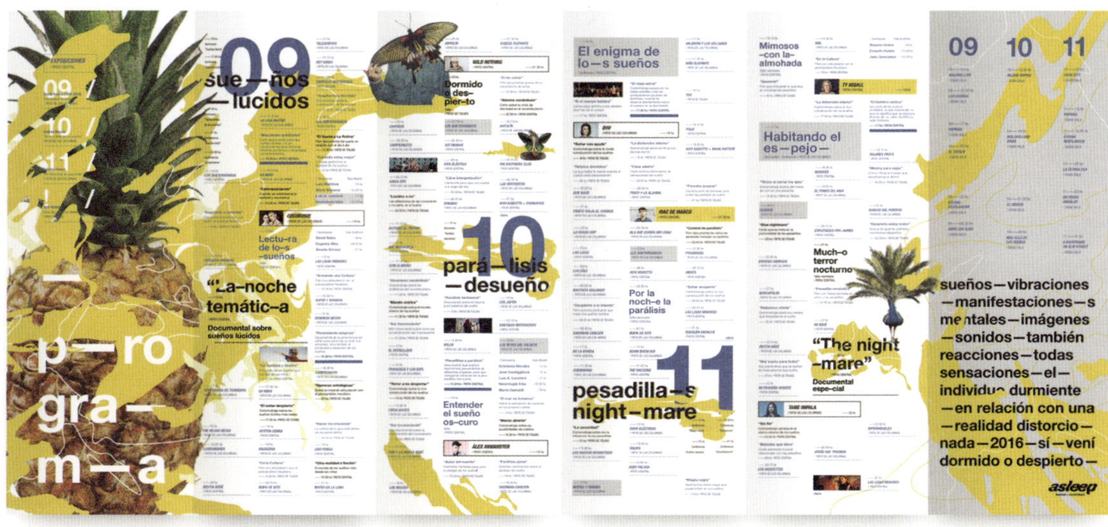
09 / 10 / 11 /
p—ro gra—m—a
09
sue—ños—lucidos
Lectu—ra de lo—s—sueños
"La—noche temátic—a
Documental sobre sueños lúcidos
Dormido o des—pier—to
10
pará—lisis—desueño
Entender el sueño os—curo
El enigma de lo—s sueños
Por la noch—e la parálisis
11
pesadilla—s night—mare
Mimosos—con la—almohada
Habitando el es—pejo—
Much—o terror nocturno
"The night—mare"
Documental espe—cial
09 10 11
sueños—vibraciones—manifestaciones—s mentales—imágenes—sonidos—también reacciones—todas sensaciones—el—individuo durmiente—en relación con una—realidad distorcio—nada—2016—sí—vení dormido o despierto—
asleep

## KIM JANSSEN—COUSINS

"Cousins" is a poetic album with lyrics full of images and symbolism. Since words and lyrics are so important, a clear and bold typeface was designed to fit the words best. The work was combined with a photo of a smoggy city, impersonal but filled with stories, from which all colors are directly derived. The typography in copper hot foil is set loosely within certain grids, just like the words in the music.

Designer: Nick Liefhebber

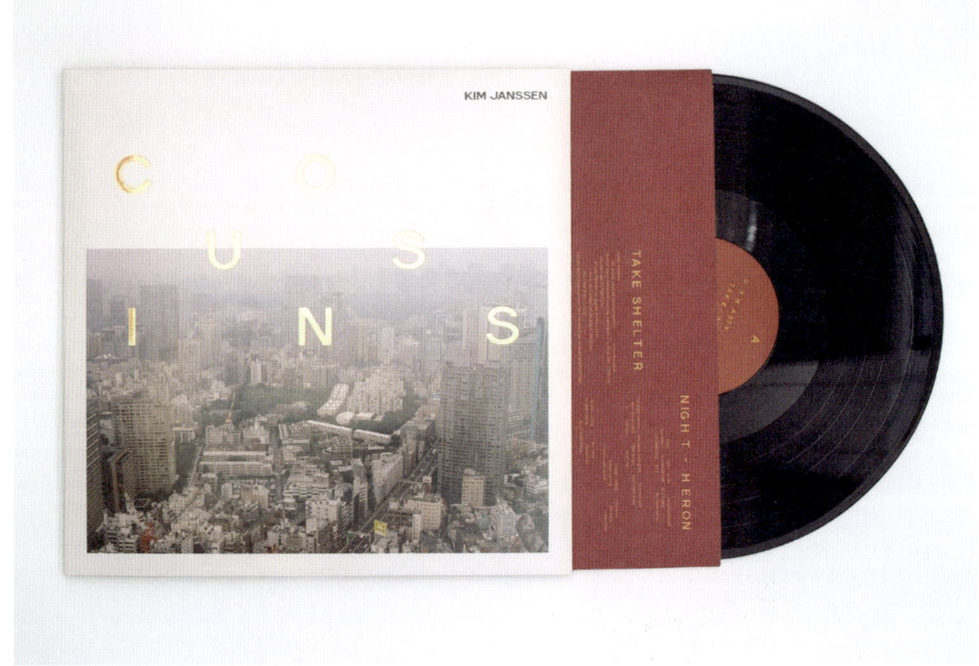


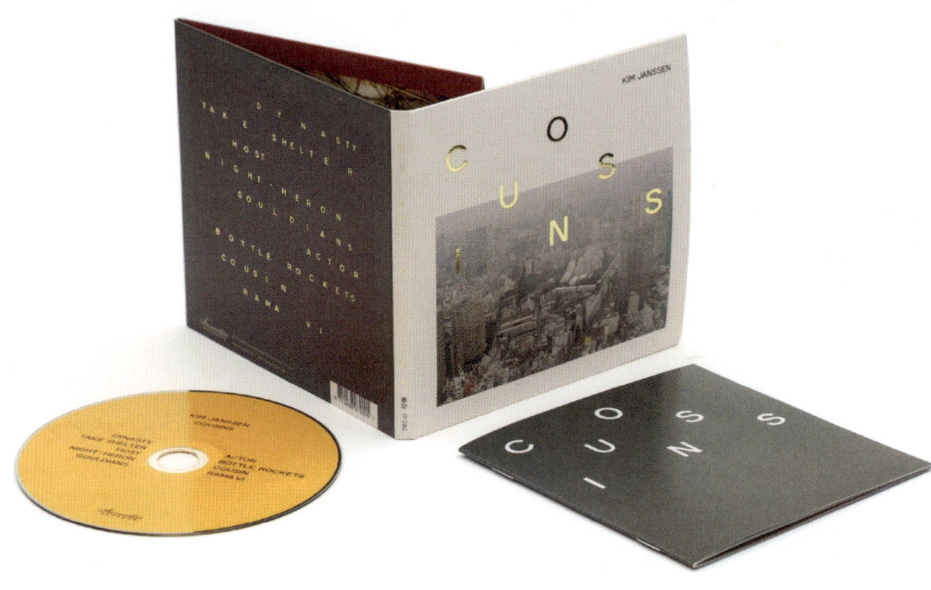

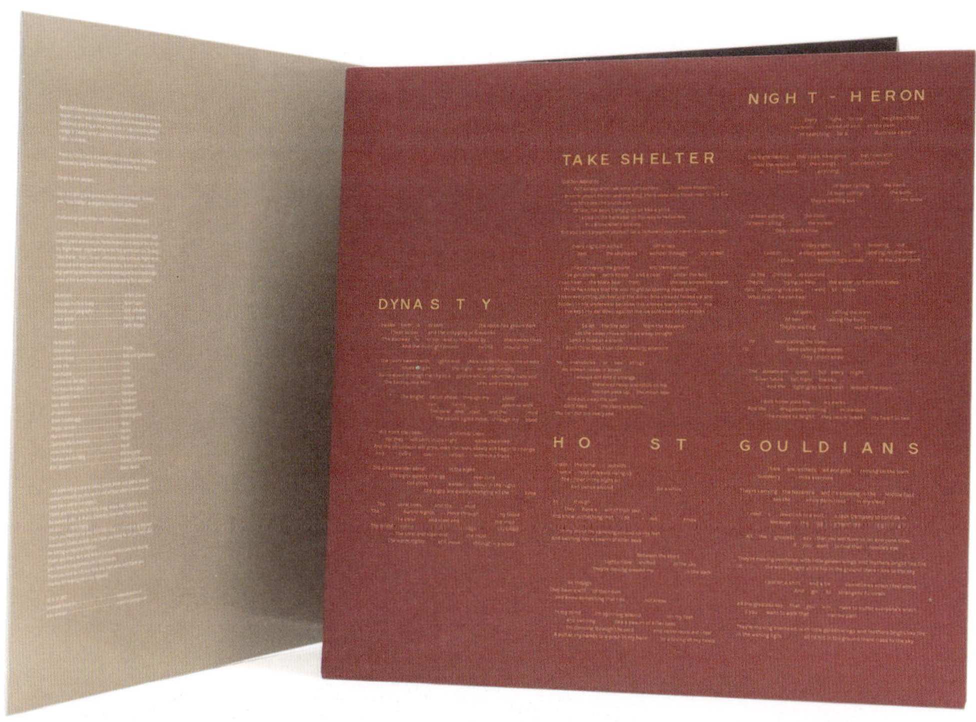
NIGH T - H ERON
TAKE SHELTER
DYNA S T Y
HO ST GOULDIAN S

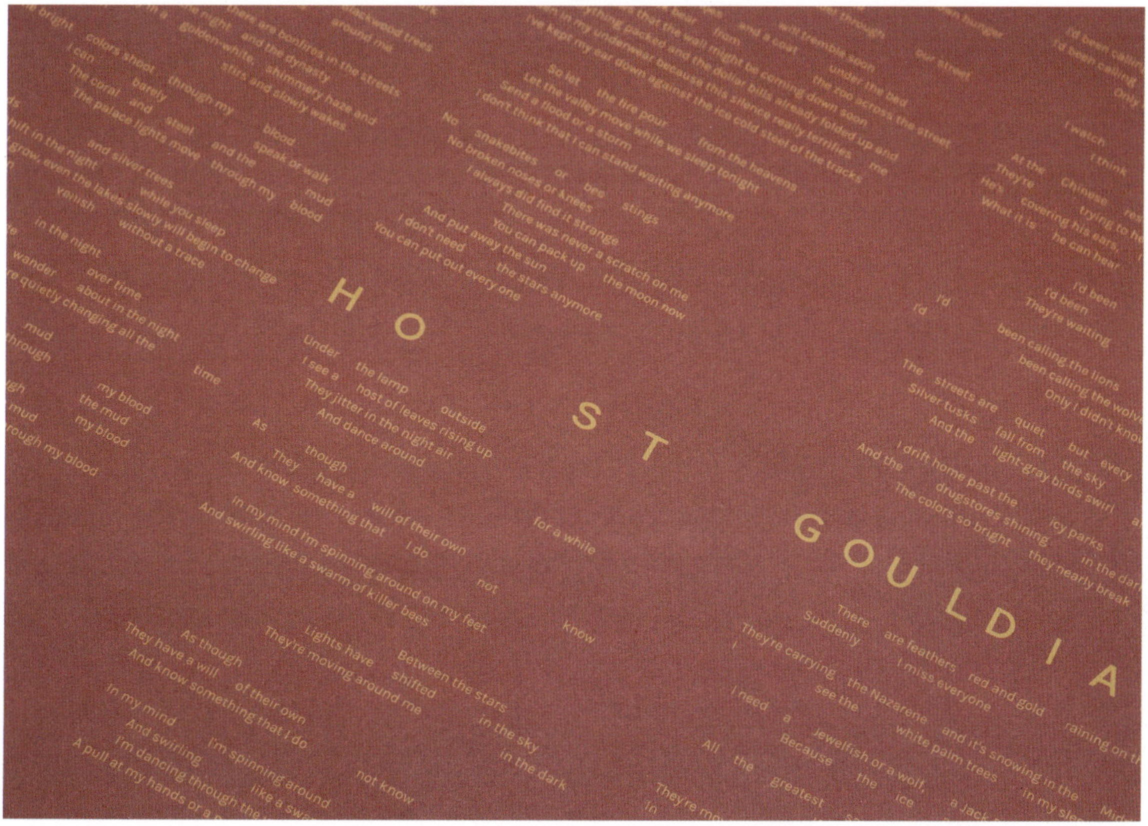

# MORE

This is an artwork for MORE, an LP from the latest album by VVHILE.

Designer: Emir Šehanović

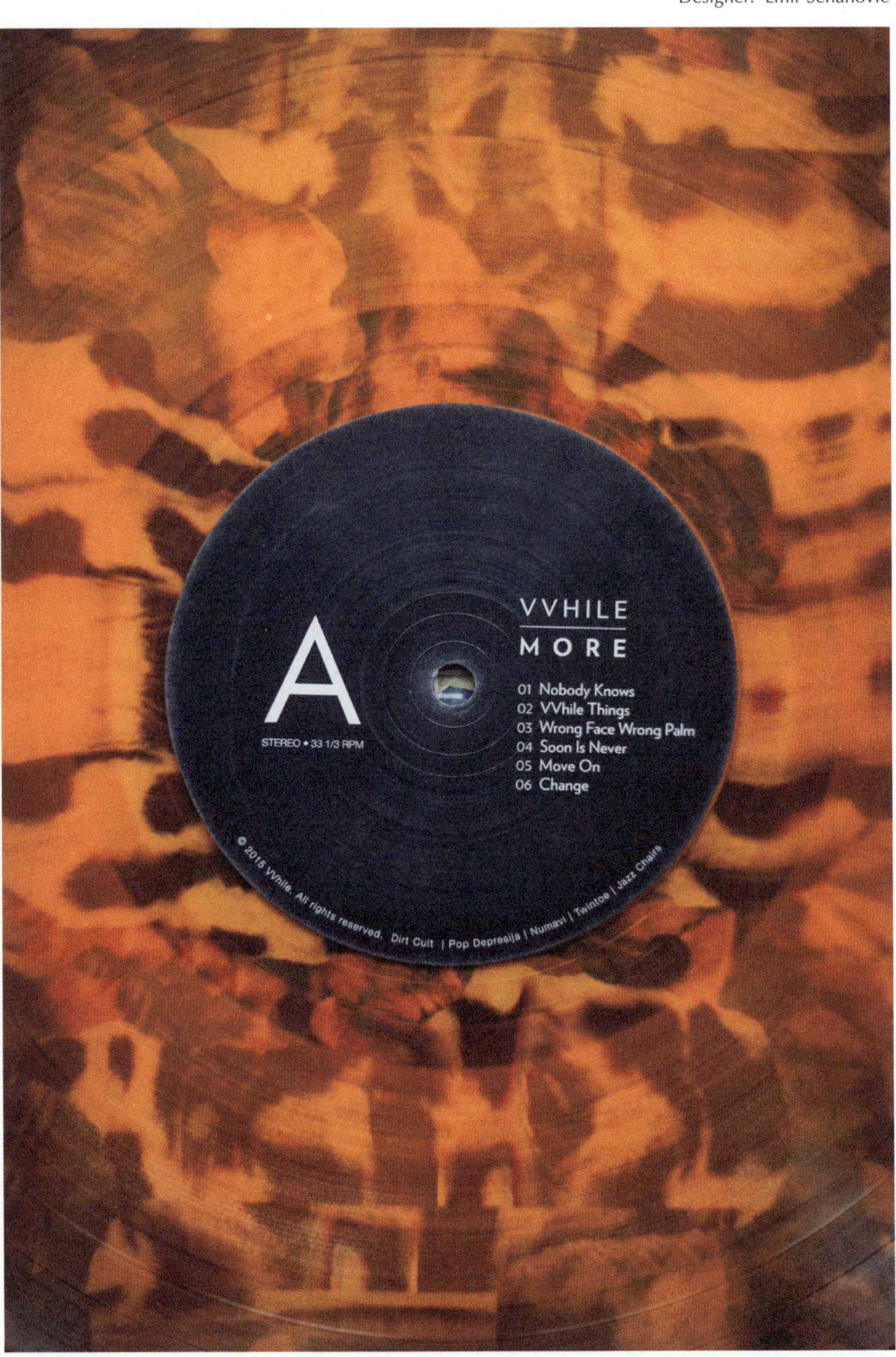

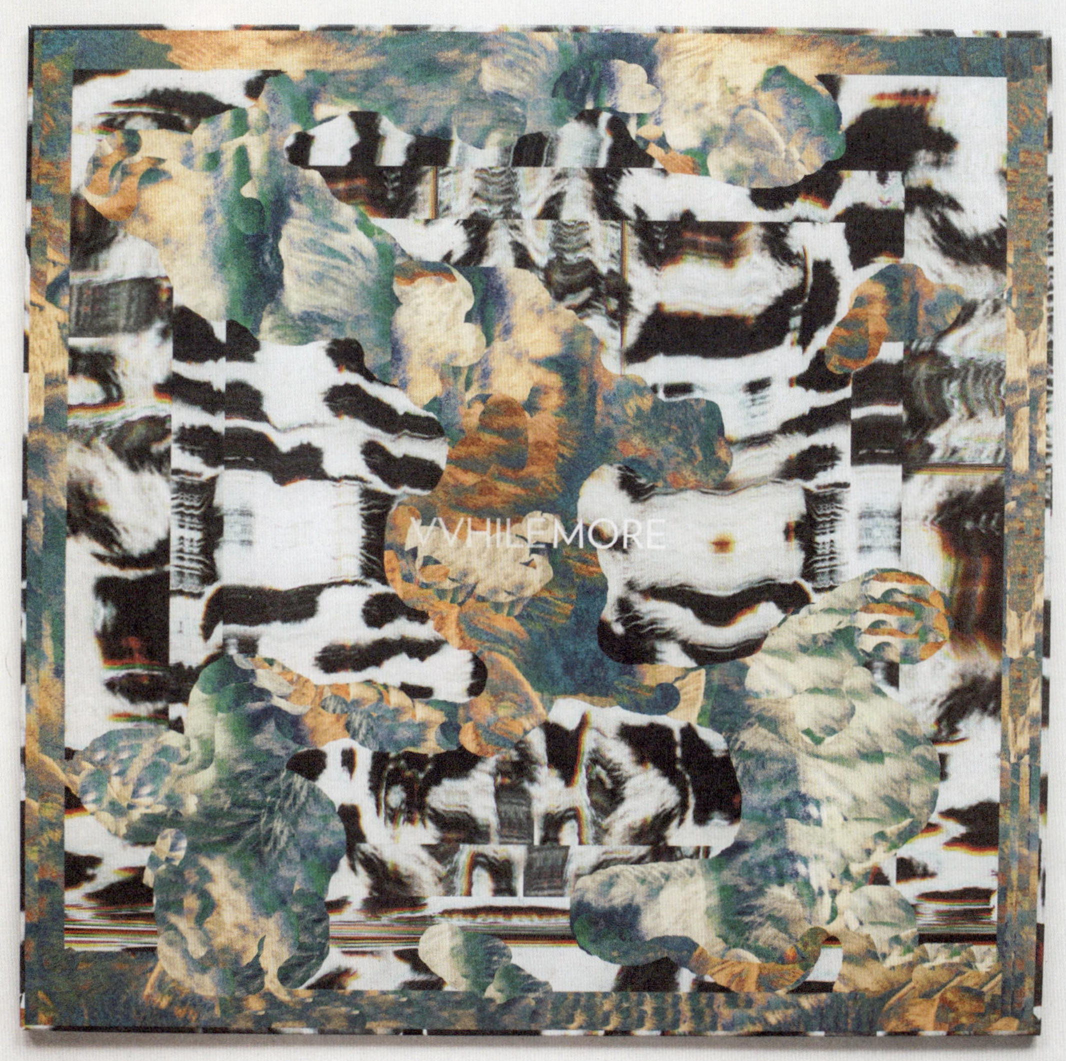
VVHILE MORE

# WASTELAND

This is a series of abstract posters. The idea behind is an imagination of a period in human history considered spiritually desolate where mother is an illusion. There is only chaos created by cannibals, dancing in the neon lights and celebrating a massive orgy. Everything is wrong, life seems to be a wasteland.

Designer: Sebastian Onufszak

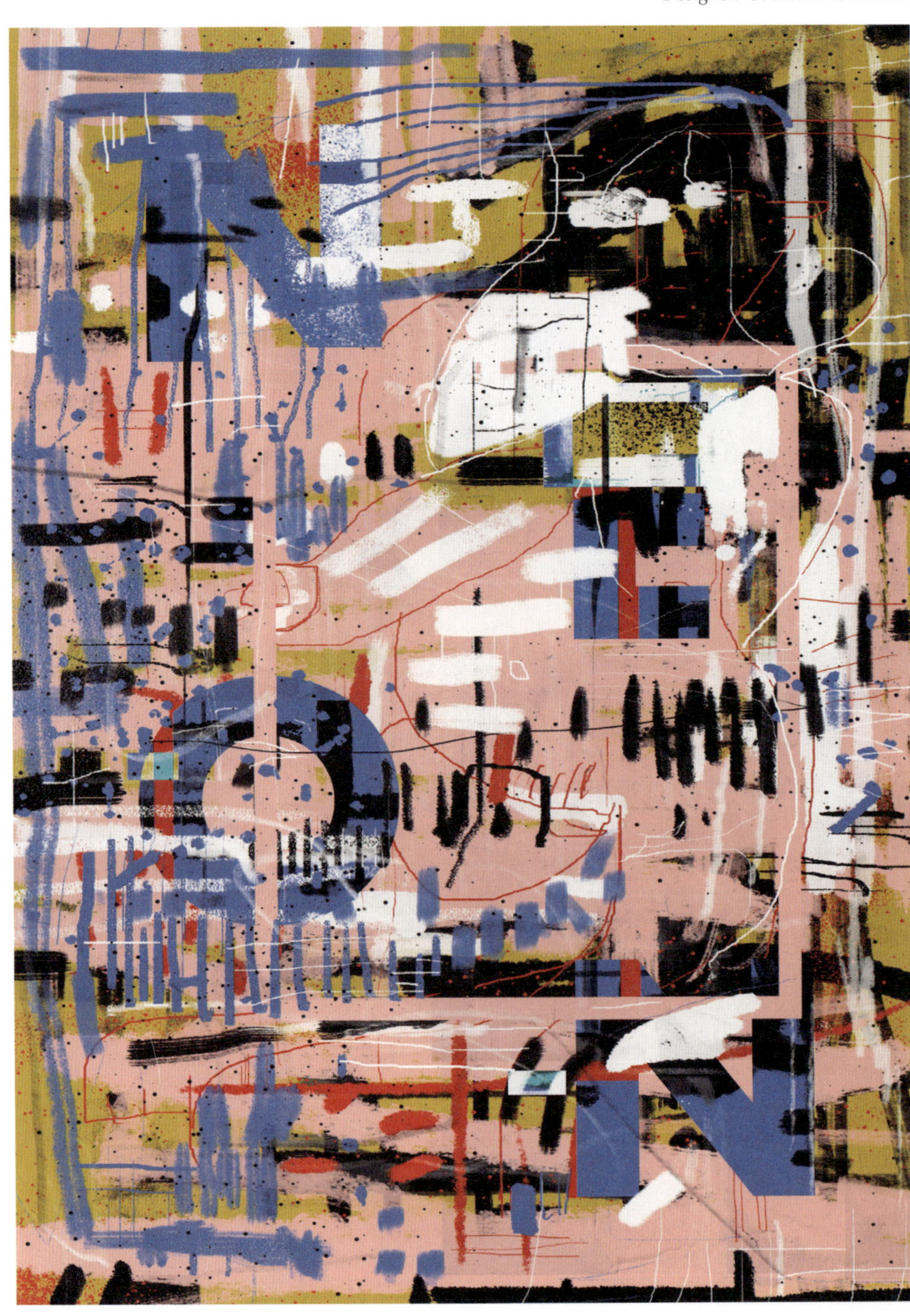

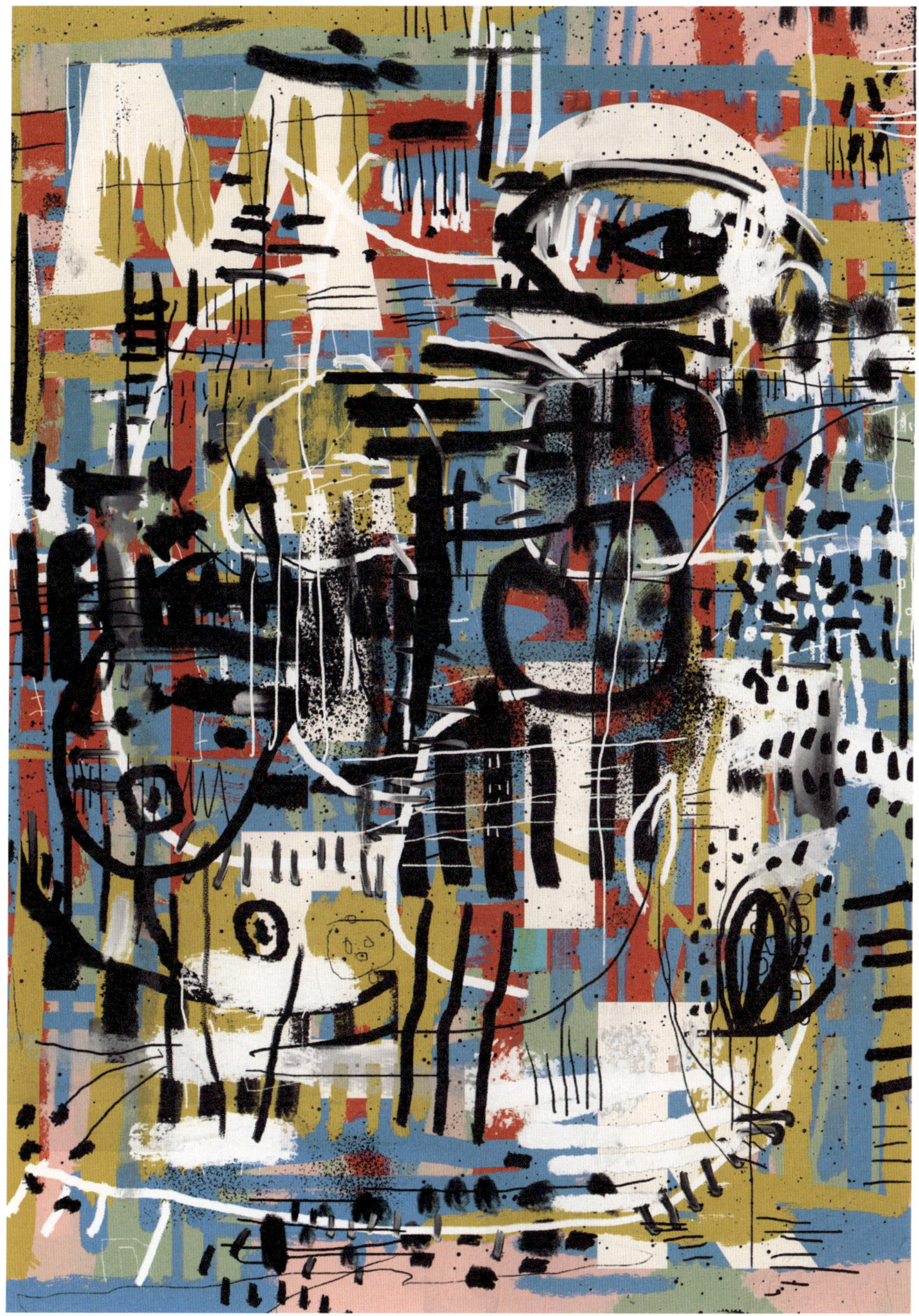

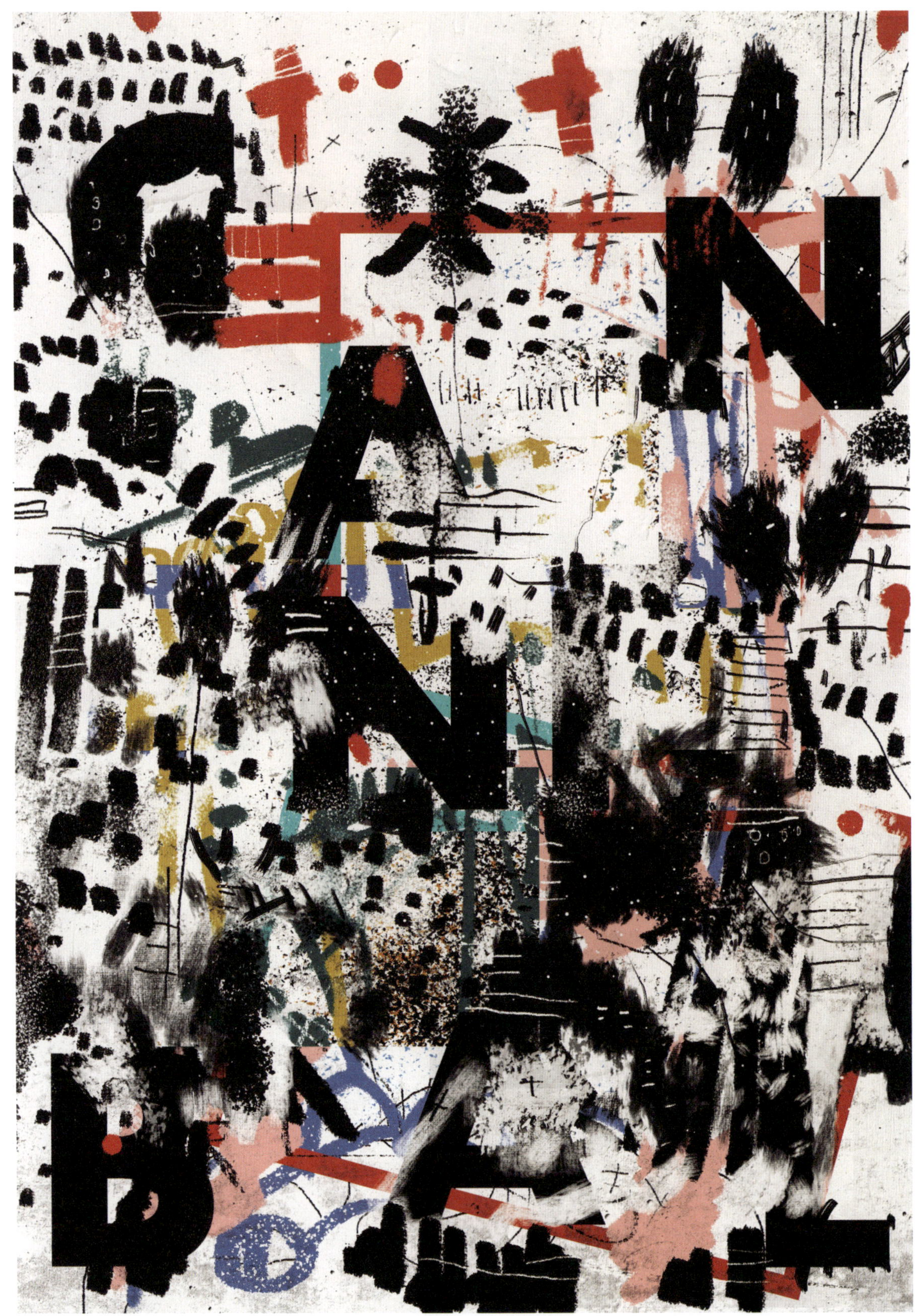

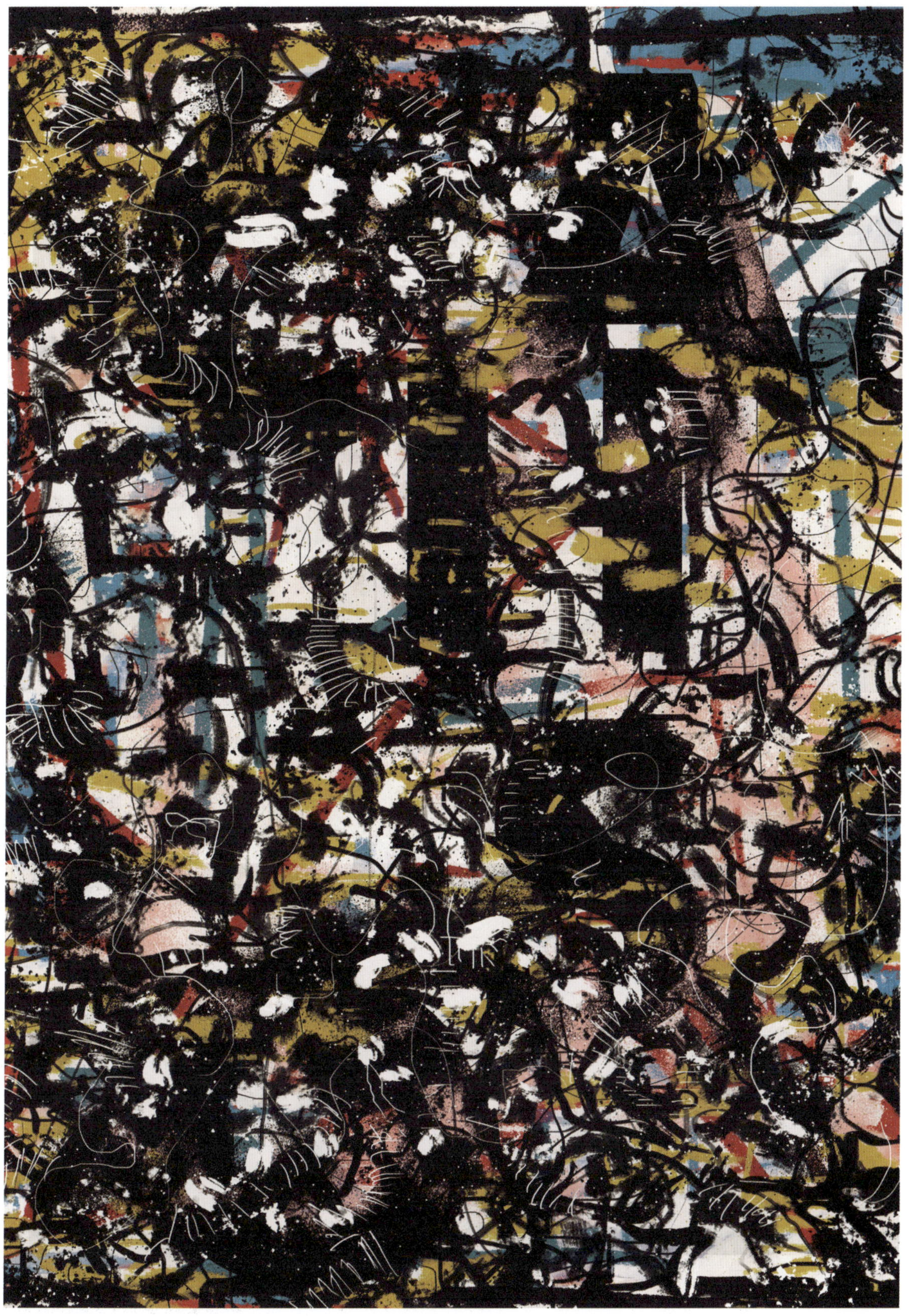

# INSIDE LOTTOZERO

This is a catalogue designed for the opening exhibition Inside Lottozero. The catalogue features 13 artists, dealing with textile design, music and performing art.

Studio: Studio Mut
Designer: Martin Kerschbaumer, Thomas Kronbichler

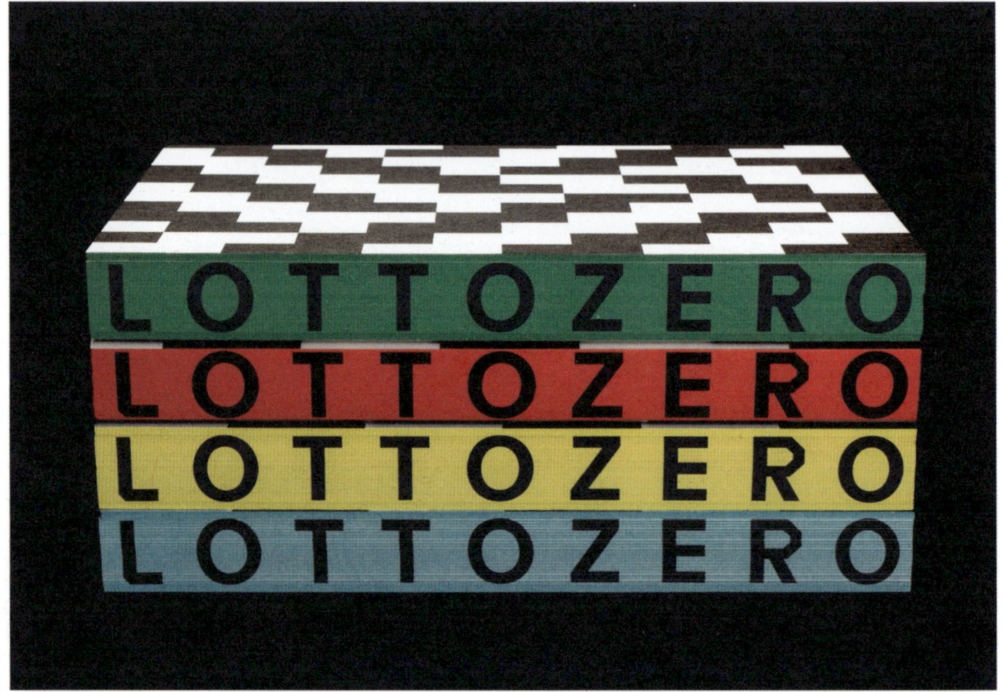


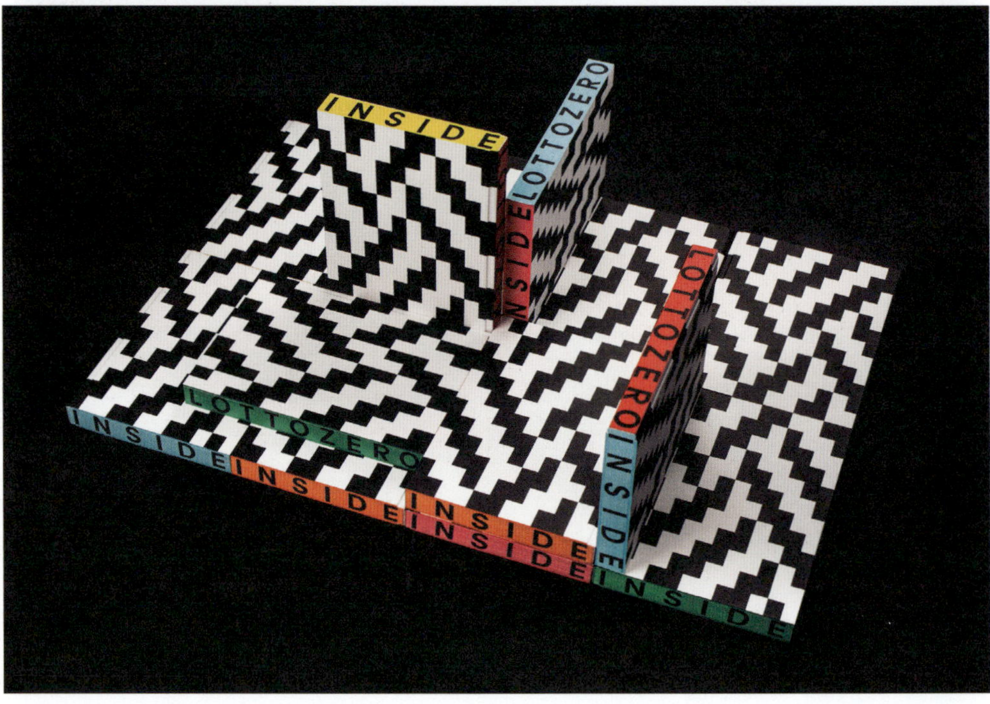

1) The format of a nocturnal concert, intended to be experienced in a state of partial or total sleep, was born in the '80s with the performance of Robert Rich, one of the most important composers of ambient music. For eight consecutive hours in his sets, using acoustic and electronic instruments, Rich modulates slow and dilated sound textures, more interested in creating an atmosphere than a musical discourse, one which acts upon our perceptual systems and resets our internal coordinates. The musicians who have been invited to be part of *Sleep Concert*, held in Kunsthalle Lana (BZ) and in the spaces of Lottozero in Prato, are: Giulio Aldinucci (IT), Paul Beauchamp (USA/IT), Alberto Boccardi (IT/EG), Gas Brown (IT), Claudio Rocchetti (IT), Sadi (IT), and Tomoko Sauvage (J/FR).

works of the thirteen Italian and foreign artists, in a variety of languages. Alongside the more traditional expressions linked to textiles, such as tapestry, costume and soft sculpture, there is also painting, photography, video, installations and sound.
The malleability of the textile medium emerges in the performative actions of the body, which assume necessarily different trajectories in the Kunsthalle Lana and in the Lottozero space in Prato. Aldo Lanzini invades the space with his masks and crocheted costumes, which adhere to the physiognomy of the wearer to reveal the otherness of the self, in a temporary abstraction from reality.

ALDO LANZINI → 42

Marjorie Chau transforms the nature of the places in which she acts, with the visual impact and dreamlike and visionary power of costumes, worn by figures on nearly four-meter-high stilts, in a mix between Chilean mythology and contemporary environmental issues.

MARJORIE CHAU → 52

The performative nature of moving cloth recalls the presence of the body even when it is not physically present, such as in the digital simulation of Zeitguised, a choreography of fabric that dances within metaphysical rooms, *as if* an invisible spirit inhabited the hollow shapes. The work of the Berlin collective introduces a dialectic between analog and digital into the exhibition. Their work contains a tension, because although it is entirely digital and created by algorithms, it demonstrates an attraction toward the analog, evident in their reiteration that their algorithms are always ‹handmade› in order to contain and control the generative fluxes of the synthetic art. It is as if the presence of fabric implies in itself a certain idea of the artisanal, intrinsic in its nature and its origin of fibers woven together by hand.

ZEITGUISED → 62

In contrast with the dematerialization of Zeitguised's images, there is the density of color which passes through the screen-printing meshes (the same ones used to print on fabric) and onto the paper of Roland Barth's works. These are animated by a chromatic, rhythmic and serial articulation, which illustrate the physicality of his relationship with painting.

ROLAND BARTH → 72

We see another analog process in Kathrin Stumreich's *Fabricmachine*, as it *plays* the fabric, using light sensors that translate the consistency of the cloth into audio signals, reading the specific characteristics of the weave of weft and warp.

KATHRIN STUMREICH → 82

The orthogonal structure of weaving, a system founded on potentially infinite repetition, lends

18 Textile as a medium

2) See Ulrich Heinen in conversation with Bazon Brock, *The Cultural Anthropology of the Textile*, in *Art & Textiles. Fabric as Concept and Material in Modern Art from Klimt to the Present*, exhibition catalogue (Wolfsburg, Kunstmuseum, 12 October 2013 – 2 March 2014; Stuttgart, Staatgalerie, 21 March – 22 June 2014), Berlin, Hatje Kantz, 2013, pp. 68–77.

itself to anthropological reflections[2], which are articulated in various ways in the works present in the exhibition. For Claudia Losi, *texture* is an interpretive principle, allowing her to simplify the complex lines of the natural landscape into a grid on which she embeds impressions and memories.

CLAUDIA LOSI → 92

The action of weaving at the heart of Mariana Sales' works instead speaks of an essential grammar of gestures with which to rediscover the body, its distances and internal functions, because the loom is housed within the body itself, using the limbs as the anchor points for the threads of the warp.

MARIANA SALES → 102

In the works of the duo Khurtova Bourlanges, the metaphor of the body is taken deeper, to a biological cellular level: the frayed and torn weaving, here realized in a knit made of threads of ceramic clay using large wooden ‹knitting needles›, represents the vulnerability of the system, physical and also social in the broader sense.

KHURTOVA BOURLANGES → 110

Nicole Miltner uses the technique of tapestry to develop a close comparison with painting, to test its limits and characteristics as a language with its own spatial dimensions, due to the three-dimensional nature of the threads and to the physical impregnation of color in the hand-dying process. The test-bed of her analysis is the depiction of a nude body, divided in shapes like a sewing pattern.

NICOLE MILTNER → 120

A similar impression of rough anatomical fragmentation occurs in Zoë Gruni's video, which references textiles by subtraction. Her body, dressed only in a head-covering of sorghum, references a previous work of wearable sculptures made of jute. These techniques and materials recall an archaic and rural dimension, as this cultural baggage which is part of the history of textiles, linked to specific traditions and culture, becomes the heritage the artists draw on to articulate their research, modifying and reinterpreting instruments, languages and prime materials.

ZOË GRUNI → 130

In the same way, Anna Rose chooses the fiber of synthetic hairs as a sculptural element to investigate certain stereotypes linked to femininity, in an intimate and symbolic work with both a social and anthropological dimension.

ANNA ROSE → 140

The textile medium, which is an integral part of human existence, can become a tool, or rather a *clue*, to undertake research that acquires a historical-social interest, like the photographic series of Virginie Rebetez, which documents

19 Alessandra Tempesti

Zeitguised è un collettivo di artisti e designer che lavorano nel campo dell'arte di sintesi, arte creata attraverso complessi processi algoritmici, *0% organic, 100% processed*, come si legge nelle note che accompagnano *geist.xyz*. Eppure i tessuti che fluttuano dentro queste stanze vuote e colorate sembrano avere a prima vista una consistenza reale, come se fossero prototipi di sofisticate ricerche e sperimentazioni hi-tech. Ogni singolo frammento del lavoro è invece interamente ricreato in digitale: la realtà non viene campionata ma simulata e in questo tentativo di rimanere entro i confini della rappresentazione emerge la specificità delle opere di Zeitguised, che progetta manualmente gli algoritmi per gestire e plasmare i flussi generativi del linguaggio computazionale, sfociando nella creazione di mondi surreali e iperreali.
In *geist.xyz* i tessuti diventano organismi viventi che volteggiano senza peso nello spazio contrapponendo le loro forme morbide e metamorfiche alle figure rigide della geometria cartesiana; i movimenti ora in espansione lenta ora concitati e ipnotici sono scanditi da un suono incalzante come quello di un metronomo elettronico che detta una sincronia intermittente. Nell'analizzare con più attenzione lo sviluppo di questa danza camaleontica di stoffe psichedeliche, si arriva a percepire la ricorrenza di alcune scene, mentre movimenti, luci, texture e schemi cromatici vengono modulati diversamente ogni volta; il lavoro si regge su una costruzione paratattica delle parti, come una tavola periodica di elementi. La dimensione temporale propria dell'immagine in movimento viene elusa a favore di una logica combinatoria, instabile, soggetta al

Zeitguised is a collective of artists and designers who work in the field of synthetic art, art created using complex algorithmic processes, *0% organic, 100% processed*, as you can read in the notes that accompany *geist.xyz*. And yet the fabrics that ripple in these empty, colored rooms seem at first sight to have a real consistency, as if they were prototypes of sophisticated research and high-tech experimentation. But every single fragment of work is entirely digital: reality is not championed but simulated, and in this attempt to remain within the confines of representation we see the characteristics of the works of Zeitguised. They manually design the handmade algorithms, in order to manage and shape the generative flows of computational language, resulting in the creation of surreal and hyperreal worlds.
In *geist.xyz* the fabrics become living organisms that vault weightlessly in space, juxtaposing their flexible, metamorphic forms with rigid geometric Cartesian shapes: the movements, now slowly expanding, now agitated and hypnotic, are scored by insistent sounds such as an electronic metronome that beats in intermittent synchrony.
On a more attentive analysis of this chameleonic dance by psychedelic fabrics, we start to see certain scenes recurring, while the movements, lights, textures and chromatic

64 Zeitguised

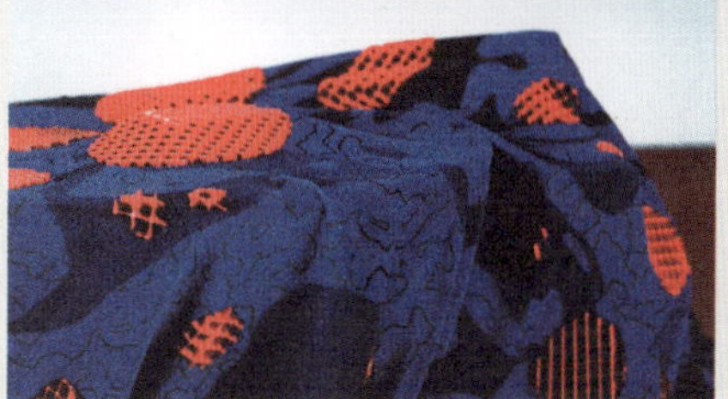

Zeitguised
*geistxyz_blue_DBr_001* and
*geistxyz_blue_D06_006*
still frames from *geist.xyz*,
digital simulation, 2'30", 2016

65

The expressive power of costume is the fulcrum of Marjorie Chau's artistic activity, at the center of a multimedia work, which combines installation, performance, film and choreography. Its scenic impact is intensified by the use of stilts, and by the grand dimensions this quasi-sculptural presence, indissolubly linked to the body that wears it. This is the origin of her astonishing and surreal figures that burst into reality with the visionary force of the fantastic, often drawing on the mythology of Chile, the artist's birthplace.

*Caleuche*, inspired by a legend from Chiloé Island in the south of Chile, is a ghost ship that appears in the night with dazzling white sails, before disappearing suddenly and continuing to navigate under the surface of the water. Its creator is Millalobo, half man and half sea lion, lord of the sea and custodian of the souls of shipwrecked people, who have become part of his crew. The work is an interactive installation, in which a large projection screen accompanies the performers who represent the characters in the story. The screen is made from sheets of plastic woven together with a Mapuche loom, in the Chilean tradition. The clothes are also made of the same material, which the artist sources directly from Chile, as it is a particular type of plastic made from packaging that is no longer produced in Europe because it is highly polluting. As a double reflection of that floating carpet of rubbish that causes the death of many animal species in the Pacific Ocean, the screen's wrinkled and translucent surface reflects the images of underwater fauna, evanescent apparitions that are accompanied by the notes of a soprano voice. Sewn from several parts, it also recalls the white sails of the ghost ship, as do the chromatic shades of the costumes. It nostalgic returns to a marine vision, the tragic image of the surface and the internal treasure chest that pulses with life.

*Caleuche* is a work which looks at Chilean stories and mythology from a contemporary viewpoint, with an explicit reference to the dramatic environmental issue of pollution in the Pacific. Compared to the artist's previous works it is also the one in which the lessons of Butoh, learned in Chile during several years of experience in a dance company, are most evident. All of Marjorie Chau's works can be interpreted as the construction of an extremely personal language, which is conferred on the costumes that unite elements of Butoh and aspects of the acrobatic world (like the use of stilts). However, in *Caleuche*, we also see on the surface a sense of spirituality that recalls that coexistence of life and death that is expressed in Butoh dance, defined by one of its founders as the ‹Dance of Darkness›[1]. This surface is also the expanse of the sea, a thin membrane that separates two kingdoms but which can easily be penetrated, when in the night the ship with the souls of the dead emerges from the abyss. Then there is no longer a separation between the internal and externals worlds, life and death.

1) The definition is credited to Tatsumi Hijikata, theoretical and spiritual guide of Butoh dance. Giorgio Salerno, *Suoni del corpo, segni del cuore. La danza Butô tra Oriente e Occidente*, Milan, Costa & Nolan, 1998.

58 Marjorie Chau

Marjorie Chau
*Caleuche*
interactive installation, woven plastic, sound, video, dimensions variable, 2014–2016

59

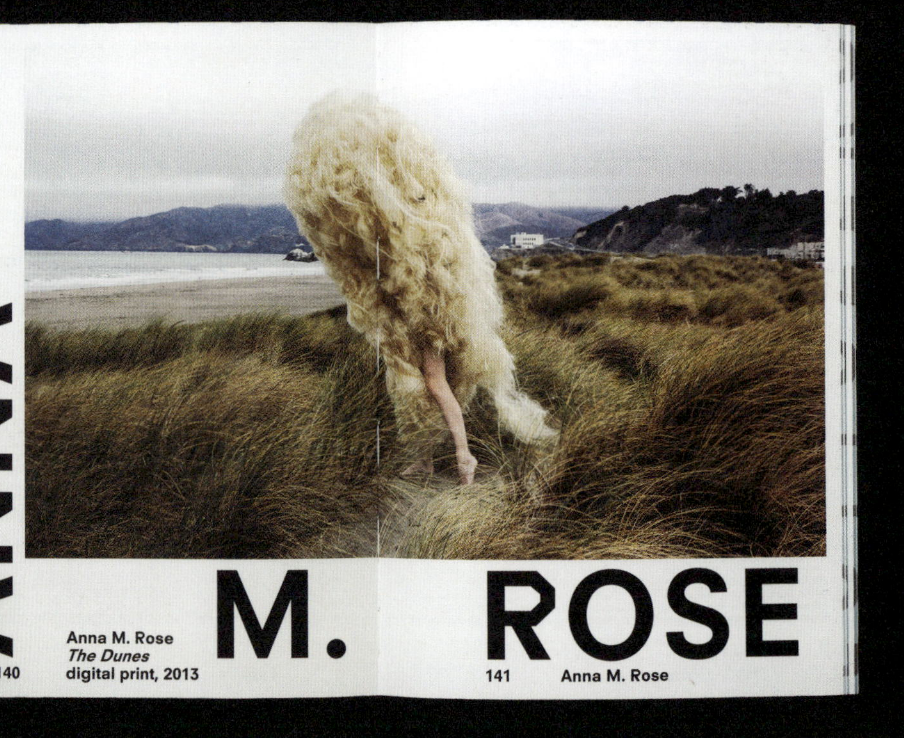

ANNA M. ROSE

Anna M. Rose
*The Dunes*
digital print, 2013

140

141 Anna M. Rose

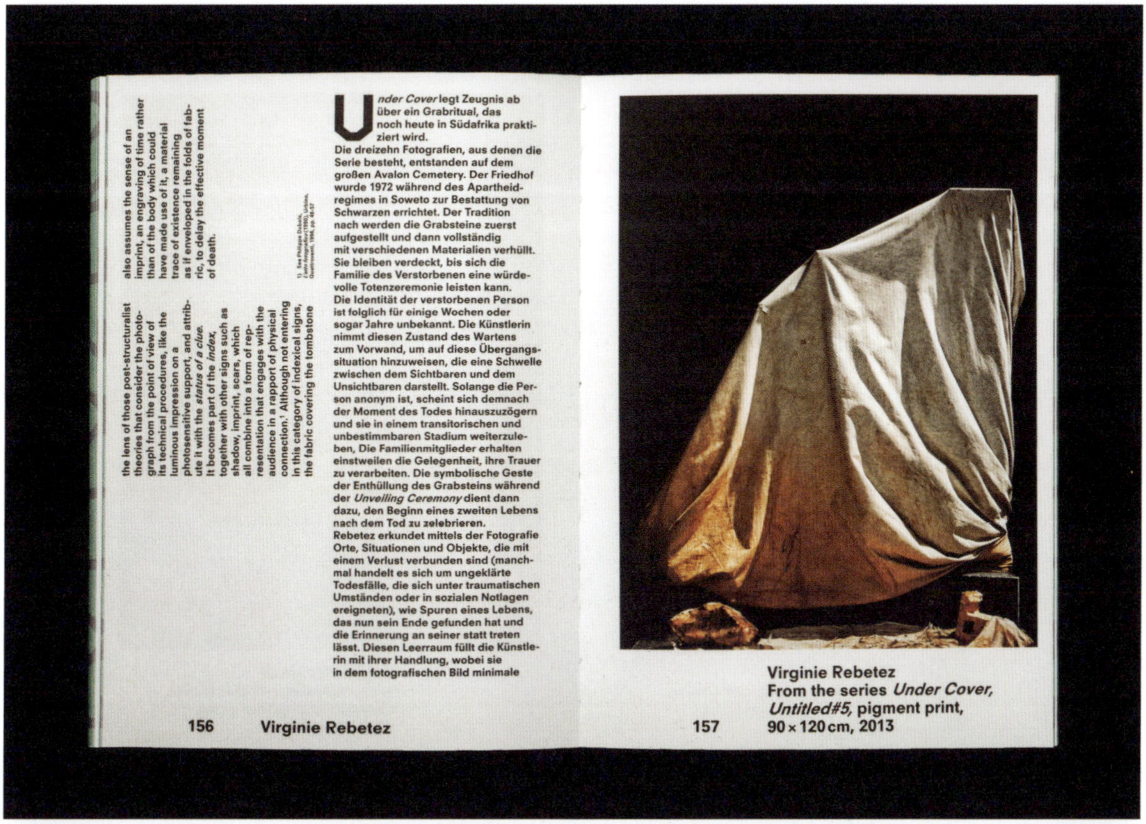

the lens of those post-structuralist theories that consider the photograph from the point of view of its technical procedures, like the luminous impression on a photosensitive support, and attribute it with the *status of a clue*. It becomes part of the *index*, together with other signs such as shadow, imprint, scars, which all combine into a form of representation that engages with the audience in a rapport of physical connection.[1] Although not entering in this category of indexical signs, the fabric covering the tombstone also assumes the sense of an imprint, an engraving of time rather than of the body which could have made use of it, a material trace of existence remaining as if enveloped in the folds of fabric, to delay the effective moment of death.

*Under Cover* legt Zeugnis ab über ein Grabritual, das noch heute in Südafrika praktiziert wird.
Die dreizehn Fotografien, aus denen die Serie besteht, entstanden auf dem großen Avalon Cemetery. Der Friedhof wurde 1972 während des Apartheidregimes in Soweto zur Bestattung von Schwarzen errichtet. Der Tradition nach werden die Grabsteine zuerst aufgestellt und dann vollständig mit verschiedenen Materialien verhüllt. Sie bleiben verdeckt, bis sich die Familie des Verstorbenen eine würdevolle Totenzeremonie leisten kann. Die Identität der verstorbenen Person ist folglich für einige Wochen oder sogar Jahre unbekannt. Die Künstlerin nimmt diesen Zustand des Wartens zum Vorwand, um auf diese Übergangssituation hinzuweisen, die eine Schwelle zwischen dem Sichtbaren und dem Unsichtbaren darstellt. Solange die Person anonym ist, scheint sich demnach der Moment des Todes hinauszuzögern und sie in einem transitorischen und unbestimmbaren Stadium weiterzuleben. Die Familienmitglieder erhalten einstweilen die Gelegenheit, ihre Trauer zu verarbeiten. Die symbolische Geste der Enthüllung des Grabsteins während der *Unveiling Ceremony* dient dann dazu, den Beginn eines zweiten Lebens nach dem Tod zu zelebrieren.
Rebetez erkundet mittels der Fotografie Orte, Situationen und Objekte, die mit einem Verlust verbunden sind (manchmal handelt es sich um ungeklärte Todesfälle, die sich unter traumatischen Umständen oder in sozialen Notlagen ereigneten), wie Spuren eines Lebens, das nun sein Ende gefunden hat und die Erinnerung an seiner statt treten lässt. Diesen Leerraum füllt die Künstlerin mit ihrer Handlung, wobei sie in dem fotografischen Bild minimale

156 Virginie Rebetez

Virginie Rebetez
From the series *Under Cover, Untitled#5*, pigment print, 90 × 120 cm, 2013

157

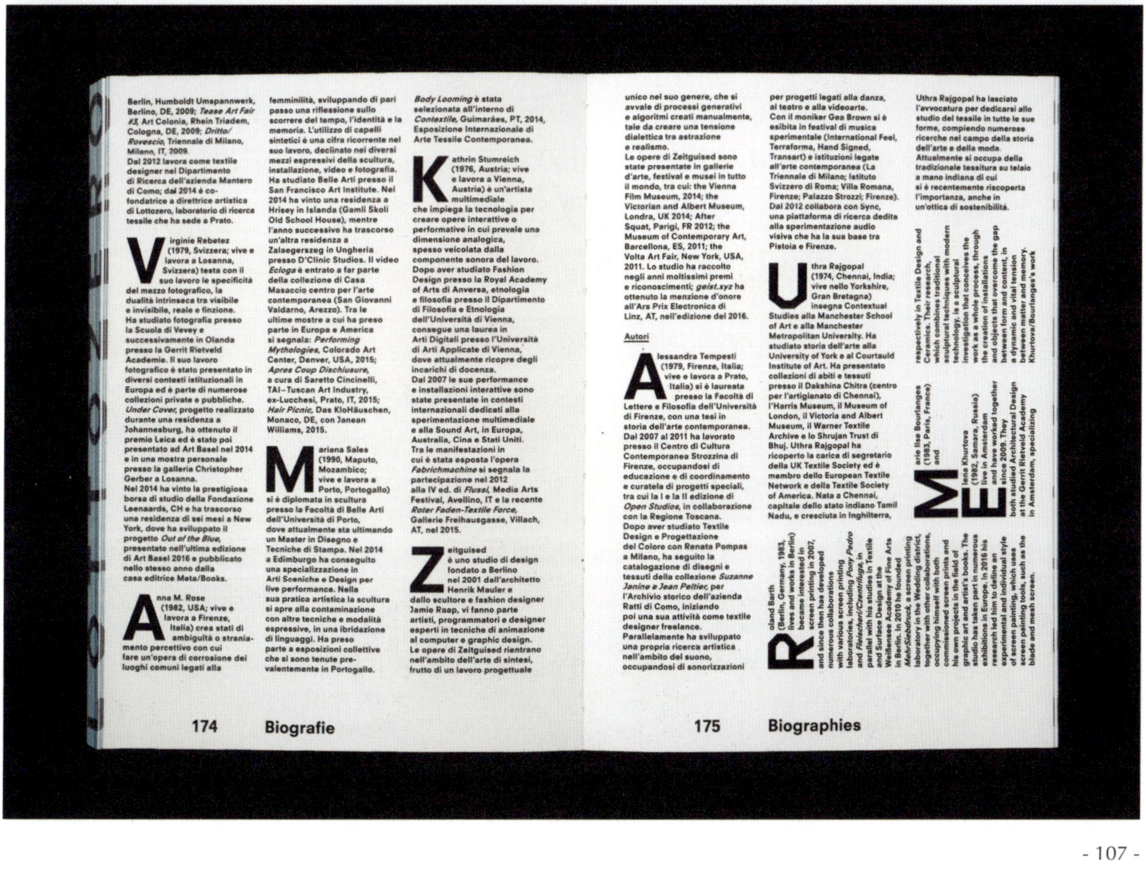

Berlin, Humboldt Umspannwerk, Berlino, DE, 2009; *Tease Art Fair #3*, Art Colonia, Rhein Triadem, Cologna, DE, 2009; *Dritto/Rovescio*, Triennale di Milano, Milano, IT, 2009.
Dal 2012 lavora come textile designer nel Dipartimento di Ricerca dell'azienda Mantero di Como; dal 2014 è co-fondatrice a direttrice artistica di Lottozero, laboratorio di ricerca tessile che ha sede a Prato.

**V**irginie Rebetez (1979, Svizzera; vive e lavora a Losanna, Svizzera) testa con il suo lavoro le specificità del mezzo fotografico, la dualità intrinseca tra visibile e invisibile, reale e finzione. Ha studiato fotografia presso la Scuola di Vevey e successivamente in Olanda presso la Gerrit Rietveld Academie. Il suo lavoro fotografico è stato presentato in diversi contesti istituzionali in Europa ed è parte di numerose collezioni private e pubbliche. *Under Cover*, progetto realizzato durante una residenza a Johannesburg, ha ottenuto il premio Leica ed è stato poi presentato ad Art Basel nel 2014 e in una mostra personale presso la galleria Christopher Gerber a Losanna.
Nel 2014 ha vinto la prestigiosa borsa di studio della Fondazione Leenaards, CH e ha trascorso una residenza di sei mesi a New York, dove ha sviluppato il progetto *Out of the Blue*, presentato nell'ultima edizione di Art Basel 2016 e pubblicato nello stesso anno dalla casa editrice Meta/Books.

**A**nna M. Rose (1982, USA; vive e lavora a Firenze, Italia) crea stati di ambiguità o straniamento percettivo con cui fare un'opera di corrosione dei luoghi comuni legati alla femminilità, sviluppando di pari passo una riflessione sullo scorrere del tempo, l'identità e la memoria. L'utilizzo di capelli sintetici è una cifra ricorrente nel suo lavoro, declinato nei diversi mezzi espressivi della scultura, installazione, video e fotografia. Ha studiato Belle Arti presso il San Francisco Art Institute. Nel 2014 ha vinto una residenza a Hrisey in Islanda (Gamli Skoli Old School House), mentre l'anno successivo ha trascorso un'altra residenza a Zalaegerszeg in Ungheria presso D'Clinic Studios. Il video *Ecloga* è entrato a far parte della collezione di Casa Masaccio centro per l'arte contemporanea (San Giovanni Valdarno, Arezzo). Tra le ultime mostre a cui ha preso parte in Europa e America si segnala: *Performing Mythologies*, Colorado Art Center, Denver, USA, 2015; *Apres Coup Dischiusure*, a cura di Saretto Cincinelli, TAI–Tuscan Art Industry, ex-Lucchesi, Prato, IT, 2015; *Hair Picnic*, Das KloHäuschen, Monaco, DE, con Janean Williams, 2015.

**M**ariana Sales (1990, Maputo, Mozambico; vive e lavora a Porto, Portogallo) si è diplomata in scultura presso la Facoltà di Belle Arti dell'Università di Porto, dove attualmente sta ultimando un Master in Disegno e Tecniche di Stampa. Nel 2014 a Edimburgo ha conseguito una specializzazione in Arti Sceniche e Design per live performance. Nella sua pratica artistica la scultura si apre alla contaminazione con altre tecniche e modalità espressive, in una ibridazione di linguaggi. Ha preso parte a esposizioni collettive che si sono tenute prevalentemente in Portogallo.
*Body Looming* è stata selezionata all'interno di *Contextile*, Guimarães, PT, 2014, Esposizione Internazionale di Arte Tessile Contemporanea.

**K**athrin Stumreich (1976, Austria; vive e lavora a Vienna, Austria) è un'artista multimediale che impiega la tecnologia per creare opere interattive o performative in cui prevale una dimensione analogica, spesso veicolata dalla componente sonora del lavoro. Dopo aver studiato Fashion Design presso la Royal Academy of Arts di Anversa, etnologia e filosofia presso il Dipartimento di Filosofia e Etnologia dell'Università di Vienna, consegue una laurea in Arti Digitali presso l'Università di Arti Applicate di Vienna, dove attualmente ricopre degli incarichi di docenza.
Dal 2007 le sue performance e installazioni interattive sono state presentate in contesti internazionali dedicati alla sperimentazione multimediale e alla Sound Art, in Europa, Australia, Cina e Stati Uniti. Tra le manifestazioni in cui è stata esposta l'opera *Fabrichmachine* si segnala la partecipazione nel 2012 alla IV ed. di *Flussi*, Media Arts Festival, Avellino, IT e la recente *Roter Faden-Textile Force*, Gallerie Freihausgasse, Villach, AT, nel 2015.

**Z**eitguised è uno studio di design fondato a Berlino nel 2001 dall'architetto Henrik Mauler e dallo scultore e fashion designer Jamie Raap, vi fanno parte artisti, programmatori e designer esperti in tecniche di animazione al computer e graphic design. Le opere di Zeitguised rientrano nell'ambito dell'arte di sintesi, frutto di un lavoro progettuale unico nel suo genere, che si avvale di processi generativi e algoritmi creati manualmente, tale da creare una tensione dialettica tra astrazione e realismo.
Le opere di Zeitguised sono state presentate in gallerie d'arte, festival e musei in tutto il mondo, tra cui: the Vienna Film Museum, 2014; the Victorian and Albert Museum, Londra, UK 2014; After Squat, Parigi, FR 2012; the Museum of Contemporary Art, Barcellona, ES, 2011; the Volta Art Fair, New York, USA, 2011. Lo studio ha raccolto negli anni moltissimi premi e riconoscimenti; *geist.xyz* ha ottenuto la menzione d'onore all'Ars Prix Electronica di Linz, AT, nell'edizione del 2016.

Autori

**A**lessandra Tempesti (1979, Firenze, Italia; vive e lavora a Prato, Italia) si è laureata presso la Facoltà di Lettere e Filosofia dell'Università di Firenze, con una tesi in storia dell'arte contemporanea. Dal 2007 al 2011 ha lavorato presso il Centro di Cultura Contemporanea Strozzina di Firenze, occupandosi di educazione e di coordinamento e curatela di progetti speciali, tra cui la I e la II edizione di *Open Studios*, in collaborazione con la Regione Toscana. Dopo aver studiato Textile Design e Progettazione del Colore con Renata Pompas a Milano, ha seguito la catalogazione di disegni e tessuti della collezione *Suzanne Janine e Jean Peltier*, per l'Archivio storico dell'azienda Ratti di Como, iniziando poi una sua attività come textile designer freelance.
Parallelamente ha sviluppato una propria ricerca artistica nell'ambito del suono, occupandosi di sonorizzazioni per progetti legati alla danza, al teatro e alla videoarte.
Con il moniker Gea Brown si è esibita in festival di musica sperimentale (International Feel, Terraforma, Hand Signed, Transart) e istituzioni legate all'arte contemporanea (La Triennale di Milano; Istituto Svizzero di Roma; Villa Romana, Firenze; Palazzo Strozzi; Firenze). Dal 2012 collabora con Sync, una piattaforma di ricerca dedita alla sperimentazione audio visiva che ha la sua base tra Pistoia e Firenze.

**U**thra Rajgopal (1974, Chennai, India; vive nello Yorkshire, Gran Bretagna) insegna Contextual Studies alla Manchester School of Art e alla Manchester Metropolitan University. Ha studiato storia dell'arte alla University of York e al Courtauld Institute of Art. Ha presentato collezioni di abiti e tessuti presso il Dakshina Chitra (centro per l'artigianato di Chennai), l'Harris Museum, il Museum of London, il Victoria and Albert Museum, il Warner Textile Archive e lo Shrujan Trust di Bhuj. Uthra Rajgopal ha ricoperto la carica di segretario della UK Textile Society ed è membro dello European Textile Network e della Textile Society of America. Nata a Chennai, capitale dello stato indiano Tamil Nadu, e cresciuta in Inghilterra, Uthra Rajgopal ha lasciato l'avvocatura per dedicarsi allo studio del tessile in tutte le sue forme, compiendo numerose ricerche nel campo della storia dell'arte e della moda. Attualmente si occupa della tradizionale tessitura su telaio a mano indiana di cui si è recentemente riscoperta l'importanza, anche in un'ottica di sostenibilità.

**R**oland Barth (Berlin, Germany, 1983, lives and works in Berlin) became interested in screen printing in 2007, and since then has developed numerous collaborations with various screen printing laboratories, including *Pony Pedro* and *Fleischerei/Czentrifuga*, in parallel with his studies in Textile and Surface Design at the Weißensee Academy of Fine Arts in Berlin. In 2010 he founded *MehrSiebdruck*, a screen printing laboratory in the Wedding district, together with other collaborations, occupying himself with both commissioned screen prints and his own projects in the field of graphic art and artist's books. The studio has taken part in numerous exhibitions in Europe. In 2016 his research led him to define an experimental and individual style of screen painting, which uses screen painting tools, such as the blade and mesh screen.

**M**arie Ilse Bourlanges (1983, Paris, France) and **E**lena Khurtova (1982, Samara, Russia) live in Amsterdam and have worked together since 2009. They both studied Architectural Design at the Gerrit Rietveld Academy in Amsterdam, specializing respectively in Textile Design and Ceramics. Their research, which combines traditional sculptural techniques with modern technology, is a sculptural investigation that conceives the work as a whole process, through the creation of installations and objects that overcome the gap between form and content, in a dynamic and vital tension between matter and memory. Khurtova/Bourlanges's work

174 Biografie

175 Biographies

# INK CATALOGUES

This is a pair of 200-page catalogs for two exhibitions that ran concurrently, featuring two highly esteemed artists, *Beauty Beyond Form—Wu Guanzhong* and *After The Rain—Chua Ek Kay*. The two books obeyed the same layout system because of the similarities in both artists but they were also intended to bring out their differences.

Studio: Somewhere Else

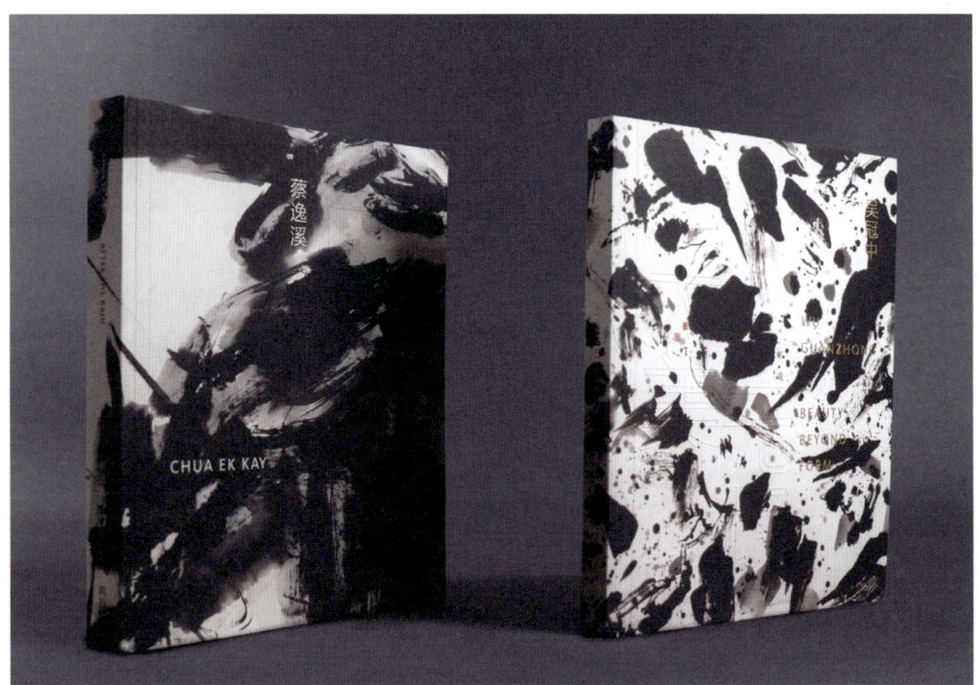


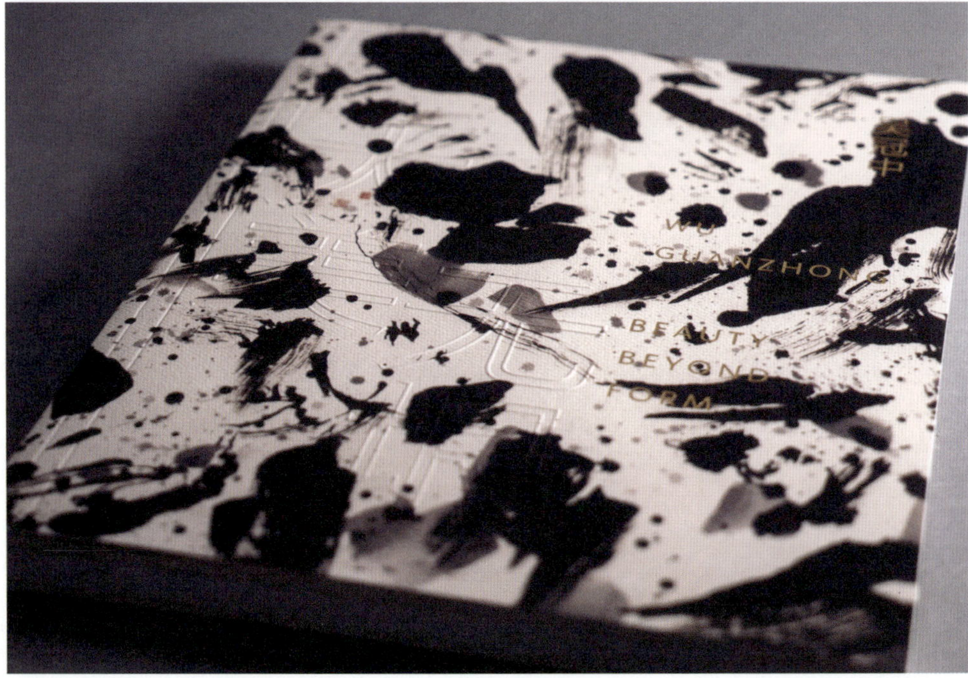

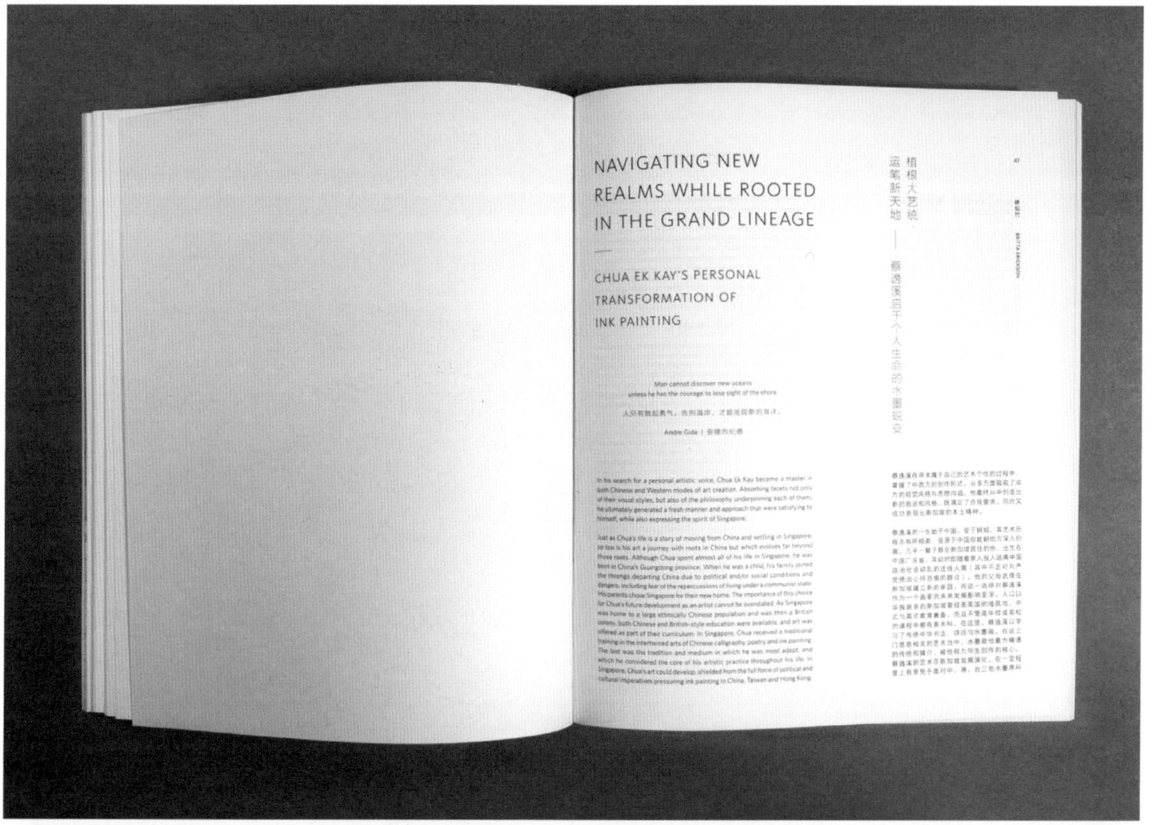

NAVIGATING NEW REALMS WHILE ROOTED IN THE GRAND LINEAGE

CHUA EK KAY'S PERSONAL TRANSFORMATION OF INK PAINTING

Man cannot discover new oceans
unless he has the courage to lose sight of the shore.

Andre Gide

In his search for a personal artistic voice, Chua Ek Kay became a master in both Chinese and Western modes of art creation. Absorbing facets not only of their visual styles, but also of the philosophy underpinning each of them, he ultimately generated a fresh manner and approach that were satisfying to himself, while also expressing the spirit of Singapore.

Just as Chua's life is a story of moving from China and settling in Singapore, so too is his art a journey with roots in China but which evolves far beyond those roots. Although Chua spent almost all of his life in Singapore, he was born in China's Guangdong province. When he was a child, his family joined the throngs departing China due to political and/or social conditions and dangers, including fear of the repercussions of living under a communist state. His parents chose Singapore for their new home. The importance of this choice for Chua's future development as an artist cannot be overstated. As Singapore was home to a large ethnically Chinese population and was then a British colony, both Chinese and British-style education were available, and art was offered as part of their curriculum. In Singapore, Chua received a traditional training in the intertwined arts of Chinese calligraphy, poetry and ink painting. The last was the tradition and medium in which he was most adept, and which he considered the core of his artistic practice throughout his life. In Singapore, Chua's art could develop, shielded from the full force of political and cultural imperatives pressuring ink painting in China, Taiwan and Hong Kong.

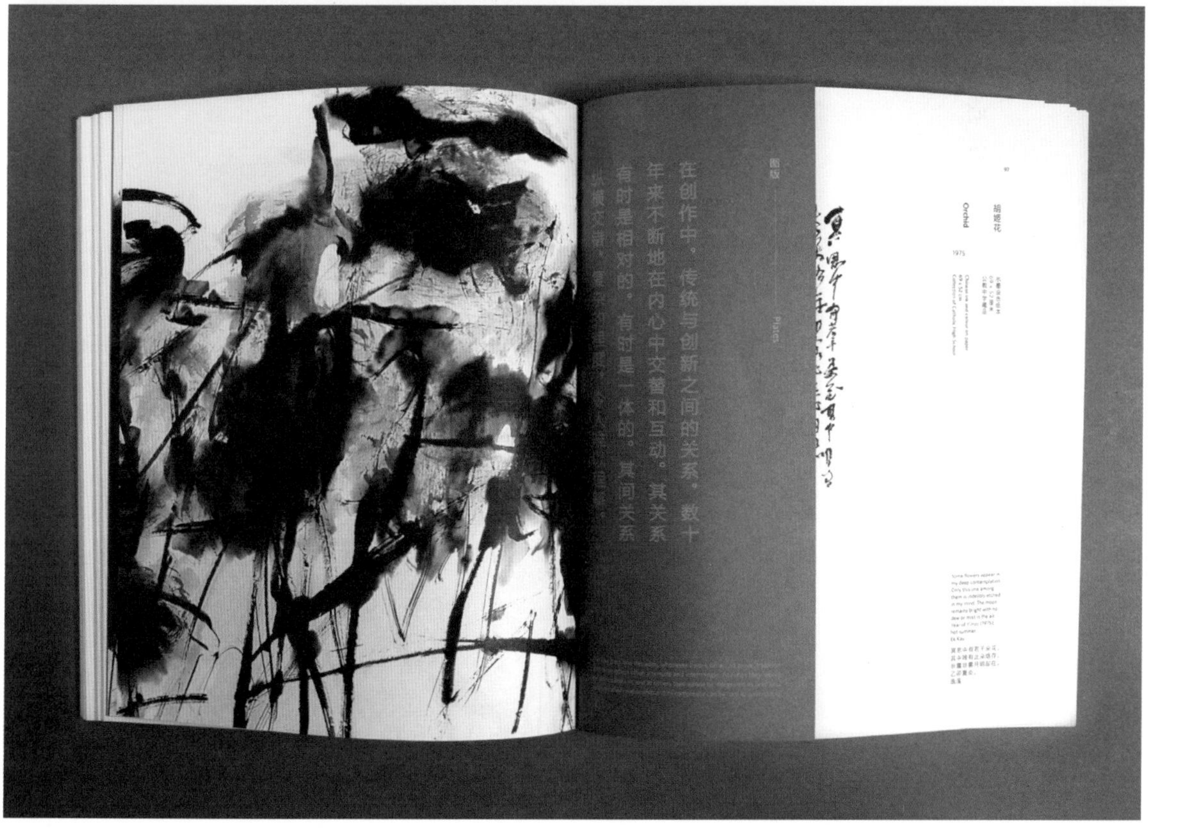

图版 Plates

在创作中，传统与创新之间的关系，数十年来不断地在内心中交替和互动。其关系有时是相对的，有时是一体的。其间关系

胡姬花

Orchid

1975

# ALICE'S ADVENTURE IN WONDERLAND

After reading the story of *Alice's Adventure in the Wonderland* for the first time, the designer felt drawn into the fictional world and all of its intriguing, vivid imagery. This inspired her to present the story through typography.

Designer: Rapas (Boong) Chamnanratanakul

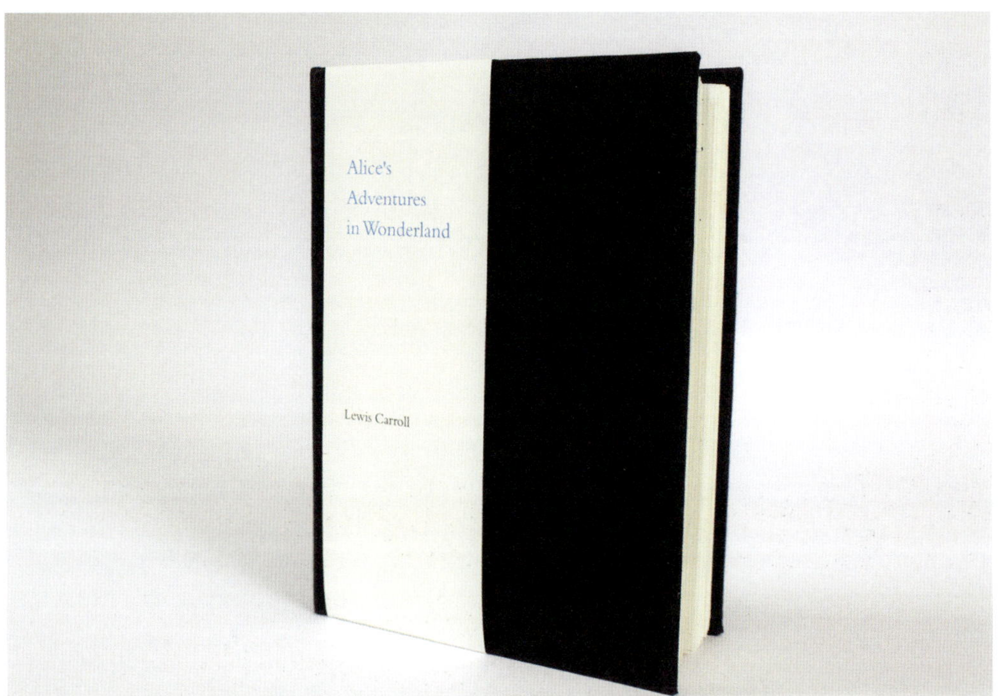


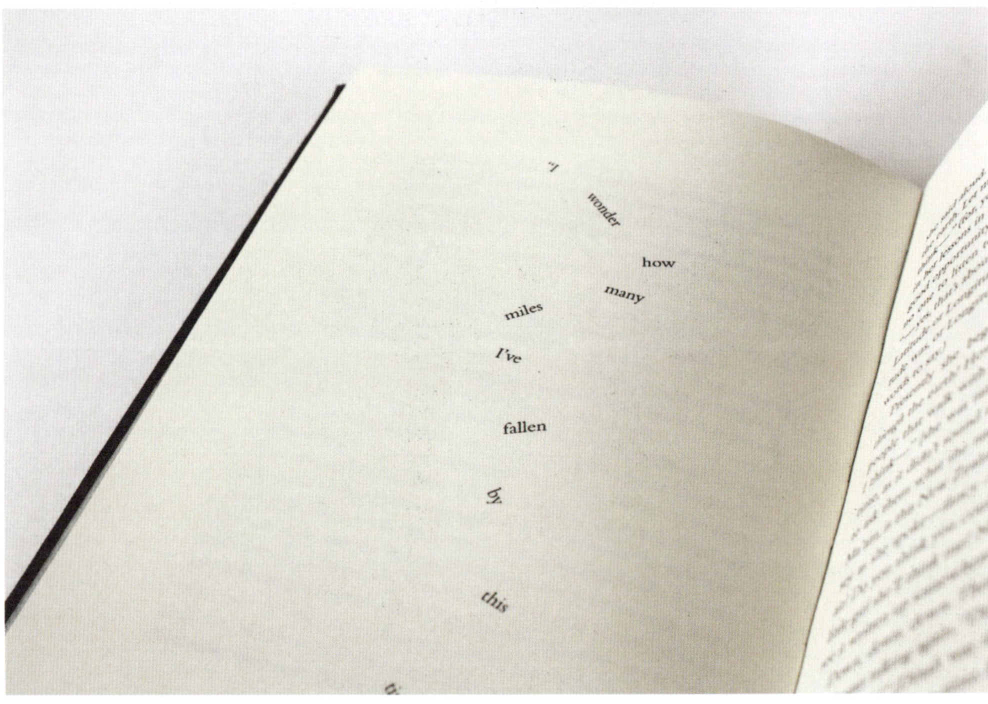

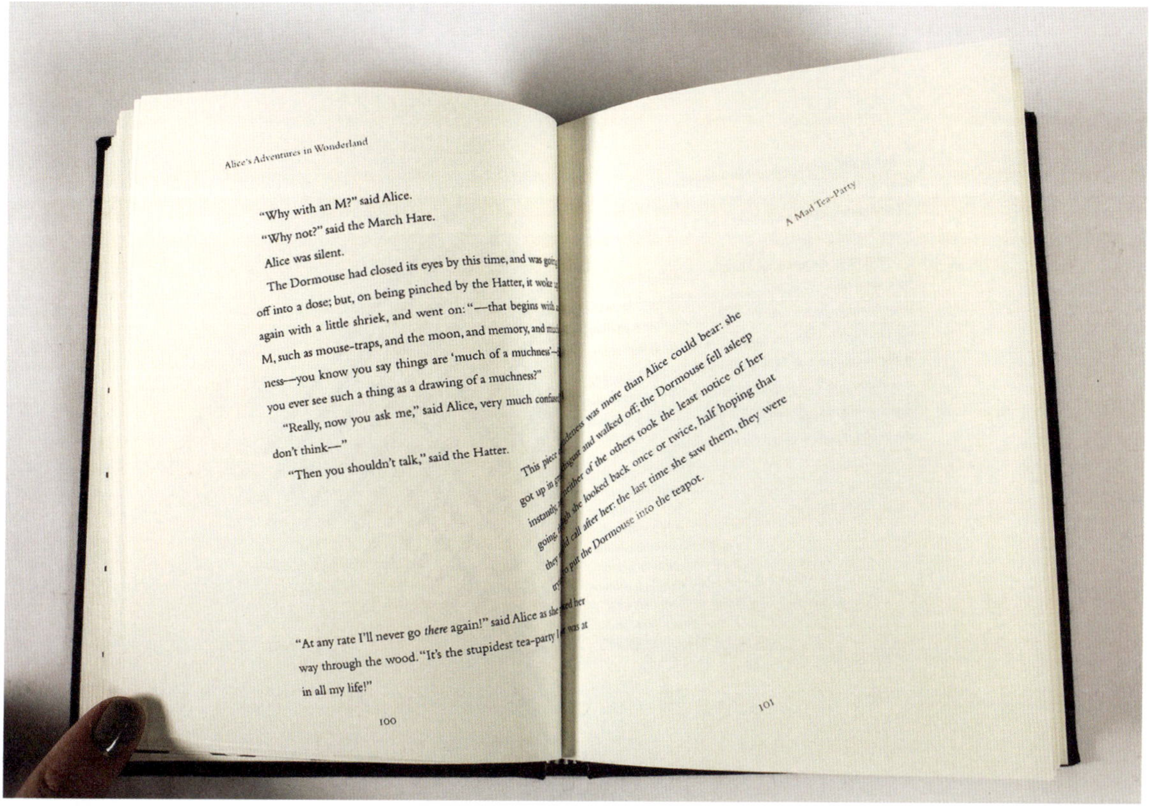

Alice's Adventures in Wonderland

"Why with an M?" said Alice.

"Why not?" said the March Hare.

Alice was silent.

The Dormouse had closed its eyes by this time, and was goin off into a dose; but, on being pinched by the Hatter, it woke again with a little shriek, and went on: "—that begins with M, such as mouse-traps, and the moon, and memory, and muc ness—you know you say things are 'much of a muchness'— you ever see such a thing as a drawing of a muchness?"

"Really, now you ask me," said Alice, very much confus don't think—"

"Then you shouldn't talk," said the Hatter.

A Mad Tea-Party

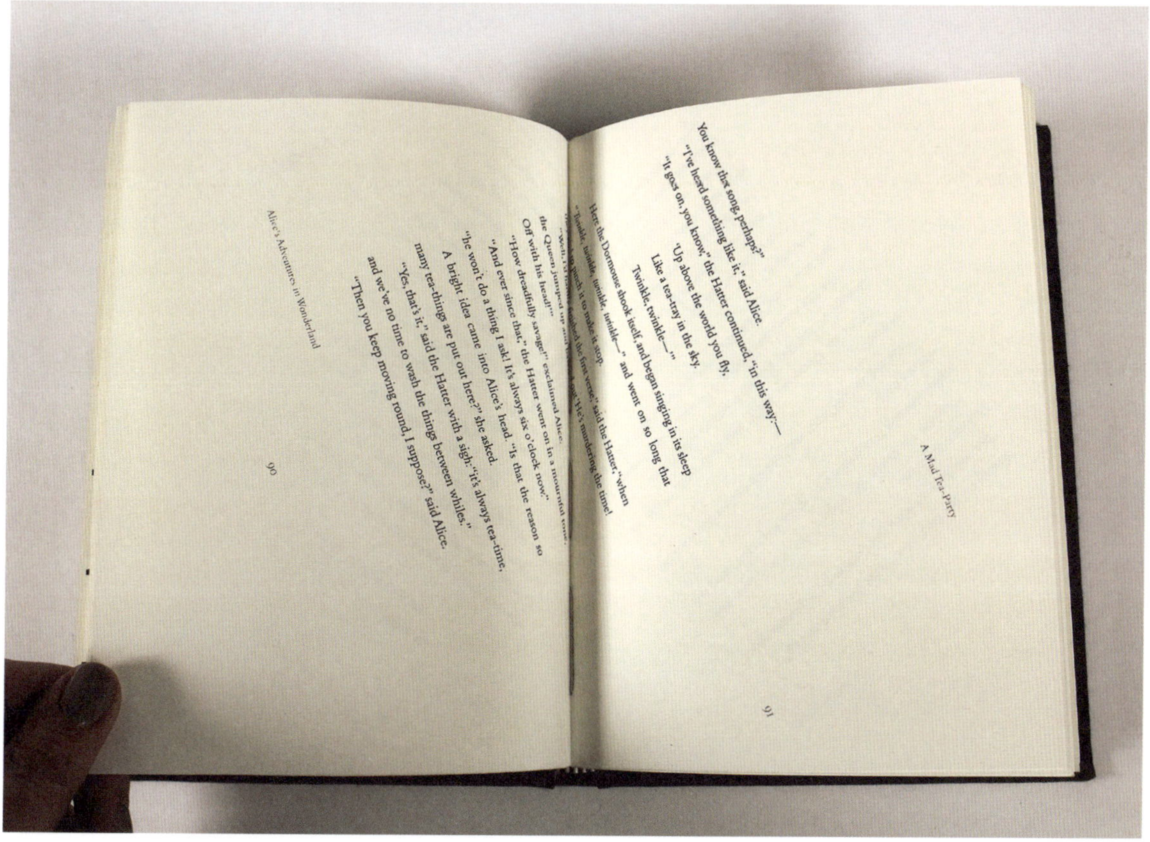

This piece ...deness was more than Alice could bear: she got up in ... and walked off; the Dormouse fell asleep instantly ... neither of the others took the least notice of her going ... she looked back once or twice, half hoping that they ... call after her: the last time she saw them, they were ... put the Dormouse into the teapot.

"At any rate I'll never go *there* again!" said Alice as she ... her way through the wood. "It's the stupidest tea-party I ... was at in all my life!"

100

101

Alice's Adventures in Wonderland

90

A Mad Tea-Party

91

# THE OLD MAN AND THE SEA

*The Old Man and the Sea* is a novel about an old fisherman, who didn't catch a fish in 80 days until when he sets out to sea again and has a fight with a giant marlin. The design of the book focuses on the simplicity of the fisherman' life, as well as on the image of the open sea.

Designer: Silva Baum

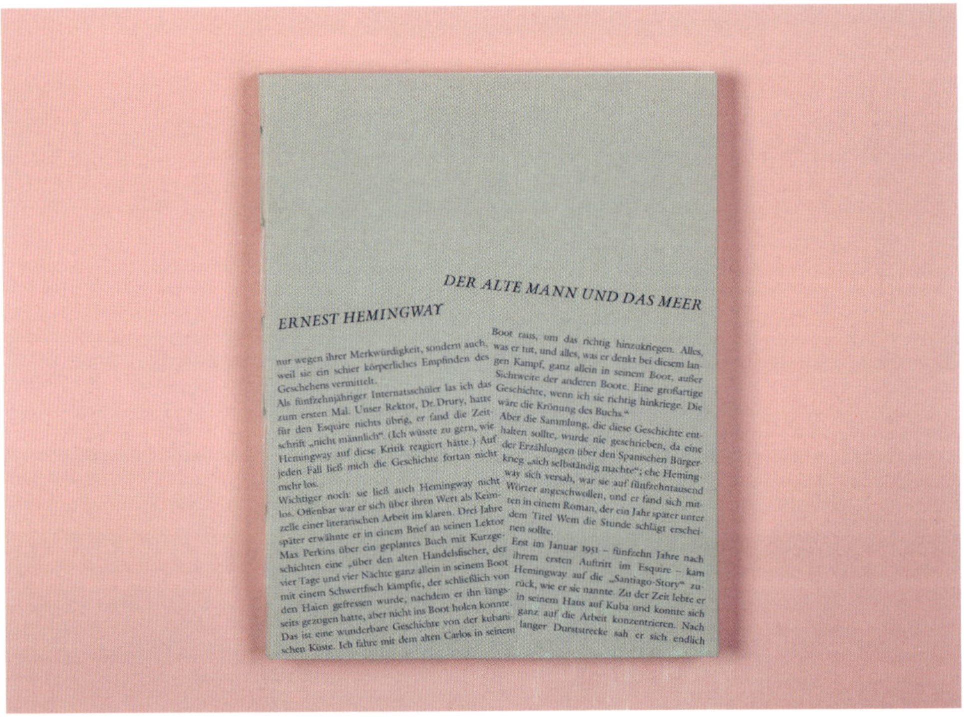

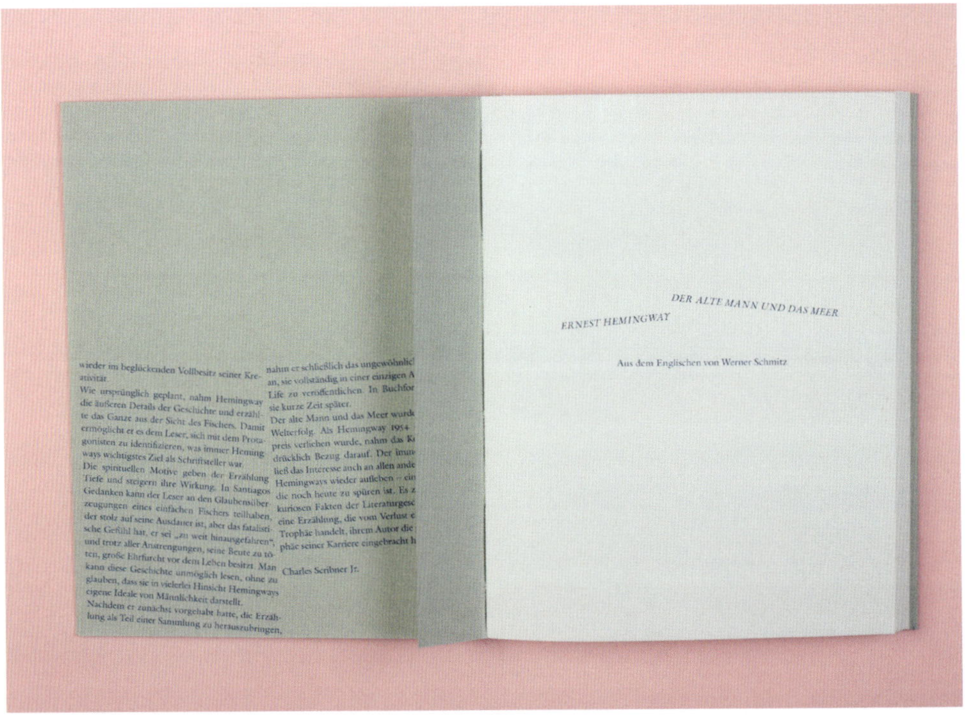

# PUNK: AN AESTHETIC

This heavily illustrated book presents an unrivaled collection of punk art and ephemera that incorporate every aspect of the movement, for example, the earliest occurrences of punk symbolism in posters and flyers for underground bands.

Studio: Triboro
Designer: Stefanie Weigler, David Heasty

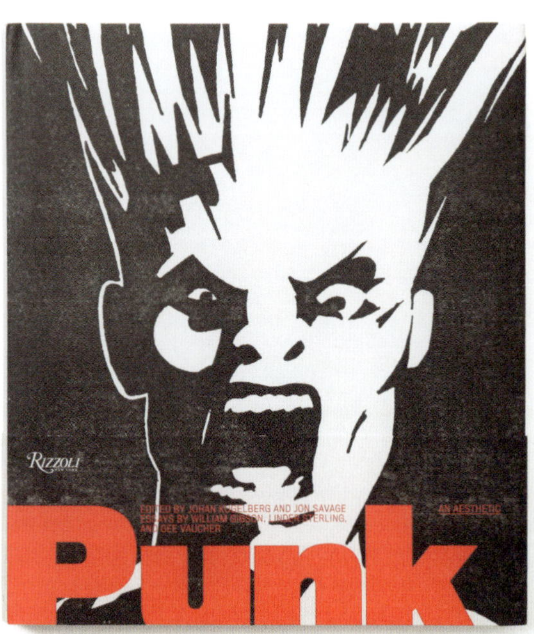


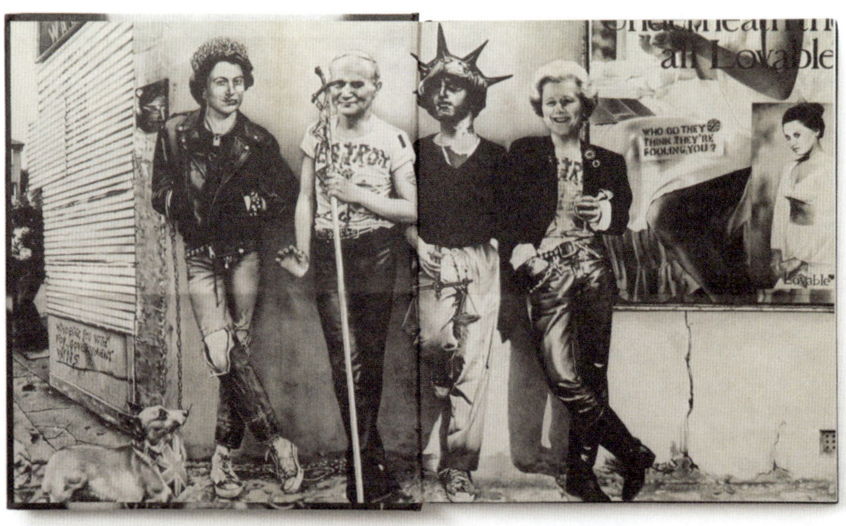

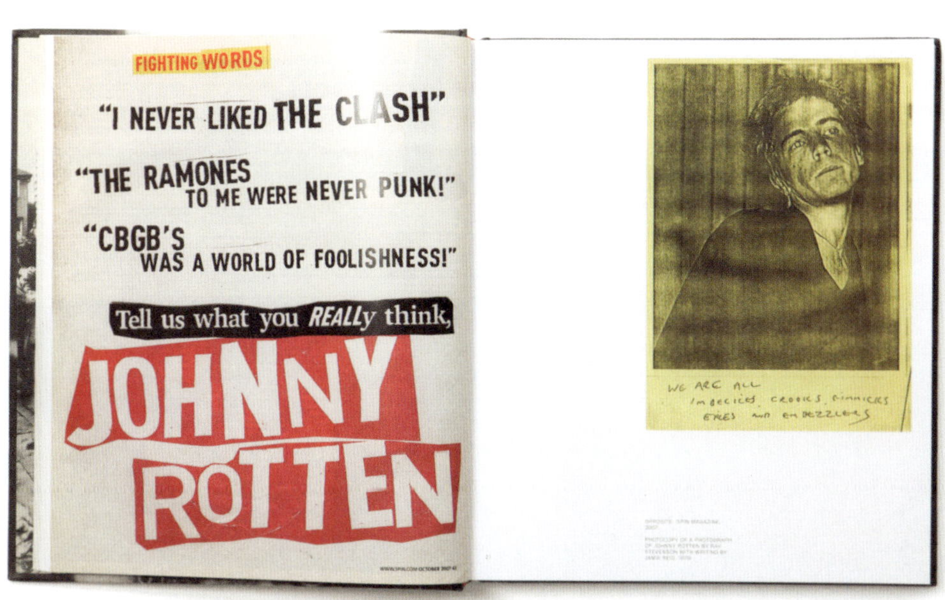

FIGHTING WORDS
"I NEVER LIKED THE CLASH"
"THE RAMONES TO ME WERE NEVER PUNK!"
"CBGB'S WAS A WORLD OF FOOLISHNESS!"
Tell us what you REALLy think,
JOHNNY ROTTEN


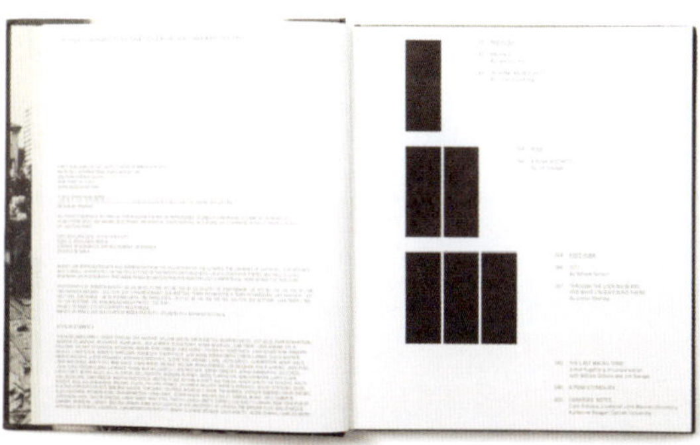

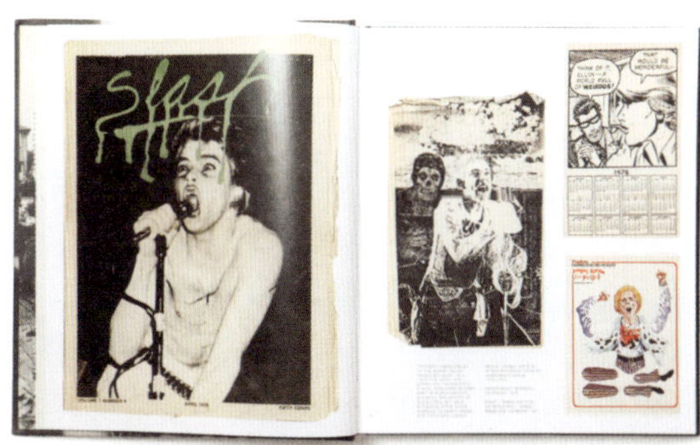

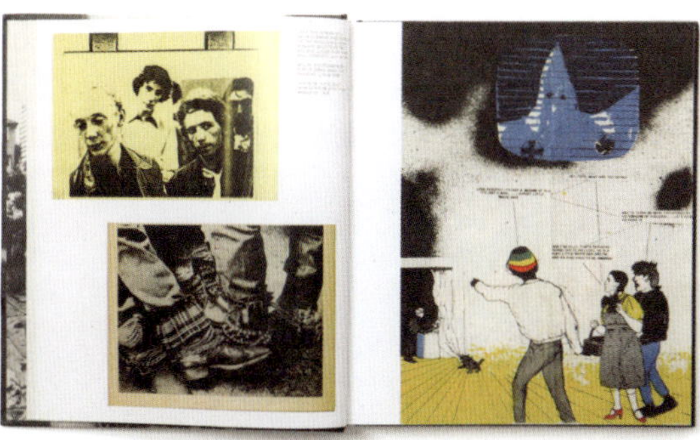

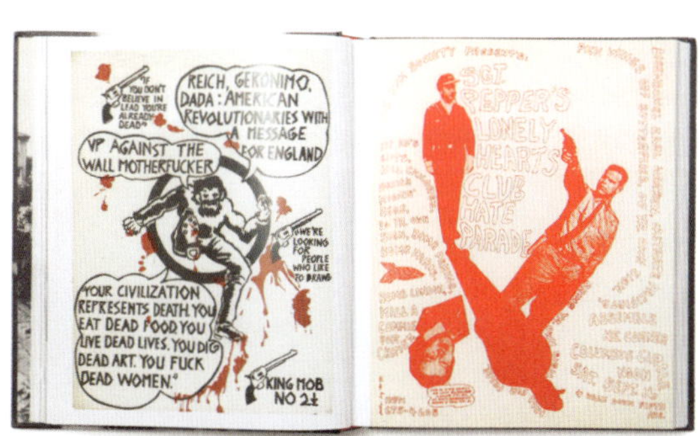

REICH, GERONIMO, DADA: AMERICAN REVOLUTIONARIES WITH A MESSAGE FOR ENGLAND
IF YOU DON'T BELIEVE IN LEAD YOU'RE ALREADY DEAD
UP AGAINST THE WALL MOTHERFUCKER
WE'RE LOOKING FOR PEOPLE WHO LIKE TO DRAW
YOUR CIVILIZATION REPRESENTS DEATH. YOU EAT DEAD FOOD YOU LIVE DEAD LIVES. YOU DIG DEAD ART. YOU FUCK DEAD WOMEN.
KING MOB
SGT PEPPER'S LONELY HEARTS CLUB HATE PARADE

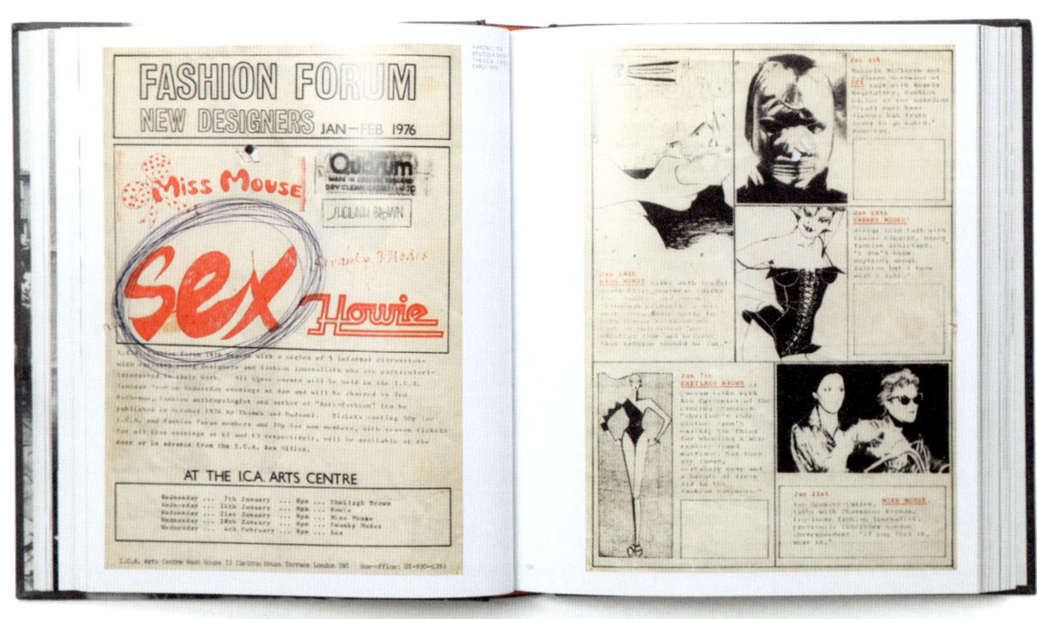
FASHION FORUM
NEW DESIGNERS JAN—FEB 1976
Miss Mouse
Quorum
SHEILAGH BROWN
Swanky Modes
Sex
Howie
AT THE I.C.A. ARTS CENTRE

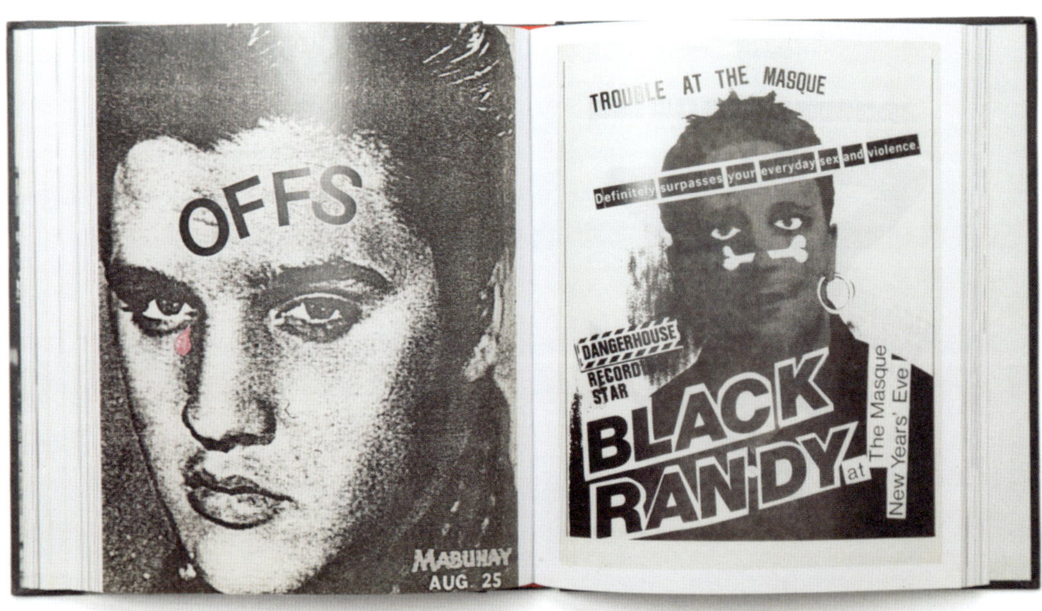
OFFS
MABUHAY
AUG. 25
TROUBLE AT THE MASQUE
Definitely surpasses your everyday sex and violence.
DANGERHOUSE
RECORD
STAR
BLACK
RAN·DY
at
The Masque
New Years' Eve

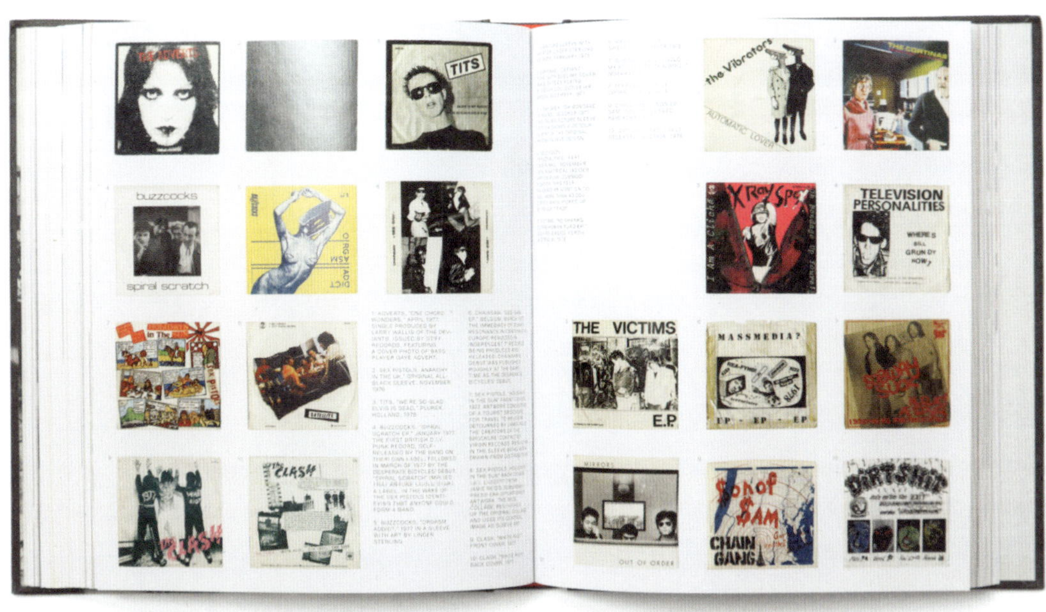
TITS
buzzcocks
spiral scratch
the Vibrators
AUTOMATIC LOVER
THE CORTINAS
X Ray Spex
TELEVISION PERSONALITIES
THE VICTIMS
E.P.
MASSMEDIA?
EP EP EP
CHAIN GANG
OUT OF ORDER

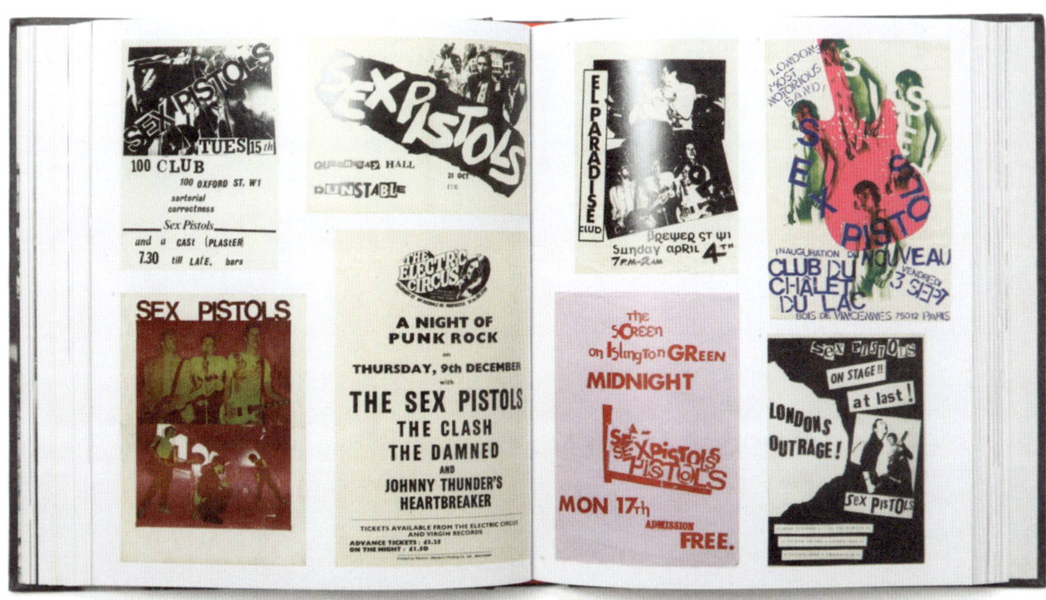
SEX PISTOLS
TUES 15th
100 CLUB
100 OXFORD ST. W1
sartorial correctness
Sex Pistols
and a CAST (PLASTER
7.30 till LATE. bars
SEX PISTOLS
DUNSTABLE
EL PARADISE CLUB
BREWER ST W1
Sunday april 4th
7PM-2AM
LONDONS MOST NOTORIOUS BAND!
SEX PISTOLS
INAUGURATION DU NOUVEAU
CLUB DU CHALET DU LAC
VENDREDI 3 SEPT
BOIS DE VINCENNES 75012 PARIS
SEX PISTOLS
THE ELECTRIC CIRCUS
A NIGHT OF PUNK ROCK
on
THURSDAY, 9th DECEMBER
with
THE SEX PISTOLS
THE CLASH
THE DAMNED
AND
JOHNNY THUNDER'S HEARTBREAKER
TICKETS AVAILABLE FROM THE ELECTRIC CIRCUS AND VIRGIN RECORDS
ADVANCE TICKETS : £1.25
ON THE NIGHT : £1.50
The SCREEN on Islington GREEN
MIDNIGHT
SEX PISTOLS
MON 17th
ADMISSION FREE.
SEX PISTOLS
ON STAGE!!
at last!
LONDONS OUTRAGE!
SEX PISTOLS

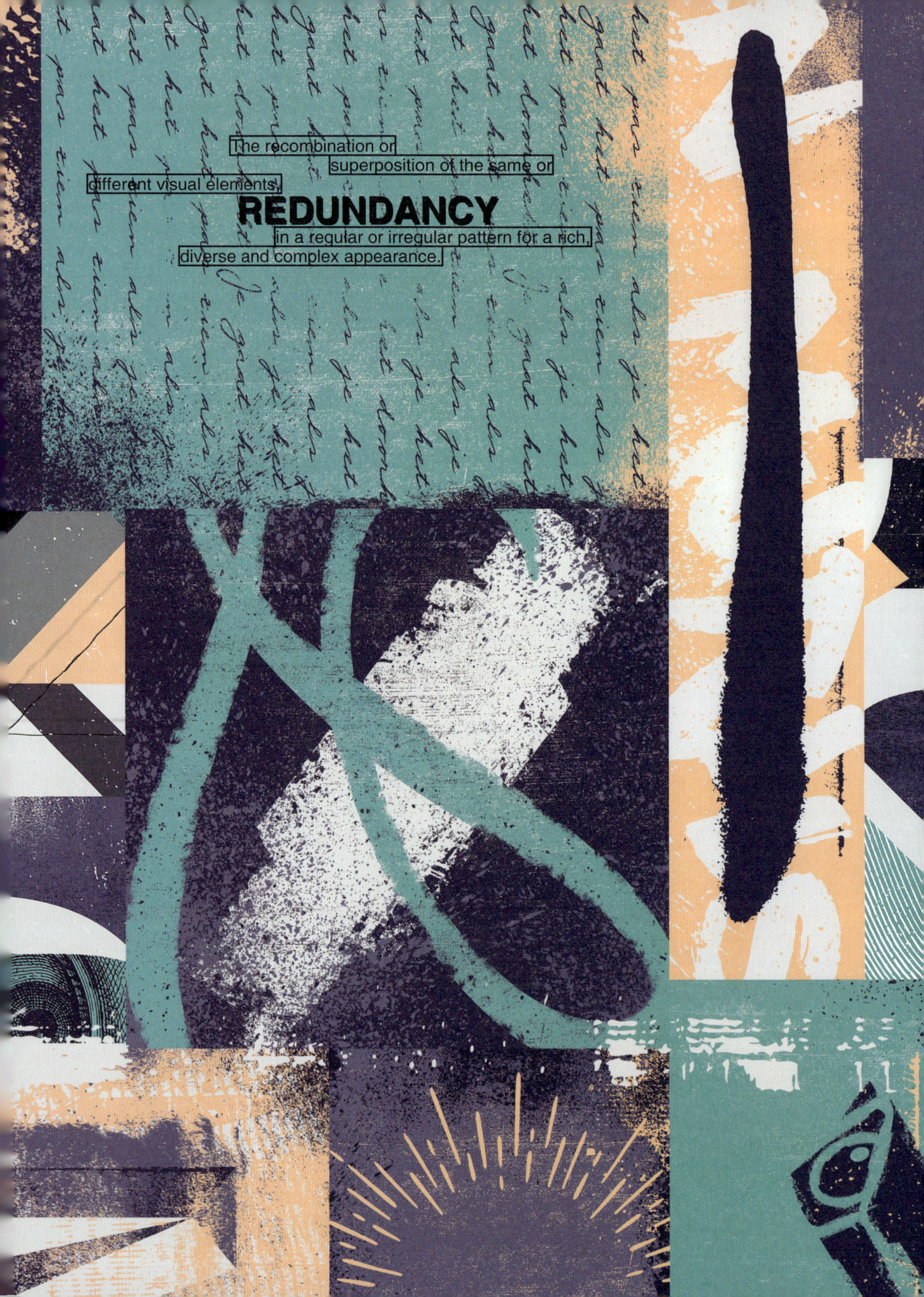
The recombination or
superposition of the same or
different visual elements,
REDUNDANCY
in a regular or irregular pattern for a rich,
diverse and complex appearance.

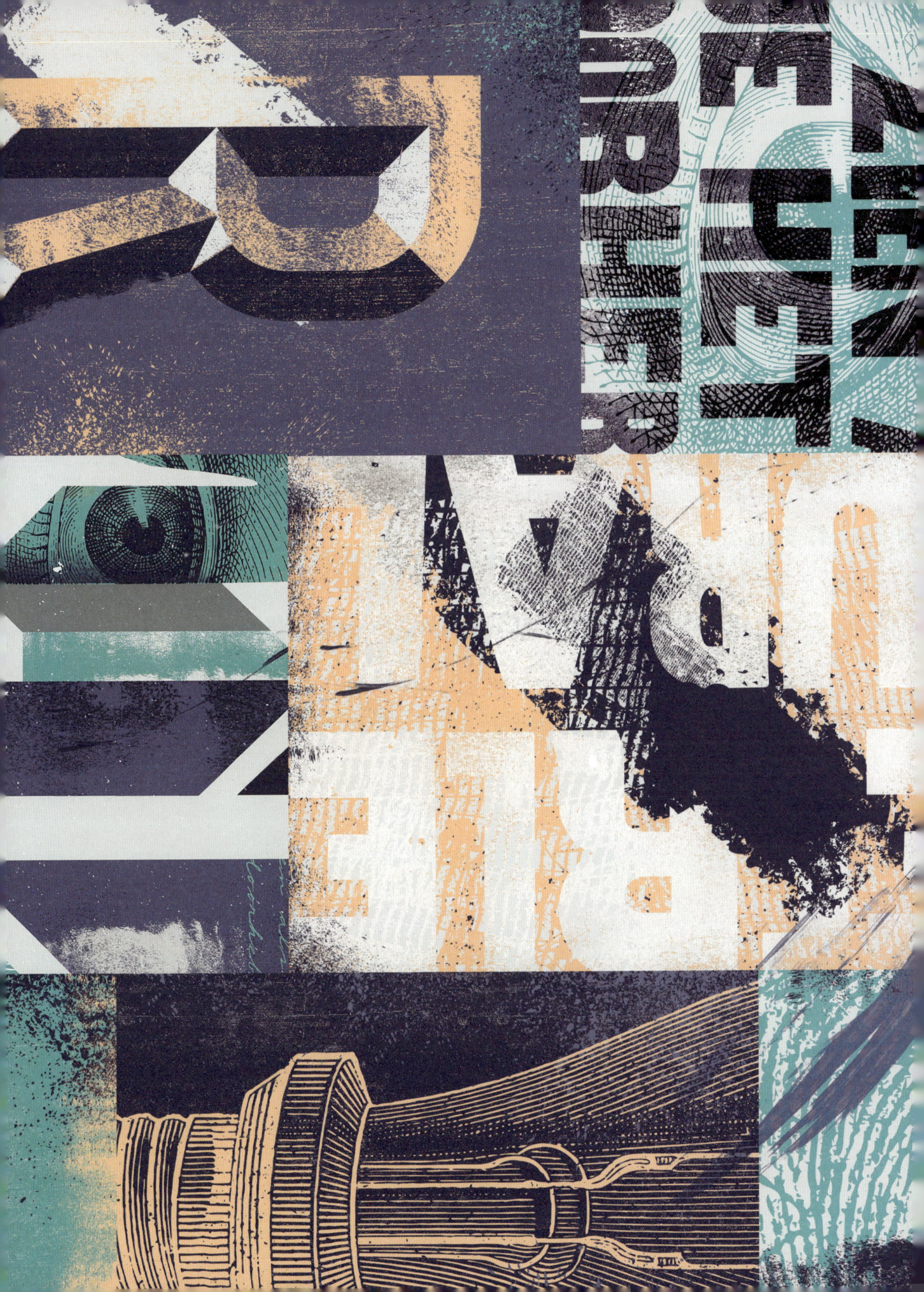

# SISTEMA: YO, ANSIEDAD

This is a design with the theme of anxiety. Every time the designer designs, he feels that the work is not good enough, thus he tends to make it again from scratch. This is what these collages are all about. The idea behind this work is simple: to seek perfection forever and never be self-satisfied.

Designer: Costa, Gabriel Alejandro

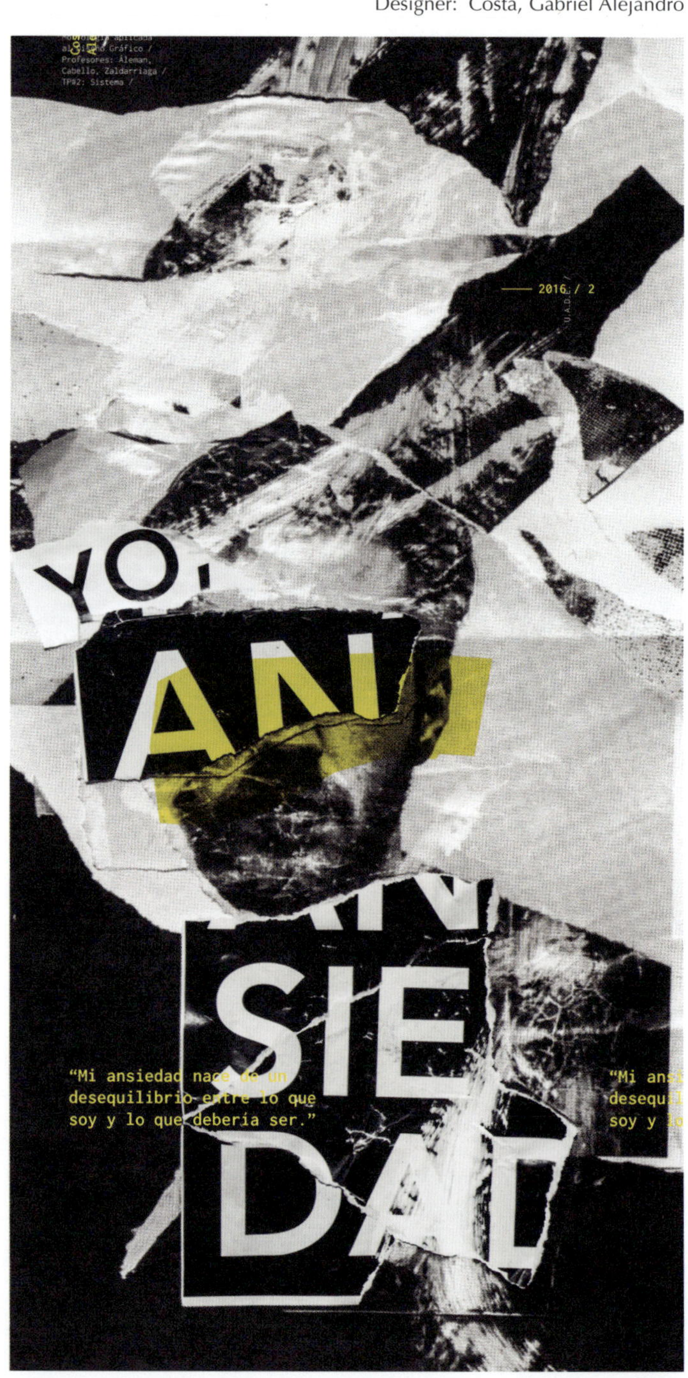


*As a kind of visual experience, what do you think about the "chaos" in graphic design?*

I think that chaos is an essential part of the unconscious mind related to our biological interaction with the universe. And this essence tends to be obliterated by the established dogmas of our society. Therefore, I think that chaos, as an inheritance of the human kind from the universe, is essential while creating visual information. Visual communication through chaotic forms, without artfully presentation or meaningless trends, should be a goal in the making process of any designer, considering design as an active tool to improve our society.

*What are your common approaches to produce a "chaotic" visual effect?*

I think that if it could be explained with words, it wouldn't be chaotic at all. As I just said, I think chaos is part of our essence, prior to our cultural and academic learning that have rooted over time. Doing something chaotic is to step out of the things that you have learned before and the things that you think are right and try to connect with your own being and with those you are communicating to. I do not believe that rules or academic learning are a complete obstacle to communicate something sincere, but they should not be taken as an absolute parameter without questioning them.

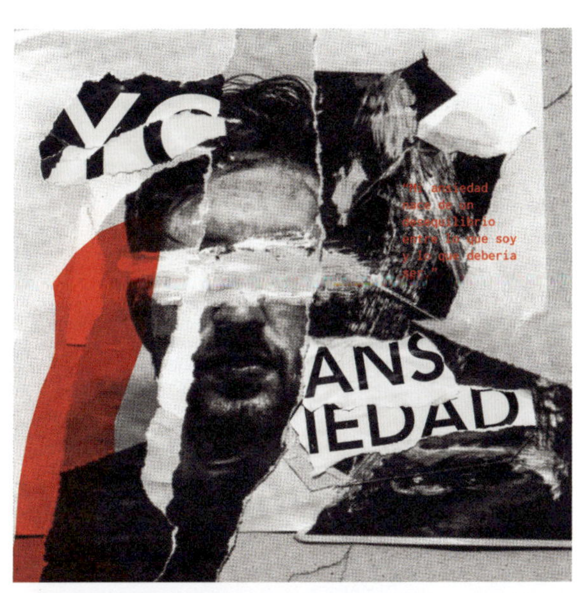

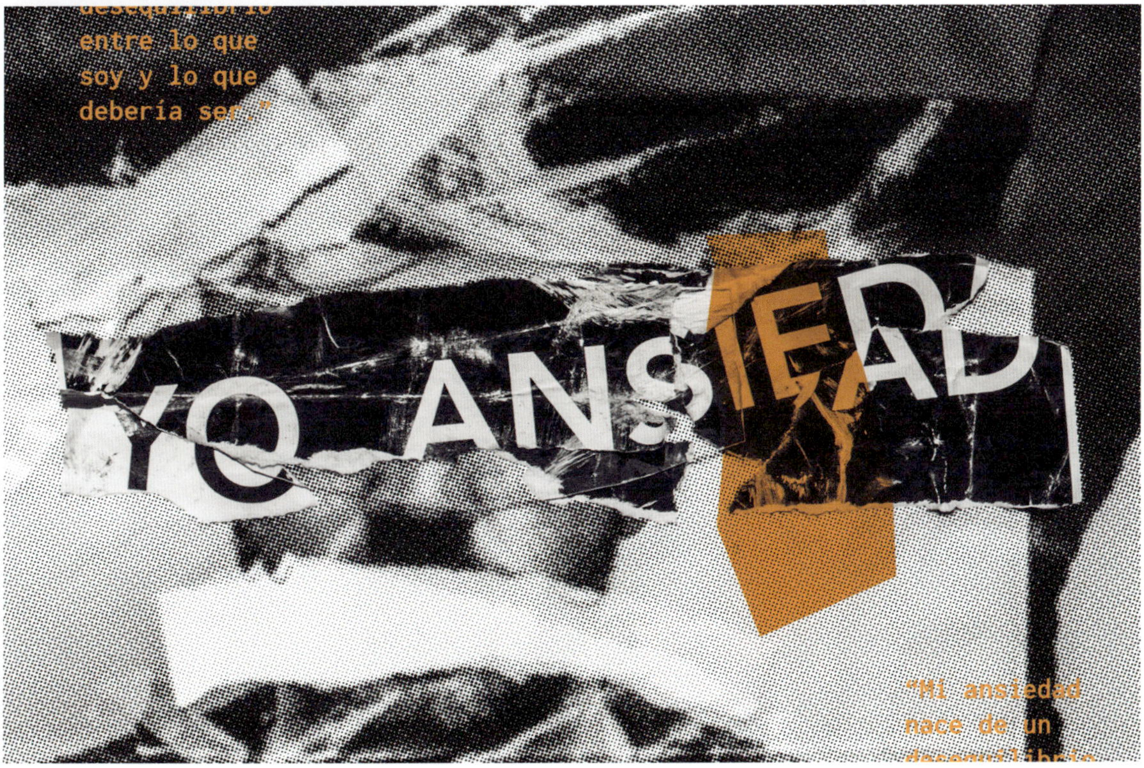

# KRAFTFELD CLUB—FLYER & POSTER SERIES

The flyer provides information about the various events at the Kraftfelt bar monthly. The arrangement of the text fields is determined by the chronology, the size and the venue of those individual events. When the flyer is unfolded, it can also be used as a small poster.

Studio: Studio am Meer
Designer: Janine Peter

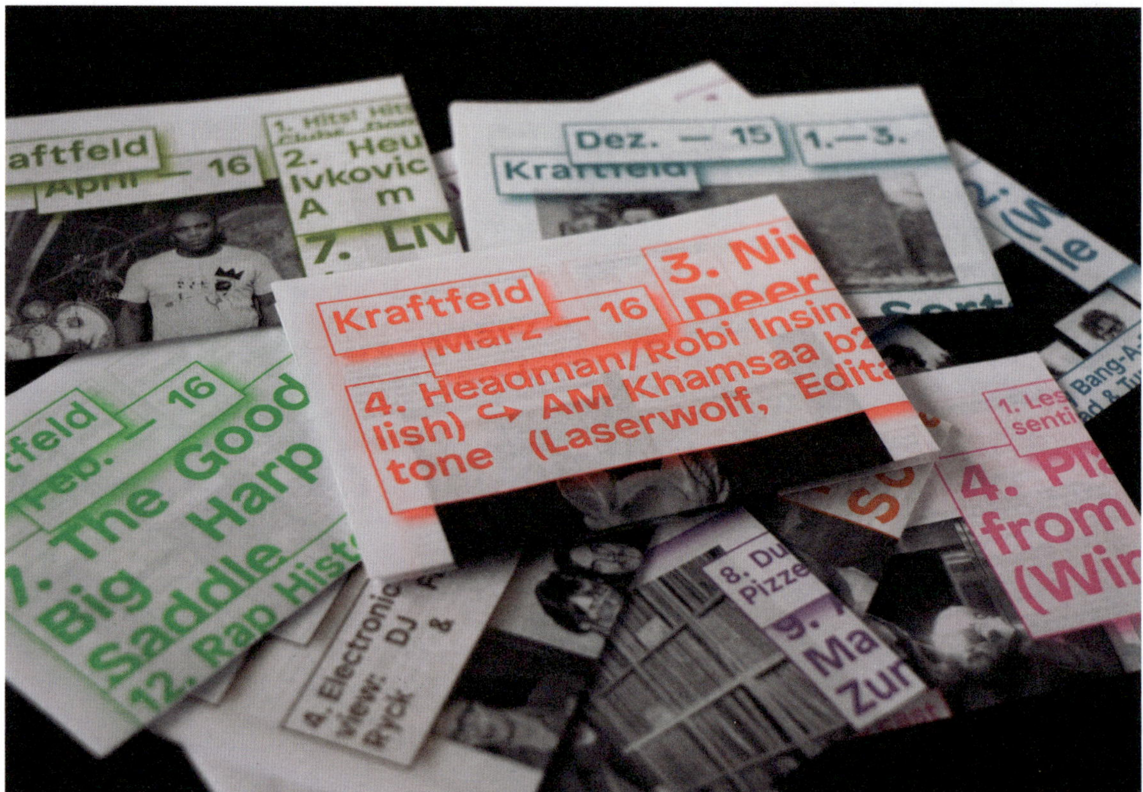


*As a kind of visual experience, what do you think about the "chaos" in graphic design?*

When I see something chaotic I can always find some kind of order behind it. For me this visual experience becomes very interesting when there is an interaction between chaos and order, then the graphic design gets really vivid.

*What are your common approaches to produce a "chaotic" visual effect?*

For an analogy, I put everything in a blender and make sure that I leave the lid open while I push the start button. The same goes for design.

Kraftfeld

März — 16

3. Nive Nielsen & The Deer Children (GL/DK)

4. Headman/Robi Insinna (Relish) ↪ AM Khamsaa b2b Auntone (Laserwolf, Editanstalt)

5. Rub A Dub Club: Real Rock Sound (SH)

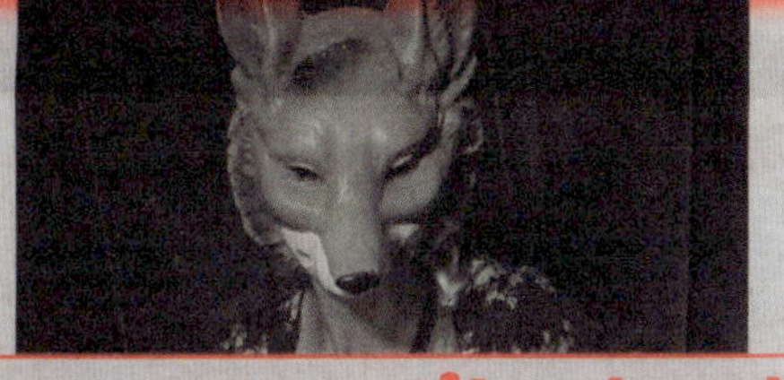

6. Sunday Mess: Siegwart (Lustpoderosa, KAUZ), Faber (Lux Rec), Omar, the Sherriff & Micha Woju (Registratur/München)

10. Wassily (SG)

11. Rap History: 1980 ↪ Professor*Innen Paul Neumann & That Fucking Sara (Berlin)

12. Flohmarkt: DJ Sir Oliver Peter & Dr. Brunner ↪ Sputnik: DJ Lounge Lizard & Ghost

19. EMR: DJ Konfront.Audio, Cut the Weazle & Cronic

18. Plattentaufe: Sebass (Winti) ↪ Trubači Soundsistema (SH)

24. Another Nice Mess: DJ Marcelle (NL/Klangbad) & new.com (Comfortnoise, Dubexmachina, Bold/Z ü

25. Trottles of the Dead (Bad Bonn)

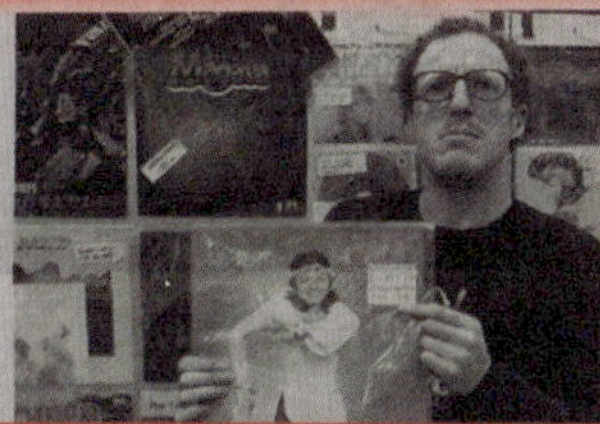

27. Manhattan Cocktail Night ↪ 6 Hours — 6 Manhattans — 99 BPM

26. B-Music: DJ Doug Shipton (UK/Finders Keepers)

31. ReadMe: Die fleischgewordene Social-Media-Plattform

KRAFTFELD

Kraftfeld / Lagerplatz 18 / Winterthur / kraftfeld.ch

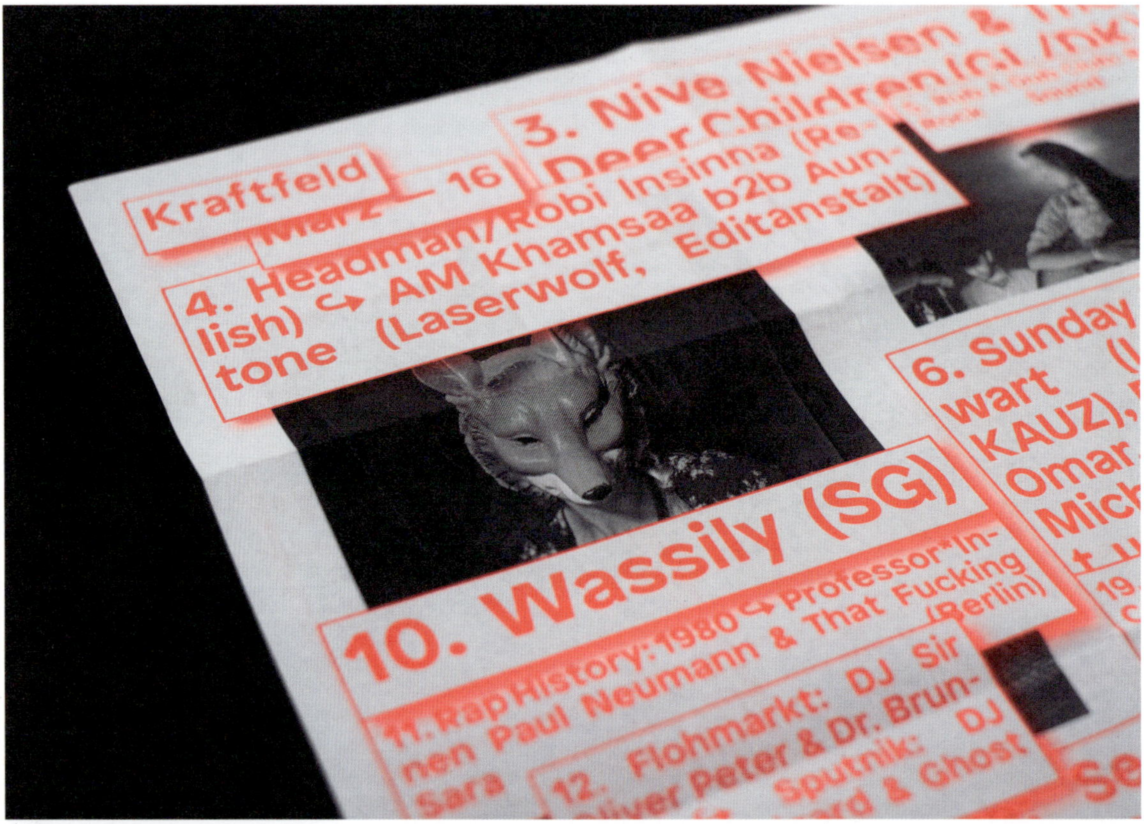
Kraftfeld
16
4. Headman/Robi Insinna (Relish) ↪ AM Khamsaa b2b Auntone (Laserwolf, Editanstalt)
6. Sunday
wart
KAUZ),
10. Wassily (SG)
Professor*In-
nen Paul Neumann & That Fucking
(Berlin)
12. Flohmarkt: DJ
Oliver Peter & Dr. Brun-
Sputnik: DJ
& Ghost

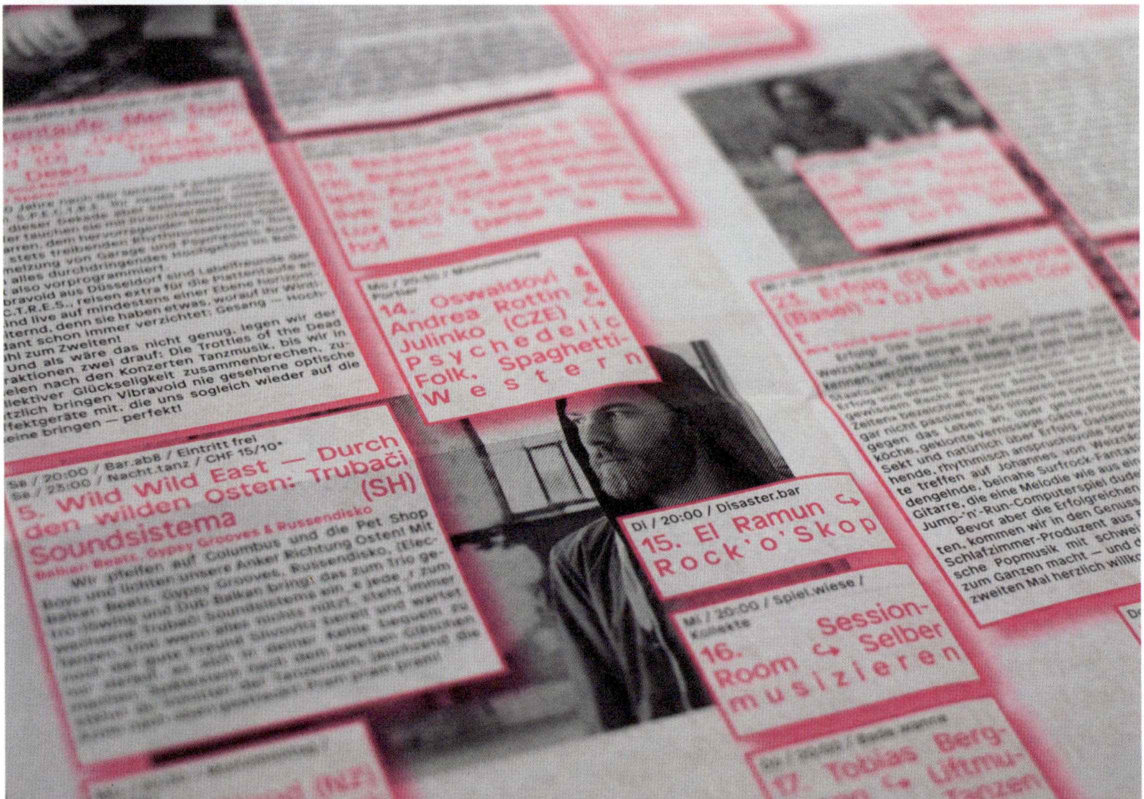
14. Oswaldovi &
Andrea Rottin &
Julinko (CZE) ↪
Psychedelic
Folk, Spaghetti-
Western
Sa / 20:00 / Bar.ab8 / Eintritt frei
Sa / 23:00 / Nacht.tanz / CHF 15/10*
5. Wild Wild East — Durch
den wilden Osten: Trubači
(SH)
Soundsistema
Balkan Beats, Gypsy Grooves & Russendisko
Di / 20:00 / Disaster.bar
15. El Ramun ↪
Rock'o'Skop
Mi / 20:00 / Spiel.wiese /
Kollekte
16. Session-
Room ↪ Selber
musizieren
17. Tobias Berg-
Liftmu-
Tanzen

Kraftfeld

Sept. — 15

1. Lesung: Coucou präsentiert REPORTAGEN

4. Plattentaufe: Men from S.P.E.C.T.R.E. (Winti) & Vibravoid (D)

5. Wild Wild East — Durch den wilden Osten: Trubači Soundsistema

11. Supertaster: iSkream (live) & DJ Shoudelistix

Dringend: Gartenzwerg gesucht! Mindesthöhe 110 cm, unbedingt pilzlos. An der Bar abgeben, Bier erhalten, vielen Dank!

12. Schlaflos in Winterthur: DJ Reezm & J. Sayne (Hum-Records)

18. Stadtfilter-Party, live: Lord Kesseli & the Drums (St.Gallen) & Dave Eleanor (Züri)

13. Backstreet Noise II: Dario Rohrbach (Gelbes Billett), Aunt One (Editanstalt), live: CCO (Endless Illusion, Lux Rec)

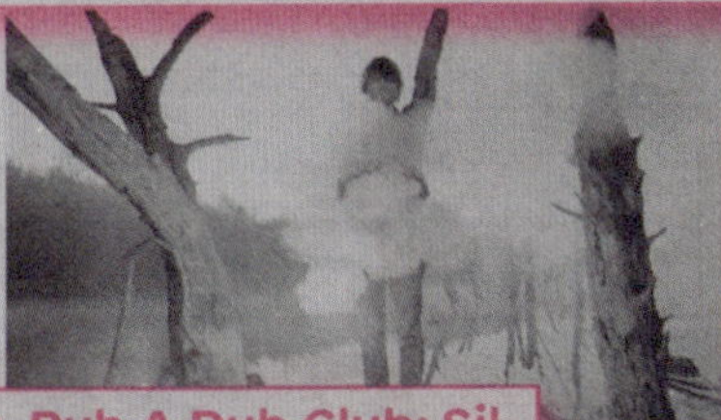

23. Erfolg (D) & Octanone (Basel)

19. Rub A Dub Club: Silly Walks Discotheque (D) & Real Rock Sound (SH)

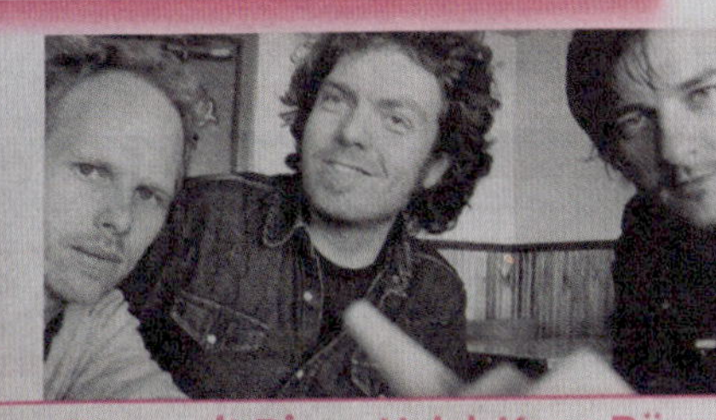

25. The Desoto Caucus (DK) & Albin (SW

26. Heute Tanz mit Disco Halal: Kaan Düzarat (FOC Edits, Istanbul), Moscoman (Correspondant, I'm A Cliché/Berlin, Tel Aviv), Mehmet Aslan (Wilde Renate, Huntleys & Palmers/Berlin), Van Nutt Psychedelic Lightshow

KRAFTFELD

Kraftfeld / Lagerplatz 18 / Winterthur / kraftfeld.ch

## FOST—FESTIVAL OF ORIGINAL SOUNDTRACKS

FOST is a festival dedicated entirely to original soundtracks of the best films around the world.

Designer: J. Marcos Carbone

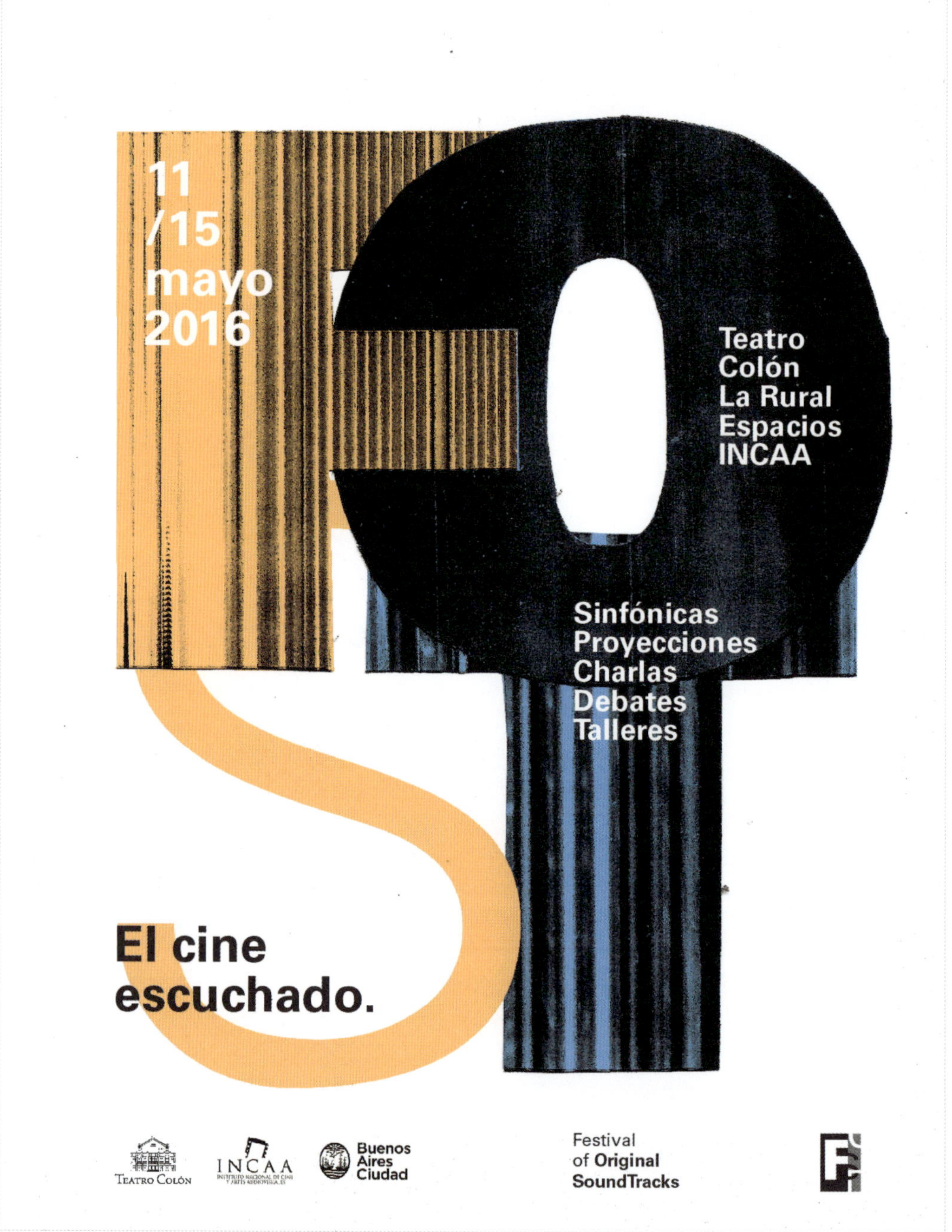

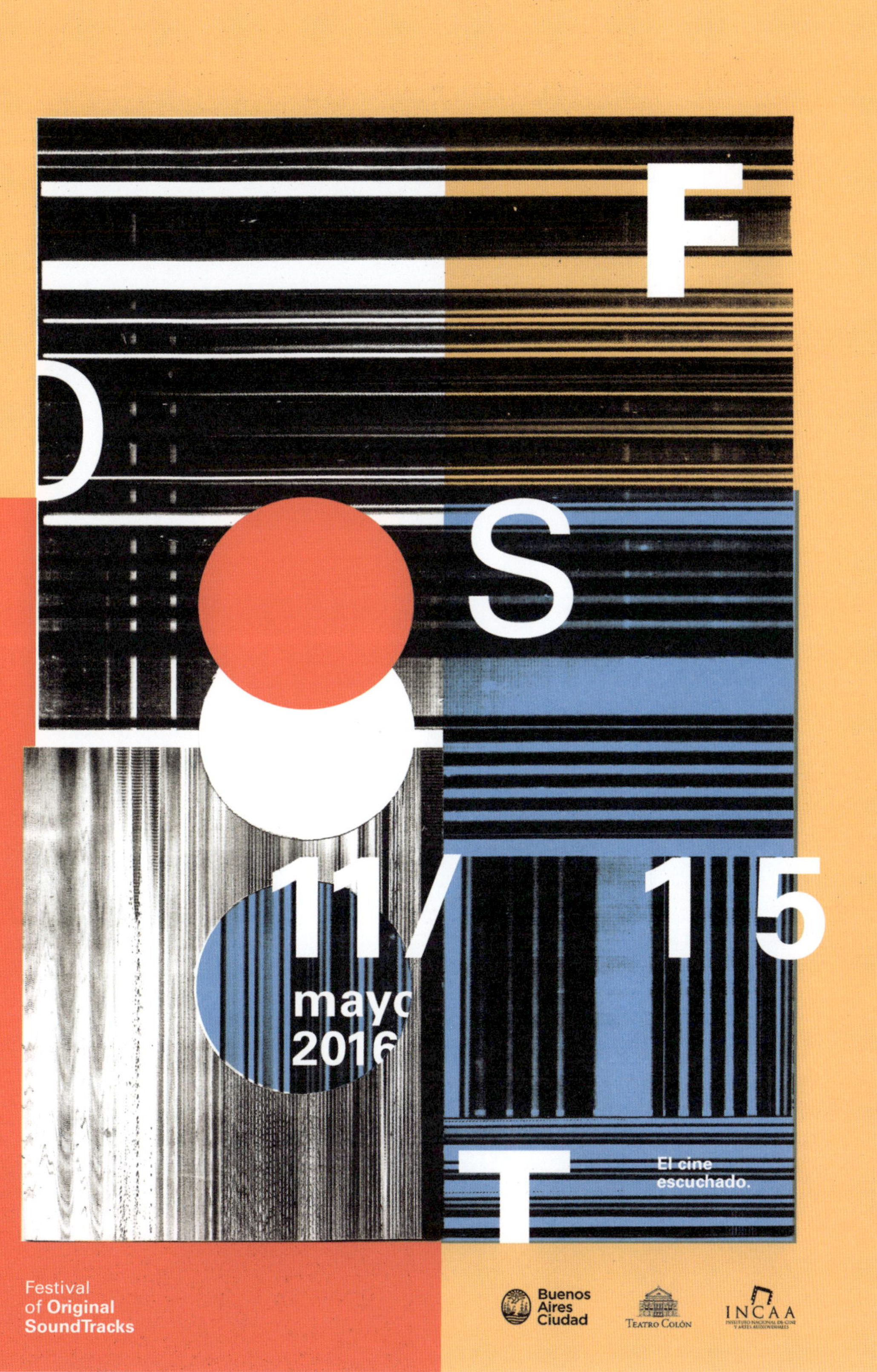
F
O
S
T
11/ 15
mayo
2016
El cine
escuchado.
Festival
of Original
SoundTracks
Buenos
Aires
Ciudad
Teatro Colón
INCAA

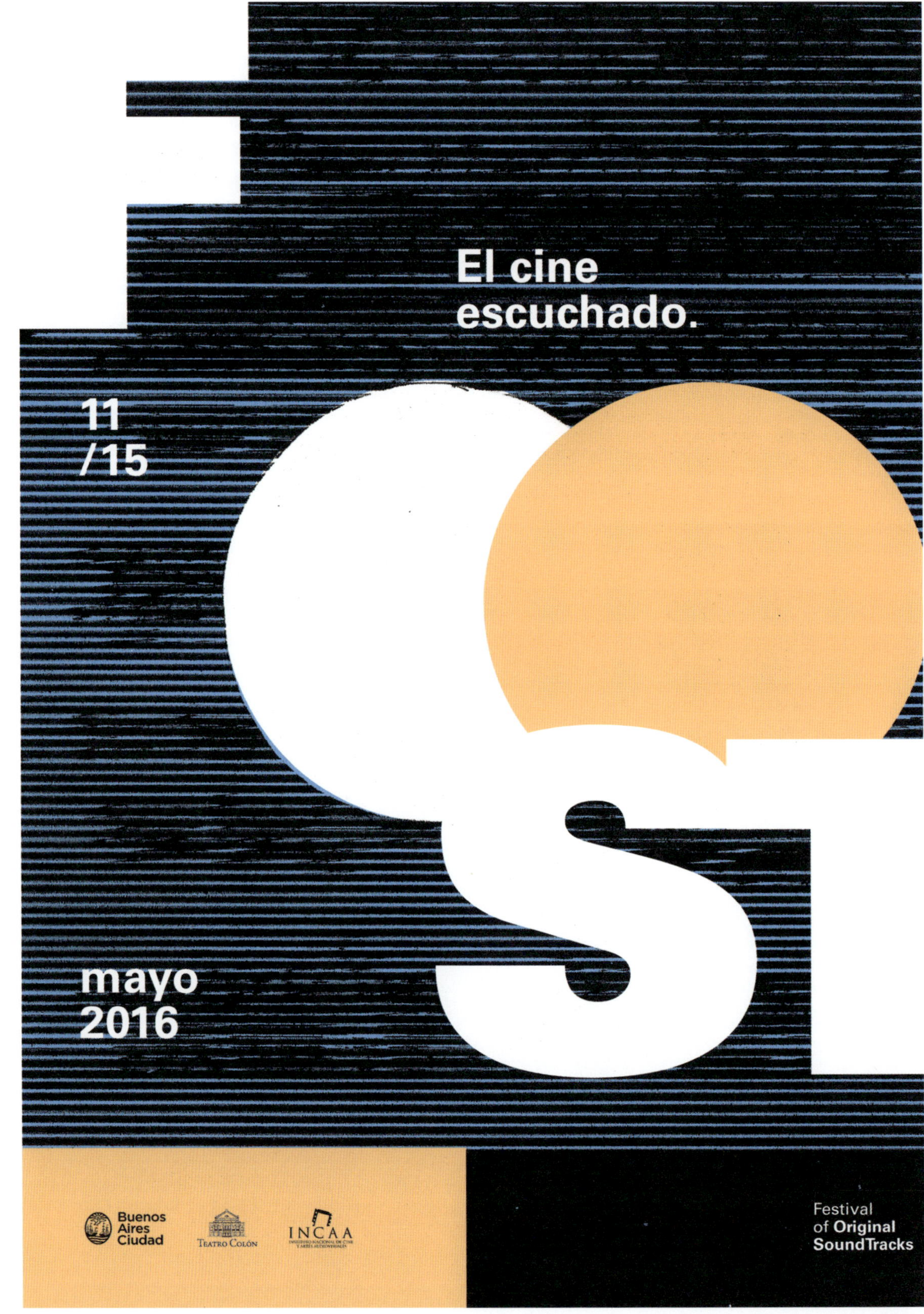
El cine
escuchado.
11
/15
mayo
2016
Buenos
Aires
Ciudad
Teatro Colón
INCAA
Festival
of Original
SoundTracks

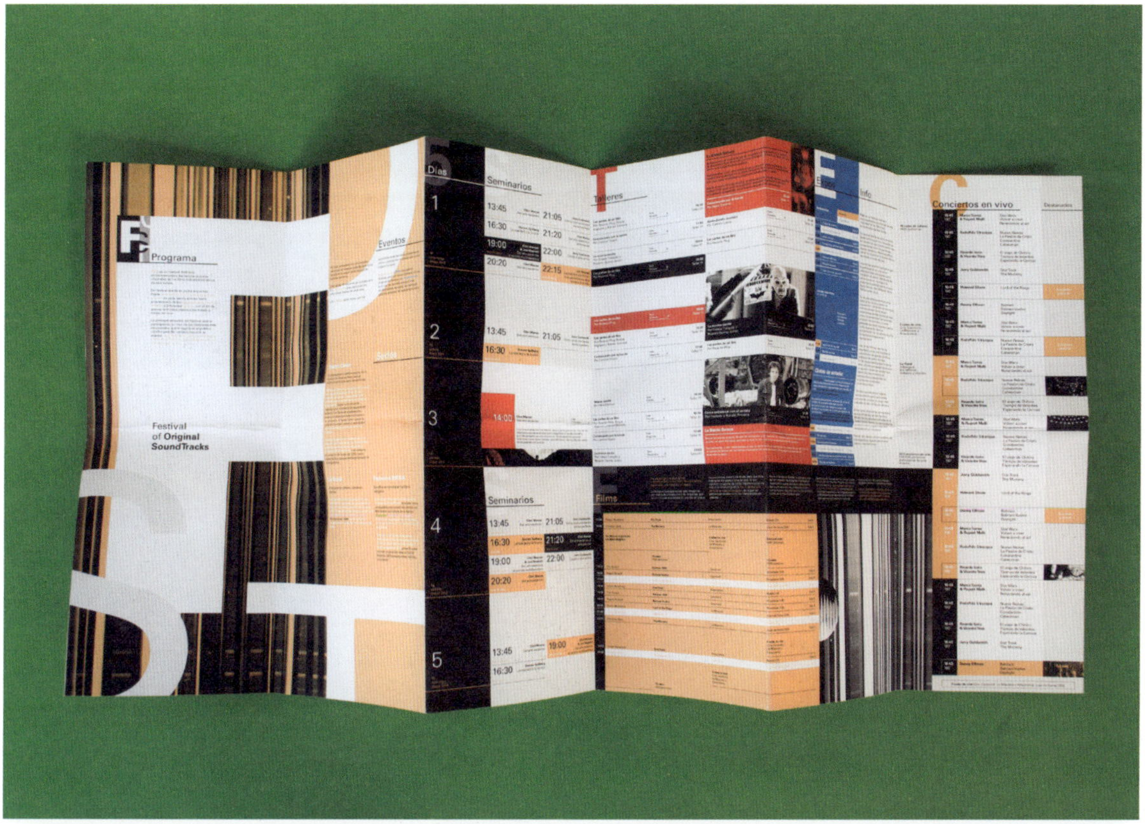
Programa
Festival of Original SoundTracks
Eventos
Días
Seminarios
Talleres
Info
Conciertos en vivo
Films

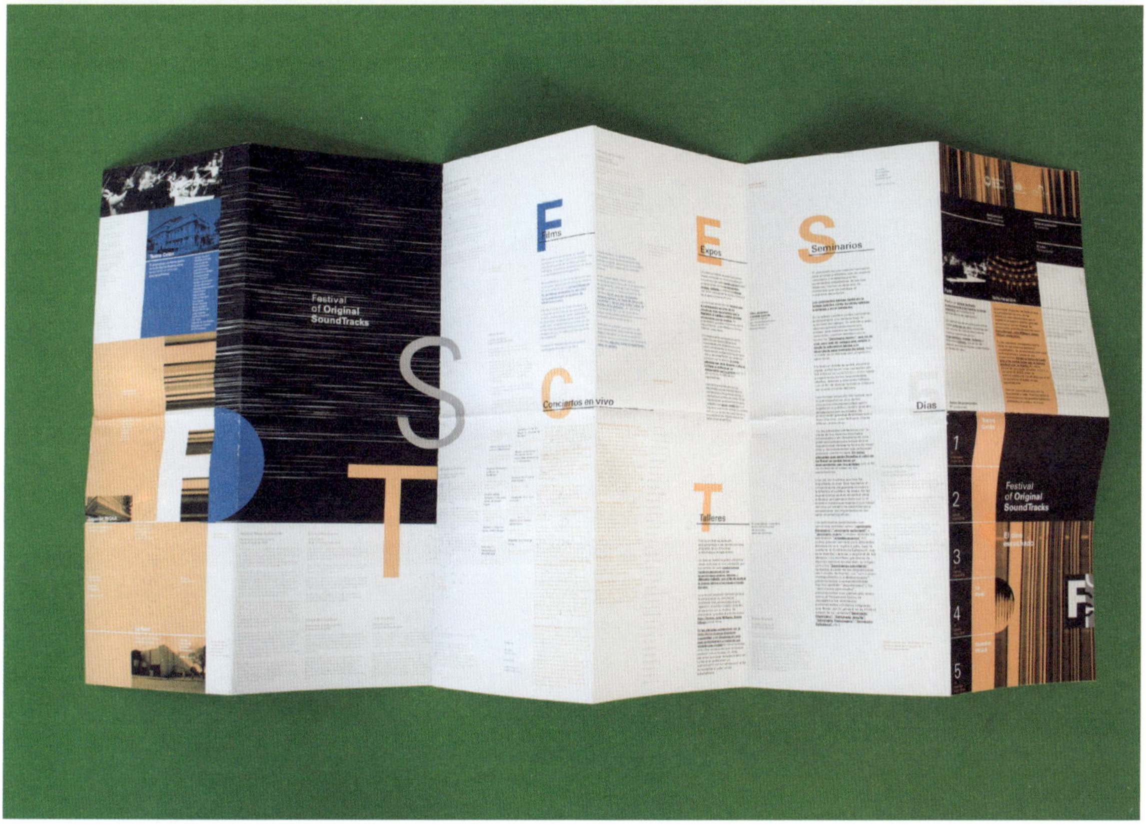
Festival of Original SoundTracks
Films
Expos
Seminarios
Conciertos en vivo
Talleres
Días

# CHÁ COM CARTAS

This project proposes a reflection on the interpersonal relationships in the contemporary world, and explores the feelings that a hand written letter can provoke. Inspired by the layers of graphic information on a mail, the series of exclusive posters was created in three stages: a direct print on the support, the use of labels and stamps, and finally, the use of several stamps for creating textures and unique compositions. The postcards were 8 sliced pieces from an artwork printed on silk in four layers of colors. The stationery is also related to the concept of layers and mail art.

Studio: Estúdio Lampejo

Designer: Filipe Costa, João Emediato

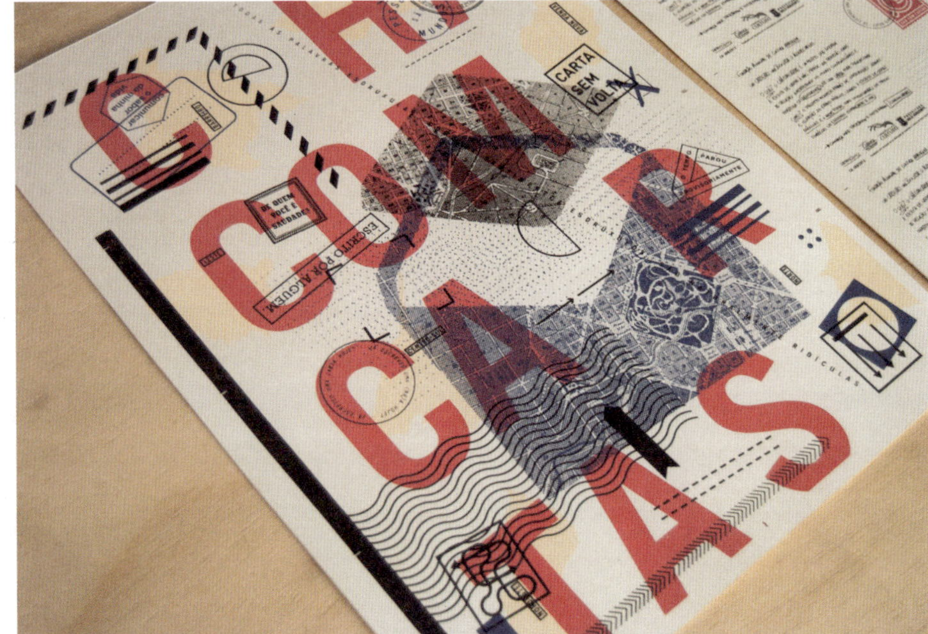


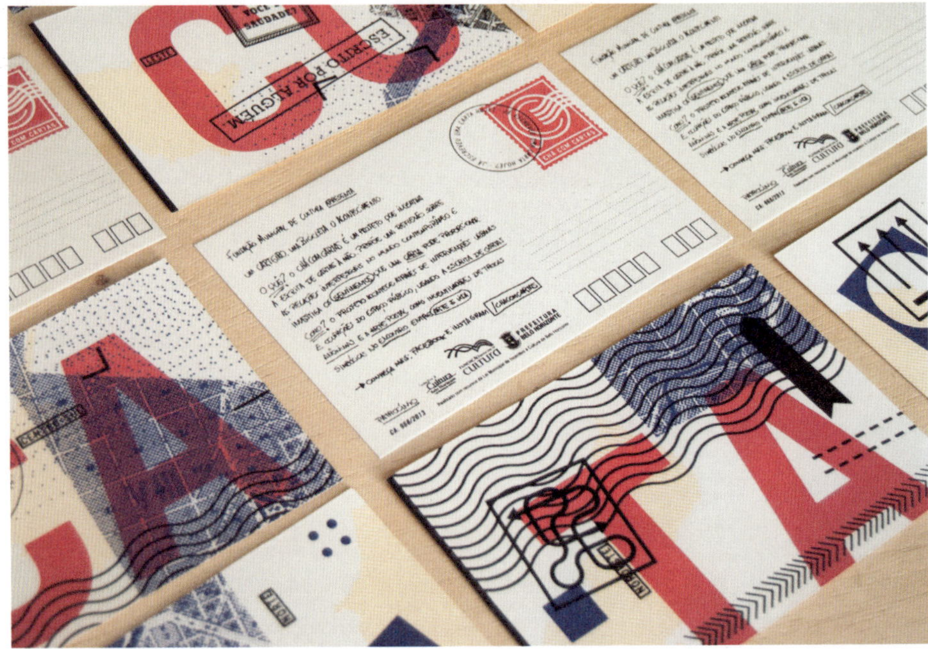

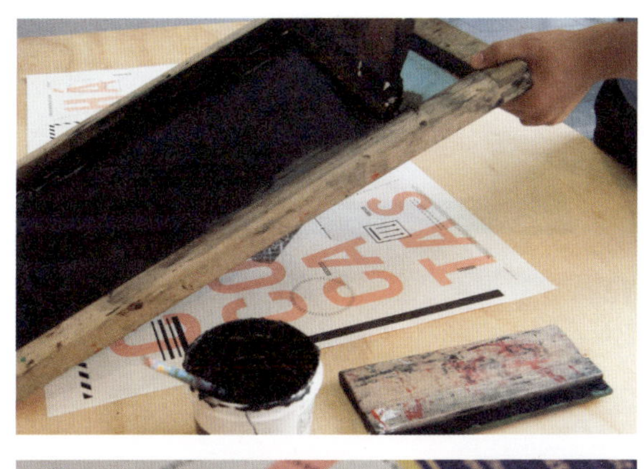

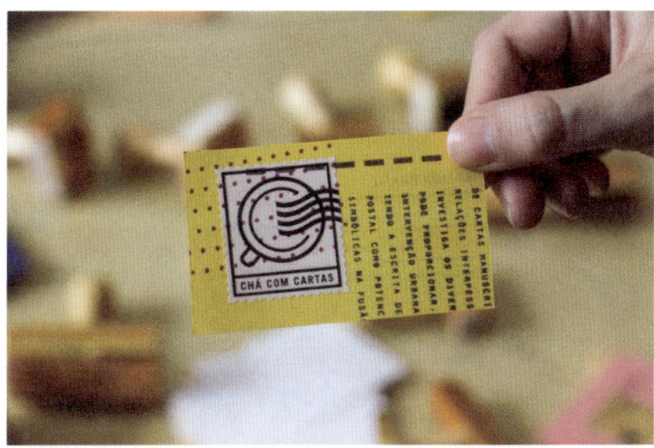
CHÁ COM CARTAS

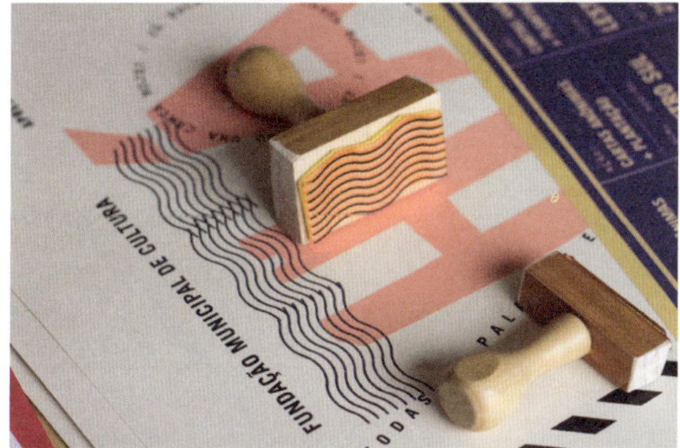
FUNDAÇÃO MUNICIPAL DE CULTURA

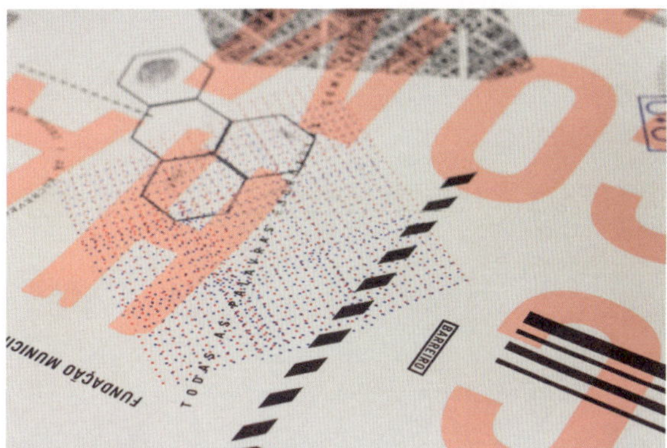
BARREIRO

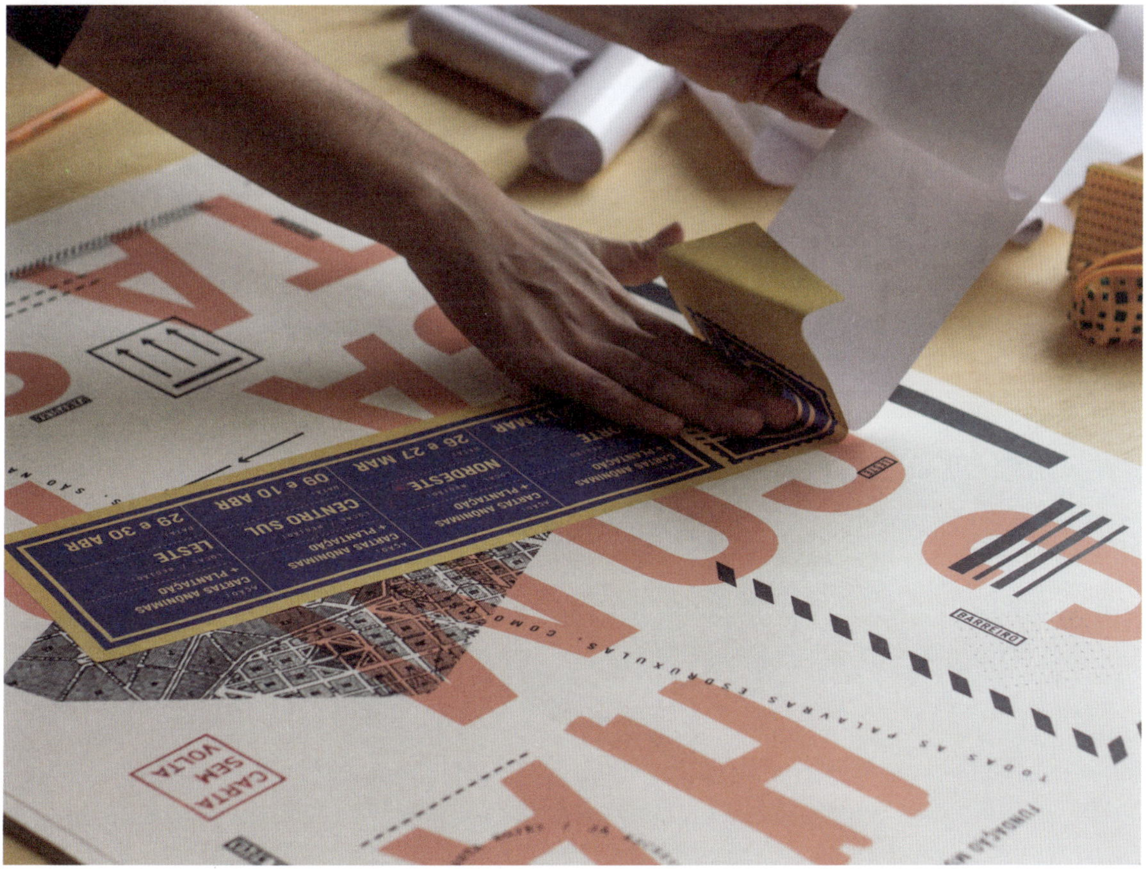

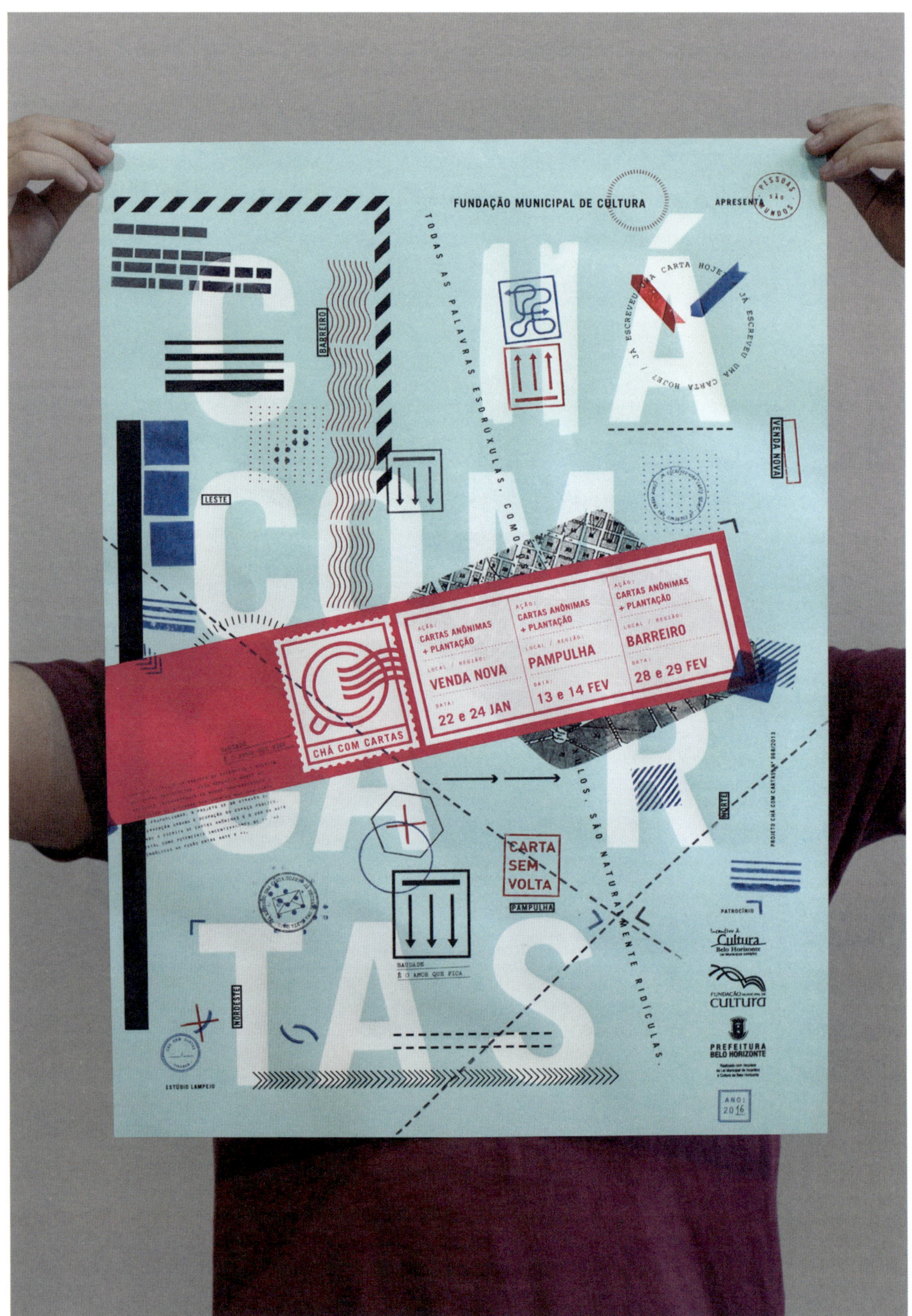
FUNDAÇÃO MUNICIPAL DE CULTURA
APRESENTA
PESSOAS SÃO MUNDOS
CHÁ COM CARTAS
TODAS AS PALAVRAS ESDRÚXULAS, COMO OS ESDRÚXULOS, SÃO NATURALMENTE RIDÍCULAS.
JÁ ESCREVEU UMA CARTA HOJE?
BARREIRO
LESTE
VENDA NOVA
AÇÃO:
CARTAS ANÔNIMAS + PLANTAÇÃO
LOCAL / REGIÃO:
VENDA NOVA
DATA:
22 e 24 JAN
AÇÃO:
CARTAS ANÔNIMAS + PLANTAÇÃO
LOCAL / REGIÃO:
PAMPULHA
DATA:
13 e 14 FEV
AÇÃO:
CARTAS ANÔNIMAS + PLANTAÇÃO
LOCAL / REGIÃO:
BARREIRO
DATA:
28 e 29 FEV
CHÁ COM CARTAS
CARTA SEM VOLTA
PAMPULHA
NORTE
SAUDADE
É O AMOR QUE FICA
NORDESTE
ESTÚDIO LAMPEJO
PATROCÍNIO
Cultura Belo Horizonte
FUNDAÇÃO MUNICIPAL DE CULTURA
PREFEITURA BELO HORIZONTE
ANO: 2016

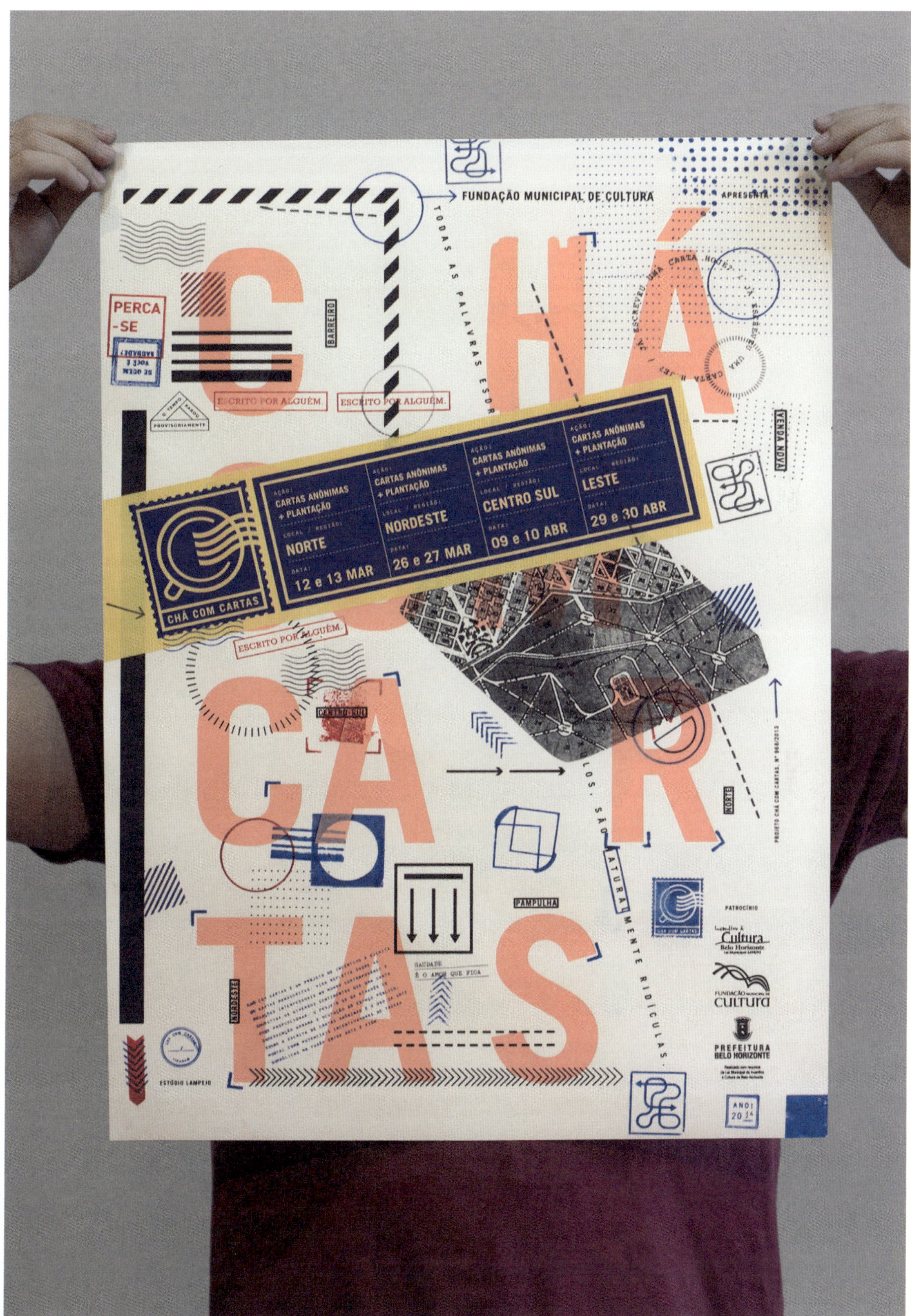
FUNDAÇÃO MUNICIPAL DE CULTURA
APRESENTA
CHÁ COM CARTAS
PERCA -SE
BARREIRO
ESCRITO POR ALGUÉM.
ESCRITO POR ALGUÉM.
AÇÃO: CARTAS ANÔNIMAS + PLANTAÇÃO
LOCAL / REGIÃO: NORTE
DATA: 12 e 13 MAR
AÇÃO: CARTAS ANÔNIMAS + PLANTAÇÃO
LOCAL / REGIÃO: NORDESTE
DATA: 26 e 27 MAR
AÇÃO: CARTAS ANÔNIMAS + PLANTAÇÃO
LOCAL / REGIÃO: CENTRO SUL
DATA: 09 e 10 ABR
AÇÃO: CARTAS ANÔNIMAS + PLANTAÇÃO
LOCAL / REGIÃO: LESTE
DATA: 29 e 30 ABR
CHÁ COM CARTAS
VENDA NOVA
ESCRITO POR ALGUÉM.
CENTRO SUL
NORTE
PAMPULHA
NORDESTE
SAUDADE
É O AMOR QUE FICA
ESTÚDIO LAMPEJO
PATROCÍNIO
Cultura
Belo Horizonte
FUNDAÇÃO MUNICIPAL DE CULTURA
PREFEITURA BELO HORIZONTE

# PROJECT K—THE KOREAN FILM FESTIVAL

This is a visual identity for the 5th anniversary of Project K—The Korean Film Festival. The number five is spelled "오" in Korean and pronounced like "oh", which could also refer to an expression of astonishment on the faces of the visitors to the festival.

Studio: Il-Ho Jung—design, interactive&motion
Designer: Il-Ho Jung, Ruth Reining

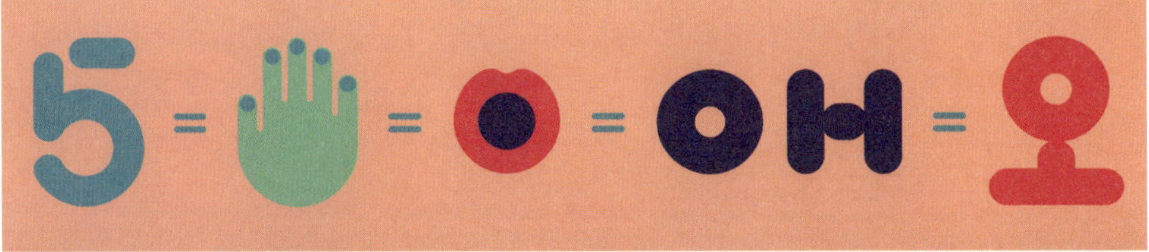


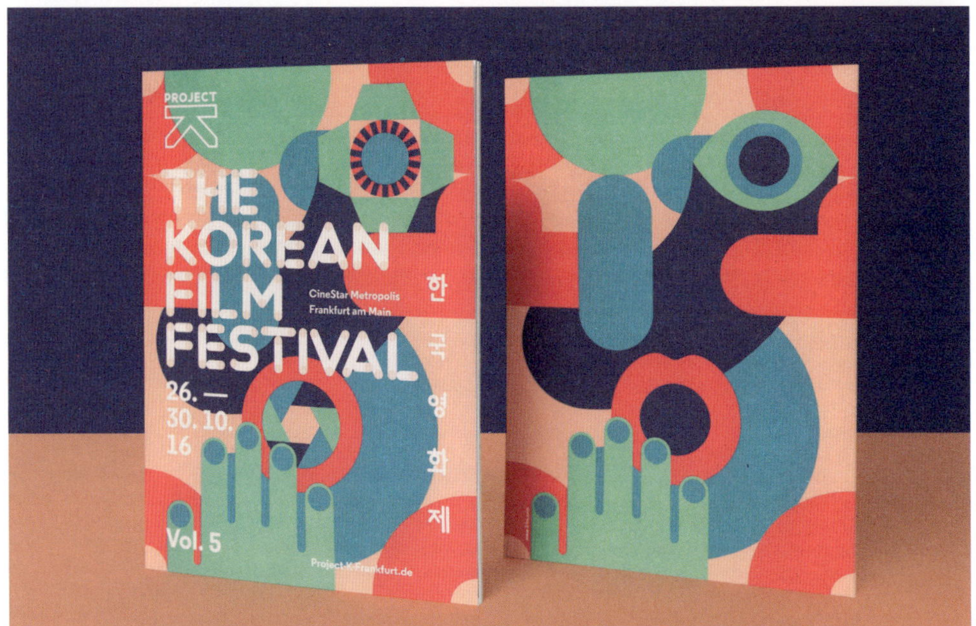


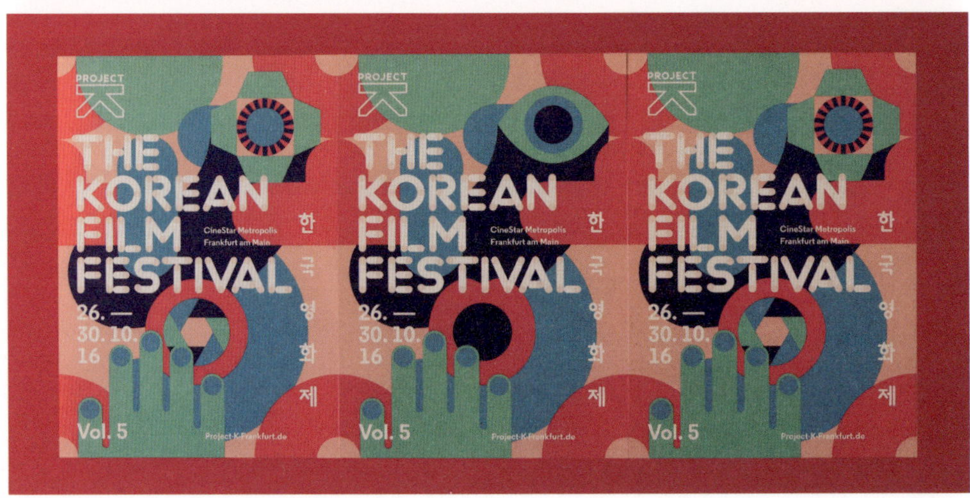

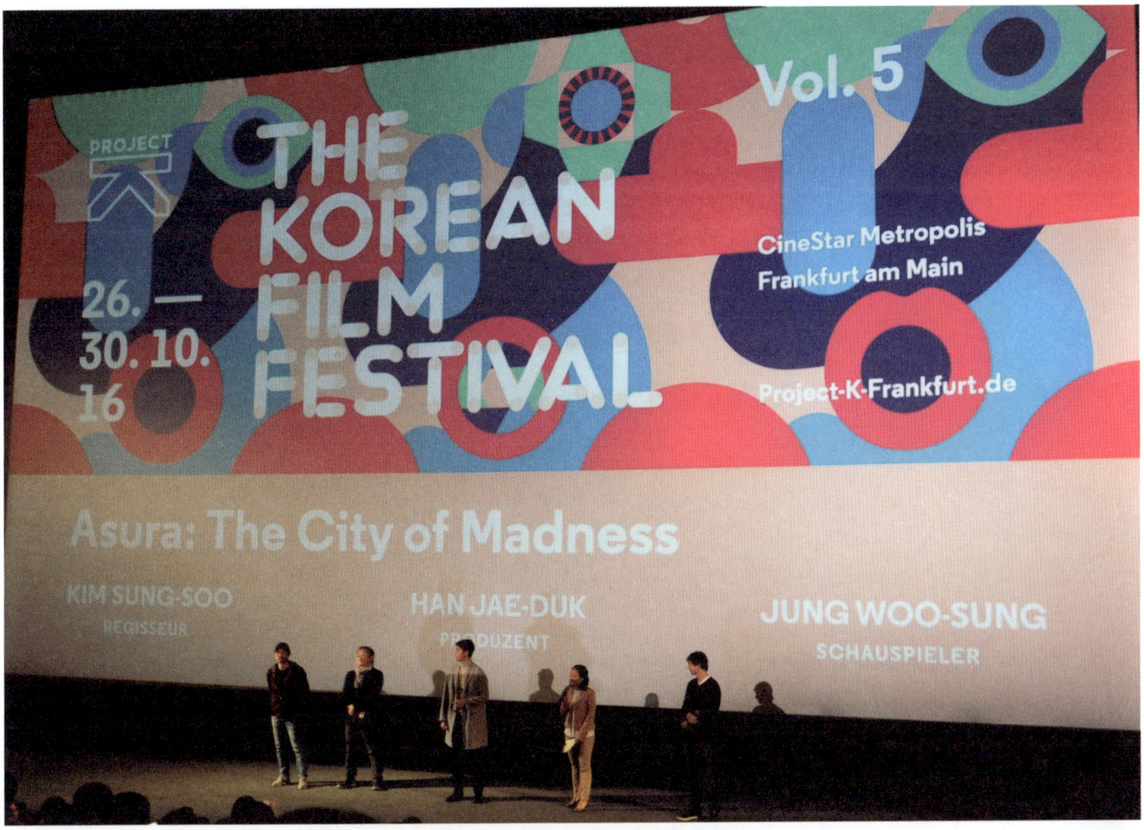
PROJECT K
THE KOREAN FILM FESTIVAL
26. — 30. 10. 16
Vol. 5
CineStar Metropolis
Frankfurt am Main
Project-K-Frankfurt.de
Asura: The City of Madness
KIM SUNG-SOO
REGISSEUR
HAN JAE-DUK
PRODUZENT
JUNG WOO-SUNG
SCHAUSPIELER

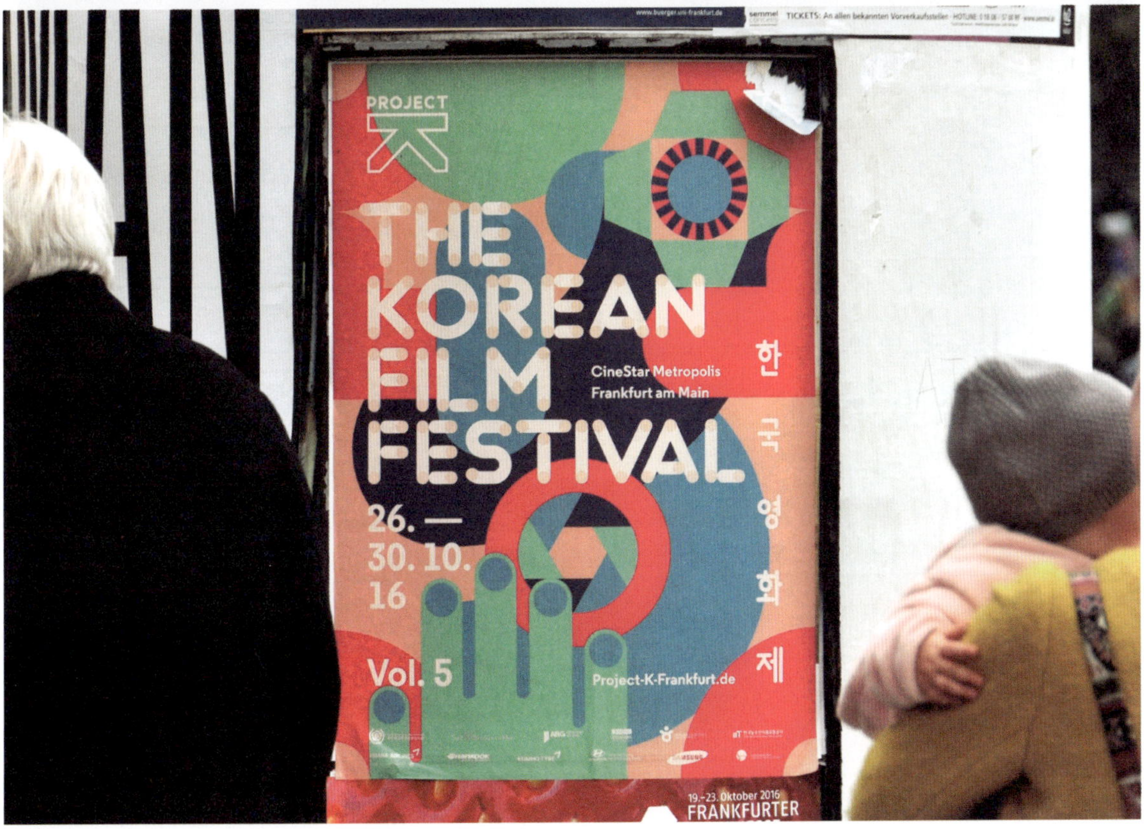
PROJECT K
THE KOREAN FILM FESTIVAL
CineStar Metropolis
Frankfurt am Main
한국영화제
26. — 30. 10. 16
Vol. 5
Project-K-Frankfurt.de
19.–23. Oktober 2016
FRANKFURTER

# WILDSCAPE IN A BOOK

This is a chapter designed for the book *The Book of Wildscape*. The designer aimed to show how "wildscape" would look like in a book.

Designer: Yasemin Cakir

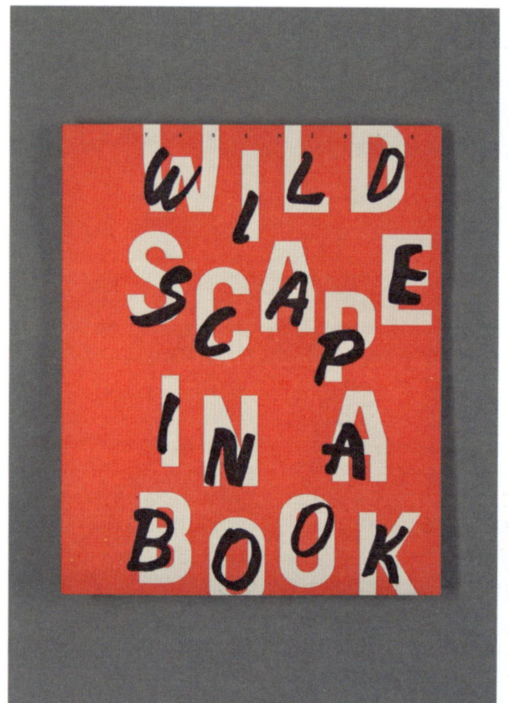


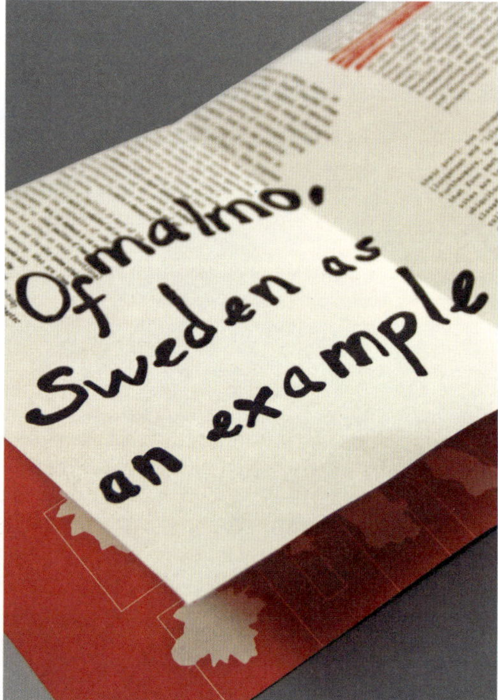


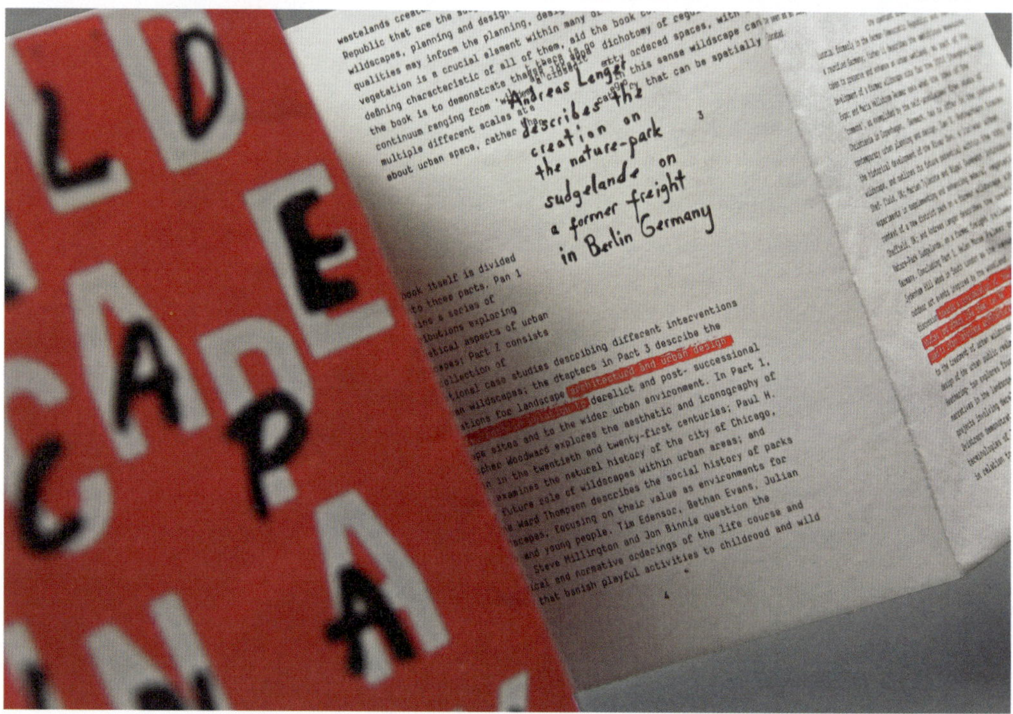

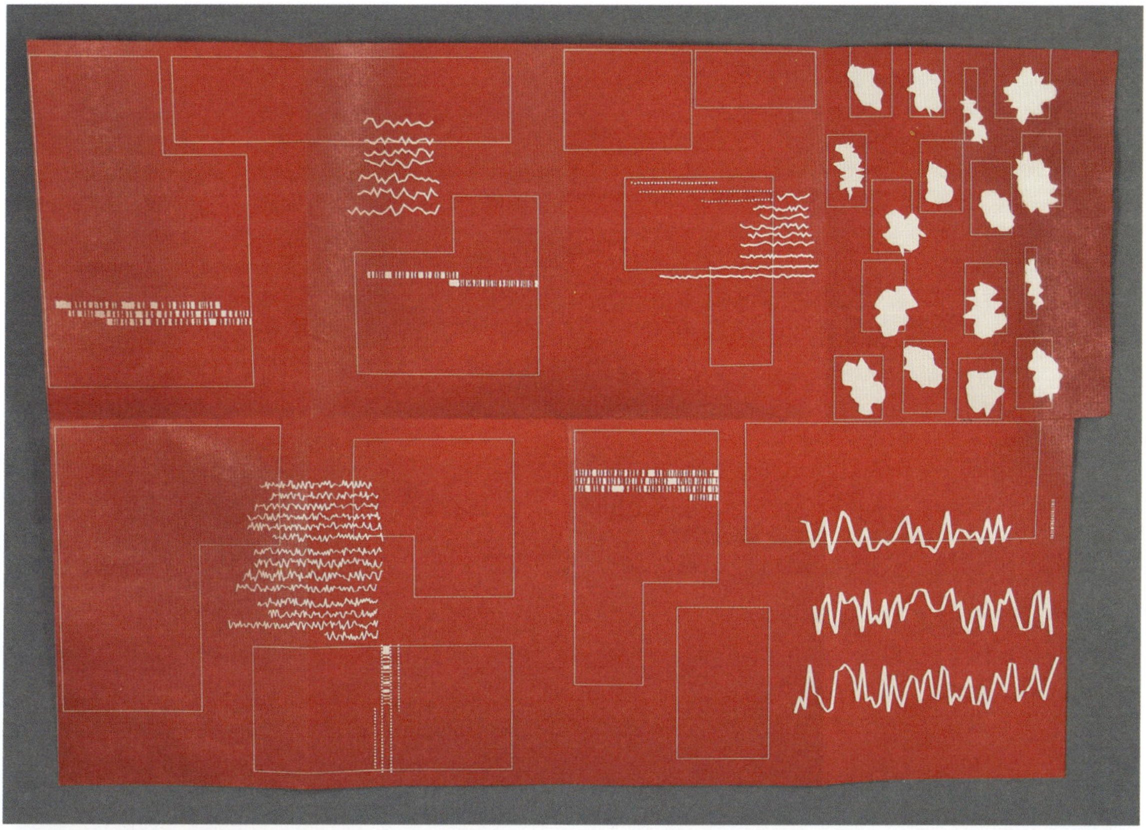

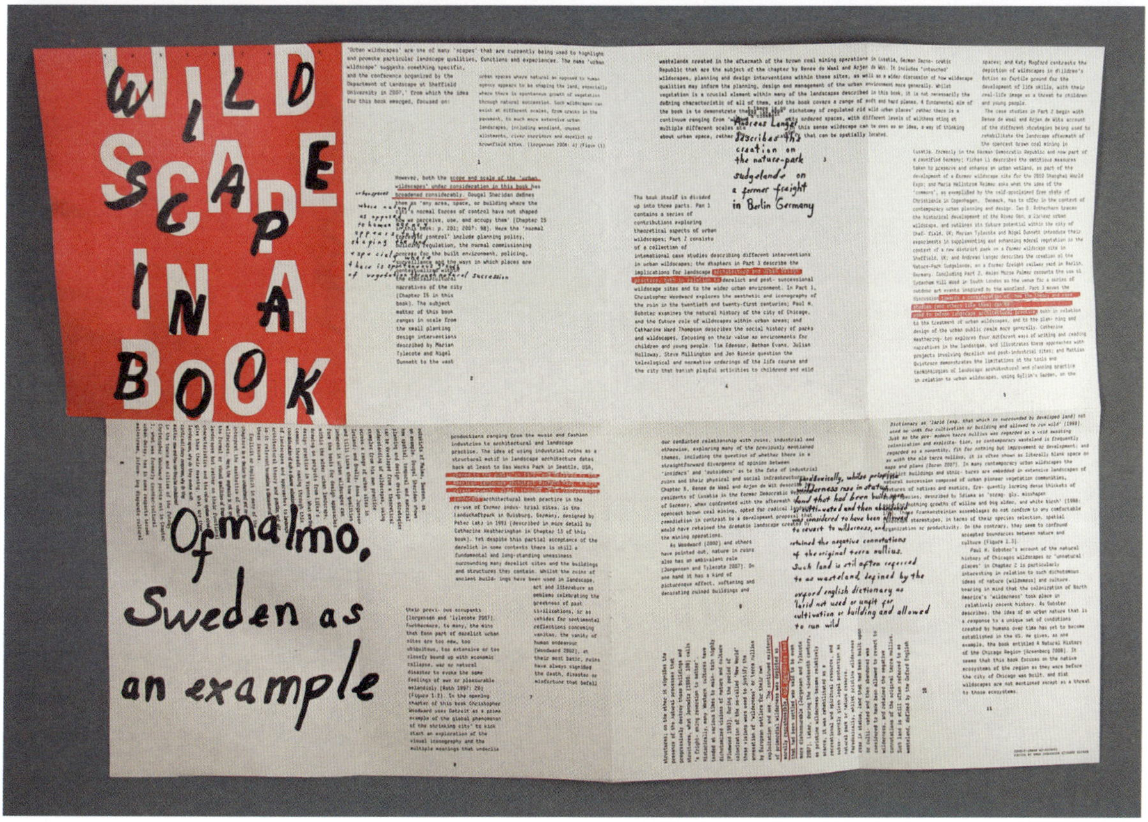

WILD SCAPE IN A BOOK

Of malmo, Sweden as an example

# NAVID IZADI—MESSIN EP

Navid Izadi is a young musician who possesses wisdom and natural flair beyond his years. Influenced by imagery from ancient Persia, psychedelic electronic music, symbolism and themes in his music, the illustrations and typography for this EP were created to build the artist's own mythological world.

Designer: Nick Liefhebber

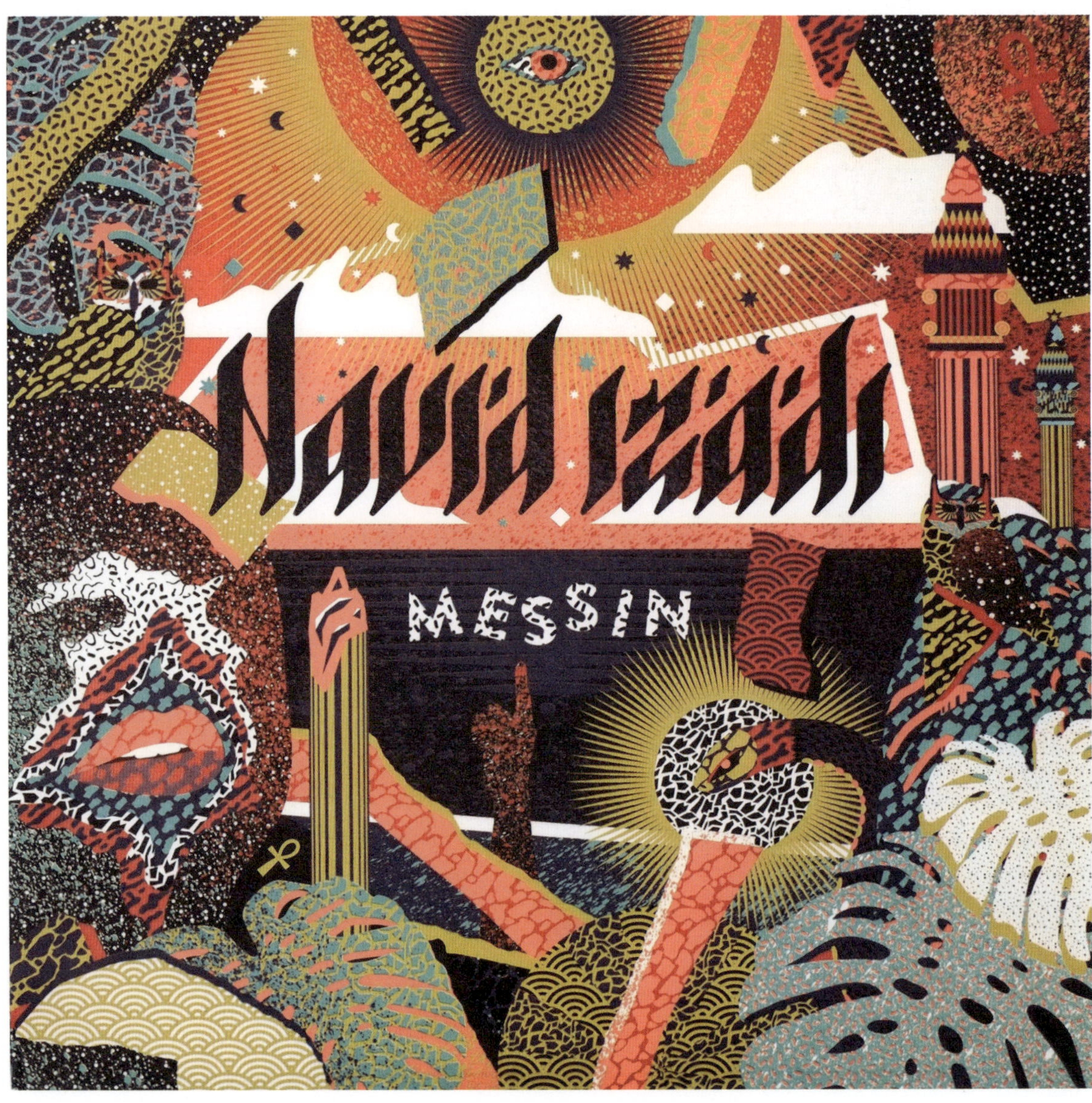

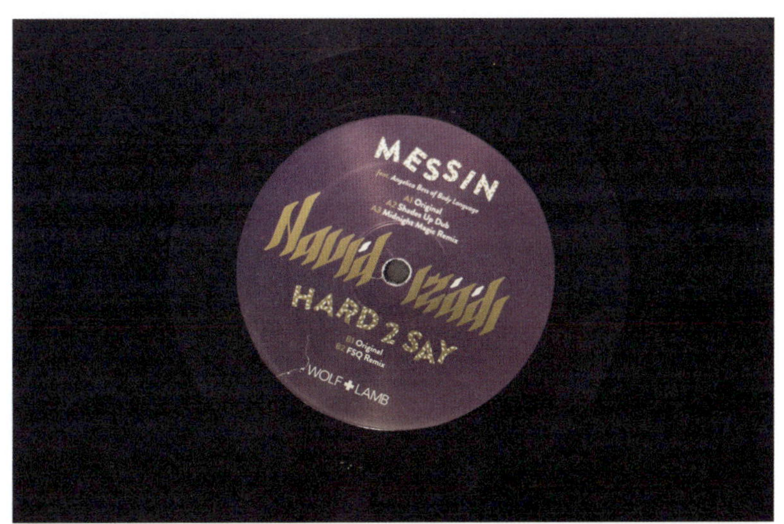

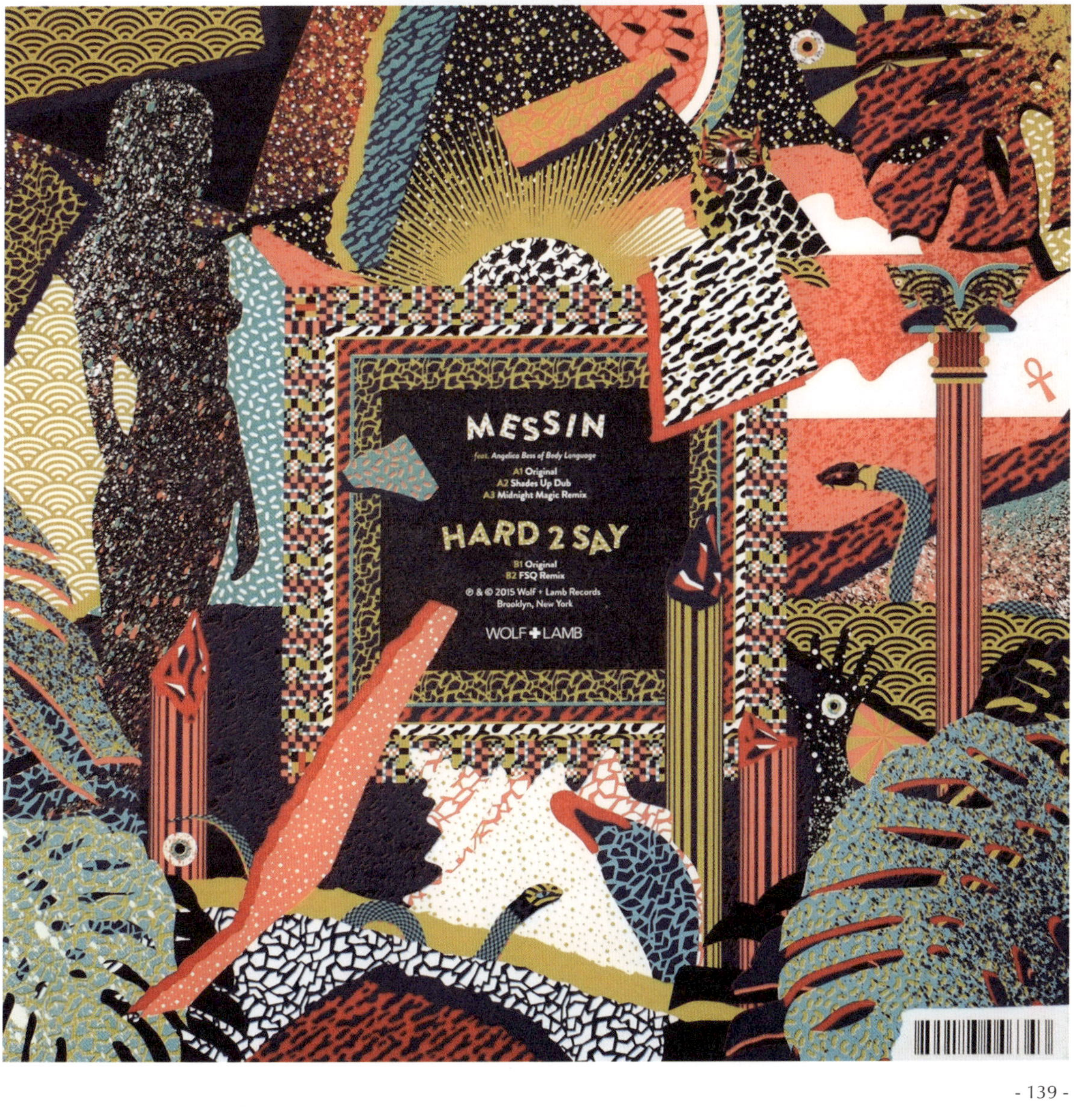

MESSIN

feat. Angelica Bess of Body Language

A1 Original
A2 Shades Up Dub
A3 Midnight Magic Remix

HARD 2 SAY

B1 Original
B2 FSQ Remix

℗ & © 2015 Wolf + Lamb Records
Brooklyn, New York

WOLF + LAMB

# HEERLEN MURALS STREET ART FESTIVAL

This work was designed for Heerlen Murals Street Art Festival, with the theme "There's more than meeting the eye". The artists were challenged to produce works that have either a worldwide or local context, and the works would be presented after a selection from around the world.

Designer: Fabian de Lange

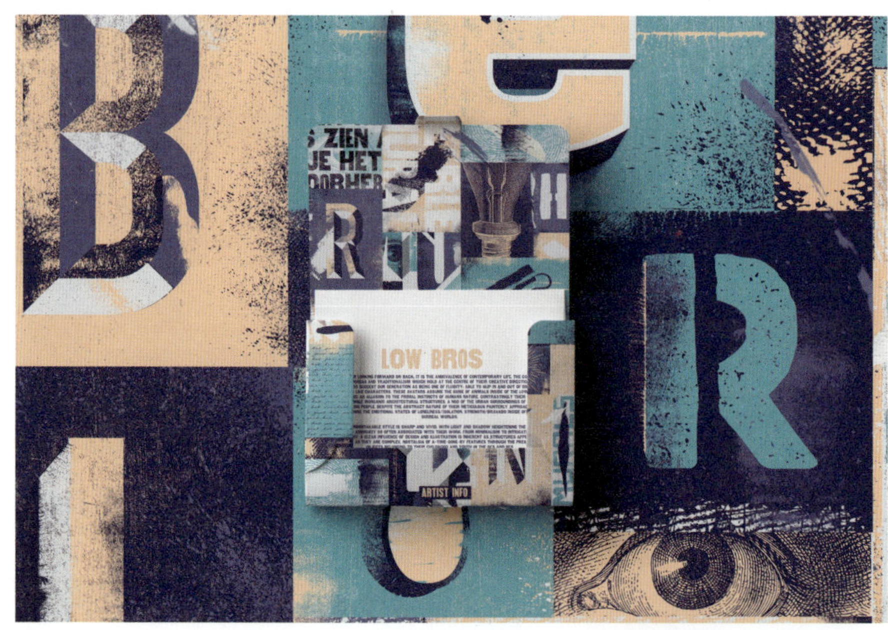

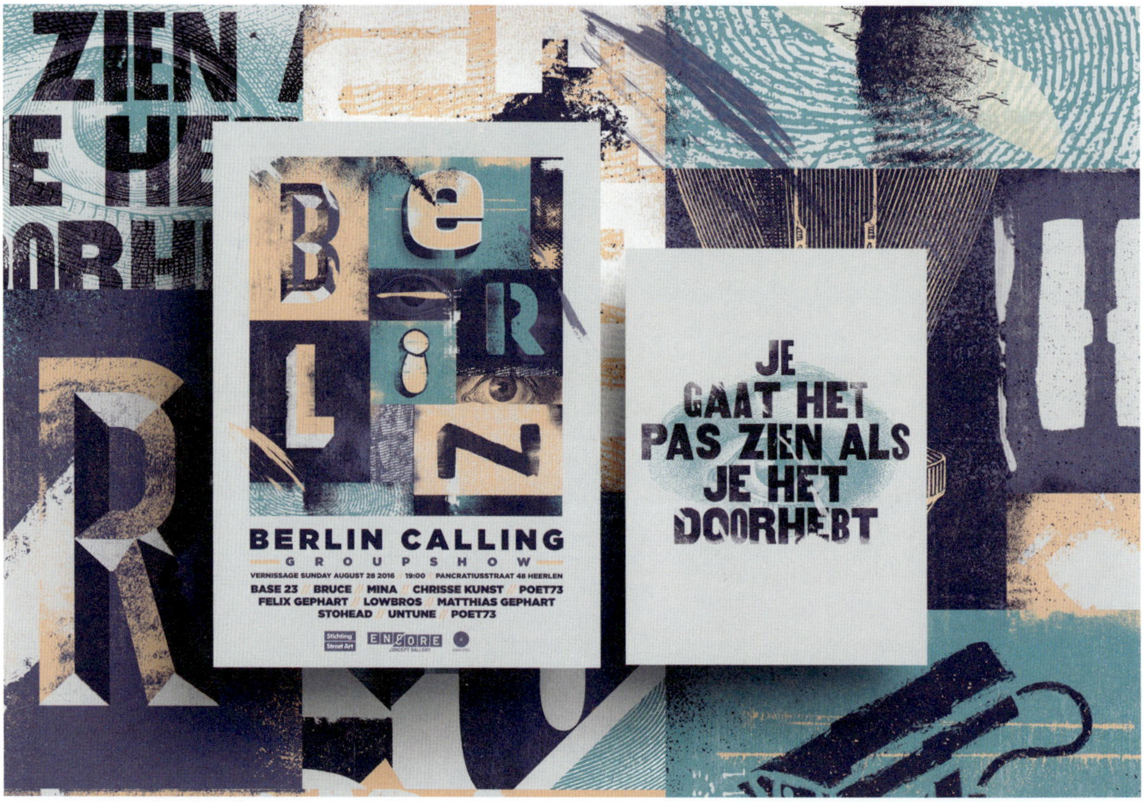

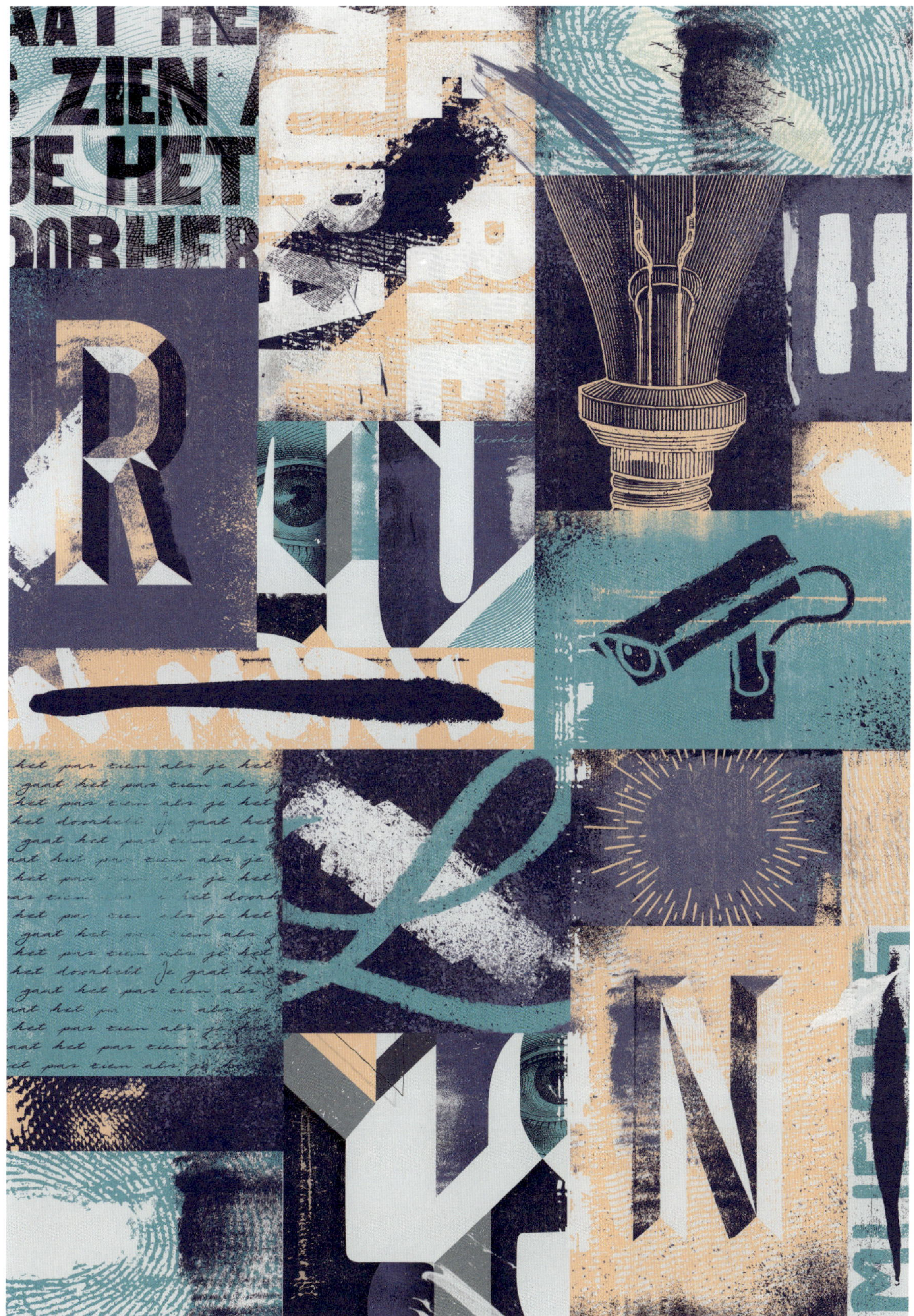
ZIEN
HET

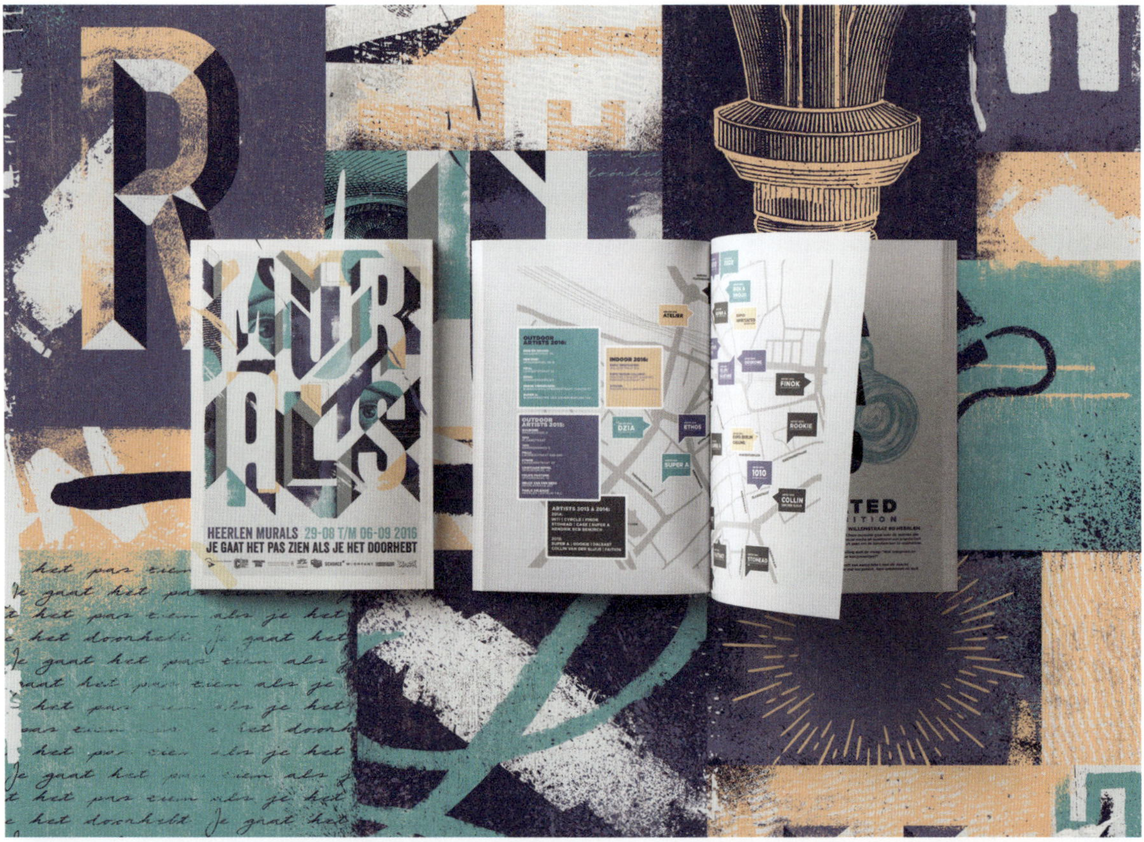

HEERLEN MURALS 29-08 T/M 06-09 2016
JE GAAT HET PAS ZIEN ALS JE HET DOORHEBT

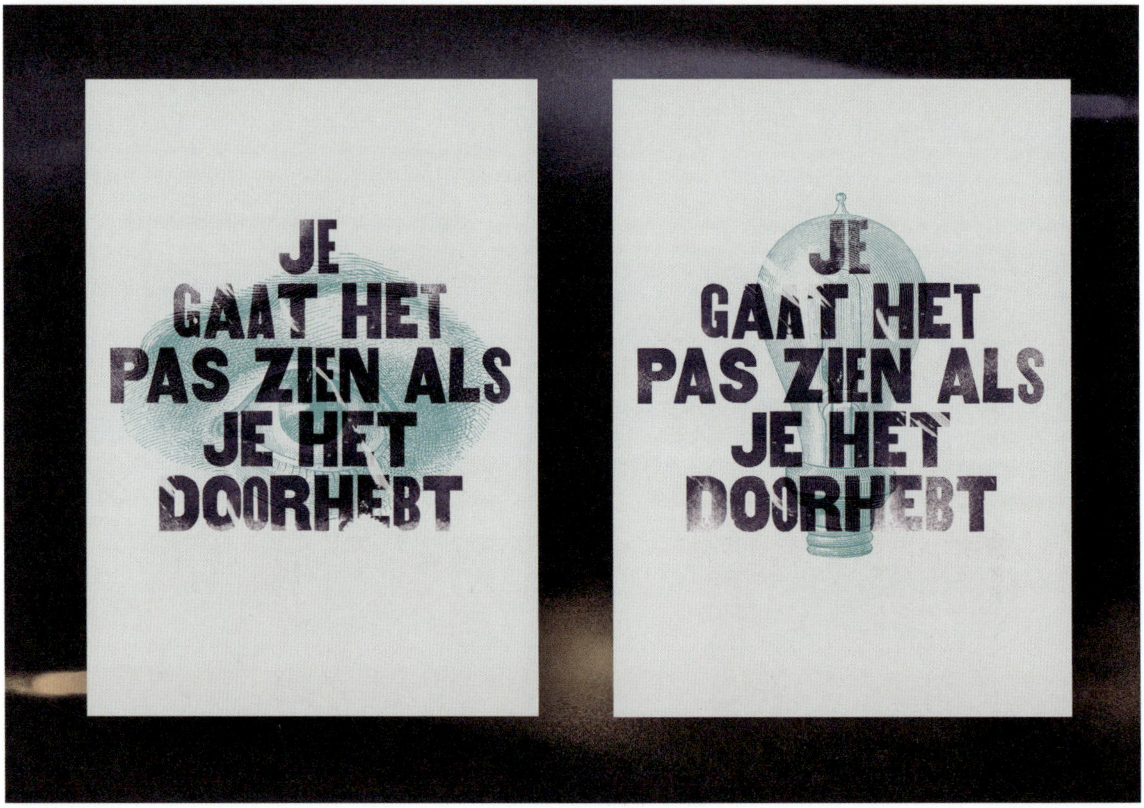

JE
GAAT HET
PAS ZIEN ALS
JE HET
DOORHEBT

JE
GAAT HET
PAS ZIEN ALS
JE HET
DOORHEBT

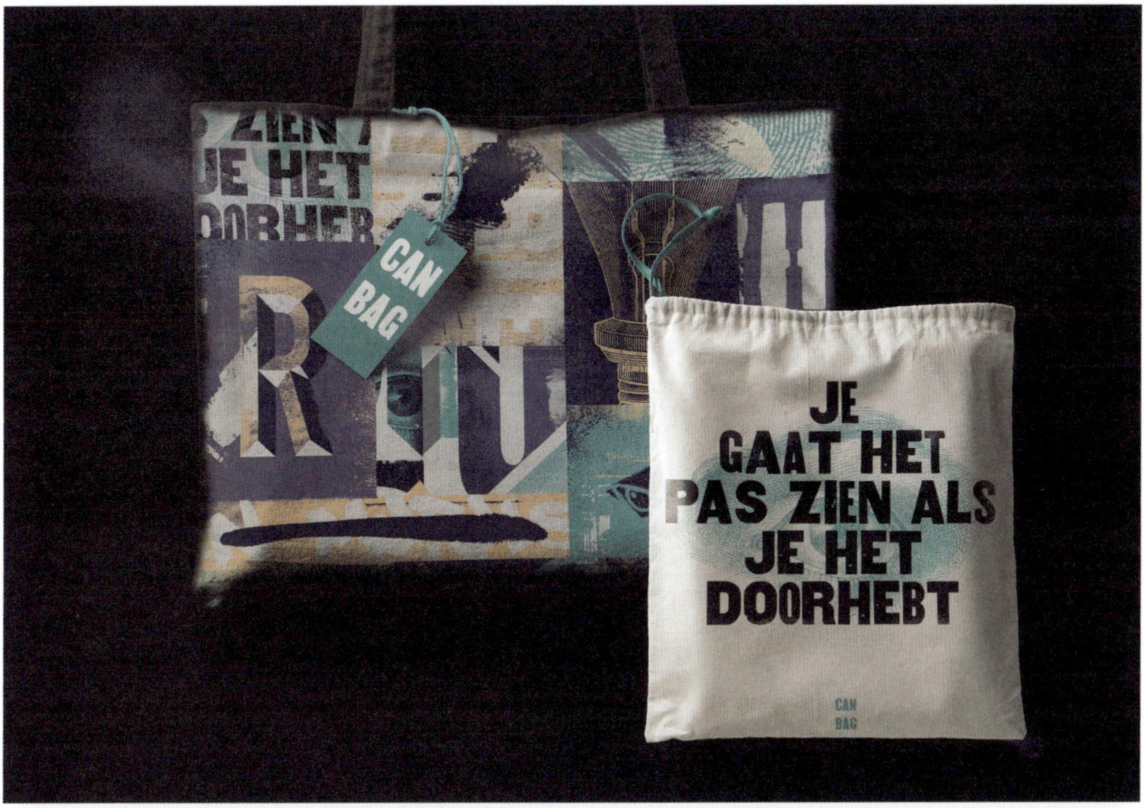

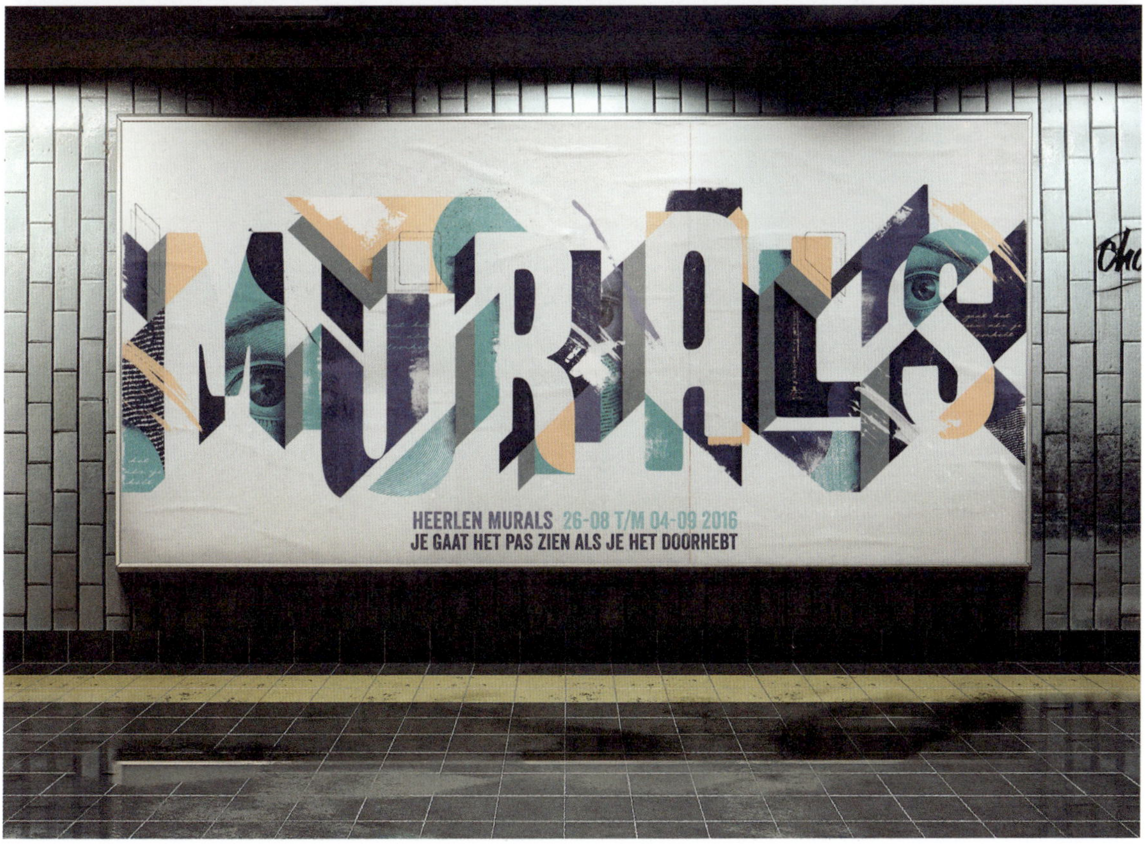

# HEADS OF PSYCHOPATHS

Inspired by Polish film posters, these are a series of illustrations showing the psychopathic characters from several iconic movies between 1976 and 1980: The Tenant(1976), Taxi Driver(1976), Eraserhead(1977), Halloween(1978), Apocalypse Now(1979), The Shining(1980).

Designer: Sebastian Onufszak

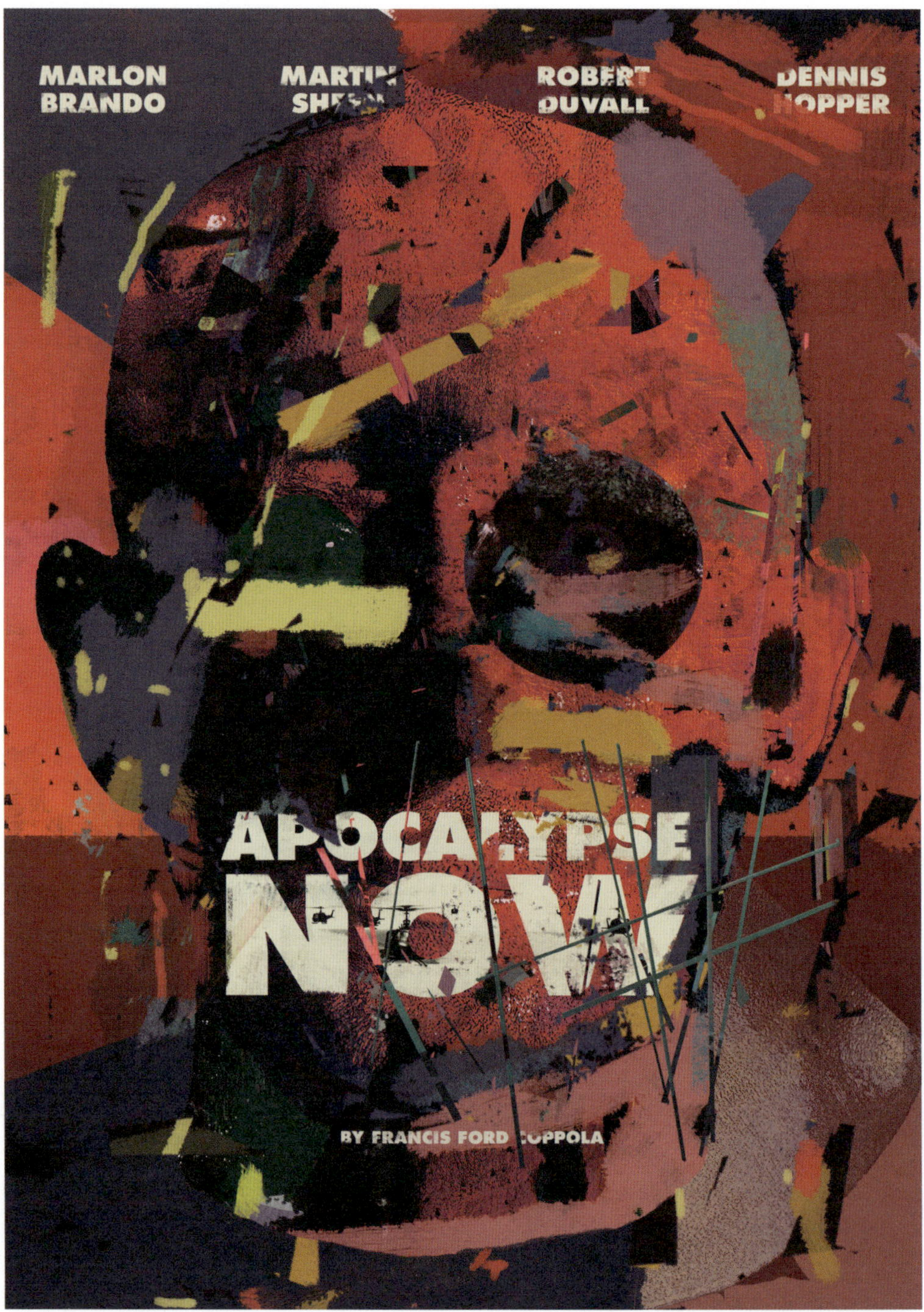

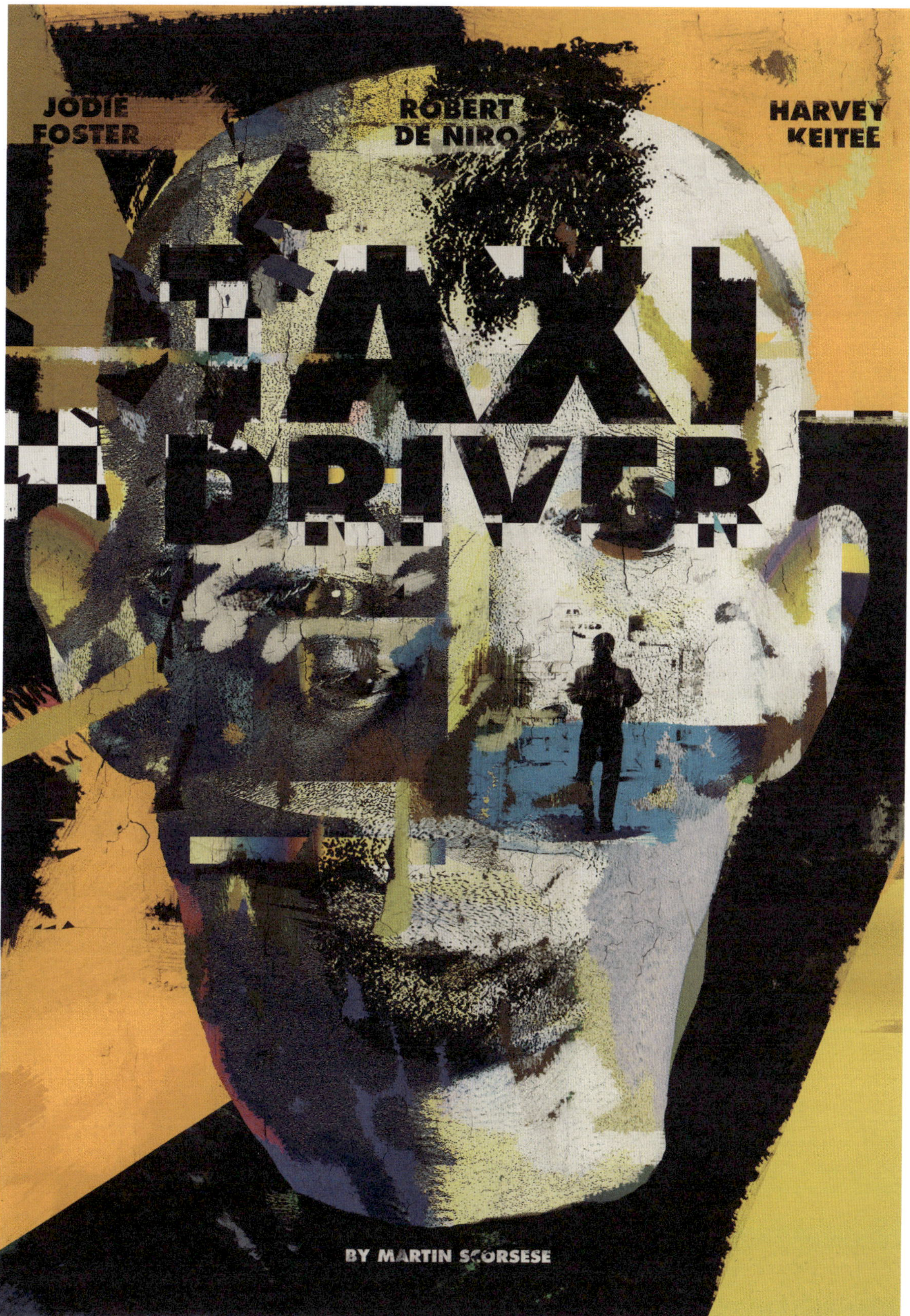
JODIE
FOSTER
ROBERT
DE NIRO
HARVEY
KEITEE
TAXI
DRIVER
BY MARTIN SCORSESE

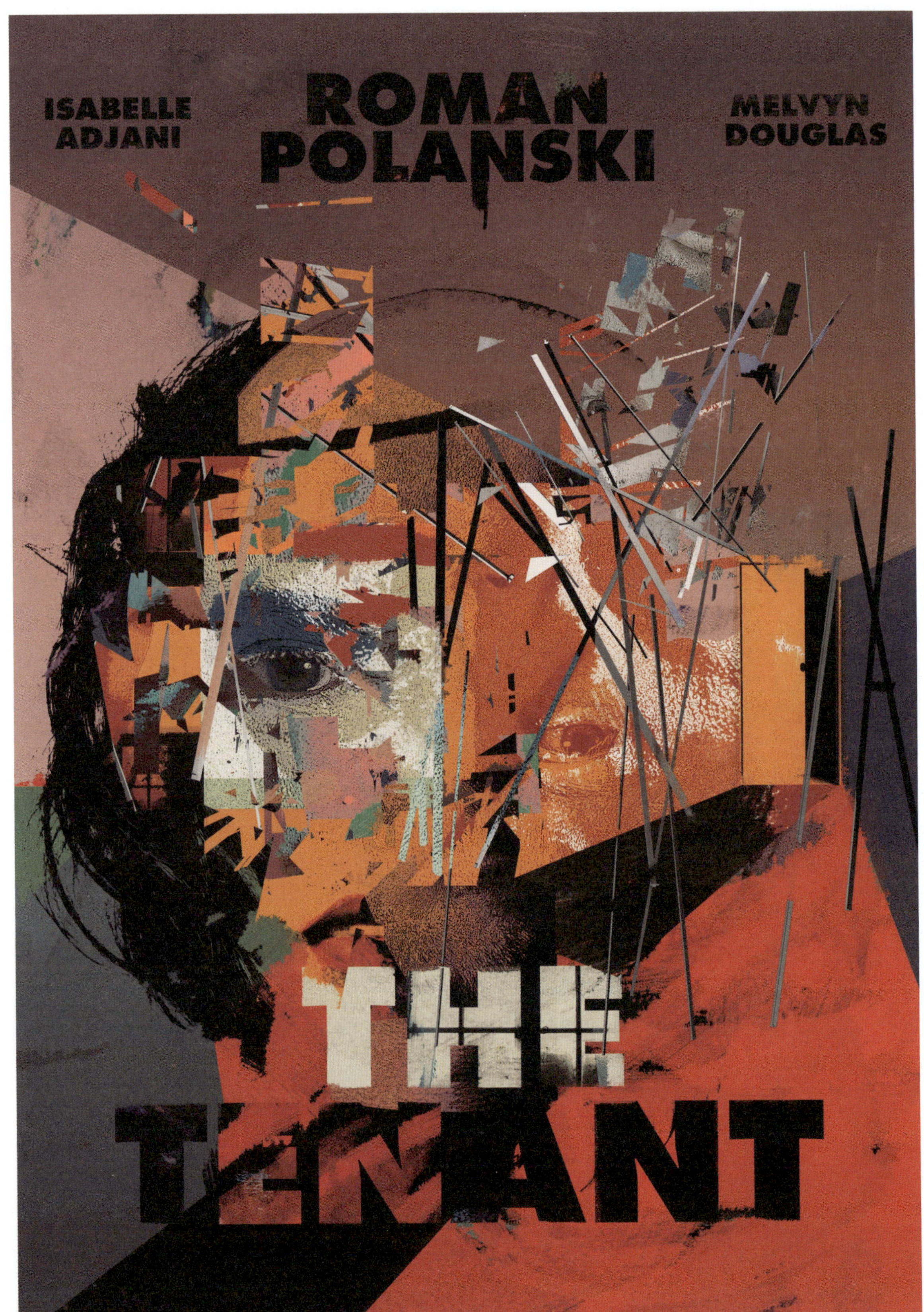
ISABELLE
ADJANI
ROMAN
POLAŃSKI
MELVYN
DOUGLAS
THE
TENANT

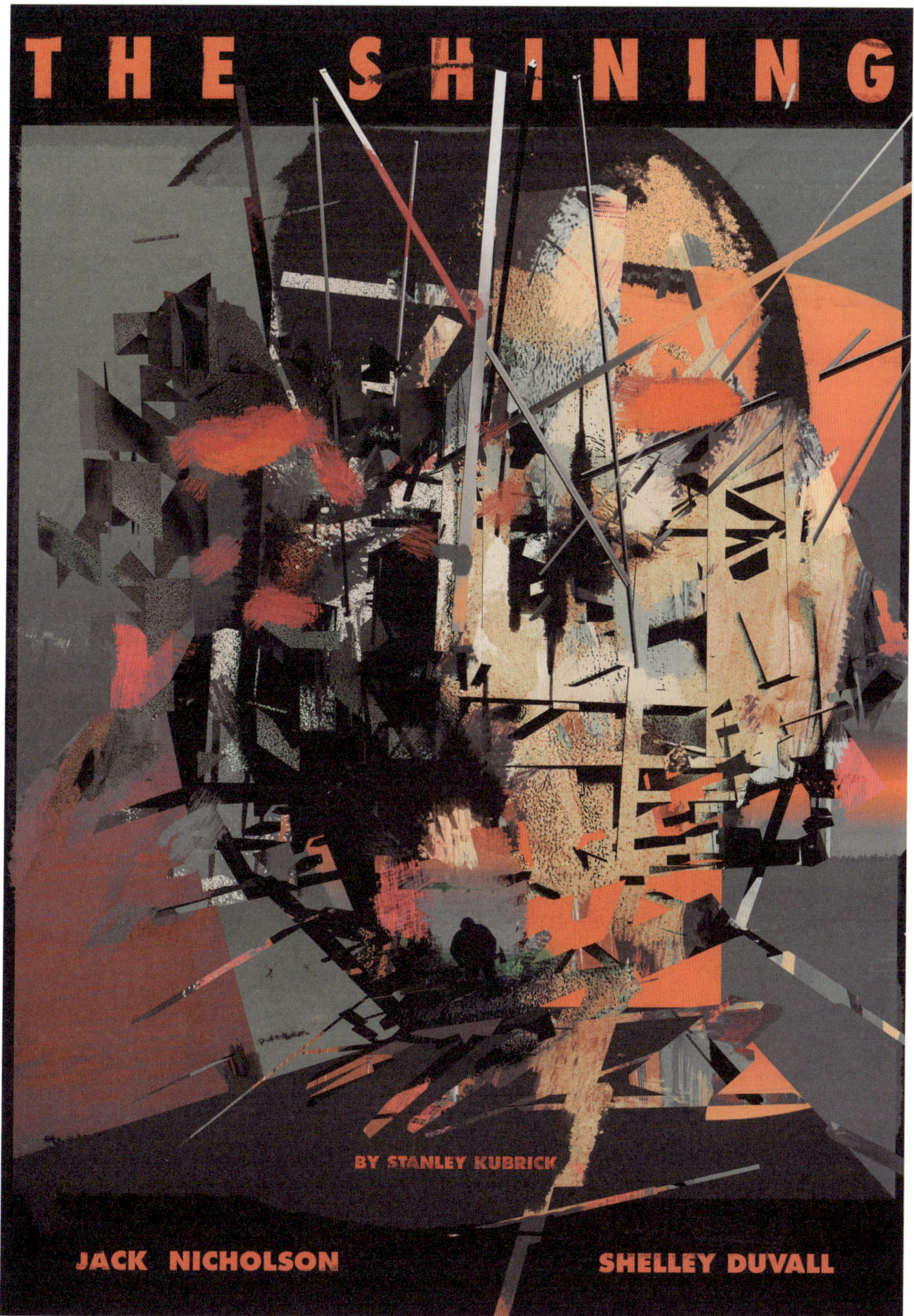
THE SHINING
BY STANLEY KUBRICK
JACK NICHOLSON
SHELLEY DUVALL

# A PROPAGANDA POEM

This is a typographical interpretation of a modern poem. The six abstract poster designs or illustrations visualized each line: *Illuminate your illusion, it's all fake, put in jail, the demagogue!, yes, we rule,* and *don't trust the truth.*

Designer: Sebastian Onufszak

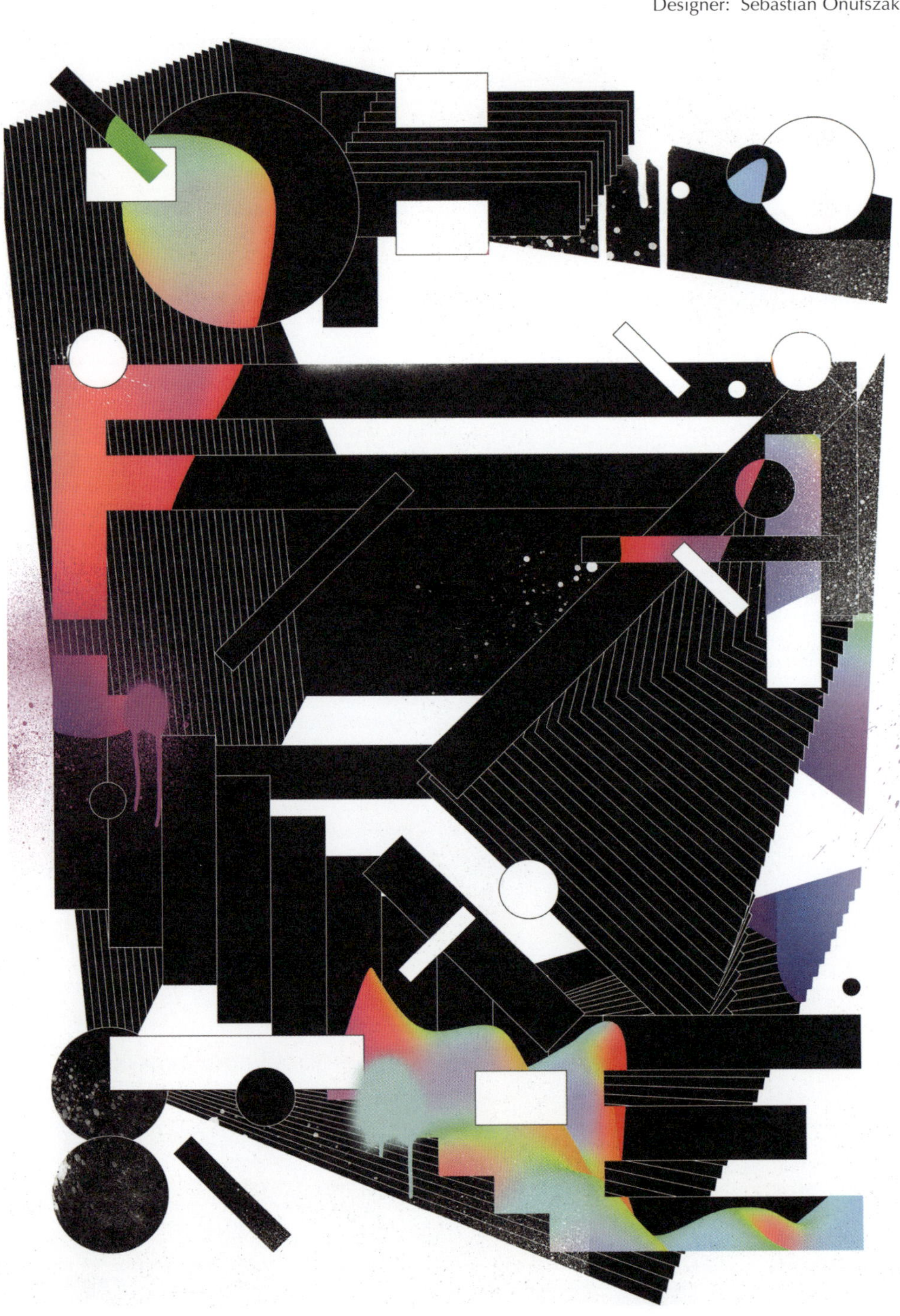

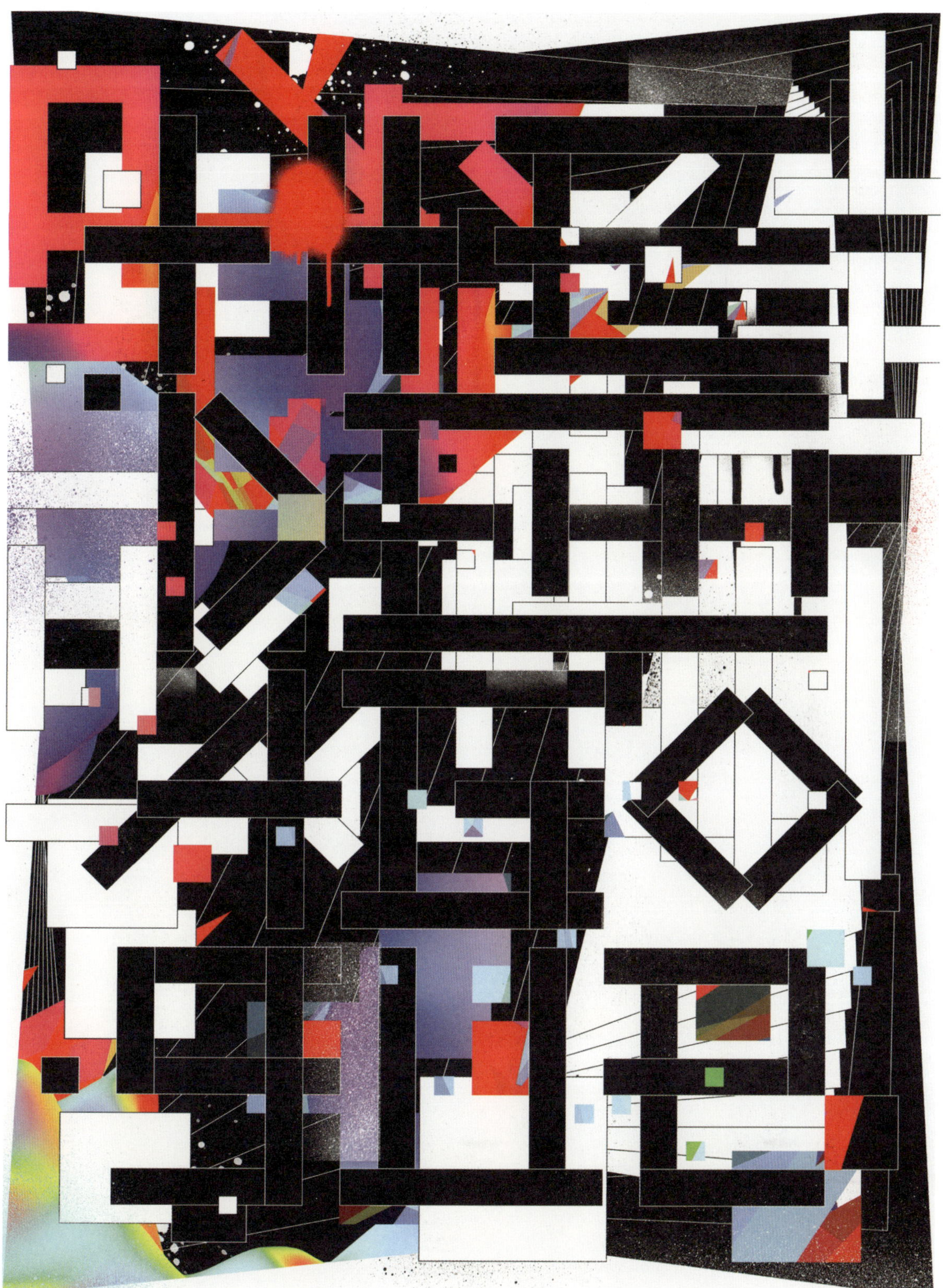

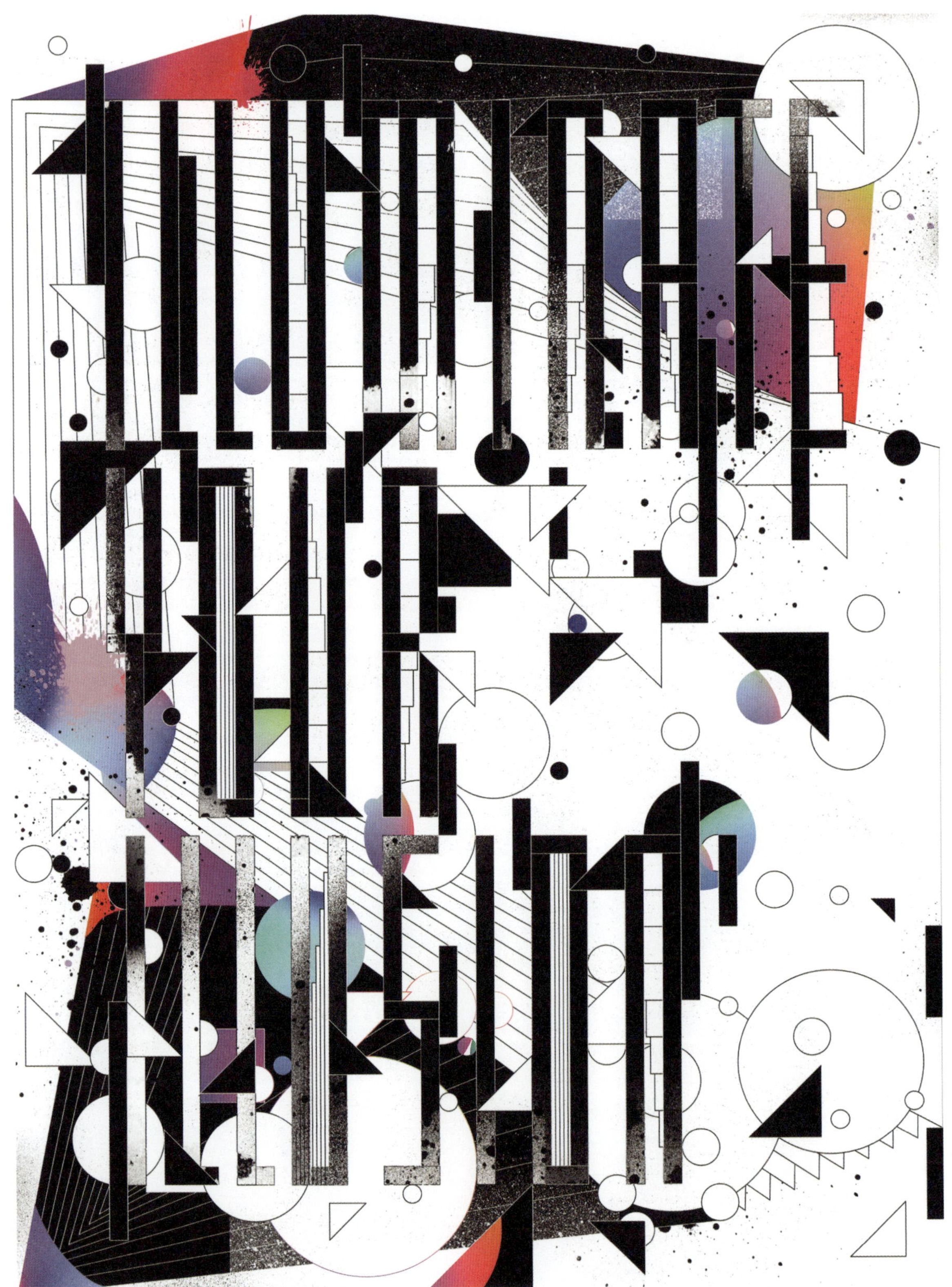

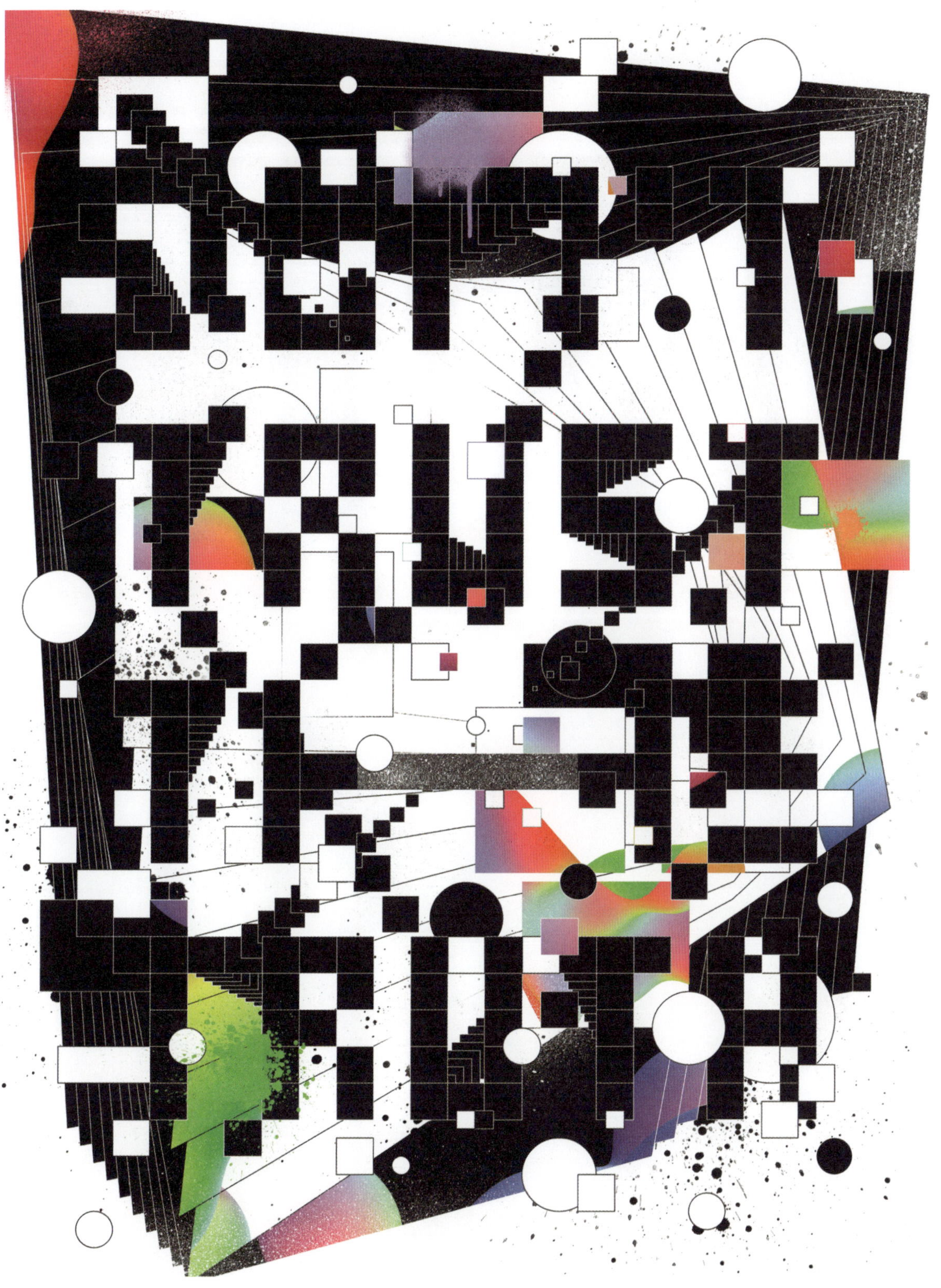

# ARCHITECTURE THINKING/TU BERLIN

This is a series of posters designed for an international symposium on philosophy and theory in architecture based in Berlin.

Studio: Studio Mut
Designer: Thomas Kronbichler, Adèle Hurbault

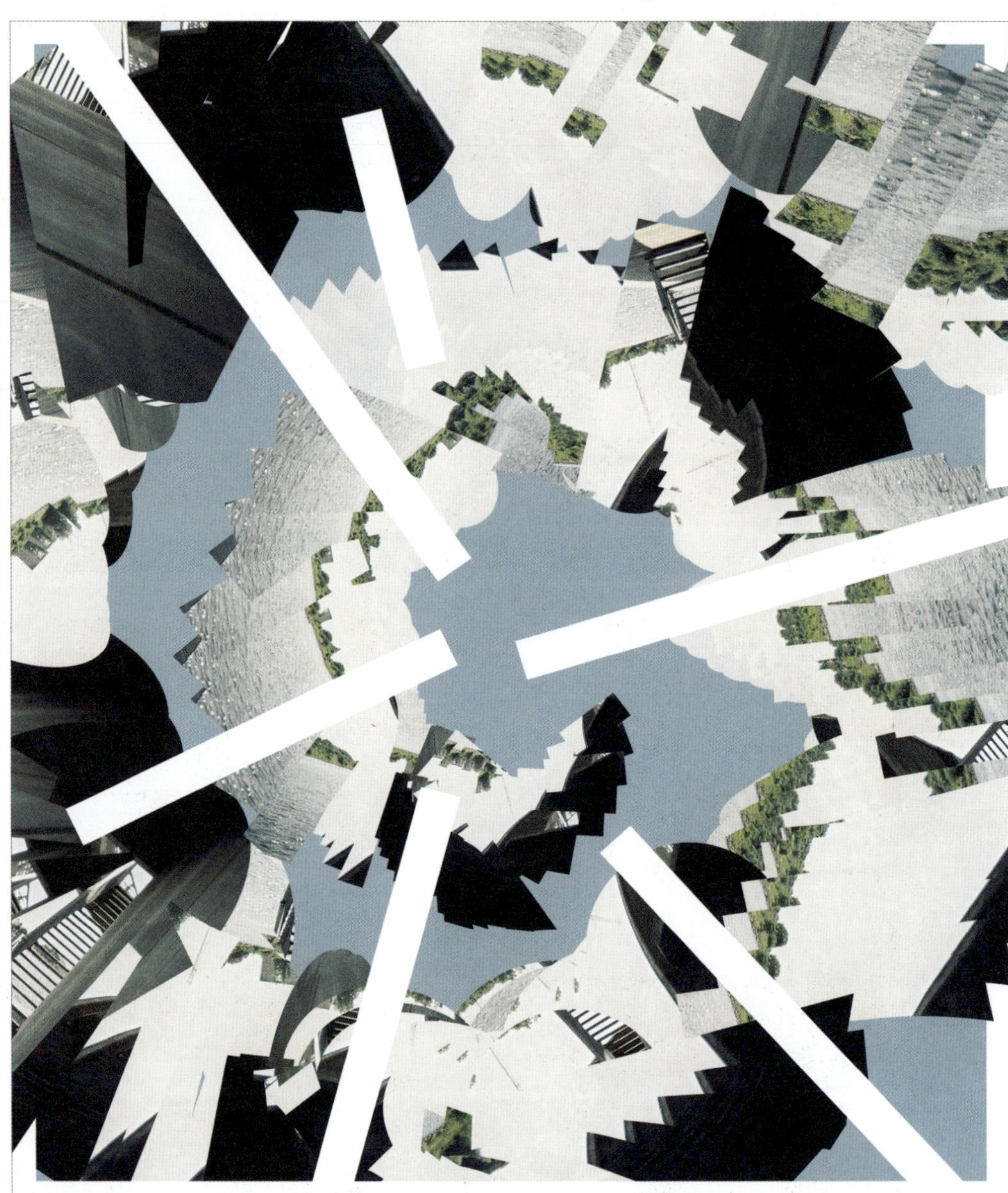

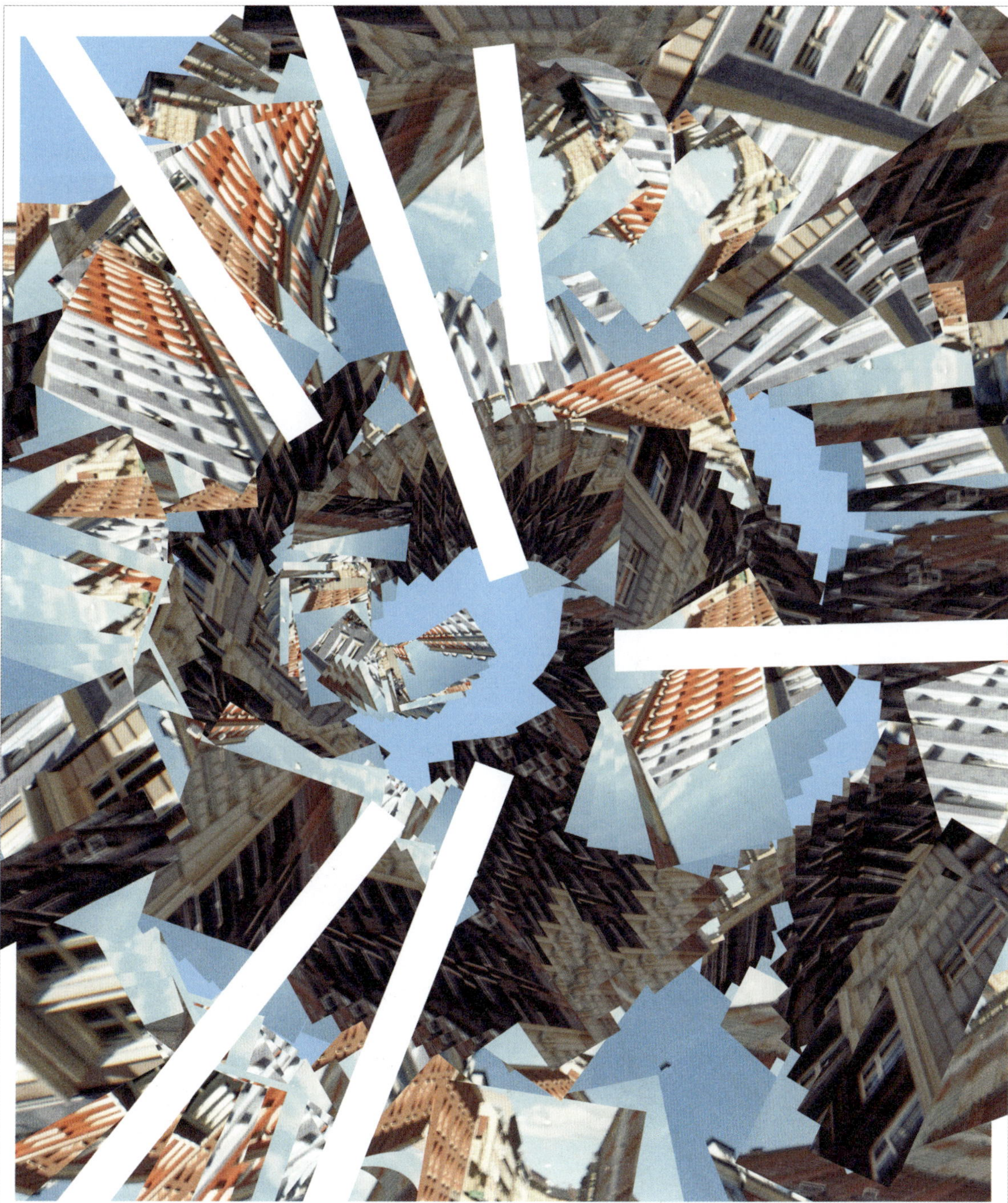

**ArchitekturDenken**
Theorie und Philosophie der Architektur

**ThinkingArchitecture**
Theory and Philosophy of Architecture

Das Symposium findet statt anlässlich der Buchpublikation *Architektur und Philosophie. Grundlagen, Standpunkte, Perspektiven*, hrsg. v. Jörg H. Gleiter u. Ludger Schwarte, Transcript Verlag Bielefeld 2015, ISBN 978-3-8376-2464-9

Symposium on the occasion of the edition of the book *Architecture and Philosophy. Basic Knowledge. Positions. Perspectives*, ed. by Jörg H. Gleiter a. Ludger Schwarte, Transcript Verlag Bielefeld 2015, ISBN 978-3-8376-2464-9

Poster: Studio Mut. Thomas Kronbichler, Martin Kerschbaumer, Adèle Hurbault

Referenten Speakers
Günter Abel *Berlin*
Iris Aravot Haifa
Petar Bojanic' *Belgrad, Rijeka*
Felicity Scott New York
Christian Bauer *Würzburg*
Christoph Baumberger Zürich
Hennes Böhringer *Berlin*
Jan Bovelet Berlin
Martin Düchs *München*
Jörg H. Gleiter Berlin
Christian Kremer *Luxembourg*
Petra Lohmann Siegen
Daniel Purdy *State College*
Ludger Schwarte Düsseldorf
Kirsten Wagner *Bielefeld*

*Organisation Organization*
Fachgebiet Architekturtheorie
Institut für Architektur (IfA)
Prof. Dr.-Ing. Jörg H. Gleiter
mit Prof. Dr. phil. Ludger Schwarte
Technische Universität Berlin
www.architekturtheorie.tu-berlin.de

Internationales Symposium
*International Symposium*

Ort Conference Venue
Forum im Architekturgebäude
Technische Universität Berlin
Straße des 17. Juni 152
10623 Berlin

29. Mai 15:00 – 18:30 *in english*
30. Mai 09:30 – 17:00 auf Deutsch

*Eintritt frei Free admittance*

Es wird keine Teilnahmegebühr erhoben.
Anmeldungen werden erbeten.
Free admission.
We kindly ask for pre-registration

Information
*Anmeldung Registration*
Dr. Tom Steinert
+49 (0)30 314 219 58
tom.steinert@tu-berlin.de

[transcript]

# VRIJ SPEL FESTIVAL

Vrij Spel is a small but well-curated music festival. During the festival, the audience is challenged to be independent thinkers. This design work for the festival was inspired by the ancient tangram puzzle.

Designer: Nick Liefhebber

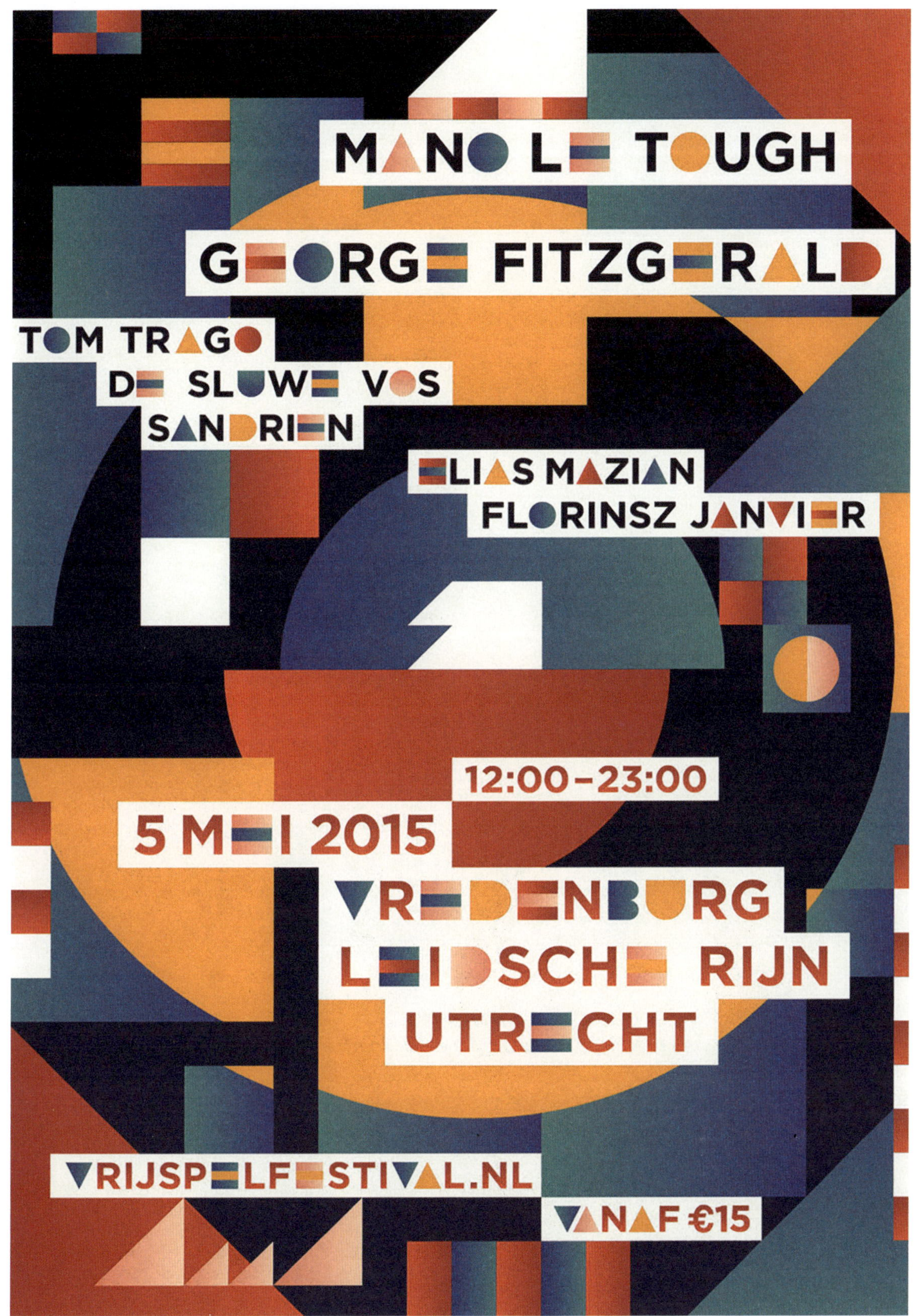
MANO LE TOUGH
GEORGE FITZGERALD
TOM TRAGO
DE SLUWE VOS
SANDRIEN
ELIAS MAZIAN
FLORINSZ JANVIER
12:00–23:00
5 MEI 2015
VREDENBURG
LEIDSCHE RIJN
UTRECHT
VRIJSPELFESTIVAL.NL
VANAF €15

# FUTURIST MANIFEST FT. PORT VINTAGE

This is a poster using Port Vintage for the context. Based on the prolific Didone environment in which the font attains its vintage feel, the designers went on to hunt: instead of following the idea of the revival times, they followed the violent reforms of the beginning of the 20th century.

Studio: Royal

1. Nós queremos cantar o amor ao perigo, o hábito da energia e da temeridade.
2. A coragem, a audácia, a rebelião serão elementos essenciais de nossa

poesia.
3. A literatura exaltou até hoje a imobilidade pensativa, o êxtase, o sono. Nós queremos exaltar o movimento agressivo, a insônia

febril, o passo de corrida, o salto mortal, o bofetão e o soco.
4. Nós afirmamos que a magnificência do mundo enriqueceu-se de uma beleza nova: a beleza da velocidade. Um automóvel de corrida com seu cofre enfeitado com tubos grossos, semelhantes a serpentes de hálito explosivo... um automóvel rugidor, que correr sobre a metral-
ais
que a
de Sa-
ia.
uere-
toar
que
vo-
uja
leal at-
a
ançada
numa
sobre o
da sua
ciso
oeta
lize
lor,
muni-
a, para
aumen ar o

entusiástico fervor dos elementos primordiais.
7. Não há mais beleza, a não ser na luta. Nenhuma obra que não tenha um caráter agressivo pode ser uma obra-prima. A poesia deve ser concebida como um violento assalto contra as forças desconhecidas, para obrigá-las a prostar-se diante do homem.
8. Nós estamos no promontório extremo dos séculos!... Por que haveríamos de olhar para trás, se

queremos arrombar as misteriosas portas do Impossível? O Tempo e o Espaço morreram ontem. Nós já estamos vivendo no absoluto, pois já criamos a eterna velocidade onipresente.
9. Nós queremos glorificar a guerra - única higiene do mundo - o militarismo, o patriotismo, o gesto destruidor dos libertários, as belas idéias pelas quais se morre e o desprezo pela mulher.
10. Nós queremos destruir os museus, as bibliotecas, as aca-

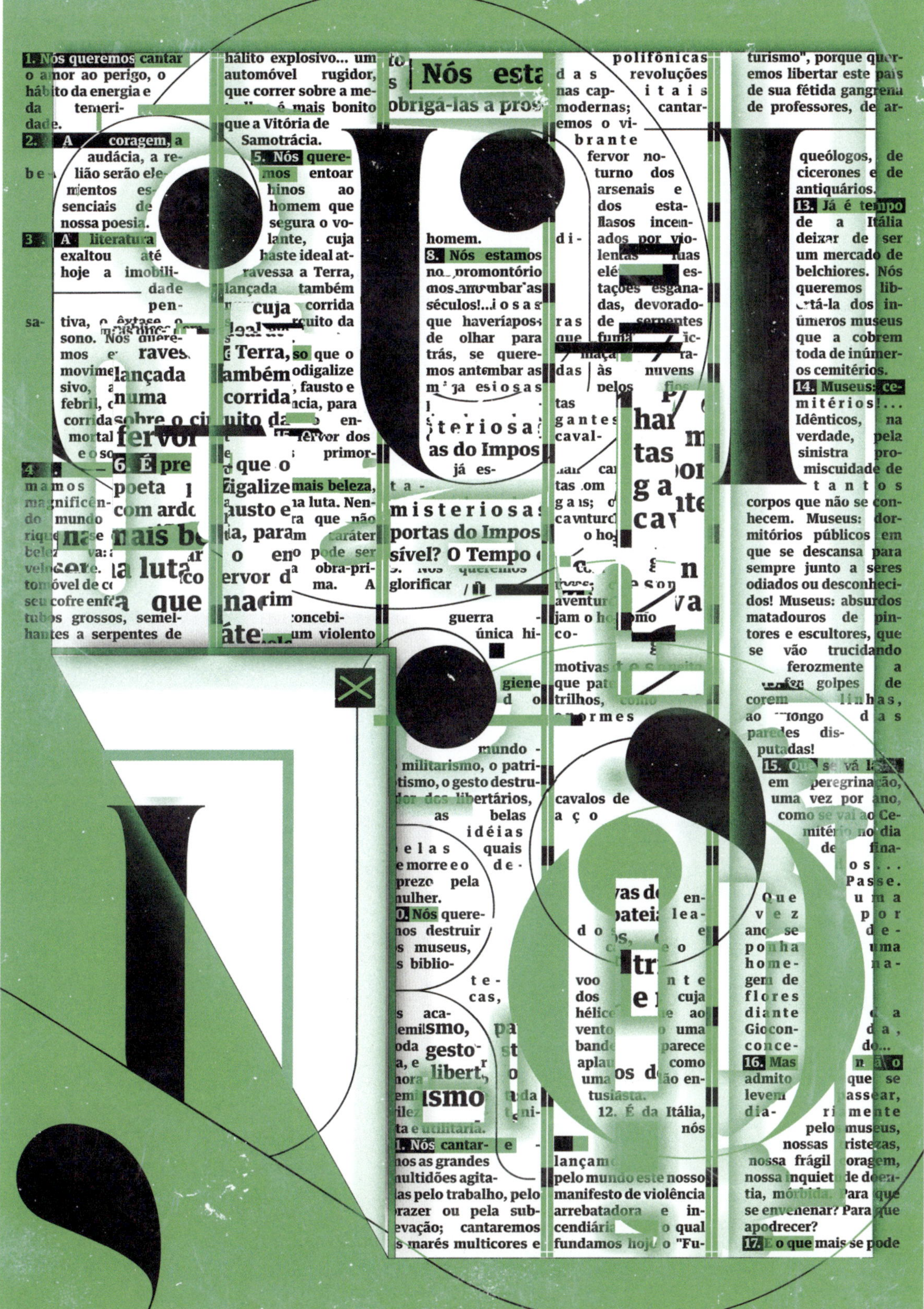

1. Nós queremos cantar o amor ao perigo, o hábito da energia e da temeridade.
2. A coragem, a audácia, a rebelião serão elementos essenciais de nossa poesia.
3. A literatura exaltou até hoje a imobilidade pensativa, o êxtase, o sono.
hálito explosivo... um automóvel rugidor, que corre sobre a metralha, é mais bonito que a Vitória de Samotrácia.
5. Nós queremos entoar hinos ao homem que segura o volante, cuja haste ideal atravessa a Terra, lançada também corrida
Nós esta
obrigá-las a pros
homem.
8. Nós estamos no promontório extremo dos séculos!... Por que haveríamos de olhar para trás, se queremos arrombar as misteriosas portas do Impossível?
misteriosas portas do Impossível? O Tempo
já es-
que o
mais beleza,
a luta. Nen-
que não
glorificar
guerra - única higiene do mundo - militarismo, o patriotismo, o gesto destruidor dos libertários, as belas idéias pelas quais se morre e o desprezo pela mulher.
Nós queremos destruir os museus, as bibliotecas, as academias
gesto
libert
ismo
Nós cantaremos as grandes multidões agitadas pelo trabalho, pelo prazer ou pela sublevação; cantaremos as marés multicores e
polifônicas das revoluções nas capitais modernas; cantaremos o vibrante fervor noturno dos arsenais e dos estaleiros incendiados por violentas luas elétricas; estações esganadas, devoradoras de serpentes que fumam; as pontes
às nuvens
cavalos de aço
12. É da Itália, nós
lançamos pelo mundo este nosso manifesto de violência arrebatadora e incendiária, com o qual fundamos hoje o "Fu-
turismo", porque queremos libertar este país de sua fétida gangrena de professores, de arqueólogos, de cicerones e de antiquários.
13. Já é tempo de a Itália deixar de ser um mercado de belchiores. Nós queremos libertá-la dos inúmeros museus que a cobrem toda de inúmeros cemitérios.
14. Museus: cemitérios!... Idênticos, na verdade, pela sinistra promiscuidade de tantos corpos que não se conhecem. Museus: dormitórios públicos em que se descansa para sempre junto a seres odiados ou desconhecidos! Museus: absurdos matadouros de pintores e escultores, que se vão trucidando ferozmente a golpes de cores e linhas, ao longo das paredes disputadas!
15. Que se vá lá em peregrinação, uma vez por ano, como se vai ao Cemitério no dia de finados... Passe. Que uma vez por ano se ponha uma homenagem de flores diante da Gioconda, concedo...
16. Mas não admito que se levem diariamente pelos museus, nossas tristezas, nossa frágil coragem, nossa inquietude doentia, mórbida. Para que se envenenar? Para que apodrecer?
17. E o que mais se pode

# F16 DESIGN WORKSHOP

F16 Workshop is a handicraft workshop specialized in lessons like silver clay, Teddy bear making, leather, ultra-light clay, etc. ranged in basic and advanced levels. These printed materials, including poster, flyer, leaflet, and postcards, were designed for their attendance at the Asia-Pacific Cultural & Creative Exhibition in Macau. The English letters and Chinese characters were interwoven in a dynamic style. The strokes of the Chinese characters were arranged uniformly but not in neat order, referring to the combination and collage approaches in handicraft work.

Designer: Tun Ho

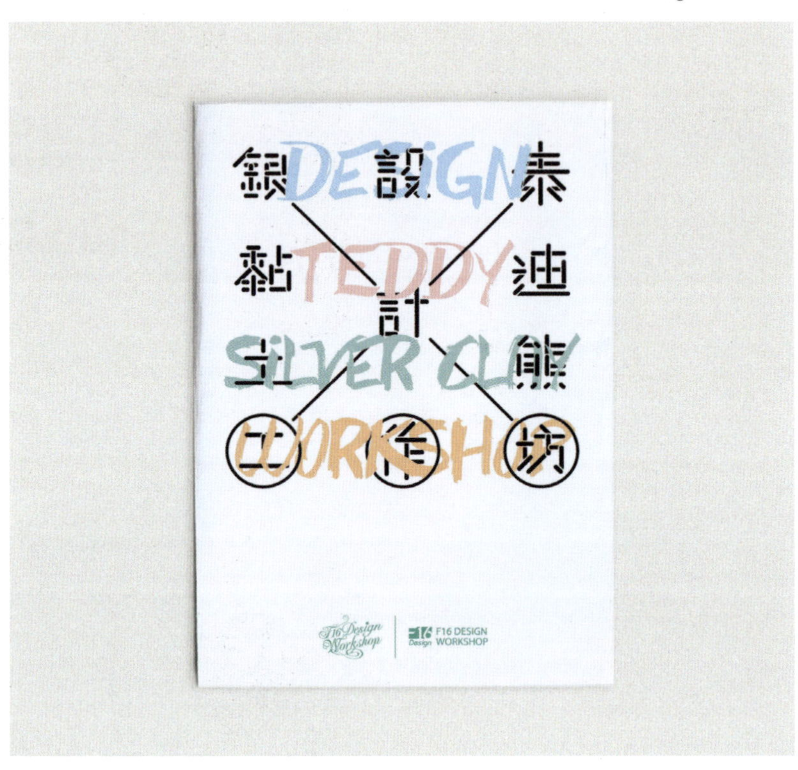


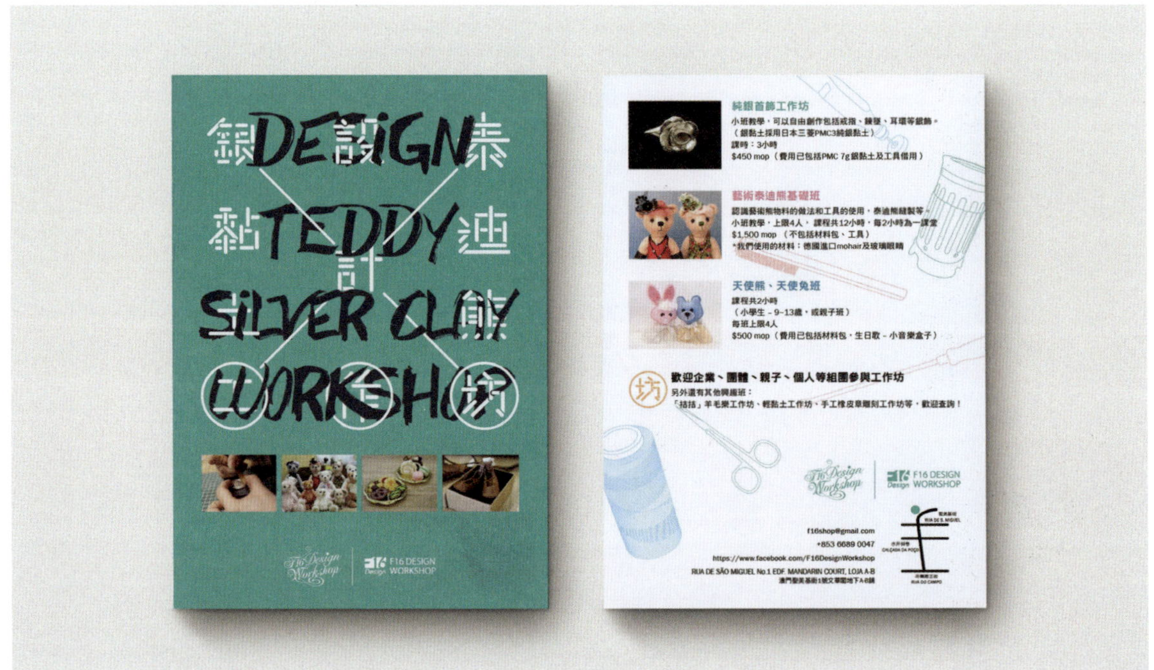

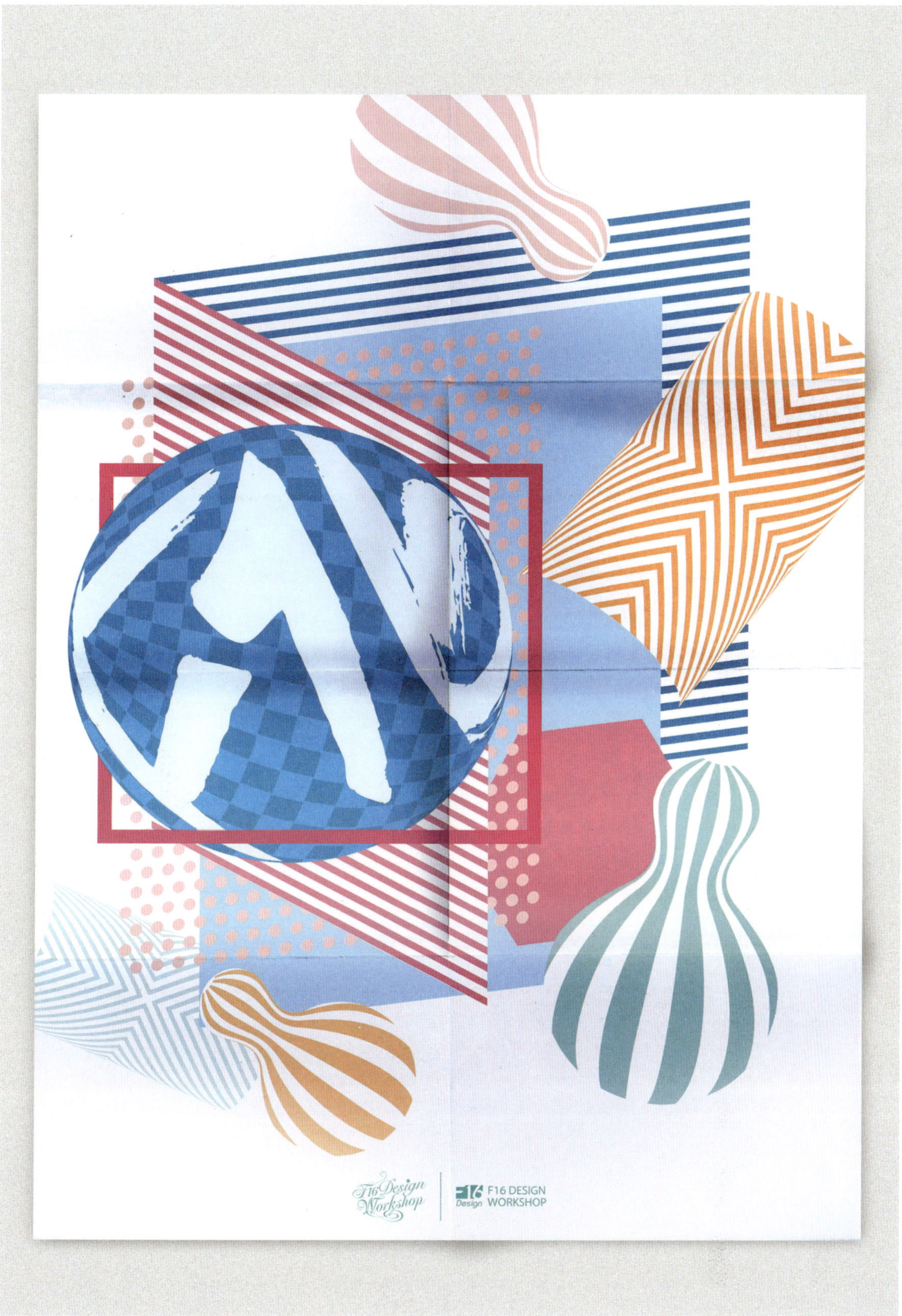

F16 Design Workshop
F16 Design
F16 DESIGN
WORKSHOP

# ABANDON

This was designed for the fashion editorial "Abandon" with the theme Stories Collective.

Designer: Adrianna Napiorkowski

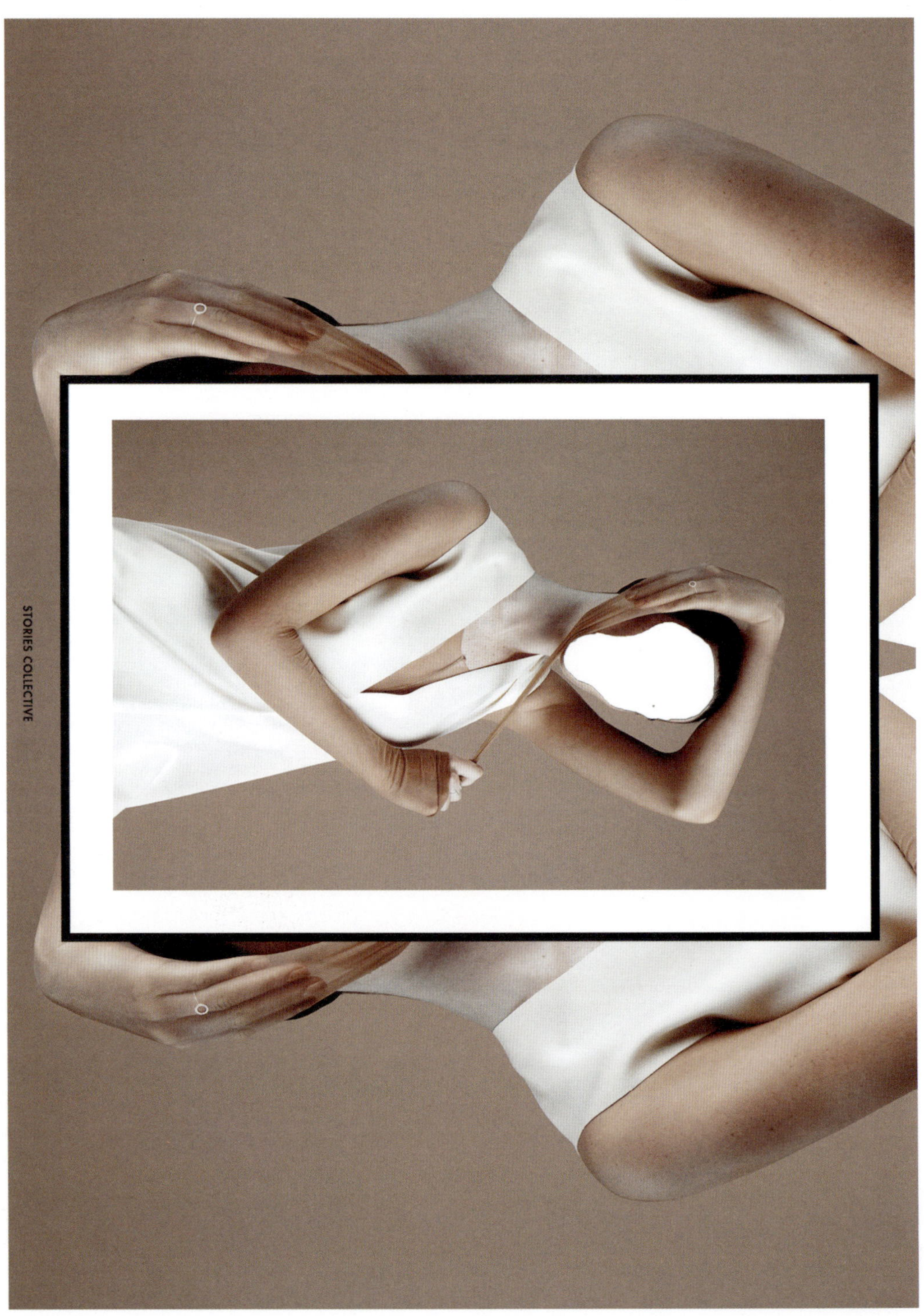

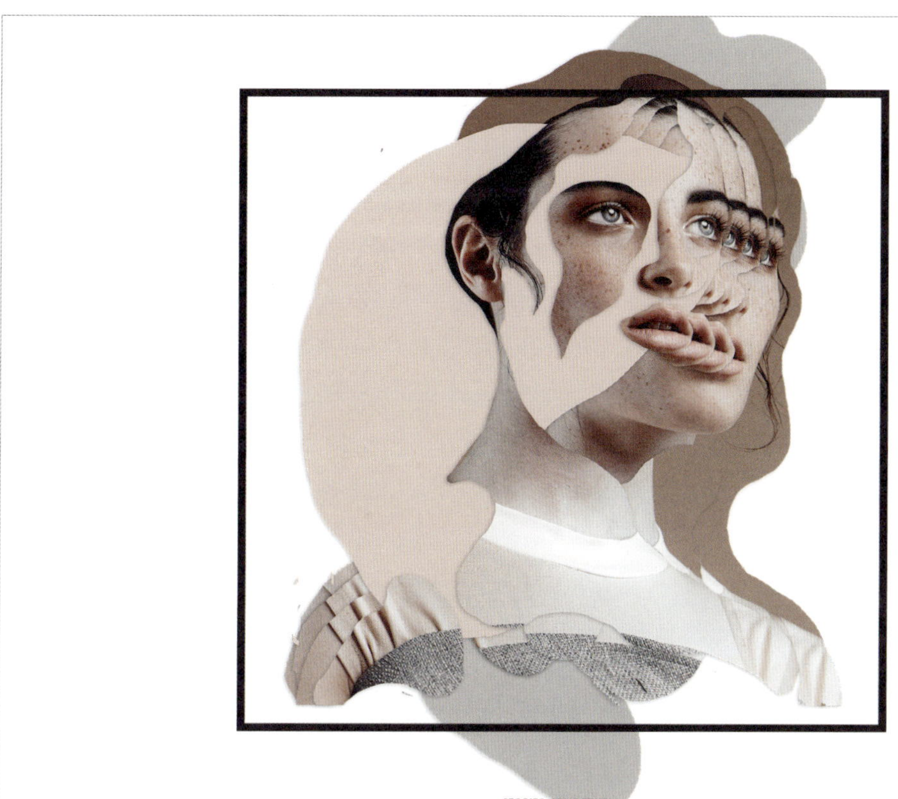

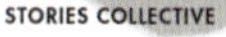

STORIES COLLECTIVE

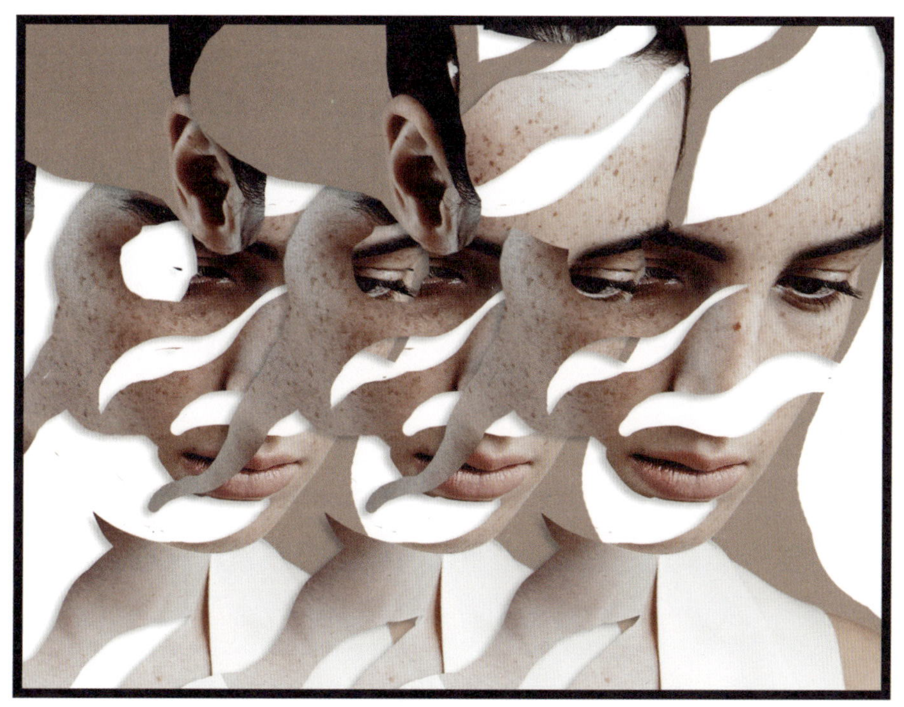

STORIES COLLECTIVE

# DIGITAL MAKER COLLECTIVE

The Digital Maker Collective is an open group of people who engage in exploring digital and emerging technologies in the context of arts, education and society. The identity was shaped by "windows" which refer to the digital world. Its flexible structure came from the way the "windows" expand in the space, reflecting the ideas of knowledge exchange, collaboration, experimentation and interaction.

Designer: Tina Touli

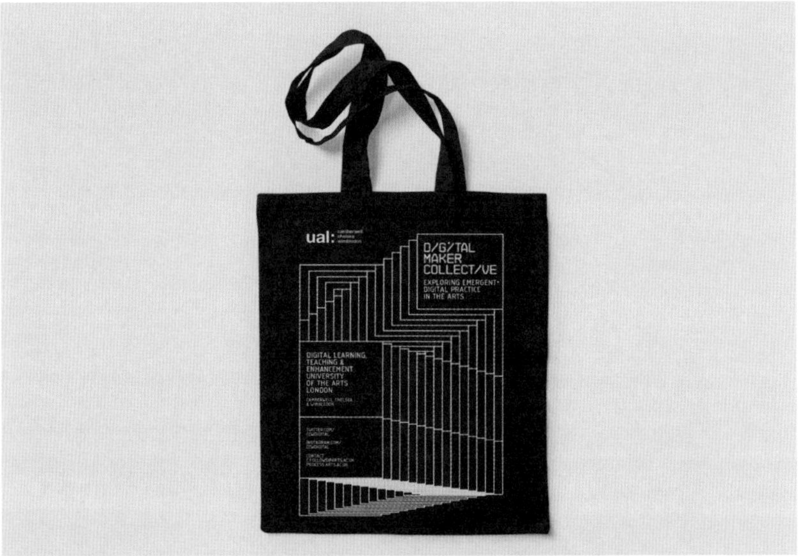

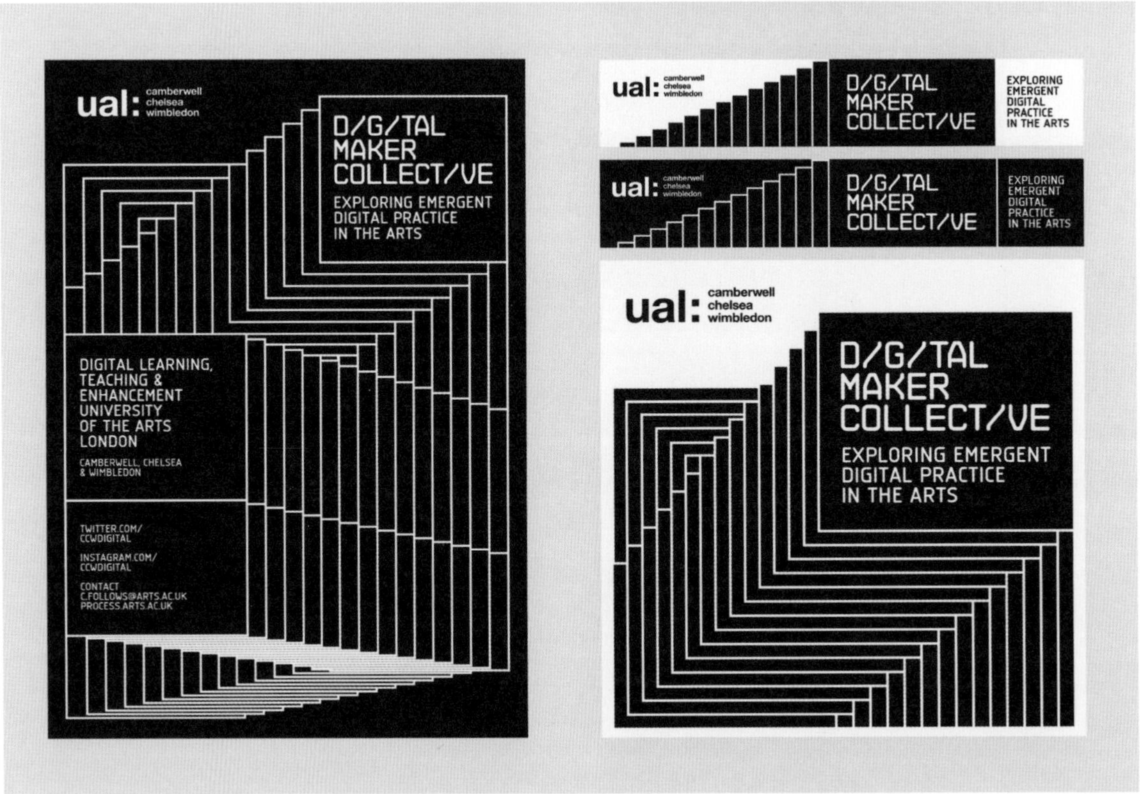

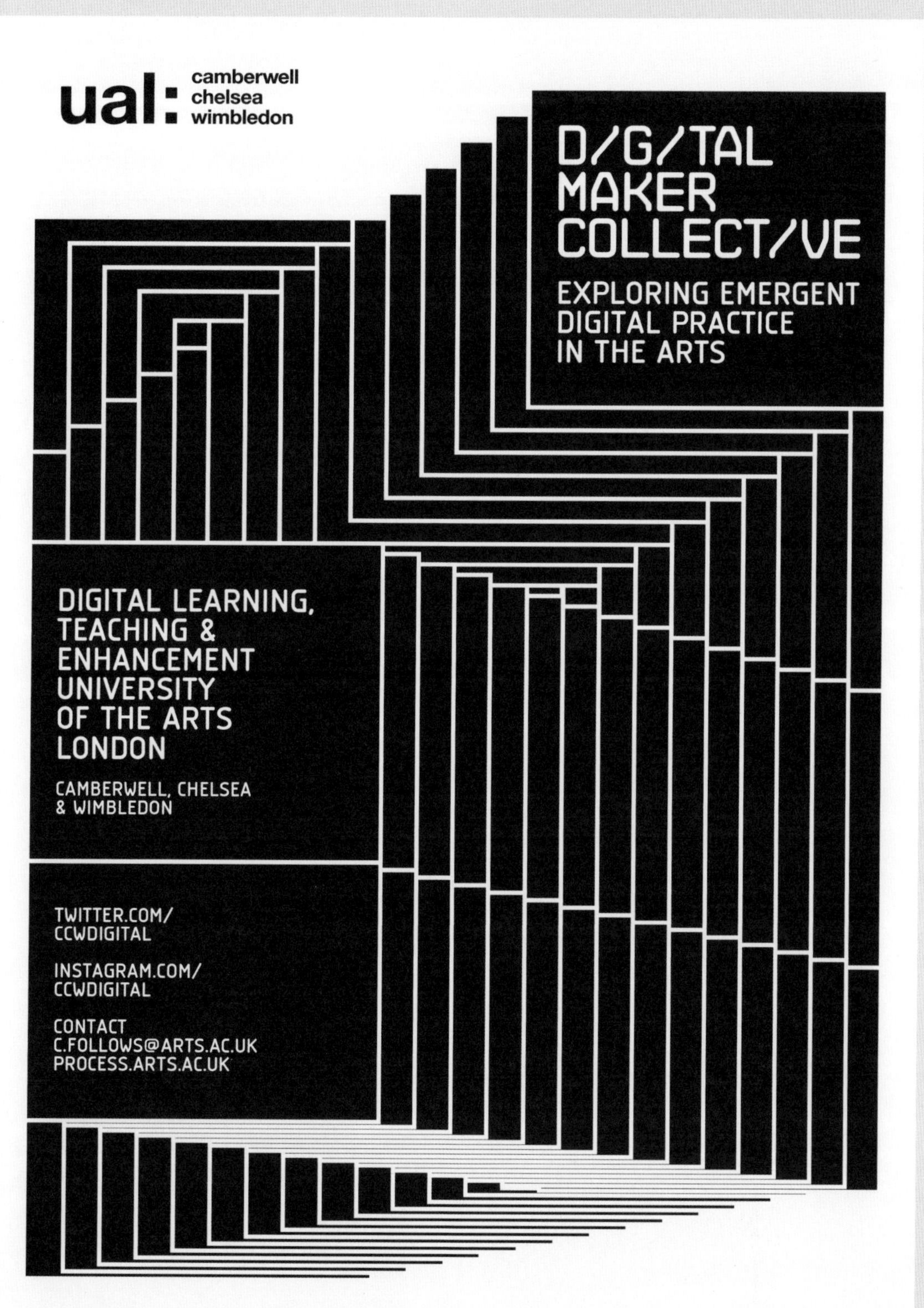

ual: camberwell
chelsea
wimbledon
D/G/TAL
MAKER
COLLECT/VE
EXPLORING EMERGENT
DIGITAL PRACTICE
IN THE ARTS
DIGITAL LEARNING,
TEACHING &
ENHANCEMENT
UNIVERSITY
OF THE ARTS
LONDON
CAMBERWELL, CHELSEA
& WIMBLEDON
TWITTER.COM/
CCWDIGITAL
INSTAGRAM.COM/
CCWDIGITAL
CONTACT
C.FOLLOWS@ARTS.AC.UK
PROCESS.ARTS.AC.UK

# PIERRE FAUCHEUX—LIFE AND WORKS

Pierre Faucheux, a famous French typographer and graphic designer, was one of the leading figures in modern French graphic design. Very interesting was his creative impulse that he deeply changed the French editorial design, and became the representative of the new school of editorial graphics in which surrealist inspiration is most present.

Designer: Brando Corradini

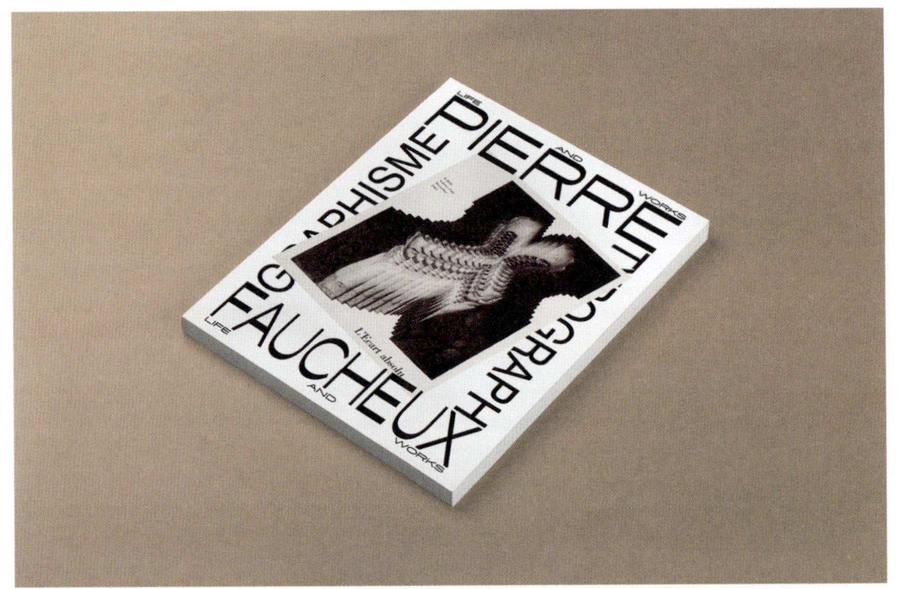


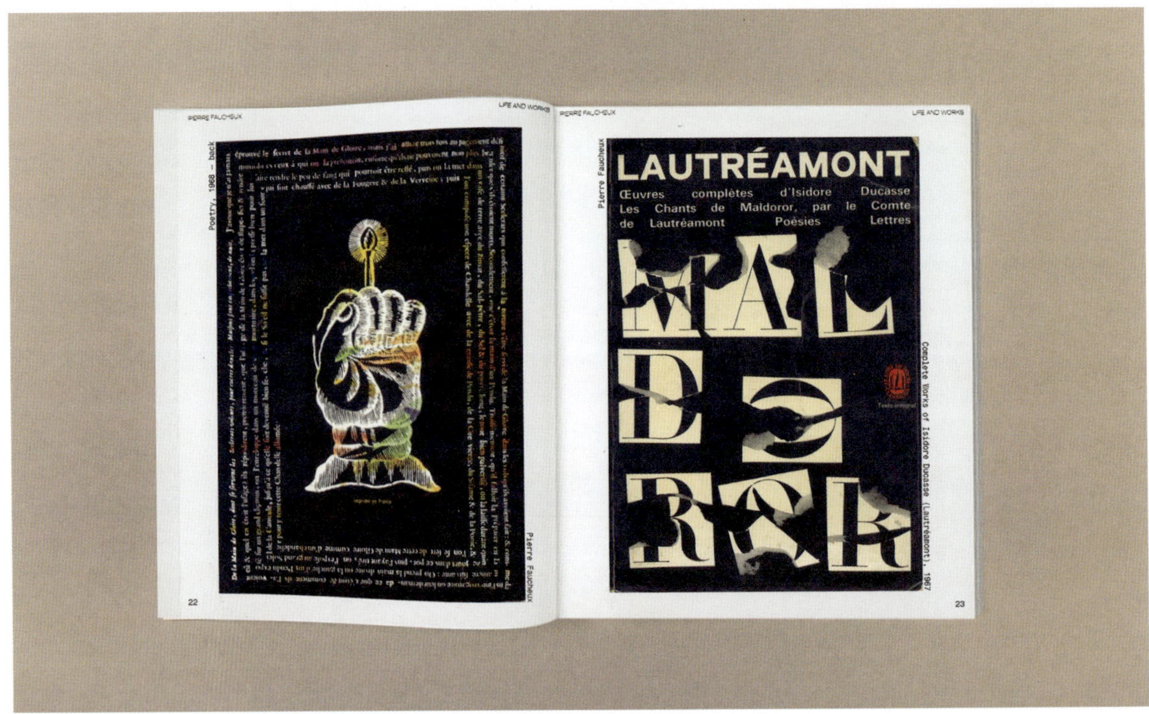

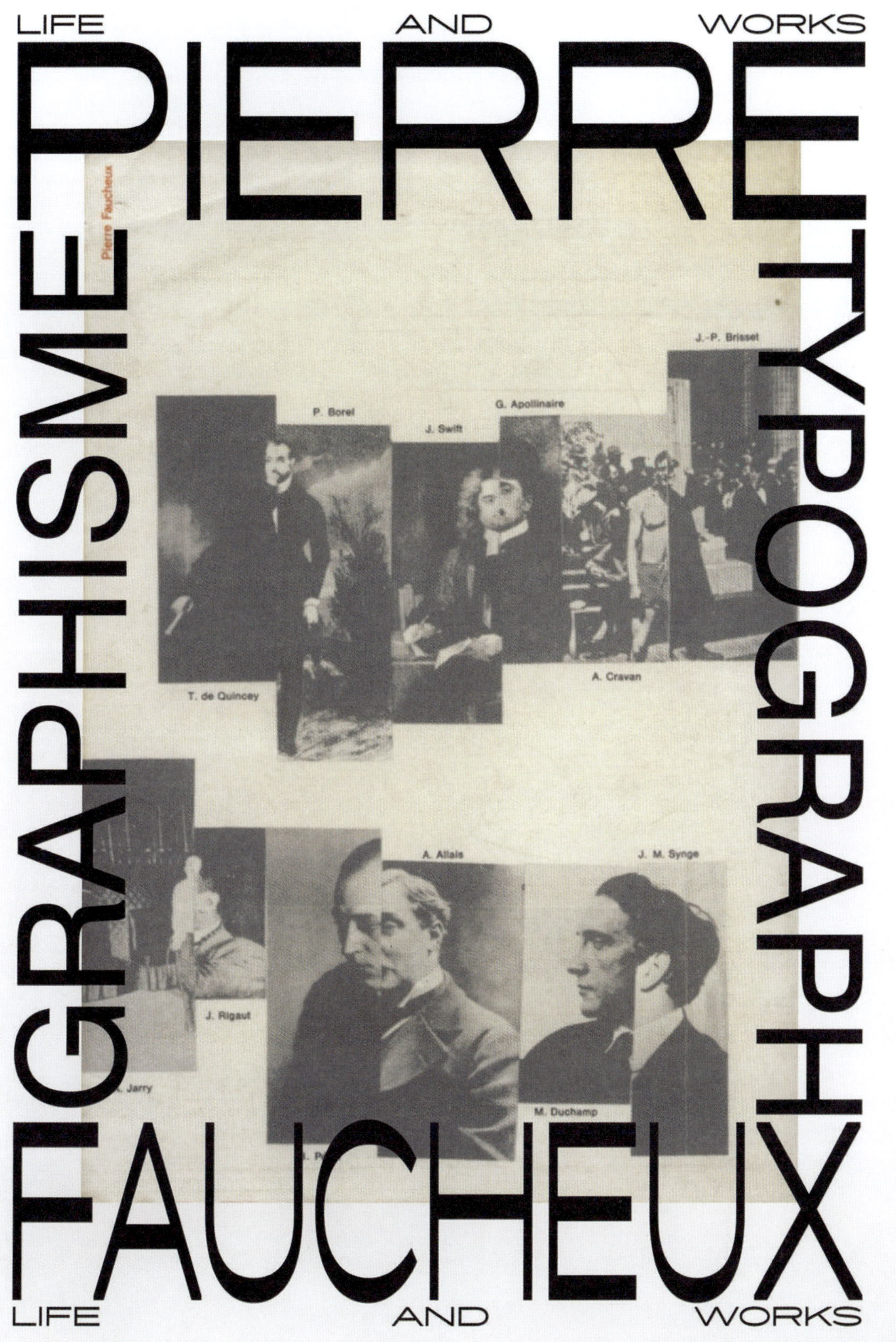
LIFE AND WORKS
PIERRE
GRAPHISME
TYPOGRAPHY
Pierre Faucheux
J.-P. Brisset
G. Apollinaire
P. Borel
J. Swift
A. Cravan
T. de Quincey
A. Allais
J. M. Synge
J. Rigaut
M. Duchamp
FAUCHEUX
LIFE AND WORKS

# APPEARANCES,DAVID LYNCH'S CINEMA SEASON

The project was about a graphic system of low complexity that aimed to compile the screen director—David Lynch's style, including three pieces: a postal system, a triptych to promote the cinema season and a poster. This work attempted to bring Lynch's sense of aesthetics to graphic language.

Designer: Micaela Nanni

DAVID
LYNCH
16 NOV
SALA / 2
23hs.
blue
VELVET
lost
HIGHWAY
17 NOV
23 hs.
wild at
HEART
18 NOV
23 hs.
CCGSM
CENTRO CULTURAL
GENERAL
SAN MARTIN

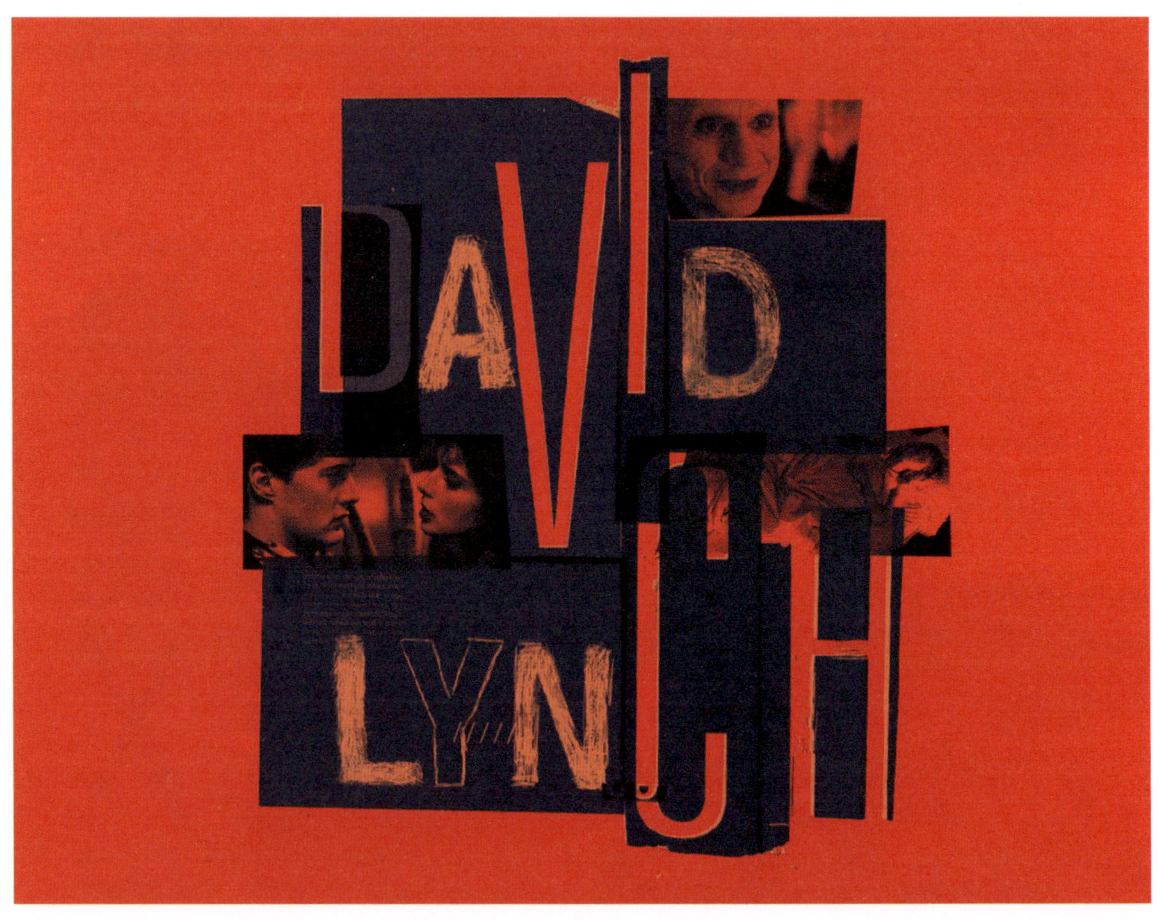

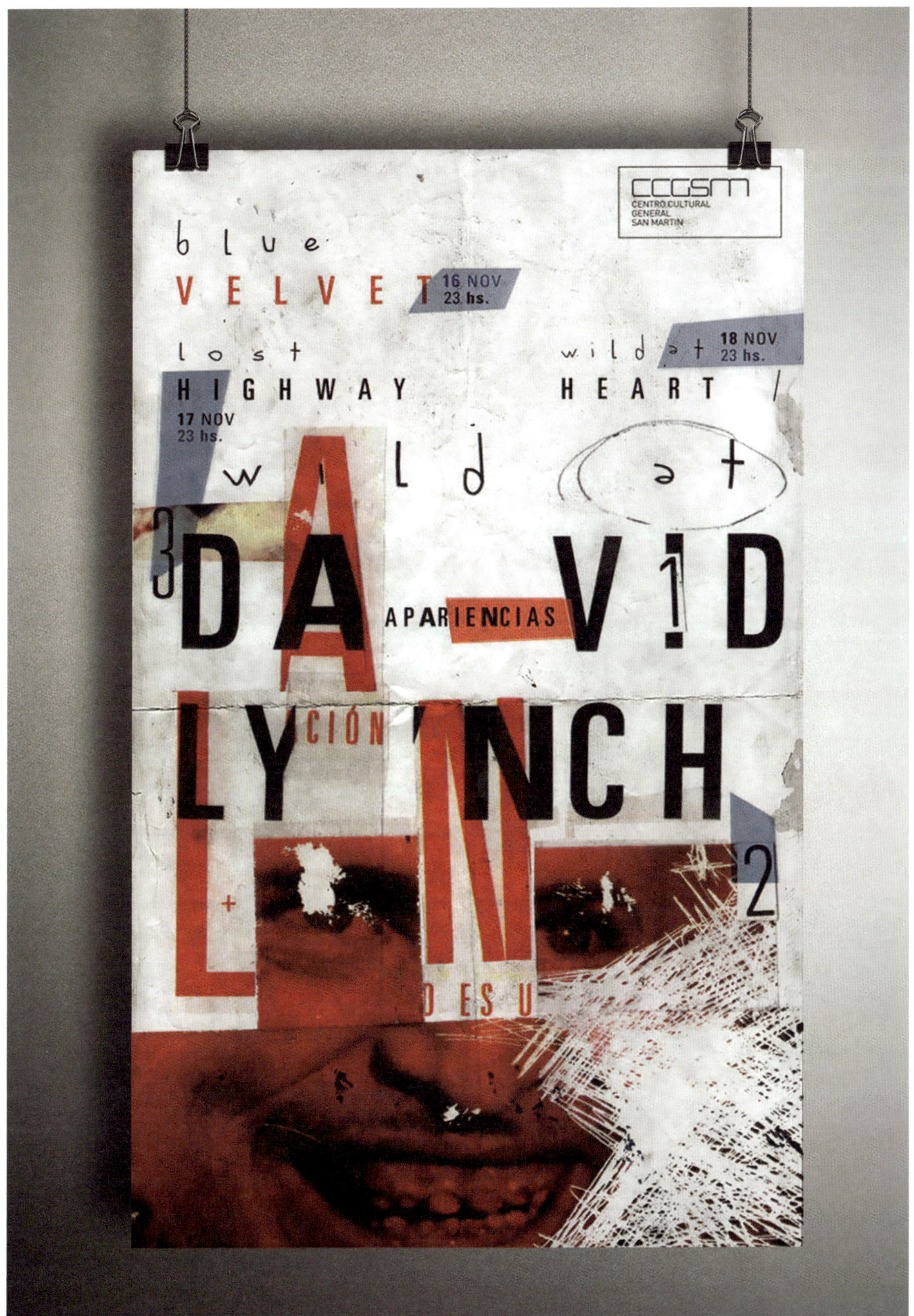
CCGSM
CENTRO CULTURAL
GENERAL
SAN MARTIN
blue
VELVET
16 NOV
23 hs.
lost
HIGHWAY
17 NOV
23 hs.
wild at
HEART
18 NOV
23 hs.
wild at
DAVID
APARIENCIAS
LYNCH
CIÓN
DESU

# d a v i d LYNCH

2

N A D A E S

Lynch es un artista múltiple, su búsqueda de imágenes bizarras que conecten con lo más profundo del subconsciente lo ha llevado a desarrollar proyectos en distintas áreas del arte, como la pintura, la fotografía, el diseño, la composición musical, la actuación, la escritura, el comic y la dirección cinematográfica.
Admirador de *Jacques Tati, Bergman y Herzog*, David es poseedor de un **estilo único**. Desde joven filmó cortos extraños con referencias del comic-art y la ilustración. Sus películas exponen una cierta **belleza siniestra y repulsiva**.

**"Hay gente a la que le gustan las películas que se entienden y hay gente a la que le gustan las películas que dejan espacio para soñar. A mí me gustan las que dejan soñar al espectador. La comprensión intelectual no tiene más importancia que la posibilidad de sumergirse en cada escena separadamente."**

L O Q U E P A R E C E

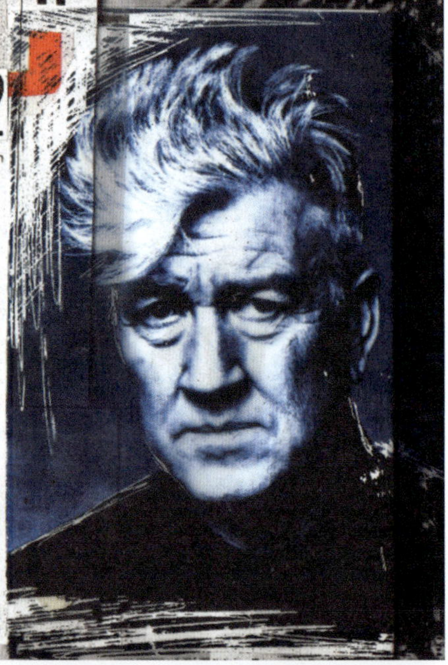

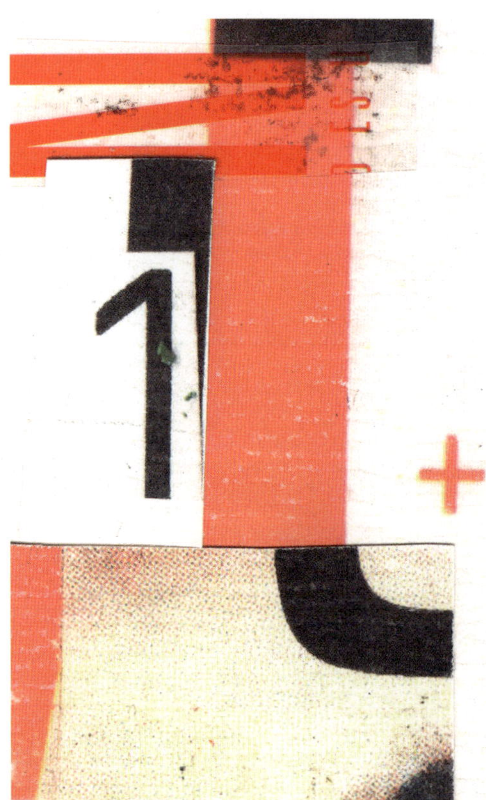


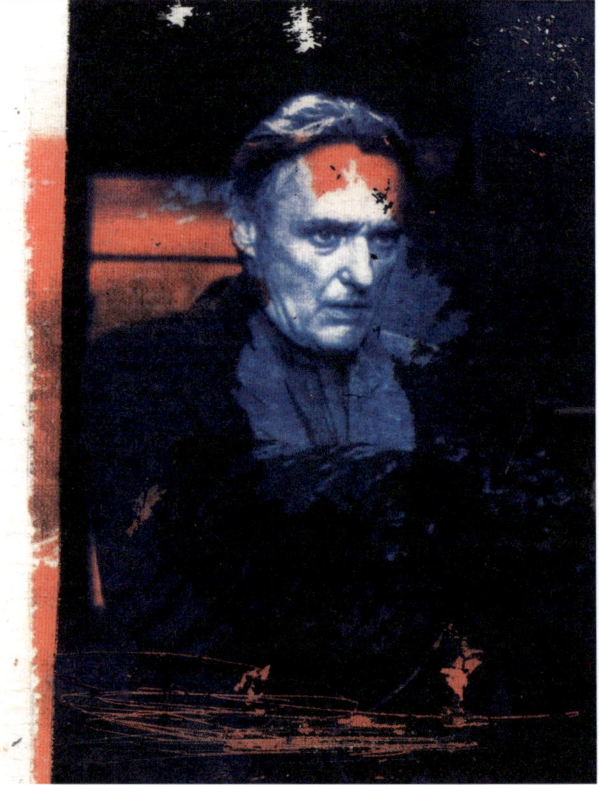

NICOLAS CAGE
LAURA DERN
WILLEM DAFOE
DIANE LADD

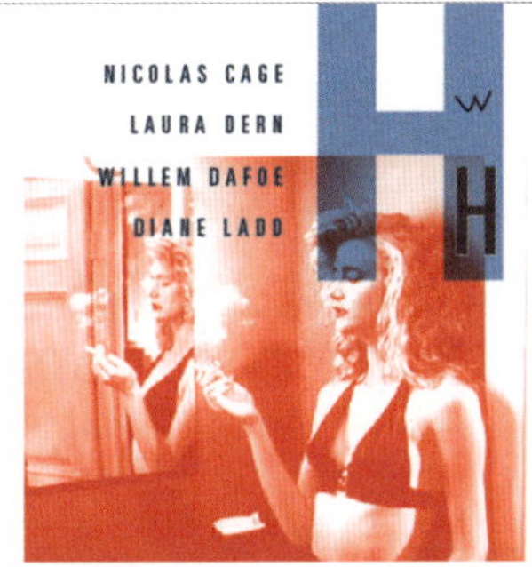

# wild at HEART

Durante un permiso que le dan en la carcel, **Sailor** va a ver a su novia **Lula** y ambos deciden huir a California. La madre de la chica, que se opone a esta relación, se pone en contacto con un mafioso para que elimine a Sailor. En realidad, quiere deshacerse de él porque el joven presenció cómo ella y su amante asesinaban a su marido. La huida de Sailor y Lula va acompañada de turbios acontecimientos y sórdidos recuerdos.

## DÍA 2 17 NOV MARTES

S A L A / 1 23hs.

GÉNERO. DRAMA
DURACIÓN. 127 MIN.
MÚSICA. ANGELO BADALAMENTI

/1990

/1997

BILL PULLMAN
PATRICIA ARQUETTE
BALTHAZAR GETTY
ROBERT LOGGIA
ROBERT BLAKE

GÉNERO. THRILLER
DURACIÓN. 135 MIN.
MÚSICA. ANGELO BADALAMENTI

## DÍA 3 18 NOV MIERCOLES

S A L A / 1 23hs.

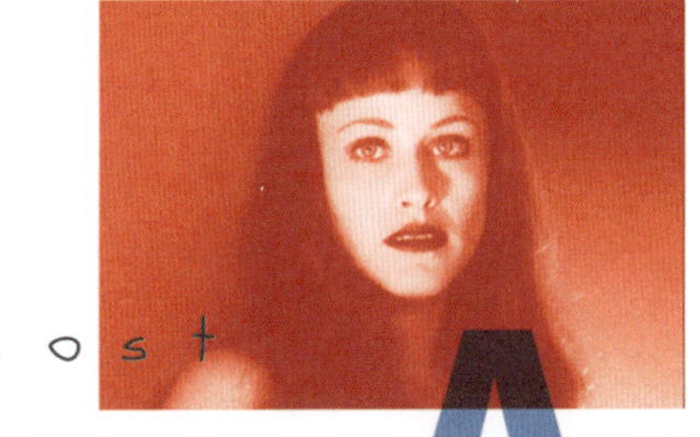

**Fred Madison**, un músico de jazz, es acusado en circunstancias misteriosas de asesinar a su esposa **Renee**. Recibe unas cintas de vídeo en las que aparece una grabación de él con su mujer dentro de su propia casa. Poco después, durante una fiesta, un misterioso hombre le dice que está precisamente en su casa en ese instante. Las sospechas de que algo raro está pasando se tornan terroríficas cuando ve la siguiente cinta de video.

# lost HIGHWAY

GÉNERO. DRAMA, MISTERIO
DURACIÓN. 120 MIN.
MÚSICA. ANGELO BADALAMENTI

KYLE MACKACHLAN
ISABELLA ROSSELLINI
DENNIS HOOPER
LAURA DERN

# BLUE TERCIOPELO AZUL

## DÍA 1 16 NOV LUNES

S A L A / 2 23hs.

Una mañana, **Jeffrey Beaumont** regresa a su idílica ciudad natal de Lumberton después de visitar a su padre en el hospital y encuentra, sorpresivamente, entre los arbustos, una ***oreja*** humana en plena descomposición. La guarda en una bolsa de papel y la lleva a la comisaría, donde lo atiende el detective Williams. Comienza así una misteriosa intriga que llevará a Jeffrey a su lado mas oscuro, acompañado de **Dorothy**, una cantante que esconde historias de las mas morbosas detrás de sí.

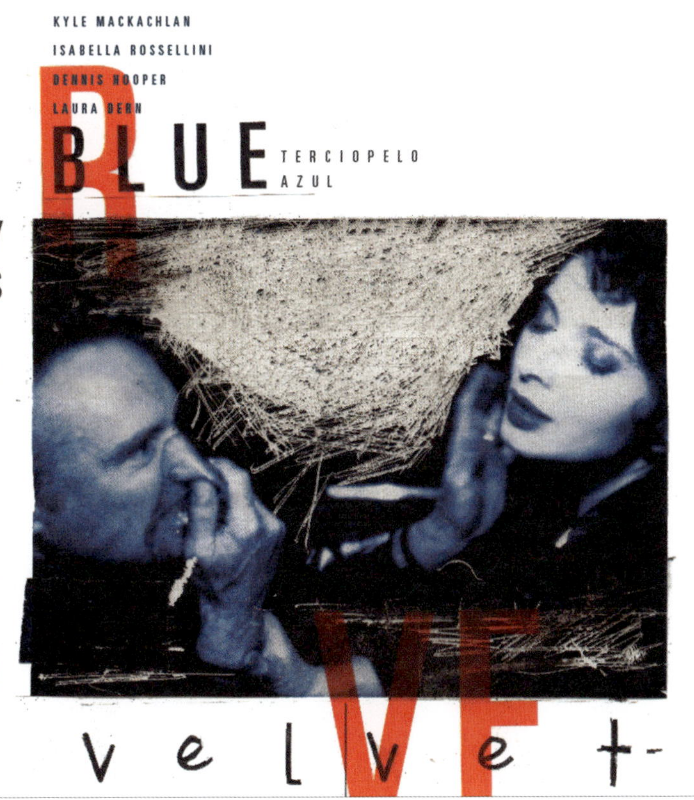

/1986

# velvet

# ADOLESER FUN PEOPLE BOX SET

This is a design project inspired by the Argentine punk rock band Fun People, who aims to represent teenagers' passion, frustrations, fears and some other struggles alike. As for the work, it's done with mixed media techniques like analog collage and stencil, with the purpose of mixing both trash and street art.

Designer: Micaela Nanni

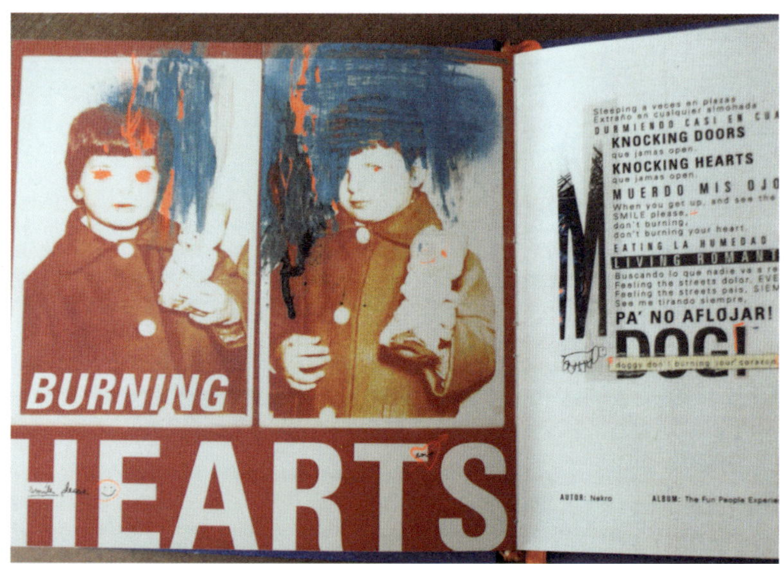

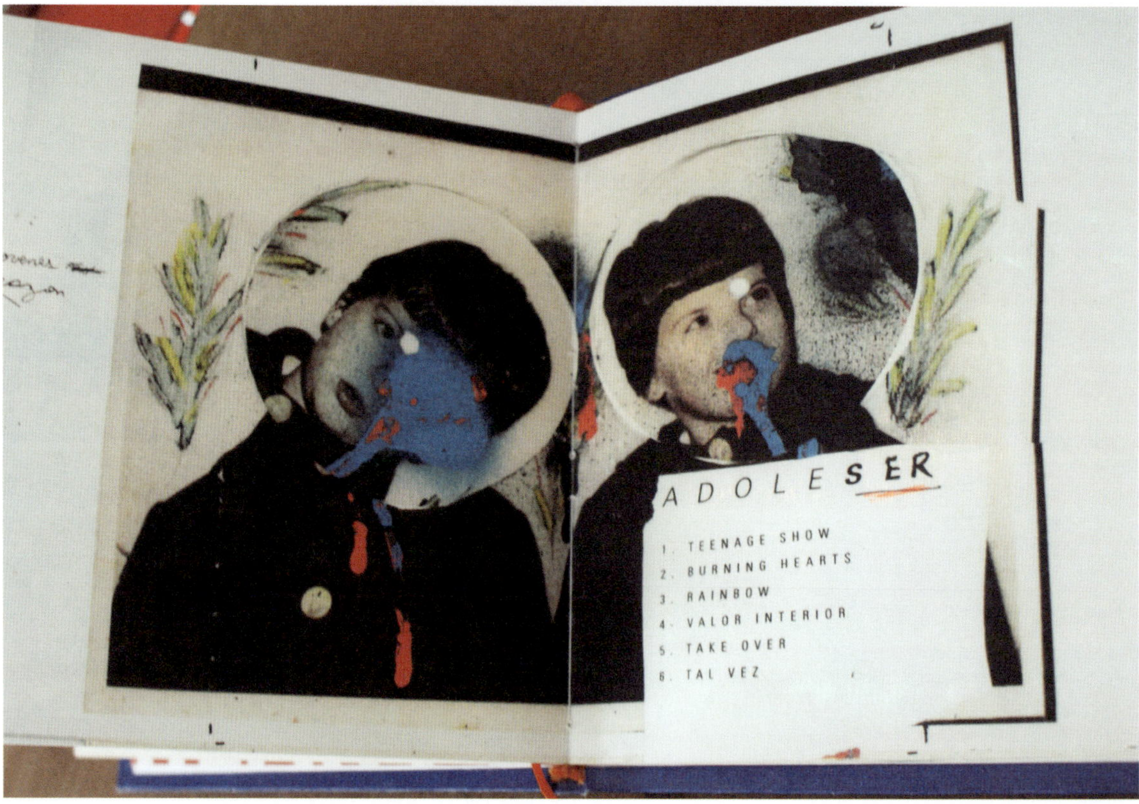

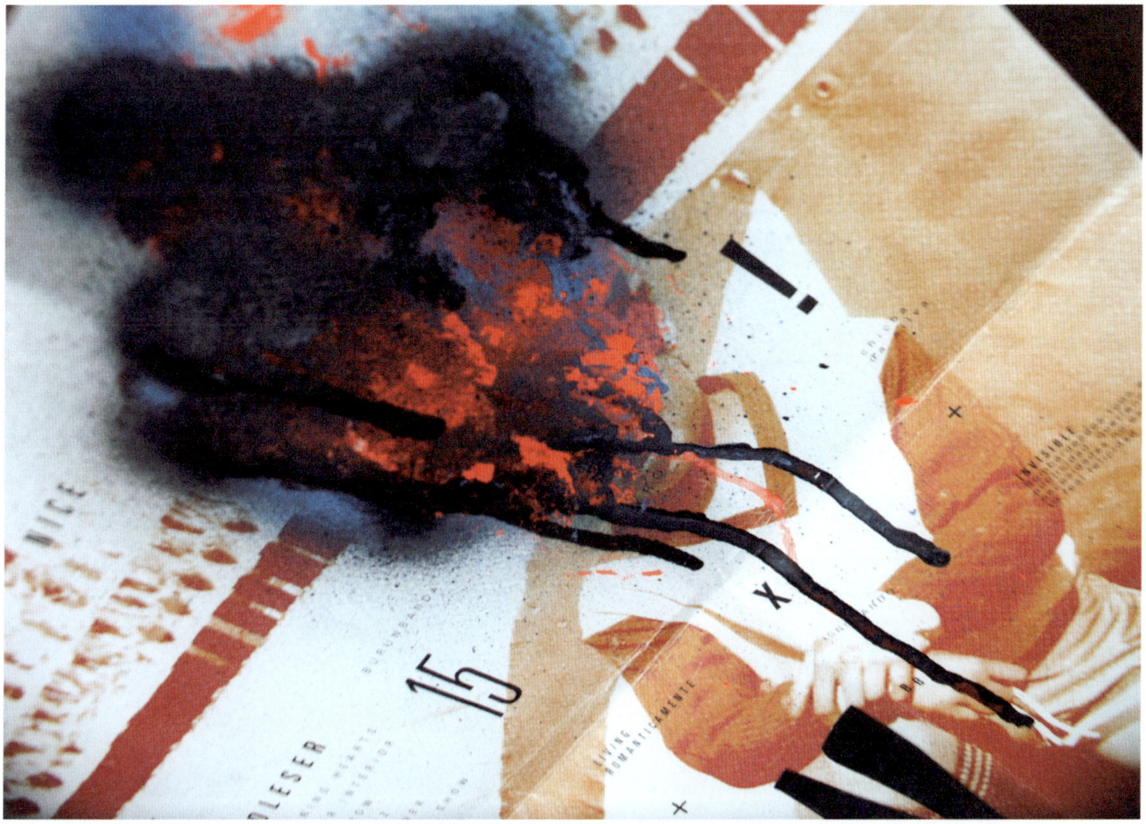

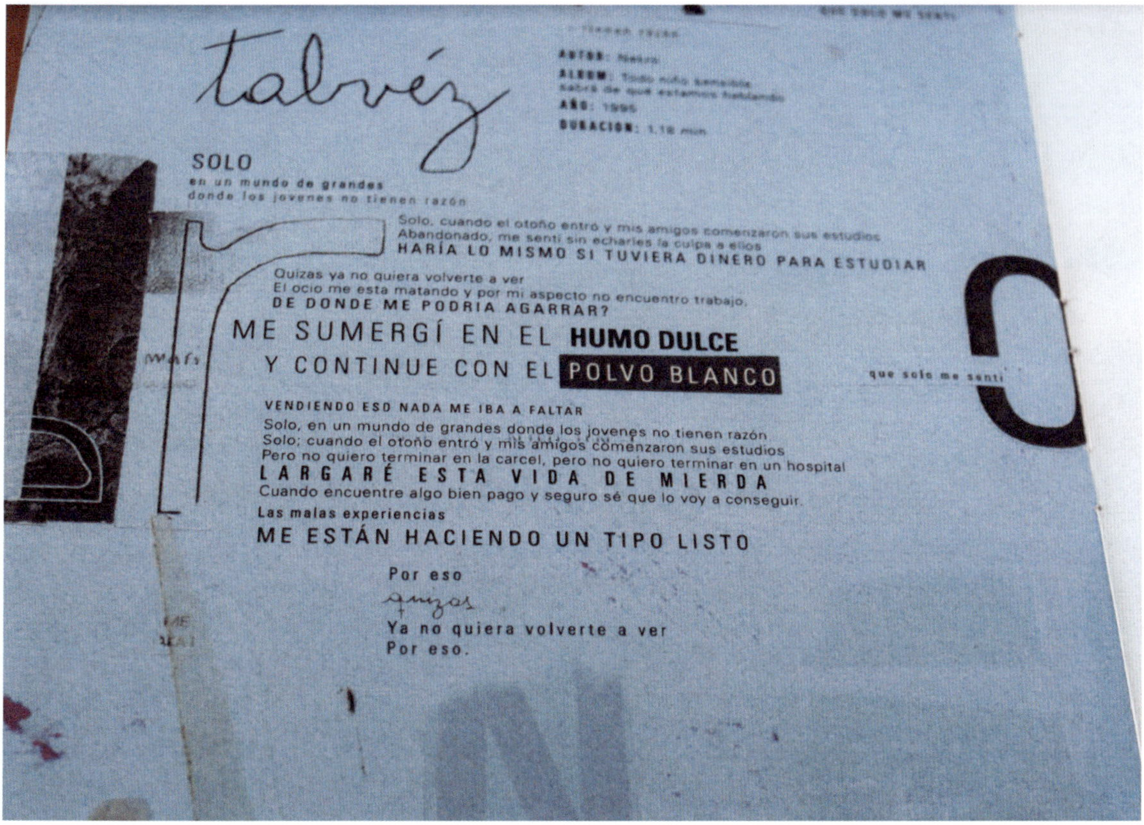

talvéz

AUTOR:
ALBUM: Todo niño sensible sabrá de qué estamos hablando
AÑO: 1995
DURACION: 1.18 min

SOLO
en un mundo de grandes
donde los jovenes no tienen razón

Solo, cuando el otoño entró y mis amigos comenzaron sus estudios
Abandonado, me sentí sin echarles la culpa a ellos
HARÍA LO MISMO SI TUVIERA DINERO PARA ESTUDIAR

Quizas ya no quiera volverte a ver
El ocio me esta matando y por mi aspecto no encuentro trabajo,
DE DONDE ME PODRIA AGARRAR?

ME SUMERGÍ EN EL **HUMO DULCE**
Y CONTINUE CON EL POLVO BLANCO

que solo me senti

VENDIENDO ESO NADA ME IBA A FALTAR
Solo, en un mundo de grandes donde los jovenes no tienen razón
Solo; cuando el otoño entró y mis amigos comenzaron sus estudios
Pero no quiero terminar en la carcel, pero no quiero terminar en un hospital
LARGARÉ ESTA VIDA DE MIERDA
Cuando encuentre algo bien pago y seguro sé que lo voy a conseguir.
Las malas experiencias
ME ESTÁN HACIENDO UN TIPO LISTO

Por eso
quizas
Ya no quiera volverte a ver
Por eso.

# KATOWICE JAZZART FESTIVAL

Katowice JazzArt Festival is a week-long international music event held in the framework of the International Jazz Day. The inspiration for the main graphic element was a piano keyboard, interwoven with loosely scattered letters that spelled the name of the event. The letters seemed to "play" the keyboard, all elements were "boiling", suggestive of the festival motto—"Hell, nobody knows where jazz is going to go."

Designer: Marta Gawin

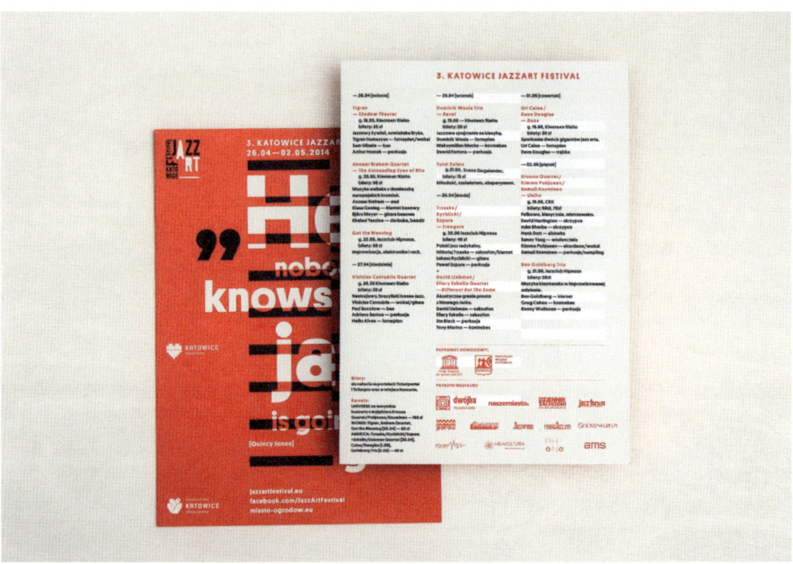

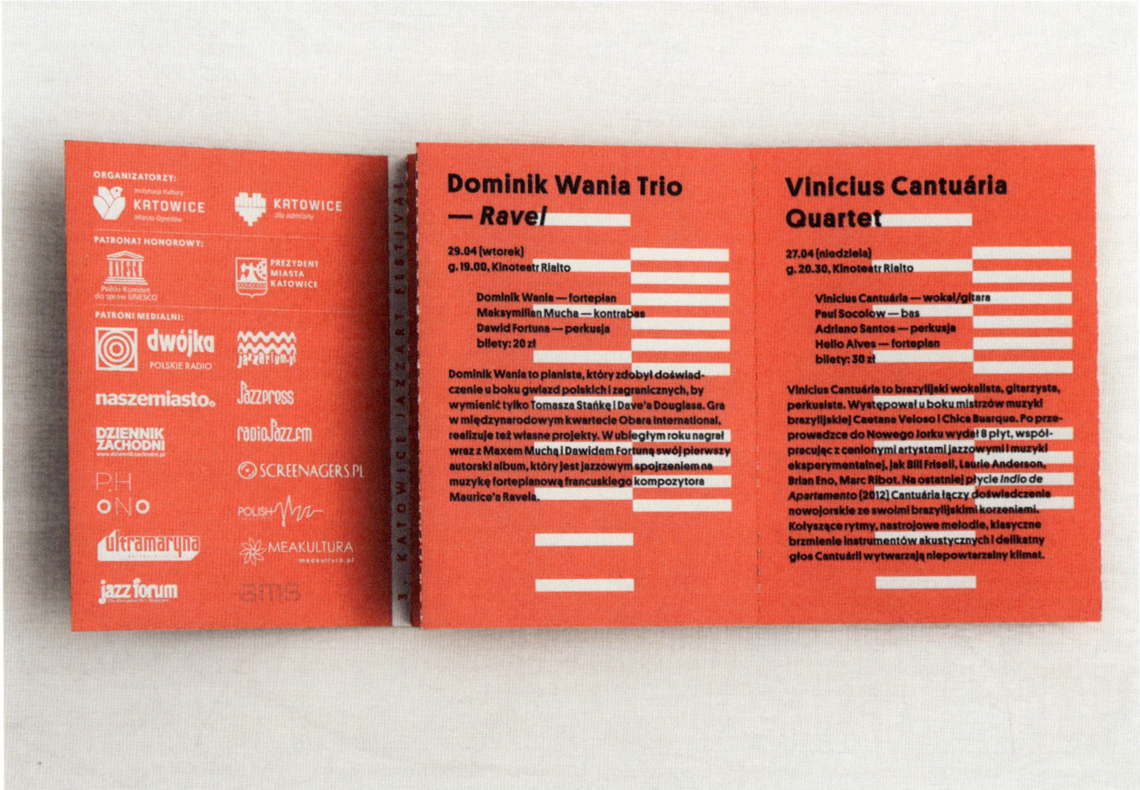

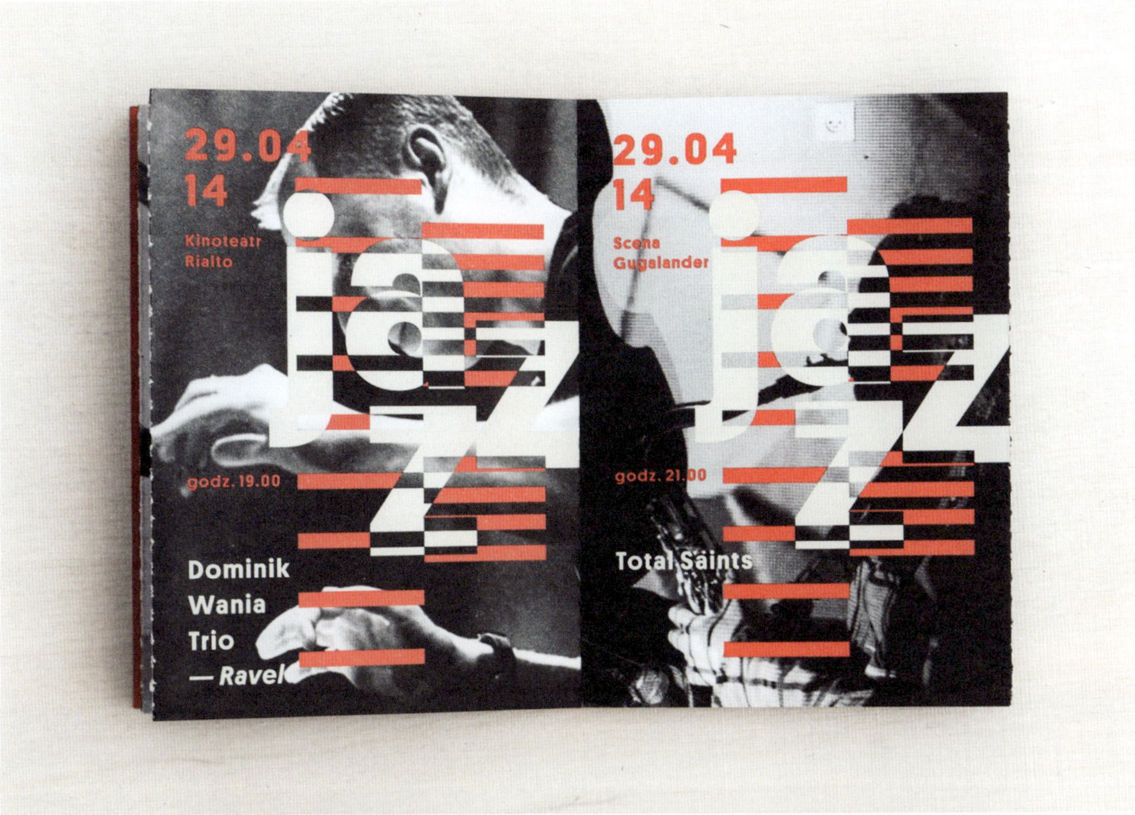
29.04
14
Kinoteatr
Rialto
godz. 19.00
Dominik
Wania
Trio
— Ravel
29.04
14
Scena
Gugalander
godz. 21.00
Total Saints

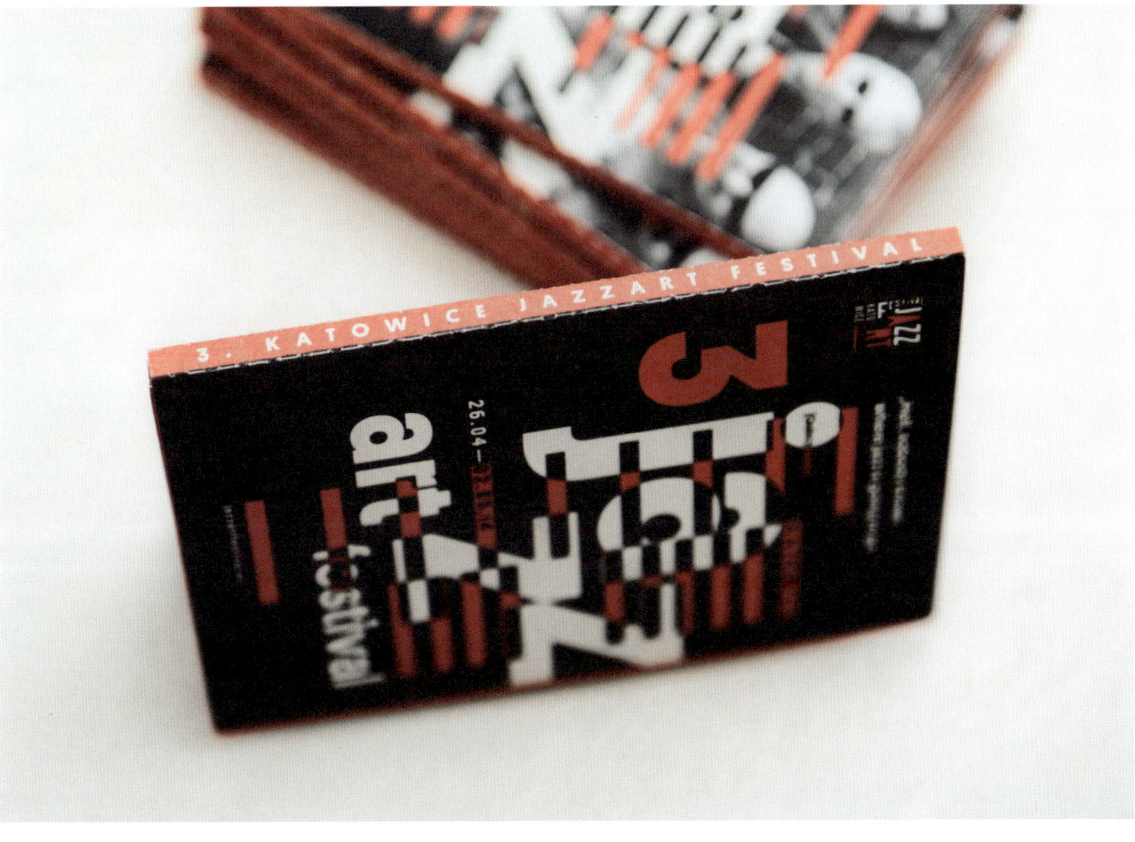
3. KATOWICE JAZZART FESTIVAL
3
art
festival

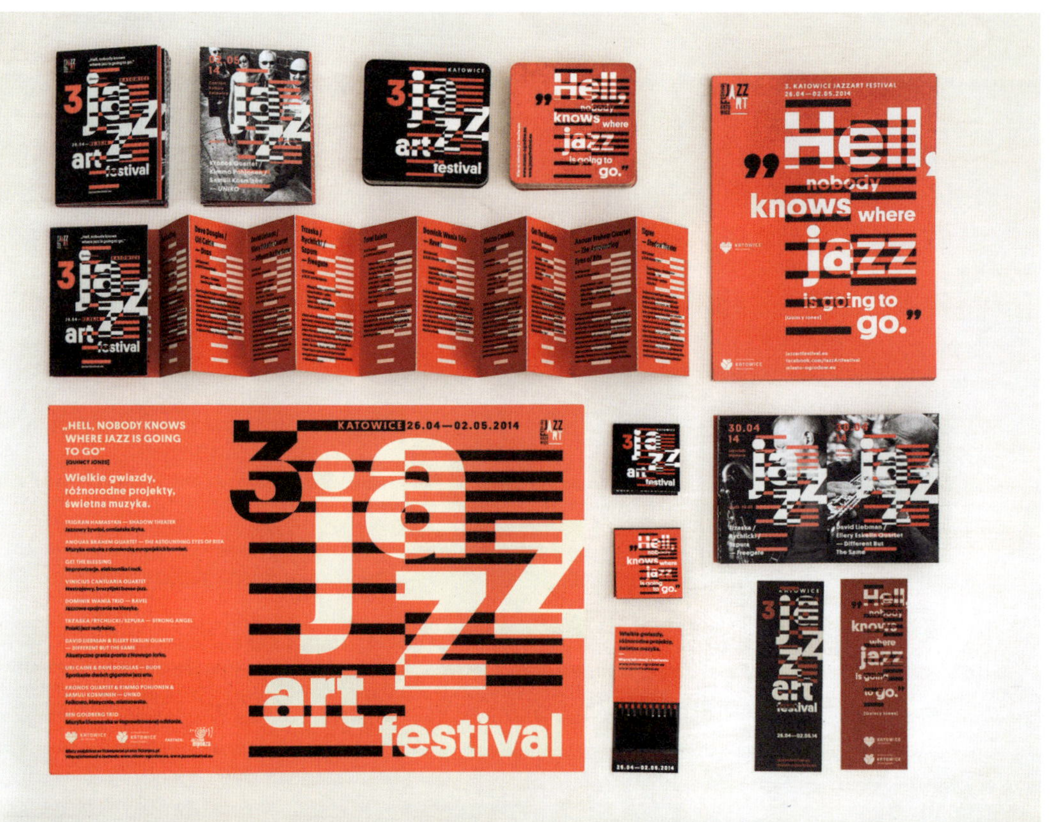
„HELL, NOBODY KNOWS WHERE JAZZ IS GOING TO GO”
Wielkie gwiazdy, różnorodne projekty, świetna muzyka.
KATOWICE 26.04—02.05.2014
3 jazz art festival
3. KATOWICE JAZZART FESTIVAL 26.04—02.05.2014
„Hell, nobody knows where jazz is going to go.”

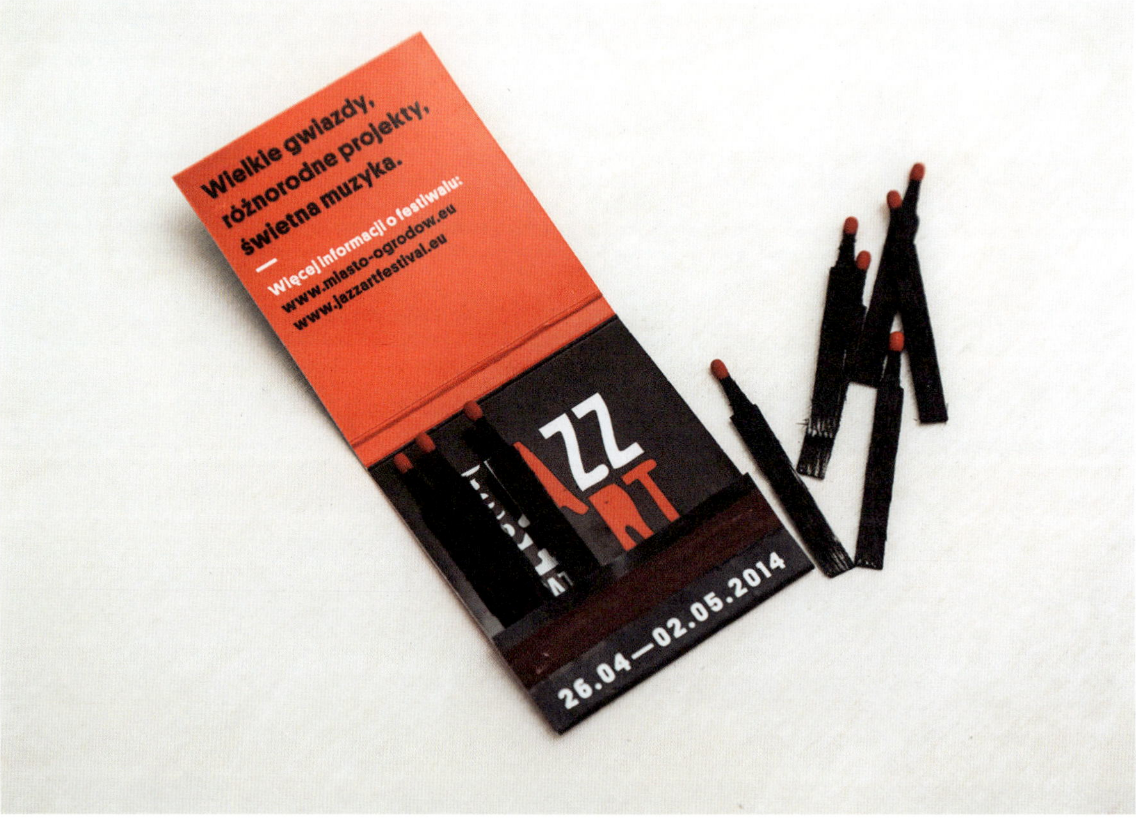

Wielkie gwiazdy, różnorodne projekty, świetna muzyka.
Więcej informacji o festiwalu:
www.miasto-ogrodow.eu
www.jazzartfestival.eu
26.04—02.05.2014

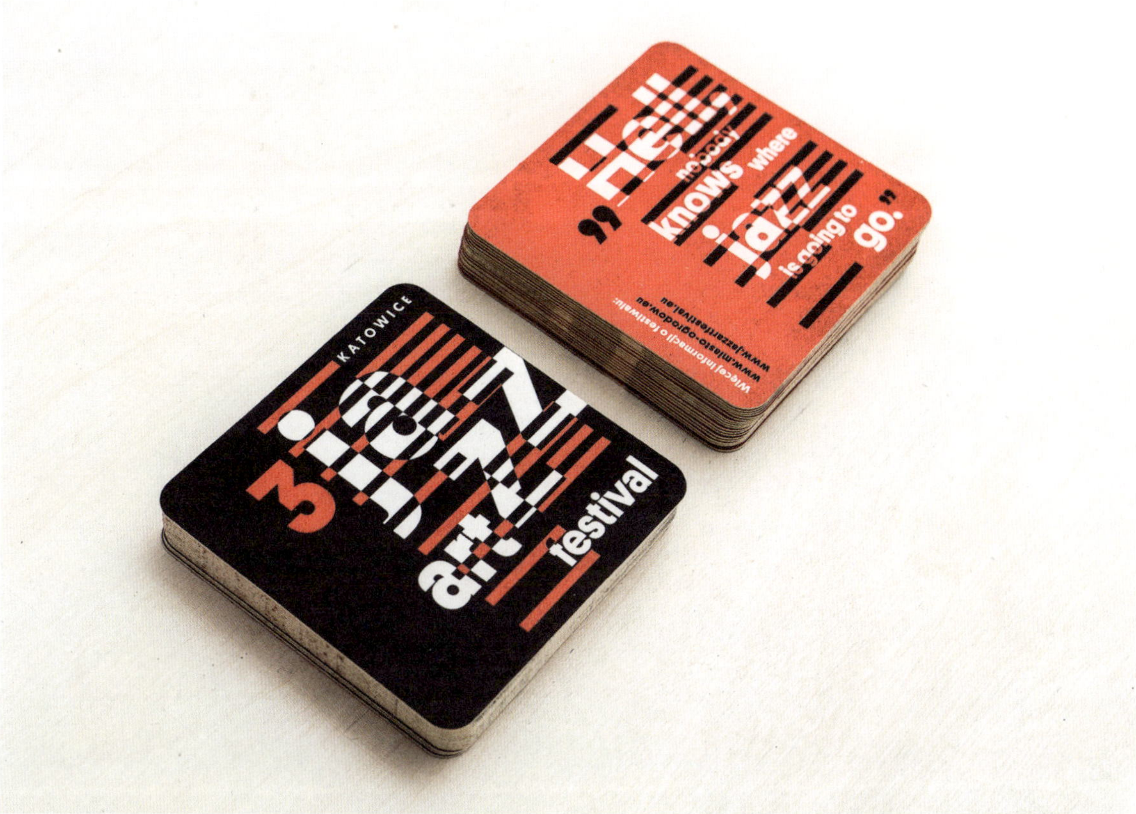
KATOWICE
3
art
festival
nobody
knows where
jazz
is going to
go.
Więcej informacji o festiwalu:
www.miasto-ogrodow.eu
www.jazzartfestival.eu

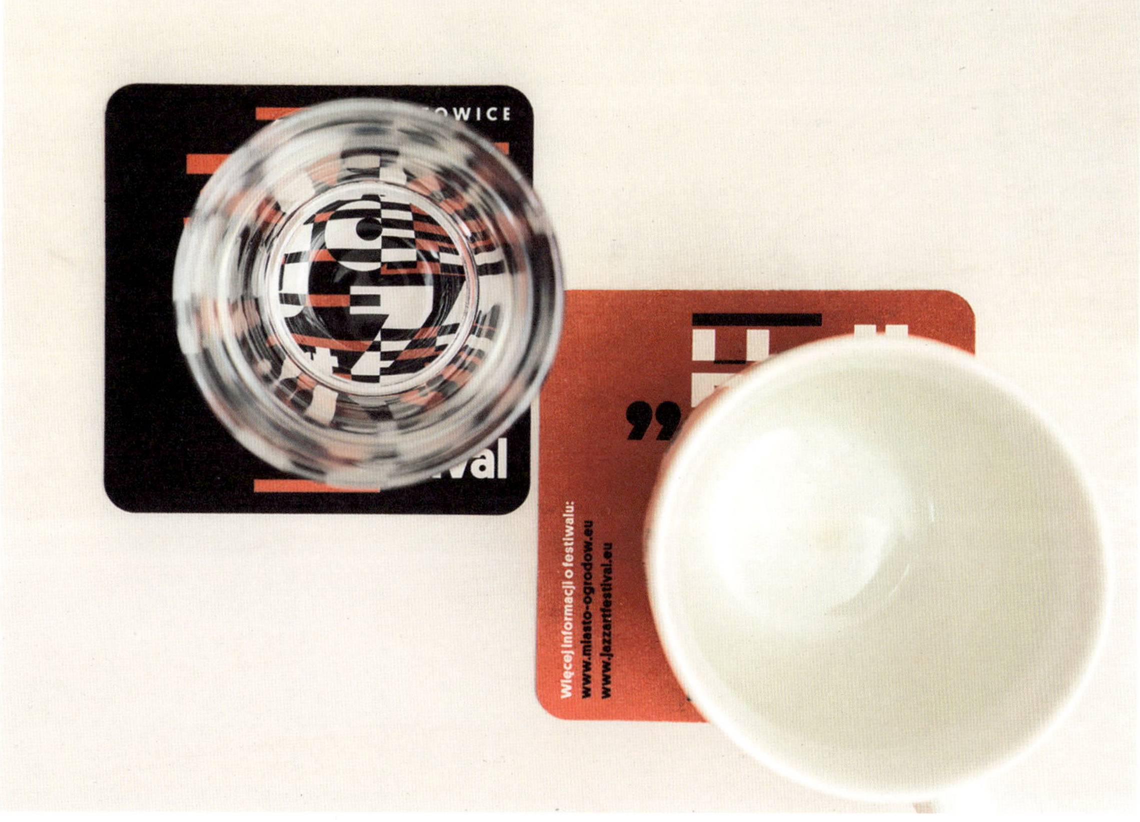
Więcej informacji o festiwalu:
www.miasto-ogrodow.eu
www.jazzartfestival.eu

# THE MAN WHO SAT ON HIMSELF

This is a design for the young curators programme at Fondazione Sandretto Re Rebaudengo, Torino, Italy. The designers collaborated with 3 curators of the programme, working on the exhibition design and the catalogue which was printed on high-gloss paper and contained artworks of 5 artists.

Studio: Studio Mut

Designer: Martin Kerschbaumer, Thomas Kronbichler

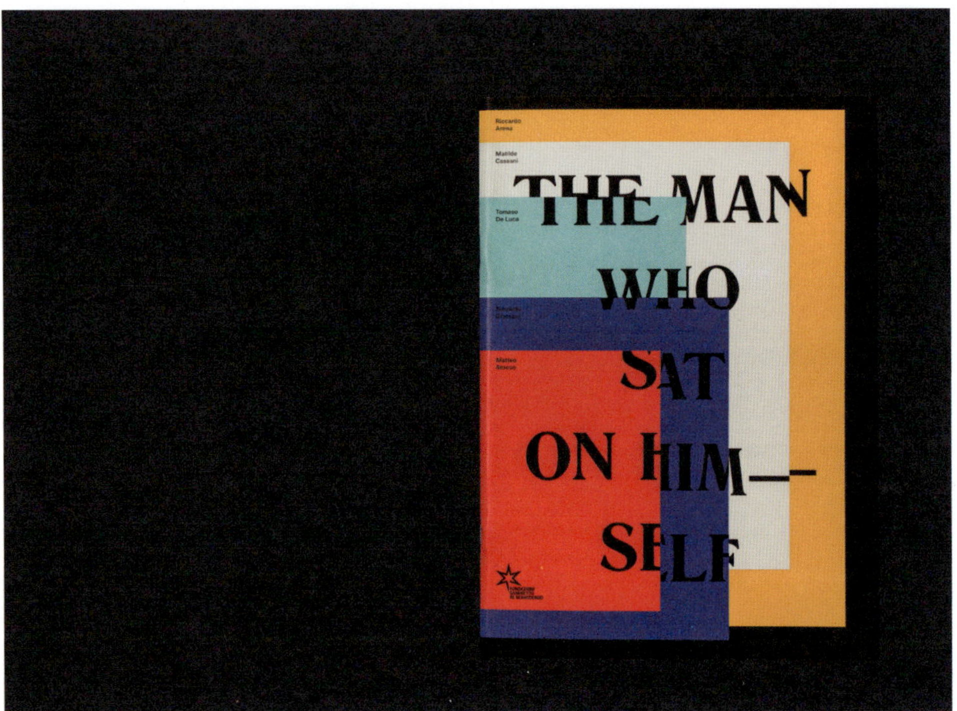


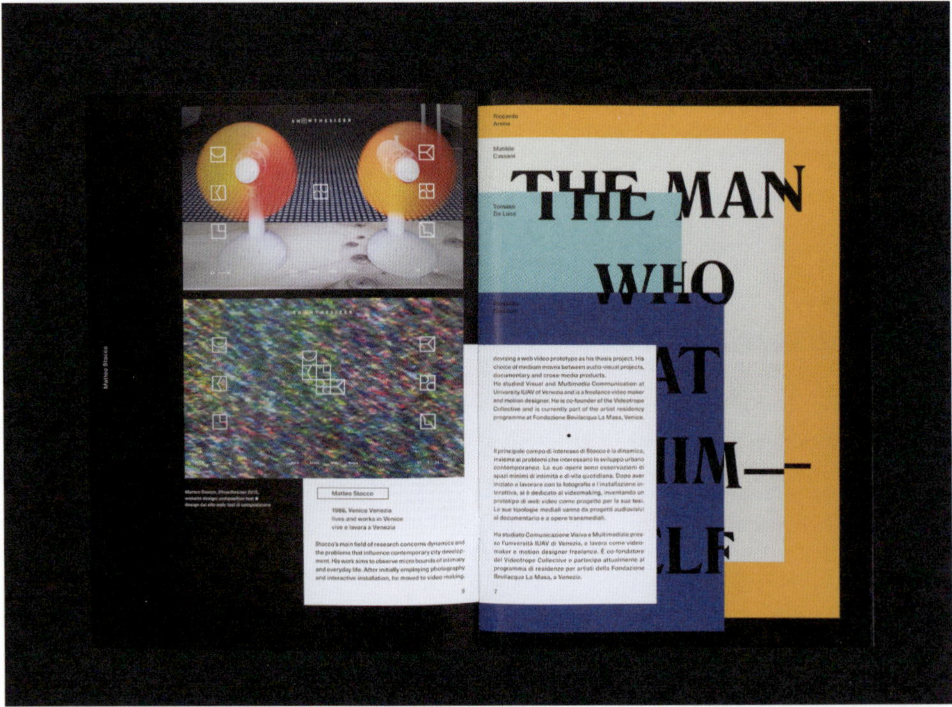

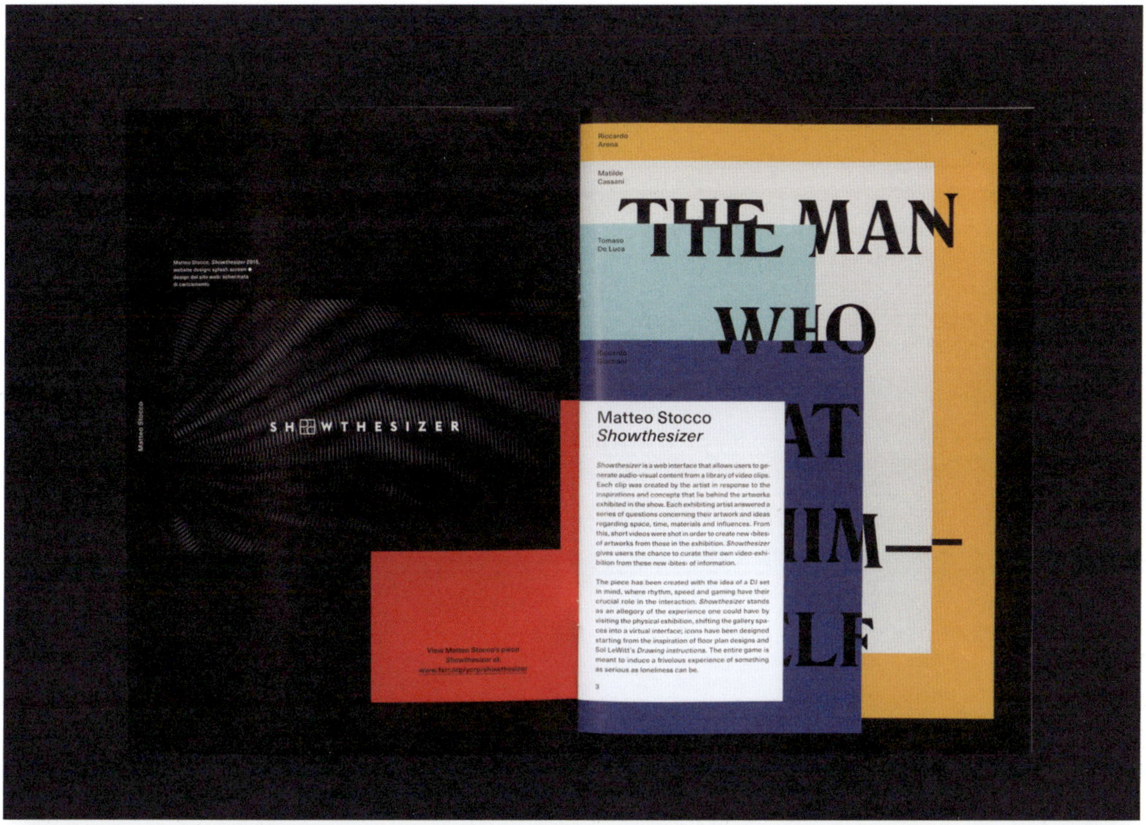

Riccardo
Arena

Matilde
Cassani

Tomaso
De Luca

# THE MAN WHO AT HIM— SELF

SH⊞WTHESIZER

Matteo Stocco

## Matteo Stocco
## *Showthesizer*

*Showthesizer* is a web interface that allows users to generate audio-visual content from a library of video clips. Each clip was created by the artist in response to the inspirations and concepts that lie behind the artworks exhibited in the show. Each exhibiting artist answered a series of questions concerning their artwork and ideas regarding space, time, materials and influences. From this, short videos were shot in order to create new ‹bites› of artworks from those in the exhibition. *Showthesizer* gives users the chance to curate their own video-exhibition from these new ‹bites› of information.

The piece has been created with the idea of a DJ set in mind, where rhythm, speed and gaming have their crucial role in the interaction. *Showthesizer* stands as an allegory of the experience one could have by visiting the physical exhibition, shifting the gallery spaces into a virtual interface; icons have been designed starting from the inspiration of floor plan designs and Sol LeWitt's *Drawing instructions*. The entire game is meant to induce a frivolous experience of something as serious as loneliness can be.

3

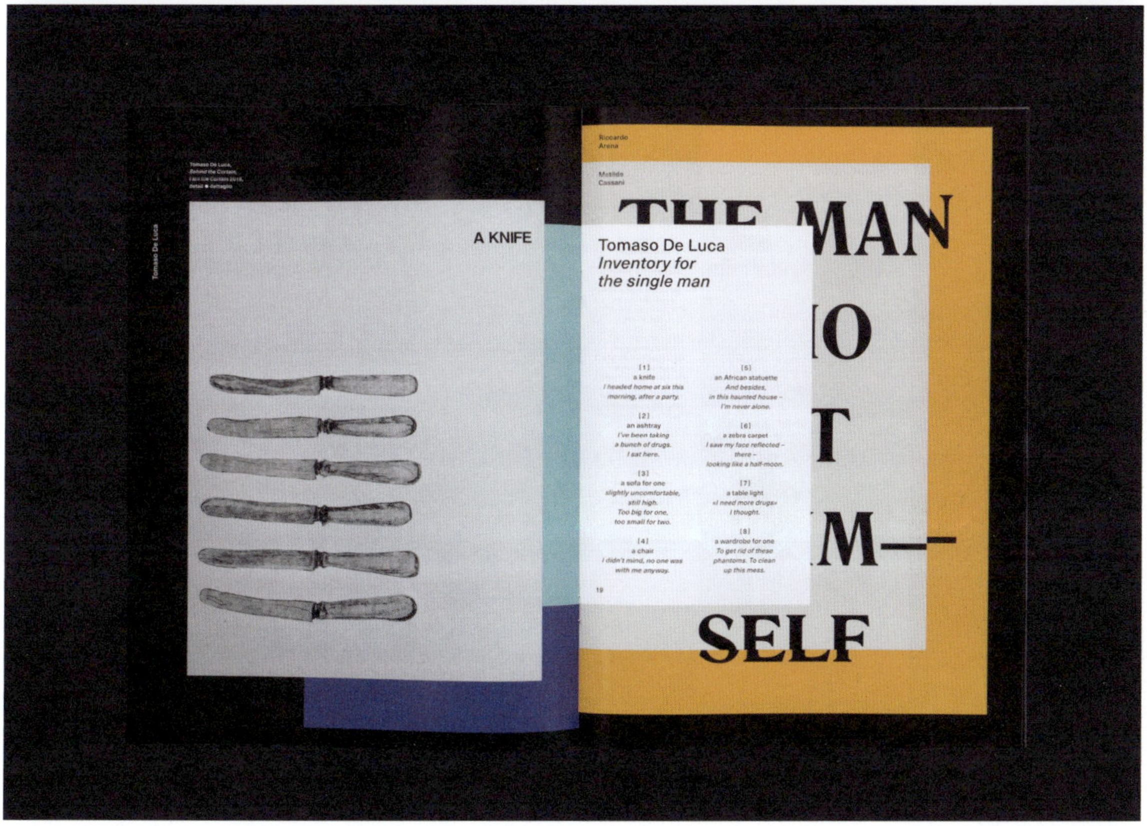

View Matteo Stocco's piece
*Showthesizer* at:
www.farr.org/ycrp/showthesizer

---

Tomaso De Luca

A KNIFE

Riccardo
Arena

Matilde
Cassani

## Tomaso De Luca
## *Inventory for the single man*

[1]
a knife
*I headed home at six this*
*morning, after a party.*

[2]
an ashtray
*I've been taking*
*a bunch of drugs.*
*I sat here.*

[3]
a sofa for one
*slightly uncomfortable,*
*still high.*
*Too big for one,*
*too small for two.*

[4]
a chair
*I didn't mind, no one was*
*with me anyway.*

[5]
an African statuette
*And besides,*
*in this haunted house –*
*I'm never alone.*

[6]
a zebra carpet
*I saw my face reflected –*
*there –*
*looking like a half-moon.*

[7]
a table light
*«I need more drugs»*
*I thought.*

[8]
a wardrobe for one
*To get rid of these*
*phantoms. To clean*
*up this mess.*

19

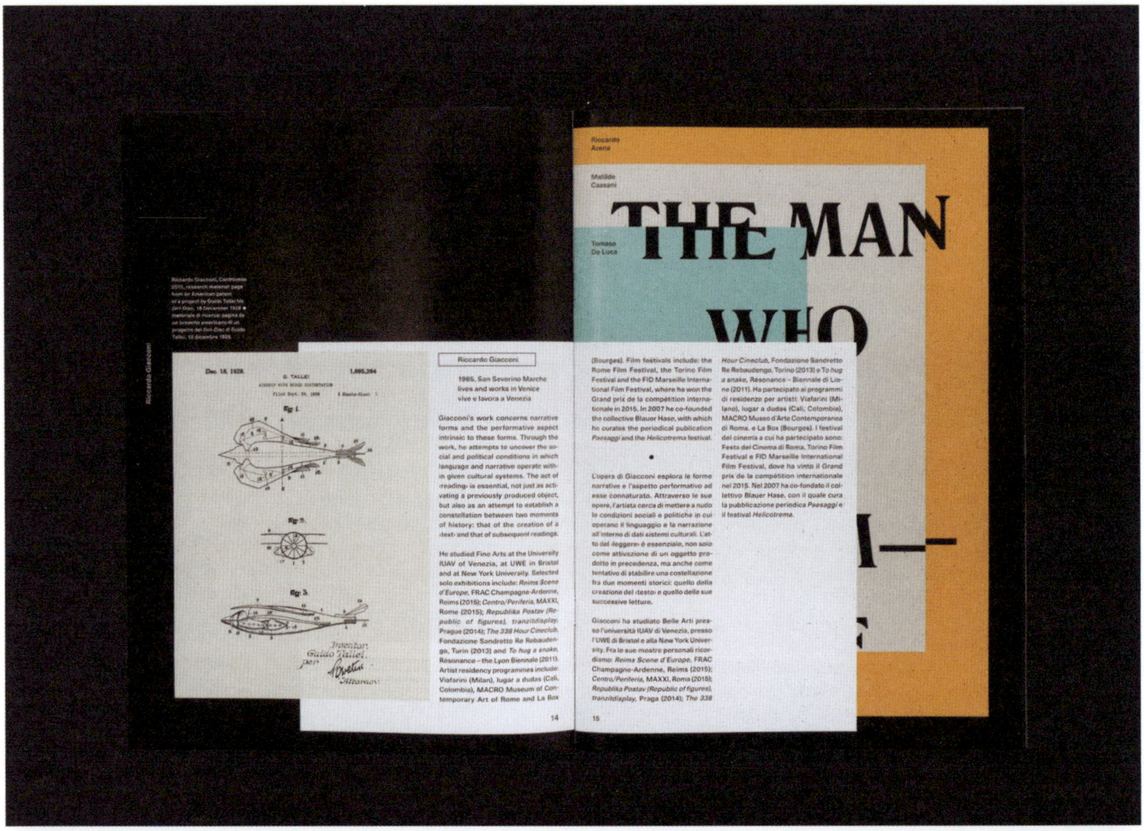

Riccardo Arena

Matilde Cassani

Tomaso De Luca

THE MAN WHO

Riccardo Giacconi

Riccardo Giacconi

1985, San Severino Marche
lives and works in Venice
vive e lavora a Venezia

Giacconi's work concerns narrative forms and the performative aspect intrinsic to these forms. Through the work, he attempts to uncover the social and political conditions in which language and narrative operate within given cultural systems. The act of ‹reading› is essential, not just as activating a previously produced object, but also as an attempt to establish a constellation between two moments of history: that of the creation of a ‹text› and that of subsequent readings.

He studied Fine Arts at the University IUAV of Venezia, at UWE in Bristol and at New York University. Selected solo exhibitions include: *Reims Scene d'Europe*, FRAC Champagne-Ardenne, Reims (2015); *Centro/Periferia*, MAXXI, Rome (2015); *Republika Postav (Republic of figures)*, *tranzitdisplay*, Prague (2014); *The 338 Hour Cineclub*, Fondazione Sandretto Re Rebaudengo, Turin (2013) and *To hug a snake*, Résonance – the Lyon Biennale (2011). Artist residency programmes include: Viafarini (Milan), lugar a dudas (Cali, Colombia), MACRO Museum of Contemporary Art of Rome and La Box (Bourges). Film festivals include: the Rome Film Festival, the Torino Film Festival and the FID Marseille International Film Festival, where he won the Grand prix de la compétition internationale in 2015. In 2007 he co-founded the collective Blauer Hase, with which he curates the periodical publication *Paesaggi* and the *Helicotrema* festival.

14

15

•

L'opera di Giacconi esplora le forme narrative e l'aspetto performativo ad esse connaturato. Attraverso le sue opere, l'artista cerca di mettere a nudo le condizioni sociali e politiche in cui operano il linguaggio e la narrazione all'interno di dati sistemi culturali. L'atto del ‹leggere› è essenziale, non solo come attivazione di un oggetto prodotto in precedenza, ma anche come tentativo di stabilire una costellazione fra due momenti storici: quello della creazione del ‹testo› e quello delle sue successive letture.

Giacconi ha studiato Belle Arti presso l'università IUAV di Venezia, presso l'UWE di Bristol e alla New York University. Fra le sue mostre personali ricordiamo: *Reims Scene d'Europe*, FRAC Champagne-Ardenne, Reims (2015); *Centro/Periferia*, MAXXI, Roma (2015); *Republika Postav (Republic of figures)*, *tranzitdisplay*, Praga (2014); *The 338 Hour Cineclub*, Fondazione Sandretto Re Rebaudengo, Torino (2013) e *To hug a snake*, Résonance – Biennale di Lione (2011). Ha partecipato ai programmi di residenze per artisti: Viafarini (Milano), lugar a dudas (Cali, Colombia), MACRO Museo d'Arte Contemporanea di Roma, e La Box (Bourges). I festival del cinema a cui ha partecipato sono: Festa del Cinema di Roma, Torino Film Festival e FID Marseille International Film Festival, dove ha vinto il Grand prix de la compétition internationale nel 2015. Nel 2007 ha co-fondato il collettivo Blauer Hase, con il quale cura la pubblicazione periodica *Paesaggi* e il festival *Helicotrema*.

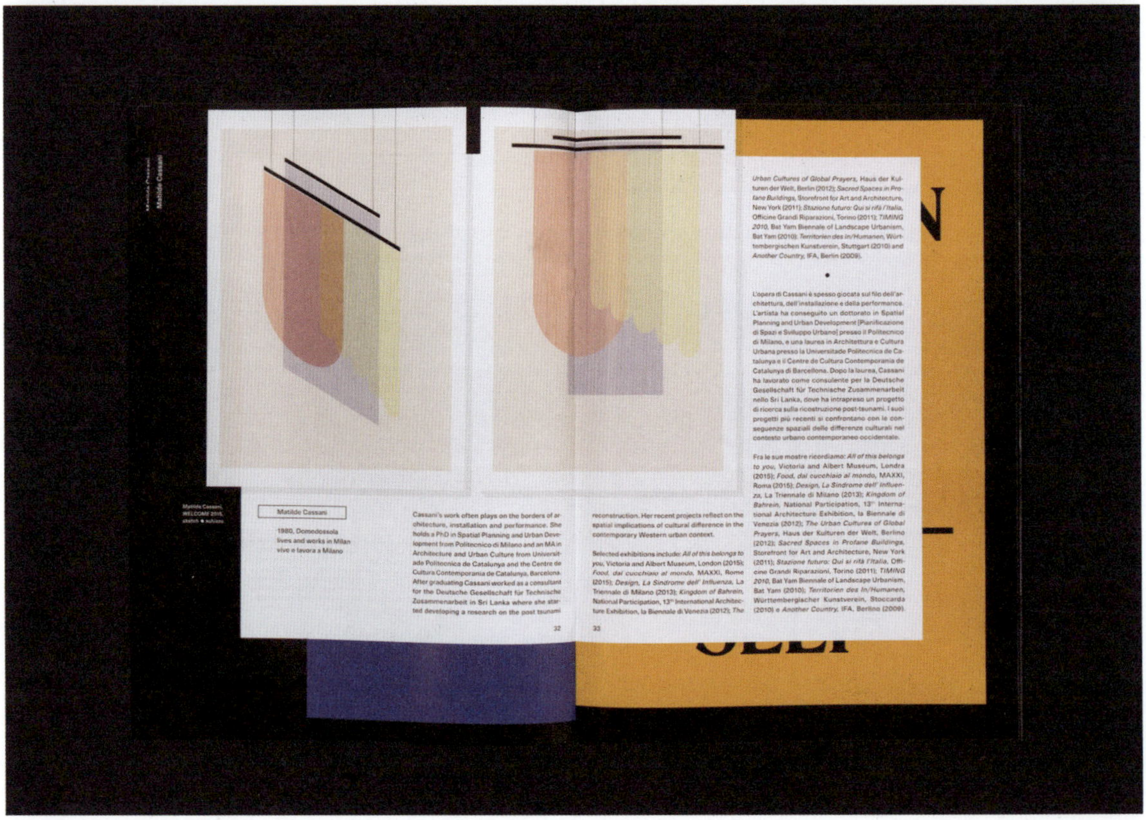

Matilde Cassani

Matilde Cassani, WELCOME 2015, sketch ● schizzo

Matilde Cassani

1980, Domodossola
lives and works in Milan
vive e lavora a Milano

Cassani's work often plays on the borders of architecture, installation and performance. She holds a PhD in Spatial Planning and Urban Development from Politecnico di Milano and an MA in Architecture and Urban Culture from Universitade Politecnica de Catalunya and the Centre de Cultura Contemporania de Catalunya, Barcelona. After graduating Cassani worked as a consultant for the Deutsche Gesellschaft für Technische Zusammenarbeit in Sri Lanka where she started developing a research on the post tsunami reconstruction. Her recent projects reflect on the spatial implications of cultural difference in the contemporary Western urban context.

Selected exhibitions include: *All of this belongs to you*, Victoria and Albert Museum, London (2015); *Food, dal cucchiaio al mondo*, MAXXI, Rome (2015); *Design, La Sindrome dell' Influenza*, La Triennale di Milano (2013); *Kingdom of Bahrein*, National Participation, 13th International Architecture Exhibition, la Biennale di Venezia (2012); *The Urban Cultures of Global Prayers*, Haus der Kulturen der Welt, Berlin (2012); *Sacred Spaces in Profane Buildings*, Storefront for Art and Architecture, New York (2011); *Stazione futuro: Qui si rifà l'Italia*, Officine Grandi Riparazioni, Torino (2011); *TIMING 2010*, Bat Yam Biennale of Landscape Urbanism, Bat Yam (2010); *Territorien des In/Humanen*, Württembergischen Kunstverein, Stuttgart (2010) and *Another Country*, IFA, Berlin (2009).

32

33

•

L'opera di Cassani è spesso giocata sul filo dell'architettura, dell'installazione e della performance. L'artista ha conseguito un dottorato in Spatial Planning and Urban Development [Pianificazione di Spazi e Sviluppo Urbano] presso il Politecnico di Milano, e una laurea in Architettura e Cultura Urbana presso la Universitade Politecnica de Catalunya e il Centre de Cultura Contemporania de Catalunya di Barcellona. Dopo la laurea, Cassani ha lavorato come consulente per la Deutsche Gesellschaft für Technische Zusammenarbeit nello Sri Lanka, dove ha intrapreso un progetto di ricerca sulla ricostruzione post-tsunami. I suoi progetti più recenti si confrontano con le conseguenze spaziali delle differenze culturali nel contesto urbano contemporaneo occidentale.

Fra le sue mostre ricordiamo: *All of this belongs to you*, Victoria and Albert Museum, Londra (2015); *Food, dal cucchiaio al mondo*, MAXXI, Roma (2015); *Design, La Sindrome dell' Influenza*, La Triennale di Milano (2013); *Kingdom of Bahrein*, National Participation, 13th International Architecture Exhibition, la Biennale di Venezia (2012); *The Urban Cultures of Global Prayers*, Haus der Kulturen der Welt, Berlino (2012); *Sacred Spaces in Profane Buildings*, Storefront for Art and Architecture, New York (2011); *Stazione futuro: Qui si rifà l'Italia*, Officine Grandi Riparazioni, Torino (2011); *TIMING 2010*, Bat Yam Biennale of Landscape Urbanism, Bat Yam (2010); *Territorien des In/Humanen*, Württembergischer Kunstverein, Stoccarda (2010) e *Another Country*, IFA, Berlino (2009).

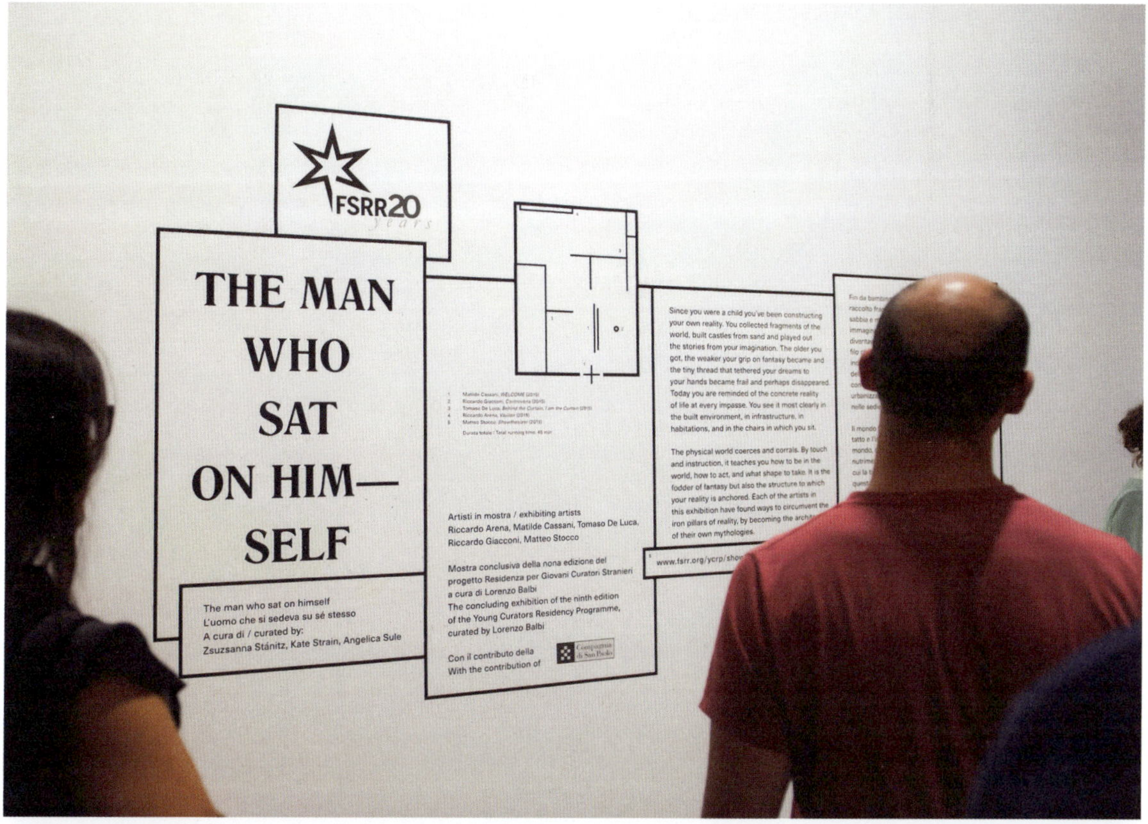

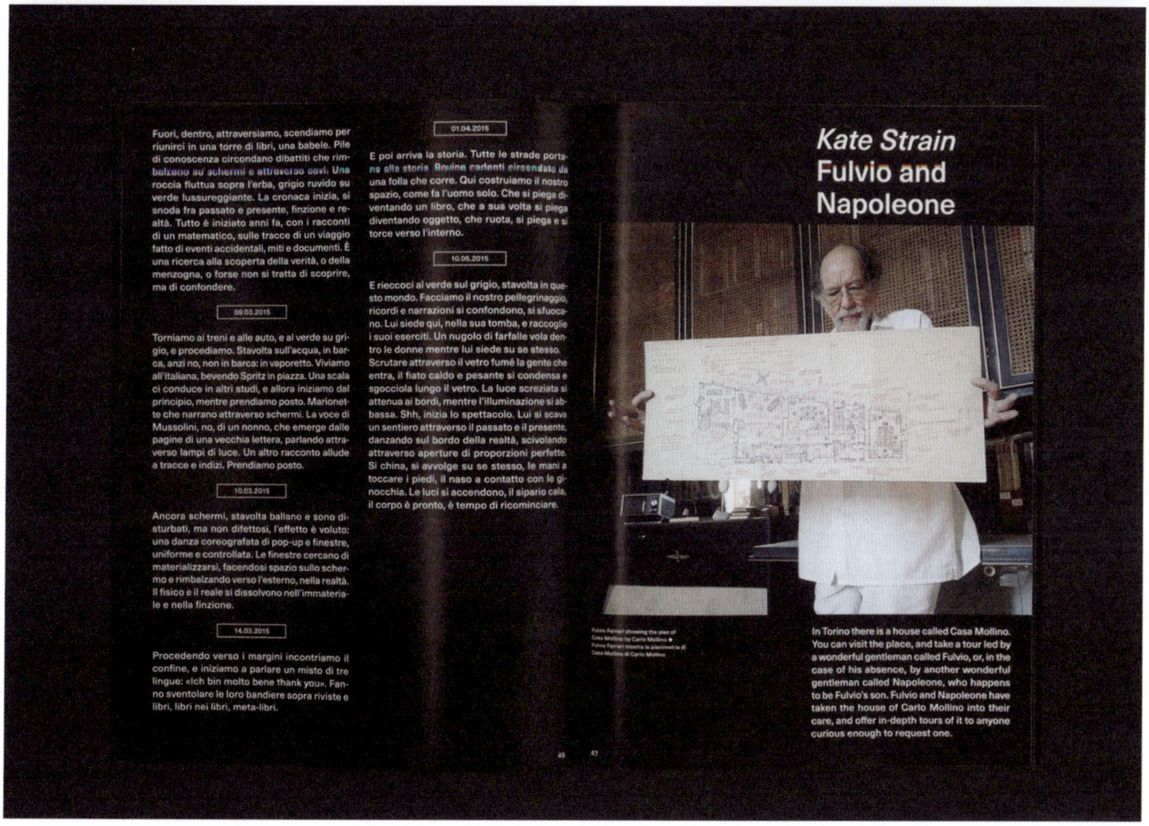

THE MAN WHO SAT ON HIM— SELF

The man who sat on himself
L'uomo che si sedeva su sé stesso
A cura di / curated by:
Zsuzsanna Stánitz, Kate Strain, Angelica Sule

Artisti in mostra / exhibiting artists
Riccardo Arena, Matilde Cassani, Tomaso De Luca, Riccardo Giacconi, Matteo Stocco

Mostra conclusiva della nona edizione del progetto Residenza per Giovani Curatori Stranieri a cura di Lorenzo Balbi
The concluding exhibition of the ninth edition of the Young Curators Residency Programme, curated by Lorenzo Balbi

Con il contributo della
With the contribution of

Fuori, dentro, attraversiamo, scendiamo per riunirci in una torre di libri, una babele. Pile di conoscenza circondano dibattiti che rimbalzano su schermi e attraverso cavi. Una roccia fluttua sopra l'erba, grigio ruvido su verde lussureggiante. La cronaca inizia, si snoda fra passato e presente, finzione e realtà. Tutto è iniziato anni fa, con i racconti di un matematico, sulle tracce di un viaggio fatto di eventi accidentali, miti e documenti. È una ricerca alla scoperta della verità, o della menzogna, o forse non si tratta di scoprire, ma di confondere.

09.03.2015

Torniamo ai treni e alle auto, e al verde su grigio, e procediamo. Stavolta sull'acqua, in barca, anzi no, non in barca: in vaporetto. Viviamo all'italiana, bevendo Spritz in piazza. Una scala ci conduce in altri studi, e allora iniziamo dal principio, mentre prendiamo posto. Marionette che narrano attraverso schermi. La voce di Mussolini, no, di un nonno, che emerge dalle pagine di una vecchia lettera, parlando attraverso lampi di luce. Un altro racconto allude a tracce e indizi. Prendiamo posto.

10.03.2015

Ancora schermi, stavolta ballano e sono disturbati, ma non difettosi, l'effetto è voluto: una danza coreografata di pop-up e finestre, uniforme e controllata. Le finestre cercano di materializzarsi, facendosi spazio sullo schermo e rimbalzando verso l'esterno, nella realtà. Il fisico e il reale si dissolvono nell'immateriale e nella finzione.

14.03.2015

Procedendo verso i margini incontriamo il confine, e iniziamo a parlare un misto di tre lingue: «Ich bin molto bene thank you». Fanno sventolare le loro bandiere sopra riviste e libri, libri nei libri, meta-libri.

01.04.2015

E poi arriva la storia. Tutte le strade portano alla storia. Rovine cadenti circondate da una folla che corre. Qui costruiamo il nostro spazio, come fa l'uomo solo. Che si piega diventando un libro, che a sua volta si piega diventando oggetto, che ruota, si piega e si torce verso l'interno.

10.05.2015

E rieccoci al verde sul grigio, stavolta in questo mondo. Facciamo il nostro pellegrinaggio, ricordi e narrazioni si confondono, si sfuocano. Lui siede qui, nella sua tomba, e raccoglie i suoi eserciti. Un nugolo di farfalle vola dentro le donne mentre lui siede su se stesso. Scrutare attraverso il vetro fumé la gente che entra, il fiato caldo e pesante si condensa e sgocciola lungo il vetro. La luce screziata si attenua ai bordi, mentre l'illuminazione si abbassa. Shh, inizia lo spettacolo. Lui si scava un sentiero attraverso il passato e il presente, danzando sul bordo della realtà, scivolando attraverso aperture di proporzioni perfette. Si china, si avvolge su se stesso, le mani a toccare i piedi, il naso a contatto con le ginocchia. Le luci si accendono, il sipario cala, il corpo è pronto, è tempo di ricominciare.

## *Kate Strain* Fulvio and Napoleone

In Torino there is a house called Casa Mollino. You can visit the place, and take a tour led by a wonderful gentleman called Fulvio, or, in the case of his absence, by another wonderful gentleman called Napoleone, who happens to be Fulvio's son. Fulvio and Napoleone have taken the house of Carlo Mollino into their care, and offer in-depth tours of it to anyone curious enough to request one.

# OMM PHOTOGRAPHIC HOURS

The second issue of FTN was focused on photography. The selected prominent photographers were separated into four parts. Each of them represented the personalized life attitude of a city and the relationship between his or her aesthetic impressions and the city.

Designer: Kristine H. Kawakubo

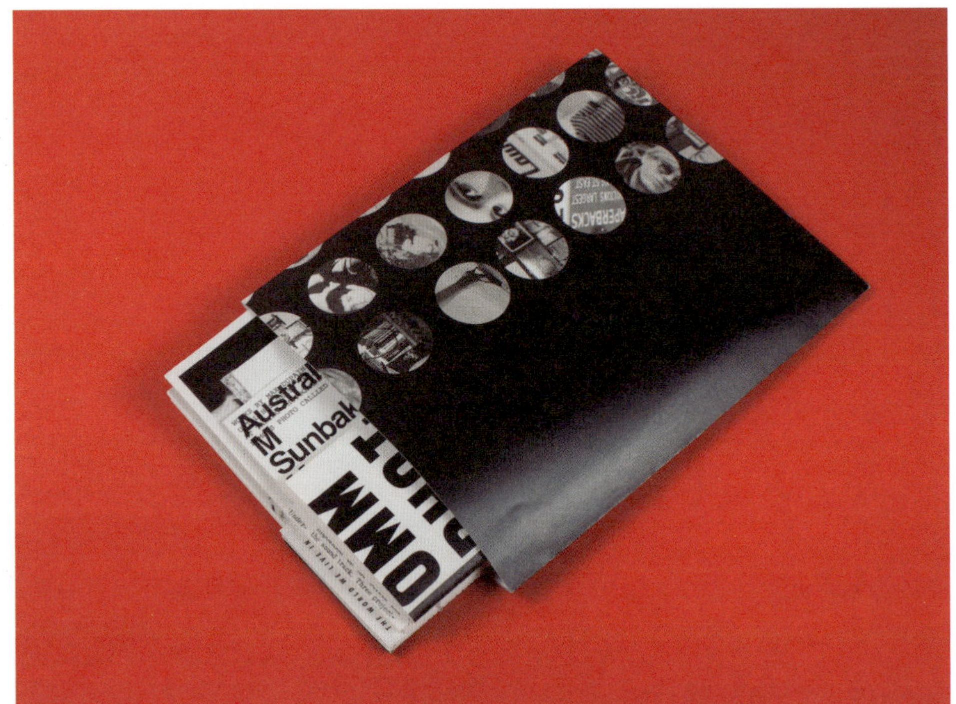


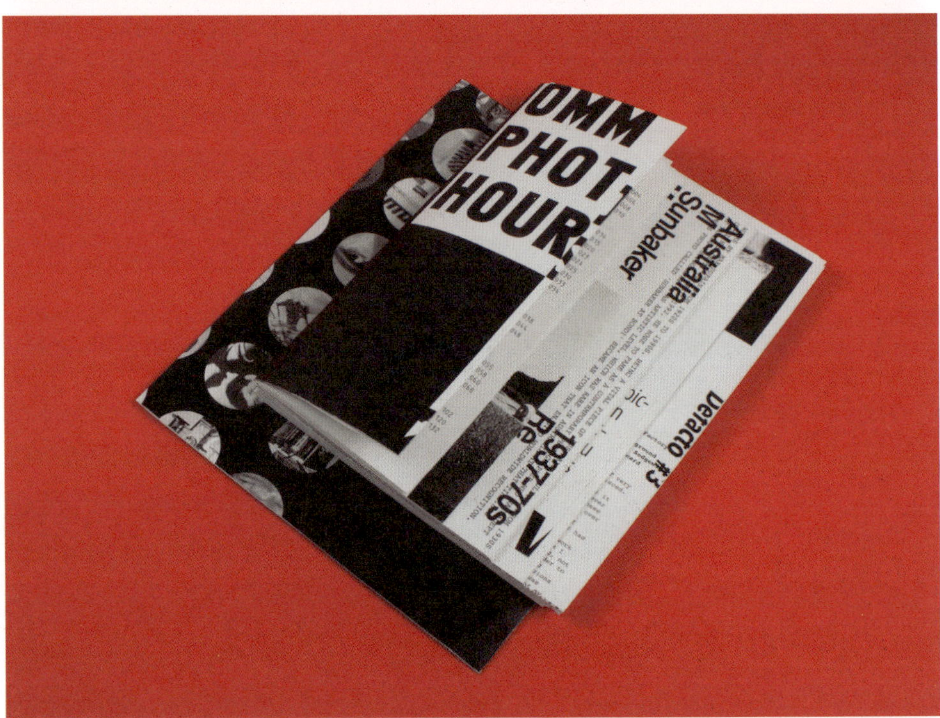

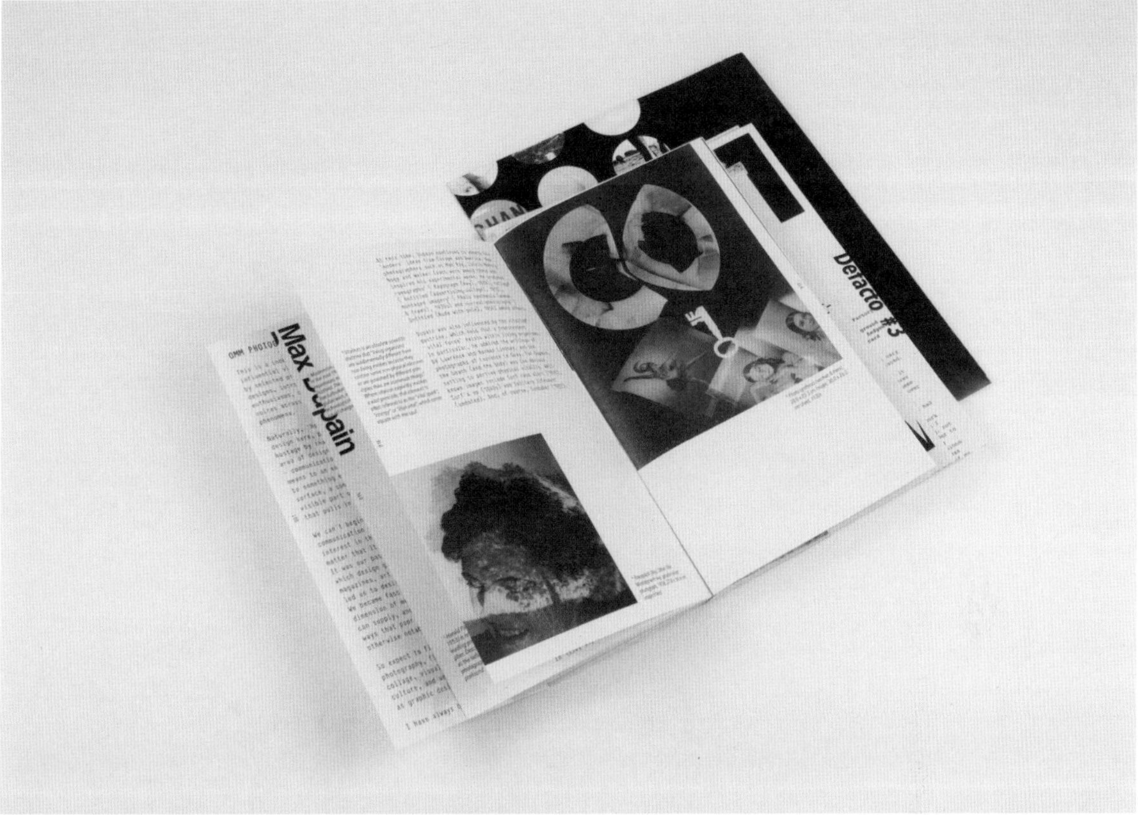

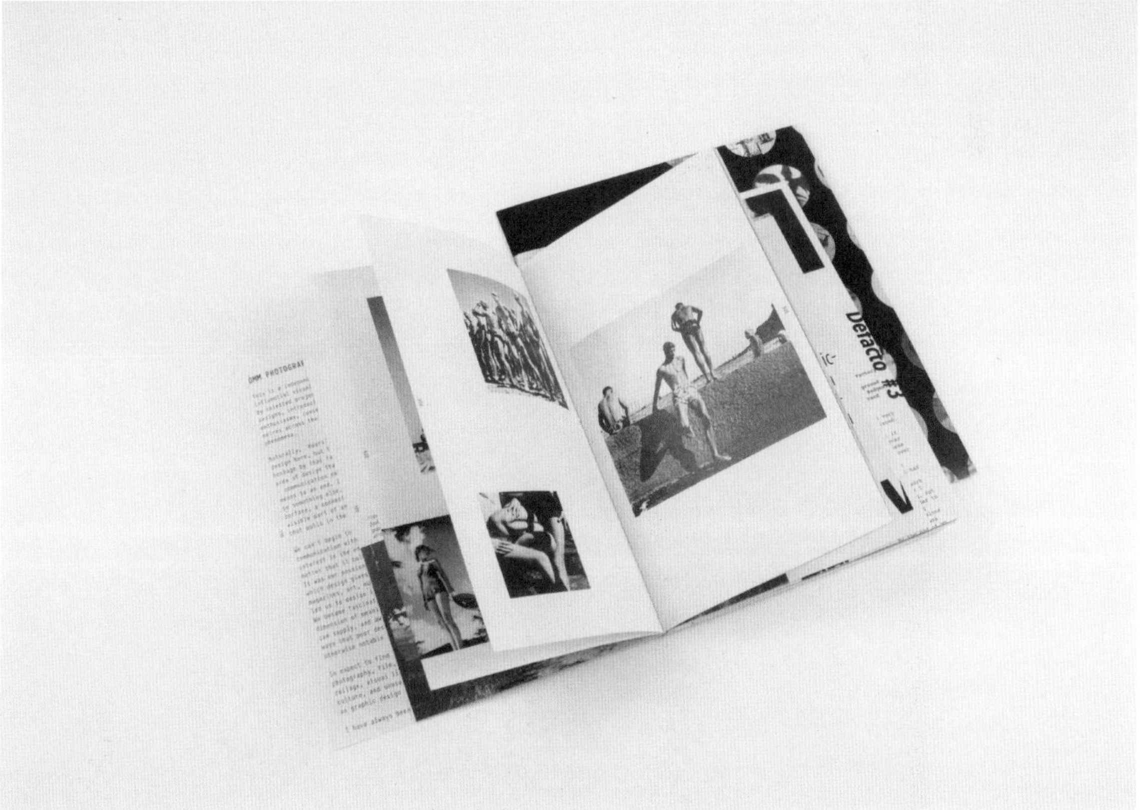

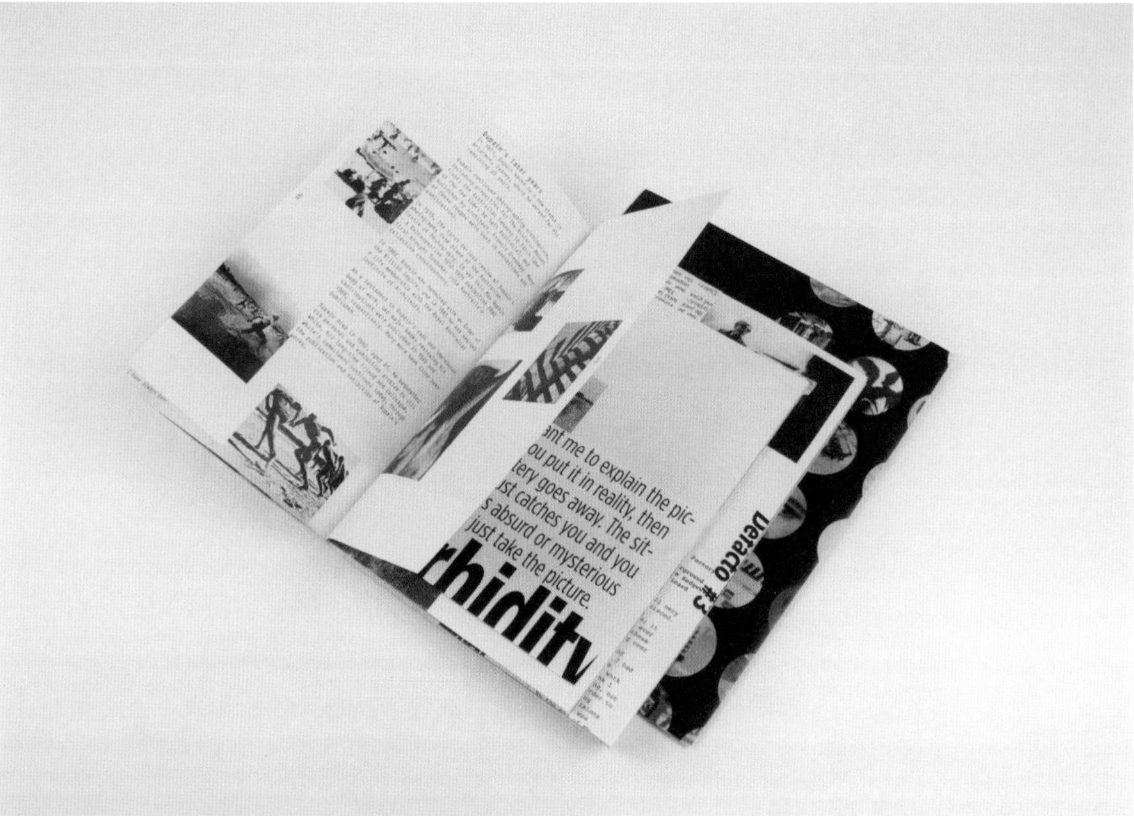

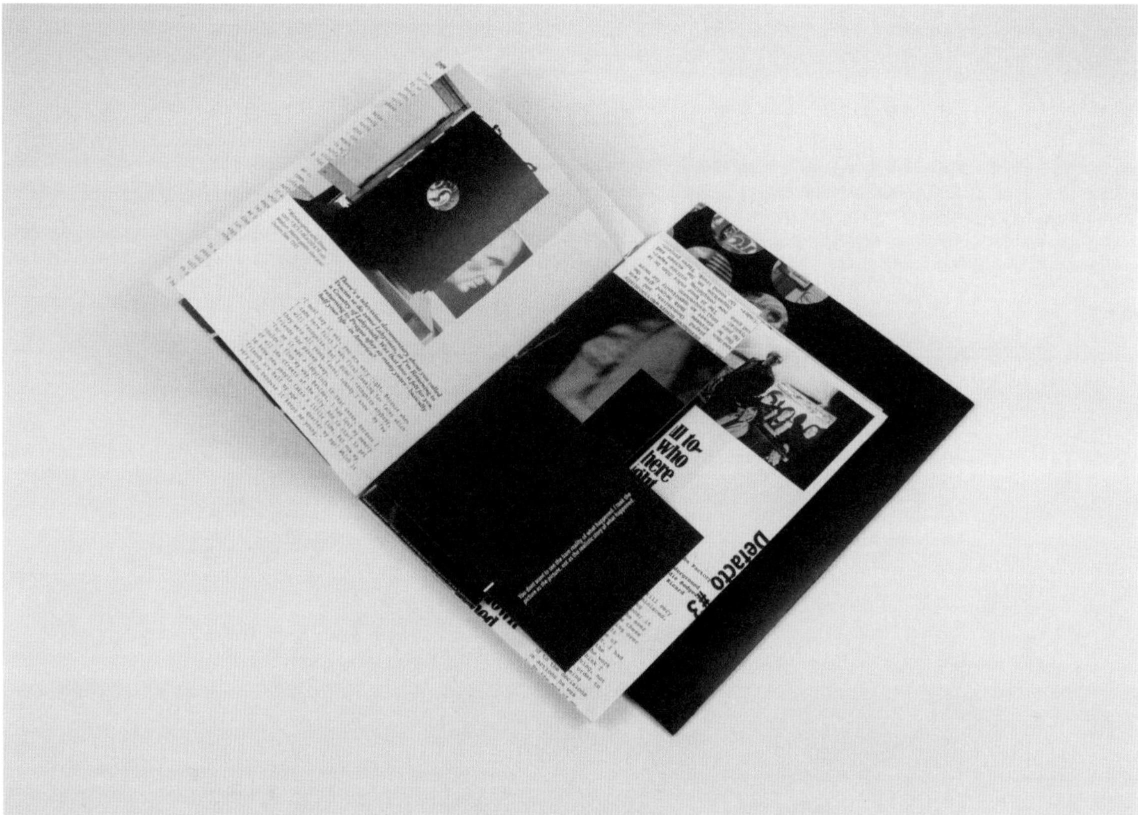

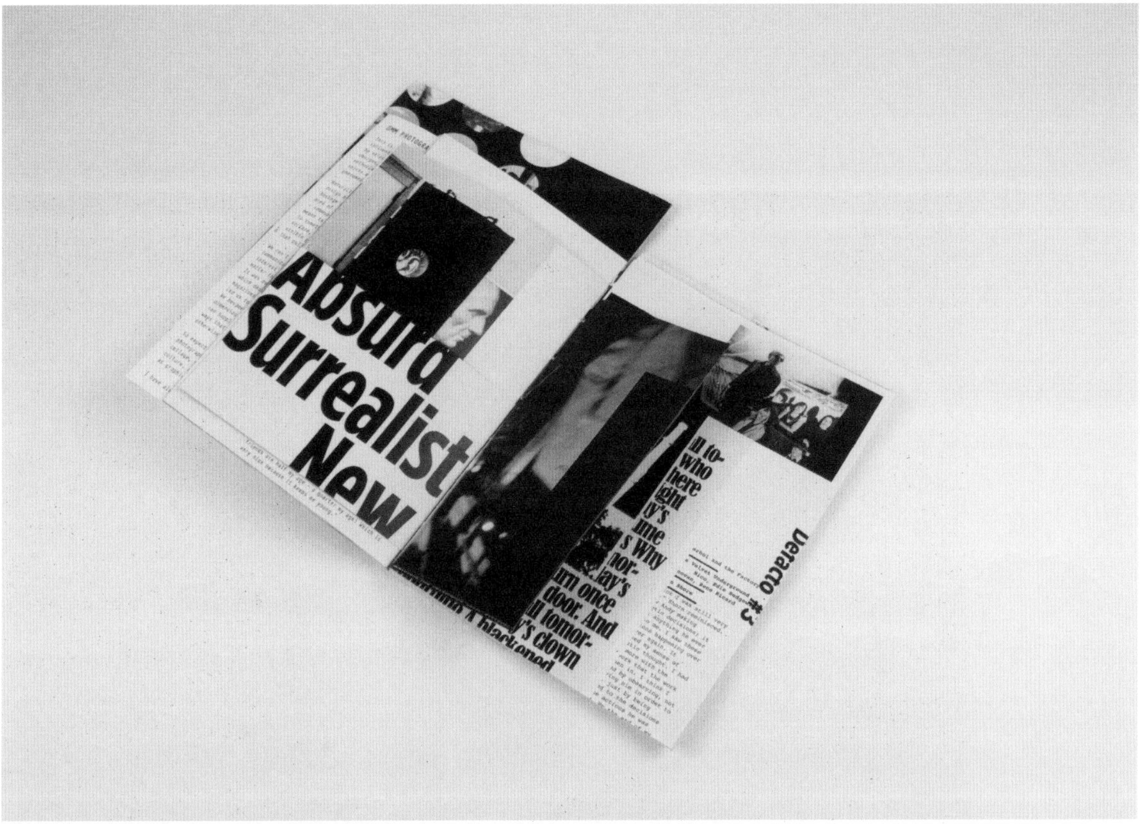

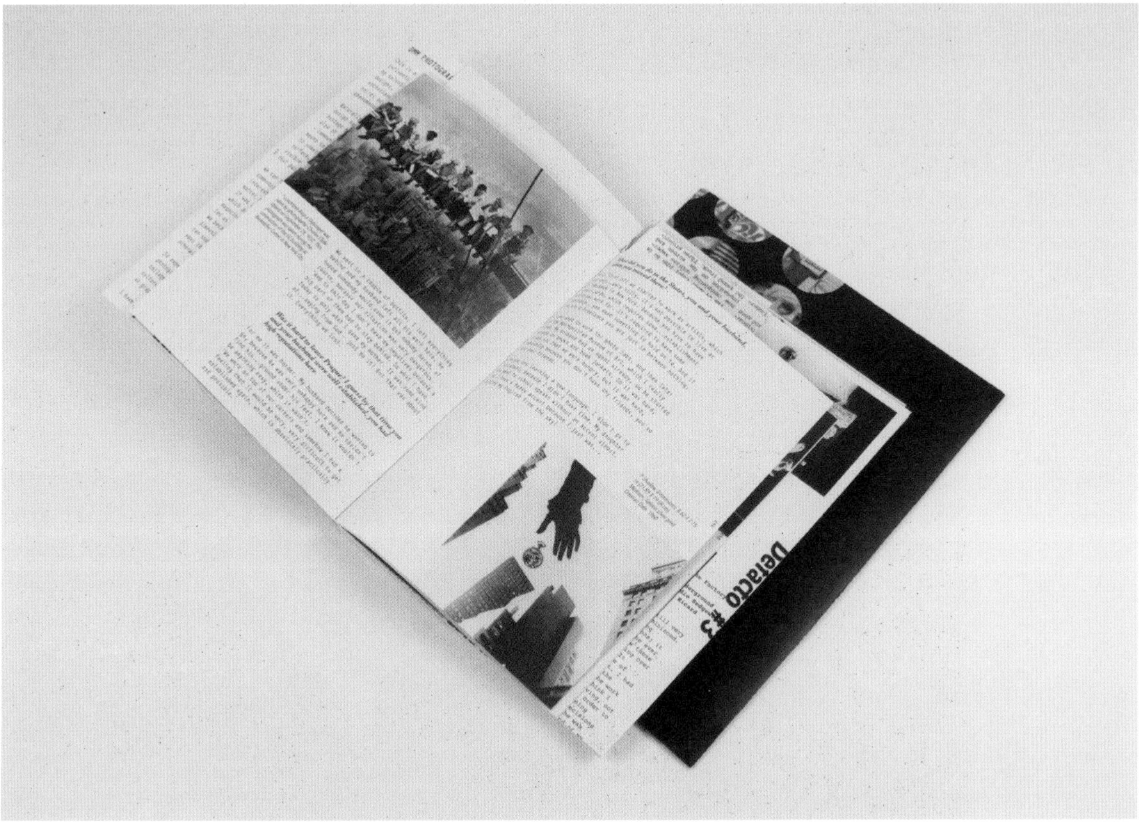

# VOLUME.3

*Volume.3* is a personal portfolio consisting of selected representative projects. The chapters are based on the different aspects of art, design and social issues, such as the discussions of post-modernism among artists and designers.

Designer: Kristine H. Kawakubo

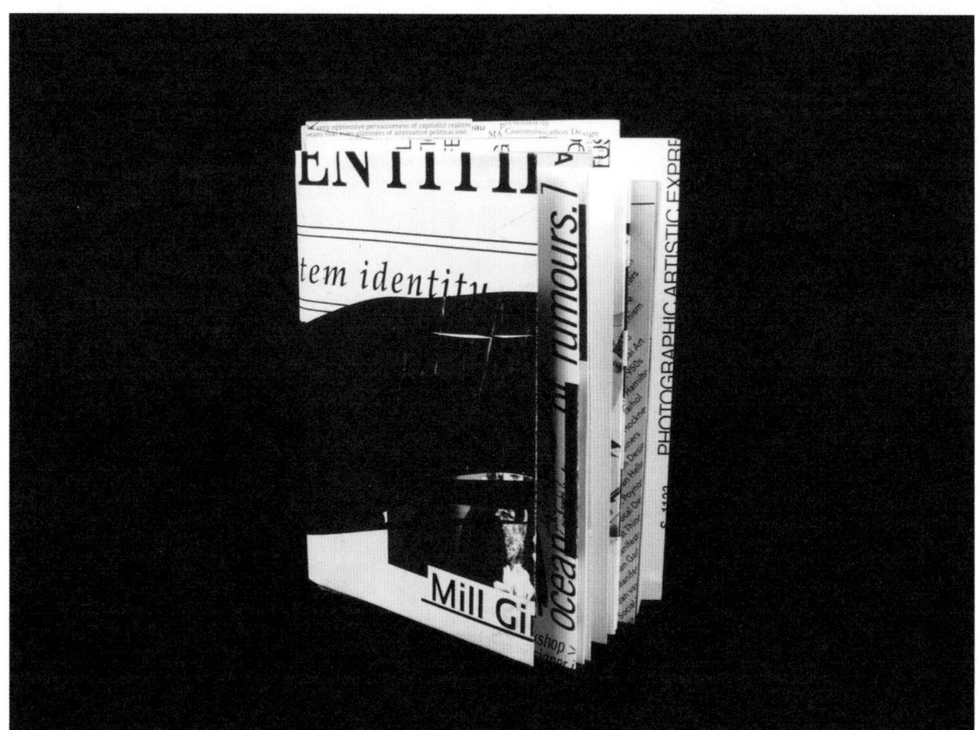

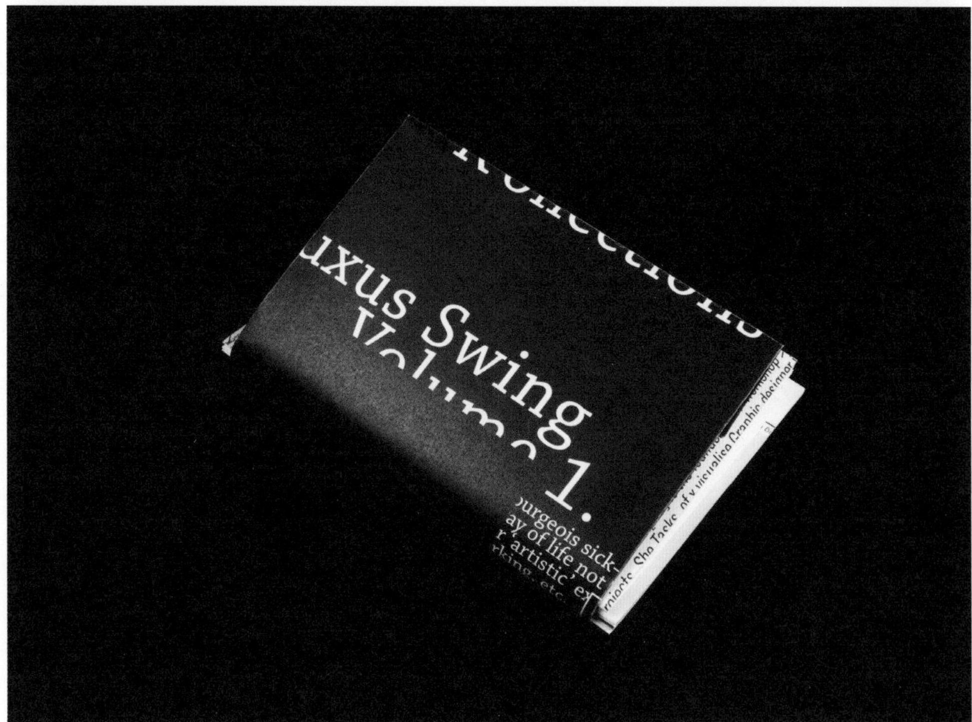

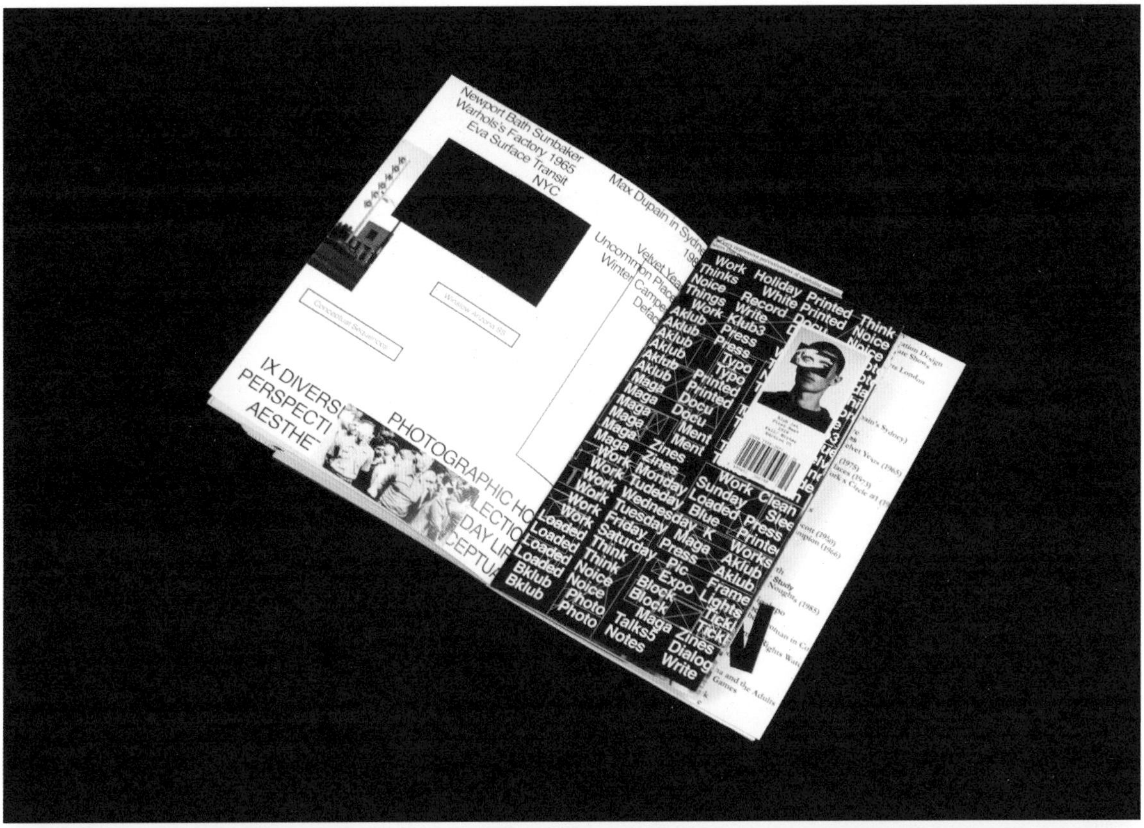
Newport Bath Sunbaker
Warhols's Factory 1965
Eva Surface Transit
NYC
PHOTOGRAPHIC
Work Holiday Printed Think
Thinks White Printed Noice
Work Clean
Sunday Loaded Press
Work Tudeday
Work Wednesday
Work Tuesday
Friday Maga
Saturday Press
Talks5 Notes
Maga Zines
Dialog
Write

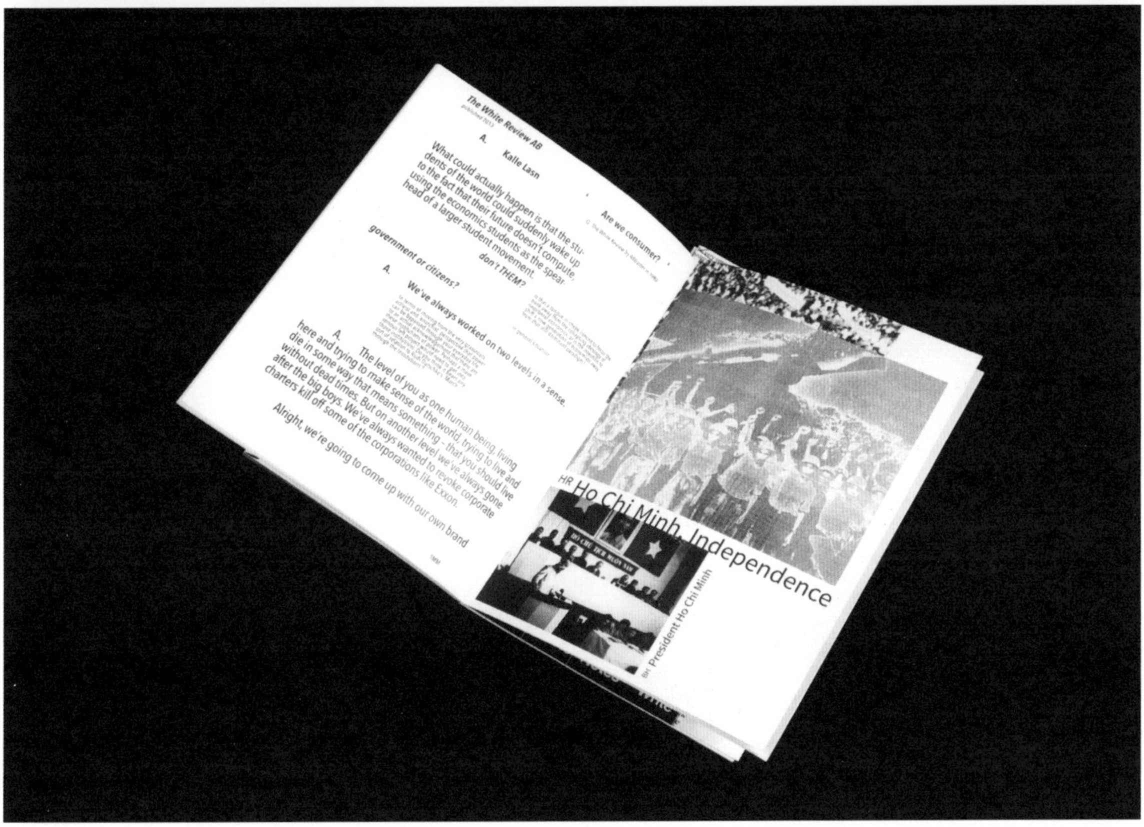
The White Review AB
A. Kalle Lasn
What could actually happen is that the students of the world could suddenly wake up to the fact that their future doesn't compute, using the economics students as the spearhead of a larger student movement.
Are we consumer?
don't THEM?
government or citizens?
A. We've always worked on two levels in a sense.
A. The level of you as one human being, living here and trying to make sense of the world, trying to live and die in some way that means something – that you should live without dead times. But on another level we've always gone after the big boys. We've always wanted to revoke corporate charters kill off some of the corporations like Exxon.
Alright, we're going to come up with our own brand
HR Ho Chi Minh, Independence
President Ho Chi Minh

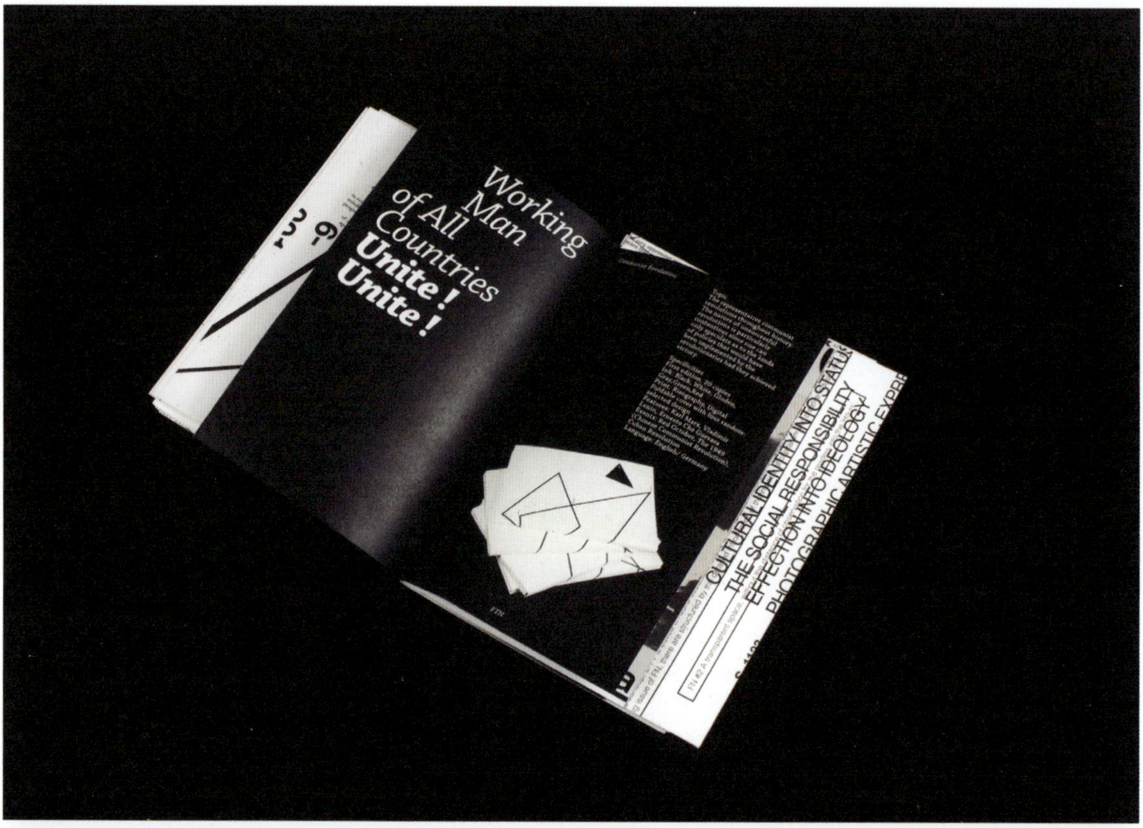

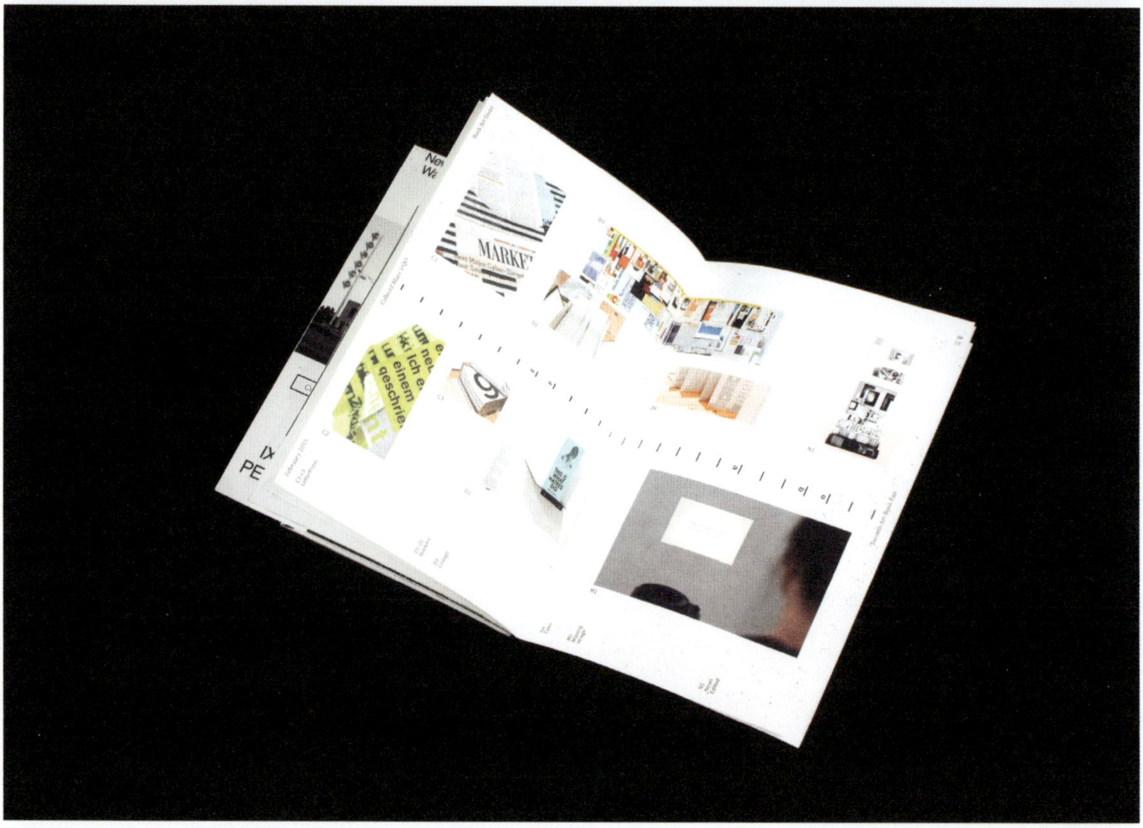

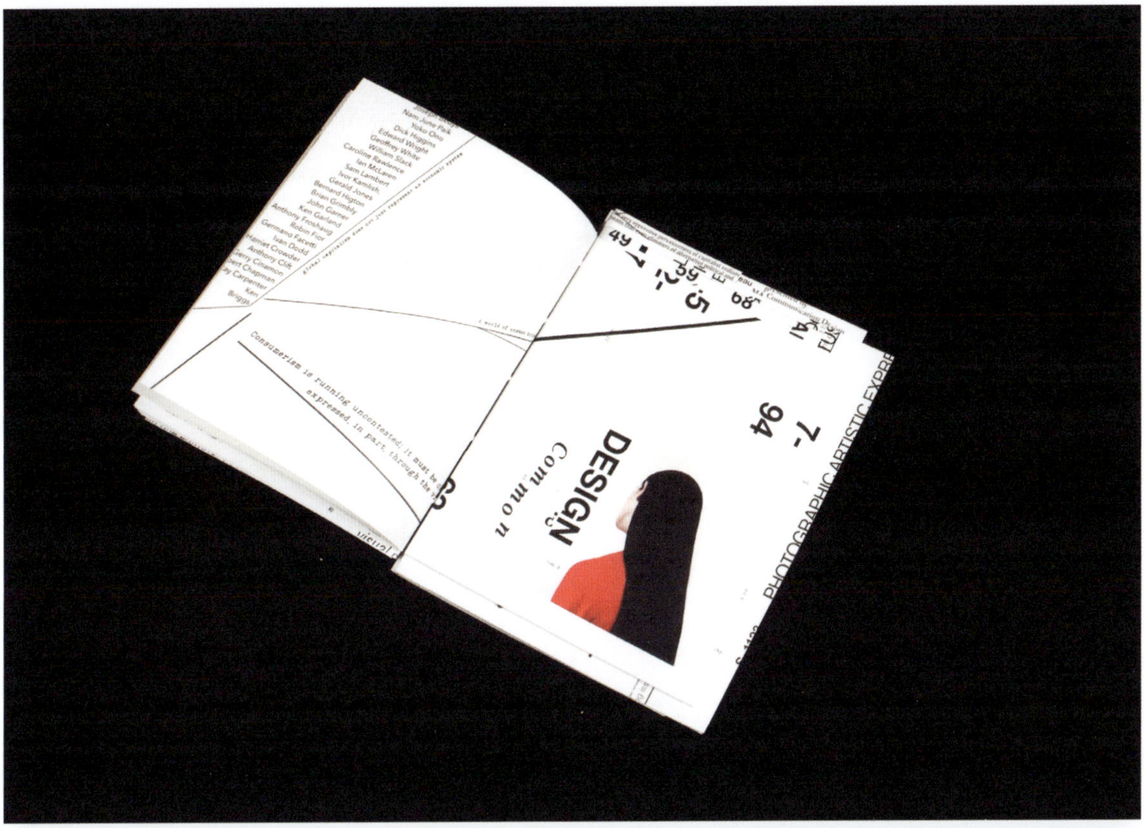

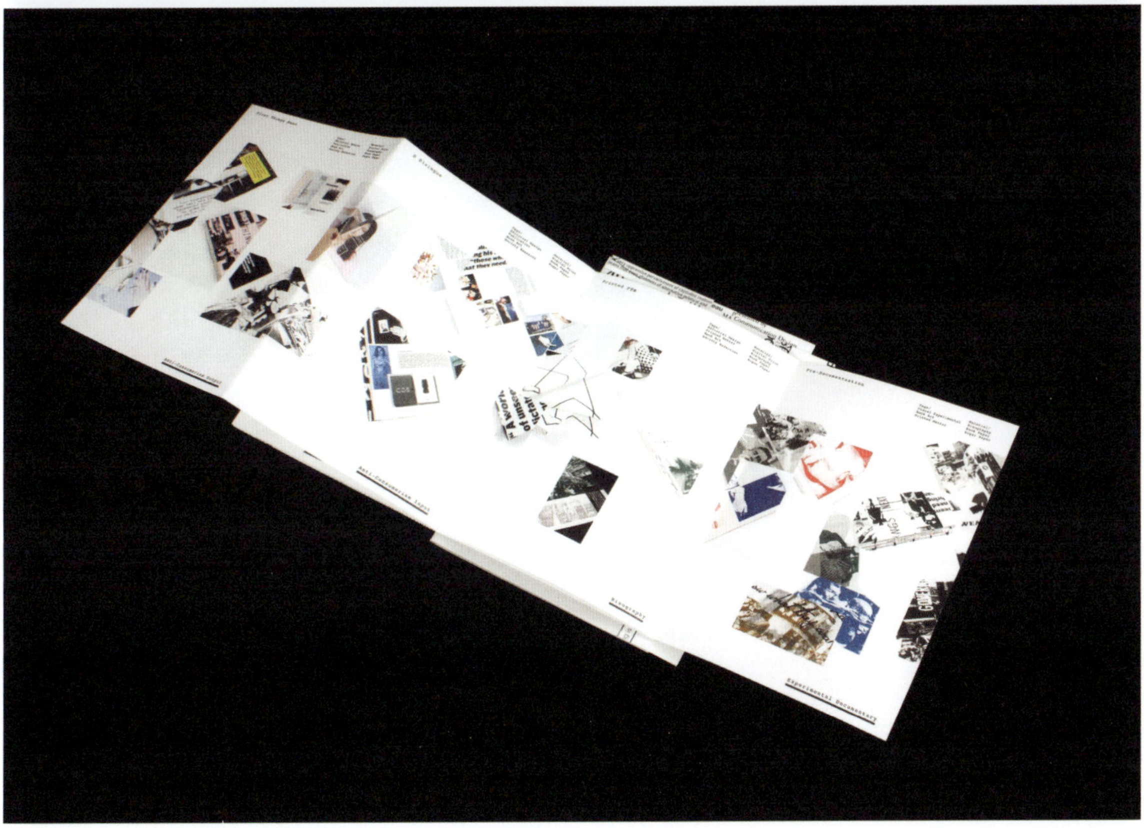

# FT#1

"FT" (First and Next) was inspired by the prominent historical manifesto "First Things First 1964". The concept of "FT" is based on the contemporary debatable visual issues related to art, design, music and public social issues.

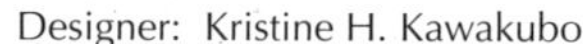
Designer: Kristine H. Kawakubo

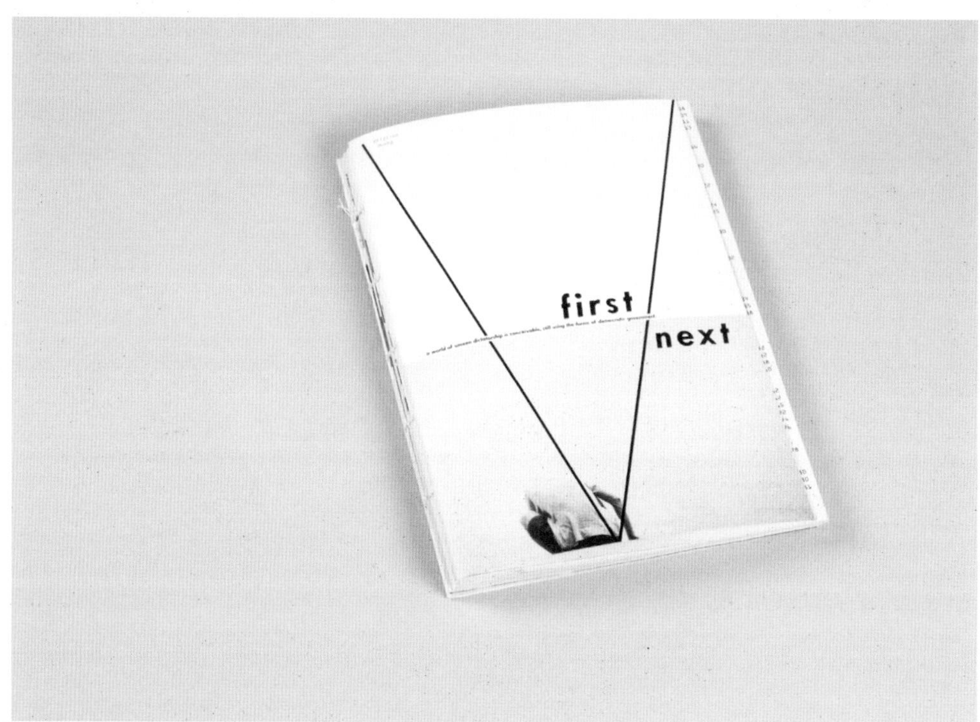


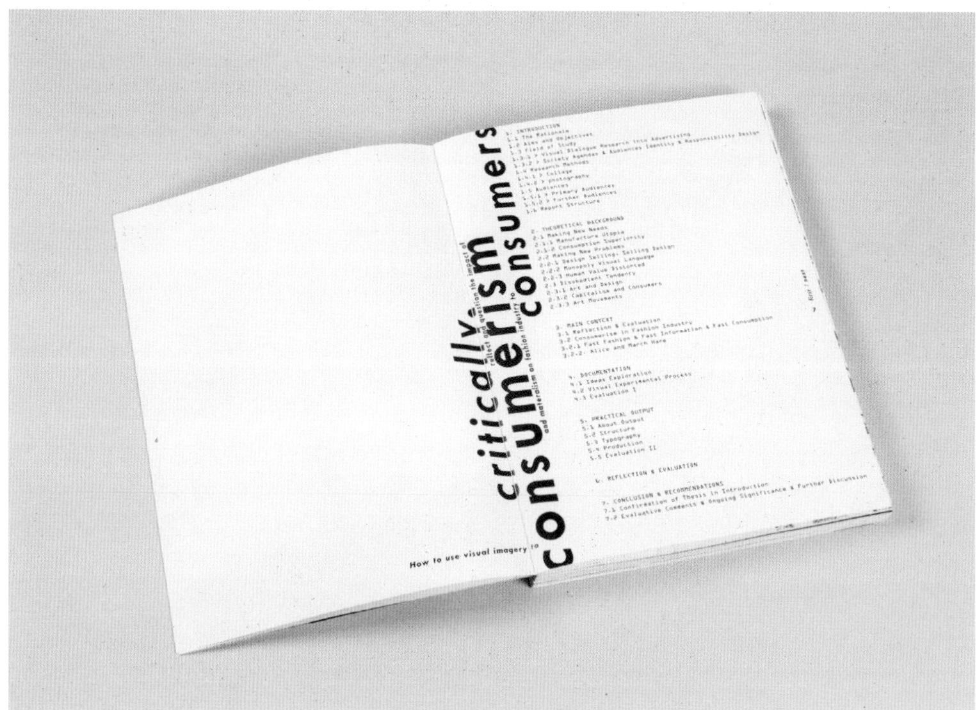

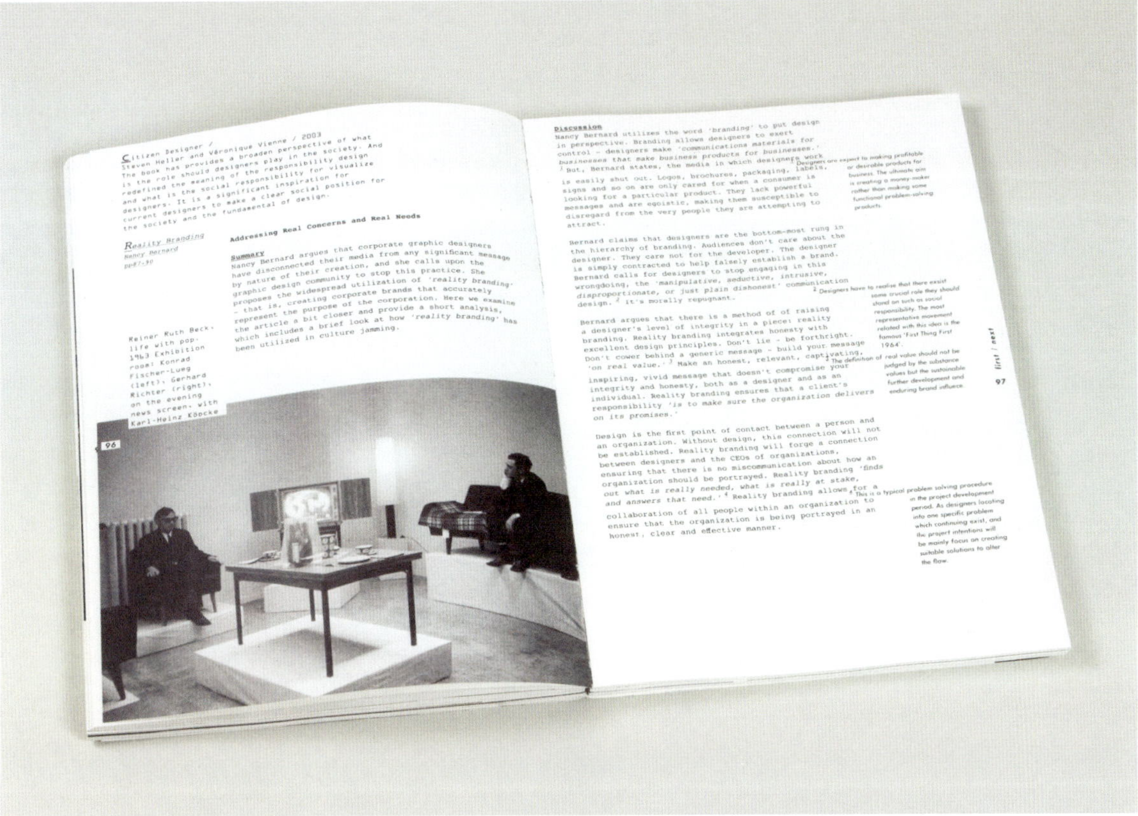

Citizen Designer / 2003
Steven Heller and Véronique Vienne / 2003
The book has provides a broaden perspective of what is the role should designers play in the society. And redefined the meaning of the responsibility design and what is the social responsibility for visualize designers. It is a significant inspiration for current designers to make a clear social position for the society and the fundamental of design.

Reality Branding
Nancy Bernard
pp87-90

**Addressing Real Concerns and Real Needs**

**Summary**
Nancy Bernard argues that corporate graphic designers have disconnected their media from any significant message by nature of their creation, and she calls upon the graphic design community to stop this practice. She proposes the widespread utilization of 'reality branding' - that is, creating corporate brands that accurately represent the purpose of the corporation. Here we examine the article a bit closer and provide a short analysis, which includes a brief look at how 'reality branding' has been utilized in culture jamming.

Reiner Ruth Beck. life with pop. 1963 Exhibition room: Konrad Fischer-Lueg (left), Gerhard Richter (right), on the evening news screen, with Karl-Heinz Köocke

96

**Discussion**
Nancy Bernard utilizes the word 'branding' to put design in perspective. Branding allows designers to exert control - designers make 'communications materials for businesses that make business products for businesses.' [1] But, Bernard states, the media in which designers work is easily shut out. Logos, brochures, packaging, labels, signs and so on are only cared for when a consumer is looking for a particular product. They lack powerful messages and are egoistic, making them susceptible to disregard from the very people they are attempting to attract.

Bernard claims that designers are the bottom-most rung in the hierarchy of branding. Audiences don't care about the designer. They care not for the developer. The designer is simply contracted to help falsely establish a brand. Bernard calls for designers to stop engaging in this wrongdoing, the 'manipulative, seductive, intrusive, disproportionate, or just plain dishonest' communication design. [2] It's morally repugnant.

Bernard argues that there is a method of of raising a designer's level of integrity in a piece: reality branding. Reality branding integrates honesty with excellent design principles. Don't lie - be forthright. Don't cower behind a generic message - build your message 'on real value.' [3] Make an honest, relevant, captivating, inspiring, vivid message that doesn't compromise your integrity and honesty, both as a designer and as an individual. Reality branding ensures that a client's responsibility 'is to make sure the organization delivers on its promises.'

Design is the first point of contact between a person and an organization. Without design, this connection will not be established. Reality branding will forge a connection between designers and the CEOs of organizations, ensuring that there is no miscommunication about how an organization should be portrayed. Reality branding 'finds out what is really needed, what is really at stake, and answers that need.' [4] Reality branding allows for a collaboration of all people within an organization to ensure that the organization is being portrayed in an honest, clear and effective manner.

1 Designers are expect to making profitable or desirable products for business. The ultimate aim is creating a money-maker rather than making some functional problem-solving products.

2 Designers have to realise that there exist some crucial role they should stand on such as social responsibility. The most representative movement related with this idea is the famous 'First Thing First' 1964'.

3 The definition of real value should not be judged by the substance values but the sustainable further development and enduring brand influence.

4 This is a typical problem solving procedure in the project development period. As designers locating into one specific problem which continuing exist, and the project intentions will be mainly focus on creating suitable solutions to alter the flow.

first / next
97

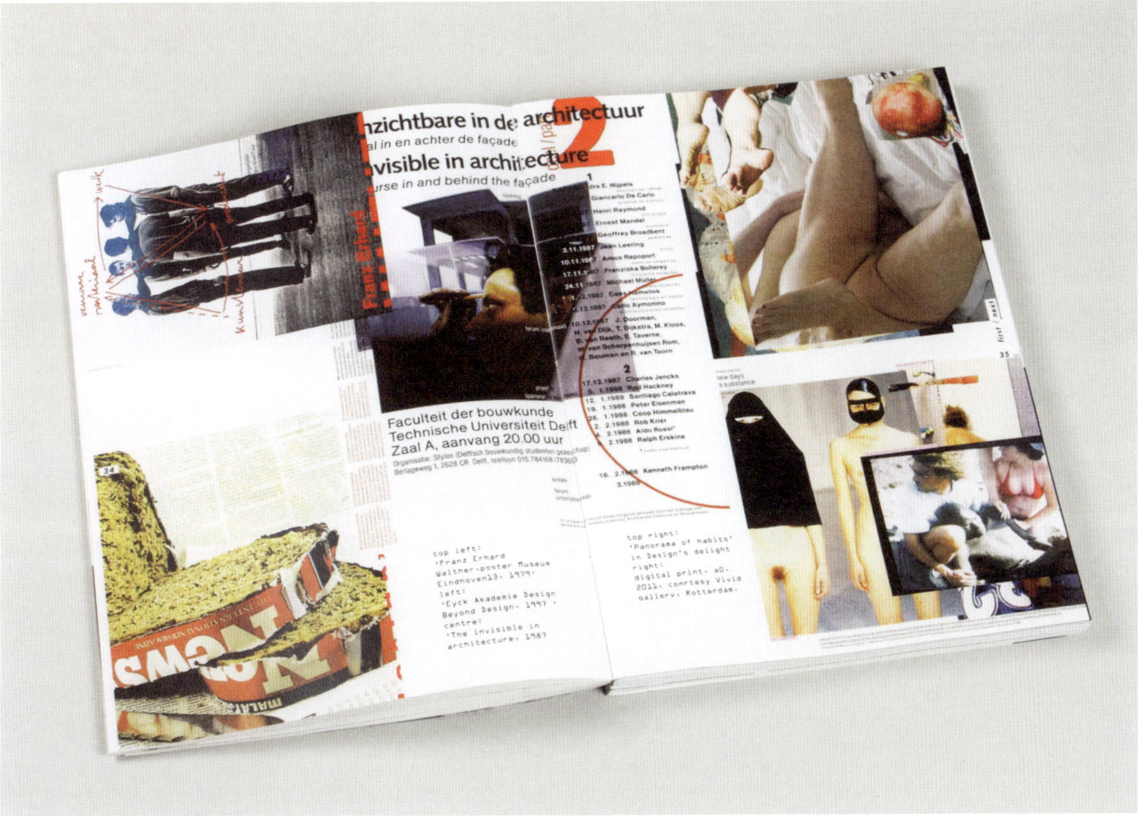

onzichtbare in de architectuur
al in en achter de façade
invisible in architecture
urse in and behind the façade

Faculteit der bouwkunde
Technische Universiteit Delft
Zaal A, aanvang 20.00 uur

top left:
'Franz Erhard Walther-poster Museum Eindhoven13, 1979'
left:
'Eyck Akademie Design Beyond Design, 1997'
centre:
'The invisible in architecture, 1987'

34

top right:
'Panorama of habits' in Design's delight
right:
digital print, A0, 2011, courtesy Vivid gallery, Rotterdam.

first / next
35

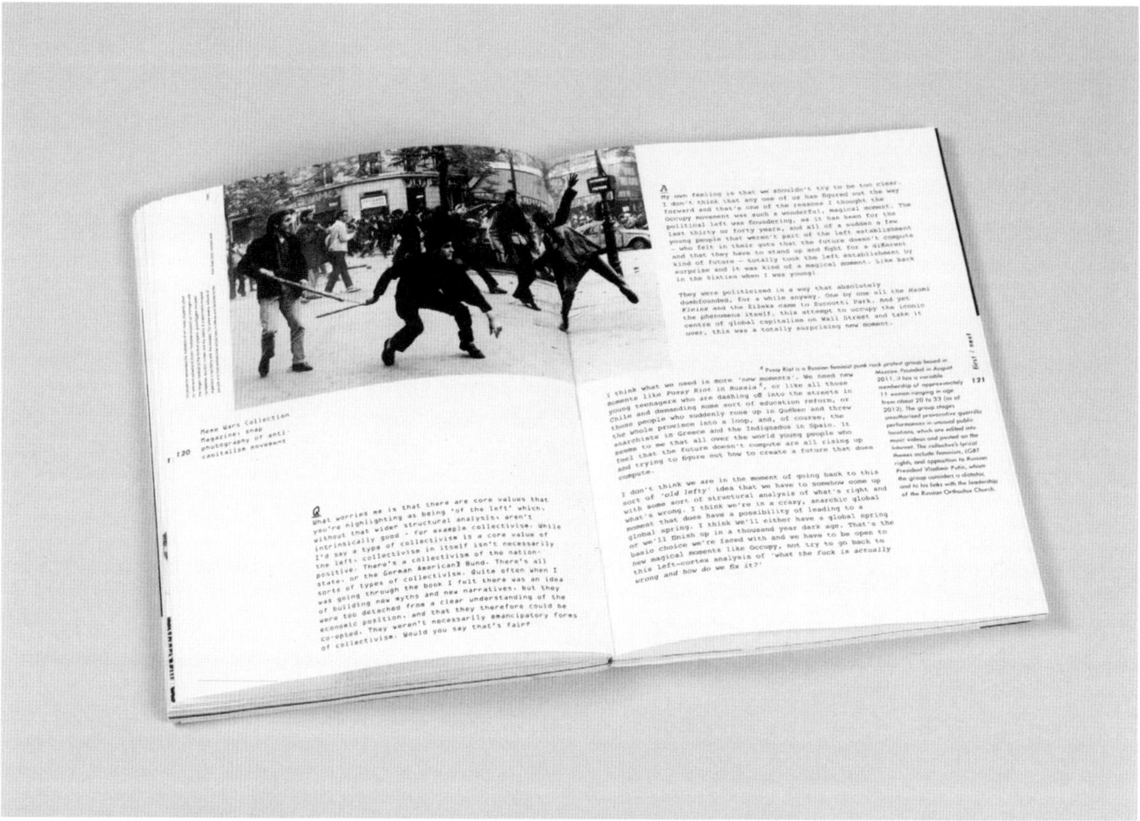
Meme Wars Collection
Magazine: snap
photography of anti-
capitalise movement
120
Q
What worries me is that there are core values that
you're highlighting as being 'of the left' which,
without that wider structural analysis, aren't
intrinsically good - for example collectivise. While
I'd say a type of collectivism is a core value of
the left, collectivism in itself isn't necessarily
positive. There's a collectivism of the nation-
state, or the German American Bund. There's all
sorts of types of collectivism. Quite often when I
was going through the book I felt there was an idea
of building new myths and new narratives, but they
were too detached from a clear understanding of the
economic position, and that they therefore could be
co-opted. They weren't necessarily emancipatory forms
of collectivism. Would you say that's fair?
A
My own feeling is that we shouldn't try to be too clear.
I don't think that any one of us has figured out the way
forward and that's one of the reasons I thought the
Occupy movement was such a wonderful, magical moment. The
political left was floundering, as it has been for the
last thirty or forty years, and all of a sudden a few
young people that weren't part of the left establishment
– who felt in their guts that the future doesn't compute
and that they have to stand up and fight for a different
kind of future – totally took the left establishment by
surprise and it was kind of a magical moment. Like back
in the Sixties when I was young!
They were politicised in a way that absolutely
dumbfounded, for a while anyway. One by one all the Naomi
Kleins and the Žižeks came to Zucotti Park. And yet
the phenomena itself, this attempt to occupy the iconic
centre of global capitalism on Wall Street and take it
over, this was a totally surprising new moment.
I think what we need is more 'new moments'. We need new
moments like Pussy Riot in Russia[4], or like all those
young teenagers who are dashing off into the streets in
Chile and demanding some sort of education reform, or
those people who suddenly rose up in Québec and threw
the whole province into a loop, and, of course, the
anarchists in Greece and the Indignados in Spain. It
seems to me that all over the world young people who
feel that the future doesn't compute are all rising up
and trying to figure out how to create a future that does
compute.
I don't think we are in the moment of going back to this
sort of 'old lefty' idea that we have to somehow come up
with some sort of structural analysis of what's right and
what's wrong. I think we're in a crazy, anarchic global
moment that does have a possibility of leading to a
global spring. I think we'll either have a global spring
or we'll finish up in a thousand year dark age. That's the
basic choice we're faced with and we have to be open to
new magical moments like Occupy, not try to go back to
this left-cortex analysis of 'what the fuck is actually
wrong and how do we fix it?'
[4] Pussy Riot is a Russian feminist punk rock protest group based in Moscow. Founded in August 2011, it has a variable membership of approximately 11 women ranging in age from about 20 to 33 (as of 2012). The group stages unauthorised provocative guerrilla performances in unusual public locations, which are edited into music videos and posted on the Internet. The collective's lyrical themes include feminism, LGBT rights, and opposition to Russian President Vladimir Putin, whom the group considers a dictator, and to his links with the leadership of the Russian Orthodox Church.
first / next
121

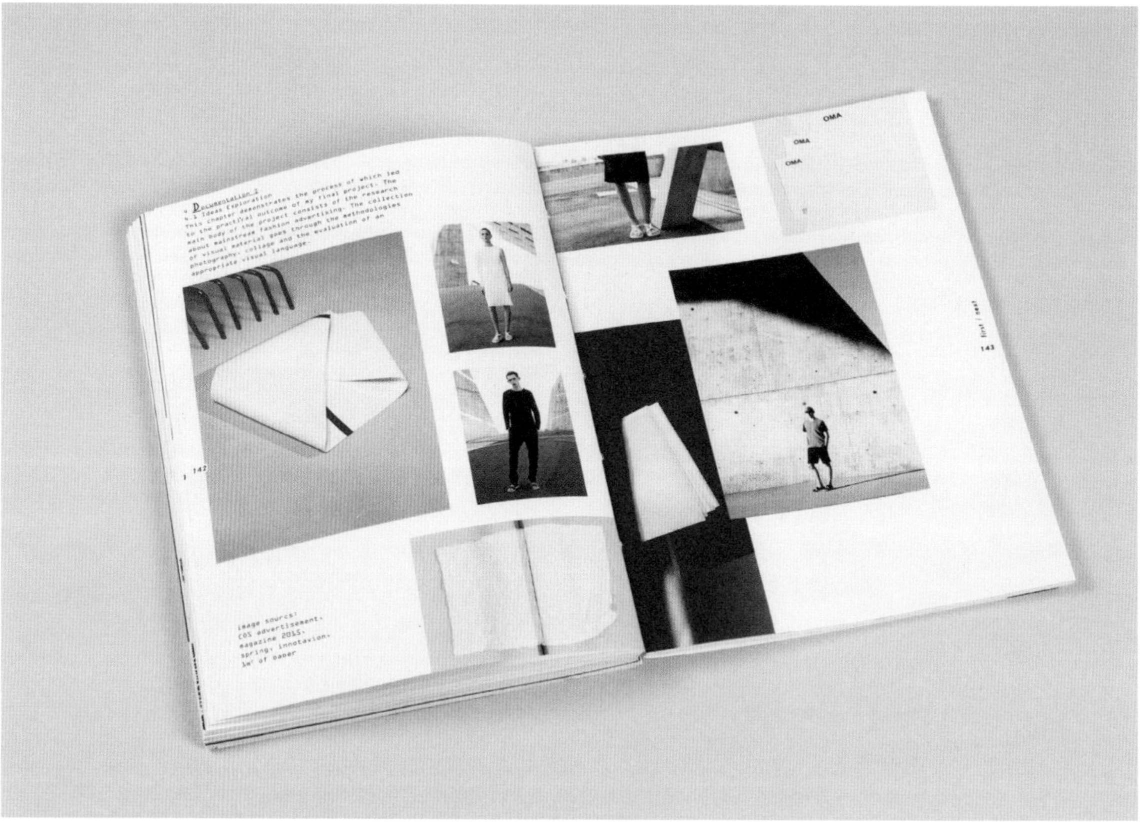
4 Documentation 1
4.1 Ideas Exploration
This chapter demonstrates the process of which led
to the practical outcome of my final project. The
main body of the project consists of the research
about mainstream fashion advertising. The collection
of visual material goes through the methodologies
photography, collage and the evaluation of an
appropriate visual language.
142
image sourcs:
COS advertisement,
magazine 2015,
spring, innotavion,
1m² of paper
OMA
OMA
OMA
first / next
143

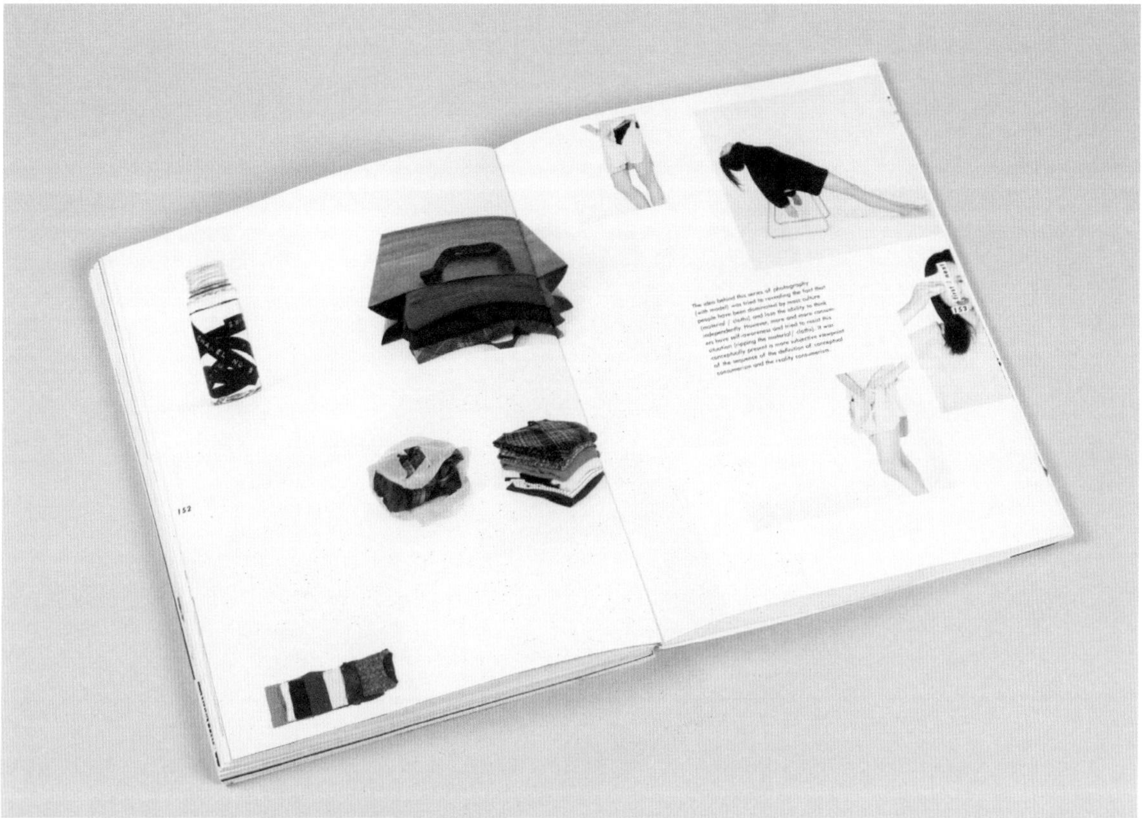

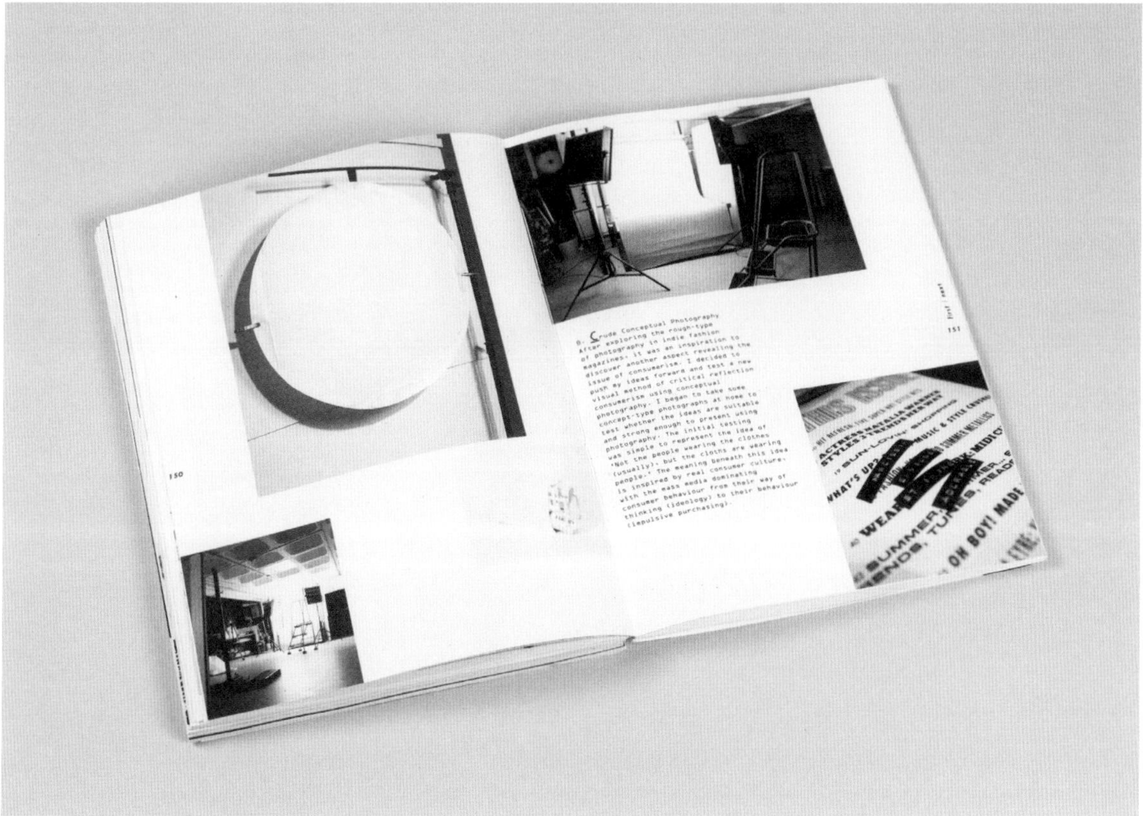
B. Crude Conceptual Photography
After exploring the rough-type of photography in indie fashion magazines, it was an inspiration to discover another aspect revealing the issue of consumerism. I decided to push my ideas forward and test a new visual method of critical reflection consumerism using conceptual photography. I began to take some concept-type photographs at home to test whether the ideas are suitable and strong enough to present using photography. The initial testing was simple to represent the idea of 'Not the people wearing the clothes (usually), but the cloths are wearing people.' The meaning beneath this idea is inspired by real consumer culture, with the mass media dominating consumer behaviour from their way of thinking (ideology) to their behaviour (impulsive purchasing).

# VIUDAS Y HUERFANAS EDITORIAL

This editorial work is a result of constructing an art installation by a team of designers. In this project, the team was asked to develop an installation around the Buenos Aires museum in order to show something about the Argentinian history, and the team, as a group of women, decided to talk about the role of female in the local literature.

Designer: Rocio Gomez

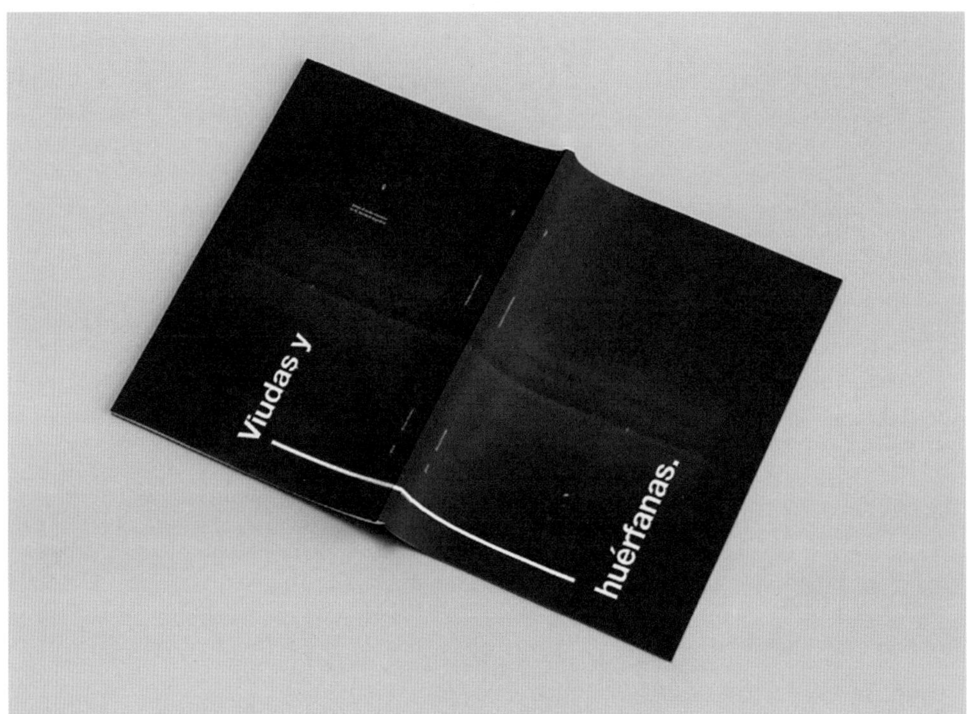


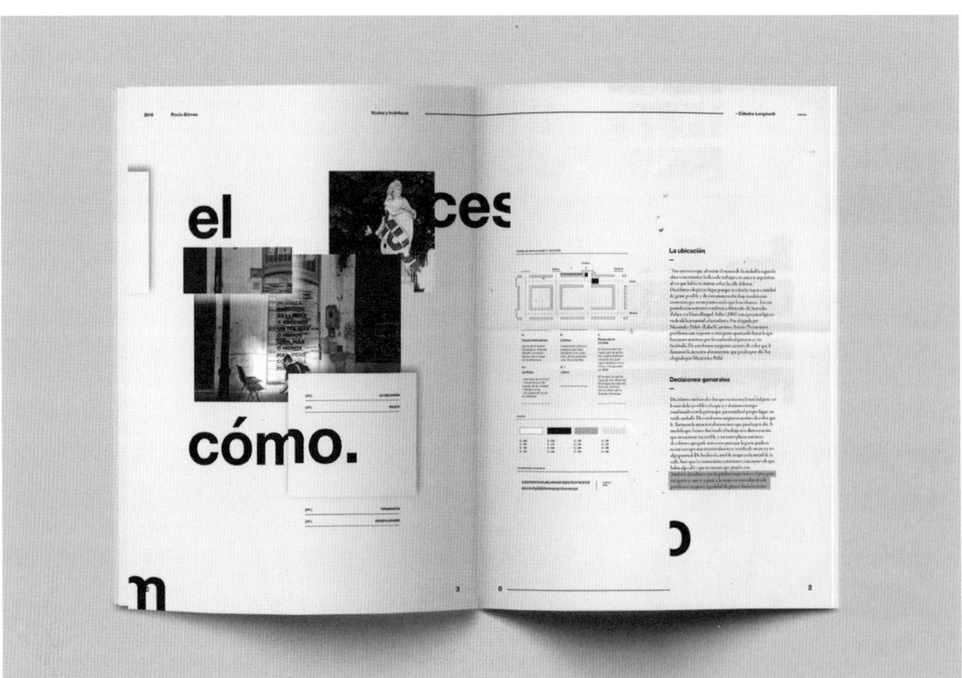

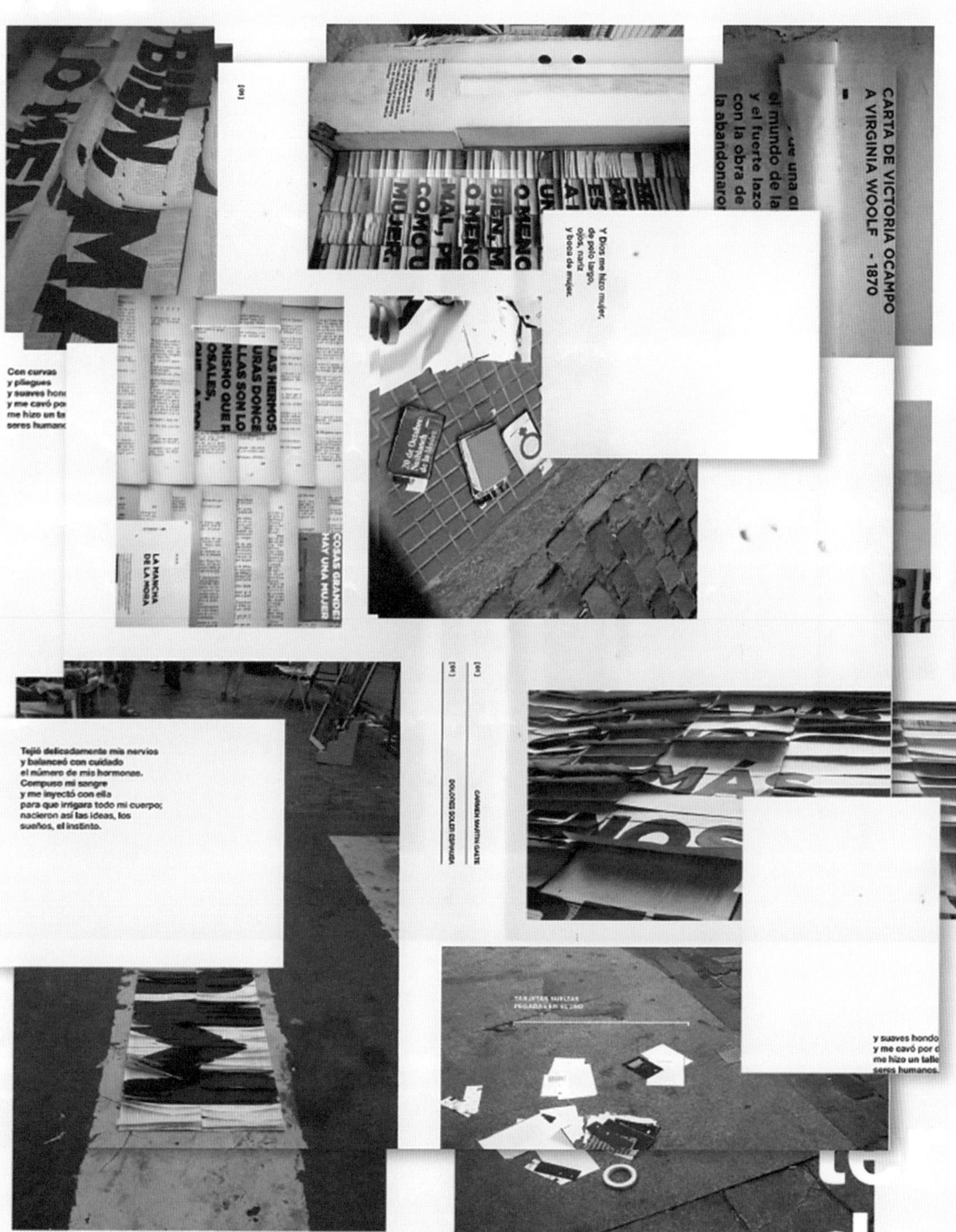
CARTA DE VICTORIA OCAMPO
A VIRGINIA WOOLF - 1870
Y Dios me hizo mujer,
de pelo largo,
ojos, nariz
y boca de mujer.
Con curvas
y pliegues
y suaves hond
y me cavó po
me hizo un ta
seres human
LA MANCHA
DE LA MORA
COSAS GRANDES
HAY UNA MUJER
Tejió delicadamente mis nervios
y balanceó con cuidado
el número de mis hormonas.
Compuso mi sangre
y me inyectó con ella
para que irrigara todo mi cuerpo;
nacieron así las ideas, los
sueños, el instinto.
CARMEN MARTÍN GAITE
DOLORES SOLER ESPIAUBA
MÁS
y suaves hondo
y me cavó por d
me hizo un talle
seres humanos.

# ESA MUJER

"Esa Mujer" is an experimental design book by the Argentine writer Rodolfo Walsh. Based on an historical fact, the story is about a man's obsession with the dead body of an iconic woman. The handmade work was done with different techniques such as collage, stencil, embroidery and pointillism. It aims to express the filth, the obsession and the morbidness of that event.

Designer: Micaela Nanni

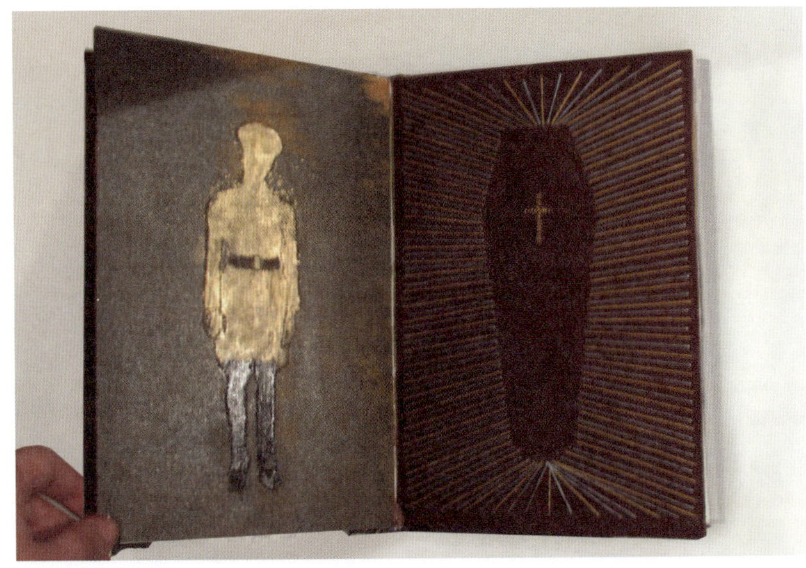

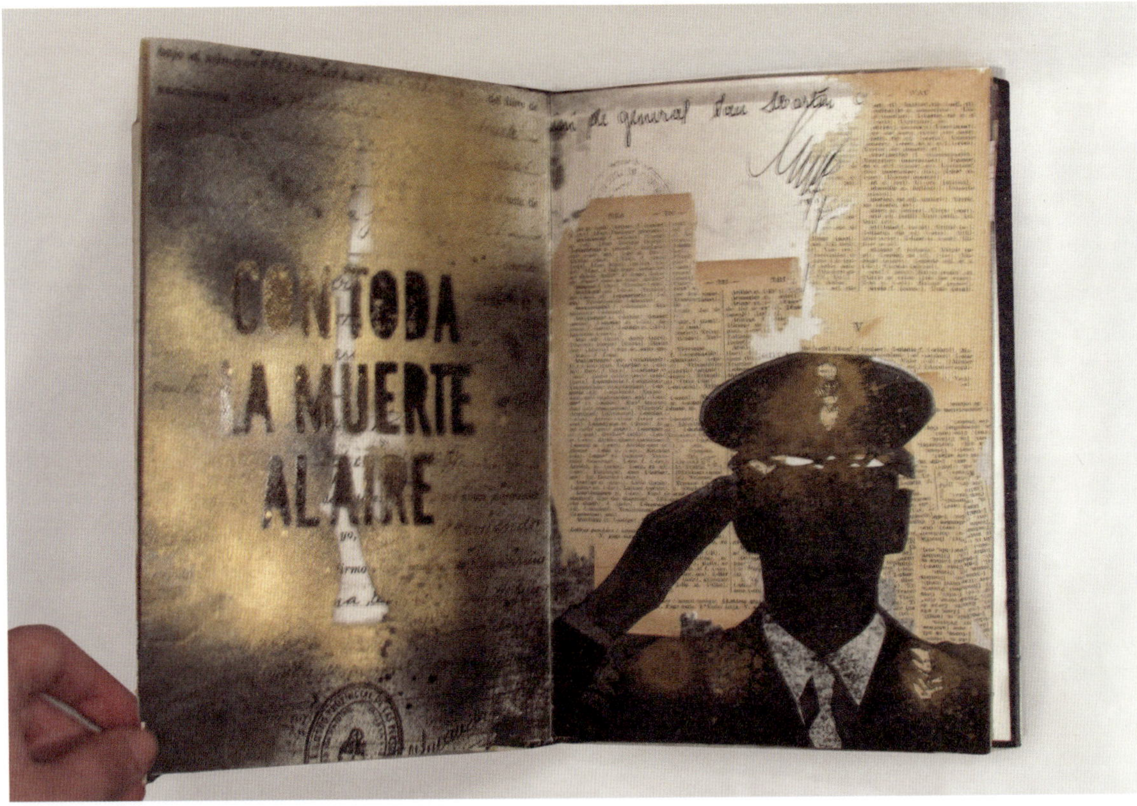

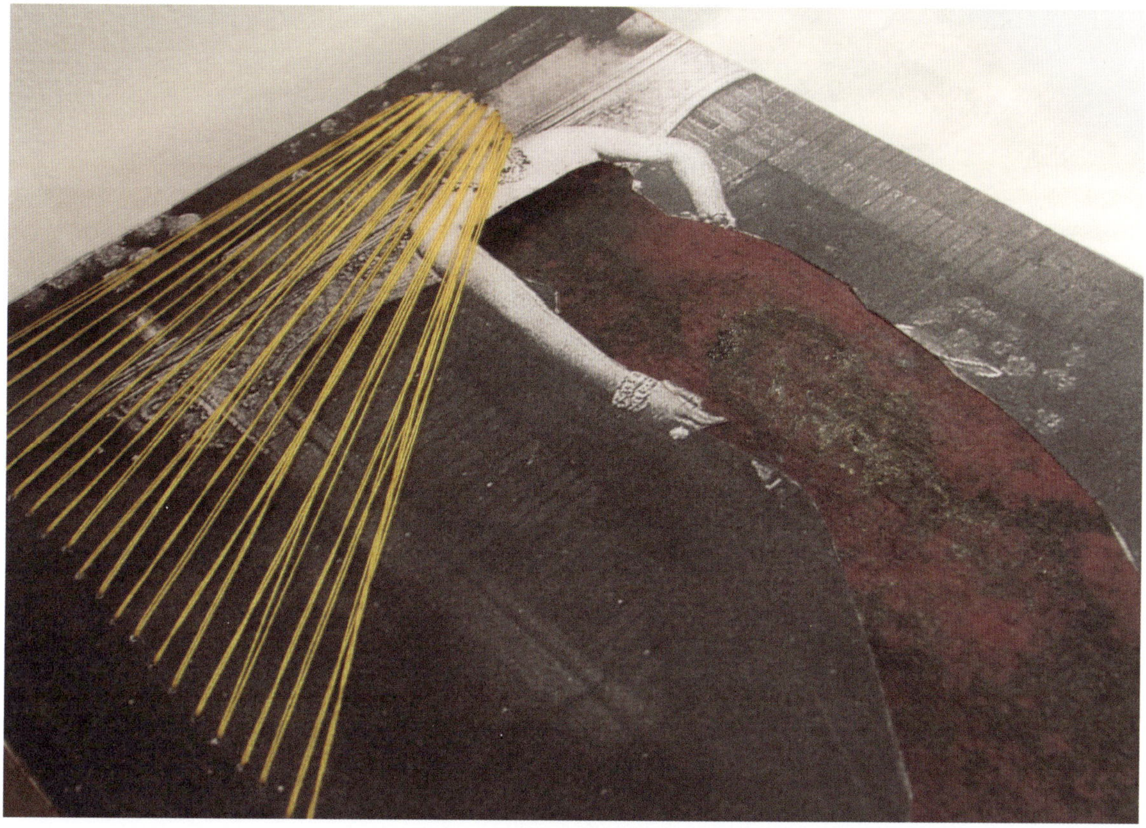

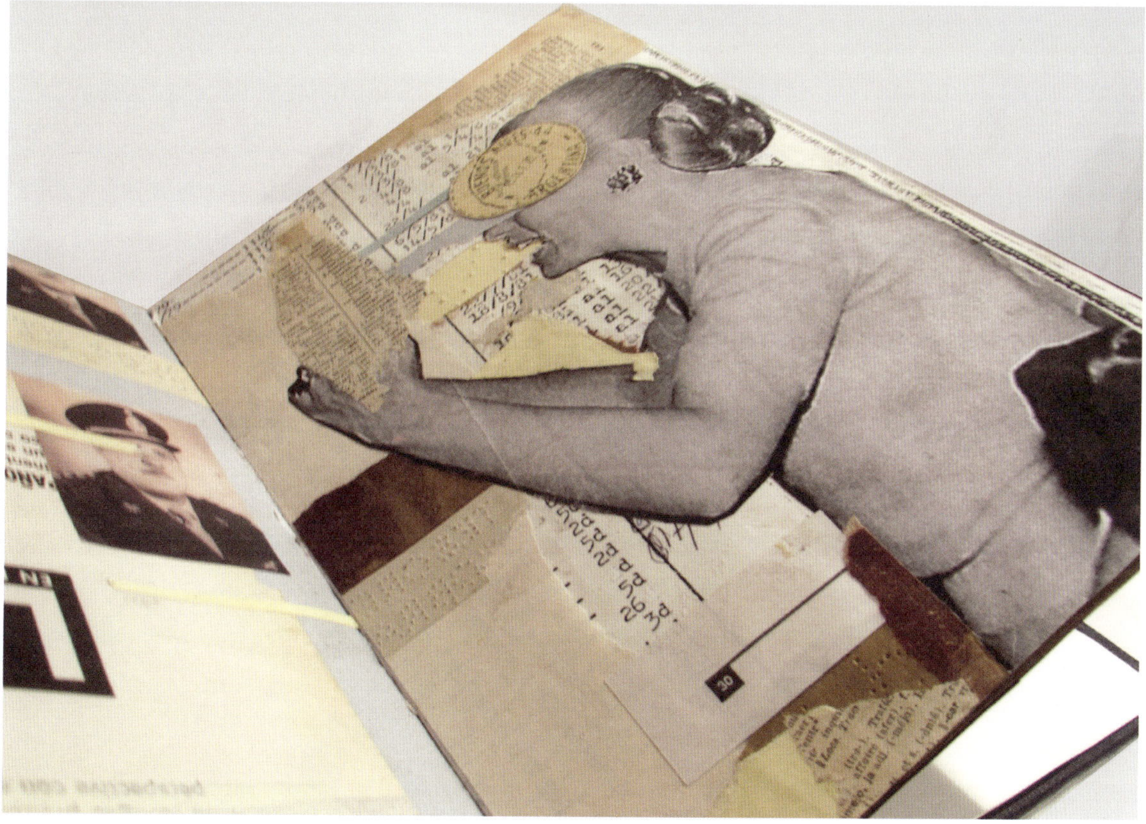

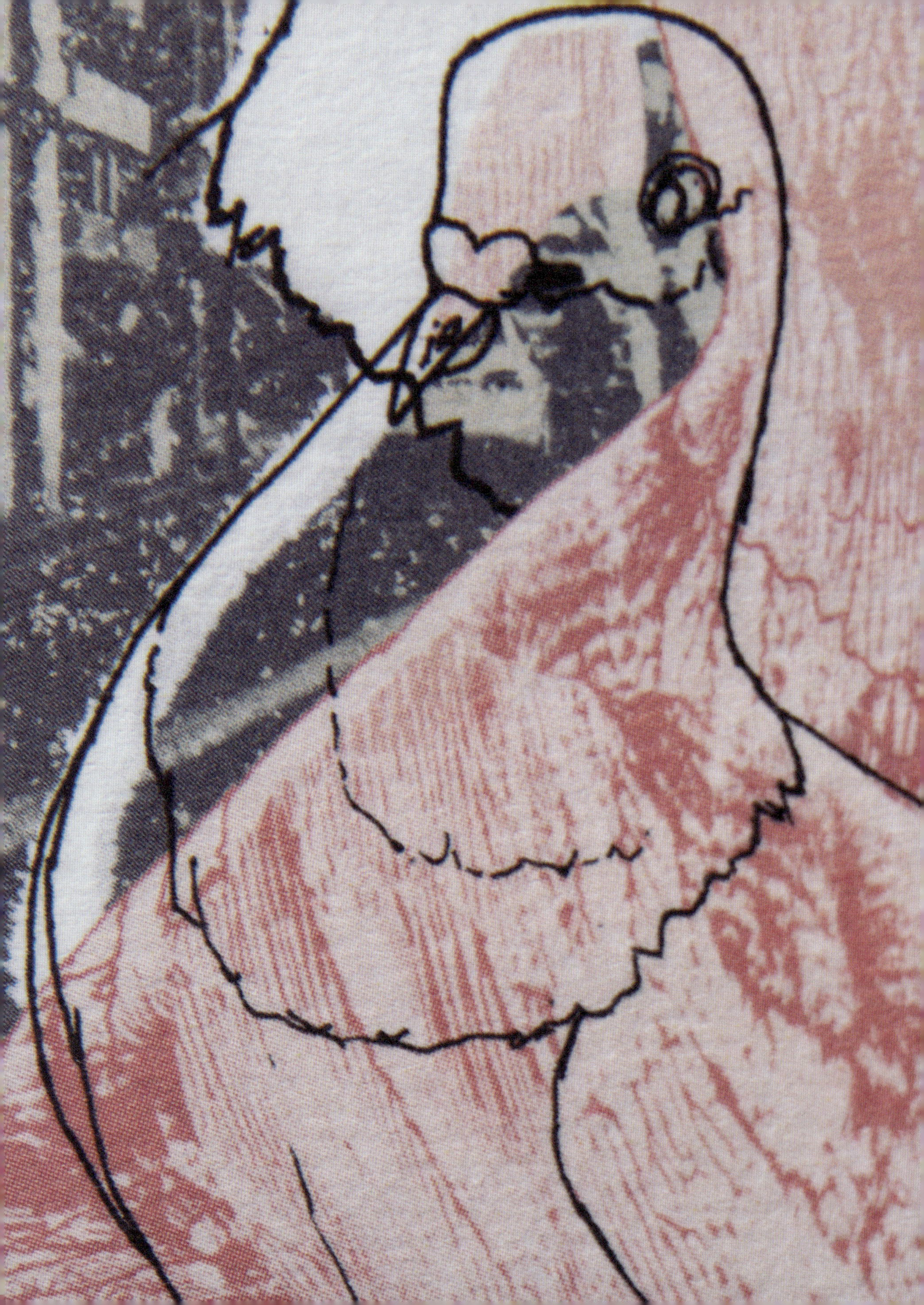

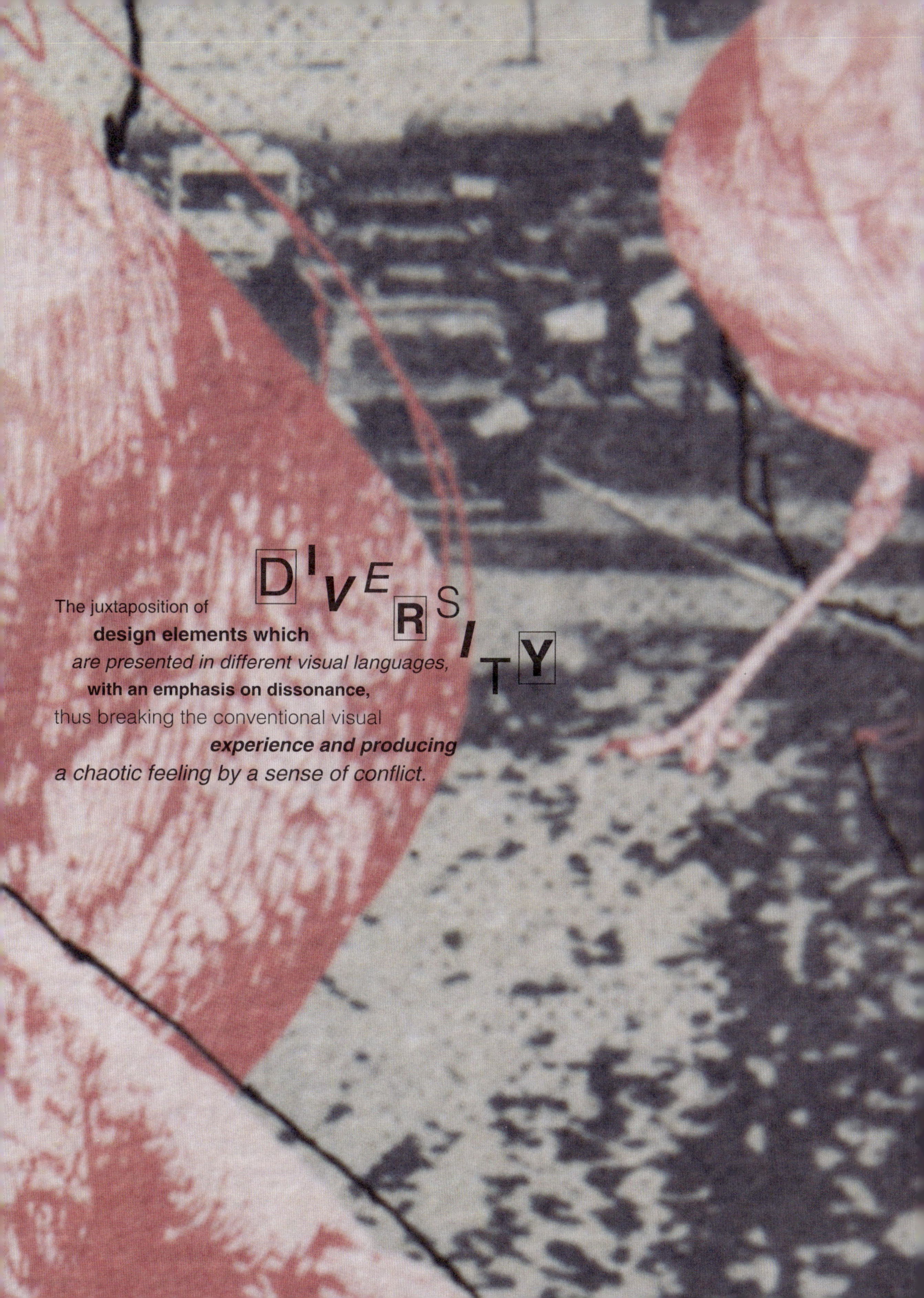
DIVERSITY
The juxtaposition of
design elements which
are presented in different visual languages,
with an emphasis on dissonance,
thus breaking the conventional visual
experience and producing
a chaotic feeling by a sense of conflict.

# NOTEBOOK II

In Notebook II, the Parisian printing house Imprimerie du Marais unites their own expertise with the work of eight talented and prestigious design studios in a set of eight notebooks. Homework Studio contributed a typographic illustration experimenting with foil, blind embossing and multi-layer embossing.

Studio: Homework

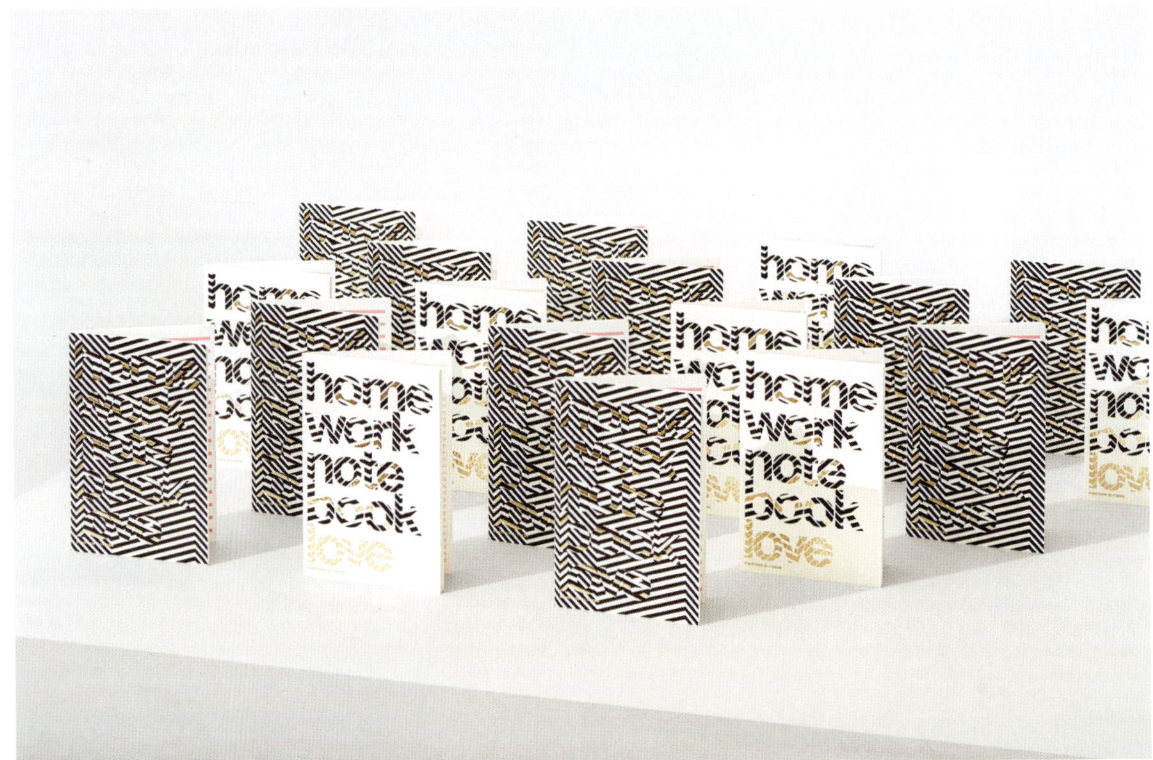


*As a kind of visual experience, what do you think about the "chaos" in graphic design?*

"Chaotic" is a way of making a mark and catching the eye. To build beautiful and dynamic brands is to challenge the way people feel and think by making design matter.

*What are your common approaches to produce a "chaotic" visual effect?*

The signature aesthetic of Homework balances both timeless and contemporary design. Catching the eye means having to find the right balance in the visual language. If everything is chaotic then nothing is noticeable—there should always be a visual hierarchy, an order, a point. You have to find the right way to play the strengths, the way that can be vivid colors, contrasts, an unusual shape or a striking print technique. Working with various styles of typography is also a great tool to make chaotic effects.

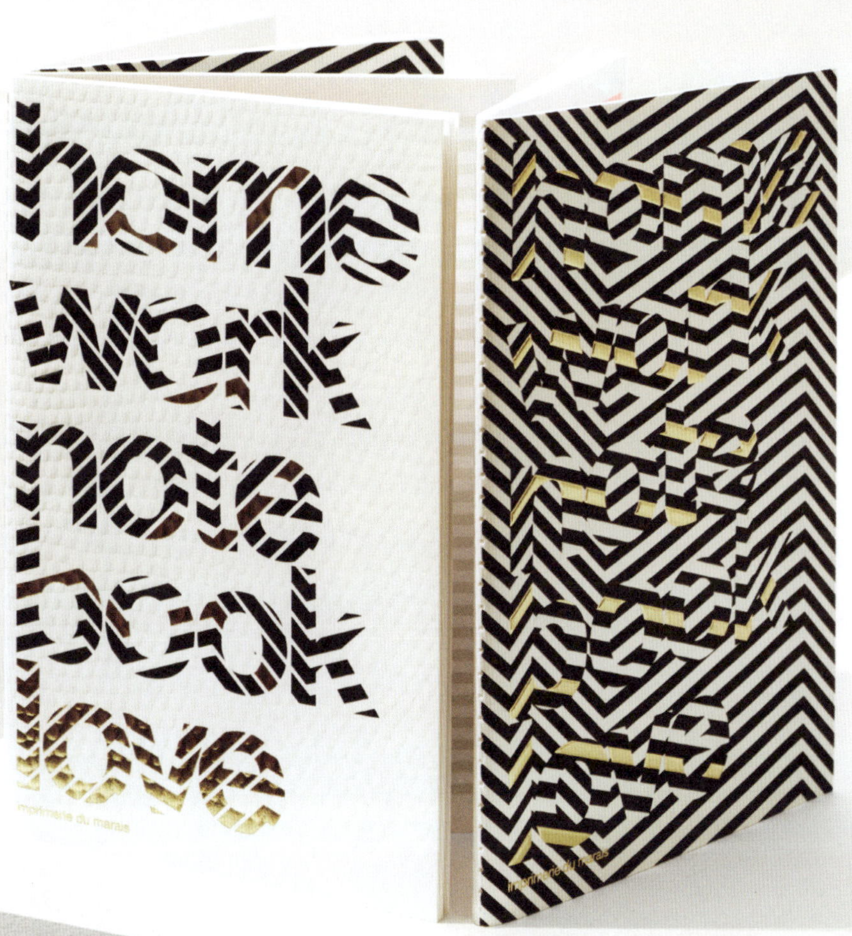

# RAD PERSONAL BRANDING

This is a branding system for the designer's personal identity, Ronnie Alley Design or RAD. He did this with a series of vibrant and colorful patterns that could then be applied to different aspects of the system, such as business cards, letterheads or envelopes, intending to keep the system fun, friendly, and energetic.

Studio: RAD
Designer: Ronnie Alley

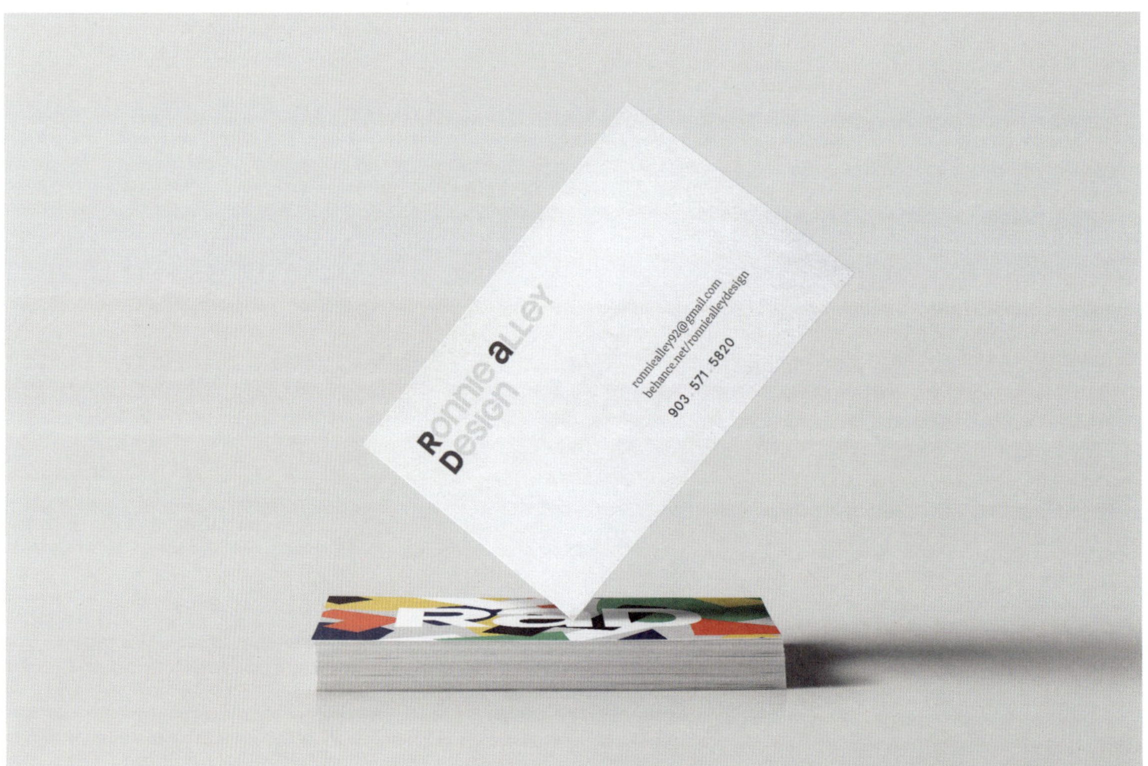


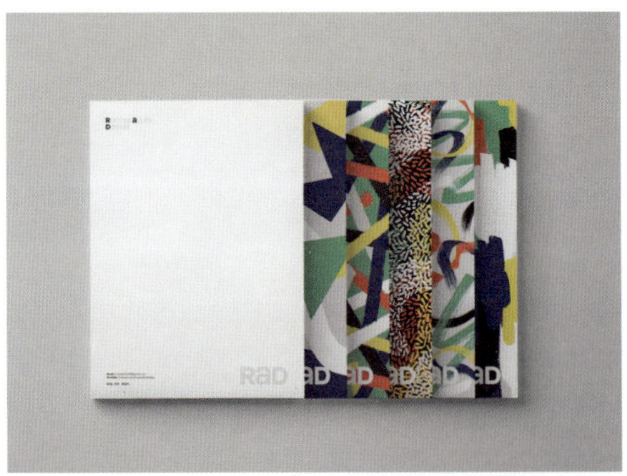


*As a kind of visual experience, what do you think about the "chaos" in graphic design?*

Whether the chaotic elements are energetic, friendly, harsh, or refined, they can represent all the emotions felt behind a project that perhaps can't be expressed through words. I believe that visual design elements can express different feelings much better and faster than merely words on a page.

*What are your common approaches to produce a "chaotic" visual effect?*

One of my favorite approaches to creat a chaotic design element is by cutting paper into random shapes. I usually create 15-30 different shapes. After they've been cut, I begin to shuffle them on the canvas I'm using until I creat a composition. Then I make a record of that composition and start to make a second, then a third and fourth. I continue this process until I'm happy with how many different patterns I've made. Once I have all the layouts finished I then begin coloring each shape in the composition to match the feeling of the project that I'm working on.

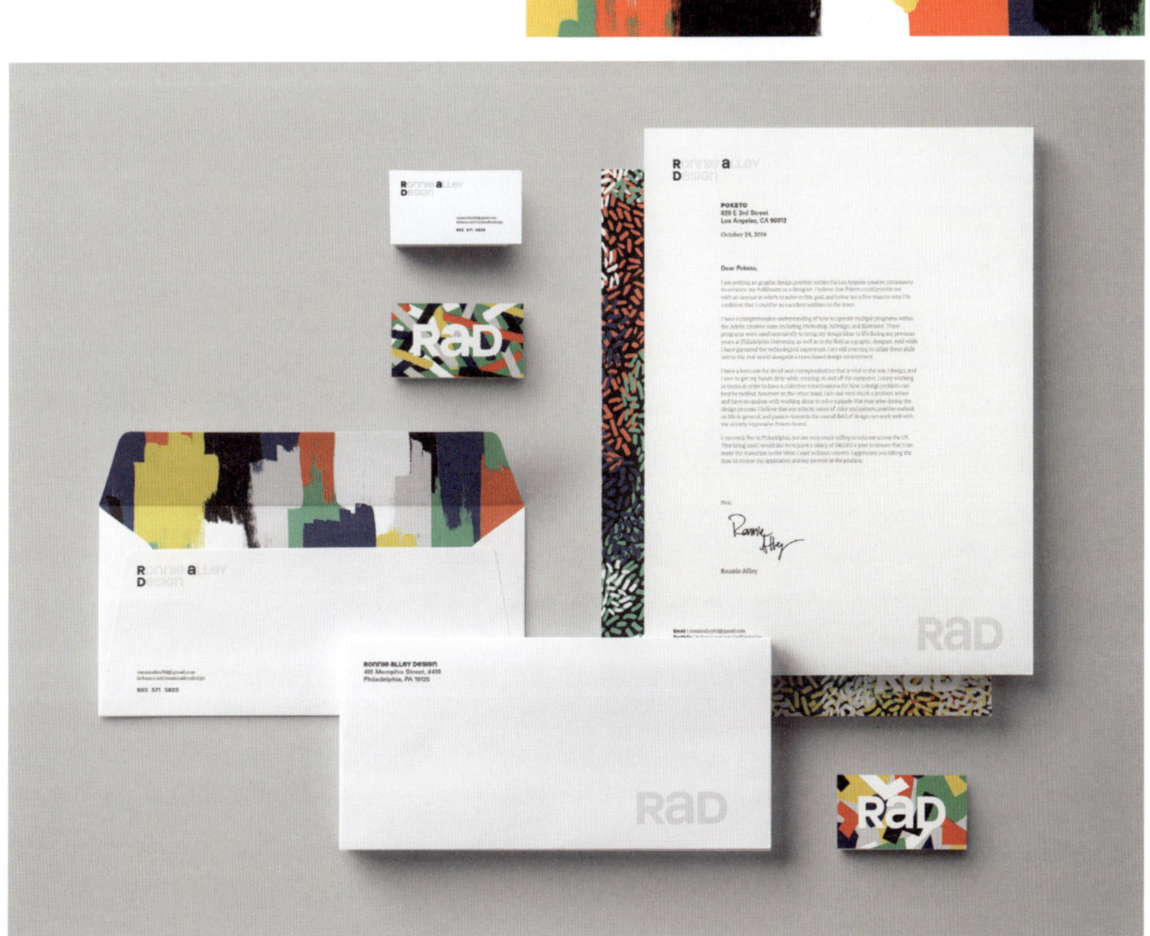

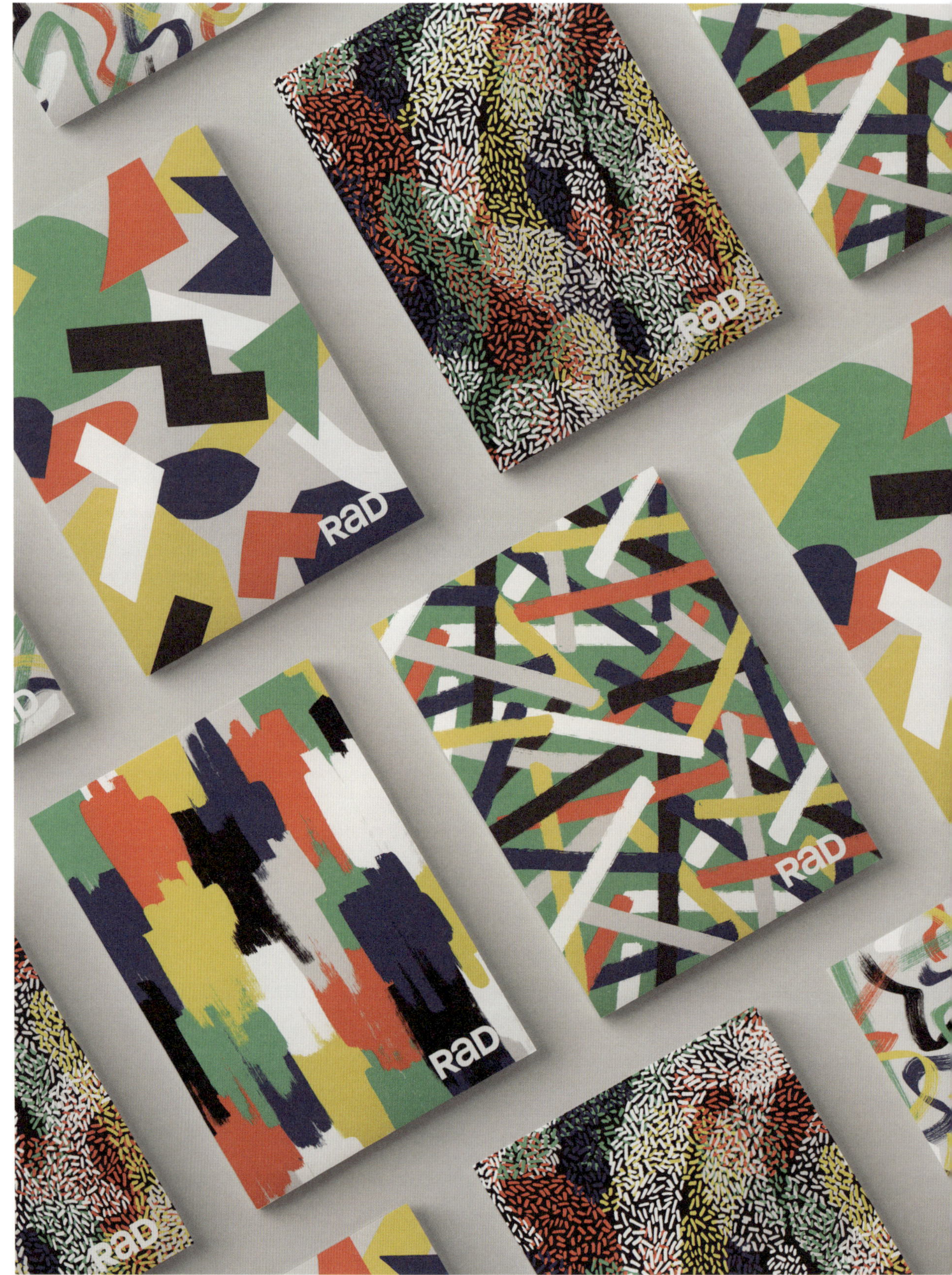
RaD
RaD
RaD
RaD
RaD

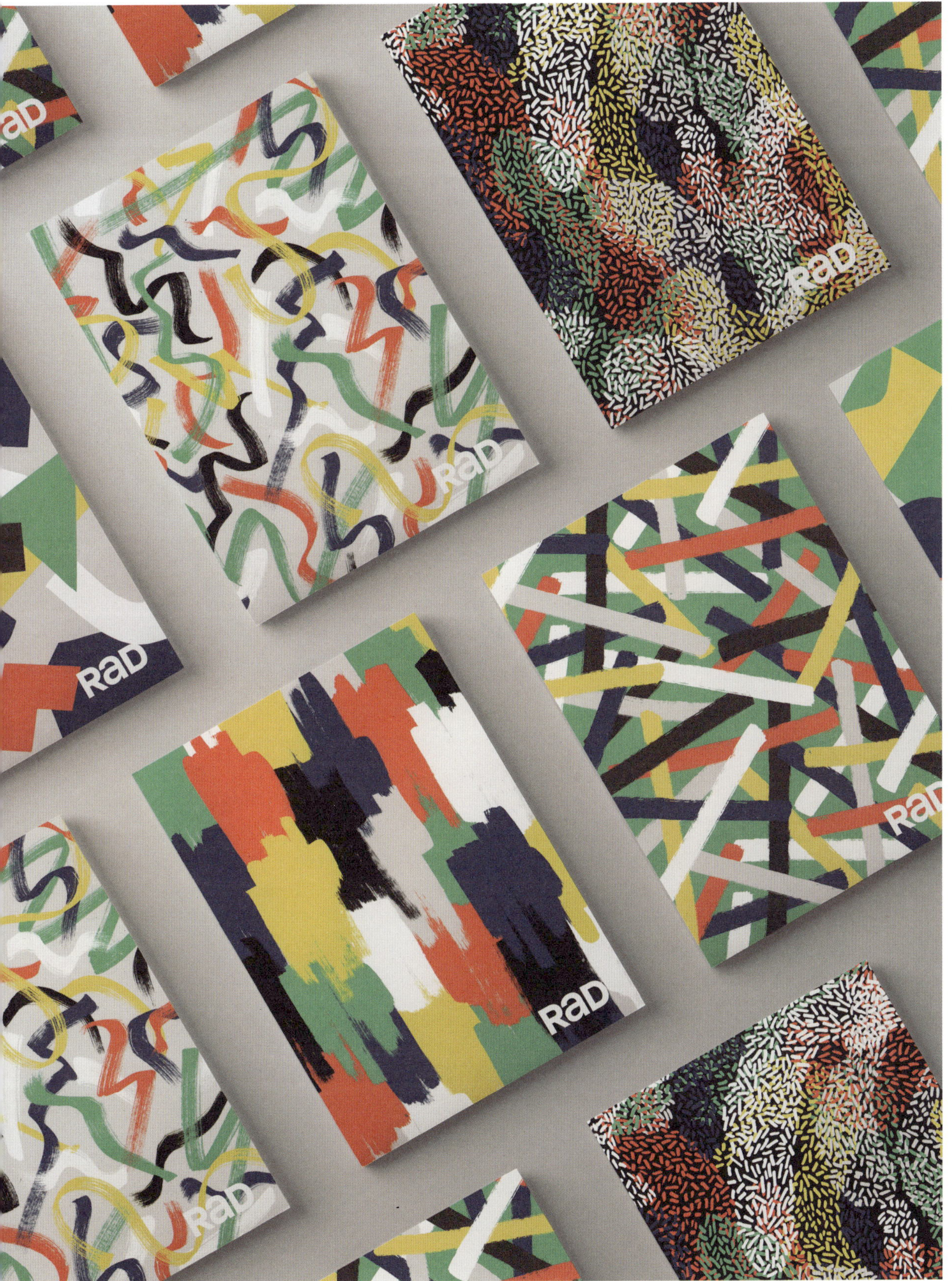
RaD
RaD
RaD
RaD
RaD

# CARNIVALESQUE REBELLION

Inspired by the daily news, "Carnivalesque Rebellion" was a unique project that uncovered the social issues about the retrogression of civilization.

Designer: Kristine H. Kawakubo

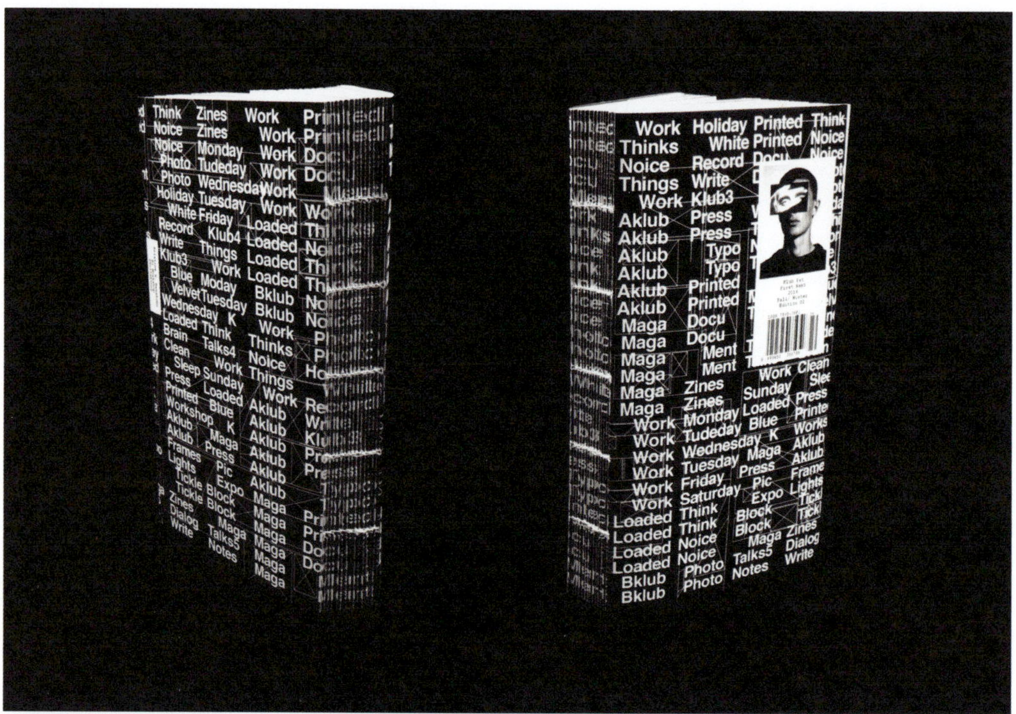

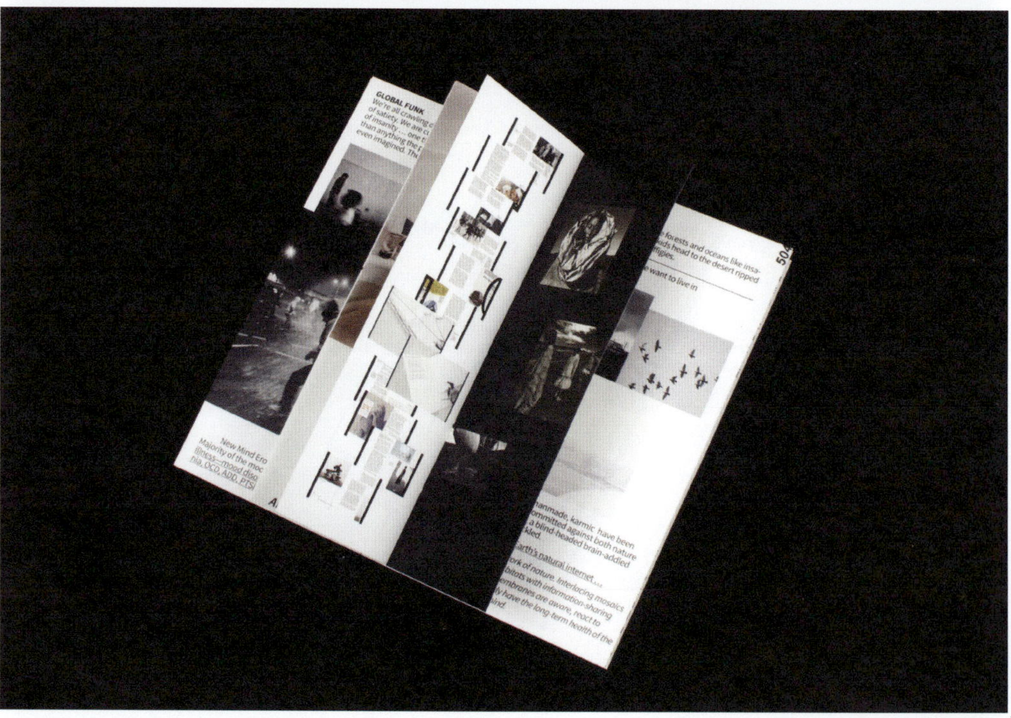

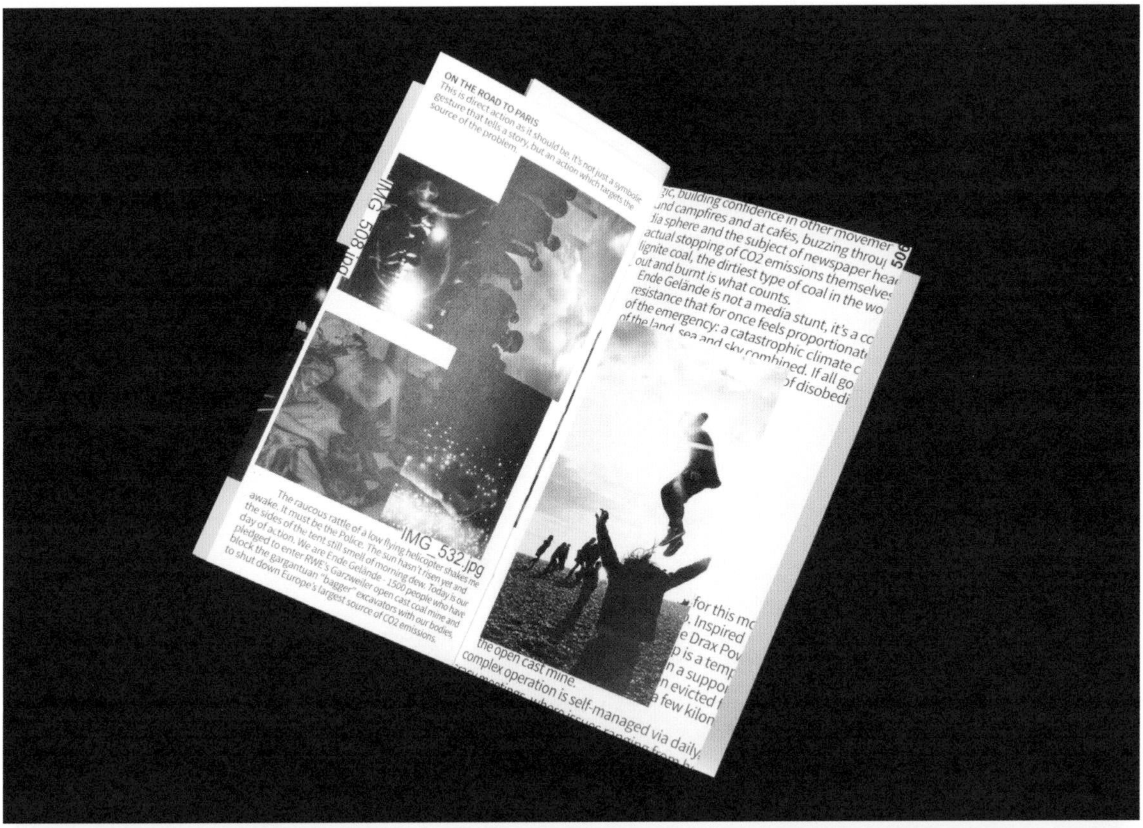
ON THE ROAD TO PARIS
This is direct action as it should be. It's not just a symbolic gesture that tells a story, but an action which targets the source of the problem.
IMG_508.jpg
IMG_532.jpg
The raucous rattle of a low flying helicopter shakes me awake. It must be the Police. The sun hasn't risen yet and the sides of the tent still smell of morning dew. Today is our day of action. We are Ende Gelände - 1500 people who have pledged to enter RWE's Garzweiler open cast coal mine and block the gargantuan "bagger" excavators with our bodies, to shut down Europe's largest source of CO2 emissions.
the open cast mine.

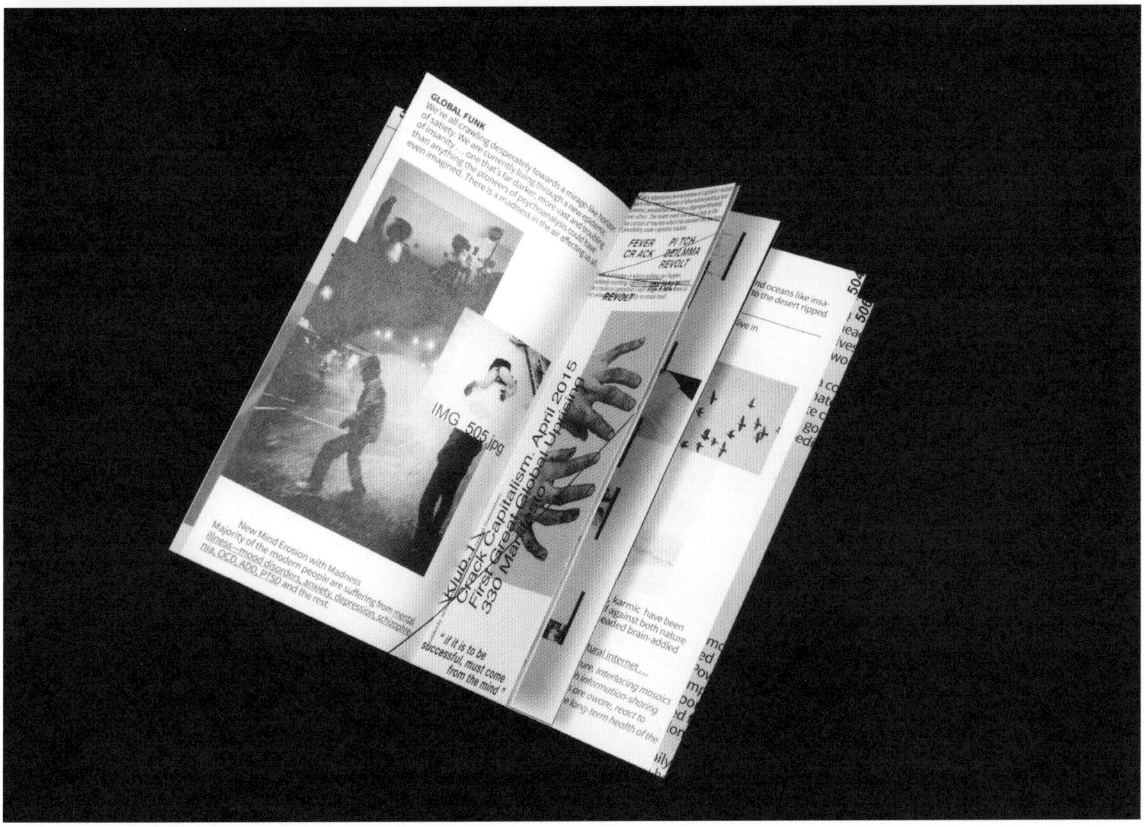
GLOBAL FUNK
FEVER
CRACK
PITCH
DEILMMA
REVOLT
IMG_505.jpg
Crack Capitalism. April 2015
New Mind Erosion with Madness
Majority of the modern people are suffering from mental illness—mood disorders, anxiety, depression, schizophrenia, OCD, ADD, PTSD and the rest.
" if it is to be successful, must come from the mind "

# FICTION: THE ENDANGERED SPECIES

*Fiction: the endangered species* is a zine that comments on and exposes fictional characters that inhabit the city. It explores discourses on such as phenomenology, flânerie, cyber culture, tradition, politics and death. This is a mixed media artwork that collages photography, illustration, design and traditional art techniques.

Designer: Matthew Tager

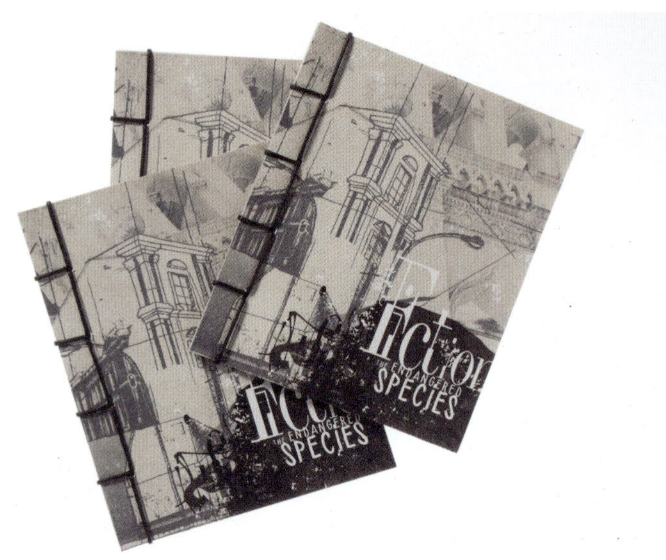

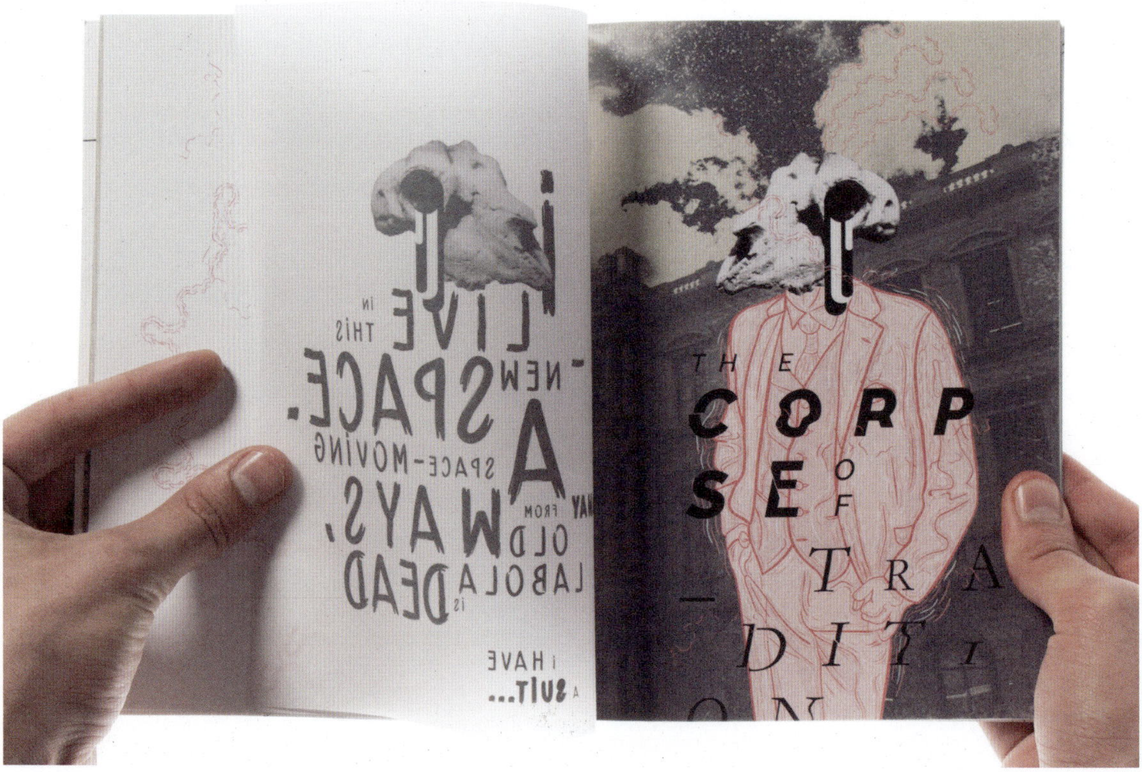

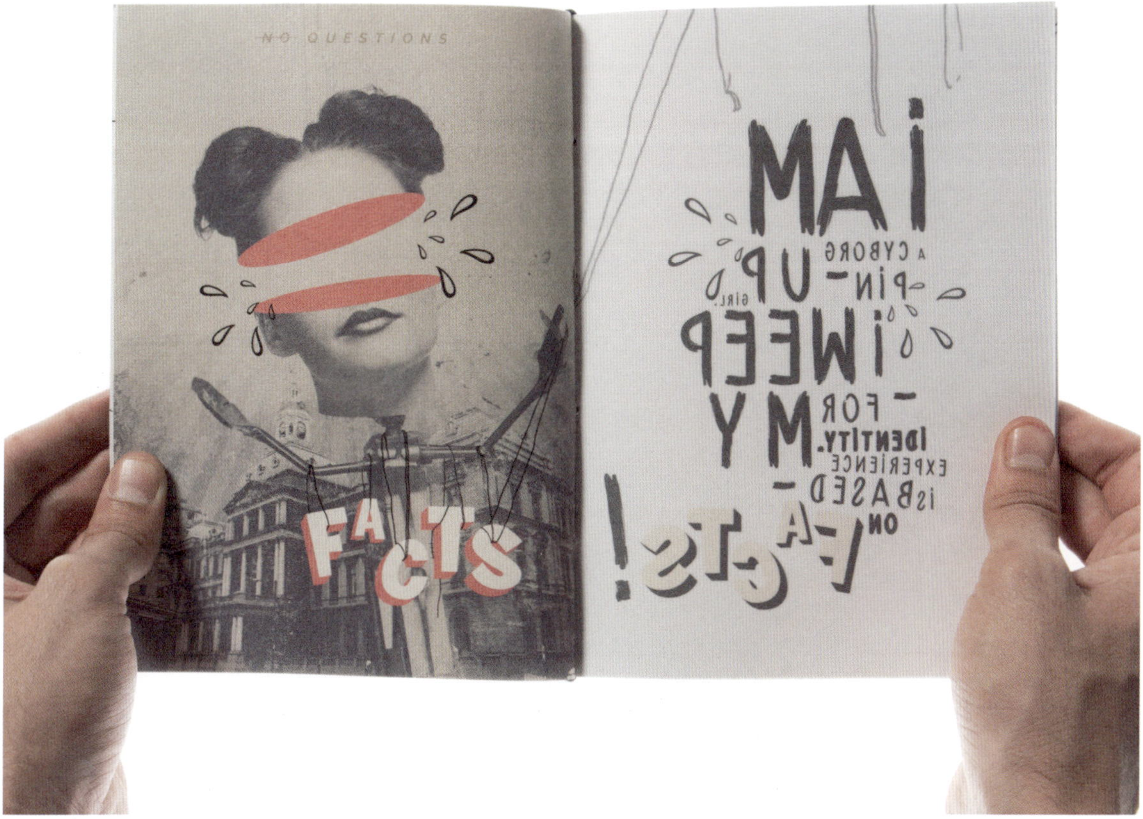

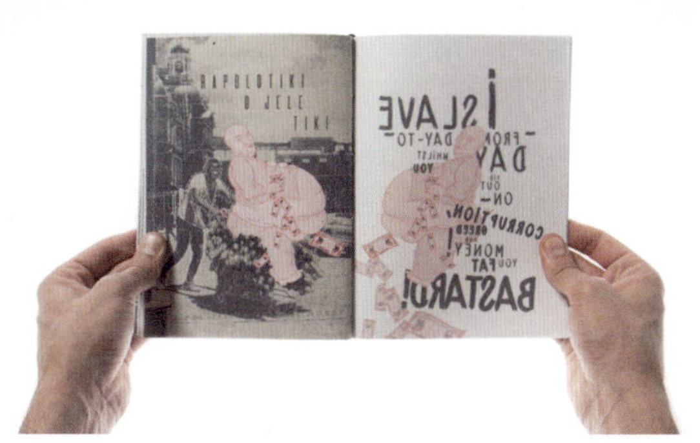

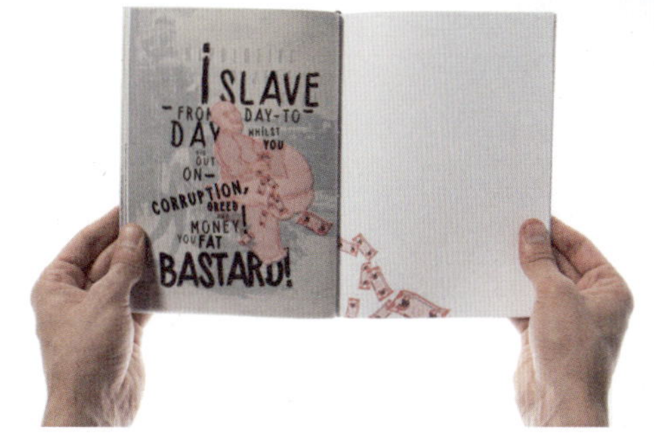
I SLAVE
FROM DAY-TO DAY
CORRUPTION
MONEY
YOU FAT
BASTARD!

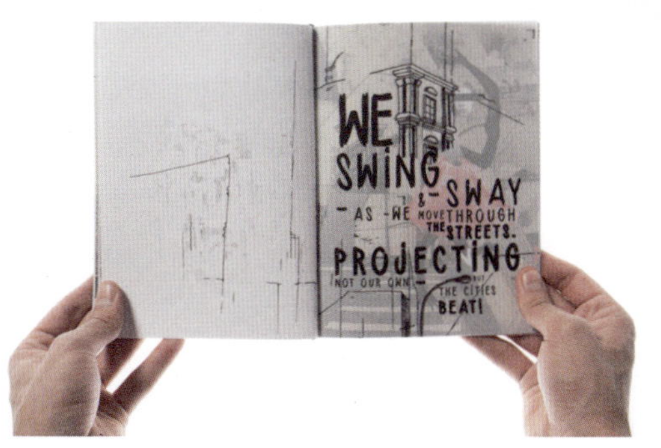
WE
SWING & SWAY
- AS -WE MOVE THROUGH THE STREETS.
PROJECTING
NOT OUR OWN
THE CITIES
BEAT!

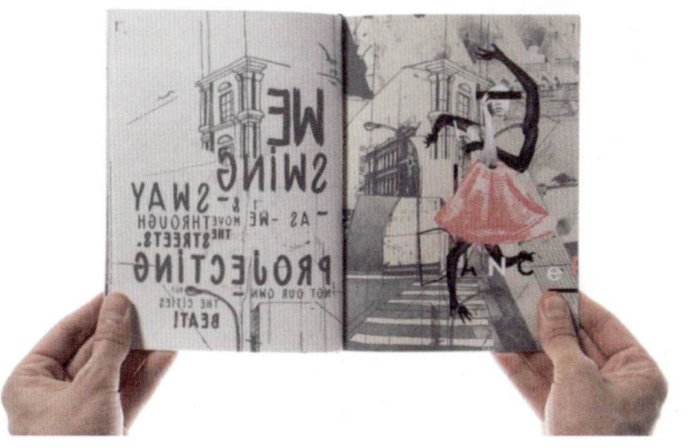

# QUEUE

"Queue" is an independent culture and art curators group. At first, the designer created a logo by superimposing the alphabet to express the continuity of the matrix which meant queue. Moreover, it was interpreted as a graphic device that adds, subtracts, multiplies, and divides the act of introducing the selected cultural arts to the public, and created a module and provided it for the guide book.

Studio: TRIANGLE-STUDIO
Designer: Kisung Jang

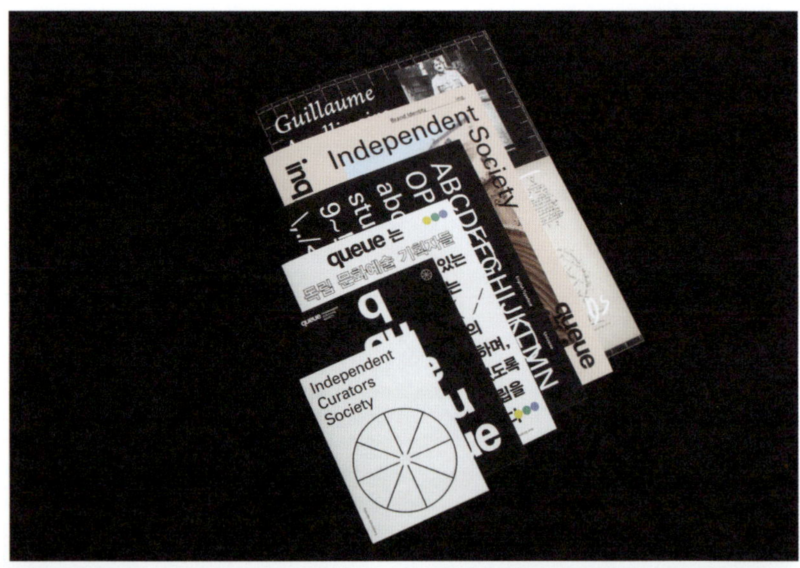

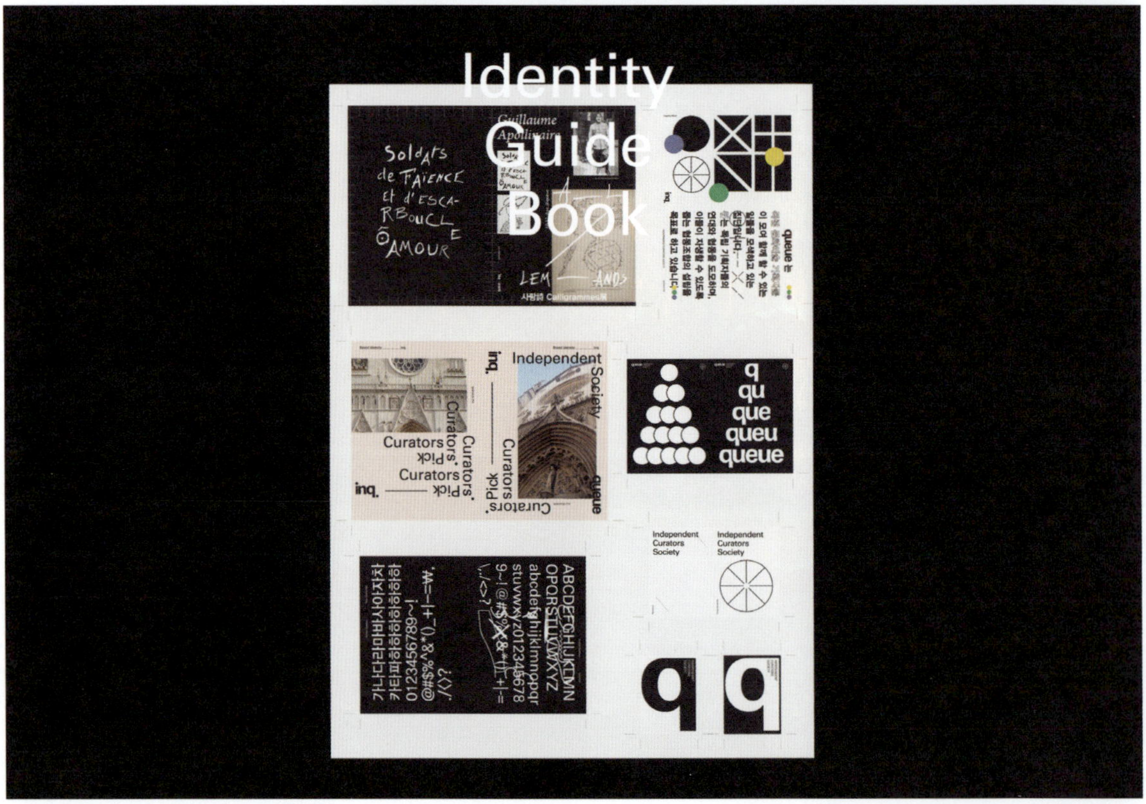

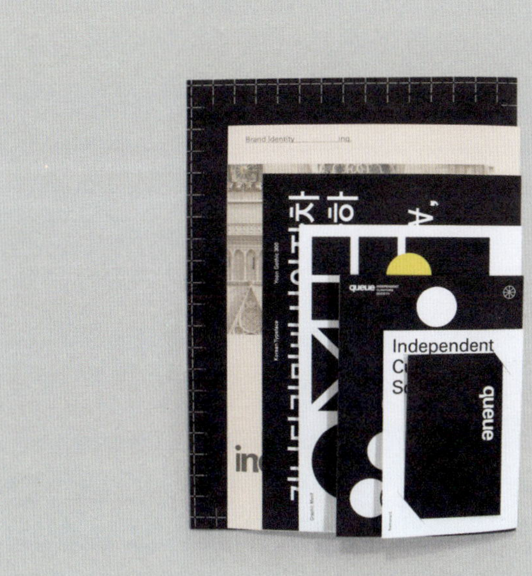
Brand Identity ing.
Independent
queue

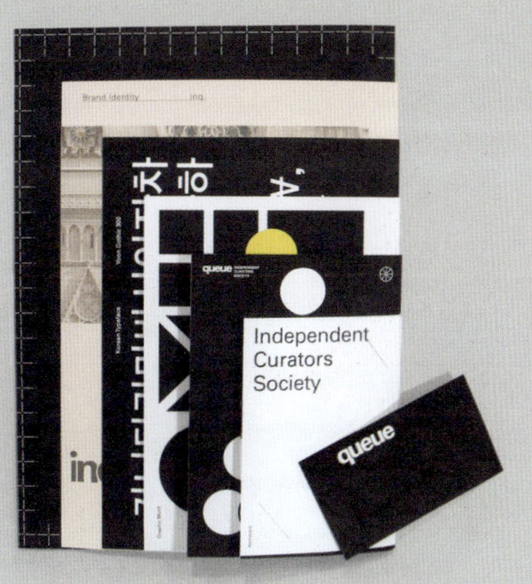
Brand Identity ing.
Independent
Curators
Society
queue

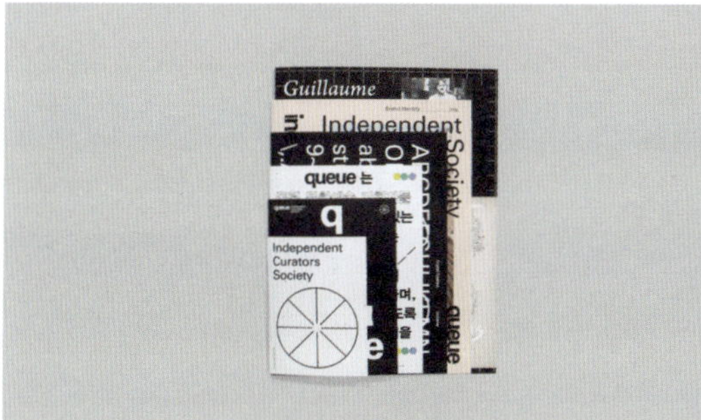
Guillaume
Independent
queue 는
Independent
Curators
Society
queue

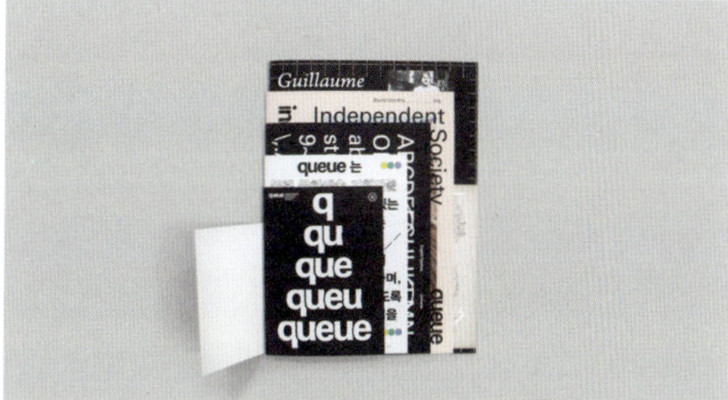
Guillaume
Independent
queue 는
q
qu
que
queu
queue

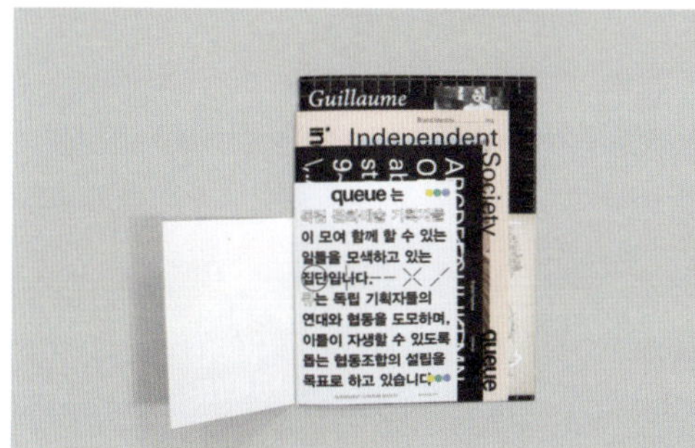
Guillaume
Independent
Society
queue 는
이 모여 함께 할 수 있는
일들을 모색하고 있는
집단입니다.
는 독립 기획자들의
연대와 협동을 도모하며,
이들이 자생할 수 있도록
돕는 협동조합의 설립을
목표로 하고 있습니다
queue

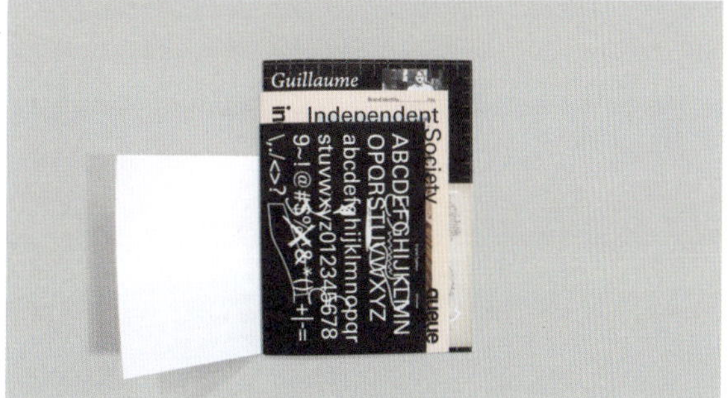
Guillaume
Independent
Society
ABCDEFGHIJKLMN
OPQRSTUVWXYZ
abcdefghijklmnpqr
stuvwxyz012345678
queue

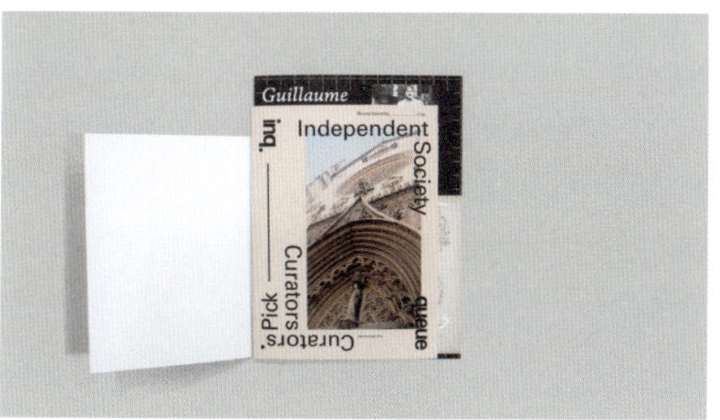
Guillaume
ing.
Independent
Society
Pick
Curators
Curators'
queue

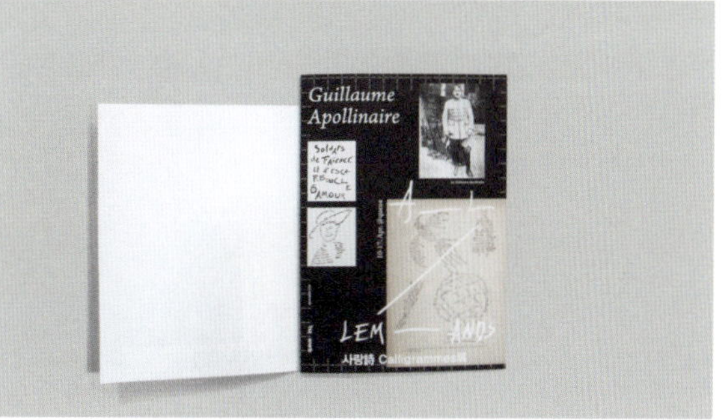
Guillaume
Apollinaire
LEM
사랑詩 Calligrammes

# CALENDARS

A series of typographic calendars.

Studio: Homework

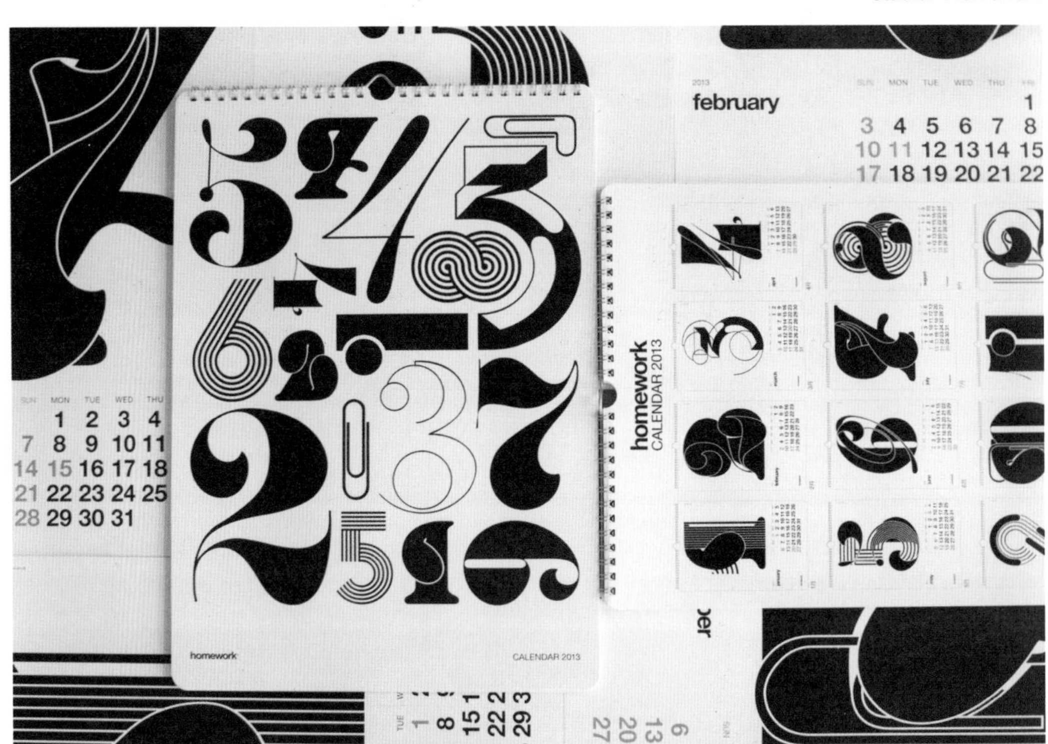


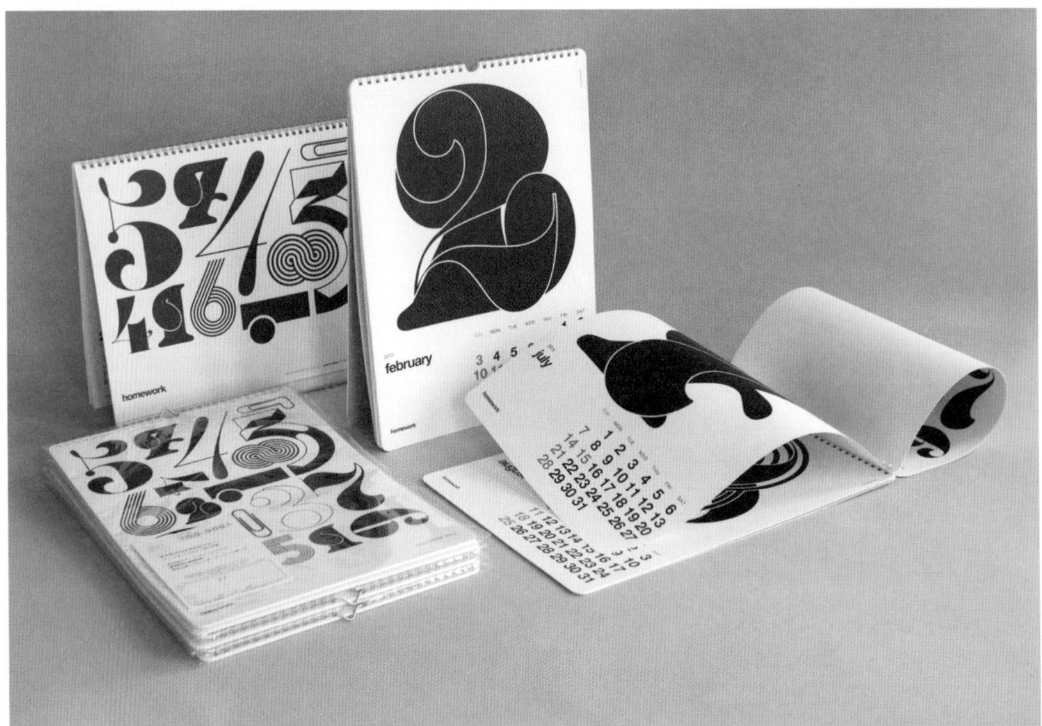

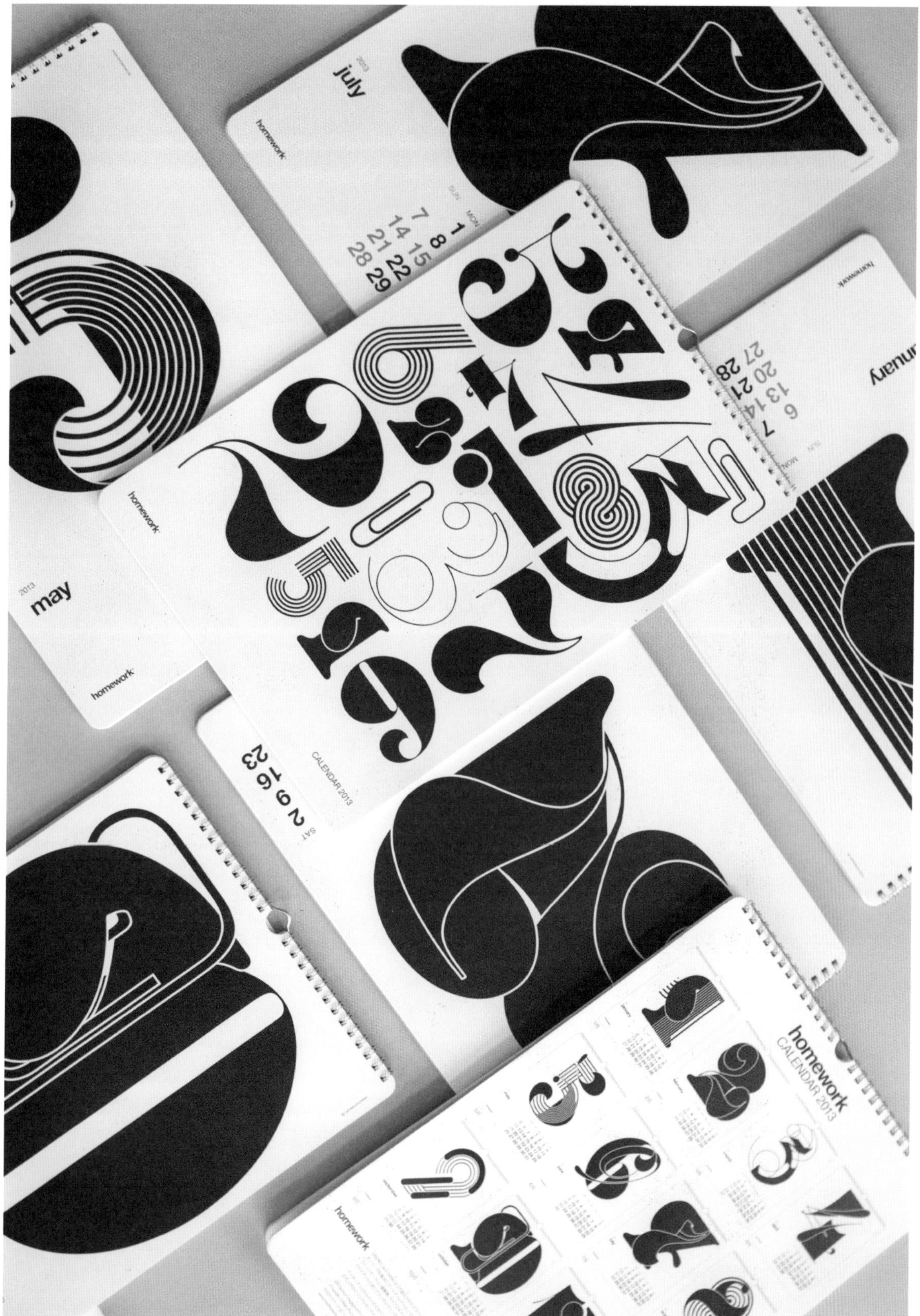
july
2013
homework
may
2013
homework
CALENDAR 2013
homework
CALENDAR 2013

# THE DIALOGUES I

This is a poster for the art gallery Alan Istanbul. The first exhibition will be held in one of the most well-known contemporary art spaces of New Jersey, MANA Contemporary.

Designer: Erman Yilmaz

THE DIALOGUES I: A COLLECTION OF TURKISH CONTEMPORARY ART IN NEW YORK

CURATOR
EFE KORKUT KURT

THE DIALOGUES

DATE
02/03
—
09/03
2017

ARTISTS
HARUN ANTAKYALI
EYLÜL ASLAN
KEZBAN ARCA BATIBEKİ
ALPER BIÇAKLIOĞLU
KADRİYE İNAL
HURİ KİRİŞ
A. CEM ŞAHİN
MERVE ŞENDİL
SAİT MİNGÜ

VENUE
MANA CONTEMPORARY
0888 NEWARK
AVE. JERSEY CITY
NJ 07306, USA

POSTER DESIGN: ERMAN YILMAZ

ALAN
ALANISTANBUL.COM

MANA
CONTEMPORARY

# NOTES IN ORIGIN

This is a poster for Fol Cinema. Canadian cinema, with some exceptions, remains mostly ignored in the history of experimental film, despite hosting a wealth of artists, and respectable institutions throughout the country. This screening aims to remedy this exclusion by showcasing a very small selection of Canadian works from artists working in different cities and contexts.

Designer: Erman Yilmaz

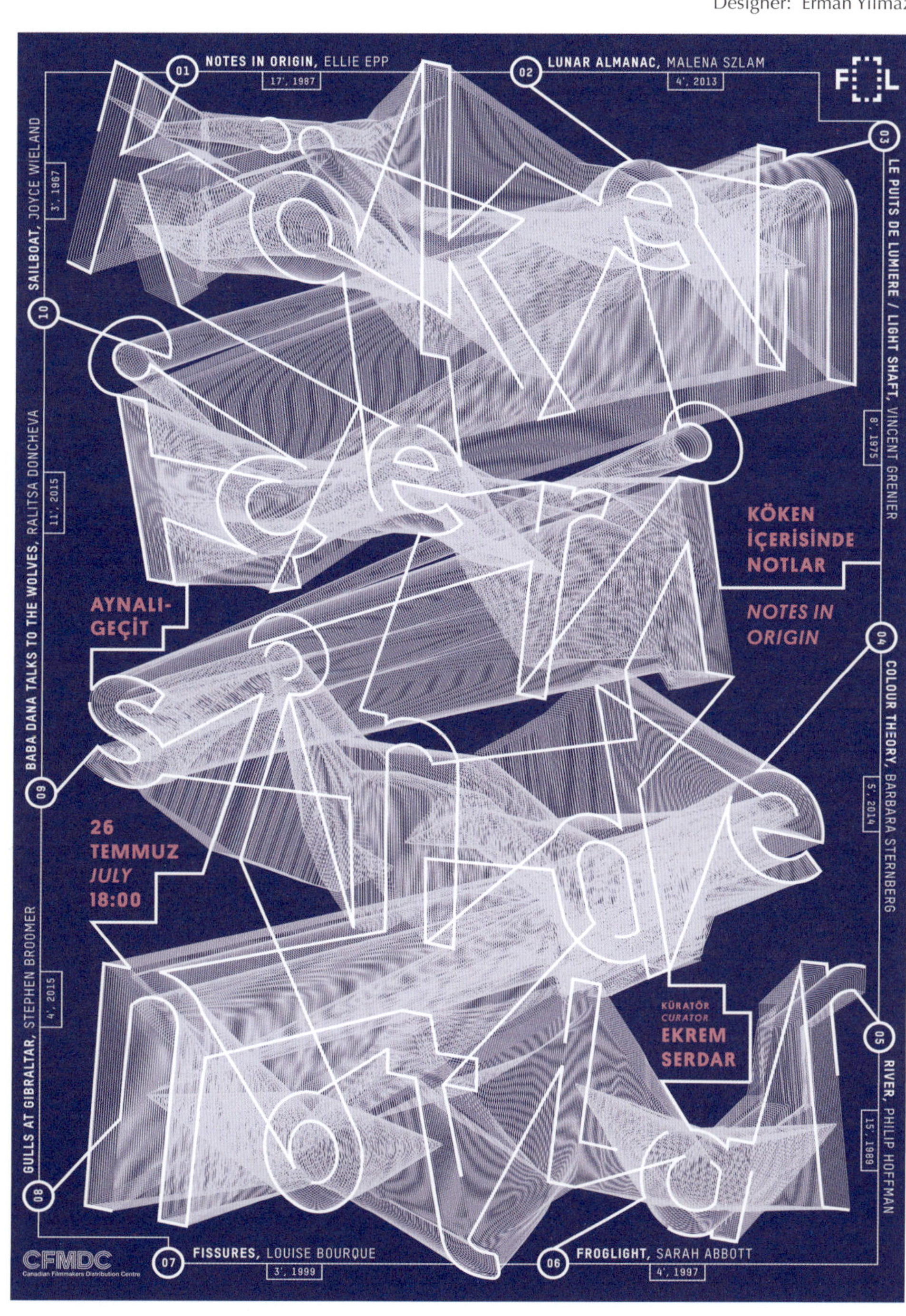

# KAMPONG

Kampong is an Indonesian and Malaysian word for "village". Inspired by ladders, a symbol of social development, this work presented the Chinese characters, which have a similar pronunciation as kampong, in a ladder form to signify the unification of different cultures in Singapore.

Studio: Fable
Designer: Jiahui Tan

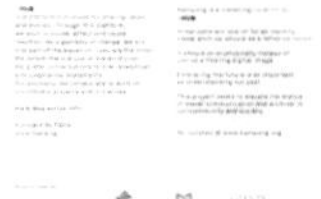

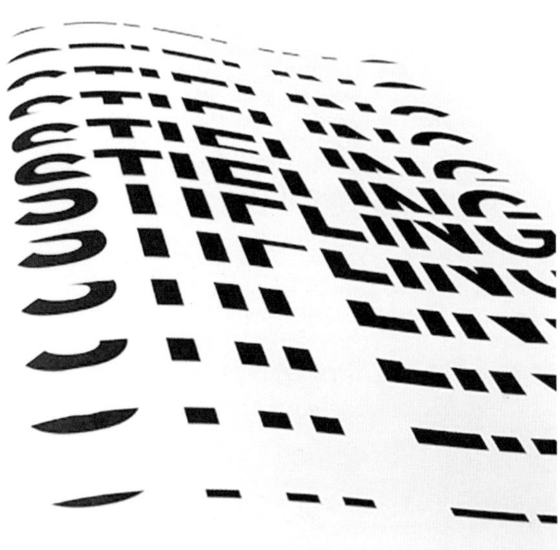

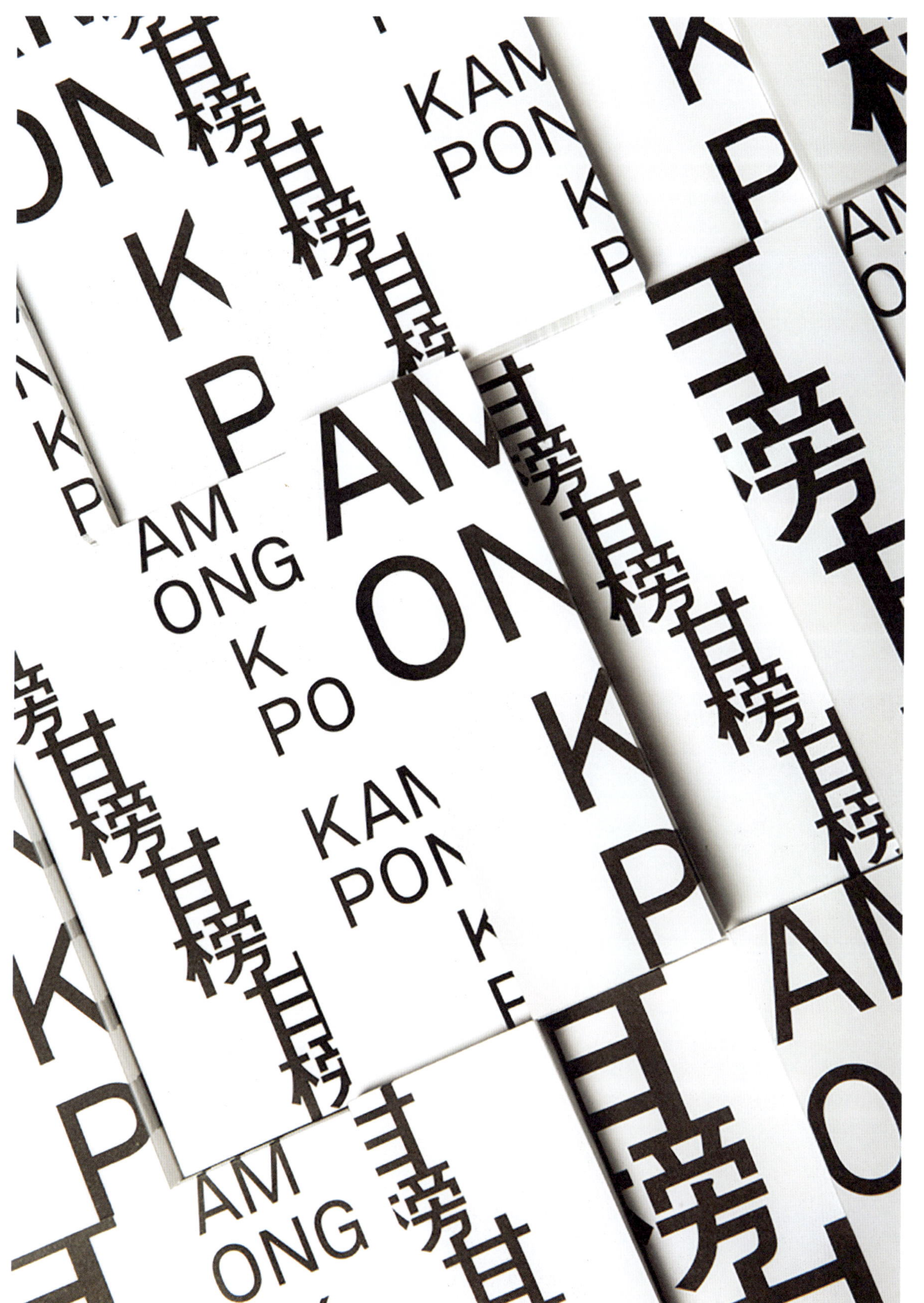
甘榜
KAM
PON
AM
ONG
K
PO

# WHAT YOU LEARNT FROM US

The designer chose a complicated, hard-to-read font to guide audiences to perceive the design as a whole idea rather than individual parts. This work intentionally utilized the emotions the audience have for certain typography in order to keep them intrigued and engaged.

Designer: Iordanis Passas

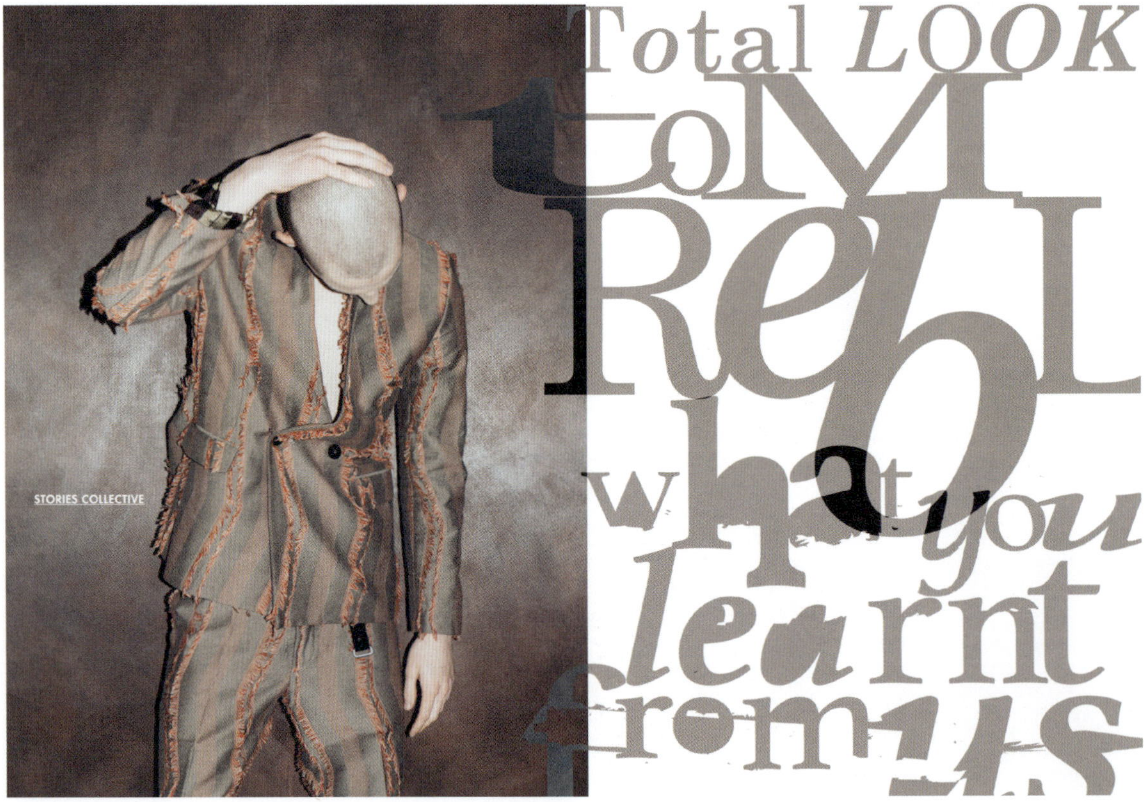

Sweater MARDON

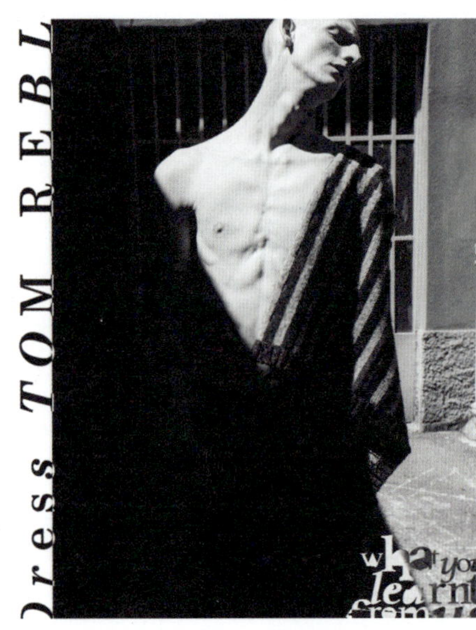


STORIES COLLECTIVE

Total LOOK
ToM
ReBL
what you
learnt
from us

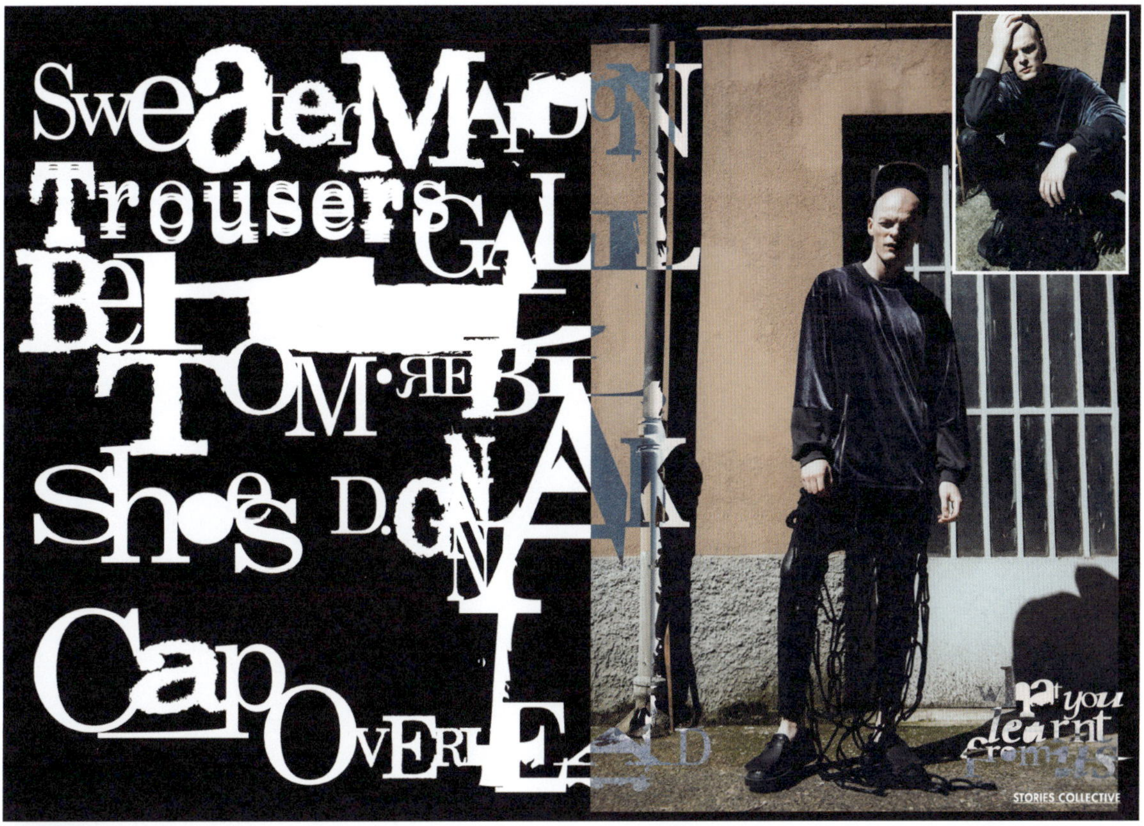

Sweater
Trousers
Belt
TOM·REBL
Shoes D.GNAK
Cap

what you learnt from us

STORIES COLLECTIVE

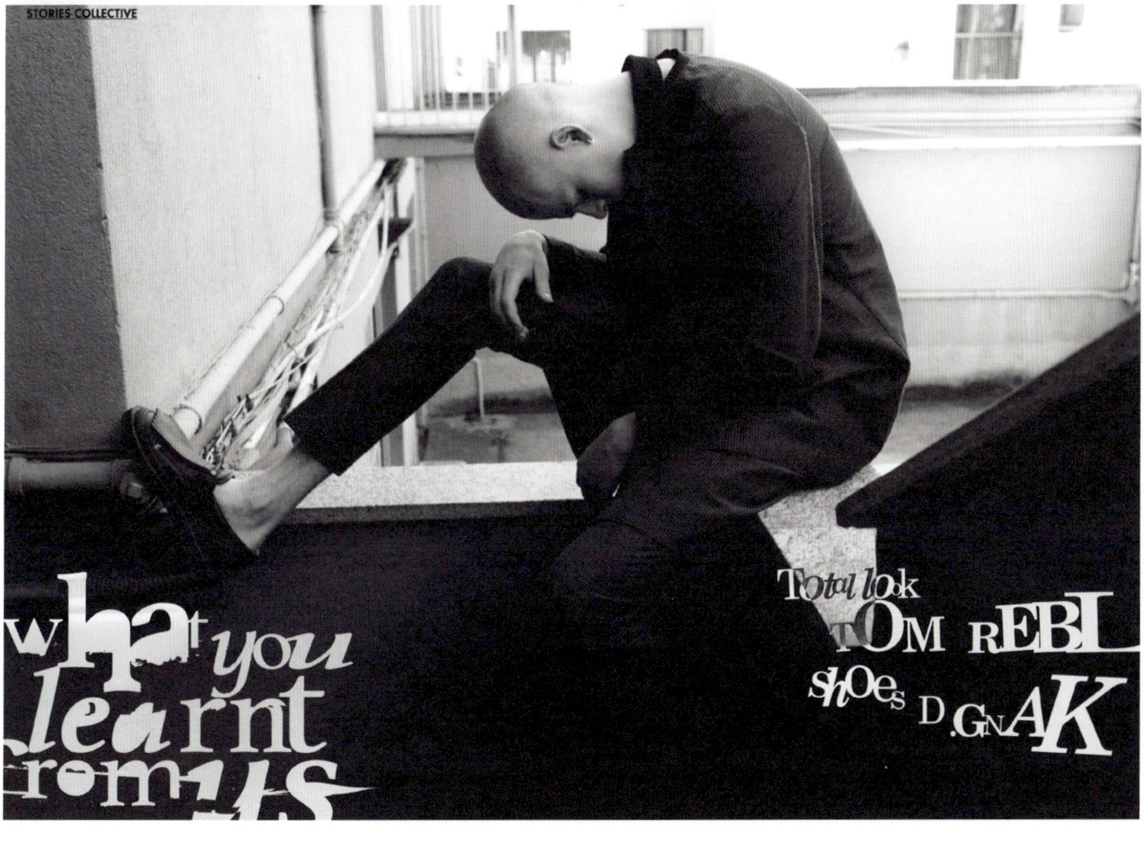

STORIES COLLECTIVE

what you learnt from us

Total look
TOM REBL
shoes D.GNAK

# ADDITION ADELAIDE COLLECTION PRESS INVITES

Addition Adelaide is a fashion and concept store in the Harajuku area of Tokyo carrying a wide range of only the best luxury brands. This is a design work to celebrate the seasons from 2015 to 2016.

Studio: Homework

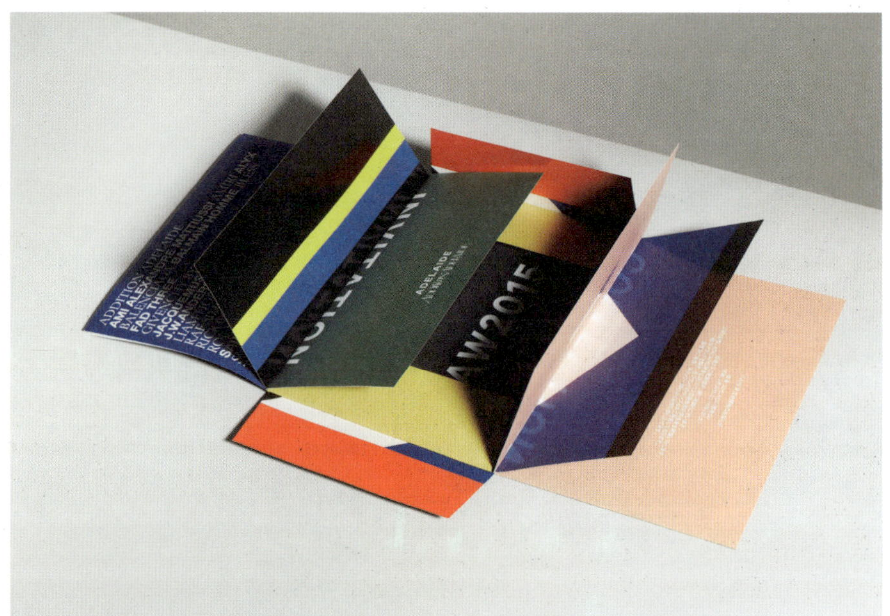

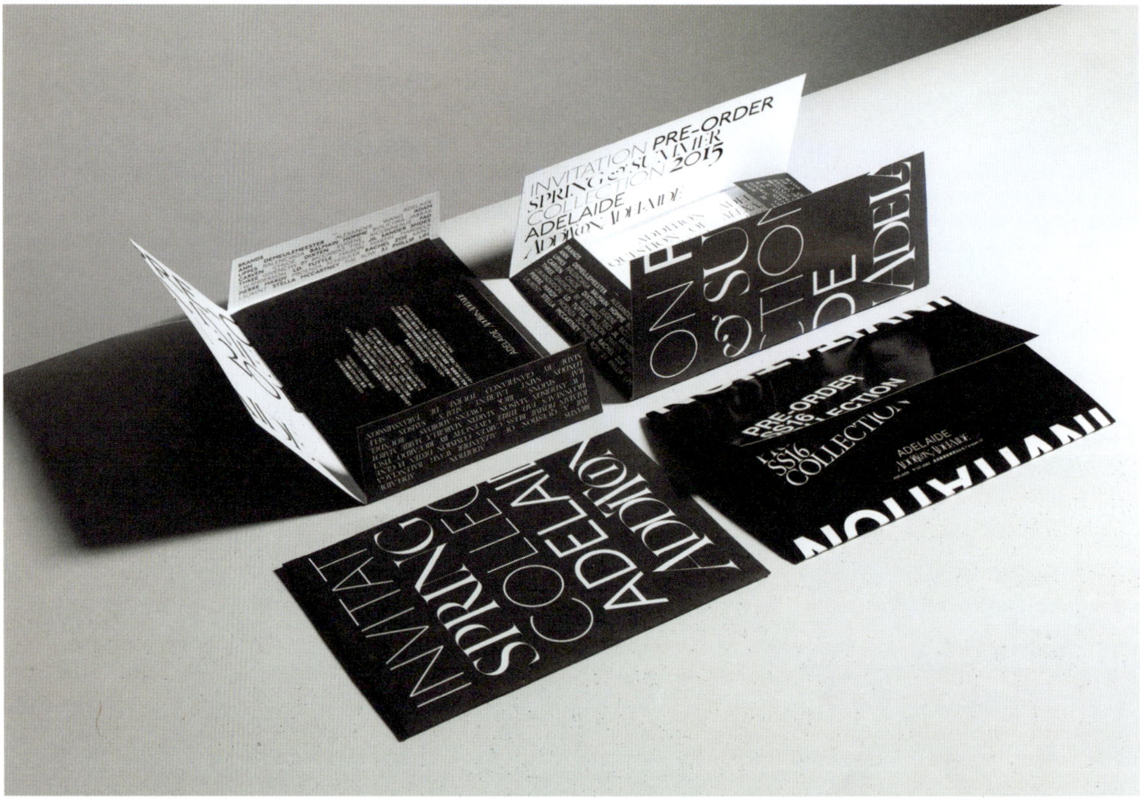

# SVEN VÄTH GREATEST HITS 1982-2017

This project came from the designer's passion for techno music. The elaborated album design is a tribute to Sven Väth, one of the greatest exponents of electronic music, collecting his major record works present in the rankings of specialized press worldwide.

Studio: Brando Corradini

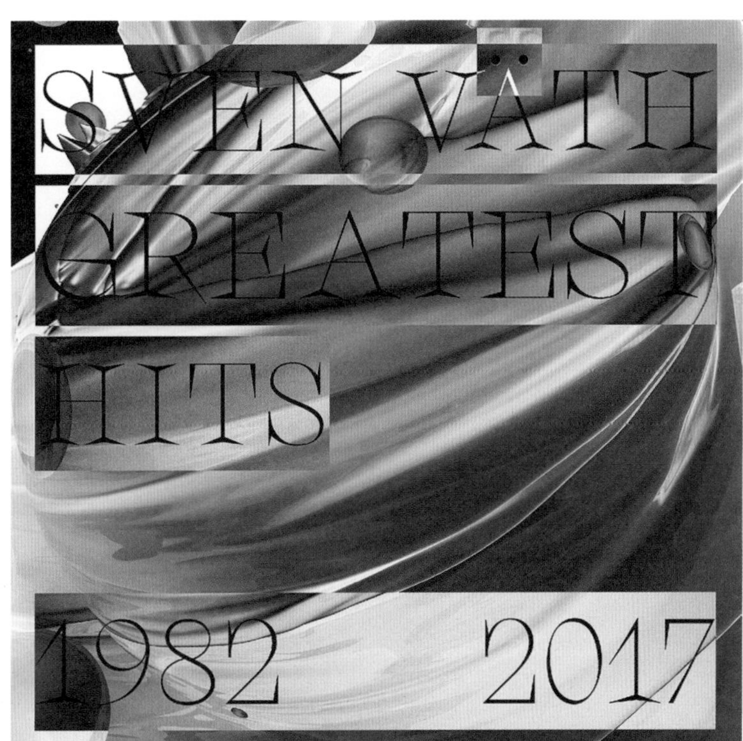


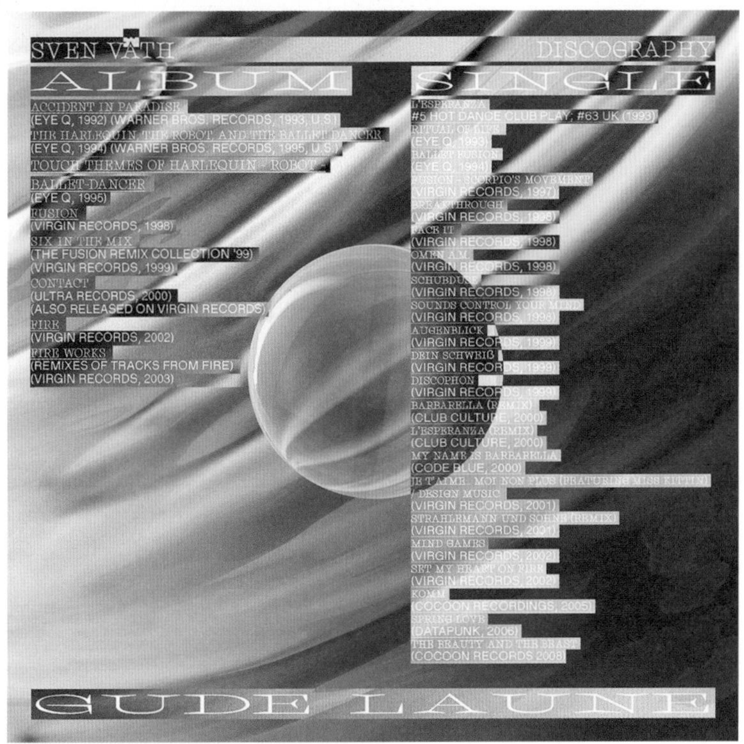

# SHUN/NI

There are two sides to everything: the ups (in Chinese: 顺, pronounced as shun) and downs (in Chinese: 逆, pronounced as ni) are closely connected. In these visual designs, the Chinese characters of "shun" and "ni" have been ingeniously interlocked that they seem to be a whole although they are in distinctly different styles, suggesting the relation between ups and downs in life.

Studio: awt design Inc.
Designer: Lok Ng

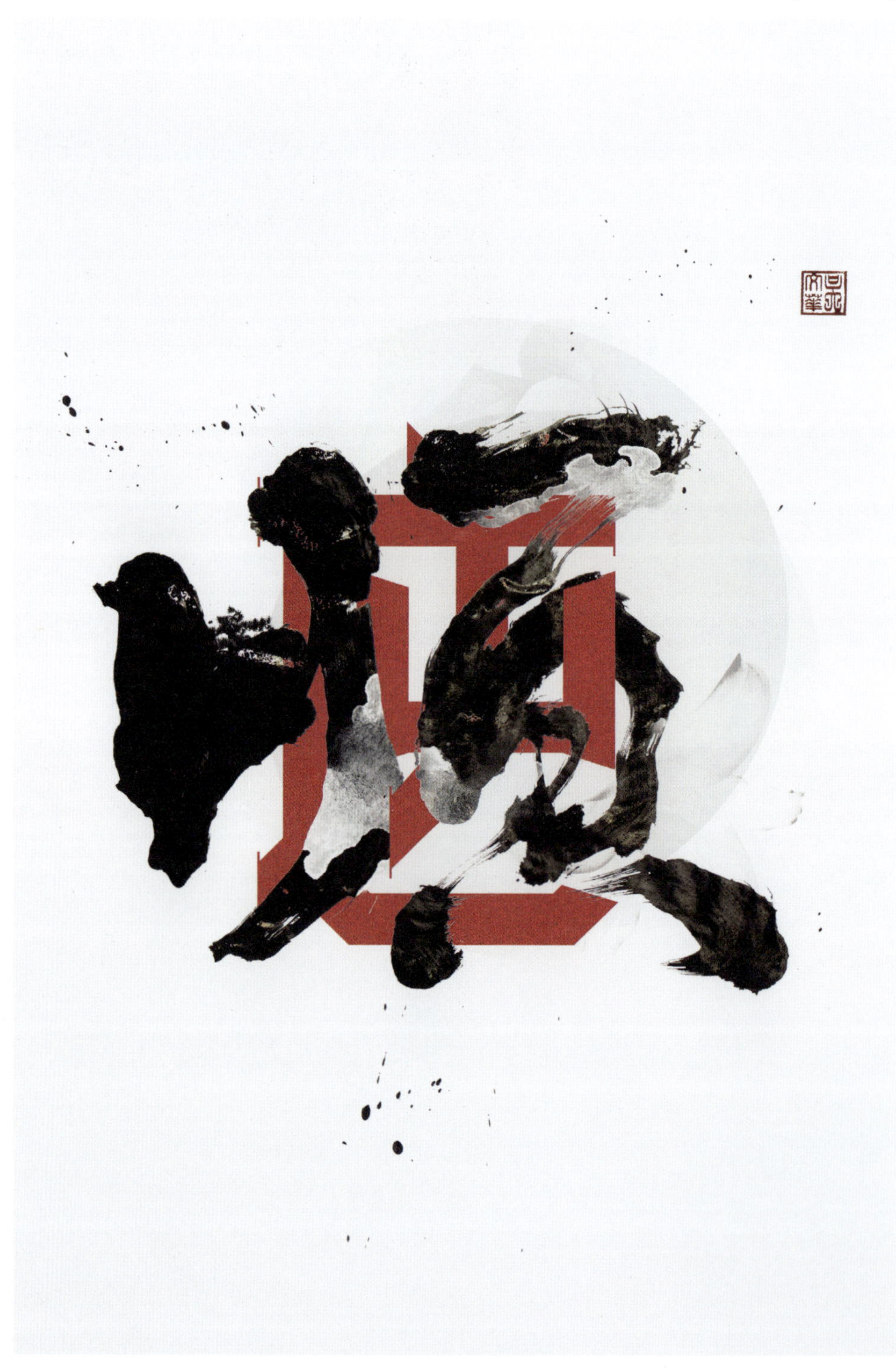

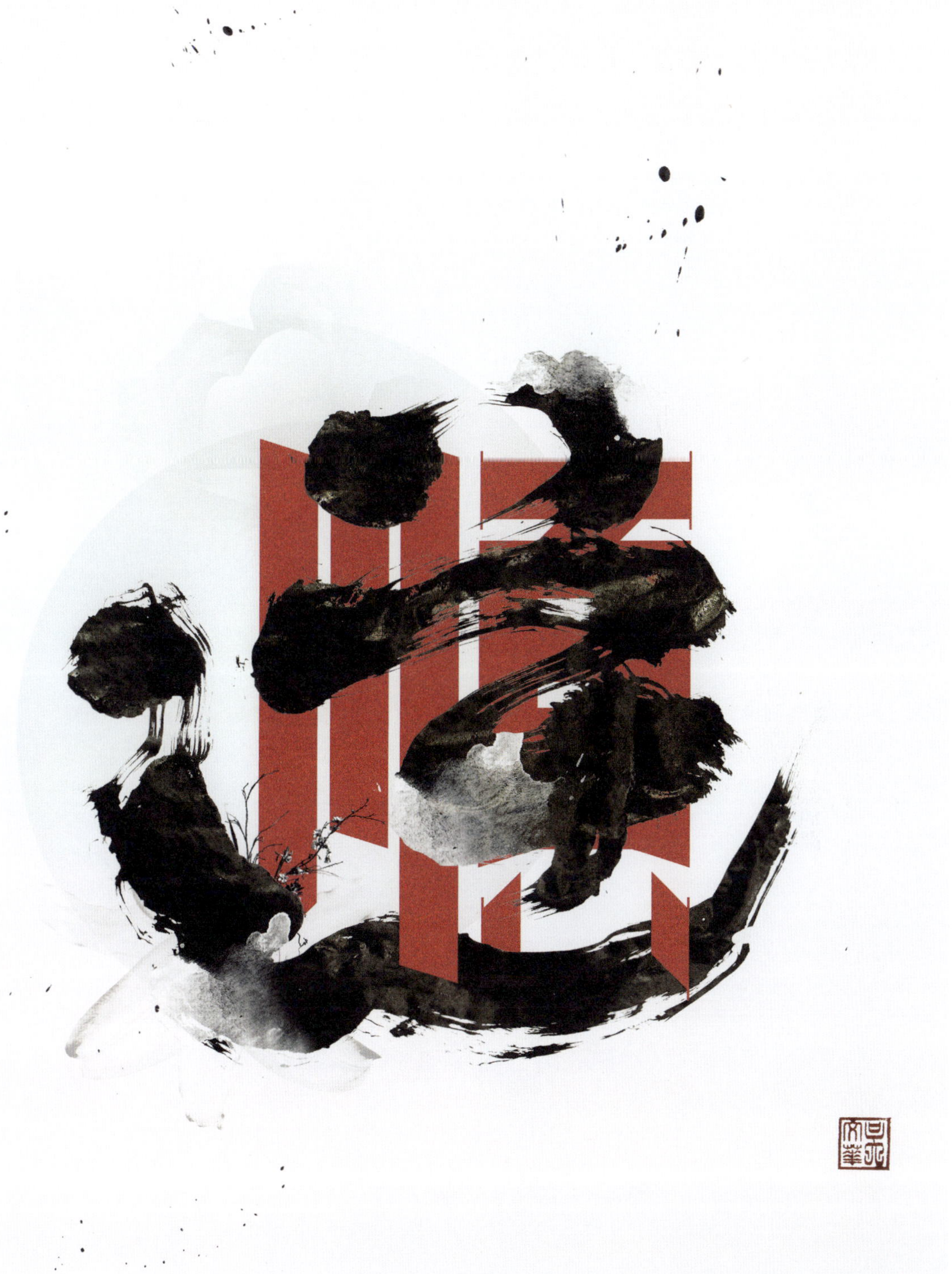

# INDEX

## L



## M



## N



## O



## R



## S



## T



## Y



## Z

# ACKNOWLEDGEMENTS

We would like to thank all the designers and contributors who have been involved in the production of this book. Their contributions have been indispensable in its compilation. We would also like to express our gratitude to all the producers for their invaluable opinions and assistance throughout this project. And to the many others whose names are not credited but have made specific input in this book, we thank you for your continuous support.

**FUTURE COOPERATIONS:**
If you wish to participate in SendPoints' future projects and publications, please send your website or portfolio to
**editor01@sendpoints.cn**